GIMME SOME SUGAR, Darlin'

By

LAURANCE DALTROFF TRIPLETTE

The SECRET LEXICON of SOUTHERNNESS

and ONE OLD BRIDE'S GUIDE to COOKING SOUTHERN

GIMME SOME SUGAR, DARLIN'
The Secret Lexicon of Southernness
and
One Old Bride's Guide to Cooking Southern

ISBN: 978-1-879958-04-3
November 2012   QVC Edition

Art direction and cover design by Brian Groppe
Layout by Kris Zediker and Laurie Triplette
Layout consultation by Carra Hewitt

The sayings, tips, and recipes contained in this book were accumulated from family and friends, and
reflect our diverse Southern cultural and ethnic heritage. Some are original, and many have been
passed along from other sources. All verbal and pictorial references to specific products and people
are personal opinion. Whenever a prior recipe source was identified, that source has been cited. No
claim is made as to the originality of the recipes in the cookbook. The author has tested them all and
tweaked many, and encourages other cooks to question and experiment with the recipes.

ON THE BACK COVER:
Black and white photo, Braswell Plantation BBQ, 1944
Photo Courtesy of the North Carolina Office of Archives & History, Raleigh, NC
Ajax Diner photo, photography permission granted
Courtesy of Amy Crockett and Randy Yates, Ajax Diner, Oxford, MS

INSIDE THE BOOK, PHOTOGRAPHY AND RECIPE PERMISSION GRANTED BY:
*3-Way Grocery & Deli, Oxford, MS; Abbott Farms, Cowpens, SC; B's BBQ in the Skymart, Oxford, MS;
Betty Davis Grocery & BBQ, Waterford, MS; City Lunch, Lincolnton, NC;
Corky's Ribs & BBQ, Memphis, TN; Craig Goldwyn (amazingribs.com), Brookfield, IL;
Craig's BBQ, De Valls Bluff, AR; Doe's Eat Place, Little Rock, AR; George's Restaurant under the I-10,
Baton Rouge, LA; Handy Andy Grocery and Market BBQ, Oxford, MS; Honest Abe's, Oxford, MS;
Jim 'n Nick's Bar-B-Q, Birmingham, AL; Just Divine Tearoom, Halls, TN;
Lodge Cast Iron, South Pittsburg, TN; Martha White Flour, Nashville, TN; Midstate Mills, Newton, NC;
Nick's BBQ & Catfish, Carlisle, AR; Old Salem Tavern, Winston-Salem, NC;
Peabody Hotel, Memphis, TN; The Rendezvous, Memphis, TN; Salem College, Winston-Salem, NC;
Stamey's BBQ, Greensboro, NC; Taylor Grocery, Taylor, MS; White Lily Flour, Nashville, TN;
The Woman's Exchange of Memphis, TN*

Printed in the USA

W I M M E R
cookbooks
A CONSOLIDATED GRAPHICS COMPANY
wimmerco.com   800.548.2537

DEDICATED WITH LOVE

To my husband, Jeff, who has always supported my obsessions and eaten everything I cooked for him ... except those Chinese meatballs;

To my children, Gabrielle and Joshua, for wanting to know how to cook it right (Joshua), or tell someone else how to cook it right (Gabrielle);

To my mother-in-law, Louise Sherrill Triplette, who always advised me to taste the leftovers first to see if they were still good, except that ONE time ("Oh honey, I wouldn't eat THAT!");

To my sisters-in-law Andrea and Dianne, who've always promised to keep little brother in line if I go first, **and to their two Garys,** who've helped their fellow outlaw with every request;

To my precious cousin Rita, who's been bird-dogging the Daltroff and Stewart family mysteries for four decades, oy vey;

And to the men and women who maintain our Southern farming, fishing, and crafts traditions, even when industrialization and Mother Nature won't cooperate.

ACKNOWLEDGMENTS

Heartfelt thanks go to the following family and friends for rounding up our recipes and photos:

Andrea Triplette Benfield, *Newton, NC*
Gary Dean Benfield, *Newton, NC*
Jill Gibbs Benfield, *Hickory, NC*
Charlotte and Don Bradley, *Hurlock, MD*
Stella Thurmond Campbell, *Red Bank, TN*
Andy Daltroff, *Fort Myers, FL*
Pat Daltroff, *Palm Springs, CA*
Rita Davidson Friend, *N. Little Rock, AR*
Henry (Trail) and Ann Jordan, *Kosciusko, MS*
Angela Kaiser, *Lincolnton, NC*
Fern Robertson Kerslake, *Radium Hot Springs, BC*
Evalyn Yancey Lipoff (and Scott), *Gainesville, FL*
Aline Thurmond Miller, *St. Petersburg, FL*
Missy Morrison, *Oxford, MS*
Rosa Lee Morton, *Oxford, MS*
Willie June Keller Noggle, *Hickory, NC*
Terri Robinson Peeler, *Oxford, MS*
Dianne Triplette Poovey, *Vale, NC*
Gary Poovey, *Vale, NC*
Randy Rosen, *New York, NY*
Ryan Russell, *Baton Rouge, LA*
Cindy Thurmond Semple, *Norcross, GA*
Ruth Callicott Thurmond, *Memphis, TN*
Loretta Phillips Triplette, *Granite Falls, NC*
Louise Sherrill Triplette, *Granite Falls, NC*
Vicki Corkran Willey, *Hurlock, MD*

To the following for their editorial advice:

Jason Derrick, *Oxford, MS*
Brian Groppe, *Memphis, TN*
Randy Rosen, *New York, NY*
Russell Schnepf, *Palm Springs, CA*
Sandy Stater, *Canton, MS*
Rachel Malone West, *Oxford, MS*
Kris Zediker, *Oxford, MS*

And to my wonderful proofreaders:

Bill Caldwell, *Oxford, MS*
Rita Davidson Friend, *N. Little Rock, AR*
Carra Hewitt, *Oxford, MS*
Rosa Lee Morton, *Oxford, MS*
Linda Sperath, *Oxford, MS*
Mary Sue Tettleton, *Oxford, MS*

And my undying thanks go to the following for permitting use of their photographic materials:

* Cotton Museum of the Memphis Cotton Exchange, 65 Union Avenue, *Memphis, TN*
* G&W Hamery, *Murfreesboro, TN*
* Ken Ross and Billy Ross Photography, *Memphis, TN (wedding photos on pages 51 and 237)*
* North Carolina Department of Cultural Resources, Office of Archives and History, *Raleigh, NC*
* Melissa Hamilton, *Thomasville, AL*
* Piedmont Craftsmen, Inc., *Winston-Salem, NC*
* Angelo Politis, Holy Trinity Greek Orthodox Cathedral, *Charlotte, NC*
* Felder Rushing, *Jackson, MS*, aka "The Gestalt Gardener" (www.felderrushing.net)

ABOUT THIS BOOK

Gimme Some Sugar, Darlin' (The Secret Lexicon of Southernness and One Old Bride's Guide to Cooking Southern) is both a family cookbook and a manifesto of Southern philosophy. In true Southern family-cookbook tradition, this book is an ode to the ancestors who instilled in my family a taste for wonderful home cooking, a bone-deep work ethic, and a communal sense of humor that, for more than 150 years, has carried us through the toughest and the best of times.

Gimme Some Sugar, Darlin' is my second compilation of family recipes. The first, which I called The Long Way Home, was printed privately for family and friends in 2008 in an edition of 100 copies. That cookbook project arose from a desperate need to organize more than a thousand recipes left by my mother, as well as a large notebook of recipes from my grandmother, both women's dog-eared, disintegrating church cookbooks, and my own recipes. The project had simmered in a large pile in my Charlotte, NC, kitchen for more than six years, almost disappearing in 2007 during my relocation to Oxford, MS.

Family and friends were supportive and enthusiastic when I finally completed The Long Way Home. A second printing was planned. But I wanted to tweak it before reprinting because essential recipes had been omitted the first time. Moreover, my children, my brothers, and nieces and nephews were requesting that I expand the culinary definitions and kitchen prep instructions. I also concluded that the dual topics of our Southern families' cooking traditions and the essence of what makes Southerners Southern needed further exploration. (We believe that to be American is a privilege; to be Southern is divine.)

Gimme Some Sugar, Darlin' is the result. It is this Baby Boomer's cockeyed, very personal essay on Southernness—my homage to four Southern families' diverse cultural and culinary heritage through our own little DNA-linked community cookbook. I call it a four-family cookbook because it represents the maternal and paternal lines of both my husband's family and my own. As with most families, though, our culinary heritage extends far beyond our parents and grandparents.

The favorite recipes contained in this book range from Tex-Mex and Cajun to Delta, Appalachian, and Low Country. All are heavily flavored with our religious preferences—from Moravian, Lutheran, and Baptist, to Catholic, Jewish, and Methodist. In these pages you will find my tweaked version of Grandmother's favorite candied sweet potato casserole with the little bitty marshmallows, Louise's chicken and dumplings, Great-Aunt Annie's favorite congealed salad, Bigmamma Rose's Matzo Ball Soup,

and hundreds of other recipes. Some of them actually contain more than five ingredients and require more than 30 minutes to cook. Others follow the classic throw-it-together tradition of using what's in the larder to get a meal on the table before the next baseball practice or music lesson.

You'll also find tips on how to modify recipes, how to stock your kitchen, and how to eat economically, along with housekeeping and culinary advice targeted to our precious, home-ec deprived 19-year-olds.

And you may just learn a teensy bit more about how we Southerners laugh our way through the ups and downs of life.

I feel better now.

TABLE OF CONTENTS

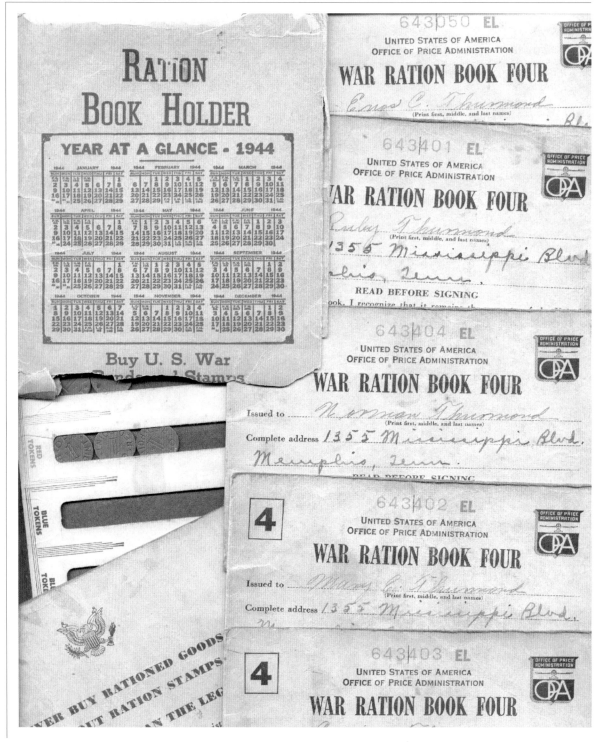

INTRODUCTION

All the recipes in *Gimme Some Sugar, Darlin'* reflect the changing times in which they were created. The cookbook includes recent concoctions, as well as heirlooms—some passed down through more than five generations of my extended family.

The extended family includes my Daltroff, Stewart, White and Thurmond blood relatives and in-laws in Tennessee, Arkansas, Mississippi, Louisiana, Virginia, Georgia, the Carolinas, Florida, Maryland, and California; my husband's Triplette, Clark, Sherrill, and Kirby blood relatives and in-laws in North Carolina and Texas; and some of our close friends. Among us, I give five stars to two: (1) my mother-in-law, Louise Sherrill Triplette, who in her day could out-cook anyone in at least Caldwell, Catawba and Alexander counties, and perhaps all of western North Carolina; and (2) my West Tennessee grandmother, Ruby White Thurmond, who could prepare a delicious three-course meal for 20—with only an hour's notice. Of course, I'm prejudiced.

Grandmother and Louise learned their culinary skills from their mothers, their aunts, and their grand-

mothers. Self-sustaining out of necessity, those Southern women and their men survived the periods between Reconstruction and World War II by growing their own fruits, vegetables, grains and meat sources. More recent family cooks, such as my father, and my brother-in-law Gary Poovey, came to the table out of a love of the art of cooking.

Culling the recipes for the cookbook enlightened me. Good home cooking is good home cooking, wherever it originated, and it all has left an indelible imprint on our culture. Thus, we have Southern culinary traditions of tamales and Tex-Mex, Italian, French, German, Kosher, Lebanese and Chinese food up and down the Mississippi River heartland; great Middle Eastern, South American and African-derived Creole foods in the Carolinas and along the Gulf; and our more recent global Southern influences from Indian, Hmong, Vietnamese, Korean, Thai, Salvadorian, and Guatamalan immigrants.

When reading a well-loved Saskatoon Unity Church cookbook inherited by my Canadian friend, Fern, I also recognized how recipes have hopscotched across the continent between communities through their church women. Fern's church cookbook contains many of the recipes claimed by our Methodist church women in West Tennessee and North Carolina.

It was impossible to identify the original sources of some of Mom's, Louise's, and Grandmother's dishes. This is not surprising, because local television cooking shows, newspaper columnists, *Southern Living Magazine* (started in 1966 by *The Progressive Farmer Magazine*), and now the internet, have contributed to the dissemination of regional favorites for more than 60 years.

The more obvious dishes to be included in the family cookbook required comparative analysis before selection. My original pile of recipes contained variations on brown sugar pound cakes, hash brown potato casseroles, and innumerable chicken casseroles passed along from cooks all over the region. (NOTE TO EVERYONE: Not all casseroles contain canned soup.) My chili bread recipes came from relatives in

Mississippi, from family friends in South Texas; and one even came from Virginia. The family's favorite Redneck Texas Caviar recipe was a gentler Southeast version of the spicier Tex-Mex version. And so on….

This cookbook contains no recipes for Spam or hominy because I don't like Spam or hominy. And there are no specific recipes for venison, squirrel or rabbit. I also omitted most bourbon recipes, considered mainstays of Southern cuisine, because I cannot bear the smell of bourbon.

Blame that on my childhood trips to the liquor store with Aunt Rosalee whenever she'd come up to Memphis for Christmas. Aunt Rosie, the football bookie, made 150-proof bourbon balls, and continued to drink Jack Daniels out of a teacup because that's what they did in Greenville, MS, during and long after Prohibition—which only ended in Mississippi in 1966. Our liquor store adventures inevitably would send my teetotaling mother into a nail-biting tizzy, but Aunt Rosie always made me laugh, even when she smelled like a distillery by 8 p.m. To this day I regret that cousins Frank, Marian, and Richard and I didn't have the nerve to stick a bottle of Black Jack in her coffin. We talked about it. It would have been so easy.

Or blame it on Deedee Hyde's wedding.

Revisiting thousands of our family recipes for this book was better than viewing home movies. Relatives and friends long gone came back to life for me, and for my children, who had never met them. And after 37 years on a thousand-mile odyssey, I understood that Thomas Wolfe was wrong. You can go home again. Despite—or perhaps because of—the cultural grittiness, the wacky weather, and the endemic wildlife teeming in this north Mississippi backyard of my youth, life here seems more special than I remember. Yet once in a while, when the wind picks up and the skies turn brilliant blue, I ache for extended family remaining in North Carolina.

How could I have realized, when sitting in Willie Sue Keller's living room at my 1973 Grace Chapel bridal shower, that the Sherrills and Triplettes sharing their recipes would come to mean as much to me as my own blood kin?

The term "family" means more than a bloodline, you know. In real life, a family's ties begin and end at the table, in the spiritual act of breaking bread together, as we share our joy, our faith, and our heartbreak. That's why it's important to preserve and share our recipes, so that wherever our loved ones put down roots, they're always at home.

The Southern culinary ties that bind my family now extend from California to the Carolinas, from Michigan to Florida, from Canada to Mexico. And every meal is prepared with love. I wish as much for you.

¡Salud!

L'Chaim!

Sláinte!

Sahtaen!

Bon Appétit!

Laissez les Bon Temps Rouler!

Photo on p. 9: James L. Thurmond Family, West Tennessee, 1920s

The

SECRET LEXICON

OF

SOUTHERNNESS

A DICTIONARY OF
SOUTHERN CULTURE
AND CONVERSATION

*One must learn about our culture
in order to understand our
Southern foodways.*

EXPLAINING SOUTHERNNESS

Southernness: A state of mind, a specific state of being. Known by all Southerners to be a sublime plane of existence.

Southernism: Saying or expression that derives from Southern culture. Usually extremely colorful, blunt, and descriptive; frequently incorporating references to livestock and dogs, intent to do bodily harm, and the right to bear arms. Often linguistically incorrect as to syntax or grammar. Makes no never mind as to social class or educational background of the user.

Southerners talk in poetic free verse. Most of us are descended from tribes with ancient singing and storytelling traditions. We take literary license in our oral relaying of events and activities. We're not lying; we're describing. Do not ask a Southerner to cut to the chase when explaining what happened, or when identifying a problem. You'll insult us to the quick, and we might take umbrage. You do not want this. Southerners tend to combine a strong streak of tacky with a bit of mean when riled up. We're awfully creative.

Do ask for additional landscape references (such as the county road number) when receiving directions from a Southerner, just in case you're "not from around here" and don't have a GPS tracking system. It's highly unlikely that you'll know where the little Abernathy boy ran down three mailboxes outside Nankipoo, or where they just laid the blacktop in Wynne, or where the factory burned down near the tracks three years ago in Hickory, or where the giant plastic bull used to be located in the Winston-Salem restaurant parking lot for 30 years.

Southernisms can be sorted into categories if one has a hankerin' for order. Most of us don't bother because life is too short, and surprises keep us looking down the road toward tomorrow. We came from chaos. We live large in chaos. We thrive in chaos, ever prepared for all of the evils that man or nature can bestow. If you have doubts, visit the Piggly Wiggly when the weatherman calls for snow. Or stop by The Home Depot three days before a hurricane. Or snoop around in the church basement until you find the radioactive fallout sign posted above the padlocked door.

Over a period of four centuries, Southerners have been beaten, burned out, relocated, enslaved, occupied, starved, and robbed. But we own the English language. And our food is everyone's guilty pleasure.

The peach water tower in Gaffney, SC, off I-85.

TYPE OF SOUTHERN PERSON (AND FOOTBALL)

It's a well known fact that our Southern religions historically have been Baptist, Methodist, and Football (except in Louisiana, where they've been Catholic, Baptist, Methodist, and Football). Our self esteem and our teams are inextricably melded. In recent decades we've expanded to include other sports such as basketball, baseball, NASCAR, tennis and golf. And other religious affiliations, too. But football rules us all.

When one refers to a Southerner by a label, one is as likely to refer to the person by his or her sports affiliation as by place of origin, personality description or general character. Darren Everson aptly described the Southern sports obsession in his December 5, 2008, *Wall Street Journal* article entitled "What the Rise of Southern Football Says about America":

"The breadth of the South's football culture creates a fanaticism that crosses all the lines. People who didn't attend the schools, or go to college at all, still support them, and will even make donations. It's a group that insiders call 'dirt-road alumni'."

My friend Sandy experienced a perfect example of dirt-road alumni culture. He has owned a vacation condo in Gulf Shores, AL, for many years. A local Gulf Shores lady had hounded him since its purchase about whether he was for Alabama or Auburn. He kept telling her he didn't have a dog in that show, being a graduate of both UVA and Ole Miss. She explained that it didn't matter. He owned Alabama real estate and therefore had to choose sides. Sandy finally told her he guessed he'd pick Alabama. "You sonofabitch," she replied.

Our teams do pretty well every season, but 2009 was a banner year for Southern football. Six of America's top 15 collegiate football programs were Southeastern Conference (SEC). Eleven Southern teams finished the season among the top 25 of the NCAA's Division I. As if that weren't enough, the NFL's New Orleans Saints set out to prove that there's life after Katrina.

Like icing on the proverbial cake, *The Blind Side* opened at movie theaters nationwide during Thanksgiving week and captured the hearts of all red-blooded Americans, particularly those who bleed SEC during football season. This true story of Ole Miss football standout Michael Oher depicted his climb from Memphis poverty to the ranks of the NFL. *The Blind Side* featured cameo appearances by many Southern coaches who had courted Oher and his adoptive family, the Tuohys, while he was still at Briarcrest Christian School. Southern fans turned out in throngs to cheer or boo the coaches who, collectively, have played collegiate round-robin.

Most importantly, the 2009 collegiate season ended with Alabama 14-0, outplaying the real second-ranked team (powerhouse Florida) at the real championship game (SEC Conference), for the right to play officially second-ranked Texas at the Rose Bowl National Championship. SEC trumped Big 12, and once again, all was right in Dixieland. Folks across the South started reminiscing about Bear Bryant and how Coach Saban, the scourge of LSU, had brought back 'Bama's glory days. On Saturday and Sunday after its big win, 'Bama placed the National Championship Coaches Trophy on display in the heart of the Crimson Tide community: The Wal-Marts in Tuscaloosa and Gardendale. 'Bama wanted to make sure Crimson Tide fans could have their pictures made with the trophy.

Football is that important around here.

TYPE OF SOUTHERN PERSON

Aggie: Texas A&M, NC A&T.

Bear: Baylor University.

Bible-Thumper: A born-again Christian who makes it his or her mission to quote Scripture to unbelievers (anyone not attending his or her church).

Bison: Howard University.

Blacklander: Someone from the Delta in southeastern Arkansas or western Mississippi.

Blue Devil: Duke University.

Buccaneer: Charleston (SC) Southern, East Tennessee State, NFL's Tampa Bay.

Bulldog: University of Georgia, Mississippi State, Louisiana Tech, South Carolina State, Samford University, The Citadel.

Bulls: University of South Florida, Johnson C. Smith (Golden Bulls).

Cajun: A Louisianian of Acadian descent (See Longfellow's "Evangeline.") Sometimes used as a derogatory appellation by non-Cajun Louisianians of French descent.

Carpetbagger: A Northern politician or adventurer who went South after the War of Northern Aggression to take advantage of unsettled conditions. A contemptuous term used even today (see Dam'yankee).

Cavalier: University of Virginia (UVA).

Chanticleer: Coastal Carolina.

Colonel: Reference to a well-known auctioneer or wheeler dealer (Think Elvis' Colonel Parker). Derived from references to Kentucky border state culture: University of Kentucky, Centre College (KY), Eastern Kentucky U, or an honorific title bestowed on gentlemen in Kentucky.

Commodore: Vanderbilt (Vandy).

Coonass: Anyone close by or otherwise affiliated with Louisiana State University. The assumption is that said persons are scavengin' Cajuns from the back bayou, and the label is stated with contempt by someone NOT in any way located close by or affiliated with LSU or Cajun culture. (Heard most frequently in the Hotty Toddy Potties at The Grove during Rebel-Tiger confrontations in Oxford, MS.) A term reviled by some, embraced by others.

Cougar: College of Charleston, University of Houston

Creole: A native-born descendant of French, Spanish, or Portuguese settlers in Latin America, the West Indies, and the Gulf and Florida areas of the United States. The term has variant applications according to region. Louisiana Creoles fall into two groups: (1) The French-speaking white descendants of the early French or Spanish settlers, many of whom still speak a variation of Louisiana French; and (2) the mixed-race descendants of free people of color (gens de coleur libre), French, Spanish and Native Americans, who speak a Creolized version of French and Spanish. In Mexico, Creoles are local-born persons of pure Spanish descent. In the West Indies, Creoles are descendants of any European settlers, white and mixed race, and in the Guianas, Creoles are descendants of African slaves. Some Caucasian Creoles in Louisiana refer to themselves as mutt French. Never confuse Creoles with Cajuns.

Crimson Tide: University of Alabama.

Damn Yankee: Pronounced as one word: Dam'yankee. Originally used by Southerners when referring to natives of all Northern states supporting the Union in the War Between the States. Nowadays, refers to anyone from north of the South who behaves boorishly or otherwise acts like a total jackass.

Demon Deacon: Wake Forest University (founded in 1834 by the NC State Baptist Convention; relocated 110 miles west from Wake Forest to Winston-Salem in 1956).

Eagles: Georgia Southern, University of the Ozarks, Tennessee Tech (Golden Eagles), University of Southern Mississippi (Golden Eagles, too).

Flatlander: Anyone not from the mountains.

Floridiot: The summer people populating the NC Highlands between June and October. Left Florida for cooler climes and barely qualify for a driver's license.

Furriner: Depending on how colloquial the community, someone not from around here. The term always applies to a Dam'yankee.

Gamecock: Jacksonville State (AL), University of South Carolina (called Gamehens or Gamechickens by disdainful sports opponents).

Gator: University of Florida.

Georgia Peach: Any lovely lady from Georgia, which is known for its succulent peach crop.

Class of 1909, Wynne (AR) High School

Good ol' Boy: A good fellow of any age who exhibits an agreeable nature, and who just wants everyone to get along.

Gullah: An African American person descended from former slave inhabitants living in the islands and coastal lowlands of South Carolina and Georgia. Retained their cultural heritage and still speak a region-specific Gullah (also called Geechee) dialect. Really cool baskets.

Halfback: The folks who left Yankeeland (Michigan, Illinois, Ohio, Rhode Island, New York and New Jersey) for Boca, but couldn't take the heat or the culture. Moved halfway back to the Carolinas as a compromise, and now make everyone else miserable whining about missing home.

Hillbilly: Person who lives in or comes from the backwoods of the mountain regions of the South; used as a derogatory term for someone ignorant. Think Li'l Abner (see Ernest T. Bass and the Darlings on *The Andy Griffith Show*).

Hokie: Virginia Tech (Virginia Polytechnic Institute).

Horned Frogs: Texas Christian University.

Hornets: Alabama State, NBA's New Orleans (originally Charlotte Hornets).

Jaguars: Southern University and A&M College (Baton Rouge), NFL's Jacksonville Jaguars.

Keydets: Virginia Military Institute.

Longhorn: University of Texas at Austin.

Mountaineer: Appalachian State, Berea College.

Majors: Millsaps.

Mustang: Southern Methodist University (SMU).

Owls: Rice, Florida Atlantic.

Panther: Birmingham Southern, Claflin, Georgia State, NFL'S Carolina Panthers.

Patriots: Old Dominion, Francis Marion (NOT New England).

Ragin' Cajun: University of Louisiana at Lafayette (formerly S.W. Louisiana).

Ram: Virginia Commonwealth, Winston-Salem State.

Rattler: Florida A&M.

Razorback: University of Arkansas.

Rebel: University of Mississippi (Ole Miss). Originally a derogatory term used by non-Southerners when referring to all Southerners after The Late Unpleasantness. Nowadays it's not proper to refer to all Southerners as Rebels.

Redneck: Originally, but nowadays not necessarily, a type of Southerner. A rube, who drinks beer, has a gut if of the masculine gender, from hanging out in honkytonks, listening to Hank Williams, Jr., and watching NASCAR from a lawn chair in the center field with the cooler of beer and fried chicken. Wears a cap to the table at the Red Lobster until someone smacks it off'n him. Wears four-inch heels with Daisy Dukes, and cowgirl boots with short skirts, if of the feminine gender. (See Gretchen Wilson's "Redneck Woman" lyrics for additional specifics pertaining to feminine-gender rednecks. Also see Tacky, tacky tacky, and beyond tacky.)

Ricecake: A person with no taste.

Ridgerunner: A person from way up yonder in the mountains.

Scalawag: A rascal. Originally coined to refer to white Southern rascals who aided the carpetbaggers or who otherwise illegally mistreated their fellows during Reconstruction.

Seminole: Florida State University.

Tar Heel: Any person native to North Carolina; University of North Carolina at Chapel Hill.

Terrapin: University of Maryland (not really Southern anymore, but included coz they're in the ACC and south of the Mason-Dixon line).

Tiger: Clemson, Louisiana State University, University of Memphis (formerly Memphis State), Auburn, Tennessee State, Savannah State, Jackson State, Grambling State, Hampden Sydney, Stillman, Sewanee (University of the South), Morehouse (Maroon Tigers).

Touron: (Tourist Moron) The winter people populating south Florida between Christmas and June. Left NC for warmer climes and zero state tax, but make no allowances for the elderly driving their El Dorados.

Trojan: Virginia State.

Volunteer: Any person native to Tennessee; University of Tennessee at Knoxville (commonly called Vols).

Wolfpack: North Carolina State University, Loyola of New Orleans.

Yellow Jackets: Georgia Tech (also Ramblin' Wrecks).

MOST MEMORABLE SOUTHERN SCHOOL SPIRIT CATCHPHRASES

And when I die I'm a Tar Heel dead, so ra-ra Carolinalina

Good Old Rocky Top

Tiger Bait!

Hook 'em Horns

Hotty Toddy Gosh A'mighty Who the Hell are We

Mother So Dear

Roll Tide

Woo Pig Sooie!

War Eagle!!!!

The sound of cowbells

Louis Bloom and Butch Daltroff, in Wynne, AR

SOUTHERN LOCATIONS DEFINED

Appalachians: A system of mountain ranges, valleys and plateaus that are divided into the Northern section, the Central section, and the Southern section, which runs from Virginia through North Carolina, Tennessee, and the northwestern corner of South Carolina into Georgia. Includes the Cumberland Plateau running through Kentucky, Tennessee, Georgia, Alabama, and Mississippi. Originally home to educated Indian tribal groups (written language, living in long houses) whom the American government tried to run off (Trail of Tears). A settlement refuge for Scots immigrants shipped over by the English in exchange for a pledge not to engage in sedition against the Crown (think Bonnie Prince Charlie vs. King George II). Southern Appalachian folkways have profoundly influenced American culture. Bluegrass. Clogging. Weaving. Pottery. Basketry. Woodworking. Metalsmithing. Glassblowing. Moonshinin'. NASCAR.

Appalachian Trail: A 2,175-plus-miles foot-trail that runs from Maine to Georgia, through 14 states; developed between 1921 and 1937.

Back 40: Farthest out-of-reach part of a person's property or geographic locale. The back 40 acres were always the toughest to get to and to work.

Bayou: A term coined by the Choctaw Indians of Mississippi, and first used by the English, who relocated the French Canadian Acadians to Bayou Lafourche and Bayou des Ecores in Louisiana. Acadians called such lowlands "bas lieu," similar to the Choctaw word "bayuck" for the region, referring to a small slow-moving stream or creek, or to lakes or pools in overflow river channels along the coast. Bayou country includes the coastal Mississippi River region between Houston and Mobile, and is centered around New Orleans.

The Beach: Galveston, Gulfport, Gulf Shores, Ocean Isle, Destin, Pensacola, Daytona, N. Myrtle, S. Myrtle, Windy Hill, Virginia, and the Islands known as South Padre, the Outer Banks, Sanibel, Captiva, Jeckyll, Cumberland, Sea, Bald Head, Kiawah and Hilton Head.

Between 4 and Plumb: Four miles from nowhere and plumb outta sight.

Big D: Dallas, TX. Home of the Cowboys, Jerry's World, and the Cotton Bowl. The Cotton Exchange moved there from Memphis in 1984, and with it the Maid of Cotton beauty competition. Over-the-top is a way of life.

Big Easy: New Orleans (pronounced N'awlins), also known as the Crescent City. Who Dat Nation. Jazz. Liquor. Food. Party Central. Even Katrina couldn't kill her off. Besides, what would the vampire cultists do without her? Where Mardi Gras started two minutes after the 2010 Saints' Super Bowl win—winding down ONLY AFTER Fat Tuesday with a N'awlins funeral for the old loser-Aints. Some folks are still celebrating.

Big Muddy: The mighty Mississippi River.

Big Orange Country: Primarily East Tennessee, or anywhere more than two Tennessee Vols congregate.

Bluegrass State: Kentucky. Considered a Southern state when it suits the politicos, but everyone knows it's a Border State, except for its bourbon, horses, and bluegrass music.

Mississippi Blues Trail marker

Blues Trail: The Mississippi Blues Trail. Marks and commemorates development of the unique blues music genre of the Southern Delta region along the Mississippi River; runs from Memphis, TN, to the Mississippi-Louisiana border. Hot music is everywhere. Where Robert Johnson sold his soul to the devil to play great guitar.

Bluff City: Memphis (pronounced Mi-fiss), high on a bluff overlooking the Big Muddy. Nashville's tough, jaded cousin. Seen it all. Done it all. Survived it all. Where for a time, raucous river-town politics were reined in under the iron-fisted benevolence of Boss Crump. Where W.C. Handy launched the Blues, which Sun and Stax Records sent forth along with Soul and Rock 'n Roll. Music still rules, but the bankers haven't figured it out yet.

Bottoms or Bottomland: Extremely fertile alluvial plains beside rivers in the valleys at the foot of the hills (see *Sergeant York*).

Catty Cornered: Diagonal, from one corner to the opposite corner.

Catty-wampus: Awry or askew, not centered. Not in a straight line.

The Club: Once upon a time, the center of every socially aspiring Southerner's golf and party activities. Not so much anymore.

Death Valley: The football stadium in the heart of Baton Rouge, on the campus at Louisiana State University (LSU), where Mike the Tiger roars loud enough to register on the Richter Scale.

Delmarva Peninsula: The peninsula of land that includes portions of Delaware, Maryland and Virginia, bordered on the west by the Chesapeake Bay, and on the east by the Delaware River, Delaware Bay, and Atlantic Ocean. The Mason-Dixon line ran right through it.

Delta: A regional term referring to the Mississippi River lowlands, running from Memphis down through southwestern Mississippi and southeastern Arkansas; the area historically farmed for the best cotton produced in the Old South.

Eastern Shore: The eastern side of the Chesapeake Bay, including the portions of Delaware, Maryland and Virginia that jut around the Bay.

Fur piece: A long way.

Glory: Heaven.

God's Acre: Sacred cemetery where one's corporeal body finds its eternal rest while the Spirit goes on to Glory. The cemetery at Home Moravian Church in Old Salem, NC, or at any Moravian church.

Hell and High Water: That place where you're between two impossible options—maybe no way out.

Highlands: The mountainous region of North Carolina between Asheville, Boone and Lenoir, centered around Mount Mitchell and Grandfather Mountain, and including Linville Gorge, Banner Elk and Blowing Rock. Geographically similar to the Blue Ridge Highlands in southwestern Virginia, which covers 14 counties running from the North Carolina line to the West Virginia line. Not to be confused with the town of Highlands, deep in the Nantahala Forest of southwest North Carolina, which, at an elevation of 4,118 feet, is one of the highest incorporated municipalities east of the Rockies, and also the coolest place in the South during the summer.

Hill Country: Rolling rugged hill region of Central Texas, housing the second largest granite outcropping in the United States. Great resort getaway and hunting region that extends between San Antonio and Austin. Not to be confused with north Mississippi Hill Country.

Hills: Includes Ozarks, Appalachians, Smokies, Blue Ridge (See The Mountains)

God's Acre in Old Salem, Winston-Salem, NC

Holler: Both a noun and a verb. A holler is that low-dipping area between mountains. To holler is to shout or yell.

Holy City: Charleston, SC, also known as Chucktown. The most romantic hurricane- and quake-prone metropolis since Atlantis; where religious tolerance has been advocated and practiced since its founding in 1670 by Anthony Ashley Cooper, namesake of the (Ashley and Cooper) rivers flanking the downtown peninsula. Whose Citadel cadets brought Antebellum North-South differences to a rolling boil. Where the parallel and perpendicular grids of downtown identify a resident's psyche: Those living south of Broad are known as SOBs, and those living Slightly North of Broad are SNOBs. Where to be Hugo'd means to be brought to your knees, but never defeated.

Hostess City of the South: Savannah, GA, the first Georgia colony settlement, established by James Oglethorpe in 1733. Whose gardens were so beautiful that General Sherman gave the city to President Lincoln as a Christmas present in 1864, rather than burn it like Atlanta. Saved again in the 1950s by local steel magnolias dedicated to historic preservation. Those eccentric gardens have lit the fantasies of book lovers everywhere. (See *Midnight in the Garden of Good and Evil.*)

Hotlanta: Atlanta, GA, the South's super city, where Peach and Peachtree are parts of at least 55 (or 71) street names. Thank Heaven for MARTA. And please, dear Lord, let us get off'n I-285 afore we get kilt. Whose Hartsfield-Jackson airport is the artsy city-within-a-city where Delta Airlines reigns supreme. (As we say down South, "Whether St. Peter sends you to Heaven or Hell, you'll have to change planes in Atlanta first.")

Just down the road: A distance away that can be short or long, depending on how fit you are.

Wetlands in Louisiana.

Kingdom Come: That distant place longed for by the devout, having reference to The Rapture in the Christian *Bible* "Book of Revelations."

Live Music Capital: Austin, the Lone Star State capital and home of the Longhorns. Where folks say Willie Nelson kicked off a citywide block party that's still going on after 30 years.

Lone Star State: Texas. Of course, the South pretty much ends at Dallas and Galveston, but we include the rest of the Lone Star State coz all Texans like a good drink, big hair, jewelry, and beauty queens, and can pitch a righteous hissy fit when appropriate. And coz the original Texian Army volunteers came from Tennessee, Louisiana, Mississippi, Alabama, Georgia, Virginia, and the Carolinas.

Low Country: That region of Atlantic coastal plains encompassing eastern South Carolina, centered around Charleston and stretching over to Savannah, Georgia. Good things come from the Low Country.

Magnolia State: Mississippi. Birthplace of America's music, the Blues.

The Mountains: The Ozarks, Smokies, Blue Ridge, Appalachians...and all the little mountain ranges in between.

Music City: Nashville, home of the Grand Ol' Opry and more stars than you can shake a stick at. The Parthenon. The Hermitage. Where the music community was already raising money for the 2010 Cumberland River flood victims while aquarium piranhas were still loose in the Opry Mills Mall.

Natchez Trace: 444-mile-long parkway on what was the original 440-mile-long Indian and animal trail from what is now Natchez, MS, through northwest Alabama and ending at the salt licks of middle Tennessee near Nashville, connecting the Cumberland, Tennessee and Mississippi rivers.

The Natural State: Arkansas. Best back woods in America.

The Old Dominion: Virginia.

The Ozarks: Divided geologically into four sections: the Springfield Plateau, Salem Plateau, Saint Francois Mountains, and Boston Mountains. The Boston Mountains, located in north central Arkansas, comprise the highest, and the Ozarks merge southward into the Ouachita Mountains of Arkansas to form the U.S. Interior Highlands, commonly called the Ozarks, which are the largest and longest mountainous terrain between the Appalachians and the Rockies. As they say in the Ozarks, "it's not that the mountains are so high, it's just that the valleys are so deep." The culture has been altered since the 1960s by the damming of various rivers for flood control and water resource management. Dogpatch's Li'l Abner, Mammy Yoakum and Daisy Mae wouldn't recognize it.

Palmetto State: South Carolina.

Peach State: Georgia.

Pearly Gates: The entrance to Glory, guarded by St. Peter, who's waiting to check you in or pass you by.

Pelican State: Louisiana.

Piedmont: The plateau region sandwiched between the Atlantic coastal plains and the Appalachians, running from New Jersey down to north central Alabama. At its broadest in North Carolina. Biggest cities in the southern Piedmont are Atlanta, Charlotte, the Triad (Winston-Salem-Greensboro-High Point), and the Triangle (Raleigh-Durham-Chapel Hill). Known for many things, including the Piedmont Blues and that danged red-clay dirt that won't wash out of anything.

Pine Hills: Areas of several Southern states where the pine forests are dense, particularly in Mississippi, Alabama, the Carolinas and Georgia.

Piney Woods: A coniferous forest region of the South that runs from southwestern Louisiana into east Texas, southern Arkansas, and southeastern Oklahoma, bounded by Mississippi lowland forests, western Gulf coastal grasslands, east central Texas forests and blackland prairies; and the Ozark mountain forests. In Mississippi, known as the place where the land, cattle and people were no good until 1909, when Dr. Lawrence Jones started the Piney Woods Country Living School under a tree.

Purt near: Fairly close by.

Queen City: Charlotte, NC, named after Queen Charlotte of England. Financial capital of the South. Where even the last Billy Graham Crusade didn't stop the orange-barrel construction brigade. Where street names start nowhere and begin again four more times somewhere else. (As folks say around here, "Just who WAS Sharon?")

Right fur: Really far away.

Right near: Really close by.

Sandhills: Strip of sandy land in the Carolinas separating Piedmont from Atlantic Coastal Plains.

Space City: Houston, TX, the fourth largest city in the U.S.; founded in 1836 and named after Republic of Texas President Sam Houston. Where residents are either inside or outside the 610 Loop. Home of NASA's manned space center, and source of modern catchphrases "Houston, we have liftoff. Houston, we have touchdown. Houston, we have a problem." Whose hospitable citizens welcomed 150,000 Katrina refugees even while having to flee their own hurricane (Rita).

Smack dab: Right in the middle of something.

Sunshine State: Florida.

Swamp: The wet, spongy marshland or bog that always has brackish water, cypress knees, egrets and herons, and that really floods during the rainy season; close by the wetlands. Full of critters such as cottonmouths and water moccasins, and an occasional alligator, depending on locale.

Mike VI at home in Death Valley, Baton Rouge, LA

Tamale Trail: A designated Mississippi food trail from Natchez to Tunica, with sidepaths over to Jackson and Corinth; centered in the Delta, most specifically Greenville.

Tar Heel State: North Carolina, sometimes called The Old North State (of the two Carolinas). Also known as the "Vale of Humility sandwiched between two mountains of conceit" (Virginia and South Carolina).

Tidewater: Although there are non-Southern locales with tidewater areas, this term generally refers to the southeastern Virginia coastal area that includes Virginia Beach, Williamsburg and Norfolk.

Tiger Country: Anywhere near LSU, whose Bayou Bengal tiger fans are referred to as swamp cats by disdainful SEC opponents; and anywhere near Clemson, SC, where the orange tiger paws mark the highway into town.

Volunteer State: Tennessee.

Wetlands (see swamp): A low-lying flat area that floods whenever it rains and that catches overflow from the nearby swamp. Also full of creepy crawlers. Loved by ducks and cattails.

Yellowhammer State: Alabama. Heart of Dixie.

Yonder: Way out there.

SOUTHERN FAMILY NUANCES

Aunt: A familial term that applies to your mama and daddy's sister, and to dear family female friends old enough to be your mama and daddy's sister. (See Uncle.)

Uncle: A familial term that applies to your mama and daddy's brother, and to dear family male friends old enough to be your mama and daddy's brother. (See Aunt.)

Brother: (1) A type of priest or preacher. (2) Male sibling, or any male with whom you have, or seek to have, a bond. Southern men sometimes are nicknamed Brother. Bubba is a derivative nickname.

Sister: (1) A type of nun or female preacher. (2) Female sibling, or any female with whom you have, or seek to have, a bond. Many families contain at least one female relative known to everyone as Sister or Sissy.

Miz (or Miss): Must be used with a woman's last name as a sign of courtesy and respect when she is not a family friend and is at least 10 years older than you. Also frequently used as a prefix before a first name, as a term of respect for a close female

Drs. Enos, Jim and Norman Thurmond, Mary Elizabeth Daltroff, Miz Lilla Callicott, Ruth Thurmond, and little Cindy Thurmond relaxing after Sunday dinner in Halls, TN

friend old enough to be your mama or your child's mama. (See Mr.)

Mr.: Must be used with a man's last name as a sign of courtesy and respect when he is not a family friend and is at least 10 years older than you. Also frequently used as a prefix before a first name, as a term of respect for a close male friend old enough to be your daddy or your child's daddy. (See Miz.)

Who are your people? Southern genealogy is complex, but we all know who's related to whom by blood, marriage and real estate. It's important to get a fix on a new acquaintance's position within the hierarchy.

Who's your daddy? Not a Maury Povich DNA question. It's a question of patriarchal job status, and also who his people are.

What's your mama's maiden name? Also couched as Who's your mama? (See Who are your people.)

Where are you from? Do not mistake this question for a geography reference to your most recent place of residence. It means, where were you born, even if you moved at age 2 months.

Kissin' kin: Any relative not jailable for potential commitment of incest with you, such as your second cousin once removed; or anyone in the Southern gene pool who can trace their family ancestry back to the same great-great-great as yours.

Where do you go to church? An important question asked of all newcomers, to properly identify where the newcomer will fit into the communal pool of social and benevolent activities. If you aren't currently affiliated, and you aren't religious, lie.

SOUTHERN PERSONALITY DESCRIPTIONS

Aggravating (pronounced aggravatin'): Acting or behaving in a manner guaranteed to annoy your family or anyone else. A situation that produces the same results.

Cussed: (pronounced cuss-ed) See Ornery.

Cute: A fair-to-middlin' ALMOST-compliment. Not always praise.

Darling (pronounced darlin'): Both a noun and an adjective. As an adjective, the term refers to someone or something quite favorable. (See Precious.) As a noun, used as a high term of endearment for loved ones, friends, recent acquaintances and

strangers toward whom you are feeling kindly at the moment.

Fast: Mostly refers to a female considered too knowledgeable about unmentionable sexual matters, who lets everyone know it, especially the good-lookin' men.

Flashy: Different from tacky, in that she wears sequins to the Steeple Chase, but knows no better, bless her heart.

Good enough for what she/he is: Not above his or her class or station in life; appropriate.

Heifer: A big ol' girl, a bit on the trashy side of proper.

High falutin': Acting too fancy for the present company or occasion (think over the top).

Honey: Both a common noun referring to the sweetness produced by bees for our use in poultices and tea with lemon, and a proper noun used as a term of endearment for loved ones, recent acquaintances and strangers toward whom you are feeling kindly at the moment, but in a smaller way than Darlin'... sometimes expanded to Honeychild or Honeybunch.

Interesting: Adjective. Vague way of NOT saying that something is boring, no account, or beneath your notice.

The Nineteenth Century Club
invites you to be present at the
Cotton Carnival Ball
honouring
Princess Amelia Russell
and
Prince William H. Williams
on Wednesday, the fourteenth of May
nineteen hundred and forty-seven
at nine o'clock
Town Club
1447 Union Avenue
Memphis, Tennessee

Cotton Carnival revolved around high falutin' moments. Like my godfather, Slick Williams, my brother Andy later served as a club prince.

Horticulturist Felder Rushing with his traveling Ford F-150 Truck Garden, complete with bottle tree lawn ornament by Stephanie Dwyer.... Friends say he's getting uppity.

PHOTO COURTESY OF FELDER RUSHING

Nice: Another oblique way to avoid saying anything negative in response to a statement or someone's appearance.

No count (no account): Worthless, having no values or upbringing, acting beneath the circumstances.

Not from around here: A term used to describe someone unfamiliar with our local ways, such as someone from three counties away or the next state over. REALLY not from around here: From Yankeeland, or from some foreign country where folks don't even speak English.

Ornery: Cranky and disagreeable, usually by genetic heritage, and therefore beyond your control, bless your heart. (See Cussed.)

Piddlin' or piddlin' around: Wasting time.

Precious: Adorable and wonderful. High praise, supreme complimentary description. (See Darling.)

Shiftless: A real lay-about, not inclined to be a productive member of society; usually by inclination as much as by heritage.

Smart as a whip: Stinging you with rapier wit and insight; if you've ever been struck by a lashing whip, you'll understand what smarts.

Sorry: Worthless and beneath contempt. (See Shiftless.) Often used to infer inbreeding in the sorry so-and-so's bloodline, sometimes with the companion observation that they have a lot of nooses in their family.

Sweet thing (pronounced thang, sometimes interchangeable with Miss Thang): An oblique barb. Not a compliment.

Tacky: Not gracious. Certainly not classy. Somewhat cheap or trashy. A fundamental concept in Southern culture that is particularly significant for Southern Belles.

Tacky Tacky: Really tacky.

Beyond Tacky: The ultimate kiss-off. Beyond redemption. Didn't your mama teach you better?

Tough as leather: Or more precisely, tough as shoe- or whet-leather. A person who's been around the block more'n once or twice whom you cannot fool, and who can take or dole out enough punishment to strip the varnish off'n a table. Usually your AP U.S. History teacher. Sometimes interchanged with "tough as nails" or "tough as a one-eared alley cat."

Trailer Trash: A negative reference to one's lifestyle and philosophy, rather than to one's financial portfolio or abode, although the implication is that living in a mobile home is less than desirable. Think tornado path. (See *My Name is Earl.*) Not to be confused with **po' white trash**, an extremely derogatory term referring to Caucasians behaving with no class whatsoever. (As the actor George Hamilton and all the cotton people used to say, "It's okay to be broke, but one must never act poor.")

Trashy: Low class, beyond beyond-tacky. Someone who may or may not hail from humble origins, but certainly behaves and lives in a manner that implies cheapness and meanness.

Triflin': Wasting everyone's time by not living up to innate potential. Capable of doing much better, unlike someone who's sorry, shiftless or no count. (See Aggravating.)

Uppity: Pretentious. Acting like someone you're not, as though trying to impress others with how much better you are.

Vulgar: Usually applies to unacceptable comportment in public by a Southern female, such as

Chewing gum or tobacco

Spitting

Smoking standing up or on the street

Eating crawfish anywhere but at a picnic

Using paper plates and plastic forks for sit-down company (See Tacky)

Using Miracle Whip instead of Duke's, Hellmann's, or homemade mayonnaise in the chicken salad, the pimiento cheese, or the aspic (also see Tacky)

Wearing white shoes after Labor Day and before Memorial Day (REFERENCE: the former Duchess of York in Houston, TX, November, 1989; see Tacky tacky)

Wearing blue eyeshadow before sundown

Wearing an ankle bracelet or visible tattoo anytime (see Beyond Tacky)

Wild as a peach orchard hog: Totally out of control. You'd better stay out of this person's way, coz nothing's coming between her and the object of her desire.

Worldly: Someone whose behavior or appearance reflects a flashy lifestyle; also one who has lost the aura of innocence. An oblique, ladylike way of referring to a woman as a trashy ho.

Wouldn't eat pie in a pie factory: Someone who acts contrary just for the heck of it. (See Ornery or Cussed.)

SOUTHERN DESCRIPTIVE PHRASES, NOUNS AND ADJECTIVES

Altar Call: The closing moments at the Baptist, Presbyterian, and Methodist church services, referring to a solicitation aimed at saving your soul.

Baby Box: A trailer or the small ranch-style homes that are lined up in neat rows on small lots with few trees, inhabited by young folks having babies.

Bag: Accessory a lady fills with her wallet and lipstick and other necessities. Also known as a pocketbook.

Beach Music: Not California surf songs; but rather, 1950s rhythm and blues songs made for dancing the Shag at Myrtle Beach, SC. (See *Bull Durham*.)

Big ol': Generic prefix to a noun.

Calaboose: The jail. The hoosegow.

Chinchy: Really stingy, as in "He's the chinchiest old coot since Jack Benny."

Clogging: A type of buckwing dancing derived from Irish dance, indigenous to the Southern mountain region.

Come-to-Jesus meeting: Mandatory confrontation during which the confrontee is going to be told something in no uncertain terms, face-to-face and eyeball-to-eyeball.

Conniption (see fit and hissy): Everyone knows one pitches a fit or hissy fit. One throws a tantrum. One may have a conniption, which is an explosive outburst just shy of a stroke. No ambulance needed. Yet.

Coot: Someone over 60 who's still frisky. In some locales, extended to "Cootie (or Cooter) Brown."

Cover/Covers: The sheet, blanket, quilt, bedspread, and other fabrics that one pulls up over one's reclining body in a bed.

Cotton Carnival Queen and her Court, circa 1946, in high cotton

PHOTO COURTESY OF THE COTTON MUSEUM, MEMPHIS COTTON EXCHANGE

Covered dish: Interchangeable with potluck, referring to a meal-time gathering to which everyone attending brings food.

Doohickey: A thingamabob. Something concrete, but indescribable.

Dresser: The three- or four-drawer piece of furniture in which a person keeps folded clothes and doohickeys. A bureau is one of those government-related agencies whose representatives need to be taken with a grain of salt or looked at with a fine-toothed comb.

Everwho: Southern reversal of pronoun and adverb (from whoever).

Eyeball to eyeball: Two or more persons talk eyeball to eyeball, or have an eyeball-to-eyeball talk. Not exactly a confrontation, but a somewhat blunt meeting of the minds in a face-to-face discussion. Capisce?

Fit: One pitches a fit, which is a tantrum guaranteed to make the pitcher embarrassed once he or she calms down (see conniption and hissy)

Happy: A little gift of something special for a person who needs their spirits lifted, or just because you like that person. Folks around here love to drop off a little happy for their friends.

Hickory: Noun or adjective. As in "Go cut me off a hickory switch so I can wear you out."

Hissy: One pitches a hissy fit. It's not pretty, and the pitchee may or may not recover. (See Conniption and Fit.)

Homecoming: The special event at high school and college football games where the most popular girl used to be crowned. Not always a girl anymore. Not always based on popularity either. Also, the increasingly popular event at a Southern church, where the church founders are honored, and former members and their families are invited back for potluck dinner.

Homemade: Usually refers to something that is the product of one's diligent creation. Occasionally not a compliment.

Hoot: Noun or verb. Something is a hoot if it is an absolutely, deliciously, hilariously wonderful situation or state of being. As in "ain't it a hoot" or "what a hoot."

Cotton Carnival Barge at Beale Street Landing, Memphis, 1930s, where folks loved puttin' on the dog

PHOTO COURTESY OF THE COTTON MUSEUM, MEMPHIS COTTON EXCHANGE

Jackleg: Adjective and noun. Refers to an unscrupulous or dishonest and generally unskilled worker, or to something temporary or makeshift. Used frequently when referring to certain television and drive-through evangelists, certain roofing companies, and certain Mississippi, Louisiana and Arkansas country lawyers. You know who you are.

Lawn or Yard ornament: The bottle tree, wind chimes, bronze sculpture, and silver ball fountain in the garden, the pink plastic flamingos flanking the front stoop, the concrete deer in the side yard, or the 30-year-old horse that's been put out to pasture. NOTE: The old tub, freezer and '69 Camaro are NOT acceptable yard ornaments. The old toilet, on the other hand, is acceptable if painted blue and planted with petunias.

Lid: The covering that one screws, snaps or positions on top of something such as a jar, bottle or box.

New English: Spanish.

Paper poke: A paper bag. Same as a paper sack.

Peaked (pronounced pee-kid): A condition in which one appears pale or wan.

Pig in a Poke: You just don't know what you're getting.

Pistol: Someone who's really good at something or unpredictable in an interesting way. Or the firearm used by that someone.

Play pretty: A noun referring to some toy or frivolous object such as jewelry.

Pocketbook: A purse.

Poke: A sack or bag.

Polecat: A skunk. A really bad person. That's why you want to skin 'em.

Pot luck: The dinner where everyone brings a dish to be shared by the group (see Covered dish); or refers to that chance a person is gonna take without knowing the outcome.

Pow-wow (also a verb): A serious sit-down meeting intended to resolve issues once and for all.

Robe Church: Just can't make it out of the house for the Sunday morning service. Instead, opt to watch the television evangelists, or listen to your preacher via the local radio broadcast.

Sack: The bag one uses to carry one's groceries home from the grocery store.

Sofa vs. couch: A couch is like a Roman recliner or lounge. A sofa is the essential long piece of furniture in the living room or family room that has arms at both ends and seats at least three comfortably.

Puny: Weak and sickly. (See Peaked.)

Store-bought: Not homemade. Depending on what it is, the term can be derogatory or a compliment.

Stuck up like a stump full of granddaddies: Refers to a person's hair (or anything) going every which way, like a tree stump full to overflowing with granddaddy long-leg spiders.

Sucker: The sticky lollipop that one licks and sucks with one's tongue and mouth. Used by folks not from around here to refer to a gullible person.

Todefrawg: Used interchangeably to refer to either a toad or a frog, the amphibian that drowned in the pool skimmer, which tastes good fried up like chicken.

Towsack: A bag used for hauling something.

Who-Shot-John: Any ol' person who thinks he or she is All That.

Y'all -- All y'all -- All y'all's: The first Southern expression picked up by folks not from around here. Y'all is singular (used when addressing a group; never used when addressing a lone individual). All y'all is plural (used when expanding the group being addressed). All y'all's is plural possessive.

SOUTHERN VERBS, ADVERBS & ACTION STATEMENTS

4-60: Environmentally green natural air-conditioning whereby one rolls down the four windows in an automobile traveling 60 miles per hour.

Badmouth: To disparage someone by opening your mouth and letting the bad words come on out.

Barking up the wrong tree: That ol' hound dog got confused.

Busy as a funeral home fan in July: When the humidity is above 90% and the temperature is above 90 degrees, air conditioning simply is not enough—those paper fans on a stick can make such a difference if one waves them fast and hard enough. (Interchangeable with Busy as a blind man at a strip show, or Busy as a bee in a field of clover.)

Carry on: To overdo your actions or make a big fuss (see Cut up).

Chunk: To throw or toss something.

Circle the wagons: What happens when like-minded friends, family and acquaintances come together to protect each other, to help someone out, or to give someone else a hard time.

Good ol' boys, belles, artists, musicians and farmers convene at the farmers' market, Taylor, MS.

Cotton to: A verb, "to cotton to" is to take kindly to someone or some situation. Remember, the historical nuances of cotton economics and cotton culture are fundamental concepts pertaining to goodness, plenty and accomplishment in the South.

Covered up: Overwhelmed.

Crank up: To start, usually referring to a motor of some sort (as in crank up the car).

Crossed, Crossed over: Has both genealogical and Biblical connotations. Refers to a person of mixed race or cultural heritage (usually Caucasian plus African or American Indian) being known for the Caucasian heritage only. Also refers to crossing between corporeal existence on the earthly plane into Heaven (or Hell, depending on the individual). Both references are interchangeable with Passed or Passed On.

Cut on/out the lights: To turn on or off at the switch.

Cuttin' the fool: Acting foolish, just joking around.

Cut up: To show off or act out.

Dogging our steps: To follow closely like a shadow (as in "to heel").

Do it up brown: Make it right, like your roux.

Dressing down/Dress him down: A blistering or scathing talking-to given to someone who needs it. Guaranteed to peel the fake right off'n him.

Druther: To prefer.

Egg on: To push into doing something probably not in the best interest of someone.

Favor: To resemble or be like. As in "he favors his daddy"

Fixing (pronounced fixin'): A noun and a verb. A fixin' or fixings would be parts that make up something such as dinner.. "Fixing to" is the statement of preparing to do something such as go.

Getting your ears lowered: A male haircut, with particular attention to shortening the hair above the ears.

Gimme some sugar: That moment when your great-aunt puts a lip lock on you and leaves you branded with her cherry-red lipstick.

Hankerin': A desire for something.

Having a dog in that show or a pony in that race: A vested interest.

He's bird-doggin' the problem: Right on top of the situation, following up with no deviation from form, like the winner of the National Field Trials at Grand Junction, TN.

Laying in, Laying by, Laying on: As in laying in supplies or laying by while someone else does the work, or laying on of hands to heal or comfort. Not to be confused with proper English differentiation between LIE, referring to the verb about a stationary (usually horizontal) thing, or the noun about an untruth; and LAY, the verb, when there is something being placed from one position (usually vertical) to another.

Lick and a promise: To do something in a hurried, perfunctory manner in order to get by—like the cleaning lady the week after you shorted her pay by $20, or when the boss calls and gives you five minutes' notice before coming over.

Like to: A Memphis-Delta twist on combining words to form an adverb substituted for Nearly. As in, "I like to have died," or "I like to been run over."

Listen up: I want you to pay very close attention to what I'm about to tell you. I may not repeat it, but I expect you to remember and act accordingly.

Look at with a fine-toothed comb: To examine and inspect closely. Think nitpicking.

Loud: Those red onions smell real loud.

Make/Make out: Not just what you did in the back seat of the '57 Chevy. What you do around the South when you need to pull together something, such as your meal. In southern Louisiana, it's what you do when you buy groceries.

Mash the button: To press for the purpose of starting.

Mind to: To have the intention of doing something, as in "I have a mind to take the hickory to you for cutting your baby sister's bangs."

Pick at: To pester or annoy, or to do something with a lick and a promise rather than a whole mind to.

Pining away: Plumb puny, wasting away with grief.

Play nice: Be good.

Play possum: Act like you're asleep or dead; pretend not to hear or notice something.

Plug in or plug up: To connect or fill something.

Put a lid on it: Bottle up that behavior right now … often stated when one of the kids is whining about how the others get treated better.

Puttin' on the dog: To make a fancy showing to impress someone.

Put up: To put something away, to prepare canned food, or to keep someone in one's home.

Recollect: To recall.

Shag: Not your shag carpet and not a sex act. Both a noun and a verb. It's a dance that one does to rhythm and blues songs such as "Sixty Minute Man." Made famous at Myrtle Beach during Sun Fun Week, and still going strong after more than 50 years. (See *Bull Durham* again)

Skin that cat: (as in polecat) Usually expressed as "There's more than one way to skin a cat."

Stir the pot: Your pickin' at the situation is gonna get everyone all fired up.

Stob: Both a noun and a verb. To stob is to accidentally hit yourself against something, such as stubbing your toe on the warped floorboard. As a noun, refers to that something that's sticking up just waiting for your toe to hit it.

Stop when it sounds expensive: When backing up a car.

Study: To ponder, to carefully consider; as in "Let me study on this a spell; I'll get back to you directly."

Take with a grain of salt: Activity or philosophy that needs a bit of seasoning to make it palatable (or even believable).

That dog won't point: Something's off, the whole concept is just wrong.

To carry: To transport.

Tolerable: Acceptable. Just barely.

Tone it down: Dial back your behavior about four clicks or the neighbors will start complaining.

Tune up: Both a noun and a verb. One gets a car tune-up. One tunes up when playing on the other's sympathy (tears) or when "harping" on a painful, unresolved circumstance.

Unlucky as a $50 bill: Even in the 21st Century, General Grant is not acceptable to folks from around here. Not even his picture.

Whistling Dixie: An essential concept regarding The Lost Cause. To perceive a situation, to engage in dialogue, or to have an attitude that's more optimistic than Real Life will allow. Pining away for the Great What Never Was, but that We Wish it Would Be.

Whole hog: Go ahead and throw the whole pig on the spit! There's no sense in being cheap or making a half-hearted effort.

Y'all come back now: Said out of courtesy to those departing, after much additional conversation.

Y'all might as well come on and go with us: Said by the departing ones to those from whom they are taking leave, when fond of them.

SOUTHERN EXCLAMATIONS, GREETINGS, THREATS AND EXPLETIVES

Southerners vocalize for every event, occasion, mishap or blip in time. It's our nature. But there are protocols we must follow. Southern ladies of a certain age never use the Lord's name in vain. If pushed to uttering an exclamation, they use imaginative alternatives when referring to the Creator and the Heavenly Host. Southern good ol' boys use descriptive expletives generally referring to their dog or intent to do bodily harm. They are not to be confused with trailer trash, po' white trash, or rednecks, who often incorporate four-letter obscenities.

Ain't that a bird dog

Bless his/her heart (Fundamental phrase of sympathy for use in all circumstances, particularly when at a loss for words to describe someone's erratic, unacceptable, inappropriate behavior, or inherent nature. The phrase may be stated as a stand-alone exclamation, but usually follows an observation about the erratic, unacceptable, inappropriate behavior, or inherent nature.)

Bless Patsy! (Bless Pat)

Dr. Hugh Crawford, Pat Daltroff, miniature schnauzer Curly, and pointers Loretta and Ralph, at Hugh's farm in Williston, TN

Bon temps (good times)

Dad burn it!

Don't lie to your mama

Fish or cut bait (interchangeable with s*** or get off the pot)

For crying out loud!

Good Lord willin' and the creeks don't rise

Goodness gracious!

Gracious mercy

Have mercy!

Hey (Southern version of saying hi or hello to an individual; hey y'all is for a group.)

Hola

Hotty Toddy (Gosh a'mighty)

I brought you into this world, and I can take you out

If things get any better I may have to hire someone to help me enjoy it

I got other fish to fry (Always used as part of an emphatic statement, as in "Make up your mind, I ain't got all day, I got other fish to fry.")

I'll be John Browned (damned)

I'll knock you clear into next week

I'll knock you into Kingdom Come!

I swan (derived from the Old English. Literally, I might swoon. Or, I swear.)

Laissez les bon temps rouler (Let the Good Times Roll)

Lord a'Mercy

Lord a'Mighty

My cow died last night so I don't need your Bull

Pshaw

Salud

Tarnation (As in what in tarnation caused you to set fire to the leaves under the swings?)

Well, butter my butt and call me a biscuit

Well, color me stupid!

Well, kick the dog and smack the cat!

Well, won't that just frost your cookies!

Whatever floats your boat

Where yat?

You'll be waiting till Kingdom Come!

SOUTHERN IDOLS REDACTED

RECENT / CURRENT DEMIGODS
Living or deceased, they're with us every day.

Louis Armstrong: Pops. Satchmo, come blow your Horn. America's Jazz Ambassador.

Drew Brees: The quarterback experts had doubted, who brought class and heart back to New Orleans and a sympathetic tear to the nation's eyes as we watched him hug his baby immediately following the Saints' 2010 Super Bowl victory.

Paul "Bear" Bryant: Alabama's winning coach from 1958 to 1982, who might be said to have spawned the SEC steamroller still ruling inter-collegiate football. (See Bryant Stadium.)

Johnny Cash and June Carter Cash: The Man in Black and the woman what saved him.

Harry Connick, Jr.: Pride of N'awlins. Old Blue Eyes' heir who never forgot his roots.

Dale Earnhardt, Sr.: No. 3 reigns forever.

William Faulkner: The Man of Yoknapatawpha County changed the literary voice of America. Page-long sentences that still sound like music. The way every self-respecting Southerner should tell a story.

Aretha Franklin: Detroit may claim her, but the Queen of Soul was born in Memphis. R.E.S.P.E.C.T.

Morgan Freeman: The Voice. Could live anywhere. So came back home to Mississippi.

Rev. Billy Graham: Born on a dairy farm in Mecklenburg County, NC; biggest global evangelist of all time, advisor to every president since Ike. Too bad some asked him afterward instead of afore they needed it.

Grand Ol' Opry: Radio programming that shaped America (We Shield Millions, WSM). Nashville's ongoing gift to the world. Bill Monroe. Flat and Scruggs. Hank Williams. Patsy Cline. Chet Atkins. On and on and on and on....

John Grisham: Mississippi lawyer turned writer. Every moviemaker's dream writer, and all the local nonprofits' best friend.

Isaac Hayes: Shaft and South Park. Cooler than cool. Brought Memphis music full circle. Neighbor to all.

Jim Henson: Miss Piggy and Kermit and the gang gave us a new way of viewing the world.

BB King: The bluesman who is to the guitar as Pavarotti was to tenors. Oh sing to us, Lucille.

William Faulkner is very much alive in Oxford, MS.

Junior Johnson: Put the NASCAR in moonshinin'.

Michael Jordan: BASKETBALL. Carolina. Bulls. Charlotte Bobcats. A smidgin of baseball.

Gov. Huey Long: The Kingfish. Raised backroom politics to a new level. As Evita was to Argentina, Huey Long was to Louisiana. Folks are still conflicted.

Mary Kay (Ash): Founder of the cosmetics firm that put the pretty in pink. Enabled thousands of women to earn a good living,

Loretta Lynn: The Queen of Country. The hard way. An inspiration to all women.

The Manning Men: Archie, Cooper, Peyton, and Eli. Football and community service all the way, including a summer youth football camp.

The Marsalis Men: Ellis. Branford. Wynton. Jason. Delfeayo. Lord only knows what other talent they're nurturing in N'awlins and the Big Apple.

Miss America: The ultimate title for many an aspiring Southern Belle. It's a scholarship program, not a beauty contest (see *Miss Congeniality*). Not to be confused with Miss USA (see "flashy").

Miss Lillian (Carter): Nobody messes with Mama.

Miss Mississippi: Launch pad for Miss America.

Oprah: Born in Mississippi, finished school in Nashville after her family fetched her back from Milwaukee. She puts her money where her mouth is. Nobody disses Oprah. Who'd wanna?

Dolly Parton: No dumb blonde jokes need apply. Hiked up her assets and then some, to promote her natural abilities, and has provided income, education and musical joy to millions.

Richard Petty: To NASCAR as Michael Jordan was to basketball.

Elvis Presley: THE KING. Spotted last week at midnight at the Malco Theater. Do I have to explain how he changed American music?

Leontyne Price: This Aida could aria down the walls of Jericho.

Charley Pride: Kiss an Angel Good Mornin'. A great thing his baseball career got eclipsed by his guitar-pickin'. This Mississippi sharecropper's son broke down barriers in Country Music.

Buford Pusser: Never let a little violence get in his way making Tennessee a safer place to live.

Anne Rice: Turned creatures of darkness into Romance. Only in New Orleans!

Dean Smith: UNC-Chapel Hill (a.k.a. Carolina), to NCAA and ACC basketball, as Bear Bryant was to NCAA and SEC football (See Dean Dome, or Michael Jordan resumé.

Elizabeth Spencer: One of the South's great literary voices, this Mississippi-born writer and teacher ended up in Chapel Hill after years in Italy and Canada. In the record books for the scandal over the Pulitzer NOT awarded for her 1948 book about racial tensions. Themes still speak to us.

Herschel Walker: Herschel in Georgia. Mr. Heisman Trophy.

General Andrew Jackson's statue rises triumphant in Jackson Square, New Orleans, LA.

HISTORICAL DEMIGODS

They changed our world, and are henceforth on a pedestal.

Dan'l Boone

Jim Bowie

George Washington Carver

Davy Crockett

W.C. Handy

Nancy Hart ("War Woman" of the Georgia Frontier)

O. Henry (William Sydney Porter)

Sam Houston

Mahalia Jackson

Rev. Dr. Martin Luther King, Jr.

General Lafayette (Gilbert du Motier, Marquis de la Fayette)

Jean Lafitte

General Robert E. Lee (late President of Washington and Lee University)

General Francis Marion (Swamp Fox)

Edward R. Murrow

Flannery O'Conner

Rosa Parks

William Travis

Booker T. Washington

President George Washington

Eudora Welty

Eli Whitney

Tennessee Williams

Thomas Wolfe

TARNISHED DEMIGODS, BUT STILL REVERED BY MANY

Time has a way of revealing the truth.

General Nathan Bedford Forrest

President Andrew Jackson (Not to be confused with pore ol' President Andrew Johnson)

President Thomas Jefferson

Charles Kuralt

Senator Strom Thurmond

REDEEMED, PREVIOUSLY TARNISHED, HONORARY LATE DEMIGODDESS

Not BORN Southern, but should have been, and would have been.

Tammy Faye Bakker Messner

SOUTHERN STATE OR CONDITION

Addled: Confused or disoriented, like Aunt Rosie by 8 p.m., after cocktails.

All het up: Worked up, possibly unduly. Interchangeable with all fired up.

All vines and no taters: All talk and no action.

Bright-eyed and bushy-tailed: Fresh and perky.

Bumfuzzled: Confused, puzzled, or stumped by a situation, like you after your 18-year-old used the Oreck vacuum cleaner to de-leaf the patio.

Fat and sassy: Feeling as good as a well fed yearling in a spring meadow.

Fair to middlin': A cotton term. Okay, not good, but not so bad.

Fine as frog hair: Doing splendidly. Just wonderful.

Goobered up: Missing a few screws, or screwed up, not by choice so much as by natural ineptitude. (See Goober Pyle, *The Andy Griffith Show.*)

Gooder'n grits: It doesn't get much better than this.

Guilty as sin: Also guilty as homemade sin, guilty as teen-age sin. (See the *Ten Commandments.*)

Hammered: Been hittin' Papa's recipe a bit too heavily. (See the Baldwin sisters in *The Waltons.*)

Happy as a clam in sand at high tide: Extremely satisfied and comfortable. In your element. Where you belong.

Happy as a pig in mud: See clams.

Happy as a tick on a lazy dog: See clams and pigs.

Hell in a handbasket: As in going to. Why don't we just pack you up and give you to the Devil like a present?

Hog heaven: As happy as a pig in slop. Or mud.

Ill as a hornet: Irritable, readily provoked into stinging unpleasantness; like Auntie Doc when she caught us spitting off the third-floor balcony of her Central Park West apartment.

In a fix: Houston, we have a problem.

In high cotton: Doing extremely fine and well fixed. Another cotton term. High cotton (tall cotton) is what you want for a good crop so it doesn't get so wet or dusty, and is easier to pick.

Jimmy-rigged: A somewhat temporary fix using what you have available —"made do," usually with baling wire and duct tape. Known in the Ozarks as hillbilly engineering.

Kick up a ruckus: To cause a noisy disturbance.

Kicking up sand: To cause a ruckus or conflict out of meanness. (See ornery or cussed.)

Like white on rice: The way it's supposed to be.

Nervous as a long-tailed cat in a room full of rockers: Just thinking about it makes me nervous.

Numerous as fleas on a dog: You can't find just one.

Outta kilter: Crooked, not working properly, like the table legs after Uncle Harry evens them up.

Ox in a ditch: Generally stated as "Well, I see you got yore ox in a ditch." Meaning a person's gotten him or herself into a tight situation, sticky wicket, or deep hole, and is having a hard time working his or her way out. Outside help may be needed.

Porely (poorly): Not doing well.

Raise the roof: Make a loud (often joyful) noise. Relates to old-fashioned barn-raisings.

Scarce as hen's teeth: Have you ever found one?

Sick as a dog: So sick all you can do is just lie there and look pitiful.

Sharp as an alligator's tooth: So keen he or she might hurt you. Made for chomping. Do not test this at home.

Stuck up: See Uppity. Refers to one's nose sticking up in the air, as in "he's so stuck up he'd drown in a rainstorm."

Andrea Triplette in 1958, named Miss Lenoir Rhyne College in 1962; has always been as pretty as a speckled pup.

Tickled pink: Just so thrilled it makes you laugh and cry at the same time. Related to "In the pink", which implies you're healthy and fine. Think high cotton without the pomp.

Tizzy: One generally is in a tizzy, which is to be highly agitated and so stressed you can't settle down and just be bothered.

Under the weather: Feeling poorly.

Up to snuff: Meeting minimal requirements for excellence (only the best tobacco was used for snuff).

Wampy-jawed: Crooked.

Who licked the red off your candy: Who put you in a foul mood? (See all het up.)

CHARACTER DESCRIPTION, PHYSICAL ATTRIBUTES AND MISCELLANEOUS SUBSTITUTIONS

Ain't worth the powder it'd take to blow his brains out: Beneath your notice. Let it go.

As country as cornflakes: So simple. Not sophisticated like granola.

Bull-headed: Intractable and not nice about it.

Crooked as a snake: Bent. Not straight on any level. Inherently evil. Interchangeable with "So crooked you can't tell if he's coming or going."

He (or she) needs killin': We all know what sorts of behavior provoke that observation. Sworn to be a valid defense in some Southern states, according to Southern historians.

Lower than a boll weevil: As low-down-dirty, sneaky, underhanded and rotten as a person can get. The boll weevil did more damage to the South than General Sherman in his march to the sea. We're still recovering.

Mean enough to hunt a bear with a hickory switch: This person's just out looking for trouble for the heck of it.

Mule-headed: Stubborn, belligerent, pridefully ignorant, intractable and contrary for the heck of it. Often also mean enough to hunt a bear with a hickory switch.

Not worth shootin': So full of barnyard manure that you're not worth the price of the bullet for shooting.

Older'n dirt: Something or someone who's been around since the beginning of time. Or seems like it. Or acts like it.

Pig-headed: Stubborn in a stupid way.

Pretty as a speckled pup: What's more adorable than a six-week-old pointer?

Rode hard and put up wet: Exhausted-looking. Appearance seems to be the result of rough living or a difficult event (see Ugly).

Rough as a cob: Harks back to before toilet paper in the outhouse.

Slick as an eel: So unctuous in presentation and talking that he or she'd slide right on by if'n you had a holt of 'em.

So dull he can't cut butter with a hot knife: Wake me up when he's gone.

Tighter than Dick's hatband: Frugal. Cheap to the point of painful. Like a belt one size too small.

Towheaded: White-blond hair on a child, usually found in the Blue Ridge region.

Ugly: Connotes misbehavior or bad character, when referring to an action, as in "Don't act ugly." The word must be used with other words when describing a physical characteristic, such as:

* Fell out of the ugly tree and hit every branch on the way down

* So ugly she looks like the dogs have been keepin' her under the porch

* So ugly he'd make a freight train take a dirt road

* So ugly the cooties have to close their eyes

* So ugly her mama had to tie a pork chop around her neck to get the dog to play with her

* So ugly his mama had to borrow a baby to go to church

* So ugly his mama takes him everywhere to avoid kissing him goodbye

* Uglier'n homemade sin

* Uglier'n six miles of homemade mud fence

DESCRIPTION OF INTELLIGENCE LEVEL OR MENTAL STATE

About as sharp as a mashed potato

A couple of sandwiches shy of a picnic

As confused as a cow on Astro Turf

Clueless or Dimwitted:

* Can't walk and chew gum

* You'd have to chew their gum for them

Dumber than (pronounced dumber'n):

* A bag of hair

* A bag of hammers

* A bag of bricks

* A box of bricks

* A rock

* Dirt

Elevator doesn't go all the way to the top

Not the brightest bulb in the lamp

Even a blind squirrel finds a nut now and then

Even a hog finds an acorn once in a while

He couldn't find his backside with both hands in his pockets or a flashlight in each hand

He couldn't pour rain out of a boot with a hole in the toe and directions on the heel

He's got a big hole in his screen door

If dumb was dirt, he'd cover about a half acre

One brick short of a full load (or two or three or four, etc.)

One fry short of a Happy Meal

Only got one oar in the water

Sharp as a tack (opposite of "Not the sharpest tack in the toolbox")

She couldn't blow her nose if all her brains were dynamite

The engine's running but no one's driving

The porch light's on but nobody's home

The wheel's still turning but that hamster's dead

Were you raised in a barn?

AVOIDANCE OF THE WORD 'VERY'

Mighty

Awfully

Plumb

Right

SUBSTITUTION OF 'D' FOR 'S' AND POSITIONED BEFORE 'N'

Bidness

Wadn't

Idn't

Dudn't

DELETION OF THE FIRST SYLLABLE(S)

Backer (bacco)

Bama (Bammer)

Coon

Gator

Tater

MEASUREMENTS AND QUANTITIES

Dab

Eensie weensie

Glob

Gracious plenty

Liddle biddy (little bitty or itty bitty)

Mean

Mess

Passel

Piddlin'

Pinch

Smidge (smidgin/smidgen)

Tad

Teensie (eensie)

Touch

Dad and his cotton buddies loved to go hunting in Arkansas and north Mississippi.

SOBRIETY

Sober as a judge

Sober as a Mormon preacher on Sunday morning

Like Pat Boone when he wakes up

Drunk as a coot/skunk

Drunker'n Cootie Brown

Liquored up (pronounced likkered up)

Snockered

Three sheets to the wind

Tighter'n a tick on a lazy dog

SOUTHERNERS AND HOLLYWOOD

BEST TV PROGRAMS SET IN OR REFLECTING THE SOUTH

The Andy Griffith Show

My Name is Earl (Camden County, Everywhere, USA, Central Standard Time, is Southern, and we all know it.)

Designing Women

Bill Dance Outdoors

Friday Night Lights

Treme

The cooking shows: Paula (Deen), The Neelys, the late Justin Wilson, Nathalie Dupree, Emeril (who adopted us and our ways), etc.

Charlie Rose (He's from the South and his good breeding shows.)

MOST ENTERTAINING MOVIES ABOUT OR SET IN THE SOUTH

Gone with the Wind

To Kill a Mockingbird

Oh Brother Where Art Thou

Jezebel

Sergeant York

Cool Hand Luke

Bull Durham

Tin Cup

The Big Chill

A Streetcar Named Desire

All the King's Men (both versions: Broderick Crawford, Sean Penn)

Cat on a Hot Tin Roof

The Miracle Worker

Shenandoah

In the Heat of the Night

The Last Picture Show

Deliverance

The Longest Yard (the original)

The Last American Hero

Norma Rae

A Soldier's Story

The Color Purple

Crimes of the Heart

The Big Easy

Mississippi Burning

Ghosts of Mississippi

My Cousin Vinny

Forrest Gump

Midnight in the Garden of Good and Evil

The Green Mile

Fried Green Tomatoes

Driving Miss Daisy

Steel Magnolias

The Grisham Movies:
- *The Pelican Brief*
- *The Rainmaker*
- *The Firm*
- *The Client*
- *The Runaway Jury*
- *The Painted House*

Drumline

Hustle & Flow

Sweet Home Alabama

Cold Mountain

The Secret Life of Bees

The Blind Side

SOUTHERN WEATHER

Weather is one of the most important facets of Southern life. It changes daily, sometimes hourly. Non-Southerners cannot comprehend the nuances of a whole culture's lifestyle ruled by pondering when the sun's gonna shine or what's behind that cloudbank. We gauge the seasons by our weather conditions: Hot, cold, wet, dry or windy. Tornadoes, hailstorms, and floods in late winter, spring and summer. Droughts when least expected. Hurricanes in autumn (accelerating in early August when school starts, and peaking 'til Thanksgiving). Sudden freezes, record-breaking snowfall, and ice storms in the early spring. It all makes life interesting for us. Remember, we thrive in chaos.

Frog choker or frog strangler: Also known as a toad strangler. So much water descending so fast that it'd drown a frog.

Gulley washer: Not as bad as a frog strangler, but enough water descending fast enough to fill all the ditches and your side yard from the too-sudden runoff.

Raining so hard the animals are beginning to pair up: It's time to get out the boat and put the photos in ziplock baggies if you aren't gonna evacuate.

It's so foggy the birds are walking: Might as well park the car and go back inside.

It's so dry the creek's only running every other day: The annual drought has begun.

It's so dry the trees are bribing the dogs: The drought has gone on a bit too long.

Dry as cracker juice: The drought has really gone on too long and we might have to lower the boat dock.

So dry the catfish are carrying canteens: See "dry as cracker juice."

Dry as the dust in a mummy's pocket: Ashes to ashes, dust to dust—we might be looking at another Dust Bowl.

The devil's beating his wife: The mixed-up weather has it storming and sunny every few minutes.

Thicker 'n molasses: 100% humidity without rain.

Cold as a banker's heart: Think 2009 and mass home foreclosures.

Cold as a cast-iron commode: Try sitting on one at 6 a.m. in January.

Colder'n blue blazes (see hotter'n): Below freezing.

Colder'n a well-digger's butt: Below freezing and the wind's a'blowin'.

Colder than a witch's teat (see "Macbeth"): Below freezing for more than two days and nights in a row, possibly with digits falling into the teens.

Hotter'n blue blazes (abbreviated to hotter'n blazes): Above 90°.

Hotter'n Hell (see Hotter'n blue blazes): Above 100°.

So hot the hens are laying hard-boiled eggs: The end of July at 3 in the afternoon on a sunny day—no shade in sight.

So hot you can fry eggs on the sidewalk: Every August.

Hot enough to peel paint off the house: The middle of September when it hasn't rained for a month. But the cotton loves it.

Record-breaking snowfall in Charlotte, NC, late February, just days before temperatures in the 70s

SOUTHERN TIME FRAMES DEFINED

When not frantically betting fortunes on the cotton market, cotton men had time to set [sic] a spell. As I grew up, I learned a lot from my daddy and the cotton men. Such as how your given word defines your character, which Scotch was the smoothest, how to keep score at gin rummy, which railroad shipper was the most dependable, where was the best duck hunting, and so on.

A coon's age: Controversial term that originated as a backwoods reference to the average two-to-three-year life expectancy of a raccoon, that creature used for stews and hats. Related to English term, "A donkey's age." Got perverted after Reconstruction, and now not acceptable for use anywhere.

A day or two: Every intention to put you next in line after the current project that's taking so long. Possibly might happen in the next week or two.

Afore huntin' season: Maybe in July.

After huntin' season: Maybe in July.

A month of Sundays: Painfully long time. In the olden days, when blue laws kept everything closed and a person couldn't get a drink, and there were at least two church services to attend, Sunday was a day that seemed like a year. Some counties still uphold the tradition.

By'n by: Eventually.

Christmas: That season of good cheer that starts the day after Labor Day, ending with the January sales.

Directly: Sooner or later.

Final Four: March Madness. Basketball.

Football Season: Starts during summer camp in July, ends after the Super Bowl for some, after spring Draft for die-hards.

Huntin' season: There's a hunting season almost every month of the year in most Southern states, with specialized restrictions and requirements pertaining to type of prey, method of hunting (such as bow or still hunting), and time of day. There might be a brief period between July and August without a hunting season open somewhere in the South, but then, that's prime fishin' season for some species.

Jiffy: Quickly.

Mañana: Every intention to do it tomorrow, but something just might get in the way so I'll get around to it by'n by.

Spell: A short time period of indeterminate length, to be gauged by the individual involved. As in "come set a spell."

Tomorrow: See Mañana.

Two shakes of a lamb's tail: Really quickly.

SOUTHERNERS AND POLITICS

The early trans-Southern gene pool was infected with the long-suffering, yet humorous approach to life embedded in the DNA of our Scottish, Irish, Scots-Irish (Ulster Irish), African, and French bloodlines. Southern politicians of all stripes and colors have embraced this heritage. You have to laugh or you might cry, is our Southern political motto. From our VAST pool of quirky Southern politicians, here are my all-time favorites:

North Carolina mountain country's legendary yellow dog political kingmaker, Zeno Ponder, who with his brother, Sheriff E.Y., set up their own Democrat sheriff's office overlooking the French Broad River (complete with firecrackers) when the Republicans placed a machine gun on the lawn and wouldn't concede the election;

Memphis Mayor Dr. Willie W. Herenton, who—in a special $1 million election being held because he had resigned shortly after winning his fifth term—filed a petition to run to replace himself because he didn't like the 25 replacement candidates.

Mind you, all astute Southerners know how to negotiate a compromise that benefits both sides of the fence. One of my favorite college roommates was married in her hometown in southern Alabama, in a lavish wedding that would do *Steel Magnolias* proud—complete with eight brides-maids dressed in candlelight white dresses with mini-trains, holding blush-pink rose bouquets on lace fans to match the bride's. Her father, a successful businessman, was a Republican in a Democrat state. Yet he was able to organize traffic control for the wedding. The Alabama Highway Patrol escorted the wedding party, and the bride and groom's getaway car was stashed at the nearby state women's prison.

SOUTHERNERS AND PATRIOTISM

Southerners tend to be flag-waving patriots, passionate about preserving our families, our independence, and our American way of life. Whether we fled from oppression somewhere else, or survived oppression on Southern soil, our personal freedoms have been won at great cost, fighting to the death for what we believe.

Our kinfolks' blood has been spilled in our back yards as well as abroad, and it's all bled red. We ain't forgot. We ain't gonna.

Catawba, Caldwell and Alexander County citizens welcome back the North Carolina National Guard's 1450th Transportation Company and the 540th Quartermaster Batallion from Operation Desert Storm, May, 1991. Jeff Triplette is second man from the far right on the truck.

SOUTHERNERS AND DEATH

Southerners have developed a culinary ritual for honoring the recently departed. When someone around here dies, we break out the phone tree(s), the cast iron, and the casserole dishes. Folks in other regions do this, too. But Southerners have been bred to do it bigger.

We certainly don't have an exclusive on death. Everybody dies. But we have arrived at a culturally intimate relationship with Death during the past four hundred years. Remember the lost colonists of Roanoke Island, the evils of slavery, entire townships wiped out by malaria, the Late Unpleasantness, and Jim Crow? And don't forget our yellow fever, typhoid, and typhus epidemics, our massive floods, tornadoes, hurricanes, and even a few geography-altering earthquakes.

Once upon a time, our spread-out families' reunions occurred only at funerals. We learned to communicate Death news quickly, and to act even more quickly to accommodate the bereaved. We still do. For example, within 30 minutes of my mother's death in our Lewisville, NC, home, art colleague Wanda Moser arrived with two homemade Moravian chicken pies. The pastor at Lewisville United Methodist Church had called her. We weren't even members of his church. When my Aunt Emily died, First Methodist Church in Halls, TN, held a post-service luncheon for the family, even though Grandmother and Granddaddy Thurmond had long since passed, and their youngest child no longer lived in Halls.

Southern funeral food must be ready-to-heat, freezable, or munch-able. Fried chicken. Chicken pie. Baked ham. Pulled pork. Potato salad. Deviled eggs. Chicken and tuna salad. Pimiento cheese. Pound cake. Angel food and sponge cake. Assorted cookies. Meat and vegetable casseroles. And the inevitable meat-and-cheese-and-fruit deli trays. The family generally provides its own iced tea and coffee. Making the beverages gives the bereaved something to do. The booze isn't brought out until the preacher leaves, unless you're Episcopalian or Catholic.

Southerners do not fear Death. Across our vast region, Death culture coexists with everyday living. It's not just a New Orleans Goth thing, or an El Dia de los Muertos thing. Granted, an above-ground city of the dead is one of New Orleans' most popular tourist attractions. But our cemeteries are the cornerstones of all Southern communities.

In Winston-Salem, my classmates met boyfriends in God's Acre for romantic trysts on Saturday nights, and studied for exams under the cemetery oak trees on Sunday afternoons. The late James Ford's public art design for the city's new Lawrence Joel Veterans Memorial Coliseum incorporated rows of three-foot-

At Dr. Hugh Crawford's wake, his sister Mary Crawford Young and nephew John Crawford Winfrey

high markers honoring Forsyth County's war dead. Wake Forest's then-athletic director provided the only design objection, stating that the markers might trip revelers leaving a basketball game. He didn't mention the tombstone symbolism.

As a child in East Memphis, I played in the grotto at Memorial Park Cemetery, where my parents, Uncle Louie and Aunt Sue Bloom, and my godfather, Judge William H. Williams, Jr. (Slick), now repose. Uncle Slick's daughter, Ginny, decorates his grave each Yuletide with a purple and gold Christmas tree honoring LSU, his alma mater. No one thinks a thing of it, except the Ole Miss, Tennessee, 'Bama and Auburn fans.

In fact, seasonal theme decoration is expected, just like the dearly departed's special instructions in the will concerning burial protocol, funeral music, wake coordination, cemetery maintenance, and why Junior wasn't named executor of the estate. (EXAMPLE: Granddaddy Thurmond's will stipulated that no plastic flowers were to be placed on his grave. Ever.)

We don't find it macabre. We Southerners coexist peacefully with our ghosts, and we all have relatives who talk to the dead—even some who don't need Lithium.

Memorial Park Cemetery in East Memphis at Christmas

ACCOUTREMENTS FOR SOUTHERN COOKING

Barbecue grilling tool set (multiple sets usually needed)

Candy and meat thermometers

Cast iron skillet (multiple sizes needed)

Celery dish (different from a relish dish and not the same as the pickle dish; must be long enough to accommodate celery ribs filled with pimiento cheese)

Cookie press (for the cheese straws)

Covered cake plate and covered pie plate (multiple plates always needed)

Cut-glass pitcher (multiples usually needed)

Deviled egg plate (multiples usually needed)

Dutch oven (multiple sizes and types needed, including enameled cast iron for indoors; cast iron with legs for outdoors)

Grease catcher (the empty Crisco can)

Grill (both charcoal and gas, turkey fryer, and a smoker)

Iced tea glasses (not to be confused with water glasses)

Iced tea spoons (a necessity at the Southern table; see six-piece silver and china service below)

Jefferson cups (best for nog or a hot toddy)

Mint julep cups (good for all sorts of hard liquor if you prefer the feel of sterling against your lips)

Pie safe (Big Granny's cupboard with the punched tin door, where she used to keep all the pies baked for dinner for the next four days, and which now all the cousins are fighting over)

Punch bowl, serving spoon and cups (see six-piece silver and china service)

Relish dish (usually cut glass, multiples always needed)

Six-piece silver and china services (Must have minimum place settings for 12. Service for 24 or 48 preferred. See Maryln Schwartz' *The Southern Belle Primer.*)

SOUTHERN FOOD TERMS

Barbecue (abbreviated to BBQ): Noun and verb. Any meat or vegetable seasoned with a spice rub and/or marinated in a concoction of sweet-and-spicy sauce based in vinegar, sugar and peppers. The Southern national dish. Proper barbecue must be roasted until falling apart over a direct, hot, steady heat source such as coals, with hickory or fruitwood added to impart proper smoke flavoring. Grilling is different from barbecuing.

Benne: Low Country Southern term for sesame seeds. The word benne is African, where the seeds originated. Benne wafers are more addictive than Girl Scout cookies.

Chit'lins (short for chitterlings): The small intestines of pigs. Stinky to cook, but edible if cooked properly, if there's nothing else to eat.

Co-cóla: Proper Southern pronunciation of the registered cola-based soft drink, whose company is still headquartered in Hotlanta.

Coke: Any carbonated soft drink (once used interchangeably by Tar Heels with "Pepsi", which was founded in New Bern, NC, but now is headquartered above the Mason Dixon Line).

Cracklin or cracklins or crackling bread: Browned or fried connective tissues that were rendered out when removing the lard from hog fat.

Holly and Linda Raney's kitchen in Oxford, MS, after a gracious plenty of red beans and rice, crawfish boil, and sweet tea

Dab of: A little bit of something, usually wet.

Dinner: The large mid-day meal.

Dressing: The tasty, complicated bread, rice or vegetable-based mixture that folks sometimes put into the cavity of dead birds before roasting them, but more often bake as a casserole side dish. Called stuffing in Yankeeland. Also refers to the wetness drizzled over salads.

Étouffé: The succulent gravy for rice made by combining roux with King Neptune's jewels—crawfish, shrimp, oysters or crabs.

Finger sandwiches: The dainty tiny sandwiches created by cutting the crusts off a regular sandwich, and then quartering the sandwich into triangles or squares (See Tea). Southern Belles take finger sandwiches to the Lenten Luncheon. Whole sandwiches with the crust on are tacky.

Goober pea: Peanut.

(A) Gracious plenty: Satisfyingly right amount.

Grits: Also known as Georgia ice cream. Plural singular: grits is good. Fine meal made by grinding dried corn; boiled in water with butter, salt and pepper; cheese, Tabasco and cayenne added on special occasions, or when served with shrimp 'n.

Half 'n half: Refers to light cream, or to a glass containing half sweet tea and half unsweetened tea poured over the ice, for those who don't like it so sweet.

Hominy: Parched corn, eaten boiled, when there's nothing better to eat.

Huckleberry: Wild blueberry (or a kissin' cousin thereto).

Iced tea: Unsweetened tea served over ice. Originated in the 19th century; popularized in the East India Pavilion at the 1904 St. Louis World's Fair, which also gave us hamburgers and ice cream cones.

Icebox: Refrigerator.

Jambalaya: The kitchen sink, bayou style, containing whatever crawled out of the Bayou or turned up in the fishing net. Never ever decline an invitation to join a Cajun for homemade jambalaya. Never ever ask what's in it.

Liver mush (Also called liver pudding): Yum. Ground pork liver and head parts, mixed with corn meal, formed into a pudding-like roll or block, to be cut into patties and fried in the cast iron skillet like regular sausage. Cleveland County, NC, holds an annual Liver Mush Expo. It's called **scrapple** on the Eastern Shore, where the town of Bridgeville, DE, holds an annual Apple Scrapple Festival and scrapple carving contest.

Mash: Both a noun and a verb. As a verb, "to mash" is to press or flatten something, such as a button or potatoes. As a noun, "mash" is the concoction made up of crushed corn soaked in hot water to form wort, used in brewing whiskey (corn likker).

Mean: A stingy amount. Why don't you ladle up a bit more of that gumbo?

Mess of: A quantity, meaning as much of something as it takes to feed a family at dinner.

Moonshine: Distilled liquor, brewed illegally, and transported by the light of the moon (or on a moonless night).

Mudbugs: Crawfish.

Pinch of: A quantity of dry ingredient, the amount captured between thumb and forefinger and flicked into the pot.

Plain flour: Unleavened flour, also called all-purpose flour.

Pone: Cornbread made without eggs or milk.

Potlikker: The broth resulting from boiling vegetables (particularly greens).

Redeye gravy: The clear reddish gravy made up from country ham drippings, usually when stirred in the pan with a bit of coffee and water. Must be consumed while hot, or the grease will separate on the plate.

Roux: A gravy-base thickener made by browning equal parts plain flour with oil, grease or pan drippings, stirred constantly until browned but not burned, before adding the broth. Basis for all good Southern meat stews, soups, gumbos and gravies. As we say around here, "It's all about the roux."

She-crab soup: A bisque or chowder soup made by combining female blue crabs (called sooks by the locals), cream, sherry and crab roe. Hence, the SHE. Unbelievably rich.

Sour milk: Buttermilk.

Supper: The light evening meal.

Sweet milk: Whole milk, not 2%, not the blue stuff that's fat-free, and not buttermilk.

Sweet tea: Tea mixed with sugar while still hot, served over ice. This Southern nectar is served year-round; we cannot comprehend why folks not from around here don't have it on their menus.

Sweetbreads: Stomach or throat of a calf used for food; edible if there's nothing else to eat.

Tea: A daytime event honoring a special occasion for someone, often an 18-year-old female who is about to graduate from high school, or a debutante during the Season, or a newly elected club chairwoman. Occasionally a Tea is given in honor of a male, but the guest of honor is his spouse (usually occurs during election season).

Vegetable plate: What you order at the local café for lunch. (See Ajax Diner menu.) A meal up of three or four vegetable "sides." Sides may include field, crowder, purple hull, or blackeyed peas in season, fried okra, red beans and rice, pintos, green beans, slaw, creamed corn or corn pudding, collard or turnip or mustard greens, and the inevitable macaroni and cheese. All good vegetable plates come with a slice of corn bread. Southern corn bread is never sweet.

White coffee: Coffee with lots of milk, not to be confused with a latté.

White lightning: The term derives from "white lightning in a jar." (See Moonshine.)

FAMILY MEMORY

Dianne Triplette, Homecoming Queen for Granite Falls High School, 1964, has co-hostessed many a Tea for young brides.

WHERE TO FIND SOUTHERN FOOD

Every Southern town has roadside vendors who sell seasonal farm-fresh produce, snow cones, ice cream, shrimp, crab and crawfish, or barbecue and tamales. Ask anyone, and they'll tell you where to find them. For actual prepared meals, the South, like other regions, offers traditional food service destinations. But around here, we also have ultra-specialized establishments catering to the locals. Often housed in a tent, a trailer, a wood hut, or an old warehouse, many of these joints coexist alongside unrelated commercial enterprise, and can be classified according to the meals in which they specialize.

The best breakfast and lunch for Southern working stiffs and students is sold at the gas station (often a Chevron), along with the fuel, the fish bait, and the Roto Rooter supplies. The best fancy dinner might be served at the old grocery store. The ladies who lunch go to the tea room located on the mezzanine of the local department store, out a country road near the cemetery, or somewhere down Main Street.

Grocery store cuisine originated at local general stores, whose proprietors added a deli counter for selling meats and cheeses, then expanded to include beer, liquor and wines when allowed, specialty take-out foods, and sit-down lunch or dinner. That's how, for example, Chinese Grocery Store Pork Roast became a favorite dish in the Delta. Southern gentrification has transformed many of these old eclectic stores into hubs of award-winning Southern cuisine. If in doubt, check out Puckett's Grocery in Franklin, TN, or Watts Grocery in Durham, NC, or American Grocery in Greenville, SC, or City Grocery in Oxford, MS.

Betty Davis Grocery & BBQ. Waterford, MS

Wall-mounted taxidermy décor is the "tell" of many gas stations and quick stops that serve good food. Station fare varies by state, but breakfast generally includes sausage biscuits, chicken biscuits, egg and bacon biscuits, country ham biscuits, Krispy Kreme or homemade doughnuts, and strong coffee. The more elaborate gas stations also serve grits. For lunch they switch to fried chicken, corn dogs, barbecue, burritos, tamales or egg rolls to go, and vegetable plates at the stations with seating. Fresh fruit is kept beside the checkout counter, along with locally made chocolate no-bake cookies or peanut butter fudge. Many stations offer

pints of homemade chicken salad and pimiento cheese for the to-go customer. These are much in demand during football season.

The typical Southern tea room specializes in home cooking such as vegetable soup, chicken pot pie or pot roast, hot pimiento cheese sandwiches, and ladies' luncheon-type fare such as congealed strawberry, orange, banana and peach salad, and chicken salad with grapes and pecans. All are served with copious amounts of fresh sweet tea.

A tea room could kill the customer with its dessert menu, which is dedicated to satisfying feminine sweet teeth (translation: sugar and chocolate cravings). Most often found on the dessert menu are Key Lime pie, fudge cake, Mississippi mud pie, pecan pie, caramel brownies, cheesecake, brûlée with raspberry, blueberry or strawberry sauce, and assorted cobblers á la mode. When dining without the presence of men, Southern women don't even pretend they want to split a tea-room dessert.

Making sorghum molasses in the North Carolina mountains did not change for over 100 years. Sorghum was made just down Grace Chapel Road from the Sherrill family farm until the late 20th century.

PHOTO: GRANITE FALLS SORGHUM-MAKING BY MARGARET MORLEY, COURTESY OF THE NORTH CAROLINA STATE ARCHIVES, RALEIGH, NC

DOWN HOME PANTRY ESSENTIALS

Baking powder

Baking soda

Beans and peas (all types, dried and/or canned, sometimes mixed)

Butter (Remember what Paula Deen says, "I'm your cook, Honey, not your physician")

Buttermilk (also called sour milk)

Cajun trinity (celery, onion, bell pepper)

Canned soup (cream-of-mushroom, cream-of-chicken, cream-of-celery, tomato, & chicken broth)

Cavender's Greek Seasoning

Cayenne pepper

Chili powder

Chow-Chow

Corn meal (yellow and white; self-rising and plain)

Crisco (Generic brands always fall short, literally. If you must substitute, use lard.)

Eggs (local)

Flour (both self-rising and plain)

Garlic

Grits

Gumbo filé

Honey (local)

Horseradish

Jelly (blackberry, raspberry, muscadine grape, pepper, pear, apple, quince)

Karo corn syrup (both light and dark)

Ketchup (also spelled catsup)

Lemons and limes

Mayonnaise (Duke's, Hellmann's, or homemade. No substitutions.)

Molasses (sometimes substituted by dark Karo)

Mustard (yellow, Creole, Dijon, and dry)

Okra

Onions (all kinds, including green, Vidalia, white, yellow and red)

Paprika

Pepper (White, black, red, and cayenne. Not to be confused with pepperS.)

Peppers (green and red bell, banana, jalapeño, cayenne, Serrano, chili, Tabasco)

Pickles (Sweet, bread-and-butter, dill, and fresh summer. May be made from cucumbers or assorted other garden vegetables and fruits such as tomatoes, watermelons, okra, peaches, cabbage, and asparagus.)

Preserves (apricot, fig, peach, strawberry, blackberry)

Relish (See chow-chow and pickles. An assortment of pickled condiments, all of them containing vinegar, peppers and sugar.)

Rice

Salt (table, kosher, sea; and rock salt for ice cream)

Soaking chips and grilling firewood (made from the hickory, cherry, apple, pear, or peach tree lost during last winter's freeze, last spring's tornadoes, last summer's drought, or last fall's hurricanes.)

Sugar (white granulated, light and dark brown, and confectioners)

Tabasco Sauce (or Louisiana Hot Sauce, or Texas Pete, or equivalent hot sauce, according to locale)

Tea (strong black tea leaves, for iced tea, green tea and specialty teas for hosting a Tea)

Tomatoes (local or homegrown)

Tony Chachere's Cajun Creole Seasoning

Vinegar (white distilled, apple cider, red wine, and rice wine)

Worcestershire sauce

TEN RULES
FOR LIFE AND COOKERY

1 ## You kill it, you clean it.

(Or pay someone else a lot of money to do it for you.)
— GRANDMOTHER THURMOND

2 ## If you never learn how to clean fish, you'll never have to.

(Or mow the lawn, or iron oxford-cloth shirts, as long as you PROVE your incompetence at the task, and can afford to pay someone else a lot of money to do it for you.)
— GRANDMOTHER THURMOND (APPENDED BY LAURIE TRIPLETTE)

3 ## Never name your food.

(This applies to pig, chicken, cow, billygoat, duck, bunny, and squirrel, even if they do "dog" your footsteps.)
—LOUISE TRIPLETTE

4,5,6 ## Protect your kitchen tools.

NEVER fry sausage in your omelet pan.

NEVER scrub your cast-iron skillet with Comet.

NEVER cut up cardboard boxes with your boning knife.
—MARY ELIZABETH DALTROFF

7 ## Never panic when your son sticks a peanut up his nose.

(If making him blow doesn't work, the nearest URGENT CARE doctor will see him in front of the head injuries.)
—KIM DALTROFF (CONFIRMED BY LAURIE TRIPLETTE)

8 ## Never store your suckers in your underwear drawer.

(The ants will find them.)
—PAPA DALTROFF

9 ## Externalize, don't internalize.

(Never let the other person make you feel bad about yourself. Most of us do a really good job of that on our own, without any help.)
—J. WILBURTA DALTROFF, M.D., PSYCHOANALYST

10 ## If you can't or won't boil water, marry someone who can or WILL.

(Or pay someone else a lot of money to do it for you.)
—LAURIE TRIPLETTE

One
OLD BRIDE'S
GUIDE
to
COOKING SOUTHERN

LET'S TALK FOOD.

My momma always said, "Darlin',
if you marry a good man, you're
a bride till the day you die."

CULINARY MEMORIES

One beautiful spring Sunday in my 11th year, my father sat me down on a kitchen stool. I had just returned from church. Dad never attended church, saying he didn't want to take sides. He had been reared in a polyglot of Southern Jewish and Methodist relatives when his mother succumbed to tuberculosis at a young age. Like the football that he grew to love, the aunties had tossed Butch around, dragging him back and forth to their homes in Arkansas, Memphis, and Mississippi. Once married and with a family of his own, Dad usually spent Sunday mornings gardening and puttering around the kitchen when not traveling for his cotton business.

Daddy announced that he was going to begin teaching me how to cook. He told me it was for my own good, and for the good of mankind, because he didn't want my future family to suffer the way he had as a newlywed when Mom learned to cook. Poor Mary Elizabeth, the sixth of seven children. By the time she came along, Granddaddy Thurmond wanted no surprises at his table. Thus intimidated from an early age, Mom remained insecure about her own skills until the day she died. She grossly underestimated her own abilities: The woman was a good cook.

That Spring Sunday was to be the first of many, dubbed by my irreverent brothers and mother as "Reform Laurie" days. Previously noted for preferring the outdoors or a book to anything domestic, I initially resented being forced to remain in the house while the other neighborhood kids were playing sandlot baseball. Eventually, though, the infinite possibilities for creativity impressed me, and I took to the cooking lessons like the Peabody ducks to their water fountain.

Daltroffs, Blooms, and Prices with Butch, circa 1933

The first recipe Daddy taught me was squash casserole. He said it contained many of the necessary techniques and ingredients for successful cooking: Lots of slicing and dicing, lots of onion, cheese and pepper, and the universal perfect food, eggs. Besides, he really loved squash casserole. An LSU Tiger, and with family history in New Orleans, Lake Providence, and Bastrup, Dad taught me the holy Louisiana trinity of celery, onion and green pepper. He preached that there's no such thing as too much garlic. Together we explored many of the regional dishes he loved—from gumbos to fricassee, and from chili to Spanish omelet sauce.

Preparation of some of Dad's favorite dishes might have been difficult if we were an ordinary Southern family. (During the early 1960s, Southern grocery stores did not stock many international foods.) My family was more fortunate than most: We were cotton people. Cotton people tended to be eccentric and somewhat outrageous, gambling fortunes on the futures market from one day to the next, wining and dining customers as a way of life.

Our family was among the even smaller group of cotton people that migrated each summer from Memphis and mill country to the lower Rio Grande Valley to buy and sell Texas long-staple cotton. Each August, before my family's Labor Day-weekend return to Memphis for the start of school, we would drive to Las Dos Republicas in Matamoros, Mexico, to stock up on a year's supply of Herdez salsa casera, canned jalapeño peppers, spiced pumpkin seeds, and other exotic fare. Next door we would enjoy a last-of-the-season great meal at the "Drive-In" (also known as the Dine-and-Dance). We children loved to order the flambéed Steak Dianne and always begged our elders to order the flaming Mexican flag (tri-color) after-dinner liqueur.

Years later, while living outside Winston-Salem, NC, I was thrilled when the Lewisville Food Lion began selling canned Herdez salsa casera and other Mexican staples for the Hispanic migrant workers in Yadkin County. But I digress.

Daddy taught me many culinary tricks that year of reform-Laurie Sundays. Perhaps the most important lesson he imparted was that a good cook must be fearless with regard to substitutions. He emphasized that sometimes our experiments succeed, and sometimes they fail. And sometimes we learn the most from our failures.

Eating at the Dine 'n Dance, Matamoros, 1962

"This," he told me, "is a lesson for living as well, and you should pass it on."

It is a lesson that keeps on giving. After 30 years of marriage, I learned that one must label all storage containers clearly, and not keep similar ingredients stored side by side in identical containers. I inadvertently battered my fried okra with a mixture of cornmeal and powdered sugar instead of cornmeal and plain flour. Some things are not meant to be combined.

In time, I also learned how to use specific cookware and appliances. There was the post-honeymoon disaster of the pressure cooker the time I forgot to cool it before checking on the pintos. Jeff and I had to scrape and repaint the rented house kitchen ceiling. One Saturday, some months later, my skillet burst into flames from overheated grease. Jeff threw Bisquick onto the fire instead of baking soda. More scraping, scrubbing and repainting followed.

It was a LOOOONG first year.

After many years of marriage, I also learned the need for proper assignment of tasks when cohabiting with other cooks. The first Christmas Mom lived with Jeff and me, we were preparing a Christmas Eve turkey dinner for company. We'd been in the kitchen for the better part of two days.

A half-hour before the guests were due to arrive, I went to remove the turkey from the oven. No turkey. The prepped turkey was in the fridge, Mom thinking I had put it in the oven, and I thinking she had put it in the oven.

That was the night we learned to fake it by broiling the turkey to brown the skin, then sticking it in the microwave in a paper bag. Old Tom Turkey was inedible that night, but he sure looked splendid.

Peabody Hotel ducks in their fountain

Butch and Andy Daltroff were members of the Memphis Cotton Exchange. In this photo from the 1930s, cotton men played dominos in the Cotton Exchange for what seemed like a month of Sundays while waiting for spot futures to commence.

PHOTO COURTESY OF THE COTTON MUSEUM OF THE MEMPHIS COTTON EXCHANGE

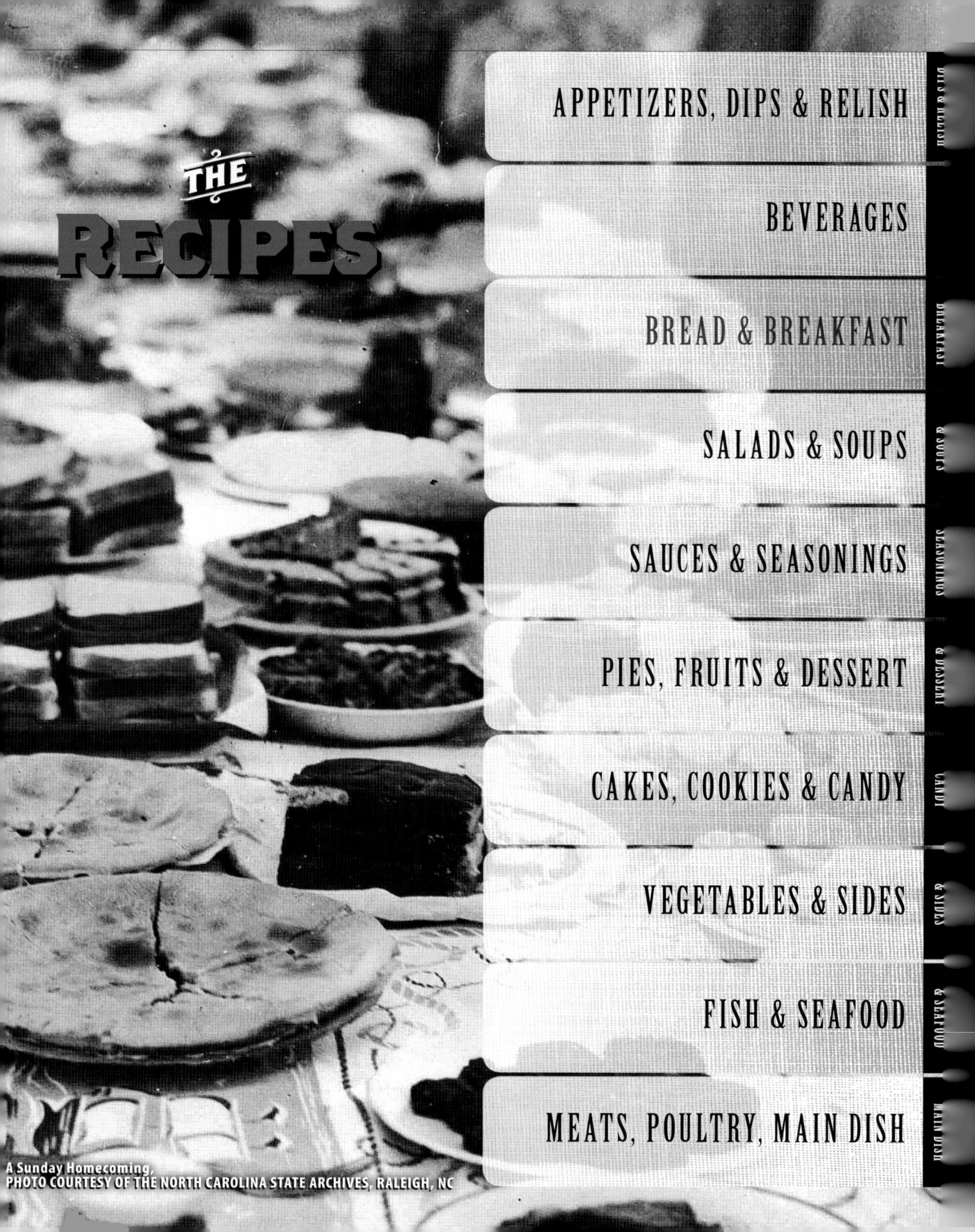

THE RECIPES

APPETIZERS, DIPS & RELISH

BEVERAGES

BREAD & BREAKFAST

SALADS & SOUPS

SAUCES & SEASONINGS

PIES, FRUITS & DESSERT

CAKES, COOKIES & CANDY

VEGETABLES & SIDES

FISH & SEAFOOD

MEATS, POULTRY, MAIN DISH

A Sunday Homecoming,
PHOTO COURTESY OF THE NORTH CAROLINA STATE ARCHIVES, RALEIGH, NC

COOKING HEALTHIER, SOUTHERN STYLE

My friend Randy, a native New Yorker, has asked me for heart-healthy conversions of ingredients used in our Southern recipes. Bless her heart, how could she know that traditional Southern cooking was as healthy as it gets? We ate what we could grow, hunt or fish, leaning heavily on seasonal leafy greens, grains, dairy, fruits, and legumes. Store-bought staples were supplemental.

Modern Southerners may have become the fattest Americans per capita, but not from overindulgence in our fundamental condiments—salt, peppers, sugar, molasses, vinegar, cream, eggs, and lard. Or in our four food groups jokingly defined as sweet, salty, fried, and au gratin by Jackson, MS, *Sweet Potato Queen*, Jill Conner Brown. It's from over-eating when most of us no longer work the Back 40 seven days a week. And it's from families on tight budgets relying too heavily on over-processed, packaged foods, which are priced cheaper in urban stores than fresh foods. Nevertheless, we've learned a few tricks for converting recipes to lighter versions ... except on big holidays.

CONVERSIONS FOR COOKING SOUTHERN LIGHT

ORIGINAL :	REPLACE WITH:
Oil or butter in baking	Applesauce or mashed banana or mashed prunes 2/3 c = 1 c of oil or butter
Butter in frying or sauté-ing	Extra-light olive oil
Peanut oil/oil in stir-frying	Chicken broth
Table salt as seasoning for vegetables	Lemon juice
Mayonnaise	Plain yogurt +lemon juice
Cream cheese	Ricotta cheese
1 c of cream cheese	4 T margarine +1 c low fat cottage cheese
1 c of heavy (whipping) cream	1 c of evaporated skim milk
1 c of heavy (whipping) cream	1/2 c plain yogurt + 1/2 c low fat cottage cheese
Frying with cooking oil or shortening + egg wash and flour dredge	Baking the meat dredged in crushed seasoned bread crumbs and drizzled with Smart Balance
White granulated sugar	Splenda, or half Splenda + half white sugar
One whole egg	Two egg whites or 2 oz egg substitute or 1 mashed banana (1/4 c)
Pork bacon	Turkey bacon
Ground beef	Ground turkey or extra lean beef + 1 tsp extra light olive oil
Whole milk or cream in baking recipes	Low-fat buttermilk
Cream in soups	Pureed vegetables, vegetable broth, or meat broth
Regular cheese	2% fat sharp or extra sharp Cheddar
Sour cream dip	Pureed veggies or beans + olive oil and cider vinegar
Buttermilk in baking	1 T distilled vinegar or lemon juice + skim milk to make up 1 c or lowfat buttermilk or plain yogurt
Pork shoulder or Boston butt	Pork tenderloin
Chuck roast or shoulder roast	Brisket or flank steak
Nuts	Toast them and use smaller amount

SLOW COOKERS

Slow cookers have come a long way since my Auntie Doc gave me my first Crock-Pot in 1973. They now come in a variety of sizes suited for making everything—from apple butter and dips, gravies, and main dishes, to side dishes, cornbread and cobbler. The sizes include 1-quart, 1.5-quart, 2-quart, 3-quart, 4-quart, 6-quart, 6.5-quart, 7-quart, and 7.4-quart. There's even a three-in-one cooker that contains interchangeable 2-, 3-, and 6-quart inserts. The larger cookers serve a family of four.

Some slow cookers are programmable. The basic ones only offer "on" or "off." Some automatically switch to "warm" once the dish has completed its cooking cycle. Oval-shaped slow cookers are best suited to cooking meats, and round slow cookers are best suited to soups and stews.

Make sure your slow cooker has a removable insert for cleaning. In my opinion, the best are heavy stoneware inserts that are easy to clean (do not use steel wool). They heat the food evenly and retain the heat longer when turned off. Some cookers have stainless steel or aluminum inserts, designed for cooking meats at a higher temperature without requiring the cook to sear (brown) the meat first.

Slow cooking is a simmer process. Slow cooking on low brings food up to 170°F. Slow cooking on high raises the temperature up to about 200°F. Better quality slow cookers bring the temperature up to at least 140°F within the first hour, which is important: Bacteria thrive in 40-140°F temperatures, known as the "danger zone" for food-borne illnesses.

If using a simple slow cooker which only offers on, off, low, medium or high, it is recommended to start the cooking on high for the first hour, then lower it to the recommended heat for the remainder of the cooking time.

Raw kidney beans and some other beans must be parboiled to kill the bean toxins before putting them into the slow cooker for long-term cooking. This is why, traditionally, one would boil, then drain and rinse the beans before refilling the pot with clean water and bringing the pot up to a long-term simmer on the stovetop.

Slow cookers love cheaper cuts of meat, which generally are tougher than expensive meats because of the connective tissues. In a slow cooker, unlike stovetop boiling, the connective tissue in the meat breaks down and the meat becomes fork tender during the slow cooking time. The cooker needs to be at least half full to avoid cooking too quickly and burning the dish. Two-thirds full is recommended. The liquid in a slow-cooker dish does not evaporate, so it is recommended not to add as much liquid as one might for stovetop cooking. Usually, one should adjust the liquid to just cover the contents.

If you prefer your meat dishes to have thick, rich gravy, allow enough pre-dinner time to make old fashioned gravy on the stovetop, using the juice from the slow-cooked meat.

See Slow Cooker recipes in various recipe sections of this cookbook. Examples: Crock Pot Apple Butter, and Slow Cooker Pulled Pork.

SIMPLE DO'S AND DON'TS WHEN USING A SLOW COOKER:

- Traditional meat-based dishes that require searing the meat as a first step should adhere to this step before placing the meat in the slow cooker. When combining meat with vegetables, try layering the vegetables first, and adding the meat on top.
- Dishes containing eggs and milk products require that the cooker interior be lightly greased with butter or cooking oil before adding the ingredients to prevent sticking.
- Some bread recipes such as gingerbread and date bread call for placing a covered can or casserole dish inside the cooker, in a shallow hot water bath.
- Add less liquid when converting stovetop soup and stew recipes to a slow cooker.
- Pre-cook pasta such as macaroni when making a dish in the cooker (such as mac'n cheese) because pasta requires boiling water to become done; OR if using small pasta such as orzo, add pasta during the last hour of cooking.
- Unless specified otherwise in a slow cooker recipe, add rice during the last hour, or it will turn into mush (I learned this the hard way).
- Add cream, sour cream, or milk only during the last 15 minutes of cooking to prevent scorching or curdling of the dairy.
- Add seafood, especially shellfish such as shrimp, during the last 13-15 minutes of cooking with cooker set on high, so it doesn't turn rubbery.
- Add thawed or fresh fish during the last 30-45 minutes of cooking.
- Do not add frozen fish or seafood to slow cooker recipes.
- Always pre-cook bacon before adding to a dish such as baked beans.
- Completely thaw frozen meat before slow cooking, or else increase the cooking time.
- Do not slow-cook frozen veggies. Prepare according to package instructions, then add to soups, stews or casseroles during the last 30-45 minutes.
- If doubling a recipe for slow cooking, double the basic ingredients, but add 1-1/2 times the liquid, and do not increase the spices.
- When slow cooking bean dishes, add salt, sweeteners (such as sugar, honey, molasses) and acidic ingredients (such as tomatoes, vinegar, citrus juice) only after the beans are soft, because these ingredients lengthen cooking time and can make the beans hard.
- Do not double or triple baked food recipes in a slow cooker.
- NEVER reheat food in a slow cooker.
- Resist lifting lid during cooking, unless recipe calls for stirring; it takes up to 30 minutes to regain proper cooking temperature.

GOOD DISHES FOR SLOW COOKER ADAPTATION:

- Vegetable- and meat-broth-based soups such as vegetable soup and Brunswick stew
- Meat dishes such as spaghetti sauce, meat balls, chili, or anything containing chicken
- Bean dishes, especially dried bean dishes such as pinto beans, red beans and rice
- Barbecued ribs and pulled pork
- Tortilla and enchilada casseroles
- Stuffed peppers (the peppers do not need to be blanched)
- Greens
- Pot roast, pork loin, turkey breast, roasting hen

CLEVER MEAL PLANNING

It's fun, healthful, and economical to plan the major (primary) household meals for the month. RULES OF THUMB FOR PLANNING:

- Buy good cuts of meat when on special at the store; freeze until needed.
- Buy long-life shelf staples such as gelatin, rice, cake mixes, and canned veggies when on sale.
- Use the slow cooker for cheaper (tougher) cuts of meat such as flank steak, and for all-in-one dish cooking when busy or on hot summer days.
- Cook multiple meals one weekend a month and freeze for weekday use.
- Convert main-dish leftovers into secondary dishes to serve on busy work days.

Several examples of ways to stretch leftovers are listed below.

Primary: A whole baking chicken, a package of chicken leg quarters, or chicken breasts. Freeze leftover chicken broth in ice-cube trays to use for sautéing, soup base, gravy.
Secondary: Chicken and rice, chicken pie, chicken soup, chicken salad

Primary: Fresh peas, green beans, butter beans or butter peas, okra, corn
Secondary: Combinations in succotash, casseroles, pot pie, soups

Primary: Fresh pot roast, eye of round, rump roast, or prime rib
Secondary: Beef and rice, salad topping, sandwiches, pot pies, soups, tamales

Primary: Cornbread
Secondary: Cornbread salad, cornbread dressing

Primary: Individual pieces of fruit (bananas, apples, peaches, grapes, oranges)
Secondary: Banana salad, banana bread, apple crisp, Waldorf salad, grape salad, peach fluff, ambrosia, gelatin fruit salad

HINTS ABOUT SALT

I developed a shellfish allergy in my thirties, and learned the hard way that iodine in any form would trigger an allergic reaction. For me, this included sea salt and regular table salt, which contain iodine unless otherwise specified. Most grocery stores sell iodine-free table salt. It is interchangeable with regular table salt.

Kosher salt is pure, containing neither iodine nor any other additives found in table salt. Kosher salt crystals are larger, and absorb meat flavors more readily than table salt, which is a good thing. Usually, kosher salt and sea salt may be used interchangeably in recipes calling for one or the other, although the texture will be different (sea salt crystals are larger). NOTE: The flavor of sea salt varies according to source. Try smoked sea salt for added flavor.

Never substitute kosher salt or sea salt in baking recipes calling for table salt. For non-baking recipes, one may substitute 1-1/2 times the amount of kosher salt as table salt. If substituting table salt for kosher salt in non-baking recipes, reduce the amount by 3/4.

NOTE: Savvy Southerners add a few grains of rice in the salt shaker to prevent table salt crystals from clumping due to humidity.

HINTS ABOUT RED SPICES AND GRAINS

In the South, where it is humid and hot, even with air conditioning, it's a good idea to store your red spices in the fridge or freezer to prevent contamination by weevils. This includes chili powder, red pepper, cayenne, and paprika.

The same goes for grains such as corn meal and grits. Flour, pasta and rice must be kept in airtight containers if stored in the pantry.

If you ever get weevils, throw out EVERYTHING, including old shelf paper. Vacuum thoroughly (empty vacuum outside into trash bag) and disinfect all surfaces, including the vacuum, baseboards and doors. Then pray. Pray hard.

DUTCH OVEN COOKING

Dutch ovens are large cooking pots with a bale handle (usually) and a tight-fitting lid. They generally are made of cast iron, although some of the fancier ones are enameled cast iron. They come in a variety of sizes, some with feet and flanged lids, for campfire cooking, and some without, for indoors cooking. The purpose of the Dutch Oven is to provide a complete heating environment for whatever it contains, either as a steam-cooker, as a bake-oven for a smaller cooking vessel within, or as a stewpot. Proper modern "Dutch oven cooking" requires an open-flame heat source generated by burning wood or briquettes.

Our Southern cooks have been relying on Dutch oven cooking pots since Colonial times, first on an open hearth fire, and gradually on the kitchen stove and in the oven. Rural cooks, furthermore, have carted their Dutch Ovens to the fields for roundups and other agricultural duties that required eating and sleeping outdoors. In my opinion, the best fricassees, stews and cobblers are made in Dutch ovens.

Gary Poovey, Dianne Triplette Poovey's husband, is a top-notch Dutch oven cook. He has studied campfire cooking since his

Gary Poovey tends dinner in the Smokies

days as an Eagle Scout, when he had to break eggs into a campfire frying pan in 28-degree weather. Gary got serious about the art of the Dutch oven in 1986, during a two-week horse-packing school in Wyoming. One-pot Dutch oven-cooked meals were part of the training. Gary has continued his studies by viewing the RFD television channel's campfire cooks, by collecting and actually reading Dutch oven cookbooks, by working with experienced campfire cooks, and by practicing on real campfires. Gary uses the hardwood coal and Kingsford charcoal briquette heating method—easily mastered by those of us who can only count up to 30 or 40.

Proper Dutch oven cooks NEVER use charcoal lighter, which taints the flavor of the oven contents and burns the briquettes too fast. Really clever Dutch oven cooks use a technique called "cooking on a volcano." The volcano is a chimney canister the height of two large bean cans with a perforated rack underneath a column that contains the briquettes. This enables the cook to ignite paper beneath the briquettes. The paper burns long enough to catch fire to the briquettes. The cook uses tongs to remove the needed number of lighted briquettes from the chimney.

When cooking in a Dutch oven, turn the pot and lid one-quarter turn, continuing to turn in the same opposite direction every 15 to 20 minutes to maintain even heat. Weather affects the number of coals needed, with extremely hot, cold, windy, or damp weather requiring more or fewer briquettes. To clean a Dutch oven after cooking in it, put water in the oven and bring it to a boil. NEVER scrub the Dutch oven with anything stronger than hot water. Moisture is the enemy of cast iron, causing rusting and sticking spots. Always wipe dry to avoid rusting. Store with newspaper or paper towels inside to absorb moisture.

GARY'S MOUNTAINMAN BREAKFAST

*Gary adapted this recipe from **Camp Dutch Oven Cooking 101 From Backyard to Backwoods**, published by Lodge Manufacturing Co., South Pittsburg, TN. Gary says it provides beginners with a fundamental understanding of how the Dutch oven campfire works.*

2 lb ground pork sausage such as Jimmy Dean (hot or regular or 1 of each)

2 lb frozen hashbrown potatoes

8 eggs, beaten with 1/4 c water

2 c grated extra sharp Cheddar cheese (8-oz pkg)

Fry and crumble sausage in 12-inch Dutch oven over a full bed of hot coals. Remove cooked sausage and drain on paper towels. Brown the potatoes in the sausage drippings, in pan, then spread them evenly in bottom of the Dutch oven. Place cooked sausage over potatoes. Pour beaten eggs over the sausage layer. Sprinkle top with cheese. Cook with 8 coals underneath, and 16 coals on top for 20 to 25 minutes, until eggs are cooked.

BOB SUMTER'S DUTCH OVEN COBBLER

This friend of Gary Poovey's was reared in Henry, NC, on his mother's Dutch oven cooking. This recipe came to Bob from his mother, and then to Gary, who cooks it for family and friends.

16 to 18 briquettes

1/2 stick butter (4 T)

2 c self-rising flour

2 c whole milk

2 c white granulated sugar

1 qt fruit of choice (strawberries, blueberries, huckleberries, blackberries, etc.)

10-inch Dutch oven, lined with foil in the bottom and up the sides. Prepare 16-18 briquettes; place 6 or 7 briquettes underneath the oven and melt 1/2 stick butter in the oven.

Mix fruit with the other ingredients and pour into the Dutch oven containing the melted butter. Cover with lid, and place 10-11 briquettes on top. Cobbler cooks in about 45 minutes to 1 hour.

DUTCH OVEN APPLE COBBLER

from Gary and Dianne Poovey

25 to 30 briquettes

4 to 6 c sliced apples (Dianne prefers Jonathans)

2 to 3 c apple juice

1-1/2 c white granulated sugar

8 T (1/2 c) salted butter, cut up and divided into 2
    batches, cut into small pieces in each batch

1-1/2 to 2 c light brown sugar, divided

1-1/2 to 3 tsp cinnamon

2 pkg Duncan Hines yellow or white cake mix

12-inch deep-dish Camp Dutch oven, lined with foil on bottom and up the sides, coated with butter.

Combine the diced apples, sugar, and juice with the cinnamon and brown sugar. Use enough juice so the apples are soaked but not swimming. Divide into two equal portions. Pour first portion into buttered oven. Mix the first 4 T of cut-up butter pieces into the apples. Sprinkle the first dry cake mix evenly over all the top of the fruit mixture.

Pour the second fruit portion over the first. Dot the top of this layer with the second 4 T of cut-up butter. Prepare the second cake mix according to the package instructions, and pour over the top layer.

Cover the Dutch oven and place over heat – about 8 to 10 briquettes on bottom. Cover with 12-18 briquettes on top. About every 15 minutes, turn the pot clockwise a quarter turn, and turn the lid counterclockwise a quarter turn. This bakes the cobbler to a golden brown. Cooks in about 45 minutes.

VARIATION: Make a Streusel topping by combining 1 cup of dark brown sugar with 3 T flour and 2 T butter until mixture is crumbly. Sprinkle over top before last 15 minutes *YIELD: 15 large servings.*

CAST IRON SKILLET TIPS

Season your new cast iron skillet in the oven by coating with lard or bacon grease (liquid cooking oils and shortening can leave a sticky residue), and heating for several hours at around 250°F.

To keep clean, rinse briefly with soapy water and wipe dry. Occasionally, a skillet must be thoroughly scrubbed and re-seasoned.

ALWAYS use separate cast iron skillets for meats and breads. The meat flavors leach into the metal and will affect the bread flavor.

DUTCH OVEN PORK AND CHICKEN

This is one of Gary Poovey's signature Dutch oven dishes. He adapted it from several meat dishes in **Dutch Oven Cooking 101 from Backyard to Backwoods***, published by Lodge Manufacturing Company Press, in South Pittsburg, TN.*

12 to 14 briquettes

White onions, coarsely chopped (2 to 3 for 3 to 6 lb of meat))

Polly Moore's BBQ sauce (enough for 3 to 6 lb of meat)

Bone-in pork chops or pork ribs (2 to 3 lb)

2 whole chickens, skinned

Extra light olive oil

Salt and pepper to taste

12-inch deep-dish camp Dutch oven. Preheat the Dutch oven with 8 to 10 briquettes underneath while prepping the ingredients.

Saute the chopped onions in olive oil, then add the pork. Smother the meat in Polly's BBQ sauce. Cook uncovered for one hour, using 12-14 briquettes, then remove 2 to 3 coals to reduce heat to a simmer and cook uncovered for another 30 minutes. Turn pot and lid 1/4-turn in opposite directions every 15-20 minutes. Cover, adding 12-14 coals on top. Simmer for another 30 minutes, turning 1/4 turn every 15 minutes.

Remove lid and add the chicken along with more Polly's BBQ sauce, and stir well to work the sauce and chicken in with the almost-cooked pork. Add salt and pepper to taste. Cover, and add coals to the top, stirring once or twice for the next 30 minutes to one hour, turning lid and pot 1/4-turn in opposite directions every 15 minutes.

Make sure there's enough liquid in the pot to prevent scorching or sticking. Add more coals underneath if needed., but do not overcook. *YIELD: 12-15 servings.*

DAILY SALT CONSUMPTION

The average American consumes about 5,000 mg of salt daily, but the recommended daily allowance is only up to 2,400 mg (about 1 teaspoon) per day. Adults age 51 and over should reduce this to 1/2 teaspoon per day (about 1,200 mg). The amount of sodium contained in one teaspoon of salt also reflects the daily recommended sodium allowance per day (2.3 grams). Remember that sodium is present in baking soda and, like salt, as a compound in other foods. To achieve the salty taste without overdoing the salt, flavor your dishes with lemon or lime juice.

DUTCH OVEN POTATOES AU GRATIN

from Dianne Poovey

19 to 21 coals, more or less, as needed for heat

12 medium to large Russet (white) potatoes

6 white onions, sliced evenly

1/2 lb bacon

Extra light olive oil

1/2 lb butter (2 sticks), cut into small pieces

Salt and pepper to taste

1/2 of a 10-3/4-oz can of cream of mushroom soup

1/2 of a 10-3/4-oz can of cream of celery soup

1/4 c chopped fresh parsley, OPTIONAL

1/4 to 1/2 c chopped bell pepper, OPTIONAL

1 lb medium-size fresh button mushrooms, sliced

1 c sharp grated Cheddar cheese

12-inch regular Dutch oven. Cook bacon in the oven over 12 coals until crisp. Leave in the oven with the drippings. Add 1/4-inch of olive oil. Position 12 sliced potatoes evenly over the oil and bacon. Cover this with onion slices and parsley. Sprinkle with optional green pepper. Dot with butter, at regular intervals. Add salt and pepper to taste. Cover. Place 12-15 coals on top. Every 5 to 10 minutes for about 20 minutes, remove lid and fold the potatoes over with a flat spatula, careful not to break the slices. At the 20-minute point, the potatoes should be partially done. Combine the two soups and spread evenly over top layer, using spatula to open up the layers and allow juices to permeate below. Leave uncovered.

Position oven lid upside down on a lid holder over 5 to 6 coals. Use lid to sauté 1 lb of sliced fresh mushrooms in just enough olive oil or butter to cook them down. While sautéing, sprinkle grated Cheddar cheese over the potatoes. Spread mushrooms over the cheese; cook 5 minutes, uncovered, using 9 to 11 coals underneath. *YIELD: 12-15 servings.*

LEGEND OF ABBREVIATIONS IN THIS COOKBOOK

T	=	*tablespoon*
tsp	=	*teaspoon*
c	=	*cup*
oz	=	*ounce*
pt	=	*pint*
qt	=	*quart*
gal	=	*gallon*
lb	=	*pound*
pkg	=	*package*
g	=	*grams*
mg	=	*milligrams*

THE
RECIPES

JELLIES, PICKLES

BREAKFAST

& SOUPS

SEASONINGS

& DESSERT

& CANDY

& SIDES

& SEAFOOD

MAIN DISH

APPETIZER BITES

ASPARAGUS CREAM CHEESE ROLL-UPS

3 oz cream cheese, softened

8 pieces of bacon, cooked and crumbled

12 slices of 9- or 12-grain bread, crusts removed

14-oz can of asparagus spears

Melted butter

Flatten the bread slightly, with a rolling pin. Mix the crumbled bacon with cream cheese and spread the mixture generously on each slice of bread. Roll bread around one asparagus spear. Place the rolled bread, seam side down, on a baking sheet. Brush with melted butter and broil until slightly brown. Cut into thirds and serve hot. *YIELD: 36 roll-ups.*

ASSORTED FRUIT APPETIZERS

Every appetizer tray needs a few fresh fruit offerings. These are great ones to serve as cocktail appetizers or as a little amuse-bouche before dinner.

Prosciutto and Cantaloupe or Pear: Slice fruit into three-inch-long slivers, lightly pepper; wrap in prosciutto and mozzarella. Secure with toothpick.

Stuffed Figs: Stuff with Gorgonzola, wrap in prosciutto; secure with toothpick. Broil until prosciutto is crisp. Just before serving hot, drizzle with a boiled honey-vinegar sauce made from a 2/3 reduction from 1 c balsamic vinegar combined with 1/3 c honey.

Stuffed Dates: Stuff cream cheese into large dates. Sprinkle lightly with kosher salt. Seasoned or stronger cheese such as feta can be used. Sweet and salty is a great combination.

Melon Balls: Use a melon baller to scoop watermelon, cantaloupe, and honeydew. Combine with lemon juice, blueberries, strawberries and pineapple. Spoon into hollowed orange halves or foil muffin cups and serve with toothpicks.

Cheese Grapes: Mix 8 oz cream cheese with 2 T blue cheese. Pinch off about 3/4 tsp at a time and form each pinch around a seedless grape. Roll cheese-covered grapes in crushed pecans, almonds or pistachios. Chill. *YIELD: About 48 cheese-covered grapes.*

Bacon-Wrapped Stuffed Dates: Make a filling of cream cheese mixed with feta or blue cheese. Stuff into date. Wrap each date with 1/3 slice of raw bacon; secure with toothpick. Broil until bacon becomes crisp. Serve immediately.

BIEROCKS (GERMAN MEAT PIES)

from Rita Davidson Friend

Cousin Rita says her mother, Sheila Daltroff Davidson, got this recipe from a German lady living in Arkansas. The recipe is similar to that of Natchez Meat Pies, made famous in Natchitoches, LA. For a Natchez meat pie, omit the cabbage, but add ground pork, minced garlic, bell pepper, green onion, and cayenne pepper to the meat filling.

BIEROCKS FILLING:

2 lb hamburger meat

1 c chopped onion

4 c chopped cabbage

2 tsp salt

Black pepper to taste

1 to 2 cloves minced garlic

Brown meat and drain. To drained meat add onions, cabbage, salt, and pepper. Cook until cabbage and onions are tender. Add garlic in last 10 minutes (too soon will over-sweeten). Set filling aside.

BIEROCKS PASTRY:

2 pkgs yeast

1 cup warm milk

2 T butter

1 tsp salt

4 cups of flour

1/4 cup sugar

1/2 cup warm water

Dissolve yeast in warm water. Add warm milk, butter, and salt. Let stand for 10 minutes. Add flour and sugar. Let double (approximately 40-60 minutes). Knead dough; roll out; cut into 6-by-6-inch squares. Spoon filling into the center of each square. Pinch the dough together as you bring each corner up to the center. Place seamed side down on very lightly greased cookie sheet. Bake at 350°F for 20 minutes until lightly browned. Serve with spicy Remoulade sauce and cold draft beer. NOTE: For alternative version, paint a thin wash of beaten egg along the pastry edges, fold pastry over filling to form triangle; pinch edges together.

BACON-WRAPPED SCALLOPS

3 T fresh lime juice

2 T chopped fresh cilantro

2 garlic cloves, minced

1/4 tsp salt

1/4 tsp black or white pepper

Dash of Tabasco or other hot sauce

1/2 c olive oil

4 lb sea scallops, rinsed and drained (about 48)

24 bacon slices (about 1 lb), cut in half

Wooden picks (the skewer kind used for kebabs, or sturdy toothpicks)

1/4 tsp salt

1/4 tsp pepper

Vegetable cooking spray such as Pam

Combine lime juice, cilantro, garlic, salt, pepper and Tabasco in a small mixing bowl. Whisk in olive oil in a slow, steady stream. Place scallops in a zip-top plastic freezer bag; add lime juice mixture. Cover or seal and chill for 30 minutes, turning once. Drain scallops, discarding the marinade.

Microwave bacon in 4 batches (covered with paper towels) on HIGH for 3 to 4 minutes, or until slightly brown. Wrap 1 bacon piece around each scallop; secure with wooden toothpick. Sprinkle evenly with salt and pepper.

Place scallops on oiled grate over charcoal flame, or on rack in pan in oven set to medium-high heat (350-400°F). If on grill, cover with grill lid. Cook 3 to 4 minutes on each side, or until bacon is crisp and scallops are done. *YIELD: about 48.*

BACON-STUFFED MUSHROOMS

8-oz pkg of cream cheese, softened

1/2 c crumbled bacon

1 tsp chopped green onion

1/4 tsp garlic powder

1 lb whole fresh small-to-medium sized mushrooms, stems removed

In a small bowl, beat cream cheese until smooth. Stir in the bacon, onion and garlic powder. Spoon into the mushroom caps. Broil 4 to 6 minutes until heated through. Serve warm. *YIELD: About 2 dozen.*

Bacon-Wrapped Scallops are always a hit with guests.

BISQUICK SAUSAGE BALLS

1 lb sausage (regular or hot)

4 c Bisquick

2 c grated sharp Cheddar cheese

Mix together and form into tiny balls. Place balls on a cookie sheet and bake at 325°F for 20-25 minutes. Store. Freeze well. *YIELD: About 4 dozen.*

CHEESE BUDS (PUFFS)

1/2 lb sharp Cheddar cheese, grated

1/2 lb butter

2 c sifted all-purpose flour

1/4 tsp red or cayenne pepper

1 egg white, slightly beaten

Pecan halves (optional)

Blend cheese and butter with mixer. Sift flour, pepper and gradually work this into the creamed mixture with a large wooden spoon. Roll out 1/4- to 1/2-inch thick. Cut into 1-inch rounds. Brush tops with egg white and place a pecan half on each top if desired. Bake on ungreased cookie sheet at 425°F for 10-15 minutes. *YIELD: 8 dozen.*

CHEESE STRAWS

Once upon a time, every Southern occasion boasted at least one type of cheese straw displayed on a crystal plate or doily-lined silver platter. We've all been known to eat them like peanuts because you can't eat just one. Or two. Or 12.

Here's my best cheese straws recipe:

Four 10-oz pkgs extra sharp Cheddar, shredded by hand

2 c (4 sticks) butter, melted (winter) OR room temp (warm weather)

4 c plain flour

Scant 3/4 tsp (mild) or 1-1/2 tsp (spicy) cayenne pepper

1 tsp salt

5 dashes of Tabasco or Louisiana Hot Sauce

Work butter by hand into the shredded cheese. Add Tabasco (do NOT overdo). Sift together the flour, cayenne and salt. Gently but thoroughly work flour mix into cheese mix, being careful not to over work (or the straws will be tough).

Put dough into cookie press with ribbon or star tip. Pipe onto parchment-lined cookie sheets in 1-1/2- to 2-inch-long strips. If you lack a cookie press, gently roll out dough between sheets of waxed paper to approximately 3/8-inch thickness. Use a sharp knife to cut into strips about 1/2-inch wide by 1-1/2 to 2-inches long.

Bake at 350°F for 10-12 minutes, until golden with dark gold flecks. If underdone, the straws will taste chewy. (Throw them back into the oven for a few minutes.) Cool completely, then store, layered in wax paper, in an air-tight metal container. *Yield: about 250 cheese straws.*

THE CHEESE STRAW LEGACY

Every Southern-based grocery store and bakery offers its own version in fancy tins during the holidays. But be careful to match the degree of spiciness to the occasion. When assigned to provide the cheese straws for Louise and Lester's 50th anniversary celebration, I ordered 10 dozen from Dewey's Bakery, which had been making cheese straws for debuts, teas, and receptions in Winston-Salem since 1930. Unfortunately, I messed up by ordering the extra spicy version instead of the regular version. They would have been better suited to tailgating with beer on Game Day than to munching with lime punch in the church education center. Thank heavens Louise loved them!

CHEESE WAFERS

from Andrea Benfield

Andrea serves this version at Christmas, and at bridal and baby showers.

1/2 lb (8 oz) grated extra sharp Cheddar cheese, room temperature

1 stick (1/2 c) butter, room temperature

1/2 tsp salt

1/2 tsp crushed red pepper flakes

1 c finely chopped pecans

1-1/4 c sifted all-purpose flour

Mix softened cheese and butter with mixer. Add flour, salt and pepper, and mix completely. Add nuts. Roll dough into 2 to 3 cylinders, wrap in waxed paper, and chill at least 24 hours. Slice into thin wafers. Place on cookie sheet greased with cooking spray. Bake at 300°F in preheated oven until lightly browned, about 10-12 minutes. *YIELD: 2 to 3 dozen.*

CHEESE STICKS

from Mary Elizabeth Daltroff

1-1/2 c sifted all-purpose flour

1/4 lb butter, softened

1 c Cheddar cheese, grated

1/2 tsp baking powder

1/4 c plain yogurt

1/ tsp salt

Dash of cayenne

1 egg yolk, beaten

With a fork, blend the flour, softened butter, cheese, baking powder, yogurt, salt and cayenne. When the ingredients are well blended, work the dough with floured hands to form a ball. Wrap in plastic wrap and refrigerate for 1 hour (or 10 minutes in freezer). Preheat oven to 325°F. When chilled, roll out dough on a floured board to 1/8-inch thickness. Brush top with beaten egg yolk. With a pizza wheel, cut the dough into strips about 1/2-inch wide by 2 inches long. Transfer to an ungreased baking sheet (I line mine with parchment paper). Bake 8 to 15 minutes, or until lightly golden. Store in loosely covered container. *YIELD: About 100.*

Laurie's cheese straws recipe was used to make these delicious wafers.

CHEX PARTY MIX

1/2 c butter or margarine

1-1/2 T Worcestershire sauce

1-1/4 tsp seasoned salt

2 c Wheat Chex

2 c Corn Chex

2 c Rice or Bran Chex

1 c salted mixed nuts

Preheat oven to 250°F. Heat butter in a 13 x 9 x 2-inch pan. Stir in seasoned salt and Worcestershire when melted. Add cereals and nuts. Mix until all are coated with the butter mixture. Bake in oven for 1 hour, stirring every 15 minutes. Spread out on paper towels or waxed paper to cool. *YIELD: 9 cups.*

CHICKEN LIVER BACON WRAPS

1-1/2 lb chicken livers

1/4 c seasoned dry bread crumbs (without cheese)

1 T Parmesan cheese

1/2 tsp dried basil

16 slices bacon, cut in half crosswise

Cut chicken livers into 1-1/4-inch pieces, making about 32 pieces. In a small bowl, combine bread crumbs, cheese and basil. Coat each liver with the crumbs. Wrap a piece of bacon around each liver and place on two 12-inch metal skewers, leaving a small space between livers. Place on rack in broiler pan. Broil 3 to 5 inches from the heat source for about 8 to 10 minutes on each side, or until bacon is cooked through. Remove meat from skewers and serve with toothpicks. *YIELD: 16 servings.*

COCKTAIL MEATBALLS

from Andrea Benfield

2 lb pre-cooked frozen meatballs, thawed,
   OR:

2 lb lean ground beef

2 eggs, beaten

1/2 c finely chopped onion

2-1/2 c bread crumbs

2 tsp pepper

2 T parsley flakes

Use thawed, precooked frozen meatballs, or mix first ingredients and form into bite-size meatballs. Brown in a large skillet. Drain grease. Mix sauce ingredients, and pour over meatballs. Stir well. Heat on medium for 20-30 minutes.

SAUCE:

1 bottle cocktail sauce

1 c grape jelly

COLD SHRIMP MARINADE

1-1/2 to 2 lb raw shrimp

1/4 c seasoned rice-wine vinegar

3 T Creole mustard

10 T vegetable oil (Canola, safflour, extra-light olive oil)

2 T extra light olive oil

1 tsp kosher salt

1 tsp fresh ground black pepper

1 c roasted red bell pepper strips

1 red onion, halved, center removed; sliced

Chopped chives (about 1/4 to 1/2 c)

Boil about 1-1/4 to 2 lb shrimp, peeled and deveined, but with tails intact. (See recipe for boiling shrimp.) Cover and cool in ice, about 10 minutes. Whisk vinegar and mustard in large bowl. Slowly add oils, whisking to blend. Whisk in seasonings. Add shrimp, bell pepper, onion, and chives. Toss and serve.

HINT: After peeling boiled shrimp to be used in a recipe, put the discarded shells and debris in a toss-away container in the freezer until garbage day. But don't forget to throw them away! This prevents them from causing odors in your kitchen or garbage cans.

DEVILED EGGS

Deviled eggs are a fundamental component of Southern pot luck gatherings. The choir members at Providence United Methodist Church in Charlotte competed every Easter to determine whose deviled eggs were best.

Fresh eggs (1 to 2 eggs per person)

Mayonnaise

Mustard

Salt and pepper to taste

Paprika

OPTIONAL VARIATIONS:

Sweet pickle relish

Chopped stuffed olives

Cayenne pepper to taste

Horseradish

Place raw eggs in a pot, cover with cold water; add 1 T white vinegar to the water. Bring to a boil and cook for a minute; lower the heat and cook for 2 more minutes, then cover, turn off heat. Let sit 2 to 3 more minutes. Drain water, fill with iced water, crack eggs, and let sit 5 minutes in chilled water. Remove and pat dry. Peel off shells. Cut each egg in half, pop hard-cooked yolk into a small bowl, and position the egg white in egg plate. Mash yolks with a fork or pastry blade until no lumps remain and yolk has a paste consistency. Salt and pepper to taste. Carefully add mayo, working it in until the paste becomes of spreadable consistency. Blend in mustard and cayenne. The spread should be stiff enough to hold a peak and not run. If adding sweet pickle relish, use less mayo and mustard. If adding chopped stuffed olives, only add enough to taste. If adding horseradish, use about 1/8 to 1/4 teaspoon. Spoon or pipe the yolk mixture into the egg centers. Sprinkle paprika over tops of the filled eggs.

EGG AND SALMON CANAPES

1 hardboiled large or extra large egg, chopped fine

1/2 c mayonnaise (I use Duke's or homemade)

2 small sweet pickles (gherkins), minced (chopped fine)

2 T fine-chopped fresh chives

1 red onion, sliced paper thin

12 party-size rye or pumpernickel slices (usually squares), lightly toasted or not, to taste

12 thin slices of smoked salmon

Hard boil the egg, then chop it fine, but do not mash. Combine mayonnaise with fine-chopped pickles, green onion, and chives, and gently fold in the chopped egg. Spread out a dollop on each bread slice. Top each with a slice of smoked salmon. Garnish with pieces of thin-sliced red onion. This canape is best served to small groups at cocktail party gatherings.

LAURIE'S HOT WINGS

This recipe can be modified to suit your personal taste, with more or less honey, more or less hot sauce, and more or less Worcestershire and soy sauce. It's also permissible to use packaged drumettes instead of whole wings.

3 lb wings, disjointed into two parts, wing tips trimmed

1 c ketchup

1/2 c water

1/2 c honey

4 T light brown sugar, packed

2 T onion powder

2 T Dijon mustard

2 T Worcestershire sauce

2 T soy sauce

4 T Louisiana Hot Sauce or Slap Ya Mama, to taste

4 to 6 garlic cloves, minced

Arrange wings evenly in a single layer on broiler sheet over broiler pan of water. Broil until lightly browned; set aside. Combine remaining ingredients in sauce pan; bring to a boil. Reduce heat, simmer 15-20 minutes. Adjust hot sauce to taste. Cool. Preheat oven to 375°F. Prepare baking sheet with cooking spray. Dip each wing in hot sauce. Place wings on greased baking sheet. Bake 35-40 minutes, turning and basting once at 20 minutes. Serve warm with ranch dressing.

MELTAWAY MUSHROOMS

1 lb fresh small white mushrooms

8-oz pkg of cream cheese, softened

1 c grated Parmesan cheese

1 tsp Worcestershire sauce

1 tsp dried dill weed

Black pepper to taste

Preheat oven to 350°F. Remove stems and wash mushroom caps in warm, salted water. Drain; place on paper towels to remove further moisture. Mix together remaining ingredients with a hand mixer until well blended. Stuff each cap with about 1 tsp of the mixture. Place on cookie sheet. Bake for 20 minutes. Serve hot. *YIELD: 8+ servings.*

HAM PUFFS

1/2 c butter

1 c water

1 c plain flour

1/2 tsp dry mustard

4 eggs

4 oz sliced ham, diced

1/2 c shredded Cheddar

Line large cookie sheet with parchment paper. Boil butter and water in saucepan on medium heat. Remove when boiling; immediately stir in flour and mustard, until forms a ball. Remove from heat and cool slightly. Add eggs, beating in one at a time, until smooth. Mix ham and cheese into batter. Drop teaspoon-sized mounds of batter onto cookie sheet, 2-inches apart. Bake about 30 minutes at 375°F, or until golden. Turn off heat; leave in oven 15 more minutes before removing.

MISSISSIPPI CHEESE CRACKERS

2 sleeves of saltine crackers

1/2 stick butter, softened (1/4 c)

8-oz pkg shredded sharp Cheddar cheese

Red or cayenne pepper to taste

Spread crackers with butter and place on a large cookie sheet. Sprinkle with grated cheese and pepper. Place under broiler until cheese bubbles. Remove from oven. When oven is cool, set at 150°F; bake crackers for 8 hours. Store in airtight metal container.

LOUISE'S OYSTER CRACKER SNACKS

1-1/2 pkg of oyster crackers

1.0-oz pkg of dry Hidden Valley Ranch dressing mix

3/4 c vegetable oil

1 T dried dill

Combine dry ingredients with the oil. Roll crackers in the oil mixture to coat. Wait 1 hour and roll crackers again. Spread the coated crackers on a cookie sheet and let dry completely. Seal in covered metal container. (Plastic containers retain moisture, causing crackers to become soft.)

PRONTO PUPS (CORN DOGS)

During my childhood, the Mid-South Fair in September always signaled the season for pronto pups (corn dogs). Many years into adulthood, my brother Andy gained a cultish fan following for his role in a crazy David Steen movie titled "The Corn Dog Man." Here's our classic Memphis version of the corn dog.

1 c all-purpose flour

1 c yellow corn meal (fine ground)

1/2 tsp baking soda

1-1/2 tsp baking powder

1/2 tsp kosher salt

1 tsp cayenne

1 egg

1-1/4 c buttermilk

1-1/2 tsp honey

1-1/2 qt vegetable oil (or enough to fill a large skillet to a depth of 1 inch)

10 hot dogs (Hebrew National Reduced Fat Beef Franks are best)

In a medium bowl, whisk together the flour, corn meal, baking soda, baking powder, salt, and cayenne. Set aside. In another medium bowl, whisk the egg until frothy. Add the buttermilk and honey; whisk again. Add wet ingredients to the dry ones, gently folding with a wooden spoon until just barely mixed (over-mixing will make the batter too dense). The batter should be very thick and slightly lumpy. Ladle batter into a tall drinking glass longer than the hot dog. In a large skillet or deep fryer, heat about 1 inch of oil to between 350°F and 375°F. Heat oven to 275°F to keep fried corn dogs hot.

One at a time, push a wooden skewer into the hot dog, about half way. Dip skewered dog into the tall glass of batter, turning slowly as pulling it out to coat evenly. Place the skewered dog into the hot fryer (skewer can go into the oil) Fry, using tongs to turn the dog to fry all sides to a golden brown. Two to three dogs can be fried at a time. Remove to paper towels to drain, then place on baking sheet in oven or in warming oven until ready to serve. *YIELD: 10 servings.*

HICKORY, NC, VERSION: Substitute Bisquick for the flour, soda, baking powder and salt.

PARTY HAM ROLLS

These are absolutely terrific for a brunch or for tailgating.

2 sticks butter, softened (1 c)

1 to 2 T Grey Poupon mustard

2 T poppy seeds

1 tsp Worcestershire sauce

1 medium sweet onion minced

3 dozen Pepperidge Farm or Rainbo finger rolls (or equivalent)

16 oz cooked ham, thinly sliced and chopped fine

2 c Swiss cheese, grated

Mix butter, mustard, poppy seeds, Worcestershire sauce and onion. Use long serrated knife to split package of rolls horizontally into two halves. Spread butter mixture on cut side of both halves of rolls. In pan, layer bottom half with ham. Sprinkle Swiss cheese on top of ham. Replace tops. Bake at 400°F for 10-15 minutes. Cool a few minutes, then use spatula to cut individual roll fingers for serving. Serve hot or cold. NOTE: These freeze well. Cut into individual rolls before freezing so a few may be used at a time. *YIELD: 3 dozen.*

PARTY ROAST BEEF ROLLS

This variation on the ham rolls is equally good for tailgating or parties.

3 dozen Rainbo or Pepperidge Farm finger rolls (3 pkgs)

1/2 c finely chopped walnuts, toasted in a skillet for 5 minutes on low heat

1 T horseradish sauce

3 T Dijon mustard

3 T mayonnaise

2 to 6T peach or apricot preserves (use more if needed)

16 oz deli Cajun roast beef, thinly sliced and chopped fine

2 c Havarti cheese, grated

Mix horseradish sauce, mustard and mayo. Split package of rolls horizontally in half with large serrated knife. Spread preserves on cut-side of tops of rolls. Sprinkle walnuts over the peach mixture. Spread mayo-mustard-horseradish mixture over cut-side of bottom layer. Layer this side with beef and cheese. Cover with top halves, peach-side down. Wrap in aluminum foil. May freeze at this point for up to 1 month. When ready to use, bake at 400° F for 10-15 minutes. Cut into individual rolls before freezing so a few may be used at a time. *YIELD: 3 dozen.*

RYE SQUARES

1 c Cheddar or Havarti cheese, grated

1 c ripe olives, chopped

1 c dried beef, grated or chopped

1 c mayonnaise

Party-size rye squares

Mix ingredients together. Spread on party rye rounds or squares. Broil until bubbly, about 5 minutes. Serve immediately.

SAUSAGE-STUFFED MUSHROOMS

1-1/2 lb white mushrooms, rinsed, patted dry

1/2 lb Italian sausage, removed from casing

1/2 c shredded mozzarella cheese

1/4 c seasoned bread crumbs

1/2 c fresh parsley, chopped fine

Remove stems from mushrooms; chop the stems fine. Set aside. Crumble and cook sausage in skillet on medium, until browned. Remove with slotted spoon to paper towel to drain. Remove all but about 2 T drippings in skillet. Cook stems in skillet about 10 minutes, until tender, stirring frequently. Remove skillet from heat; stir in sausage, cheese and crumbs. Fill mushroom caps with mixture. Place in 10-1/2-by-15-1/2-inch pan. Bake 15 minutes at 450°F. Serve hot on a platter.

SCALLOPED OYSTERS

1 qt raw oysters, shucked, but liquor reserved

2 T butter

1 onion or 3 shallots, chopped fine

1 T all purpose flour

2 tsp dry mustard

2 tsp lemon juice

1/2 tsp white vinegar

1-1/2 tsp Worcestershire sauce

Salt to taste

1 T minced fresh parsley

1/2 c heavy cream

Heat oysters slightly, drain into original liquor; combine liquor and enough water to make up 1 cup. Cook onion in butter, add flour and stir constantly. Whisk in seasonings, liquor, and cream in this order. When very hot, pour over oysters and serve on toast or in patty shells. *YIELD: 8 servings.*

SHRIMP REMOULADE

This was one of Mom's favorite ladies' luncheon offerings, served on a bed of lettuce alongside Rose of Sharon congealed salad.

1 lb boiled shrimp, peeled

3 green onions, minced

3 sprigs parsley, minced

2 ribs celery, minced

2 T creole mustard

4 T olive oil

1 T lemon juice

3/4 tsp paprika (not smoked)

Salt and pepper to taste

Cut shrimp into pieces and toss with all minced ingredients in large bowl. Mix remaining ingredients and add to shrimp, toss well. *YIELD: 4 servings.*

SPINACH BALLS WITH SAUCE

2 pkgs frozen, chopped spinach, cooked and drained

4 eggs, beaten

1-1/2 sticks of butter or margarine (3/4 c)

1/2 c Parmesan cheese

2 c Pepperidge Farm herb stuffing mix

1 large onion, chopped fine

1/2 tsp ground thyme

1/2 tsp garlic salt

1 tsp black pepper or cayenne

1/2 tsp Italian seasoning

3/4 c cooked rice

Combine all ingredients. Chill for 2 hours. Roll into quarter-sized balls. Bake on a cookie sheet for 20 minutes at 350°F.

DIPPING SAUCE:

1 c mayonnaise

1/4 tsp prepared mustard

4 T lemon juice

1/3 c milk (or less)

Mix well all ingredients. Serve on the side with the spinach balls.

DIPS

BEAN DIP (REFRITOS)

This recipe works better in the microwave than the stovetop. Ingredients tend to stick to the pot.

21-oz can of pinto beans, rinsed and drained

6 T chopped onion

2 garlic cloves, peeled and minced

1 tsp chili powder

1 tsp cumin powder

1/4 tsp cayenne pepper

2 whole green chilies, chopped

2 T salsa casera

1/2 c Fiesta Blend Mexican shredded cheese

Put all ingredients but cheese into a food processor or blender with a small amount of water. Process until smooth. Pour into greased casserole dish. Stir shredded cheese into the mixture. Microwave, covered with waxed paper, for 3 minutes on high heat. Stir, and repeat microwave heating in 1 minute segments until all cheese has melted and bean mixture begins to bubble. Stir between heatings. Do not overcook. Serve with heated tortilla chips or with soft tortillas and diced fresh tomatoes.

CARAMEL APPLE DIP

from Terri Robinson Peeler

I got this recipe from my Oxford neighbor, Terri, who makes it for Ole Miss tailgates in The Grove. Note that you have the option to use either confectioners or white granulated sugar, and either toffee bits or pecans.

Two 8-oz blocks of cream cheese, room temperature

8 oz confectioners sugar or 3/4 c white granulated sugar

Mrs. Richardson caramel topping (ice cream topping sold in squirt bottle)

8-oz pkg Heath toffee bits, OR chopped roasted pecans

Tart apples such as Rome, Granny Smith, or Winesaps

Use mixer to blend cream cheese and sugar until fluffy. Spread in shallow dish. Spread with caramel topping. Evenly top with Heath brickle bits or with fine-chopped pecans. Refrigerate until 30 minutes before time to use. Wash and slice the apples for dipping.

CHILI CON QUESO (HOT CHEESE DIP)

Long before prepackaging and national advertising for Rotel, every good Texan knew how to make this most addictive of dips. It's why my family stocked up on Herdez and Rotel in Matamoros. Jeff Triplette became hooked after his first trip to Harlingen in 1973.

QUICK VERSION:

2 lb Velveeta cheese

1 jar of Herdez Salsa Casera OR

10-oz can of Rotel, mild, medium or hot to taste

Cut Velveeta into cubes or strips. Place in large microwavable casserole dish. Melt in microwave on high for 2 minutes. Stir (will not be completely melted). Add Herdez or Rotel; microwave in 2-minute increments between stirrings, until completely melted and bubbly. NOTE: Over-cooking will cause the cheese to harden. Store unused dip covered in fridge. Reheat in microwave or double boiler.

SCRATCH VERSION:

2 lb Velveeta cheese

1 small can evaporated milk

16-oz can diced tomatoes, drained

8-oz can diced green chilies, drained

1 medium white onion, chopped

1 tsp salt

Dash of garlic powder

Combine all ingredients except Velveeta. Cut up Velveeta into smallish chunks and stir into sauce. Melt in double boiler on medium heat, stirring until bubbly.

DEVILED HAM DIP

This is a quick dip or spread for when you're in a pinch. When I was growing up, my mother's friends in East Memphis called this spread Frayser hors d'oeuvres, referring to another part of town.

1/2 c mayonnaise

7-oz can of deviled ham

2 T chopped pimientos

8-oz pkg cream cheese, softened

1 T grated onion

1 tsp chopped parsley, fresh or flakes

Worcestershire sauce to taste

Salt and pepper to taste

Combine all ingredients; mix well. Spoon into serving dish. Serve with crackers.

FABULOUS HOT CHIPPED BEEF DIP

Adjust salt to taste. Dried chipped beef is very salty.

2-1/2 oz dried beef, grated fine

8-oz pkg of cream cheese

2 T milk

1/4 c finely chopped green bell pepper

1/2 tsp garlic powder

1/4 tsp pepper

2 T dried onion flakes

1/2 c sour cream

1/2 c chopped pecans or walnuts

2 T melted butter

1/2 tsp salt

Combine first seven ingredients and mix thoroughly. Fold in sour cream. Sauté nuts in butter in a saucepan, add the salt. Sprinkle over the beef mixture and bake in a Pyrex dish for 20 minutes at 350°F. Serve with corn chips, crackers or toast.

In our family, proper tailgating preparation includes a referee and a mediator. The appetizers and munchies are ALMOST as important.

TRIPLETTE'S TOUCHDOWN TAILGATING TIPS

In the South, appetizers and munchies are essential food groups during football and baseball season. We've developed an entire culture surrounding the tailgate on game day. Here's how to make your tailgating fun and trouble-free.

Keep your game-day essentials in a tailgate bag on rollers, and maintain a tailgate-essentials checklist.
Know your parking location and all rules or restrictions at the location where you plan to set up your tailgate.
Anticipate where to secure your tailgating accoutrements during the game (they are prohibited in all stadiums).
Prepare your make-ahead components the day before, and run the checklist:

- Grill-ready foil packets containing cookout food; casserole food ready to bake prior to the game
- Veggies for dipping, stored in cooler-ready baggies or refrigerator containers
- Desserts and munchies, stored in cooler-ready baggies
- Bottles of water frozen in advance to pack in the cooler(s) for no-mess cooling
- Disposable cups, plates, cutlery and napkins
- Trash bags, paper towels, wet wipes, toothpicks
- Grilling supplies, matches, butane lighter (where flames are allowed); sterno warmers ready to light
- Spices (salt, pepper, pepper sauce, condiments)

FRESH CHICKPEA HUMMUS

My mother grew up with several neighbors of Lebanese descent who became lifelong friends. Lebanese Middle Eastern cuisine such as hummus and tabouli are old favorites up and down the Mississippi.

FOR THE CHICKPEAS:

2 c chickpeas

1/2 c water

1/2 tsp coarse salt

FOR THE HUMMUS:

4 T tahini (sesame paste)

1/2 c olive oil

3 T lemon juice (juice of 1 lemon)

3 cloves of fresh garlic

1/2 tsp ground cumin

1/4 tsp ground coriander

Salt and ground pepper, to taste

Place chickpeas in a colander and rinse under cold water. Remove any pods or pod pieces. Put water, salt and beans in a small pot, cover, and place over high heat until water boils. Turn down heat and simmer for 2 to 4 minutes until beans are tender. Drain and let cool.

Place hummus ingredients and chickpeas into a food processor or blender. Puree, scraping down the sides. Refrigerate. Serve with crackers or toasted pita bread cut into wedges. *YIELD: About 3 cups.*

GUACAMOLE

Avocados are interesting. Different varieties taste completely different. Haas avocadoes are the small ones that turn really black when over-ripe. Haas make the best guacamole in my opinion, if not TOO ripe. Save the large green avocados for salads and soups. Authentic guacamole relies on lime juice to enhance the flavor, so go easy on the salt. Some people prefer to dice, not mash, the avocado. NOTE: To prevent browning, place avocado pit in center of prepared guacamole.

2 to 3 ripe avocados (skin not too black and not too soft)

Juice of 2 to 3 limes

6 to 8 green onions, chopped fine, including some greens

2 to 3 cloves garlic, crushed and minced, OPTIONAL

Salt to taste (be conservative)

2 medium tomatoes, peeled and diced, or 1 c halved cherry tomatoes

Salsa casera or diced green chili peppers, OPTIONAL

Fine-chopped cilantro, OPTIONAL

To prepare avocados, use a paring knife and cut lengthwise all around, down to the seed. Using both hands, twist the two halves in opposite directions to break apart. Use paring knife to lift out the seed. Scoop the meat out from inside the avocado skin.

Mash the avocado in a small bowl. Squeeze lime juice over the avocado, add the garlic and onion, and continue mashing with a ricer or pastry blender. When smooth, or almost smooth, add the salt and tomatoes. Add salsa casera or diced chili pepper for hot pepper kick, with cilantro, if desired. *YIELD: 4 to 6 servings.*

SEAFOOD DIP

from Andrea Benfield

2 c cooked shrimp

12 oz crab meat, picked and cleaned

1 can cream of shrimp soup

1 tsp black pepper

1/2 c mayonnaise

2 c fresh grated Parmesan cheese

3 celery ribs, chopped fine

1 green bell pepper, chopped

1 white onion, chopped

Mix first 6 ingredients together in a large bowl. Sauté the celery, green pepper and onion in butter or olive oil. Drain. Add to the seafood mixture and mix well. Pour into a casserole dish and bake at 325°F for 20-25 minutes until bubbly and brown. Serve hot with crackers or toast points. Andrea serves this at her Christmas Open House.

SHRIMP DIP

from Mary Elizabeth Daltroff

2 cans of shrimp (or 20 boiled, medium-sized shrimp, peeled and chopped)

8-oz pkg of cream cheese

Juice of 1 lemon

1 small onion, chopped fine

3 ribs of celery, chopped fine

1/2 c mayonnaise

1/4 c ketchup

Tabasco sauce to taste

Worcestershire sauce to taste

Salt to taste

Mix all ingredients together. Serve with crackers.

HINT: Best way to chop onions: Remove all loose papery covering, but retain root. Slice onion in half from top to the root, pull remaining outer onion skin down toward root. With flat cut side down, slice onion from top toward root, then cut across the slices.

SPINACH DIP

Two 10-oz pkgs frozen, chopped spinach

1 tsp salt

1 c chopped parsley

Small bunch of scallions or green onions, finely chopped

1 pt of sour cream

2 c mayonnaise

2 to 3 T lemon juice (to taste)

3 T dill

1/4 c chopped chives

Garlic salt to taste

Thaw spinach and squeeze out water. Combine with other ingredients. Cover and refrigerate overnight. Serve in a "boat" carved from an oblong loaf of bread. Place chunks of rye bread or other breads around the boat for dipping. May also serve with dipping veggies, and may also serve the spinach dip in a hollowed head of purple or green cabbage.

QUICKIE VARIATION: Add 2 pkg (1.4 oz each) of Knorr vegetable soup mix, and omit the parsley, dill and chives.

VIDALIA ONION DIP

2 to 3 T light olive oil

2 lb Vidalia onions, sliced into thin rings

8 oz cream cheese, softened

1 c sour cream

1 T red wine vinegar

1 lb thick-sliced bacon, crisp-cooked, crumbled

1 tsp thyme

Salt and pepper to taste

Heat oil over medium heat. Add onions, sauté about 15 minutes. Cover, reduce heat to low. Cook, stirring frequently until golden brown, about 20 minutes. Cool, then coarsely chop the cooked onions. Mix cream cheese and sour cream until smooth. Reserve 1 slice crumbled bacon, stirring remaining bacon, onions, vinegar, thyme, salt and pepper into cream cheese mixture. Top with reserved bacon. Chill 30 minutes before serving.

SPINACH ARTICHOKE DIP

4-1/2 c whole milk

1 tsp ground mustard

1 tsp garlic powder

1/2 to 1 tsp cayenne pepper

1/4 tsp red pepper flakes

1 c finely chopped yellow onion

1 to 2 T butter

2 T plain flour

4 T butter

8 oz sharp Cheddar cheese, shredded

4 oz Monterey Jack cheese, shredded

8 oz Velveeta cheese, cubed

Two 6-oz jars artichoke hearts, well drained

Three 10-oz boxes frozen chopped spinach, thawed overnight in fridge

1-1/2 c Monterey Jack cheese

Heat milk and spices in 4-qt saucepan on medium heat just to a boil. Reduce heat and simmer. Sauté onion in 1 to 2 T butter until transparent, add to saucepan. Melt 4 T butter in small sauce pan, then whisk in flour until smooth. Cook on low heat until golden brown and thickened (add more butter if needed to make proper roux). Whisk roux into milk; mix well. Cook until sauce thickens, whisking as needed.

Add Velveeta, Cheddar, and Monterey Jack cheeses to saucepan, stirring with wooden spoon until completely melted and blended. Make sure not to scorch on bottom of pot. Remove from heat. Cool 15 minutes.

Drain artichokes and squeeze out excess water. Cut into 1/4-inch strips. Set aside. Squeeze water out of thawed spinach. Place in sieve and squeeze more. Add drained spinach and artichokes to cheese sauce; mix until completely blended. Pour into 11-by-9-by-2-inch casserole pan. Top with 1-1/2 cup grated Monterey Jack. Bake at 350°F 12-20 minutes until bubbly. Serve hot with pita chips or crusty bread.

FAMILY MEMORY

Grandmother Thurmond, a former teacher, always advised me to marry a tall man with good teeth and small feet. I took her advice.

NUTS

FROSTED PECANS

from Rosalee Hyam

A member of the Pilot Club in Greenville, MS, and with her own pecan trees, Aunt Rosie was always my Memphis family's in-house source for a year's supply of pecans.

2-1/2 c pecan halves

1 c white granulated sugar

3 T water

1/4 tsp salt

1-1/4 tsp vanilla extract

1 tsp cinnamon

Toast the pecans in moderate oven for 8 minutes. Mix other ingredients in a saucepan. Cover and bring to a boil. Boil until reaches the soft ball stage. Remove mixture from heat, add nuts and stir until the syrup covers the nuts and looks frosty. Turn onto waxed paper to cool. Separate the nuts while still warm.

VARIATION: Fold toasted pecans and spices (omit vanilla) into 2 egg whites, beaten stiff. Spread out on buttered cookie sheet and bake about 30 minutes at 325°F, tossing frequently. Cool, then break apart.

Jeff Triplette and Rosalee Bloom Hyam, June 2, 1973

ROASTED PECANS

My biggest regret when packng the cars for the move to Oxford from Charlotte was that the jumbo bag of pecans from Louise and Lester's farm wouldn't fit. It was the crowning, 11th-hour, move-related crisis: Pick either the pecans or the toy poodle for that last square foot of car space. I chose the dog; still miss those nuts!

1 c pecan halves

1 T butter

1/2 tsp salt

1/4 tsp cayenne pepper

Pinch of white granulated sugar

Cover pecans with water, bring to a boil for 30 seconds, then heat butter and spices in a saucepan. Scoop up the pecans from the water and mix into the spice butter. Stir until dark and glossy (4 to 5 minutes).

SPICY PECANS

2 c pecan halves

1/2 c brown sugar

1/4 c butter, softened

1/4 tsp cayenne pepper

1 tsp kosher salt

1 tsp chili powder

Preheat oven to 350°F. Mix softened butter and spices. Melt in 9-by-13-inch pan, remove from heat, toss in pecans. Cover in foil. After a few minutes, uncover and toss pecans and spice mixture again. Spread pecans in one layer on a baking sheet. Roast for 15 minutes, tossing several times to keep from burning or roasting unevenly. Remove from oven and cool on a wire rack. Store in a tightly covered metal container.

TOASTED GARLIC OR CURRY PECANS

1/4 c butter, melted

4 tsp Worcestershire sauce

1 T garlic salt

Dash of Tabasco

4 c pecan halves

Stir butter and spices; mix with pecans. Spread out in large flat pan and toast at 250°F for 30 minutes. Stir occasionally while toasting. Use slotted spoon to spread on paper towel to cool and drain. Store in tightly sealed metal container once cooled (3 to 4 hours).

VARIATION: Add 1 tsp curry powder.

SPREADS

BUTTER SPREADS FOR FANCY TEA SANDWICHES

The spreads below are only a few examples of what can be combined to create elegant and tasty appetizers served with tea or cocktails. Skim the spread lightly over a piece of bread, cover it with a second piece of bread, then use cookie cutters to cut out decorative mini sandwiches. Cream cheese may be substituted for butter.

LEMON BUTTER: Cream 1/4 c butter with 2 tsp lemon juice and 1 tsp lemon zest

CHEESE BUTTER: Cream 1/4 c butter with 1/4 c fine-shredded extra sharp cheese and 1 to 2 dashes of paprika

CHIVES BUTTER: Cream 1/2 c butter with 1 to 2 tsp fine-minced chives.

ONION BUTTER: Cream 1/2 c butter with 1 to 2 tsp fine-minced onion (juice squeezed out).

SHRIMP BUTTER: Cream 1/4 c butter with 1/4 c finely minced cooked shrimp, 1 tsp lemon juice, and a dash of paprika.

PARSLEY BUTTER: Cream 1/4 c butter with 2 T finely minced fresh parsley.

PESTO BUTTER: Cream 1/2 c butter with 1 to 2 tsp pesto.

Six-year-old Sheila Daltroff, Baby Louis, and Eula May Daltroff, Spring, 1927

CHEESE BALL—WITH VARIATIONS

BASIC CHEESE BALL:

Two 16-oz pkgs extra sharp Cheddar cheese (NOTE: packaged grated cheese is okay)

8-oz pkg muenster cheese

8-oz pkg of another light and mild cheese (Colby or Monterey Jack)

Four 8-oz pkgs cream cheese

1/8 to 1/4 tsp cayenne pepper

6 shakes of powdered garlic

3 shakes of onion salt

1 tsp lemon juice

1 squirt Worcestershire sauce

Soften the cream cheese. Grate the other cheeses; blend by hand into cream cheese. Mix and knead like dough until thoroughly mixed. Blend in spices and lemon juice; continue working by hand.

To complete, choose one of the following:

· Roll cheese ball or log in up to 1/2 c finely chopped walnuts or pecans.
· Roll log or ball in chopped bacon bits or grated chipped beef.
· Sprinkle paprika over outside of cheese ball or log.

YIELD: 3 to 4 balls or logs.

Variation 1: PINEAPPLE CHEESE LOG OR BALL:

Add 1/4 c finely diced bell pepper, 1/4 to 1/2 c finely diced sweet onion, and 1 small can crushed pineapple, well drained.

Variation 2: SPICY CHEESE LOG:

Mix in 1 small can of chopped green chilis, or a fine-chopped jalapeño pepper (with seeds removed).

Variation 3: HAM AND CHEESE LOG:

Combine 1/4 c sour cream with 1 small can of deviled ham spread, and mix thoroughly. Add 1/4 c finely chopped nuts (walnuts or pecans). This makes up more of a cheese spread than a log.

Variation 4: SALMON CHEESE LOG:

Add 1/4 c sour cream, 1 small can of drained and picked-out salmon (all fat, bones and skin removed), finely chopped celery, and 1/4 c finely chopped almonds.

CHICKEN LIVER PATÉ

from Laurie Triplette

Chopped liver, Southern style. I developed this because I love chicken livers. I call it paté because by adding unflavored gelatin to the cooked paste, one can mold it in a small loaf pan and serve cold, sliced, with Creole mustard, midget pickles and crusty bread. It works best, though, as a hot paste on toasted, sliced multi-grain or peasant bread.

20-oz container of frozen chicken livers

1-1/2 tsp salt

1/4 tsp black pepper

Pinch of thyme

2 c all-purpose white flour

1-1/2 sticks of butter (3/4 c)

1 c medium or hot chow-chow (amount of heat to taste)

1/8 to 1/4 c of cognac

Cayenne pepper to taste

Thaw chicken livers in refrigerator overnight. Rinse, drain and pat dry. Mix the salt, pepper and thyme with the flour in a bowl, and dredge the livers in the flour mixture. Place coated livers on a cookie sheet to set.

Melt butter or chicken schmalz (fat) in a skillet, and add the coated livers. Cook for 2 to 3 minutes on each side. When the livers begin changing colors and juices start running clear instead of red, start "worrying" them with the spatula or spoon. Keep pushing the livers around, making sure to keep flour from burning at the edges and on the sides of the skillet.

As the livers start to crumble, mash them and keep on until they have been mashed evenly, turning the heat down to medium or medium-low. Keep turning the liver mixture in the pan. Sprinkle a dash of Cayenne and add sherry or dry white wine. Add the chow-chow. Stir completely and keep stirring for about 5 minutes. The mixture should have the consistency of a liver mush.

Remove from heat and pour into a covered terrine or chafing dish. May serve immediately or heat in oven at 325°F for 30 minutes. Serve with toast or crackers. Just as good at room temperature. Freeze leftovers up to 1 month.

VARIATION: Chop and sauté two yellow onions, in the butter before adding the livers.

Cucumber finger sandwiches and spread are an old-fashioned treat.

CHICKEN LIVER EN CROÛTE

CRUST:

6 c all-purpose flour

2 tsp salt

1-1/2 c shortening

2 eggs

3 c water

Work with fingers to get crust to the consistency of coarse cornmeal. Make a "well" in the center of this blended mixture and break two eggs, one at a time into the center, working the dough into the egg from the sides. Gradually add 3 cups water, working dough with your fingers. Roll the dough into a ball and chill, covered, for at least 1 hour. Roll out with a rolling pin when ready to use. Mold dough into greased, floured terrine or loaf pan, flapping edges over the sides.

PATÉ:

Laurie's chicken liver paté (*see recipe, page 79*)

1 pkg unflavored gelatin

2 T boiling water

Make Laurie's Chicken Liver Paté. Combine 1 pkg unflavored gelatin with 2 T boiling water until granules have dissolved. Mix into pate while both are still hot. Ladle paté into dough-lined terrine. Cover with more crust dough, crimping and sealing all edges. Make decorative slits in top. Place dish in a pan of water and bake uncovered at 350°F until crust is golden brown, about 30-45 minutes. Cool 20 minutes, flip out. Slice and serve. Refrigerate unused portion.

BACON VARIATION: Position overlapping bacon strips inside a terrine or loaf pan, flapping over the edges of the pan. Make sure bacon completely covers pan with no gaps. Fill with paté, and fold bacon strips over the top. Place dish in oven and bake uncovered at 350°F until bacon is crisp, about 35 minutes to 1 hour. Let cool, then flip out onto serving plate, using a spatula to loosen from pan. Chill. Slice and serve.

CUCUMBER SANDWICH SPREAD

6 to 12 medium-size gourmet seedless cucumbers, OR 6 to 12 Kirby cucumbers, OR 2 large English cucumbers

1/2 c finely diced sweet onion (drained on paper towel)

1 T lemon juice

Two 8-oz pkg cream cheese, softened

2 to 3 T mayonnaise

1/2 tsp salt

3 to 4 shakes of cayenne pepper (about 1/8 tsp)

2 turns of black pepper mill

Two loaves of white bread (about 20 bread slices)

Peel the cucumbers. Quarter them and finely dice. Drain them. If the Kirby cukes have noticeable seeds, scoop the seeds out of the centers before dicing. Add the chopped onion and mix.

Using a hand mixer, beat the cream cheese until softened and smooth, then add the mayo, lemon juice, salt and black pepper. Beat in the cucumber and onion mixture. When thoroughly blended, add the cayenne pepper to taste. Drain any excess liquid that might accumulate from the cukes. Seal tightly and refrigerate overnight in a covered container. Just before serving, punch bread rounds with a biscuit cutter (makes approximately 2 rounds per slice of loaf bread). This amount of spread will require 2 loaves of bread rounds. Spread the cucumber mix on one side and clean up the sides after adding the "top" slice. Or, spread on slices of bread, top, and remove crusts, quartering the sandwiches into triangles. Spread is good served as a dip with crackers or toast points.

FALLBACK OLIVE SPREAD

This recipe dates back to the early 1960s. It's a safe standby to whip up when company's coming and supplies in the larder are low.

6 oz cream cheese (from 8-oz pkg), softened

1/2 c mayonnaise

1 c chopped green olives (buy the inexpensive jar that says chopped salad olives)

Dash of ground pepper (NO SALT)

1/2 c chopped pecans

Combine the cream cheese and mayo. Add the juice from the olive jar, and the dash of pepper. Fold in the pecans and the olives. Serve with toast points or crackers.

HOLIDAY CHEESE RING

from Andrea Benfield

Andrea serves this at her annual holiday Open House.

1 lb sharp Cheddar cheese, grated

1 c mayonnaise

1 c chopped pecans

1 small white onion, finely diced

1 c strawberry preserves

Mix first 4 ingredients well. Press into a round glass pie plate. Refrigerate overnight. Top evenly with chilled strawberry preserves before serving.

OLD-FASHIONED PIMIENTO CHEESE

from Ruth Thurmond, a Callicott family recipe

Aunt Ruth inherited this really old recipe from her family. Try this for a reminder of the good old days.

1 hard-cooked egg, chopped

1/2 lb grated sharp Cheddar cheese

1-1/2 T diced pimiento, drained

2 T finely chopped white onion

1/4 T salt

1 T butter

1 T white granulated sugar

1 T all-purpose flour

2 T white distilled vinegar

1/2 c evaporated milk

Dash of cayenne pepper

Combine cheese, pimiento, onion and salt with chopped egg in a bowl. Melt butter in double boiler, add sugar and flour, and blend. Add vinegar, milk and cayenne; cook until thickened, stirring. Cool slightly and combine with the cheese mixture. Blend well. Refrigerate.

HINT: Best way to chop or crush garlic: Place unpeeled garlic clove on its side on cutting board. Place flat side of chopping knife on top, then pound once with fist to crush the clove. Outer paper comes loose and can be easily removed, and the clove is flattened enough to chop fine.

SOUTHERN PIMIENTO CHEESE

2- to 4-oz jar of diced pimientos (drained), to taste

8 oz extra-sharp Cheddar cheese, shredded

1-1/2 tsp white granulated sugar

1/2 c Duke's mayonnaise, or homemade mayo

1/4 c finely chopped onion

1/2 to 1 tsp Worcestershire sauce, OPTIONAL (less, not more)

Dash of cayenne pepper, to taste

Combine pimientos and cheese in a bowl and mix. Add sugar and mayo to mixture. Add onions (juice squeezed out through paper towel), and optional Worcestershire, to taste. Stir with hand mixer if you want the mixture soft and spreadable, or use a hand whisk if you prefer it chunky. Scrape down the sides of the bowl as you mix. Chill at least 2 hours. Ages well.

RELISHES

LAURIE'S BRUSCHETTA

Traditional Spanish bruschetta calls for rubbing raw garlic over toasted bread before topping with tomatoes, basil, and olive oil. This recipe is my interpretation of the Americanized relish version of bruschetta.

Roma, Campari or Plum tomatoes, diced, with skins on

1 large bunch of fresh basil leaves

4 to 6 green onions, chopped, with green part

4 to 6 cloves of garlic, minced fine

2 T of sweet onion, minced

2 to 3 T Parmesan cheese, grated fine

Olive oil

Apple cider vinegar

Salt and pepper to taste

Toasted slices of French or Italian bread

Chop the basil leaves, onion, garlic, green onion and tomatoes and mix well in a small metal bowl. Whisk in the Parmesan until it starts to form a paste. Pour in olive oil, stirring briskly, until completely blended. Pour in a bit of vinegar at a time, whisking or stirring briskly, until oil and vinegar are completely mixed. Add salt and pepper to taste. If too pasty to spoon over toasted French or Italian bread, add more oil and vinegar. The tomatoes will naturally thin the mixture as it sits. Serve with sliced mozzarella and loose basil leaves, to taste. *YIELD: 4 to 8 servings.*

CHOW-CHOW

Chow-Chow relish, served as a side for meats and veggies, is a Southern staple, particularly in the Appalachians and Piedmont. Louise made this version.

2 qt cabbage (medium to large head)

1/2 c to 1-1/2 c sweet onion

1/2 c red or green bell pepper

2 T salt

Cayenne pepper, OPTIONAL

2 c white distilled vinegar

1-1/2 c white sugar

2 tsp dry mustard

1 tsp turmeric

1/2 tsp ground ginger

2 tsp celery seed

2 tsp mustard seed

Shred cabbage in box grater. Chop onion fine, and peppers more coarsely. Combine, and sprinkle veggies with salt. Let stand 4 to 6 hours in fridge. Drain well. Combine spices, sugar and vinegar in large pot, simmer for 10 minutes. Add salted, drained veggies to pot and simmer another 10 minutes. Bring to a boil. Then pack into sterilized, heating canning jars while boiling. Leave 1/8-inch space at top. Place canning lids and rings on jars, and tighten. Turn jars upside down while hot to ensure heat seal. Edible as soon as jars cool.

ROYAL CHOW-CHOW (SPANISH PICKLE OR PICCALILLI)

4 c chopped cabbage

3 c chopped cauliflower

2 c chopped onions

2 c chopped green tomatoes

2 c chopped green bell peppers

3 T salt

2-1/2 c white vinegar

1-1/2 c white sugar

2 tsp dry mustard

1 tsp turmeric

1/2 tsp ground ginger

2 tsp celery seed

1 tsp mustard seed

Same instructions as Chow-Chow. *YIELD: 4 pints.*

CORN RELISH

Grandmother Thurmond made this as a topping.

1/3 c white granulated sugar

1 T cornstarch

1 tsp instant minced onion

1 tsp turmeric

1/2 tsp celery seed

1/4 c white distilled vinegar

1/4 c water

12-oz can of vacuum packed kernel corn (or 1-1/2 c fresh-cut corn)

2 T finely chopped green bell pepper

1 T finely chopped pimiento

Combine first 8 ingredients in a saucepan. Cook and stir over medium heat until mixture thickens and boils. Remove from heat to cool. Stir in green pepper and pimiento. Chill. *YIELD: 1-3/4 cups.*

CUCUMBER RELISH

from Andrea Benfield

Andrea makes this in summer to eat with various beans. It's also good with pork.

10 large cucumbers, peeled and chopped

8 green bell peppers, cored, seeded, and chopped

5 medium onions, diced

2 T salt

1 pt white distilled vinegar

3 c white granulated sugar

1 T mustard seed

1/2 tsp turmeric

1/4 tsp celery seed

Combine chopped cucumbers, peppers and onion. Cover with salt and let stand 4 hours. Squeeze off water. Bring the vinegar, sugar, mustard seed, turmeric and celery seed to a boil. Add the chopped vegetables; continue for 1 minute. Ladle into hot, sterilized jars to seal. No need for hot water bath; the jars will seal themselves. *YIELD: 8-1/2 pints.*

Christmas Relish (7 pts.)

5 Red Bell Peppers
5 Green "
5 Medium white Onions
4 hot peppers (optional)
1 qt. vinegar
2 lbs. sugar
3 Tb. Salt
(This is full sweet.
Add less sugar if
you like it Better
not so sweet.)

Wash peppers & remove
Peel onions & wash
Grind peppers & onions
Put in colander.
Pour boiling water over
them; let drain 10 min.
Measure salt, sugar and
vinegar in steamer.
Place over medium heat
to dissolve.
Add pepper mixture and
cook until light in color
(30 or 35 min)
Seal in sterile jars.

GRANDMOTHER'S CHRISTMAS RELISH

This was written by my Grandmother, Ruby White Thurmond, in her own hand to my Aunt Aline, Norman Thurmond's wife, on a postcard dated September 28, 1965. Granddaddy loved relish in any form, but particularly Grandmother's Christmas Relish and her chili relish. Grandmother's Christmas relish is like the South's traditional Sweet Pepper Relish, but on steroids.

5 red bell peppers

5 green bell peppers

5 medium white onions

4 hot cayenne or tabasco peppers

1 qt white vinegar

2 lb (4 c) white granulated sugar

3 T salt

Wash peppers and remove seeds. Peel onions and wash. Grind peppers and onions in chopper. Put in colander. Pour boiling water over them, and let drain for 10 minutes. Measure salt, sugar and vinegar in large stock pot. Place over medium heat to dissolve. Add pepper mixture and cook until light in color, 30 or 35 minutes. Seal in sterile canning jars.

NOTE FROM GRANDMOTHER:
"This is full sweet. Add less sugar if you like it better not so sweet."
Does anyone else find this hilarious?

LOUISE'S SWEET PEPPER RELISH

from Louise Sherrill Triplette

Grandmother Thurmond's Christmas Relish was a sweeter version of this one.

12 green peppers

12 red peppers

12 small onions, about the size of an egg

2 c white vinegar

2 c white granulated sugar

3 T salt

Chop peppers and onions. Cover with boiling water. Let stand for 15 minutes, then drain. Bring vinegar, sugar and salt to a boil. Add pepper and onion mixture and boil for 5 minutes. Pack this into jars and seal.

MAJOR GREY-STYLE CHUTNEY

What's the difference between chutney and relish? Chutney is a spicy relish made with fruit instead of veggies.

4 c peeled, chopped mangoes

1 c dark brown sugar

1 c apple cider vinegar

1 c yellow onion, chopped

3/4 c golden raisins

1/2 c lime, seeded, chopped

1/2 c ginger root, grated

1/2 c orange, peeled, seeded

1/2 c molasses

1/4 c peeled, seeded, chopped lemon

3 cloves garlic, minced

1 T mustard seed

1 T red pepper flakes

1 tsp ground cinnamon

1/4 tsp ground cloves

1/4 tsp allspice

2 T minced cilantro

Combine first 13 ingredients in large stainless steel pot. Bring to a boil, stirring constantly, cooking 30 minutes. Add last 4 spices, stir well, cook 10 more minutes, until chutney begins to thicken. Ladle into hot, prepared half-pint canning jars, using standard canning techniques. Process in hot water canner for 10 minutes. Store in dark cool place.

JALAPEÑO SALSA

from Andrea Benfield

1/2 bushel Roma tomatoes

3 lb. white onions

6 to 12 jalapeño peppers, seeded

1 T garlic powder

2 large cans tomato paste

1 c white granulated sugar

2 c white vinegar

1/2 c salt

6 T paprika

6 T chili powder

2 T cumin powder

Peel and chop tomatoes, onion and peppers. Mix all ingredients and cook 10 minutes in a large stock pot. Fill sterilized pint jars and seal. Process in hot water bath 15 minutes. NOTE: The quantity of peppers determine the "heat" of the salsa. *YIELD: 18 pints.*

PICO DE GALLO

The first time my brothers and I ever had pico de gallo was in the Rio Grande Valley in the 1950s.

2 slicing tomatoes, or 4 Plum tomatoes, diced and seeded

1 large or two small ripe avocados, diced

1/4 c diced white or red onion *(I prefer red)*

1/4 c chopped green onion

2 to 4 T diced yellow or red bell pepper

1 Serrano or large jalapeño pepper, seeded and chopped

1/4 c fine-chopped fresh cilantro, OPTIONAL

1 clove garlic, minced, OPTIONAL

2 to 4 T fresh lime juice

1 T extra virgin olive oil, or extra light olive oil

Salt to taste

Combine all ingredients in a glass or stainless steel bowl. Refrigerate at least 30 minutes before serving. Best served the day it's made, but keeps up to 4 days if sealed. Also tastes great on tossed salad greens or large Romaine lettuce leaves with strips of smoked chicken. (NOTE: Romas or plum tomatoes actually work best.)

JAMS AND JELLIES

APPLE BUTTER (SLOW COOKER)

Old fashioned apple butter was our ancestors' way to salvage damaged apples. The classic calls for leaving the apples unpeeled. Modern cooks can still make it this way, or can use unsweetened applesauce as a short cut. Definitely use a slow cooker. The Scratch and Applesauce versions both adapt well to peaches, pears, and apricots.

SCRATCH APPLE BUTTER

4 lb tart cooking apples (Jonathans or Winesaps)

2 c apple cider

3 c granulated sugar

2 tsp cinnamon

1/4 to 1 tsp ground cloves (to taste)

1/8 tsp allspice, OPTIONAL

Stem and core apples. Chop. Combine with cider in large slow cooker. Cover; cook 10 hr. Stir in sugar and spices. Cook additional 1 to 2 hours, until thickened and darkened. Remove from heat; cool, stir to blend skins. Freeze or pour into sterilized jars and seal. *YIELD: 4 to 5 pints.*

APPLESAUCE VERSION

7 c (3-1/2 pt) unsweetened applesauce

2 to 3 c granulated sugar, to taste

2 tsp cinnamon

1/8 tsp ground cloves

Combine all ingredients in slow cooker. Cover, but place layer of paper towels under lid to prevent condensation from dripping. Cook on high 8-10 hr. Butter will condense and turn dark. Remove lid during last hr; stir occasionally. Cool; freeze or pour into sterilized jars; seal. *YIELD: 2 pints.*

VARIATIONS: Use canned peaches, pears or apricots instead of apples.

WHEN DESEEDING HOT PEPPERS

Some peppers are so hot they will burn your skin. To deseed hot peppers, wear gloves. Be sure to remove all the seeds, which are the major source of heat. Use milk and lemon or lime juice to remove all the pepper capsaicin from your hands afterward.

BLACKBERRY JAM

6 c crushed blackberries

1 pkg powdered pectin

8-1/2 c white granulated sugar

Sort and wash fully ripe blackberries. Remove any stems or caps. Crush them, and if very seedy, press through a sieve to remove the large seeds. Measure the crushed berries into a large pot; add pectin and stir well. Place on high heat and bring quickly to a rolling boil, stirring constantly. Boil at a rolling boil for 1 minute, stirring constantly. Remove from heat, skim the top and stir alternately for 5 minutes. Ladle into hot canning jars and seal immediately. *YIELD: About 14 each, 6-oz jars.*

FERNIE'S CARROT MARMALADE

from Fern Robertson Kerslake

3 oranges

4 c water

3 c grated carrot

3 T lemon juice

4 c white granulated sugar

1/2 tsp ground ginger

Peel oranges, cut peel into strips, cut pulp into small pieces. Cook peel in the 4 cups of water until tender, Let stand overnight. Add grated carrot; boil 10 minutes, then add remaining ingredients; boil until sugar is clear and starts to thicken. Pour into sterilized pint jars and seal with hot water bath.

FIG PRESERVES

All old-time Southerners know to plant their fig trees in the sun on the south side of the house, against a wall, for added protection during inevitable winter freezes. After freeze-backs, our fig trees grow back as hearty shrubs, stronger than before.

2 to 5 pts fresh ripe figs, washed, blemish-free

1 pt white granulated sugar for every 1 pt of figs

1 T water per every 1 pt of figs

In a large boiler, combine sugar with just enough water to wet the sugar. Heat on low until sugar dissolves, making a thick syrup. Add figs and increase heat. Bring to a moderate boil until figs are pink and transparent, about 10 minutes. Pack figs into sterilized, hot jars, cover figs with fig syrup, and seal. Process in hot water bath 10 minutes.

GREEN PEPPER JELLY

This recipe is fun to make, even for those of us who do not can and preserve other fruit and vegetables. Tastes fantastic on cream cheese with crackers.

3 whole green bell peppers, cored, seeded, chopped

3 to 5 smallish jalapeño peppers (or other hot variety), seeded and diced

6-1/2 c white granulated sugar

1-1/2 c apple cider vinegar

6-oz bottle of Certo

Green food coloring

Half-pint canning jars sterilized according to jar instructions

Paraffin, OPTIONAL

Cut up bell peppers and put into blender. Add hot peppers, cut up, and puree until milky looking. Put sugar and vinegar in a large pot and add the pureed peppers to this. Bring to a roaring boil. Add Certo. Return to a rolling boil for 60 seconds. Remove from heat. Scrape off excess scum from top. Add food coloring. Pour into hot, sterile, half-pint jars. Seal with paraffin if desired. The jars will seal themselves due to heat, but process in hot water bath (without paraffin) if unsure. *YIELD: 6 half-pint jars.*

VARIATION: Use red bell peppers instead of green to make red pepper jelly.

ORANGE MARMALADE

from Ruby White Thurmond

3 oranges

1-1/2 lemons

Water

White granulated sugar

Leave rinds on lemons and oranges. Cut in half and remove seeds. Grind fruit very fine. Add 3 cups of water and 1 cup of sugar for every cup of ground citrus. Cook until jellied. Pour into hot sterilized pint jars. Seal. Process 10 minutes in hot water bath.

FOR A MORE EXOTIC FLAVOR

Top figs with thin-sliced lemon or ginger before sealing and processing.

CEDAR OAKS

Cedar Oaks Historic Home is an 1859 antebellum house preserved and maintained since 1963 by two Oxford sister organizations, The Cosmopolitan Club and The Centennial Study Club. One autumn day while working at Cedar Oaks with fellow Cosmopolite Lorraine Wagster, I realized that the property still contains several mature quince trees, which were fruiting like crazy.

STRAWBERRY PRESERVES

2 heaping qt fresh strawberries

2 c white granulated sugar + 3 c white granulated sugar

2 T lemon juice

Wash and cap the strawberries. Drain and pat dry. Put in large pot and add the sugar and lemon juice. Heat on low until all sugar dissolves, Stirring only with wooden spoon.

Bring to hard boil; boil 5 minutes. Remove from heat, add 3 more c sugar, and return to low heat. Let all new sugar dissolve; bring again to hard boil and time it for 10 minutes minimum (may take longer). Skim scum off surface. Test for doneness: When 2 drops run together from silver spoon, the preserves are done.

Remove pan from heat. Pour preserves into shallow Pyrex dish, cover airtight with Saran wrap. Let dish stand for 12-24 hrs, shaking dish from side to side every few hours to even-up juice. Remove wrap, skim off remaining foam. Ladle into hot, sterilized half-pint jars. Cover with hot lids; process jars 5 minutes in boiling water bath. Cool. If any of the lids fail to seal, refrigerate and use immediately. NOTE: Old instructions advise the cook to seal in jars with melted paraffin without using a hot water canning bath. This has been deemed by the canning industry to be less than failsafe.

QUINCE JELLY

Lorraine and I dug out our old family recipes, and also consulted the internet for helpful hints on how to make old-fashioned quince jelly. We learned the hard way to ignore vintage instructions to omit pectin. Definitely DO ADD pectin to insure proper jelling. The result is a beautiful, rose-colored jelly that tastes tart but sweet, with a flavor both perfumey and piquant.

3 to 3-1/2 lb quinces, halved and deseeded, peels on

7-1/2 c white granulated sugar

3 fluid oz liquid pectin (Certo)

4-1/2 c water

1/4 c lemon juice

Nine 1/2-pt canning jars and lids

Select quinces, about three-fourths fully ripe, and one-fourth under-ripe. Sort, wash, remove stems and blossom ends. Some recipes say not to pare or core, but I recommend it because the seeds are slightly poisonous.

Sterilize 9 jars in boiling water at least 5 minutes, drain on sterilized rack. Have new lids in warm but not boiling water from the sterilization.

Place quinces in a large pot, pour in water. Bring to a boil on high heat. Reduce heat and simmer, covered, about 25 minutes, Strain off 4 cups of the juice. Mix juice with sugar and lemon juice in heavy pot. Bring to a boil over high heat, stirring constantly. Stir in pectin and return to boil. Continue stirring constantly, until jelly temperature reaches 8 degrees above the boiling point of water, which is 212°F at sea level. You'll know it's ready when mixture sheets off spoon or when a half teaspoonful on a chilled plate wrinkles when pushed with your fingertip,

Remove from heat and skim off foam. Immediately pour into jars, filling to 5/8 inch from top rim. Wipe off any residue with sterile damp rag. Position sterilized warm lids over the jars and screw on. Do not over-tighten. Prepare in hot water bath for 5 minutes. Do not re-tighten lids. Cool upright on towel for 24 hours. Each lid will pop as the seal is created during cooling.

Quinces before the first frost at Cedar Oaks

PICKLES

DILL PICKLES

20-30 large pickles (for 6 to 8 qt)

BRINE FOR EACH QUART JAR:

2 heads dill weed

1 clove garlic

1 tsp red pepper flakes

Grape leaf

1/8 tsp alum

1 qt white distilled vinegar

1 c pickling salt

3 qt water

Wash cucumbers carefully, let stand overnight in cold water. Pack in hot sterilized quart jars, alternating with sprigs of dill. To each jar, add alum, garlic clove, red pepper. Combine vinegar, salt and water; heat to boiling. Fill jars with liquid, add 1 grape leaf. Seal.

GARLIC DILLS

8 to 10 pickling cucumbers

4 to 10 garlic cloves, peeled

About 4 heads of fresh dill

1 scant c pickling salt

1 c white distilled vinegar

3 c water

Wash cucumbers carefully. Soak overnight in cold salt water. Drain and dry. Put head of dill and several garlic cloves in each qt jar. Pack cucumbers in hot sterilized jars, near stove to keep jars warm. Bring salt, vinegar and water just up to a boil in a pot; pour into packed jars, leaving about 1/4-inch at top. Seal.

Setting out pickles and relish at the Braswell Plantation BBQ, Sept. 1944. PHOTO: By John Hemmer. COURTESY of the North Carolina State Archives, Raleigh, NC

ROSA LEE'S REFRIGERATOR PICKLES

from Rosa Lee Morton

My Oxford neighbor, Rosa Lee, is a Delta girl who's lived all over Tennessee, Arkansas, and Mississippi. She's a wonderful cook, and we're always consulting each other when trying to remember family heirloom versions of regional dishes. Rosa Lee swears these pickles would keep for years in the fridge, but are eaten too quickly to test the theory.

1/2 c white distilled vinegar

1 c white granulated sugar

1 tsp salt

1/4 tsp celery seed

1/4 tsp turmeric

1/2 tsp mustard seed

Medium white onion, sliced thin

3 medium cucumbers, unpeeled, cut into 1/4-inch rounds

Fill a 4-liter microwave-safe bowl (Corning or Pyrex) with sliced cucumbers and onions. Mix up remaining ingredients for pickling brine; pour over onions and cukes in bowl. Cover with microwavable plastic wrap; microwave on high 7 to 8 minutes. Remove from microwave, toss onions and cucumbers, cover again, and nuke again 2 to 3 minutes, checking, tossing, and nuking until onions become translucent. Let cool to room temperature. Use a sterilized utensil to spoon ingredients into sterile canning jars. Seal lids and refrigerate.

BARBARA TEAGUE'S SWEET PICKLE STICKS

from Louise Sherrill Triplette

Large, firm Kirby cucumbers

3 c water

3 c white distilled vinegar

3 c white granulated sugar

4-1/4 tsp celery seed

4-1/4 tsp turmeric powder

2 tsp mustard seed

1 tsp pickling salt

Scrub cucumbers, careful not to break skin. Slice into spears. Pack into quart jars. Boil remaining ingredients for 5 minutes. Pour over cold cucumbers in jars. Seal. Place in hot water bath for 2 to 3 minutes.

LOUISE'S SACCHARIN PICKLES

from Andrea Triplette Benfield, from Louise Triplette

Absolutely, no one could make these small sweet and sour pickles like Louise. The secret was in the crisp, heirloom white cucumbers containing very small seeds, and the pure well water on the farm. Seeds for heirloom small white cukes can still be found for sale in western North Carolina and in Kentucky. Andrea says Louise always prepared a gallon of vinegar water at a time.

1/2 gal white distilled vinegar

1/2 gal soft water

1 qt small pickling cucumbers (as fresh as possible)

PER JAR:

Three 1-grain saccharin tablets

2 tsp pickling salt (not table salt and no iodine)

2 to 4 dashes red pepper flakes

1/8 scant tsp alum

Scrub cucumbers, being careful not to break skin. Drain and dry. Sterilize wide-mouth canning jars and lids. Remove jars, top up; leave lids and seals in simmering water to keep hot. Put 1 tsp pickling salt in bottom of each hot jar. Pack half full with cucumbers, then add saccharin, remaining salt, pepper, and alum. Mix equal parts vinegar and water, heat up to boiling, pour over cucumbers. Fill each jar to about 1/4-inch below rim. Place lids and rings over top, seal, pressing down on center of lids. Do not reheat in hot water bath or cucumbers will become soft. Lids should make a slight pop sound within 20-30 minutes, which indicates they have sealed. After 24 hours, remove rings and check to ensure lids have sealed. If lids did not seal, refrigerate and consume like refrigerator pickles.

PICKLED BEETS

10 pt beets, peeled and sliced evenly

1 qt white distilled vinegar

3-1/2 c water

4 tsp pickling salt

1 T pickling spice

1-1/4 c white granulated sugar

Bring pickling salt, spice and sugar to a boil in water and vinegar. In another pot, cook beets in water, drain, and drop into pickle juice, return mixture to a boil. Pack beets and mixture into sterilized wide-mouth canning jars. Seal. Process in warm water bath.

GREEN TOMATO PICKLE

from Nellie Triplett

Nellie Triplett, wife of Lester's much older brother Walter, gave me this recipe at my Grace Chapel bridal shower.

4 qts thinly sliced green tomatoes

1 qt thinly sliced white onion

1/3 c pure granulated salt (no iodine)

3 c white distilled vinegar

1 tsp whole allspice

1 T black peppercorns

1 tsp celery seed

1 T mustard seed

1/8 tsp cayenne pepper

1 lemon, thinly sliced

3 c packed brown sugar

Put tomato and onion in large bowl and sprinkle with salt. Cover and let stand overnight. Drain. Bring remaining ingredients to a boil and add tomatoes and onion, stirring gently several times, about 10 minutes. Pour into 5 hot sterilized pint jars; seal process 5 minutes.

PICKLED OKRA

I can't remember who gave me this recipe, but it was someone in the Triplette family at my bridal shower.

3 lb whole, young, and tender okra

Celery leaves

Garlic cloves

Dill seedheads

1 qt water

1 pt white distilled vinegar

1/2 c salt

Pint jars

Place okra in hot, sterilized jars with a few celery leaves, a garlic clove, and a dill seedhead for each jar. Make a brine of water, vinegar and salt. Heat to boiling. Pour over okra. Seal and let stand 4 weeks. *YIELD: 6 pints.*

VARIATION: Add 2 tsp hot pepper sauce to mixture.

PICKLED PEACHES

from Ruby White Thurmond

8 c white granulated sugar

3 tsp whole allspice and cloves

2 sticks cinnamon

1 c white distilled vinegar

2 c water

4 qts whole peaches, peeled

Put spices and sugar in bag and mix. Combine spice mix with water and vinegar; boil for 20 minutes. Pour boiling mixture slowly over the peeled peaches. Place peaches with liquid into sterilized jars. Seal.

WATERMELON PICKLE

7 lb watermelon rind (see below)

7 c white granulated sugar

2 c white distilled vinegar

1/2 tsp oil of cinnamon (drugstore or health store)

1/2 tsp oil of cloves (drugstore or health store)

Cut up watermelons and consume pink part. Trim off outer skin from rind and discard. Cut rind into pieces or small strips and weigh. Need 7 lb of rind. Cover with cold water, cook until clear but not mushy. Drain. Place in crock such as crockpot. Boil other ingredients. Pour over rind. Let stand overnight. Drain off syrup and heat it again. Pour back over rind. Let stand overnight (second night). Bring rind-in-syrup to boil, then put in sterilized, hot jars; seal. *YIELD: 4 pints.*

Watermelon season at Edenton, NC, circa 1915
PHOTO COURTESY OF THE NORTH CAROLINA STATE ARCHIVES, RALEIGH, NC

RECIPES

ABOUT THOSE PUNCH RECIPES...

Before manufacturers offered us canned punch coolers, every homemaker and club leader knew how to create punch libation for a gathering. All punch recipes call for some sort of fruit juice—sometimes two or three fruit juices—in combinations with lemons or limes, and often with a carbonated beverage. Really festive recipes for girlie gatherings include orange, lemon, lime, raspberry or pineapple sherbet in the punch.

Chef, cookbook author, and humorist Robert St. John (himself a Methodist) researched numerous church-issued cookbooks in identifying standard church punch recipes. He expounded on the subject in one of his weekly *Clarion-Ledger* (Jackson, MS) newspaper columns. According to St. John, the basic lime punch is modified to suit the liturgical season. A member of my church's altar guild, I was curious, so I checked it out, and verified the seasonal ecumenical colors. The color for Advent is purple, so grape gelatin is substituted for the lime. Easter and Christmastide both are symbolized by gold or white, so pineapple gelatin is substituted for the green. Pentecost and All Saints Day are red, so strawberry or cherry gelatin is substituted.

Lebanon United Methodist Church, Crockett County, TN, founded in 1844 in the home of Samuel Conyers, Laurie's great-great-great grandfather

PHOTO, PREVIOUS PAGE: Andrea Benfield serves lime punch to Vickie and Robin Annas, Grace Chapel United Methodist Church, 2008.

PUNCH

PUNCH ICE RING

An ice ring keeps the punch properly chilled and is prettier than ice cubes. The day before the event, prepare the ice ring by first boiling 7 cups of water. Boiling eliminates cloudiness that would occur in tap water. Pour 3 cups of the water into a 6-cup ring mold. Freeze. Set remaining water aside.

Embellish the ring by making lemon, lime or orange slices, and citrus roses. To make a rose, cut a thin slice from the bottom of the citrus fruit using a sharp paring knife. Discard this slice. Beginning at the top, begin peeling a continuous 1/2-inch-wide strip. Curl the strip, starting with the first portion cut, coiling tightly to form the center and then loosening up toward the outer edges.

Alternate positioning the citrus roses with half-slices of fruit and sprigs of mint on top of the frozen ring. Gently fill the mold to the top with the remaining half of boiled water. Freeze. To unmold, let mold sit at room temperature for 5 minutes, then carefully turn out into the punch bowl.

BASIC CHURCH PUNCH

4 c cranberry juice, chilled

4 c pineapple juice, chilled

1 T almond flavoring

1-1/2 c white granulated sugar

2 qt ginger ale, chilled

Combine juices, flavoring and sugar, stir to dissolve sugar. Add ginger ale just before serving. Float an ice ring of frozen cranberry juice, and a sprig of mint. *YIELD: 20 punch cups.*

CHAMPAGNE PUNCH

2 c white granulated sugar

2 c lemon juice (not frozen)

20-oz can pineapple chunks and juice

1-1/2 qts chilled sparkling water

1 qt chilled sauterne wine

1 qt bag whole frozen strawberries

2 bottles chilled champagne

Mix well and chill first 3 ingredients. Just before serving,. add remaining ingredients. Float ice ring in serving bowl to keep chilled. *YIELD: 30 servings.*

GET-TOGETHER PUNCH

Two 46-oz cans of Hawaiian Punch (Juicy Red), chilled

2/3 c of pineapple juice

6-oz can frozen lemonade concentrate, thawed

12 oz club soda, chilled

Lemon slices, mint leaves or white orchids

DAY ONE: Pour 1 can of the Hawaiian Punch into a 1-1/2 qt ring mold and freeze. Mix remaining punch with the pineapple juice, lemonade concentrate and club soda in a punch bowl. Cover, and refrigerate overnight.

DAY TWO: Just before time to serve, carefully loosen the frozen punch from the mold and gently place it into the punch bowl containing the punch. Place lemon slices around the outside edge of the frozen punch ring. Fill the center of the frozen ring with the mint or white orchids. *YIELD: 2 quarts. Serves about 16.*

HOLIDAY FRUIT PUNCH

from Ruby White Thurmond

This is the old-fashioned fruit-juice recipe used before the advent of commercial punch drinks.

2 qts boiling water

1/4 c loose tea leaves

2 c white granulated sugar

2 c lemon juice

1-1/2 qts cranberry juice

1 qt water

1 qt ginger ale

1 lemon, sliced

2 limes, sliced

Maraschino cherries

Bring 2 quarts of water to a full rolling boil. Immediately pour this over the tea. Let steep for 5 minutes, then strain to remove the tea leaves. Set the tea aside to cool at room temperature. Combine with sugar, fruit juices and 1 quart of water. Chill.

Just before serving, pour into a punch bowl over an ice ring. Stir in ginger ale and embellish with sliced lemons, limes and Maraschino cherries.

YIELD: 5 quarts.

LIME PUNCH

3-oz pkg lime-flavored gelatin (ore other flavors)

2 c white granulated sugar

2 c boiling water

2 c lemon juice

Two 46-oz cans pineapple juice

12-oz can frozen orange juice concentrate, thawed and undiluted

1/2 tsp green food coloring

2-liter bottle ginger ale, chilled

Combine the gelatin, sugar and boiling water in a large stock pot, stirring until the sugar dissolves. Add lemon juice and next 3 ingredients, stirring until blended. Cover and chill. When ready to serve, pour the chilled mixture into a large punch bowl. Stir in the chilled ginger ale. *YIELD: 1-1/2 gallons.*

RED VELVET PUNCH

12-oz can frozen cranberry juice concentrate, thawed and diluted

7.5-oz bottle of frozen lemon juice, thawed

6-oz. can frozen orange juice concentrate, thawed and diluted

6-oz can frozen pineapple juice concentrate, thawed and diluted

2 c brandy

Two 750-milliliter bottles of champagne, chilled

Combine first 5 ingredients, stirring until blended. Chill mixture. To serve, pour mixture into punch bowl and add champagne. Add an ice ring made of fruit juice. Place an orchid in the center of the ring for flourish. *YIELD: 5 quarts.*

RUBY RED FROST PUNCH

1 pint bottle of cranberry juice cocktail

1-1/2 c lemon juice

1 c white granulated sugar

Two 28-oz bottles of chilled ginger ale

1 pint of raspberry sherbet

Lemon slices

Combine cranberry cocktail, lemon juice and sugar, blending well. Chill. To serve, pour over ice in a punch bowl. Add chilled ginger ale and sherbet. Garnish with lemon slices. Serve at once. *YIELD: 24 cups.*

SPICED CRANBERRY PUNCH

1 c white granulated sugar

1 c water

1/4 c whole cloves

Three 3-inch sticks of cinnamon

2 qts cranberry juice cocktail, chilled

46-oz can of orange-grapefruit juice, chilled

46-oz can of pineapple juice, chilled

1/2 c lemon juice

2 qts ginger ale, chilled

Combine first 4 ingredients in a saucepan; bring to a boil. Reduce heat and simmer for 10 minutes. Remove from heat, let cool completely. Strain, discarding the cloves and stick cinnamon.

To serve, combine the sugar mixture, fruit juices and ginger ale in a large punch bowl. *YIELD: 7 quarts.*

COLD DRINKS

LEMONADE

from Mary Elizabeth Daltroff

Mom inherited this recipe from Grandmother Thurmond. The more usual method is to squeeze the juice from the lemons and combine with a simple syrup of sugar and water. Grandmother's version has more bite because of the mashed lemon peel.

4 lemons

2 c white granulated sugar

1/2 c water

Lemon slices and Maraschino cherries, OPTIONAL

Cut lemons into thin slices, place in a bowl, and cover with sugar. Mash thoroughly until all juice has been extracted. Add water. Let stand for 1 hour. Strain. Allow 1 or 2 T of the strained lemon juice for each serving. Pour into a glass filled with shaved ice and add water. Garnish the glass with a maraschino cherry and a slice of lemon. *YIELD: 3 to 4 servings.*

(HOP) SKIP AND GO NAKED

Cousin Willie June Keller Noggle made lifelong friends of strangers when she got to Tulane. On a budget, she made "cheap" punch, by stirring a 12-oz can of frozen pink lemonade (or limeade), a lemonade can full of gin (or vodka), and 1 bottle of decent beer into a punch bowl of ice. Tastes like lemonade. But watch out!

BLOODY MARY MIX

This mix works for either a Bloody Mary (with vodka) or a Virgin Mary (without vodka).

1 qt (46 oz) tomato juice

2 T lemon juice

1 tsp Worcestershire sauce

1 T fresh horseradish

Several drops of Tabasco

1 tsp salt

Dash of celery salt

Place all ingredients into a blender and mix thoroughly, or put into a gallon jug and shake until completely blended. Refrigerate for at least 2 hours. FOR Bloody Marys: Add 2 c good, chilled vodka and shake well. Serve over ice with a stalk of celery. *YIELD: 6 to 8 servings.*

HOMEMADE KAHLUA

1/2 c instant coffee (freeze-dried)

3 c white granulated sugar

2 c boiling water

2 c good vodka (1 pint, 80 proof)

1 vanilla bean

Mix coffee and sugar together and then pour boiling water over the mixture. Let cool. Add vodka. Pour this combination into a half-gallon jug with vanilla bean. Close up and set aside at room temperature for 30 days. ¡Salúd!

MARGARITAS

3 jiggers lime juice

1 jigger lemon juice

1 T white granulated sugar

4 jiggers good tequila

1-1/4 jigger triple sec

Crushed ice

Salt

Blend these ingredients until smooth. Use "margarita-style" glasses. Rub slice of lime around the rims of the glasses, and then twist the wet rims in salt. Pour margarita into the glasses and serve. *YIELD: 4 servings.*

VARIATION: Add 1 jigger orange juice instead of lemon juice. Serve on the rocks.

LAURIE'S KILLER (*TO HELL WITH CHOLESTEROL*) EGGNOG

I developed this many years ago due to my distaste for bourbon. Even bourbon lovers will like this eggnog.

12 pasteurized eggs or locally grown organic eggs

1 lb confectioners sugar

1 c dark rum

1 c B&B Brandy

1 to 2 c Kahlua

1-1/2 qt half and half cream

1/2 qt whipping cream

1/2 tsp table salt

Separate the egg yolks and egg whites into two metal bowls, careful not to get any yolk with the whites. Refrigerate whites. Beat the 12 egg yolks together until light and fluffy. Gradually beat in 1 lb confectioners sugar. Slowly beat in the dark rum and brandy. Let stand for 1 hour in the fridge.

While waiting, whip the 2 quarts of creams. Mix into the egg and booze mixture until completely blended. Add Kahlua last. Refrigerate immediately and for at least 3 hours.

When ready to serve, beat the 12 egg whites with the salt in chilled bowl with very clean beaters, until mixture forms stiff peaks. Fold the beaten egg whites into the eggnog mixture. Pour into punch bowl. Sprinkle individual servings with fresh-grated nutmeg.

Unused nog can be kept in the refrigerator for days, re-beating prior to serving each time. NOTE: For a thinner eggnog, use whole milk instead of cream.

MIMOSAS

Known a generation ago as the Magnolia. By any name, a Mimosa is a refreshing brunch beverage.

Crushed ice

1 part orange juice (OJ)

3 parts champagne

Splash of Grand Marnier

Pour 1 part OJ over small amount of crushed ice. Add champagne, leaving room at the top for a splash of Grand Marnier. The key to success is good champagne. Serve in a large flute or wine glass. *YIELD: 1 serving.*

BEVERAGES

MINT JULEP

This is my big bourbon exception in this cookbook. How can we have Southern beverages without the mint julep?

The quintessential Southern drink, the mint julep links Kentucky's two most famous products: bourbon whiskey and horses. The julep's origins go back to the ancient Persians, who mixed infusions of flowers and herbs with sugar and spirits. The julep may have arisen in the Virginia colony as a medicinal draft, but certainly didn't evolve until Kentuckians learned how to make bourbon whiskey. The mint julep as we know it today was introduced to America at the Round Robin Bar of the Willard Hotel in Washington, D.C., by Kentucky's famous 19th century orator, Senator Henry Clay. More than 120,000 mint juleps are served each year by the bourbon sponsor at the Kentucky Derby, the state's most famous horse race.

The two basic versions of the mint julep vary primarily in the type of sugar component. One calls for sugar and water added to bruised mint leaves. The other calls for mint-leaf-infused simple syrup. NOTE: Mint is a tender leaf, and your goal in bruising it is to release the mint oils. Beating the mint into pieces goes too far, releasing slightly bitter chlorophyll. Proponents also quibble about whether to add the simple syrup before the bourbon, or after the bourbon like a snow cone. The most important thing to remember about mint julep preparation is to use a delicate touch. No one wants the julep to taste too minty, too sweet, or too boozy. Disregard the tacky Tom Collins-glass versions containing cubed ice. The only proper way to enjoy a mint julep is to serve it in a sterling mint julep cup, filled with "snowy" ice crushed in a bag with a mallet. Connoisseurs have differing opinions about whether to stir or not to stir the julep. Either way, the goal is to frost the cup more than to blend the flavors, which accomplish that on their own.

Mint Juleps should be served properly, in a sterling julep cup.

SUGAR VERSION

"Muddle" (bruise) 1 to 4 fresh mint leaves in julep cup with a wooden spoon or stick (muddler). Add 1 tsp powdered or granulated sugar and 2 tsp water; muddle some more to dissolve the sugar. Fill cup with shaved or crushed ice. Pour 2 to 2-1/2 oz good bourbon (about 1/4 of the cup) over the ice and top with more shaved ice. Give a gentle shake or swirl to frost the cup. Garnish with more mint. When drinking, hold cup by the rim or base to retain frost. Drink through a short straw.

MINTED SIMPLE SYRUP VERSION

Boil together 2 cups water and 2 cups white granulated sugar. Cool, and add 6 to 9 sprigs fresh mint. Cover, and refrigerate up to two weeks. To prepare julep, place 1 sprig fresh mint in bottom of cup, add shaved ice. Gently pour about 2 oz bourbon over the ice. Add 1 to 2 T simple syrup over the ice. Top with a bit more crushed ice and slightly bruised sprig of mint. Swirl the cup gently to frost.

Sangria is as pretty as it is tasty.

RAMOS GIN FIZZ

This recipe was one of Dad's brunch secrets, written on "Ship by Southern" bill-of-lading paper by a New Orleans bartender. The cream and gin must be cold.

2 oz lemon juice (or 1 oz lemon juice and 1 oz lime juice)

4 oz half and half (light cream)

2 oz whipping cream

4 tsp superfine sugar or confectioners sugar

1 tsp orange flower water (use less rather than more)

4 oz gin (Tanquerey), chilled

Splash of club soda, OPTIONAL (Dad omitted this)

    Mix in a blender or shaker, adding the gin last. Blend or shake until frothy. *YIELD: 4 to 6 servings.*

VARIATION: Add 1 beaten egg white or 1 T powdered egg white. Some people also blend in ice at the end.

PEACH COOLER

This is a Low Country beverage for brunches and wedding receptions.

5 medium peaches, unpeeled but quartered

6-oz can of frozen lemonade concentrate

6 oz vodka or gin (Smirnoff or Tanqueray)

    Combine all ingredients in blender and fill with ice cubes. Blend and serve. Garnish with fresh mint.

NON-ALCOHOLIC SANGRIA

True sangria is the product of natural fruit fermentation and wine. This is a G-rated variation.

3/4 c commercial lemonade mix (yellow or pink)

1 qt (4 c) cranberry juice cocktail

1 c cold orange juice

1 T fresh lime juice

3 c club soda, cold

2 medium oranges, sliced

2 medium limes, sliced

    Put drink mix into large pitcher. Add juices. Stir until drink mix is completely dissolved. Refrigerate until ready to serve. Stir in club soda and fruit when serving. Serve in tall glasses with ice cubes and fruit slices in each glass. *YIELD: 8 servings of 1 cup each.*

SAZERAC

1 tsp simple syrup

1 tsp Pernod

2 dashes bitters

2 oz bourbon

    Stir or shake well and serve chilled, or on the rocks.

SYLLABUB

5 c white granulated sugar

12 c apple cider

12 T grated lemon rind (zest)

1 c lemon juice

4 tsp light corn syrup

2 tsp aromatic bitters

8 egg whites

8 c whole milk

2 pt half and half (light cream)

    Combine 4 cups of sugar, the cider, lemon juice, zest, corn syrup and bitters in large bowl. Stir to dissolve. Let chill overnight. Make meringue by beating the egg whites and gradually adding remaining 1 c sugar until stiff peaks form. Place individual puffs of meringue on cookie sheet and freeze. To Serve: Beat milk and cream into cider mix with whisk until frothy. Pour into punch bowl and float the meringues on top. Serve a Swiss meringue puff with each cup of syllabub (*see recipe, page 185*). *Yield: 50 punch cups.*

BEVERAGES

TEA BEVERAGES

SWEET TEA

All good Southern sweet tea comes with lots of lemon or lime, and occasionally a sprig of mint. When in the Carolinas and the Deep South and ordering at a restaurant or fast-food place, "ice tea" refers to unsweetened tea—except in lower Louisiana, where they don't sweeten the tea as a matter of course.

3 qt or 8 qt cold water

2 to 4 family size Luzianne tea bags

2 c granulated sugar for every 8 c water

Sliced lemon or lime to taste, or 1/4 to 1/2 c juice

Bring cold water to a boil in stainless cooking pot that is not used for anything BUT boiling water or making tea. Once water has come to a boil, remove pot from heat and add the appropriate number of tea bags Let the bags steep until lukewarm. Before the water cools, remove tea bags and pour liquid into container over 2 cups of sugar for every 8 cups of water. Stir well.

VARIATION: Some cooks make a simple syrup of sugar dissolved into boiled water. They keep the sugar syrup separate and add to the tea before serving.

ARNOLD PALMER ICED TEA

We consider Mr. Palmer our adopted NC son, since his days as a Wake Forest Demon Deacon golfer. Versions of this refreshing drink made famous by him have been around forever. New Englanders called it the Nantucket. Californians called it Teamonade or California Iced Tea. Some Southerners called it Sunshine Tea, Swampwater, or Half and Half, not to be confused with Sweet Tea half 'n half (made of half sweet, and half unsweet tea).

Tall glass of ice

1 part lemonade

1 part iced tea (either sweetened or unsweetened)

Which goes in first over the ice affects the appearance of the Arnold Palmer. If the tea is poured over the lemonade, the beverage retains two layers. If the lemonade is poured over the tea, the two beverages mix, and should be stirred.

Salem College in Winston-Salem, NC

SALEM COLLEGE ICED TEA

Salem Academy and College, the oldest American school for females still in continuous operation on the same site, is renowned for its Colonial cuisine. I learned this recipe while attending Salem. It was later published in an alumnae cookbook titled **Soup's On At Salem**.

4 sprigs fresh mint

8 to 12 whole cloves

3 qt water

1 oz tea leaves

Juice of 8 lemons

Juice of 6 oranges

46-oz can pineapple juice

2 c white granulated sugar

Add mint and cloves to water and bring to a boil. Simmer for 10 to 15 minutes. Remove from heat. Add tea and steep for 10 to 15 minutes. Strain, and while still hot, add fruit juices and sugar. Stir to dissolve the sugar. Makes about 4-1/2 qt. Serve over ice in tall glasses.

ABOUT OUR SWEET TEA

What can be said about this most Southern of beverages? Every cook has his or her preferred method for achieving the final result, which should impart an uplifting hit of caffeine with a bite of tannic acid. The sweet tea should not taste bitter, and must be sweet ALMOST to the point of toothache. Some cooks still adhere to the old English steeping method that requires rinsing a porcelain teapot with boiling water to heat, and then pouring boiling water into the teapot over loose black tea leaves or teabags. Some cooks make sun tea by placing a large jar containing fresh water and tea leaves in the hot midday sun to steep for several hours.

BEVERAGES

SPICED TEA MIX (RUSSIAN TEA)

1 c instant tea (no sugar or lemon)

1 c white granulated sugar

2 c instant orange breakfast drink (Tang)

3-oz pkg of pre-sweetened lemonade

1 tsp ground cloves

1/2 tsp cinnamon

Mix all ingredients together. We Southerners store it in a jar, and cover the lid with decorative fabric. Instructions: To make spiced tea, use 2 tsp with 1 cup hot or boiling water. *YIELD: 32-48 servings.*

HOT DRINKS

HOT COCOA (SCRATCH)

1-1/2 T cocoa powder

2 T granulated sugar

A few grains of salt

1/2 c boiling water

4 c milk

Combine dry ingredients in saucepan. Boil water in a kettle or other pan, and add 1/2 cup boiling water to dry ingredients. Heat on medium-high, and boil for 3 minutes to dissolve the sugar and salt. Add milk, stirring, and heat to just below boiling. Beat with hand mixer or whisk. Remove from heat and serve. *YIELD: 6 cups.*

HOT COCOA MIX

from Mary Elizabeth Daltroff

This was one of Mom's standby beverage mixes for the children. It's the homemade version of commercially prepared hot-cocoa packets.

2 c nondairy coffee creamer

1-1/2 c white granulated sugar

3/4 c cocoa powder

1/2 c instant nonfat dry milk powder

1/4 tsp salt

Mini-marshmallows

Mix all ingredients. Store in a covered jar. To make, place 2 T of mix in mug and add boiling water. *YIELD: 32 servings.*

HOT FRENCH CHOCOLATE

2 oz unsweetened chocolate

1/2 c cold water

3/4 c white granulated sugar

A few grains of salt

1/2 c whipping cream, whipped (no sugar added)

Stir chocolate and water over low heat until chocolate melts. Add sugar and salt, stirring, until thick, about 10 minutes. Remove from heat. Cool. Fold whipped, unsweetened cream into chocolate mixture.

To serve, heat 1 qt whole milk. Pour hot milk into individual mugs. Add 1 T chocolate cream and stir well. This is an old French-American hot chocolate recipe. It's my favorite version of hot chocolate. *YIELD: 6 servings.*

FAMILY MEMORY

My mom, Mary Elizabeth, always encouraged my flights of fancy, but wouldn't let me take typing or work as a waitress. She was a closet feminist. She's probably laughing her wings off at the thought that I wrote a cookbook. *On a computer.*

Mary Elizabeth holds Laurie, while Preston Smith and Rita Kay Davidson sort of watch the animals at the Memphis Overton Park Zoo.

BEVERAGES

HOT SPICED CIDER

2 qts apple cider

1 tsp whole allspice

2 sticks cinnamon

2 to 3 whole cloves

1/4 c lemon juice

2 T orange juice

Light brown sugar to taste

Simmer the cider, allspice, cinnamon and cloves for 20 minutes. Add the lemon juice and orange juice. Continue to simmer until ready to serve. Strain. Add a small amount of brown sugar if the cider is not sweet enough. *YIELD: 10 servings.*

PERCOLATOR PUNCH

from Ruby White Thurmond

This was one of Grandmother Thurmond's church meeting staples, made in a 30- to 48-cup coffee percolator. It's GREAT for Christmas!

9 c cranberry cocktail or cranberry juice

9 c pineapple juice

4-1/2 c water

1 c brown sugar

4 T whole cloves

4 sticks of cinnamon

Put liquid ingredients in the percolator. Place sugar and spices in the percolator basket. Cover and percolate. Serve hot.

MORAVIAN LOVE FEAST COFFEE

Don't wait for Sunday services to make this. Nothing tastes as good as Love Feast Coffee on a chilly winter morning. Add some sugar cake or a sweet roll, and you're sittin' pretty.

1 lb ground coffee

1-1/4 lb white granulated sugar

9 qt water

1/3 gal whole milk plus half and half light cream

Bring water to a boil in a large stock pot. Bag the coffee grounds in white cotton and drop into the boiling water for 15 minutes. Remove bag. Just before removing pot from heat, mix in sugar and milk. Pour into pre-warmed kettle for serving. Serve coffee in stoneware mugs (made by a Carolinas potter). *YIELD: Serves a crowd.*

IRISH COFFEE

2 sugar cubes

2 jiggers hot coffee

2 jiggers Irish whisky (Bushmill's or Jameson's)

Dab of whipped cream

Put sugar cubes in large mug. Add hot coffee, then whisky. Top with whipped cream. Do not stir.

Hot Spiced Cider is perfect during the dark, cold days of winter.

SWEET DESSERT PARTY MEMORIES

One of my favorite hosting memories is of a dessert party, held in 1985 for exhibiting members of the Guild of Piedmont Craftsmen, Inc.

During the 1980s, my art appraisal and consulting firm was one of several urban pioneering arts groups occupying a former flop house in downtown Winston-Salem. Located just two blocks away from the city's convention center, the two-story building dated to the turn of the 20th century, and was renovated by developer David Shannon. The first floor storefronts housed Master Potter Ron Propst, who also was the Old Salem Potter, and Artworks Gallery, a cooperative of area painters, sculptors and printmakers. The second floor, embellished with multiple skylights, consisted of individual studio rooms occupied by an intriguing mix of artists such as Joyce Teta, one of America's best calligraphers, and a four-room central suite, occupied by my firm. In this grand space, even the full-moon winos and crack-house prostitutes didn't bother us. It was a live-and- let-live neighborhood.

The annual fall Piedmont Crafts Fair weekend had become one of Winston-Salem's major destination events. People traveled from all over the United States to attend. The exhibiting craftsmen always worked frantically up to the last minute before the fair's opening at the Convention Center. By the end of the PCI members-only preview on Thursday night, they would be exhausted. We occupants of 213 West Sixth Street—most of us heavily involved with the Guild and the crafts fair—decided the exhibiting craftsmen deserved some TLC. So we invited all several hundred of them to a post-opening dessert party.

I don't remember what Ron and Artworks offered downstairs. But upstairs, we served Kahlua and coffee and Irish Coffee made with Bushmill's and fresh whipped cream, along with home-

The Piedmont Crafts Fair is held in Winston-Salem every October.
PHOTO: 1980s Piedmont Crafts Fair, COURTESY OF PIEDMONT CRAFTSMEN, INC.

made banana bread, cranberry-date bread, and pumpkin bread, topped with hand-churned butter made by Louise Triplette with cream from Paul Sherrill's dairy cows. Jeff, Mom, and many of our friends pitched in to serve the hungry, tired craftsmen.

Despite the late hours, and the long weekend ahead, the craftsmen joined us in howling at the moon that night. Not a crumb and nary a drop remained when we locked the doors around 3 a.m.

BEVERAGES

FAUX WASSAIL

1 gal apple cider

46-oz can pineapple juice

46-oz can apricot nectar

1 c cranberry juice

1 c lemon juice

1/2 c white granulated sugar

1 T whole cloves

1/2 box stick cinnamon

Splash of dark rum or rum flavoring, OPTIONAL

Simmer all ingredients together for 1 hour. Add rum flavoring or real rum for alcoholic version of this ancient English winter punch. *YIELD: 12-15 servings.*

GENUINE WASSAIL

12 apples, cored and baked

1 c water

4 c white granulated sugar

1 T grated nutmeg

2 tsp ground ginger

1/2 tsp ground mace

6 whole cloves

1 tsp allspice

1 stick cinnamon

12 stiff-beaten egg whites

12 beaten egg yolks

4 bottles sherry or Madeira wine

2 c brandy

Combine water, sugar, and spices in saucepan. Boil 5 minutes. Fold the beaten egg yolks whites into the beaten yolks in a large bowl.

Strain spiced liquid into eggs, mixing quickly to prevent eggs from curdling.

Heat the two liquors separately, starting with the sherry. Blend slowly into the egg mixture.

Add brandy last while mixture is foaming. Carefully add baked apples. Ladle servings into punch cups.

TO BAKE APPLES: Remove cores with apple corer. Place apples upright in baking pan in 1/2 to 1 inch of water. Bake at 350°F for 30 minutes up to 1 hour, until soft.

NEW ENGLAND WASSAIL

2 c water

2 c white granulated sugar

6 whole cloves

2 cinnamon sticks

3 allspice berries

1 T ground ginger

5 oranges, sliced, seeded,

4 lemons, sliced, seeded

2 c apple cider

Boil sugar and water 10 minutes to syrup stage. Add spices and ginger. Let stand covered one hour. Strain. Add oranges, lemons, and cider. Bring to boil and serve at once.

Patrons at George's neighborhood restaurant under the I-10 in Baton Rouge enjoy sports, great home cooking, and the liquid cameraderie. It's one of my favorite stops in Tiger Country.

THE RECIPES

BREAD & BREAKFAST

BISCUITS

ANGEL BISCUITS

This version of biscuit is indigenous to Tennessee, where buttermilk and yeast go hand-in-glove for all baked goods.

5 c self-rising flour

1/4 c white granulated sugar

3/4 c shortening, chilled

1 pkg active dry yeast, dissolved in 2 T warm water

2 c buttermilk

Sift flour, add sugar, and cut in shortening. Add yeast and buttermilk. Knead and place in refrigerator. Make biscuits as needed. Not necessary for biscuits to rise before baking—they do it in the oven. Bake in preheated oven at 400° to 425°F for 15 minutes, or until golden brown.

BISCUIT TIPS

Making light biscuits is science AND art. Low gluten flour works best for biscuits because it's softer wheat. That's why some flours are marketed as biscuit flour. Self-rising flour works better than plain flour because the leavening agents of baking powder and baking soda have been thoroughly mixed into the flour. If your flour is old, it will result in dryer, tougher biscuits. Buttermilk makes more tender biscuits than plain milk. And all older Southern cooks know that lard makes softer, fluffier biscuits than shortening. Remember the following tips:

- Use buttermilk rather than regular milk.
- Do not handle dough any more than necessary (fold over and press with heel of hand two times).
- If the dough does not stick to your fingers, it's too dry.
- Roll out dough about 1/2- to 3/4-inch thick.
- Cut out biscuits by pressing straight down and back up; DO NOT twist when cutting.
- Always fully preheat oven; bake at high temperature; higher oven temps make the biscuits rise fluffier.
- For fluffier biscuits, place them with sides touching.
- For crispier biscuits, leave 2-inch space between them.

PHOTO, previous page: Brandon Jones at Cafe du Mond, New Orleans, LA

CAROLINA BISCUITS

Southern Biscuit Flour® is produced by Midstate Mills, Newton, NC. It's the Carolina version of the classic light Southern winter red wheat flour. Midstate's Formula L® version is like Bisquick for gourmets. Andrea recently mailed me some at Jeff's request. He was desperate.

2 c self-rising Southern Biscuit Flour®

1/4 c shortening or lard, chilled

2/3 to 3/4 c buttermilk or milk

2 T melted salted butter

Preheat oven to 450°F. Spray baking sheet with cooking spray. Measure flour into bowl. Cut shortening or lard into flour with pastry cutter or hands, until flour forms pea-size beads. Stir in milk just until flour is moistened. Do NOT over-stir. Make sure dough is sticky to touch. If not, add more milk. Turn dough onto lightly floured surface. Shape into a ball with floured hands. Press to flatten slightly then fold in half 2 to 3 times. Lightly roll out with floured rolling pin. Cut out biscuits with 2-inch biscuit cutter. Arrange on pan, touching for softer, or slightly apart for crisp. Bake 10-14 minutes until browned. Remove from oven, brush tops with melted butter. *YIELD: 12 biscuits.*

WHITE LILY BISCUITS

The cooks in my Memphis and Tennessee family always swore by White Lily Flour of Knoxville. Known by all as the "Sunday Flour," its ultra-sifted, chlorine-bleached winter red wheat flour was the lowest-protein flour available. The traditional White Lily rule for measuring: When baking recipes not issued by White Lily, measure 1 cup plus 2 T for every 1 cup of flour in the recipe.

Use exactly the same recipe as the Carolina biscuit recipe, but substitute with White Lily flour, and pre-heat the oven to 500°F. Bake 8 to 10 minutes.

MISSISSIPPI CHEESE BISCUITS

There are a number of variations of this recipe, which is popular across Mississippi.

1 stick (1/2 c) margarine, softened

1/3 lb sharp Cheddar cheese, grated

1 c self-rising flour, sifted (*I always used Martha White*)

Dash of cayenne pepper

Combine margarine and cheese. Stir in flour and cayenne. Mix thoroughly. Shape into marble-sized balls. Bake in preheated oven at 400°F for 10-12 minutes. Serve hot.

MARYLAND BEATEN BISCUITS

Beaten biscuits are indigenous to southern Maryland and the Eastern Shore. A variation traveled westward to the Tennessee mountains. The concept originated on colonial plantations, whose settlers had little access to leavening ingredients. Without soda or baking powder, the only way to get the biscuits to rise was to beat the dough vigorously with a hammer or axe-back to force air into the dough. According to Orrell's, the Wye Mills, MD, company which has carried on the beaten biscuit tradition, most old recipes called for the dough to be beaten 30 minutes for family, and 45 minutes for company!

Our Hurlock, MD, friend, Vicki, shared her grandmother's heirloom recipe and her mother's updated version. Once a "must" on the Eastern Shore for Thanksgiving Dinner, beaten biscuits are soft in the middle, crusty on the outside, and addictive when slathered with butter.

VICKI'S NOTES: "When my grandmother made Maryland biscuits, they used a biscuit block similar to a butcher's block on legs on which to beat the biscuits. I had my own biscuit board which we put on the kitchen table and my own rubber mallet. I got quickly tired and bored with beating the dough, but my grandfather usually rescued me."

MILDRED ISENBERG'S OLD ORIGINAL VERSION

from Vicki Corkran Willey

SIFT TOGETHER:

6 c flour (a full sifter unsifted)

1 tsp salt

Pinch of soda and 2 pinches white granulated sugar

CUT IN:

8 T Crisco

ADD:

1 c water

This dough makes up very stiff and must be beaten for 25 minutes on a butcher block or biscuit board with a rubber mallet, hammer or axe. Section if too bulky to beat all at once; beating each until dough blisters. Fold dough and repeat process for 25 minutes per section. Form walnut-sized balls. Place on ungreased cookie sheet. Prick tops with fork. Bake 10 minutes or until browned in oven preheated to 500°F. *YIELD: About 42 biscuits.*

ANN ISENBERG CORKRAN'S UPDATED VERSION

Vicki's mom developed the following version, which "cheats" by adding baking powder, and thus avoiding the need to beat the dough.

3 c White Dove flour (this flour is like White Lily and other "light" Southern flours)

1/2 tsp baking powder

1 T white granulated sugar

1/2 tsp salt

1/4 c shortening

2/3 c of ice water

Insert metal blade into food processor. Add flour, salt and sugar. Pulse twice. Add shortening. Process until mixture is like cornmeal. Pour ice water through feed tube in a steady stream while processing; continue running until mixture forms a ball. Process 2 additional minutes. Form walnut-sized balls. Bake on double cookie sheets (to prevent bottoms from burning) at 450°F for approximately 20 minutes, until light brown.

BREAKFAST GRAINS

BEIGNETS

Homemade doughnuts can't compete with fresh Krispy Kreme. Beignets can and should!

1/2 c boiling water

2 T vegetable shortening

1/4 c white granulated sugar

1/2 tsp salt

1/2 c evaporated milk

1/2 pkg yeast

1/4 c warm water

1 egg, beaten

3-1/4 c of all-purpose flour, sifted

Vegetable oil for frying (not peanut oil)

Confectioners sugar

Pour boiling water over shortening, salt and sugar. Add milk and let stand until warm. Dissolve yeast in warm water and add to milk mixture with beaten egg, Stir in 2 cups of flour. Add enough flour to make a soft dough. Place in a greased bowl, and gently grease the top of the dough. Cover with waxed paper and then a cloth over the paper. Chill until ready to use. Roll dough to 1/4-inch thickness. Do not let dough rise before frying. Cut dough into squares and fry a few at a time in a deep fryer heated to 360ºF. Brown on one side, turn, and brown on the other. Remove and drain on paper towels. Sprinkle with confectioners sugar while still hot. Serve at once.

CHEESE DANISH COFFEE CAKE

CHEESE FILLING:

8-oz pkg cream cheese, softened

1/4 c granulated white sugar

2 eggs

1/4 tsp almond extract

Cream together in a mixer set on medium speed.

CAKE:

2 T melted butter or margarine

1-1/2 c Bisquick

1 egg, beaten

2 T white granulated sugar

1/2 c whole milk

2 T vegetable oil (canola)

1/2 tsp almond extract

1 c confectioners sugar

2 to 3 T water

1/4 c finely chopped roasted pecans or walnuts

Preheat oven to 350ºF. Prepare cheese filling and set aside. In oven, melt butter in a 9-by-13-by-2-inch baking pan. Mix Bisquick, egg, sugar, milk, oil and almond extract in a bowl, beating vigorously for at least 30 seconds. Spread batter in pan over the melted butter. Pour cheese filling evenly over the batter, and cut through the batter about 10 times with a spatula. Bake 20-25 minutes or until toothpick comes out clean. Cool 15 minutes. Drizzle with a powdered sugar glaze made up of 1 cup of confectioners sugar and 2 to 3 T of water. Sprinkle finely chopped pecans or walnuts over glaze.

CARAMEL ROLLS

36-count pkg frozen dinner rolls, unthawed

Pkg of butterscotch pudding mix

1 stick (1/2 c) margarine (not butter)

1/2 c light brown sugar

6 oz walnuts or pecans, chopped or halved, OPTIONAL

The night before, grease bottom and sides of a 9-by-13-inch pan. Sprinkle nuts evenly across pan bottom. Position frozen rolls evenly in pan. Sprinkle with dry pudding mix. Melt margarine and mix with brown sugar. Pour evenly over pudding-covered dough. Cover. Let rise overnight. Bake the next morning in preheated oven at 350 ºF for 30 minutes. When browned, invert onto a cookie sheet. Serve hot.

CREAM CHEESE BRAID

from Andrea Benfield.

Andrea got this old recipe from Helen Pitts. Andrea makes this for Christmas breakfast and gifts to friends.

DOUGH:

1 c sour cream

1/2 c white granulated sugar

1 tsp salt

1/2 c margarine or butter

1/2 c warm water

2 pkgs yeast

2 eggs

4 to 6 c all-purpose flour

FILLING:

Two 8-oz pkgs cream cheese

3/4 c white granulated sugar

1 beaten egg

Pinch of salt

2 T vanilla extract

Raisins, OPTIONAL

Chopped Nuts, OPTIONAL

Scald sour cream, stir in sugar, salt, butter and then cool to lukewarm. Measure warm water into a large, warm bowl. Sprinkle in the yeast and stir. Add lukewarm sour cream mixture, eggs and flour. Mix until well blended. Cover tightly and refrigerate overnight.

Divide dough the next day into 4 pieces. Roll each into a rectangle 8-by-12 inches.

Mix first 5 filling ingredients until smooth. Spread on each dough rectangle, not touching edges. Sprinkle with raisins and nuts, if desired. Roll up and pinch ends together or turn under. Place on greased cookie sheet and cut slits on top. Allow to rise until dough doubles in size. Bake in preheated oven at 375°F for 10-20 minutes. Remove from oven.

Top with a powdered sugar glaze: Mix until smooth 2 c powdered sugar, 2 tsp vanilla extract, 5 T milk. Dribble the glaze over the braid.

TO SCALD SOUR CREAM OR MILK:

Heat slowly in a heavy sauce pan or double boiler. When it reaches 198°F (just below boiling), it has scalded and small bubbles will rise at the sides. Cool back down to 110 to 115°F to add to yeast for breadmaking. Also scald milk, cream or sour cream to achieve creamier texture in custards. NOTE: The film that forms on top of the scalded milk or custard is coagulated protein.

EASY APPLE DUMPLINGS

from Andrea Benfield, from Beulah Benfield

10-pc can of refrigerator biscuits

5 tart apples, peeled and halved (Rome, Granny Smith)

1 stick (1/2 c) butter

1 c light brown sugar

1/2 tsp cinnamon

1 c water

Stretch biscuits around halved apples. Heat just to boiling the other ingredients and pour over the dumplings in a baking pan. Bake in preheated oven at 350°F for 30 minutes.

FRENCH TOAST

One-inch-thick slices of Italian, French or Challah bread

Eggs (1 for every 2 to 3 slices)

Splash of whole milk

Pinch of salt per egg

White granulated sugar

Splash of vanilla extract added to egg, OPTIONAL

Butter (1 to 2 T at a time, avoiding too much)

We always made French toast like scrambled eggs, using the dump method. Whisk eggs in a bowl, adding salt, splash of milk, and 1/2-tsp sugar per egg used. Soak bread slices in egg mixture while melting butter in skillet on medium-high. Brown slices about 10-12 minutes per side until golden brown. Do not drown the bread in butter. Serve hot, with a dusting of confectioners sugar and maple syrup.

VARIATION: Position slices over 1/2 c maple syrup spread in 9-by-13-inch baking pan. Cover bread with beaten egg and milk mixture. Refrigerate overnight, covered. Bake at 350°F about 20-30 minutes. Slice hot.

FERN'S RELATIVELY LOW-FAT GRANOLA

from Fern Robertson Kerslake

4 c old-fashioned rolled oats

1 c sliced almonds

1/2 c raw sunflower seeds

1/2 c wheat germ

1/2 tsp ground cinnamon

1/2 c light brown sugar

1/3 c honey

Rind and juice of 1 lemon

Rind and juice of 1 orange

2 c fine-chopped dried fruit (cranberries, apricots, peaches, banana chips, apples, dates)

Combine oatmeal, seeds, nuts, wheat germ and cinnamon in large bowl. Combine sugar and honey in saucepan, bring to boil on medium heat Remove from heat; add lemon and orange rinds and juices. Toss liquid mixture with dry mixture. Spray large, edged baking sheet with PAM, spread out mixture in pan, bake at 300°F for 30 minutes, stirring every 10 minutes until even golden brown. Cool. Add dried fruits. Store in airtight container. *YIELD: about 7 cups.*

FROSTED CINNAMON ROLLS

This popular recipe tastes just like Cinnabon at the Mall.

DOUGH:

1 c whole milk (room temperature or warmed to 70-80°F)

1/4 c warm water

1/4 c butter, softened

1 egg

1 tsp salt

4 c bread flour

1/4 c instant vanilla pudding mix

1 T white granulated sugar

1 T active dry yeast

FILLING:

1/4 c (4 T) butter, softened

1 c packed light brown sugar

2 tsp ground cinnamon

FROSTING:

4 oz cream cheese, softened

1/4 c (4 T) butter, softened

1-1/2 c confectioners sugar

1-1/2 tsp whole milk

1/2 tsp vanilla extract

In bread machine pan, place first nine ingredients in order of listing. Select dough setting. Check dough after 5 minutes of mixing; add 1 to 2 tablespoons water or flour if needed. Do not use timer. When dough cycle is completed, turn dough onto lightly floured surface. Roll into a 17-by-10-inch rectangle. Spread with butter; sprinkle with brown sugar and cinnamon. Roll up, jelly-roll style, starting from a long side. Pinch seam to seal. Cut into 21 slices.

Place 12 slices, cut side down, in a greased 13-by-9-by-2-inch baking pan, and nine rolls in a 9-inch-square baking pan. Cover; let rise in a warm place until doubled (about 45 minutes).

Bake at 350°F in preheated oven for 20-25 minutes, or until golden brown. Cool on wire racks for 5 minutes. In a mixing bowl, beat frosting ingredients. Frost warm rolls. Store in refrigerator. *YIELD: 21 rolls.*

MADELINE'S SWEET ROLLS

from Madeline Bradley

Madeline Bradley is the mother of Jeff's Wake Forest roommate, Don. During our visits with Don and his wife Charlotte, in his hometown of Hurlock, MD, we always stayed with his parents Madeline and Merton. Madeline made these rolls for breakfast. She was a terrific cook, and showed me that this recipe can be modified from sweet rolls to ham rolls.

1 cake compressed yeast (I use 2 pkg active dry yeast)

2 c lukewarm water

1/2 to 3/4 c white granulated sugar

1 tsp salt

1 egg, beaten

7 c all-purpose flour

3 T melted shortening (up to 1/2 c)

1 stick butter, melted (use only what is needed)

3/4 c white granulated sugar

Put yeast in mixing bowl and add lukewarm water. Add sugar and salt. Add beaten egg. Add 3 cups of flour. Add shortening. Fold in rest of flour gradually until mixed. Cover with a damp towel and set in a warm place until dough doubles in size. Roll out and spread with melted butter and sugar, then roll up. Cut across to make 1-1/2-inch thick spirals, and put in a lightly greased pan to rise again. Cook at 400°F in preheated oven until tops are golden brown.

VARIATION 1, SPIRAL REGULAR ROLLS: Omit the melted butter and sugar rollup. Roll out and roll back up to cut into spirals, or knead the risen dough and pinch off tablespoon-sized bits, and let rise in lightly greased pan.

VARIATION 2, HAM ROLLUPS: Spread rolled-out dough with melted butter and country or baked ham. Roll up like a jellyroll. Cut into 1-1/2-inch spirals and let rise again before baking.

MORAVIAN SUGAR CAKE

A member of Home Moravian Church in Winston-Salem gave me this heirloom recipe in 1979. It is the same recipe used by Salem College when I attended the school. Sunday was Moravian sugar cake morning. It was an honor for anyone to be invited to Sunday breakfast at Salem. Make it the day before, then heat it up to serve!

1/2 c hot mashed potatoes

1/2 c shortening (Crisco)

1/2 c white granulated sugar

2 eggs, beaten

3/4 c potato water, lukewarm

2 pkg active dry yeast

4 scant c flour, sifted

1/2 tsp salt

Light brown sugar, to taste

1 stick butter, cut into 1/2-inch squares (or less, to taste)

Dash of cinnamon

Grease four 11-by-7-by-2-inch pans or three 8-inch pans. Preheat oven to 375°F. Using a large bowl, add shortening and sugar to hot mashed potatoes. Add beaten eggs. Dissolve yeast in lukewarm potato water (the water in which the potatoes were cooked) and add sifted flour and salt and yeast mixture to other ingredients in bowl. Beat well. Cover and let rise until dough doubles in bulk.

Divide dough, pat and stretch into greased pans to no more than a half-inch thickness. Let rise 1 hour, until doubled. Sprinkle dough generously with light brown sugar, sliced-thin margarine or butter, and a dash of cinnamon. With thumb and index finger, make indentations in dough at 2-inch intervals, pressing all the way to the bottom of the pan. Bake at 370-375°F for approximately 20 minutes, if oven cooks slowly. If it cooks hot, bake at 350°F. When dough is light brown, remove from oven. If removed from oven before dough is cooked to medium brown, it will reheat well in toaster oven. Once cooled, the sugar cake may be wrapped in plastic wrap, placed in freezer bags, and frozen for later use. To reheat frozen sugar cake, remove from plastic wrap, wrap loosely in foil, and heat for 20 minutes in oven set to 350°F.

ABOUT MORAVIAN SUGAR CAKE:
The tradition among Home Church members is that a baker's generosity can be determined by seeing how deep the dimples are in his or her sugar cake. If the dough dimples indent almost to the pan, allowing for bigger pools of buttery sugar, then the baker is a very generous soul. If the dimples barely indent the surface, then pity those living with the baker.

APRICOT PASTRY

from Mary Elizabeth Daltroff, from Willa Hand

1 pkg refrigerated crescent rolls

1/2 c apricot jam

1 c sour cream

1 beaten egg

1 T white granulated sugar

1/2 tsp vanilla extract

Unroll crescent rolls. Pat into the bottom of a buttered 12-by-9-by-2-inch baking dish. Spread with jam. Bake at 425°F for 15 minutes. Remove from oven. Reduce oven heat to 325°F. Combine remaining ingredients; pour evenly over the rolls. Return to oven and bake 5 to 6 minutes longer. Cut into bite-sized bits. Serve warm. These freeze well.

TIP: Be creative! Use canned biscuits to make your own coffee cake by dipping the biscuits into butter, rolling them in sugar (with or without cinnamon), layering them in a bundt or tube pan, and combining with cream cheese, nuts, or fruit.

EASY MONKEY BREAD

This was yet another use my mom's friends found for refrigerator biscuits.

1/2 c chopped pecans (I chop toasted nuts)

1/2 c white granulated sugar

1 tsp ground cinnamon

Three 10-oz cans refrigerated buttermilk biscuits

1 c firm packed light brown sugar

1/2 c butter or margarine, melted

Preheat oven to 350°F. Generously grease Bundt pan with shortening or cooking spray. Sprinkle chopped pecans evenly in bottom; set aside. Combine sugar and cinnamon. Cut biscuits into quarters, roll each piece in sugar mixture, place in pan, layering. Combine brown sugar with butter; pour over dough. Bake 30-40 minutes. Cool 10 minutes in pan; invert onto serving platter. *YIELD: 12 servings.*

NUTTY ORANGE COFFEE CAKE

This recipe has been passed around the family for about 20 years. Yet another use for canned biscuits!

3/4 c white granulated sugar

1/2 c chopped pecans

2 tsp grated orange rind

1/2 pkg (4 oz) of reduced-fat cream cheese

Two 11-oz cans refrigerated buttermilk biscuits

1/2 c butter or margarine, melted

1 c sifted confectioners sugar

2 T fresh orange juice

Combine first 3 ingredients in a small bowl and set aside. Place 1 T cream cheese on half of each biscuit; fold biscuit over cheese, pressing edges to seal. Dip folded biscuits in melted butter and dredge in sugar mixture. Place dredged biscuits, curved side down, in a lightly greased 12-cup Bundt pan, spacing them evenly. Drizzle any remaining butter over the biscuits, and sprinkle with any remaining sugar mixture. Bake at 350°F about 40 minutes. Immediately invert onto a serving plate while still hot. Combine powdered sugar and orange juice, stirring well, and drizzle over the warm coffee cake. Serve immediately.

MUFFINS AND BREADS

APPLESAUCE MUFFINS

2 sticks (1 c) butter or margarine, softened

2 c white granulated sugar

2 eggs

1 tsp vanilla extract

4 c all-purpose flour

3 tsp cinnamon

1 tsp cloves

2 tsp allspice

1 c chopped nuts, OPTIONAL

16-oz jar of applesauce (natural)

2 tsp baking soda

Cream margarine or butter with sugar until light. Add eggs and vanilla. Blend well. Sift the flour and 3 spices together; add to the butter mixture. Add nuts if desired. The batter at this stage is very stiff. Mix applesauce and baking soda together, add to batter last. Bake in muffin cups at 450°F in a preheated oven until done (tops spring back or toothpick comes out clean). Batter will keep in fridge for a week. Muffins freeze well. *YIELD: 4 dozen.*

BLUEBERRY MUFFINS

Joshua has pointed out to me that this muffin has a roll-like texture. These muffins are well suited for drizzling with butter and local honey.

1/4 c vegetable shortening

1 egg

1/3 c white granulated sugar

2 c all-purpose flour

1/2 tsp salt

2 tsp baking powder

3/4 c whole milk

15-oz can of blueberries, drained, or generous 1-1/2 c fresh blueberries

Cream together the shortening, egg and sugar until light and fluffy. Sift together flour, salt, and baking powder. Alternating flour mixture with milk, add 1/3 at a time to creamed mixture. Gently fold in thoroughly drained blueberries. Fill greased muffin tins half full. Bake at 400°F in preheated oven for 20 minutes. *YIELD: 1 dozen.*

BRAN MUFFINS

from Rita Davidson Friend

This is for my neighbor, Polly Williams, who asked for a bran muffin recipe. The recipe came from my cousin Rita, who still uses Aunt Sheila's old **Watkins Cookbook,** *published in 1945.*

2 T shortening

2 T molasses

2 T light brown sugar

2 egg yolks, lightly beaten

1 c whole wheat flour

1 c bran

3 tsp baking powder

1/2 tsp salt

1/2 tsp baking soda

1 tsp warm water

1 c sour milk (buttermilk)

2 egg whites, beaten stiff

Melt shortening. Add molasses, sugar, egg yolks. Dissolve soda in warm water and add to mixture. Set aside. Sift all dry ingredients together; add alternately to batter with buttermilk. Fold in beaten egg whites, stirring in only one direction. Pour into greased or lined muffin tins. Bake in very hot preheated oven set to 425°F, about 20-30 minutes until done. Cool 30 minutes before turning out.

Fresh Blueberry Muffins and Old Salem Pumpkin Muffins

HINT: Vegetable soup, chili, spaghetti sauce, banana bread, pumpkin muffins, apple tea cake, zucchini bread, and coconut cake all taste better after having been frozen.

OLD SALEM PUMPKIN MUFFINS

This classic Moravian recipe is served at the Old Salem Tavern, and has been one of my signature recipes since the mid-1970s. The recipe works well in loaf pans as pumpkin bread and freezes well. (Note: I have doubled the pumpkin quantity.)

1-2/3 c sifted all-purpose flour

1/4 tsp baking powder

1 tsp baking soda

1/4 tsp salt

1 tsp pumpkin pie spice

1/8 tsp ground cloves

1/3 c golden raisins, OPTIONAL (I add them)

1/3 c butter, melted

1-1/2 c sugar

1/3 c water

15-oz can pumpkin

2 eggs

Old Salem Tavern in Winston-Salem, NC

Grease and lightly flour a muffin tin (you can use Pam spray and Wondra gravy flour), or use liners. Sift all the dry ingredients together and set aside. Mix wet ingredients thoroughly; add the dry ingredients in about 3 batches, until blended. NOTE: Use plain pumpkin. Fold in raisins. Bake at 350° F in preheated oven until golden brown, about 35 minutes. NOTE: If your muffins are too moist, cut back to about 1 generous cup pumpkin. *YIELD: 12 to 18 muffins, or 1 loaf.*

TO TRIPLE:

4-1/3 c sifted flour

3/4 tsp baking powder

3 tsp baking soda

3/4 tsp salt

3 tsp pumpkin pie spice

3/8 tsp ground cloves

1 c golden raisins, OPTIONAL

1 c butter (two sticks)

4-1/2 c sugar

1 c water

6 eggs

ALMOST three 15-oz cans of pumpkin

RAW APPLE MUFFINS

from Aline Thurmond Miller

2 c diced apples

1/2 c granulated sugar

1 egg, beaten slightly

1/4 c oil

1 tsp vanilla extract

1 c all-purpose flour

1 tsp baking soda

1 tsp cinnamon

1/2 tsp salt

1/2 c raisins

1/2 c broken nuts

Mix apples and sugar. In separate bowl, blend egg, oil, and vanilla with mixer; pour over apples. Mix dry ingredients together then blend into wet mixture. Add raisins and nuts. Spoon into greased muffin pans. Bake in preheated oven at 325°F for 25 minutes.

ZUCCHINI-CARROT MUFFINS

1-1/2 c plain flour

1/2 tsp salt

2 eggs

1 c sugar

2 T oil

3/4 c Coca-Cola® soft drink

1-1/2 tsp vanilla

2 c fine-grated carrots

1/2 c fine-grated zucchini

1/2 c raisins, OPTIONAL

1/4 c chopped nuts, OPTIONAL

Mix dry ingredients through a sieve. Whisk together egg, sugar, oil, cola and vanilla in a separate bowl. Fold wet and dry ingredients together, a bit at a time. Add grated veggies, raisins, and nuts until just combined. Spoon batter into greased muffin tin. Bake at 350°F in preheated oven for 20 minutes. *YIELD: 1 dozen.*

QUICK BANANA BREAD

1-3/4 c all-purpose flour, pre-sifted

2-1/4 tsp double acting baking powder

1/2 tsp salt

1/3 c shortening

2/3 c white granulated sugar

3/4 tsp grated lemon rind

1 extra-large or 2 large eggs, beaten

1-1/4 c ripe banana pulp

1/2 c broken nuts, OPTIONAL

1/4 c chopped apricots or dates, OPTIONAL

Have all ingredients at room temperature. Preheat oven to 350ºF. Lightly oil and flour an 8-1/2-by-4-1/2-inch loaf pan. Sift flour before measuring, then resift with the baking powder and salt. Blend until creamy the shortening, sugar and lemon rind. Beat in the beaten eggs and banana pulp. Add the sifted ingredients to the wet ingredients in about 3 parts. Beat the batter after each addition until smooth. You may fold in nuts and/or chopped apricots or dates. Put batter in the greased and floured pan. Bake about 1 hour or until toothpick inserted in center comes out clean.

QUICK LEMON POPPY SEED BREAD

1 box white cake mix

Two pkgs instant sugar-free low-fat lemon pudding mix

1 c warm water

4 eggs

1/2 c extra light olive oil

4 tsp poppy seeds

Combine cake mix, pudding mix, water, and oil in large bowl on low speed for 30 seconds. Add eggs one at a time, blending on medium speed 2 minutes. Pour into two greased 9-by-5-inch loaf pans. Bake at 350ºF in preheated oven for 35-40 minutes, until toothpick comes out clean. Cool on rack about 1 hour, then turn out. These freeze well. *YIELD: 2 loaves.*

HINT: When measuring flour and other dry ingredients for a recipe, assume that it is a LEVEL measure unless the recipe specifies HEAPING or ROUNDED or SCANT. To achieve a level measurement, spoon the dry ingredient such as flour into the cup or measuring spoon, then use a knife to scrape across the top. VOILA! It's level. A scant measurement is not quite filled to level.

Make banana bread with browning bananas. Freeze it for more flavor.

ZUCCHINI BREAD

from Aline Thurmond Miller

You will want to make more than one loaf at a time. It's that good.

3 c all-purpose flour

2 tsp baking soda

1 tsp salt

1/2 tsp baking powder

1-1/2 tsp cinnamon

3/4 c fine-chopped walnuts or pecans

3 eggs

2 c granulated sugar

1 c vegetable oil

2 tsp vanilla extract

2 c coarsely shredded zucchini

8-oz can crushed pineapple, drained

Combine dry ingredients, add nuts, set aside. Beat eggs in large mixing bowl, add sugar, oil and vanilla; beat until creamy. Stir in zucchini and pineapple. Mix in dry ingredients until moistened. Spoon into two 9-by-5-by-3-inch greased loaf pans. Bake at 325ºF in preheated oven for 1 hr and 15 minutes. Cool 10 minutes on rack before turning out from pans. Cool. Wrap well in plastic wrap or foil. Freezes well. *YIELD: 2 loaves.*

GRIDDLE

BUCKWHEAT CAKES

from Mary Elizabeth Daltroff

I found this in Mom's files, on the back of an unsigned note from a friend, referring to it as a recipe her mother used to make.

1/3 c breadcrumbs (white bread)

2 c scalded whole milk

1/2 tsp salt

1/4 pkg yeast

1/2 c lukewarm water

1-1/4 c buckwheat flour

1 tsp molasses

1/2 tsp baking soda

1/4 c warm water

Soak breadcrumbs in scalded milk 30 minutes. Add salt. Dissolve yeast in first water, add to crumb mix. Stir in buckwheat flour. Cover with cloth; let rise overnight. Add molasses in the morning, plus baking soda dissolved in second water. Mix thoroughly. Bake on hot griddle.

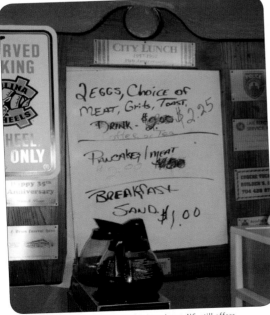

Angela Kaiser's City Lunch in Lincolnton, NC, still offers multiple breakfast deals, especially to Tar Heel fans.

SCRATCH PANCAKES

from Emma Nichols

*This recipe is included in the **Nichols Family Recipes and Remembrances "Seasoned with Love,"** 1954, published in Kearney, NE, by Morris Press. Wayne and Emma Nichols were friends of Lester and Louise, and Lester's brother Lawrence and his wife Hilion. Lester and Lawrence used to go pheasant hunting in Nebraska. Wayne and Emma, also farmers, visited the Triplettes in North Carolina as well.*

1 egg, beaten

2/3 c soured milk (add 1 T vinegar to whole milk to sour it, or use buttermilk)

3/4 c all-purpose flour

1 tsp baking powder

1 T white granulated sugar

2 T oil or melted shortening

1 tsp baking soda

1/2 tsp salt

Blend together beaten egg, milk and shortening. Stir dry ingredients together, then mix into the egg and milk mixture. Grease a griddle and heat to 400°F (point at which a drop of water will sizzle). Ladle batter onto the griddle. Turn the cakes over as they puff up and bubble but before the bubbles break. Do not stack.

SCRATCH WAFFLES

2 eggs, separated

1 c all-purpose flour

3/4 tsp salt

1 c whole milk

4 T butter

2 heaping tsp baking powder

Sift the flour and salt together. Set aside. Beat egg whites until fluffy. Set aside. Beat egg yolks in a large bowl, add milk and flour alternately to blend with the yolks. Beat in melted butter, and then add baking powder. Fold in the beaten egg whites until completely mixed. Spoon onto heated waffle iron and cook. *YIELD: 3 to 4 waffles.*

TRUE GRITS (not those instant faux grits) require 20 minutes on medium heat and constant stirring. (See *My Cousin Vinny.*) Southern grits are never crunchy from lack of stirring, or as thin and tasteless as watered-down oatmeal; and grits are NEVER sweetened like cream of wheat.

EGGS, MEAT, CASSEROLES

BRUNCH KUGEL

from Rose Ackerman Daltroff

Great dish any time, or upon breaking a religious fast such as Yom Kippur.

8 oz wide egg noodles, boiled and drained

4 large eggs, beaten

1/2 c white granulated sugar

1 tsp cinnamon

1-1/2 c fruit cocktail, or canned, sliced peaches, drained

1/2 c margarine

1/2 c light brown sugar

1 generous c of cornflakes, lightly crushed

Drain and rinse cooked noodles in cold water. In large bowl, combine beaten eggs, sugar, cinnamon, and fruit. Mix in noodles. Pour into greased casserole dish. Melt margarine. Combine with brown sugar; toss in crushed cornflakes. Sprinkle evenly over casserole. Bake uncovered about 1 hour or more, at 350°F, until knife inserted in center comes out clean.

CHIPPED BEEF ON TOAST (SOS)

from Butch Daltroff

Dad often served his children SOS for breakfast. We loved it. A World War II Navy veteran, Dad told me SOS stood for Sink or Swim. I never knew otherwise until my husband, an Army veteran, explained the real meaning of the acronym. I'm not telling; ask your own veteran.

2-oz jar dried beef, chopped, or shredded with box grater

1/4 c all-purpose flour

1/4 c butter

2 c milk or cream

Sliced mushrooms, OPTIONAL

Melt butter in pan, whisk in flour and until flour begins to thicken and turn light brown. Whisk in milk. Add chopped beef and mushrooms and cook, stirring, until bubbling hot. Some people add Worcestershire, cheese, and onion. It's a matter of personal taste. Serve over toast, biscuits, or English muffins.

CHEESE GRITS FOR A CROWD

I learned through trial and error to do these grits in a slow cooker for choir on Easter and Palm Sunday. Pour 1 to 2 cups of boiling water into a slow cooker set on low. Add cooked cheese grits. To keep the grits thin enough for serving, add more boiling water as needed.

1 gal + 3-1/2 qt water in a large, well-seasoned stock pot

1 T salt

7 c quick grits

8-oz pkg of sharp shredded Cheddar cheese

8-oz pkg shredded cheese blend (Mexican 4-cheese)

1/2 stick butter (4 T)

Dash of cayenne pepper

Dash of Tabasco, OPTIONAL

Bring salted water to a rolling boil and add the grits, being careful not to splash yourself. Stir constantly, lowering the heat to reduce potential for scorching. When grits consistency gets thick and creamy, add butter, and continue stirring until butter is completely blended. Lower heat again, and begin adding cheese, cayenne and Tabasco, stirring constantly. Add boiling water to keep consistency of mashed potatoes. When cheese has been blended in, pour into slow cooker (*see above*). Stir occasionally. *YIELD: 28 servings.*

SOUFFLÉ VARIATION: Grease a 3-qt casserole dish. Cook 2 c quick grits in 6 c water. Remove from heat to cool. Scald 2 c whole milk and 4 T salted butter, stir into grits in dish. Temper 4 large beaten eggs with some of the hot grits, then stir into grits with 3 to 4 tsp salt. Add 1/2 c grated Havarti cheese and a dash of cayenne. Bake at 350°F for 1 hour and 15 minutes.

Butch Daltroff, 1945, in the U.S. Navy

COUNTRY HAM CHEESECAKE

This recipe shared with me by a choir mate in Charlotte is a terrific brunch recipe.

6 T butter, melted

3 c soup-and-oyster crackers

1 c fresh grated Parmesan cheese

Four 8-oz pkgs cream cheese, room temperature

7 large eggs

2 c grated Swiss cheese

1 c of half-inch cubes of country ham, cooked

1/2 c chopped chives

1 tsp salt

1/4 tsp ground white pepper

Preheat oven to 300ºF. Brush 9-inch springform pan with 1 T melted butter. Finely grind the oyster crackers in a food processor. Mix the cracker crumbs, Parmesan and 5 T melted butter in a medium bowl to blend. Reserve half the crumb mixture for topping. Press remaining crumb mixture on bottom and up sides of prepared pan. Refrigerate while preparing the filling.

Beat cream cheese and eggs in a large bowl with a mixer, until smooth. Mix in remaining ingredients. Pour filling into chilled crust. Sprinkle reserved crumb mixture over top. Place cheesecake on a rimmed baking sheet. Bake until the filling no longer moves in center when the pan is gently shaken, about 2 hours. Cool 30 minutes. Serve warm or at room temperature. Can be prepared a day ahead.

NO-FAIL OMELET

My family had the ultimate dream vacation in 2004, at the newly opened 5-star Singita Lebombo Lodge of the Sabi Sands Reserve, South Africa, on the Mozambique border. Among fewer than 32 guests, we were the only Americans. Joshua and I taught one of the eight chefs how to make a Western omelet. What a way to rough it!

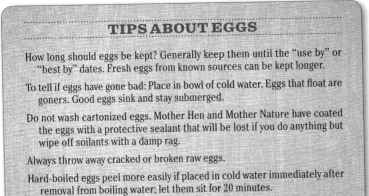

Fresh eggs (2 to 4)

Salt and pepper

Water

2 T butter

OPTIONAL:

- **Dash of garlic**
- **Dried basil**
- **Grated cheese (Monterey Jack or Colby)**
- **Dash of cayenne pepper**
- **Other condiments such as chopped mushrooms, ham, onion, bell pepper, diced tomatoes, green chilies**

Break eggs into a small mixing bowl. Stir vigorously with a whisk until frothy. Add seasonings to taste and whisk again. Add a splash of water and whisk again to keep frothy. NOTE: Do NOT use milk, which makes omelet too dense, and tends to scorch.

Melt butter in omelet pan on medium-high heat. As soon as butter begins to bubble, remove from heat and pour in frothy egg mixture (re-whisk just before cooking). Return to heat and lower to medium.

Use spatula or turner to lift edges of egg as it begins to firm up, rolling pan slightly to allow uncooked egg to go under cooked portions. Keep doing this until only center remains runny.

Sprinkle cheese or other condiments over runny center; cover for a minute with lid, gently moving pan over burner to keep egg from sticking.

Uncover and shake in pan to free from bottom, then turn out onto plate. Top with Spanish Omelet sauce, if desired. *YIELD: 1 to 2 omelets.*

TIPS ABOUT EGGS

How long should eggs be kept? Generally keep them until the "use by" or "best by" dates. Fresh eggs from known sources can be kept longer.

To tell if eggs have gone bad: Place in bowl of cold water. Eggs that float are goners. Good eggs sink and stay submerged.

Do not wash cartonized eggs. Mother Hen and Mother Nature have coated the eggs with a protective sealant that will be lost if you do anything but wipe off soilants with a damp rag.

Always throw away cracked or broken raw eggs.

Hard-boiled eggs peel more easily if placed in cold water immediately after removal from boiling water; let them sit for 20 minutes.

To avoid curdling when adding raw eggs to a hot mixture, begin by beating the eggs, and slowly adding a small amount of the hot mixture to the beaten eggs to raise the egg temperature. Then stir into the hot mixture.

Cold eggs separate more easily than room-temperature eggs.

QUICK BREAKFAST SAUSAGE MUFFINS

1 lb regular pork sausage

12 canned buttermilk biscuits

2 eggs

3-oz pkg cream cheese, softened

Shredded extra sharp Cheddar

Spray muffin tin with cooking spray. Preheat oven to 375°F. Brown sausage like ground beef; drain grease. Flatten each biscuit with rolling pin between waxed paper sheets. Line greased muffin tin with each biscuit. Combine eggs and cream cheese with hand mixer or in blender. Fill each muffin cup. Spoon sausage evenly into each cup. Top each with cheese. Bake until golden brown. *YIELD: 1 dozen.*

SAUSAGE-EGG-CHEESE CASSEROLE (STRATA)

This is a classic Carolinas breakfast casserole. It's our favorite at Easter, served with fresh fruit and muffins. For a variation, use crumbled cooked bacon, onion and bell pepper instead of sausage.

2 lb of ground pork sausage (Jimmy Dean or Tennessee Pride; *I combine 1 lb regular and 1 lb hot*)

9 slices white or honey wheat bread, crust removed

1 stick butter (1/2 c), softened

2 c shredded cheese (*I use Cheddar and Monterey Jack mixture*)

8 eggs, beaten

2-1/2 c half and half cream (or whole milk)

1-1/2 tsp salt, or less, to taste

1-1/2 tsp dry mustard

Cook sausage over low heat until done and crumbly, breaking it up by constantly stirring and turning. Drain sausage and set aside. Spread butter on de-crusted bread and cut the bread into cubes. Place cubes into a 13-by-9-inch Pyrex dish. Sprinkle sausage on bread, and cheese over the sausage. Whisk milk, salt and mustard together; whisk into beaten eggs. Pour evenly over cheese. Chill at least 8 hours overnight. Bake in preheated oven at 350°F for 40-60 minutes, until brown or until toothpick comes out clean.

TO ENLARGE RECIPE: For a 10-by-15-inch Pyrex dish: increase bread to 11 slices, the butter to 1 stick plus 2 T, the eggs to 10 eggs, the sausage to 3 pounds, the milk to 3 cups, and the cheese to 2-1/2 to 3 cups.

Shirred Egg Cups

SHIRRED EGG CUPS

4 large eggs

8 slices deli ham (sliced on #1 cut)

1/2 to 3/4 c grated Baby Swiss cheese

Pinch of dry mustard for each egg

Dash of cayenne pepper for each egg

Dashes of salt and black pepper, to taste

Whipping cream

Line 4 oven-proof custard ramekins with the sliced ham, 2 slices per ramekin overlapped to form a nest. Break one egg into the center of each ham-lined ramekin. Sprinkle dash of cayenne and dry mustard over each egg yolk. Bake ramekins on cookie tray in preheated oven set at 350°F. When egg whites begin to turn opaque, remove from oven. Sprinkle cheese over each cup; pour whipping cream over cheese almost to the ramekin lip. Sprinkle with salt and pepper. Quickly return to oven for about 10 more minutes, until cheese and cream are bubbly. *YIELD: 4 servings.*

Start your morning with this delicious
Sausage-Egg-Cheese Casserole (Strata)

BREAKFAST GRAVIES

CHOCOLATE GRAVY

My immediate family never ate chocolate gravy for breakfast, but some of our Arkansas, Louisiana, and mountain relatives did. The origin of this regional breakfast treat is loosely attributed by historians to the Spanish-Mexican connection, brought from Louisiana to the Tennessee mountains and the Ozarks. Recipes have been handed down in mountain families as far north as Kentucky and West Virginia. Some family recipes call for starting the gravy like a béchamel white sauce, with butter or bacon grease. Most, however, call for stirring in butter and vanilla once cooked. My chocolate gravy version is as good a way to end the day as it is to start—it makes a great hot sauce on homemade or Blue Bell vanilla ice cream!

3 T plain flour

2 T cocoa

2 c whole milk

1 T butter

1/2 tsp vanilla extract

Combine dry ingredients in saucepan, then whisk in milk until smooth. Cook on low heat, stirring frequently with wooden spoon. Sauce takes a while to thicken (unlike the version where the flour and butter are cooked together first). Remove from heat when thick and glossy like gravy. Stir in butter and vanilla until completely blended. Ladle over hot biscuits or ice cream. Store leftovers in fridge. Reheat in microwave in short bursts of 30 seconds.

SAUSAGE GRAVY

Sausage pan drippings

2 c coffee, divided

Water

2 T plain flour dissolved in 1 c cold water

Salt and pepper to taste

Add 1 c coffee to pan when sausage is almost done. Stir up drippings and simmer. Add about 1 c water and repeat, letting cook down halfway. Add 1 more c coffee just before removing sausage, and simmer down a bit. Remove sausage to plate; scrape pan drippings into the liquid. Whisk in the flour water, stirring until gravy thickens. Add salt and generous amount of pepper. Serve immediately over sausage and biscuits or toast.

LAURIE'S SPANISH OMELET SAUCE

from Butch Daltroff

Dad and I concocted this sauce for omelets. The hot version is our sure-fire cure for sinus infections. Sauce will keep in freezer about 6 months, tightly sealed.

1 medium to large onion, chopped

1 c of celery heart and leaves, chopped fine

1 small can of green chilies chopped

8-oz can of tomato paste

28-oz can of tomato puree

14-oz jar Herdez salsa casera (mild, medium or hot)

1 pkg of small white mushrooms, stemmed and chopped

1 green bell pepper, chopped

Cayenne pepper to taste

Tabasco sauce to taste

1 tsp salt

1/4 tsp black pepper

1 stick (1/2 c) butter, or 1/4 to 1/2 c cooking oil

Sauté the onion and celery with the salt and pepper in butter or oil until transparent. Add the mushrooms and bell pepper and continue cooking for 5 minutes. Add the tomato puree, pour the Herdez salsa in the tomato puree can and mix in the tomato paste. Add to celery and onion mixture and continue stirring. Add the green chilies and seasoning. Simmer for at least 30 minutes on medium-low, stirring to keep from scorching When ready to serve, ladle onto omelet sprinkled with grated cheese. (NOTE: Tomato paste contains sugar, and will cause the mixture to burn easily, especially in a previously scorched pot.)

TOMATO GRAVY1/4 C BACON DRIPPINGS (OR COOKING OIL)

1/4 to 1/3 c plain flour

28-oz can diced tomatoes, or 2 lb fresh tomatoes, peeled, cored, seeded and chopped fine(may substitute tomato paste)

1 small yellow onion, chopped fine

2 cloves garlic, minced fine

1-1/2 tsp kosher salt, plus more to taste

1/2 tsp fresh ground black pepper, plus more to taste

2 tsp fresh chopped thyme, OPTIONAL

1 c evaporated milk, or cream

Heat bacon drippings in 12-inch skillet (cast iron preferred) over medium-high heat. Add onions and cook, stirring until transparent, about 10 minutes. Add garlic, 1 tsp salt, pepper, thyme, and cook, stirring occasionally until flavors meld; about 2 minutes. Whisk in flour, stirring continuously until it makes a dark golden roux. Stir in tomatoes and mash into the roux, adding remaining salt. Cook until tomatoes begin to soften; about 6 minutes. Heat milk, whisk in slowly and cook, stirring, until gravy thickens. Add salt and pepper to taste.

SPICY VARIATION: Add 1 can of Rotel.

CORN MEAL

CORN FRITTERS

2/3 c whole milk

1 egg

1-1/2 c self-rising flour

17-oz can whole kernel corn, drained

2/3 c oil for frying

Heat oil in fry pan. Combine milk and egg in medium bowl; beat slightly. Lightly spoon flour into measuring cup and level off to measure. Gradually add flour, mixing after each addition. Stir in corn. Drop batter by tablespoon into 2 to 3 inches of hot oil. Fry until golden on each side (about 1-1/2 to 2 minutes per side). Drain on paper towel. Dust with powdered sugar. Serve with honey.

SKILLET CORNBREAD

1/4 c bacon drippings or shortening

1 to 2 eggs, lightly beaten

1-1/2 c yellow corn meal (not self-rising)

1/4 c sifted plain flour

1 tsp salt

1/2 tsp baking soda

1 tsp baking powder

1-1/4 c buttermilk

Preheat oven to 450°F. Melt bacon drippings or shortening in a 9-inch cast iron skillet heated in the oven while the oven is preheating. The drippings will melt while you mix the batter. Pour cornbread batter into the skillet, and bake about 20 to 25 minutes. The cornbread will pull away from the sides when done.

VARIATION 1: 1-3/4 cup of self-rising yellow or white corn meal, 2 c buttermilk, 1/4 c plain flour, 1 beaten egg, 2 T melted butter; 1 T sugar, OPTIONAL.

VARIATION 2: 1 cup white corn meal, 1/2 cup flour, 1 egg, 1-1/2 tsp baking powder but no soda, 1/2 tsp salt, 1 cup of milk and 1/2 cup of buttermilk, 1/4 cup bacon drippings.

ROSE'S CHILI CORNBREAD

from Rose Price May

Rose, a daughter of Florence Daltroff, would visit the Memphis relatives about once a year. Rose and her husband, Walter Dent May, lived in Natchez; Rose had served as a Mississippi state historian. Rose particularly favored Mexican-Mississippi-Louisiana cuisine.

1 c corn meal

1 c creamed corn

3/4 c whole milk

1/2 tsp baking soda

1/3 c canola oil

2 eggs

Pinch of salt

Cheddar cheese, shredded or grated

Diced green chili peppers

Mix ingredients together except the chilies. Spread half of batter into a prepared baking pan, and spread with green chilies and Cheddar cheese. Spread remaining batter on top and cover with more grated or shredded cheese. Bake at 400°F in preheated oven for 30-40 minutes, until toothpick comes out clean.

MISSISSIPPI HUSHPUPPIES

2 c self-rising corn meal

2 T all-purpose flour

1 tsp sugar

1 tsp black pepper

2 c buttermilk

1 egg

1/2 c green bell pepper, chopped

1 white onion, chopped

4 oz strong or dark beer

Mix all dry ingredients, then add buttermilk, egg, bell pepper, onion, and beer. Mix well. Let mixture sit in the fridge for about 1 hr. before cooking. Have oil ready (shortening or peanut oil in a Fry Daddy). Drop puppies in by the spoonful. Do not overcrowd in the oil. Cook until they float, then remove and drain on paper towels.

ROSE'S HUSHPUPPIES

from Rose Price May

Baldwin and Helen Newman, Rose's sister, lived in Vicksburg, and this was a favorite recipe of Helen's. When I was growing up, Vicksburg still didn't celebrate the Fourth of July due to the brutal Siege of Vicksburg during the War of Northern Aggression.

1-1/2 c self-rising corn meal

1/2 c self-rising flour

1 large onion (blended)

2 large eggs

1/2 c cream-style yellow corn

1 tsp granulated white
    sugar

1/2 c diced jalapeño
    pepper, OPTIONAL

3 to 4 oz beer (not lite)

Mix, refrigerate overnight. Drop by the tablespoon into hot fish-frying oil, AFTER frying the fish. *YIELD: 10 servings.*

VARIATION: Add 1/4 c chopped green onion.

CHEESY SPOONBREAD

1 can condensed Cheddar cheese soup

1/2 soup can of milk (3/4 c)

1/2 c plain yellow cornmeal (not self rising)

1/4 c butter or margarine

3 eggs, separated

1/2 tsp salt

1/4 tsp baking powder

Stir soup until smooth in a saucepan, gradually blending in the milk. Bring to a boil, stirring occasionally. Lower the heat and gradually add the cornmeal, stirring until just thickened. Remove from heat, stir in butter. Beat egg yolks until thick, and stir in a few tablespoons of the soup mixture. Blend yolks into the remaining soup. Combine salt and baking powder, sprinkle over the egg whites. Beat the egg whites until stiff but not dry, Fold the beaten whites into the soup mixture. Turn out into a 1-1/2-quart soufflé dish. Bake at 350°F for 1 hour.

MOM'S HONEY SPOON BREAD

from Mary Elizabeth Daltroff

1 c white corn meal

1-1/2 tsp salt

4 T butter or margarine

1-1/3 c boiling water

3 eggs

1 T baking powder

1-1/3 c hot milk

2 tsp honey

Vicksburg, MS, fell on July 4 during the Civil War.

Grease 2-qt casserole dish. Mix corn meal and salt; blend well. Add butter, pour into boiling water, stirring constantly. Allow to cool. Beat eggs with baking powder until light and fluffy. Add to corn meal mix. Stir in milk and honey and mix thoroughly. Pour into casserole dish. Place dish in shallow pan of hot water; bake in preheated 350°F oven for 35-40 minutes. Serve hot by the spoonful. *YIELD: 6 servings.*

ROLLS

BECKY SHERRILL'S ROLLS

from Becky Sherrill

This recipe from Aunt Becky, Uncle Paul's wife, is in the Grace Chapel UMW cookbook.

1 pkg active dry yeast

1 c warm water

1 well beaten egg

2 T sugar

1/4 c of oil

3 c self-rising flour

Dissolve yeast in 1 cup of warm water (NOT hot). Add egg, sugar, and oil to the yeast and water mixture. Add the flour to the wet mixture. Work it in a bit. Cover and let rise for 1 hour. Roll out dough on a lightly floured surface, and cut into circles with a biscuit cutter. Dip each roll in melted butter and fold the circle into "pocket book" shapes. Put pocketbooks into lightly greased 9-by-13-inch pan, slightly apart. Let rise for 2 hours. Bake in hot oven at 450°F for 8 minutes or until browned. *YIELD: 28 rolls.*

CHEDDAR CRESCENTS

1 pkg (1/4 oz) active dry yeast

1/2 c warm water (100-110°F)

2-1/2 c Bisquick

1-1/4 c (5 oz) shredded Cheddar cheese

1 large egg, beaten

Stir together yeast and warm water in large bowl; let stand 5 minutes. Stir in Bisquick, cheese and egg. Stir until soft dough forms. Turn out onto well floured surface; knead 20 times. Place in a bowl coated with cooking spray; turn dough to grease top. Cover; let rise 20 minutes. Divide dough into 4 equal portions. Roll out 1 portion at a time into 8-inch circle on lightly floured surface. Cut circle into 8 wedges; roll up, starting at wide end, to form crescent. Place point side down on greased baking sheet. Repeat with rest of dough. Bake at 350°F in preheated oven for 10-12 minutes, until golden brown. *YIELD: 8 servings.*

Paul Sherrill and his older brother, Hugh, during World War II

DOUBLE QUICK DINNER ROLLS

1 pkg active dry yeast

3/4 c warm water

1/4 c white granulated sugar

1 tsp salt

2-1/4 c all-purpose flour, divided

1 egg, beaten

1/4 c (1/2 stick) butter, softened

Dissolve yeast in warm water. Add sugar, salt and half the flour. Beat for 2 minutes. Add beaten egg and butter; beat in the remaining flour until smooth. Put in large bowl and let rise for 30 minutes in a warm place. Stir down. Put in greased muffin tins and bake at 425°F in a preheated oven for 15 minutes.

GRANDMOTHER THURMOND'S ROLLS

from Stella Thurmond Campbell

Cousin Stella Thurmond Campbell sent me this recipe. Grandmother taught it to Stella's mother, Ann, upon her marriage to my Uncle Enos. Aunt Ann, a wonderful cook, became noted in Jackson, TN, for "HER" rolls. Stella says the only reason we now have this recipe is because one of her non-Thurmond cousins documented the "pinch of this" and "dab of that" as Aunt Ann made rolls for her.

1/2 c white granulated sugar

2 c whole milk

1/2 c vegetable shortening (Crisco)

1 to 1-1/2 c all-purpose flour, sifted

1 pkg active dry yeast

3 to 4 T lukewarm water (about 110°F)

1/2 tsp salt

1 c all-purpose flour

1 tsp baking powder

1/2 tsp baking soda

Mix the sugar, milk and shortening in a saucepan and bring to a boil on medium heat. Allow to cool for 50 minutes. Sift the 1 to 1-1/2 cup of flour. Set aside. In another bowl, sift together 1 cup of flour with the salt, baking soda and baking powder. Set aside.

Dissolve 1 package of dry yeast in a small amount of warm water. Add yeast to the milk-sugar mixture in a large bowl, along with the 1 to 1-1/2 cup of sifted flour, working in a little bit of flour at a time. This makes a thin dough. Cover with a damp cloth and set in a warm place until it doubles its bulk (about 1 to 2 hours, depending on the weather).

Sift together the second flour (1 cup) with the baking powder and soda. After the thin mixture has risen, work in the additional flour-baking powder-soda mixture. Roll out onto a lightly floured board just like biscuit dough. If too sticky, dust in additional flour. Cut out rolls and place into a greased pan with sides almost touching. Cover with dampened cloth and let rise again. Bake in preheated oven at 450°F until golden brown. These rolls taste like angel biscuits. *YIELD: About 20 rolls.*

LOUISE'S QUICK ROLLS

1/2 c whole milk

1 T shortening

1 T white granulated sugar

1/2 tsp salt

1 pkg yeast

1/4 c lukewarm water

1 egg

1-3/4 c all-purpose flour

1 T butter, room temperature, on the butter wrapper

Scald milk. Add sugar, salt and shortening. Cool to lukewarm, add yeast dissolved in lukewarm water. Add egg; beat well, add flour until blended. This is a soft dough. Cover. Let rise about 30 minutes. Grease baking pan. Pinch pieces of dough and roll into balls. Place in pan, sides not quite touching. Let rise 30 minutes. Bake at 400°F for 15 minutes until browned. Remove, rub butter wrapper over top. *Yield: 12-15 rolls.*

LOUISE'S POTATO YEAST ROLLS

1/2 c lukewarm water

1 pkg active dry yeast

3 T instant potato flakes

3 T white granulated sugar

1 scant T salt

4-1/2 to 5-1/2 c all-purpose flour, sifted

1/2 c shortening, plus 1/4 c melted in dish

Add yeast to lukewarm water in a quart-size canning jar. Add potato flakes, sugar and salt to yeast water. Add lukewarm water until jar is half full. Keep jar warm; allow to rise to about 3/4 full in jar. Cut 1/2 cup shortening into flour. Shake yeast mixture well; mix into flour. Knead, or fold well with spatula (dough is sticky). Put dough into greased bowl; cover with damp cloth. Let rise to double, about 1-1/2 hour. Knead again. Flour hands and dough enough to make little rolls. Dip each into melted shortening. Place into greased 9-by-13-inch pan in 5 rows. Let rise again, 1-1/2 hours. Bake at 350°F about 35 minutes until brown; drizzle with melted butter. *YIELD: 20-25 rolls.*

HOW TO USE YEAST: Active dry yeast is sold in packets of 0.25 oz each, or in jars, and requires two risings for the dough. Bread Machine Yeast (Rapid Rise Yeast) is sold in jars or 0.25-oz packets, is more finely ground, and absorbs moisture faster than active dry yeast, acting quickly with only one rising. Its yeast aroma and flavor are less pronounced. One may substitute Rapid Rise for active dry yeast, if one shortens the rise time. Do not use active dry yeast in bread machine recipes. Cake yeast is fresh yeast, compressed while moist. Equivalent measures: 1 pkg active dry yeast = 2/3 of a cake yeast; and 1 pkg of Rapid Rise yeast = one cake of yeast. 1 packet of active dry or rapid rise yeast= 2-1/4 teaspoons.

MARY ELIZABETH'S ROLLS

from Mary Elizabeth Daltroff

MIX TOGETHER:

1 c shortening

1 c boiling water

3/4 c white granulated sugar

Let cool to lukewarm temperature.

MIX TOGETHER IN ANOTHER BOWL:

2 pkgs active dry yeast

1/2 c warm water

Let sit for a few minutes, then add the lukewarm shortening-water-sugar mixture.

MIX IN ANOTHER BOWL:

1 c cold water

2 eggs

IN A LARGE BOWL, COMBINE THE FOLLOWING:

6 c all-purpose flour, unsifted

1 tsp salt

The yeast-sugar-shortening mixture

The egg mixture

Cover with dampened cloth or towel and let sit in a warm place until dough doubles in size. Remove from bowl onto lightly floured surface and knead with palms of hands for 2 to 3 minutes. Pinch off and roll into balls, place on lightly greased baking pan, sides almost touching. Let rise again and bake in preheated oven at 350-375°F until golden brown.

Brothers David and Enos III, with cousin Cheri Thurmond, holding the puppies of Mary Elizabeth's red cocker spaniel, Taffy, at Grandmother and Granddaddy Thurmond's home in Bells, TN, 1951

MAYONNAISE ROLLS

This is one of those 20th century recipes that everyone used for its quickness.

1 c self-rising flour

1/2 c buttermilk

2 T mayonnaise

Combine all ingredients, blending well. Drop onto a lightly greased or oiled cookie sheet. Bake at 425°F in a preheated oven for 10 to 12 minutes, until light brown. *YIELD: 8 to 10 rolls.*

QUICK TINY ROLLS

2 c Bisquick

1 stick melted butter

1 c sour cream

Mix together and drop into the small-sized muffin tins (sprayed with Pam). Bake for 15 minutes at 400°F in preheated oven. *YIELD: 3 dozen small rolls.*

EMERGENCY BAKING SUBSTITUTIONS

Out of baking soda? For 1 teaspoon, combine:
1/4 tsp baking powder + 1/2 tsp cream of tarter
Out of self-rising flour? For 1 cup, combine:
1 c plain flour + 1/2 tsp salt + 1 tsp baking powder
Out of "Southern-style" flour? For 1 cup, sift:
1/2 c cake flour + 1/2 c regular all-purpose flour

MORAVIAN LOVE FEAST BUNS

1 cake yeast (equivalent of 1 pkg Rapid Rise dry yeast)

1/4 cup warm water

1 cup sugar

2 eggs, beaten

1/2 cup softened butter

1 tsp salt

1/4 to 1/2 cup warm mashed potatoes (1 Russet potato)

1 to 2 c lukewarm potato water

5-1/2 to 6-1/2 c of all-purpose flour, sifted

Melted butter or cream for glazing

Peel and cube a Russet potato. Boil in 3-qt sauce-pan of water until tender. Drain, saving water. Mash potato. Dissolve yeast in 1/4 cup warm water. Add sugar to beaten egg, then softened butter, salt, warm mashed potatoes, and yeast mixture. Alternate adding flour and warm potato water. Makes soft, sticky dough. Turn out onto lightly floured surface; fold over and knead until smooth. Cover with clean, warm cloth; set in warm place to rise. When doubled in bulk, punch down dough and make into rolls 3 to 4 inches in diameter. Place, not touching, on greased sheets. Cover with warm cloth and let rise again. Bake in pre-heated oven at 400°F until brown, about 20 minutes. Brush with cream or melted butter to glaze as soon as removed from oven. (I combine 3 T melted butter with 3/4 cup whipping cream.) *YIELD: 12-15 rolls.*

SWEET POTATO ROLLS

1 pkg active dry yeast

1 tsp white granulated sugar

1/4 c warm water

1/2 c white granulated sugar

1/2 c shortening

1 tsp salt

2 c mashed, cooked sweet potato (canned is okay if drained)

1 egg

4 c (approximately) of plain flour

Dissolve yeast and 1 tsp sugar in the warm water in a small bowl. Let stand.

Cook fresh potatoes about 1 hour, drain, remove skins, mash (or use canned). In a large metal or glass mixing bowl, mix 1/2 cup of sugar, the shortening, and salt into the hot mashed potatoes. Let potato mixture cool, then stir in the yeast and egg. Add flour, a little at a time. Dough should be slightly stiff when all added. Cover with a dampened cloth and let rise in a warm place such as the oven with its light on.

Mash down risen dough, and roll out as if for cutting biscuits; OR hand-shape into rolls. Place each roll into a well greased pan with the roll sides almost touching. Let rise until double in bulk. Bake for about 20 minutes at 375°F on rack farthest from the heat source (bottoms burn easily). Dough will keep in fridge for about 3 to 4 days. *YIELD: 2 dozen rolls.*

Home Moravian Church in Old Salem, NC

SOUTHERN JEWISH FOOD MEMORIES

My dear friend, Randy Rosen, has quizzed me about Jewish cooking traditions in the South. I'm no expert, as my Jewish ancestors intermarried and many crossed over before my birth. Only a few family recipes have survived from Dad's Jewish relatives, who celebrated every occasion over food, just like my mother's Methodist family. But Randy's question led me to ponder the fascinating assimilation of Jewish food culture into Southern traditions, where pork and shellfish endlessly commingle with dairy and meat.

The first Jewish immigrants settled our Southern coastal areas in the late 17th century. By the 18th century, Jews had begun immigrating in earnest, founding Congregation Mickve Israel, in Savannah, GA, in 1733. It is the second oldest religious institution in this colonial city. By 1749, enough Jews had settled in nearby Charleston, SC, to establish their own synagogue. New Orleans, founded in 1718, established its first synagogue in 1826 and 1827.

By the 1840s, Jewish immigrants from Germany and France, including my ancestors, had fanned out across the Southern states, with lively Jewish communities anchored in Memphis, the Arkansas and Mississippi sides of the Delta, Houston, New Orleans, Savannah, Atlanta, and Charleston. Mini-trans-Southern Jewish migrations outward occurred during the various cholera and yellow fever epidemics in New Orleans and Memphis in the 1870s. Another migration out of the Delta occurred in the last quarter of the 20th century, as young Jews left our rural areas for work in urban areas.

Historically, Southern Jews have always had a strong sense of place and the appropriateness of regional foodways to kashrut (kosher laws). Jewish food culture across the South, as elsewhere, was imprinted with their roots in Europe and the Mediterranean.

Marcie Cohen Ferris, author of *Matzoh Ball Gumbo*, brilliantly enumerates the culinary similarities and differences between Southern Jews and their Gentile black and white neighbors. Food, family and religion were the focus of Southern Jewish and Gentile families alike. The greater difference, according to Ferris, was between city Jews and country Jews. Urban Jews could establish a Jewish community and access to kosher foods. Country Jews had to travel to the nearest big city for kosher supplies. Jewish cooks, influenced in many instances by their servants, adapted to available materials within the region. Thus, we have kosher Cajun delicatessens, kosher Chinese take-out, barbecued brisket, greens seasoned with chicken schmaltz, and gumbo ya-ya made with chicken and kosher smoked-beef salami. And what could be more Southern AND Jewish than a dish called pecan kugel?

The Memphis of my childhood offered satisfying Jewish cuisine. My family, like many local Jewish and Gentile families, loved the deli food from Halpern's or Rosen's. We regularly purchased delicious challah bread from Mr. Jewel's bakery oven in East Memphis, or in a pinch, from Seessel's grocery deli.

These are all long gone, but the women of the Margolin Hebrew Academy (formerly the Memphis Hebrew Academy), located just five blocks from my childhood home, have collected the region's kosher Southern recipes in a popular cookbook titled *Simply Southern with a Dash of Kosher Soul*. Above all, in Memphis, Jewish humor and foodways prevail, as in the annual ASBEE-Kroger Kosher BBQ Cooking Contest and Festival, sponsored by Anshe Sphard-Beth El Emeth Congregation and Kroger Grocery. No pig allowed.

CHALLAH BREAD

Challah is Sabbath bread, the rich, brioche-like Jewish egg bread. Traditionally, one prepares two loaves of challah—one for Friday, and the second for Saturday (the Sabbath), when no cooking is to be done. Challah, like many other international foods, has crossed ethnic and religious boundaries. Everyone in America knows that leftover challah makes the best French toast this side of Heaven.

1/2 c warm water (110-115°F)

2 tsp active dry yeast

1 T white granulated sugar

5 large eggs

1 c vegetable oil

2 tsp salt

1 c sugar

2/3 c warm water (110-115°F)

7 c plain flour

1 large egg yolk

1 T water

Combine warm water, yeast and 1 T sugar in small bowl. Stir to dissolve yeast. Let set in warm spot until foamy (10+ minutes). Beat eggs with electric mixer in large bowl until foamy; add dissolved yeast, oil, salt and 1 cup of sugar. Beat until pale yellow and slightly thickened. Add 2/3 cup of warm water; beat to blend. Mix in flour with dough hook, 1/2 cup at a time, until dough no longer sticks to bowl.

Turn out onto lightly floured surface; knead until smooth and elastic (5 to 7 minutes). Add 1 tsp flour at a time if too sticky. Turn dough into lightly oiled large bowl, turning once to coat. Cover with plastic wrap. Wet a clean towel with warm water and microwave it for 30 seconds. Place warmed towel over plastic-wrapped bowl. Let dough rise in warm, draft-free spot (such as an open microwave oven) until doubled in bulk, about 1 hour. Punch down, cover as before, and let dough rise again for 30 more minutes.

Grease 2 medium baking sheets. Turn risen dough onto lightly floured surface and divide in half. Divide each half into 3 equal pieces and roll into 9-inch ropes. To shape the challah loaves, arrange 3 dough ropes side by side on each of the 2 baking sheets. Start in center and braid out toward each end, pinching ends together to seal. Cover each loaf with towel and let rise again until almost doubled, about 30 minutes.

Preheat oven to 400°F. Whisk 1 egg yolk and 1 T water. Brush mixture on risen loaf tops. Let rise another 20-30 minutes, and brush on more egg yolk, sprinkling with poppy or sesame seeds if desired. Bake on center rack 30-40 minutes, or until golden.

PASSOVER ROLLS

Southern mainstream Christians, seeking a connection to the life of Jesus, have begun participating in Passover Seders conducted by our patient Jewish neighbors. For Passover Seder instructions, see **www.jewfaq.org** *and your local rabbi.*

2 c matzo meal

1c water

1/2 c vegetable oil

1 T white granulated sugar

1 tsp salt

4 large eggs Stir matzo meal, salt, and sugar in mixer bowl. Boil water and oil in saucepan; remove from heat; add to matzo mixture. Blend with mixer, adding eggs, one at a time on low speed, then beat on medium. Let stand 30 minutes, OR chill in fridge for 20 minutes. Pour oil into palms & form golf ball-sized rolls. Place on greased baking sheet, 2 inches apart. Re-oil hands as needed. Bake in preheated oven at 375°F for 45 minutes. Dough freezes up to 3 months. *YIELD: 12 rolls.*

FAMILY MEMORY

My great-grandmother, Rose Ackerman Daltroff, was Shields Daltroff's second wife. Shields was a second generation Jewish Southerner from Louisiana who moved to Arkansas. His first wife, Willie Malone, was a Methodist minister's daughter, and gave Shields three daughters: Willie Florence, Bettye, and Fredricka (Freda). Rose married Shields after Willie died. She produced a second family for Shields. Willie's daughters, the older half sisters, helped  rear them. The younger siblings included my grandfather Sol, Lee, Wilbur (who died as a child), and Wilburta, who was named after her deceased older brother. As folks around here used to say, Rose came from a good Jewish family with Memphis and Philadelphia ties. Her sister Tilly had been married to Shields' brother, my great-great Uncle Louis. Even before my Protestant grandmother, Eula May Stewart, married Sol, the family was a religious hodge podge. But Jew or Gentile, everyone loved Bigmamma Rose's family recipes.

THE RECIPES

SALADS & SOUPS

CONGEALED & MOUSSE

APPLE CRANBERRY SALAD

from Mary Elizabeth Daltroff

1 pkg cranberries, ground on "round hole" of grater (or in chopper)

1 c chopped apples, Rome or Braeburn

2 c mini-marshmallows

1 c chopped pecans

1 c white granulated sugar

1 small can evaporated milk

Mix first 5 ingredients and chill in refrigerator overnight (8 hours). Whip a small can of evaporated milk that has been chilled in the freezer for 1 hour. Fold the whipped evaporated milk into the other chilled ingredients; pour into a lightly oiled rectangular 11-by-7-inch or 8-inch square pan. Chill. *YIELD: 8 to 10 servings.*

CRANBERRY RELISH (It's a chutney): 4 c cranberries, chopped, 1 orange chopped, w/peel, 1 c chopped roasted pecans, 4 large apples, peeled, and chopped, 1-1/2 c sugar, Combine fruit; stir in nuts and sugar. Refrigerate.

CRANBERRY CREAM MOLD

from Louise Triplette

2 c cranberry juice cocktail

1/4 c white granulated sugar

1 envelope unflavored gelatin

1/4 c cold water

1-1/2 T lemon juice

1 c whipping cream, whipped

Combine cranberry juice cocktail and sugar in a saucepan. Bring to a boil over medium heat, boil until cranberry juice is reduced to 1 cup. Sprinkle gelatin over cold water, let stand for 1 minute. Add gelatin mixture and lemon juice to condensed cranberry mixture. Cook over medium heat, stirring constantly until gelatin is dissolved. Remove from heat and once cooled, pour into a metal mixing bowl. Chill until mixture congeals to the consistency of unbeaten egg white. Beat on medium speed with electric mixer until light and fluffy. Fold in the whipped cream. Spoon mixture into a lightly oiled 4-cup mold. Cover and chill until firm, at least 4 hours. *Yield: 6 servings.*

CRANBERRY FREEZER SALAD

1 can jellied cranberry sauce

1/2 c nuts, chopped (pecans or walnuts)

1/2 pt whipping cream

Two 3-oz pkgs of cream cheese

8-oz can of crushed pineapple, drained

2 T mayonnaise

2 T white granulated sugar

Whip the cream and refrigerate. Blend cranberry sauce, mayonnaise, sugar and cream cheese in mixer (starting with the cream cheese). Add drained pineapple and nuts, then fold in whipped cream. Freeze in an 8-inch square pan. Cut into squares when ready to serve. *YIELD: 8 to 10 servings.*

FRESH CRANBERRY SALAD

My mom Mary Elizabeth Daltroff, my mother-in-law Louise Triplette, and my sister-in-law Andrea Benfield, ALL gave me this identical recipe. Louise and Andrea omit the celery because Michael Triplette hates celery. Prepare ahead and keep chilled.

Two 3-oz pkg cherry gelatin

1/2 envelope unflavored gelatin

1 c hot water

2/3 to 1 c white granulated sugar

1 T lemon juice

15-oz can crushed pineapple, juice reserved

2 c fresh whole cranberries, chopped to equal 1 c of chopped berries

1 orange, chopped

1 c celery, chopped, OPTIONAL

1 to 1-1/2 c chopped pecans

Dissolve cherry and unflavored gelatin in hot water. Add sugar and lemon juice. Drain the juice from the pineapple and add pineapple to the gelatin mixture. Stir well to dissolve all the sugar. Coarsely chop the cranberries in a food processor. Cut orange into sections, removing center membrane and seeds before chopping finely in the food processor. Chop celery and nuts. Add all the chopped ingredients and pineapple juice to the gelatin mixture. Spoon into a single large prepped (oiled or wet) mold, or into 15 individual molds. Chill until firm, at least 2 to 4 hours. Cover tops of molds with wax paper before refrigerating to prevent tough skin from forming.

HOLIDAY CRANBERRY SALAD

from Louise Triplette and Mary Elizabeth Daltroff

3-oz pkg cherry gelatin

3 c boiling water, divided

16-oz can of whole-berry cranberry sauce

1/2 c chopped pecans

3-oz pkg lemon gelatin

3-oz pkg cream cheese, softened

15-oz can unsweetened, crushed pineapple, well drained

16-oz can of pear halves, undrained

3-oz pkg lime gelatin

Dissolve cherry gelatin in 1 cup boiling water. Stir in cranberry sauce and pecans. Pour into oiled 12-by-8-by-2-inch dish; chill until firm. In separate bowl, dissolve lemon gelatin in 1 cup boiling water. Use electric mixer to beat in cream cheese until smooth. Stir in pineapple; chill until congealed to consistency of unbeaten egg white. Pour over cranberry layer. Chill until firm. Drain pear halves, reserve 3/4 cup liquid; chop; set aside. Dissolve lime gelatin in remaining 1 cup of boiling water. Stir in chopped pears and reserved liquid. Chill until partially congealed; spoon over pineapple layer. Chill, covered, 4 hours, until firm. *YIELD: 12 servings.*

BLUEBERRY DESSERT

6-oz pkg blackberry gelatin

2 c boiling water

16-oz can blueberries, undrained

20-oz can crushed pineapple, drained

8 oz cream cheese, softened

8 oz sour cream

1/2 c white granulated sugar

1 tsp vanilla extract

1/2 c chopped pecans or walnuts

In large mixing bowl, dissolve gelatin in boiling water. Mix in undrained can of blueberries and drained pineapple. Pour into 9-by-13-inch dish and chill thoroughly (about 4 hours). Blend together the cheeses, sour cream, sugar, and vanilla, until smooth. Spread evenly over firm-set gelatin. Sprinkle nuts over top. Cut into squares to serve. Keep refrigerated.

FRUIT COCKTAIL SALAD

1 T unflavored gelatin

2 T lemon juice

3-oz pkg cream cheese

1/4 c mayonnaise

2/3 c whipping cream (one small carton)

1/2 c white granulated sugar

15-oz can fruit cocktail in heavy syrup

1/2 c walnuts or pecans, chopped)

Soak gelatin in lemon juice and dissolve in double boiler. Blend cream cheese and mayonnaise with mixer; add dissolved gelatin. In another bowl, whip cream until stiff, adding sugar during beating; fold into cheese mixture. Drain fruit cocktail. Fold fruit and nuts into whipped cream and cheese mixture. Pour into decorative mold or tray; refrigerate until firm. Cut into squares for individual servings, or turn out onto a platter to serve. *YIELD: 8 servings.*

GINGER ALE FRUIT SALAD

2 T unflavored gelatin

1/4 c cold water

1/2 c boiling fruit juice (apricot nectar, pineapple, apple, or peach)

1/2 c white granulated sugar

1/8 tsp salt

2 c ginger ale

Juice of one lemon

1/2 lb skinned, seeded grapes (Tokay recommended)

1 orange, peeled and sliced into even circles

Segments from 1 grapefruit

6 slices canned pineapple, cut into pieces

2 tsp candied ginger

Soak the gelatin in the cold water and dissolve into the 1/2-cup of boiling fruit juice in a bowl. Add the sugar, salt, ginger ale, and lemon juice, and mix. Chill this mixture, which is a jelly, until almost set, about 2 hours. Combine the fruit gelatin mixture with the fruit and candied ginger, then pour into a prepared mold (wet or oiled). Chill for at least 4 hours, then unmold onto a bed of lettuce on a platter. Serve with a dollop of mayonnaise and a spray of parsley in the center as garnish.

HIDDEN PEAR SALAD

from Aline Thurmond Miller

16-oz can of pears, drained, liquid reserved

3-oz pkg lime gelatin

3-oz cream cheese, softened

1/4 tsp lemon juice

1 envelope whipped topping mix such as Dream Whip

Lettuce leaves

Bring pear liquid to a boil in saucepan. Stir in gelatin until dissolved. Remove from heat; cool at room temperature until syrupy. While cooling, puree pears in blender. Beat cream cheese with lemon juice with mixer until fluffy and smooth. Add pureed pears; mix well. Prepare whipped topping according to directions, fold into pear mixture. Fold in cooled gelatin. Pour into oiled 4-1/2-cup mold. Chill overnight. Unmold salad onto lettuce-lined platter just before serving. *YIELD: 6-8 servings.*

AUNT HILION'S GOOD DESSERT

from Hilion Sherrill Triplette

Aunt Hilion, wife of Lester's older brother Lawrence, gave me this recipe at my Grace Chapel bridal shower. Aunt Hilion was Louise's first cousin on the Sherrill side, the daughter of Grandpa Clarence Sherrill's brother Charlie. Hilion was Louise's second cousin on her mother's side, daughter of Fannie Starnes Sherrill, who was Grandma Grace Kirby Sherrill's first cousin. Must be Southern!

16-oz container Cool Whip

6-oz pkg of orange gelatin

20-oz can chunk pineapple, drained well

8-oz can mandarin orange slices, drained

1 c fresh frozen coconut

Sprinkle orange gelatin powder over Cool Whip in a bowl, then mix well to dissolve. Stir in remaining ingredients. Chill in a mold or 11-by-7-inch freezer-proof dish for at least 3 to 4 hours. *YIELD: 8 to 12 servings.*

BEULAH'S TWELVE-HOUR SALAD

from Beulah Benfield

Andrea's mother-in-law, Mrs. Clyde Benfield, gave me this recipe at my Grace Chapel bridal shower in Willie Sue Keller's home, where so many new family members shared their favorite recipes.

1 c mandarin oranges, canned, drained

1 c crushed pineapple, drained

1 c flaked moist coconut, canned

1 c miniature marshmallows

1 c sour cream

Mix all ingredients together and refrigerate in a glass serving bowl or 11-by-7-inch pan for 12 hours before serving. *YIELD: 8 to 10 servings.*

ORANGE SALAD MOLD

from Mary Elizabeth Daltroff

3-oz pkg orange gelatin

1 c boiling water

1 c orange juice

2 cans mandarin oranges, drained

1/2 c slivered almonds

Small curd cottage cheese

Mayonnaise

Pour boiling water over gelatin in medium bowl. Stir until completely dissolved. Add orange juice. Place bowl into a larger bowl containing iced water, stirring occasionally. As mixture begins to gel, add oranges and almonds. Pour into ring mold; refrigerate overnight. Turn out onto a platter and surround with lettuce leaves. Fill center with cottage cheese. Serve with dollops of mayo. *YIELD: 8 servings.*

Hilion Sherrill Triplette, late 1920s or early 1930s

GRACE SHERRILL'S SALAD

This recipe was given to me at my Grace Chapel bridal shower by Forney Sherrill's wife Grace, not to be confused with Louise Sherrill Triplette's mother, Grace. Forney was Aunt Hilion Sherrill Triplette's brother, and a son of Clarence Sherrill's brother, Charlie Sherrill.

6-oz pkg flavored gelatin (cherry, strawberry, lemon, or orange work well)

Regular size container of Cool Whip

20-oz can of chunk pineapple, drained well

1/2 c flake coconut

32-oz container of small-curd cottage cheese

15-oz can of Mandarin oranges, drained, or segments from two fresh Clementine oranges or tangerines

Make up the gelatin according to package instructions, using the version that accommodates addition of fruit. Before gelatin sets, mix in container of Cool Whip. Add drained chunk pineapple, cottage cheese, and flake coconut. Fold in canned Mandarin oranges or the segments of two fresh small citrus fruit. Chill in a 9-by-13-inch pan. *YIELD: 15 squares.*

HELEN'S FROZEN FRUIT SALAD

from Great-Aunt Anne Thurmond

This recipe was passed along to me by my Great-Aunt Anne Thurmond. It came to her from the Susanna UMW Circle in Brownsville, TN, where she and Uncle Gene lived after his retirement as a Methodist minister.

Two 8-oz pkgs of cream cheese

2 T mayonnaise

2 T pineapple juice

24 regular marshmallows, quartered

1 c sweet seedless grapes, halved (Red Flame or Thompson's Seedless are best)

20-oz can of chunk pineapple, drained

1/2 pt whipping cream

1/2 c chopped pecans or walnuts

Beat cream cheese with beater until softened. Whip cream and add to cream cheese; beat in mayonnaise and juice until blended. Fold in marshmallows, grapes, chunk pineapple, and nuts with a paddle blade on mixer, or by hand with a spatula, until well mixed. Pour into 9-by-13-inch tray and freeze. Cut into squares and serve on lettuce leaves. *YIELD: 12-16 servings.*

MOLDED AMBROSIA

from Great-Aunt Anne Thurmond

1 c graham cracker crumbs

1/4 c butter or margarine

9-oz can crushed pineapple

3-oz pkg orange gelatin

1/3 c white granulated sugar

1 c hot water

1 c sour cream

1/4 tsp vanilla extract

1 c diced orange sliced

1/2 c flaked coconut

Combine crumbs and butter; reserve 1/3 cup of crumbs for topping. Press remaining crumb mixture into an 8-by-8-by-2-inch baking dish. Drain pineapple, reserve syrup. Dissolve gelatin and sugar in hot water. Stir in syrup. Chill until partially set; add sour cream and vanilla. Whip until fluffy. Fold in fruit and coconut; pour over crumbs in dish. Sprinkle top with reserved crumbs. Chill until firm; cut into squares. Top with maraschino cherries. *Yield: 9 servings.*

LIME FLUFF CONGEALED SALAD

from Mary Elizabeth Daltroff

This always was my personal favorite congealed salad.

14 large marshmallows, cut up

3 oz cream cheese

3-oz pkg of lime gelatin

1 c celery, chopped fine

1 c walnuts or pecans, chopped

15-oz can crushed pineapple, drained

1 T mayonnaise

1/2 pt whipped cream, unsweetened

Dissolve marshmallows and cream cheese in 1 cup of boiling water. Add gelatin and stir until dissolved. Add next four ingredients. Mix completely. Fold in whipped cream. Pour into oiled mold. Refrigerate 2 to 4 hours before serving. To serve, place mold in hot water about 30 seconds to loosen. Flip onto serving plate.

PINEAPPLE LIME COTTAGE CHEESE SALAD

20-oz can crushed pineapple in syrup

Reserved pineapple syrup PLUS water to make 2 cups

Two 3-oz pkgs lime gelatin

2 c small curd cottage cheese

1 c undiluted evaporated milk

1 c chopped celery

1 c chopped pecans or walnuts

Drain pineapple, reserving the syrup. Add water to the syrup to make up 2 cups. Heat syrup-water mixture to boiling; dissolve the gelatin in boiling mixture in a metal bowl. Chill to the consistency of unbeaten egg whites. Stir in evaporated milk, cottage cheese, pineapple, celery and nuts. Pour into a 7-1/2-by-12-by-2-inch baking dish. Chill until firm. Cut into 15 squares.

SOUTHERN BELLE SALAD

During my childhood, every bridge club and women's luncheon offered this congealed salad, also known as Cherry Coke Salad in some areas.

16-oz can pitted Bing cherries (now called dark, sweet)

8-oz can crushed pineapple, drained (juice reserved)

3-oz pkg black cherry gelatin

3-oz pkg red raspberry gelatin

3-oz pkg cream cheese, cut into small cubes

12-oz bottle of cola soft drink (2 small 6-oz bottles in original recipe)

1 c chopped pecans or walnuts

Drain cherry juice into cup; combine with water and pineapple juice to make 1-1/2 c. Boil liquid; pour over gelatin to dissolve. Mix in cream cheese. Let cool, add cherries, pineapple, nuts and cola. Chill in an 8-inch square dish until thickened.

PINEAPPLE MARSHMALLOW SALAD

from Louise Triplette

2 pkgs lime gelatin

2 c boiling water

24 large marshmallows

2 small cans crushed pineapple, drained

1 c mayonnaise

8-oz pkg cream cheese, or 1 c small-curd cottage cheese

1 pt whipping cream

Black walnuts, halved or chopped

Dissolve marshmallows and gelatin in 1 c boiling water. Mix in cream cheese (cottage cheese may be substituted), crushed pineapple and mayonnaise. Chill until partially congealed. Whip the cream and fold into the partially congealed gelatin mixture. Pour into oiled 8-inch or 7-1/2-by-12-inch baking dish Sprinkle top generously with black walnuts. Chill several hours before serving.

ROSE OF SHARON SALAD

from Ruby White Thurmond

This is a Tennessee congealed luncheon salad, one of dozens with quaint names.

1/2 c water

1/2 c white distilled vinegar

1 c white granulated sugar

Two 3-oz pkgs raspberry-flavored gelatin

1 pkg unflavored gelatin, dissolved in 3 T water

2 c tomato soup

1 green bell pepper, chopped

2 c grated cabbage

1 white onion, chopped

1 c finely chopped celery

Dash of black pepper

Salt to taste

Combine water, vinegar and sugar and bring to a boil. Add the raspberry-flavored gelatin and stir until dissolved. Let cool. Combine dissolved unflavored gelatin with tomato soup. Add remaining 6 ingredients ingredients, and mix with raspberry gelatin mixture. Pour into a mold, or square dish. Refrigerate overnight. If molded, turn out onto a plate lined with lettuce or spinach leaves. *YIELD: 6 to 8 servings.*

Southern Belles do lunch. Mary Elizabeth Thurmond, far left, and her four friends Jane, Jean, Barbara and Betty, at the Hotel Peabody Skyway and Plantation Roof in Memphis, circa 1948.

LOBSTER MOUSSE

from Mary Elizabeth Daltroff

BOWL 1:

3/4 c finely chopped celery

1-1/2 c canned or cooked lobster meat

2/3 c minced apple, OPTIONAL

Salt and paprika to taste

BOWL 2:

1 T unflavored gelatin

1/4 c water

3/4 c mayonnaise

3 T lemon juice

1 tsp dry mustard, OPTIONAL

1/2 clove pressed garlic, OPTIONAL

Tabasco to taste, OPTIONAL

1/3 c unsweetened heavy cream, whipped

Whip the 1/3 cup of whipping cream, and set aside. Soak the unflavored gelatin in the 1/4 cup of water. Dissolve it in a double boiler over boiling water.

Set aside while preparing Bowl 1. Combine the ingredients in Bowl 1 in sequence. Set aside. Add remaining Bowl 2 ingredients to gelatin in the double boiler bowl. Fold this mixture into the Bowl 1 lobster mixture, along with the whipped cream. Spoon out into a wet or oiled mold.

Chill thoroughly for at least 4 hours. Unmold onto a platter. Garnish with mesclún greens and cucumber circles. Enhance individual serving plates by drawing a circle of sauce around the mousse.

SAUCE FOR LOBSTER MOUSSE:

1 c tomatoes (use canned, crushed)

1/2 c olive oil

1/2 tsp white granulated sugar

1/2 tsp salt

1 T chopped fresh parsley

Fresh pepper to taste

1/2 tsp Worcestershire sauce

Simmer the tomatoes until they reduce to a half-cup in volume. Then chill for at least 1 hour. Add the olive oil and remaining ingredients. Mix well.

SALMON MOUSSE

1/4-oz pkg unflavored gelatin

1/2 c cold water

16 oz canned or fresh-steamed salmon

1/2 c mayonnaise

3/4 c sour cream

1/2 tsp salt

1 T lemon juice

1-1/4 c celery, finely chopped

1 T capers

Sprinkle gelatin over 1/4 cup of cold water to soften. Dissolve this in 1/4 cup boiling water. Let cool. Put the gelatin mixture and all other ingredients except celery and capers into a blender; whip until smooth. Stir in the capers and celery; pour into a buttered mold or into individual molds. Chill and serve with cucumber dressing and saltine crackers.

TOMATO ASPIC

2 c tomato juice

1 T lemon juice

1/2 tsp salt

1 tsp sugar

1 Bay leaf

2 whole cloves

1-inch-stick of cinnamon

1/2 c sliced white onion

1/3 c celery + leaves

1/2 tsp chili powder

1 T unflavored gelatin

1/4 c cold water

1 c grated carrots

Salad greens

Mayonnaise

Mix tomato juice and lemon juice, salt, sugar, Bay leaf, cloves, cinnamon, onion, celery and chili powder. Heat to a boil, then simmer 5 minutes. Strain. Soften gelatin in water. Add softened gelatin to hot tomato liquid and stir until dissolved. Add 1 cup coarsely grated carrots to thicken. Pour into a large oiled mold and chill until firm. Unmold onto a bed of greens on a platter. Top with a dollop of mayonnaise.

DRESSINGS & SAUCES

ASIAN DRESSING

3 T honey

1-1/2 T rice wine vinegar

1/4 c mayonnaise

1 tsp Dijon mustard

1/8 tsp sesame oil

Mix in a small bowl. Refrigerate until ready to use.

BLUE CHEESE DRESSING

1/2 c mayonnaise

1/2 c sour cream

3 T whole milk

2 T lemon juice and 1/4 tsp garlic powder

2/3 c crumbled blue cheese

Combine all ingredients. Chill. *Yield: about 2 cups.*

BUTTERMILK DRESSING

2 c buttermilk

2 c real mayonnaise

1 T dried or 2 T fine-chopped fresh parsley

1/2 tsp salt

3/4 tsp garlic powder

3/4 tsp ground black pepper

1/2 tsp garlic salt

1/2 tsp onion salt

Combine in blender. Refrigerate at least 2 hours.

CUCUMBER DRESSING

1/2 c whipping cream, whipped without sugar

1 c mayonnaise

2 T lemon juice

1/4 tsp salt

1/8 tsp white pepper

Dash of cayenne pepper, OPTIONAL

1 small cucumber, chopped fine, and well drained

Fold whipped cream into mayo; stir in lemon juice, spices, and cucumber. Chill. *YIELD: 4 servings.*

SALADS & SOUPS

FRENCH DRESSING

1 c white granulated sugar

1 tsp salt

1 tsp dry mustard

1/2 tsp pepper

2 tsp Worcestershire sauce

1/2 c ketchup

1/2 c white vinegar

1 c salad oil (light olive oil)

Combine in a blender until thickened. Refrigerate at least 1 hour.

NO-OIL SALAD DRESSING

from Mary Elizabeth Daltroff

1 clove garlic, crushed

1 c red wine vinegar

1 c tomato juice

1 tsp salt

1-1/2 tsp black pepper

1/4 tsp dry mustard

1-1/2 tsp sugar, or 8 saccharine tablets

Italian seasoning to taste

Mix all ingredients in a large bowl and whisk until completely blended. Store in refrigerator in a jar.

POMEGRANATE-BALSAMIC VINAIGRETTE

1/4 c sweet balsamic vinegar

1/4 c fresh pomegranate juice

1/2 c orange juice

3 to 6 T white granulated sugar

1 tsp honey

1/4 tsp black pepper

1 tsp salt

3/4 to 1 c extra light olive oil

1/2 c finely minced Vidalia (sweet) onion

2 to 4 fresh basil leaves, shredded fine

Whisk all ingredients together in bowl, adding the minced onion after the sugar has dissolved. Serve on fresh spinach or spring mix salad with crumbled feta or fresh mozzarella cheese, roasted pecans, and fresh strawberries.

POPPYSEED DRESSING

from Louise Sherrill Triplette

1 c honey

1 c salad vinegar

1 c vegetable oil (Canola or light olive oil)

1 T poppyseeds

3 slices red onion, chopped fine

Blend together. Store in stoppered vinaigrette bottle or covered canning jar. Will keep in the refrigerator for several weeks. Excellent on fruit or spinach greens.

RUSSIAN DRESSING

1 c mayonnaise

1 T grated horseradish sauce (plain horseradish in a jar works fine)

1/4 c ketchup

1 tsp finely grated white onion

1 tsp Worcestershire sauce, OPTIONAL

Mix all ingredients and keep refrigerated. Serve chilled with eggs, salad dishes, or shellfish. *YIELD: 1-1/2 to 1-3/4 cups.*

STRAWBERRY DRESSING

10-oz pkg frozen strawberries, thawed, drained

2/3 c mayonnaise

8-oz carton strawberry-flavored yogurt (1 cup)

Puree first 2 ingredients in blender, strawberries first. Fold in yogurt. Chill covered for 1 hour. Serve with fresh melon. *YIELD: 2-1/3 cups.*

CRANBERRY SAUCE

1 pkg (4 c) fresh cranberries, washed

1-1/2 c white granulated sugar

1 T lemon juice

3 c water

1 pkg unflavored gelatin, dissolved in 2 T warm water

Combine berries, sugar, and water in saucepan. Bring to boil over medium heat, stirring constantly, until berries pop and liquid thickens. Mix in lemon juice and gelatin, remove from heat. Pour into bowl. Chill.

VARIATION: Strain through sieve to make jelly.

SALADS

BANANA FRUIT SALAD

from Aline Thurmond Miller

I was thrilled when Aunt Aline sent me this really old family recipe. It's a delicious change—sweet and salty.

2 eggs

1/2 to 3/4 c white granulated sugar

3/4 c water

1 tsp cornstarch

1 tsp yellow mustard

1/4 c lemon juice

Chopped salted peanuts

2 to 4 bananas

Mix ingredients in saucepan and cook, stirring constantly until thickened. Chill. Slice bananas lengthwise and arrange on platter. Pour chilled sauce over bananas. Top generously with chopped, salted peanuts. Serve at once. The lemon juice prevents discoloration. *YIELD: 4 to 8 servings.*

MARINATED BRUSSELS SPROUTS

4 to 6 c whole Brussels sprouts

1 bottle Italian dressing of choice

Rinse Brussels sprouts. Trim off remains of stems. Steam sprouts 5 to 8 minutes. Leave covered in steamer another 10 minutes. Cool. Place sprouts in sealable plastic container. Cover with salad dressing. Toss lightly to coat. Cover and chill at least 3 hours. Will keep in fridge up to 4 days. *YIELD: 8 to 10 servings.*

BROCCOLI AND BACON SALAD

1/2 to 1 lb bacon

4 to 6 c fresh broccoli, chopped

2-oz pkg sliced almonds

1 c gold raisins, OPTIONAL

Large red onion, chopped

4-oz pkg salted sunflower seeds, or 1 c roasted peanuts

2 T red wine vinegar

2 T white granulated sugar

1 c Miracle Whip Salad Dressing

Fry bacon and crumble. Let cool. Combine next 5 ingredients in large bowl; refrigerate. Mix vinegar, sugar and Miracle Whip to make dressing. Toss salad in dressing one hour before serving, adding bacon.

CAESAR SALAD

from Ruth Callicott Thurmond

1 clove of garlic

1/2 c olive oil

1 c cubed French bread

2 heads washed Romaine lettuce, torn in 2-inch lengths

1-1/2 tsp salt

1/4 tsp dry mustard

3 to 5 twists of fresh-ground black pepper

5 fillets of anchovies, cut up small or mashed into a paste

2 to 3 drops of Worcestershire sauce

3 T white wine vinegar

6 T of the remaining garlic-infused oil

1 large egg

Juice of 1 lemon

Fresh grated Parmesan cheese, quantity to taste

Peel and slice the garlic. Soak the sliced garlic in the olive oil for 24 hours to infuse the oil.

Sauté the cubed French bread in 2 T of the garlic-soaked olive oil.

Mix lettuce, salt, pepper, mustard, anchovies, Worcestershire, vinegar, remaining olive oil, and Parmesan in a large bowl. Mince and add oil-soaked garlic.

Cook 1 egg in simmering water for 1 to 1-1/2 minutes, or use raw (if pasteurized). Crack and drop the egg from the shell onto the lettuce and other ingredients in the bowl. Do not stir or mix. Squeeze juice of 1 lemon over the egg. Add the croutons and 2 to 3 T of Parmesan cheese. Toss well to coat the lettuce. Serve at once. *YIELD: 4 servings.*

CARROT SALAD

This salad represents a last-ditch effort by parents to convince their children to eat carrots. During my childhood, carrot salad without nuts was the fall-back dish when the school cafeteria was running low on food supplies.

4 large carrots, scraped

1/2 c seedless raisins

1/2 c chopped peanuts or pecans

3/4 tsp salt

Black pepper to taste

1 T lemon juice

1 c low-fat sour cream or mayonnaise

Chill carrots on ice for 1 hour. Coarsely grate carrots into large bowl. Mix in next 5 ingredients and toss. Add sour cream or mayonnaise, and mix well. Keep chilled.

Corn Salad

COPPER CARROTS (COPPER PENNIES)

I got this recipe at a family luncheon or at a Mother's Day luncheon at Grace Chapel United Methodist Church. I know one of the Sherrill aunts shared it with me. Wish I could remember which one!

2 pounds of carrots, cleaned, scraped, and sliced

10-3/4-oz can tomato soup

1 medium white onion, chopped

1/2 c green bell pepper, chopped

3/4 c white distilled vinegar

1/2 c extra light olive oil or canola oil

1 tsp Worcestershire sauce

1 tsp prepared mustard

1 c white granulated sugar

Salt and pepper to taste

Cook sliced carrots in salt water until tender but still firm. Plunge into ice water to cool. In another pan, heat tomato soup with vinegar, oil, sugar, Worcestershire Sauce, mustard, and spices. Drain the carrots. Gently toss with the onions and bell pepper. Pour tomato soup mixture over the vegetables. Chill at least 24 hours. Better served after several days. Serve cold or at room temperature. Keeps up to 2 weeks.

VARIATION: Add small cooked shrimp and several slices of red onion before serving.

CORN SALAD

2 c blanched fresh corn, cut off cob

8 cherry tomatoes, quartered

1 medium salad cucumber, peeled, seeded and diced

1/2 c green bell peppers, chipped

1/2 c red bell peppers, chopped

1/2 c celery, chopped

1/2 c Vidalia onion, chopped

1/2 tsp salt and 1 tsp black pepper

To blanch fresh corn, bring a pot of water to a rolling boil and drop the corn into it, and boil for 1 to 3 minutes. Remove corn and submerge immediately in an ice bath for about 5 minutes. Drain, pat dry, and hold ear in position in center hole of a Bundt pan while cutting off kernels with sharp knife. Combine all ingredients in a large bowl, seasoning with salt and pepper to taste. Add just enough dressing to mix but not drown, and toss well. Refrigerate at least 1 hour. Serve with tortilla chips or fresh rolls.

DRESSING FOR CORN SALAD:

1/4 c red wine vinegar

2 T extra virgin olive oil

1 tsp white granulated sugar

2 T mayonnaise

1 T sour cream

Combine vinegar, olive oil and sugar in a small bowl, whisking until sugar is dissolved. Add mayo and sour cream. Gently stir until blended.

SOUR CREAM CUCUMBER SALAD

from Andrea Benfield

6 c (more or less) cucumbers, peeled and either sliced or diced

2 to 3 c Vidalia or other sweet onion (slice cucumbers into rings, or dice big)

1/3 c sour cream

1/4 c mayonnaise (homemade, Duke's or Hellmanns)

1/4 to 1/3 c apple cider vinegar

Salt and pepper to taste

Use either white cucumbers or other pickling cucumbers (Kirby) if available. If not, use seedless, or deseed the cukes. Mix all ingredients together. Let the mixture season for at least 1 hour. Refrigerate.

BROCCO-CAULI MARINATED VEGGIES

SALAD:

3 to 4 bunches broccoli, cleaned, broken into florets

Head of cauliflower, cleaned, broken into florets

16-oz pkg white mushrooms, stems removed, sliced

2 to 4 large carrots, scraped and sliced

Green bell pepper, deseeded, sliced and diced (both)

Large red onion, loosely chopped

Campari tomatoes, quartered, or cherry tomatoes, halved

Fresh mozzarella, cubed, or sliced on the side

MARINADE:

3 bunches of green onions, chopped, including greens

1/2 c finely chopped fresh parsley

1/4 to 1/2 c grated Parmesan cheese (do not overdo)

1-1/2 to 2 c extra light olive oil

About 1 c apple cider vinegar

Large bunch of fresh basil, chopped

1 tsp salt (sea salt works well)

1/8 tsp black pepper (or about 10 turns of a pepper mill)

6 to 8 cloves of regular garlic, minced in a garlic press

Combine all veggies except tomatoes in over-sized bowl. For marinade, combine chopped green onion, parsley and basil in small bowl. To this, mix in Parmesan and minimal amount of salt and pepper. Mix in crushed garlic. Moisten with the olive oil, adding enough to make thick paste. Whisk in enough vinegar to achieve consistency of a loose paste. If marinade looks too dry and thick, add more oil and

vinegar. Once moist enough, pour marinade over the veggies; toss to blend thoroughly, then seal tightly and refrigerate overnight. Before serving, stir again, and add the fresh tomatoes. Serve with fresh mozzarella and fresh Italian, French or sourdough bread slices. NOTE: It is impossible to add too much basil or garlic. *YIELD: 15 to 20 servings.*

CORNBREAD SALAD

from Rebecca Sherrill Pittman

6 c yellow cornbread baked thin, stale and crumbled

1 c chopped green pepper

1 c chopped white or red onion

2 stalks celery, diced

1/2 c dill pickle

3 c chopped ripe tomatoes (Romas hold up best)

1 lb crispy-cooked bacon, crumbled

1 c mayonnaise

1/2 c pickle juice

1/2 c chopped, toasted pecans

Mix the mayonnaise and dill pickle juice to make a dressing. Mix all the veggies together. LAYER the cornbread, mixed vegetables, crumbled bacon and dressing as follows cornbread, then the veggies, then crumbled bacon and top these three layers with half of the dressing. Continue layering. Top with pecans.

VARIATION: Omit pickles but add pimientos; or add jalapeños and green chilies.

OVERNIGHT 7-LAYER SALAD

1 head of iceberg lettuce, cleaned and cut up

1/2 c celery, chopped

1 c green bell pepper, chopped

1 onion, sliced

10-oz pkg of frozen English peas

1 c mayonnaise

2 T white granulated sugar

4 oz grated sharp Cheddar cheese

8 slices of bacon, fried crisp and crumbled

Layer the first 5 ingredients in a large bowl that will be used at the table. Spread the layers with mayonnaise and sprinkle with sugar. Sprinkle crumbled bacon and grated cheese on top of the mayo and sugar layers. Cover tightly and refrigerate overnight. Cut through all the layers for each serving.

NAPA SALAD

Dr. Bob Ward, my friend and client from Rock Hill, SC, passed this along to me.

Two 3-oz pkgs ramen noodles, discard seasoning packets

1/2 c sesame seeds

2-oz pkg of sliced almonds

1/2 c butter

1 Napa cabbage (also known as Chinese cabbage)

5 green onions, chopped

1/2 c white granulated sugar

1/2 c vegetable oil

1 tsp soy sauce

1/4 c white distilled vinegar

1/4 tsp salt

Sauté the sesame seeds, noodles, and almonds in the butter until lightly browned. Remove from pan to prevent over-browning, and chill. Chop cabbage and onion. Set aside. Blend oil, sugar, soy sauce and salt. Toss with the other ingredients just before serving. It is not necessary to use ALL of the dressing.

NASTURTIUM SALAD

from Ruby White Thurmond

Grandmother always grew nasturtiums among her other flowers in the vegetable garden. Church ladies in her day grew flowers to use for Sunday altar arrangements. They also looked good in the landscape. Some, like nasturtiums, were edible, and others, such as marigolds, kept away undesirable insects.

4 c fresh nasturtium leaves

1/8 to 1/4 c chopped olives

2 hardboiled eggs

2 small gherkin pickles

Fresh nasturtium blossoms

Salt and pepper to taste

Boiled mayonnaise dressing (*see recipe, page 166*)

Pick the leaves and blossoms just prior to preparation for serving. Rinse gently. Crisp in cold water a few minutes. Shake dry. Place into salad bowl. Chop the eggs and gherkins, toss with leaves. Serve on salad plates. Sprinkle with olives and top with a dollop of dressing. Garnish each plate with gently rinsed blossoms, which also are edible. *YIELD: 4 servings.*

STRAWBERRY ORANGE SALAD

DRESSING:

3/4 to 1 c white granulated sugar

1-1/2 T poppy seeds

1 tsp dry mustard

1 tsp salt

1/3 c apple cider vinegar

1-1/2 tsp onion juice or 2 tsp grated onion

1 c canola or light olive oil

SALAD:

9-oz pkg romaine lettuce, torn into bite size pieces

3 c baby spinach leaves

11-oz can mandarin oranges, drained

20 strawberries, halved

6 green onions, chopped

1 c roasted and salted or sugared almonds

Blend sugar, poppy seeds, mustard and salt with a mixer at low speed. Add vinegar and onion; beat at medium speed for 3 minutes. Add oil in a steady stream until mixture is thick. Refrigerate covered, until 30 minutes before serving. Combine romaine, spinach, oranges, strawberries and green onions in a large bowl. Add almonds. Shake dressing, pour half over salad. Toss gently. Serve immediately. Refrigerate remaining dressing. *YIELD: 12 servings.*

NOTE: See Veggies & Sides section for Potato Salad Recipes

SHRIMP SALAD

1-1/2 c finely chopped cooked shrimp

1/2 c finely chopped celery

1 tsp caraway seed, OPTIONAL

2 tsp lemon juice

3/4 c of mayonnaise or salad dressing

Salt and pepper to taste

Combine ingredients and mix well. Refrigerate for at least one hour. *YIELD: 2 servings.*

SHRIMP, CRAB, AND RICE SALAD

2 pkgs imitation crabmeat or two 15-oz cans crabmeat

1 lb medium-size shrimp, boiled

1-1/2 c cooked rice

3/4 c chopped green pepper

3/4 c chopped onion

3/4 c chopped celery

1 c mayonnaise, to taste

4 tsp French dressing

Lemon and tomato wedges for garnish

Mix all ingredients in large bowl except the lemon and tomato. If using canned crabmeat, pick out shell and drain before using. Chill for at least 2 hours or overnight. Serve on a lettuce leaf with a slice of bread or roll, and add tomato and lemon garnishes. Of course you may prefer to use genuine crabmeat, but the imitation has more of the same texture as the shrimp.

COUSCOUS SALAD

2 c couscous, cooked according to package directions

2 green onions, chopped

1/2 c red pepper, seeded and chopped

1/2 c sliced celery (about 2 stalks)

1 c diced cucumber, seeded if it's the type with big seeds

1 medium tomato, seeded and diced

1/4 c chopped fresh basil

1/4 c freshly squeezed lemon juice

2 tsp Dijon-style mustard

2 T extra-virgin olive oil

2 T toasted pine nuts

Prepare couscous according to package directions to yield 2 cups. If package refers to browning couscous in olive oil, omit this step and continue cooking by adding boiling water. Place couscous, chopped vegetables and basil in a medium bowl. Toss gently to blend. In a small bowl, whisk together the lemon juice, Dijon mustard, and olive oil until blended. Pour over salad and toss gently to blend. Sprinkle with pine nuts just before serving. Serve at room temperature just after making it, or chilled. *YIELD: 8 servings.*

TABBOULEH (TABOULI)

This is a great cold salad dish. Some of the boxed ready-to-mix varieties work as well, if fresh tomato, cucumber, parsley and green onions are added.

2/3 c bulgur wheat

2 c hot water

2 medium tomatoes, diced

1 c chopped parsley

1/2 c thinly sliced green onions

1/4 c chopped fresh mint

1 clove garlic, minced

1/4 c fresh lemon juice

2 T extra light olive oil

1/4 c chopped cucumber, seeded

Bring water and bulgur wheat to a boil. Remove from heat and let sit 15 minutes. Drain and fluff with a fork. Transfer to a large bowl. Add tomatoes, parsley, green onion, mint, cucumber and garlic. Mix well. Add lemon juice, olive oil and salt. Stir well and chill before serving.

WILD RICE, ARTICHOKE AND SPINACH SALAD

from Mary Elizabeth Daltroff

*Mom got this recipe from **The Commercial Appeal** years ago. Wild rice is a delicacy in the Delta, the Mid-South, and central USA. I never encountered it much east of the Appalachians. The French-style vinaigrette used in this recipe works well with other salads: Double the recipe and save half in a salad dressing bottle.*

SALAD MIX:

2 boxes wild rice and white rice pilaf mix

8- to 12-oz can of quartered artichoke hearts (about 1 c), drained

4-oz jar diced pimientos, drained, or roasted red peppers, drained and diced

4 green onions, chopped

1 small bag (or 6 hands full) baby spinach leaves

VINAIGRETTE:

1/4 c red wine vinegar

2 tsp Dijon mustard

1 tsp white granulated sugar

1 small clove garlic, minced

1/2 tsp salt

1/2 tsp pepper

3/4 c olive oil

Cook the rice according to package instructions and cool completely. In a large bowl, mix together the cooled rice blend, artichoke hearts, peppers, and green onions. In a jar or bottle with a tight-fitting lid, combine the vinaigrette ingredients and shake until completely emulsified. Pour the vinaigrette to the bowl of rice and mix thoroughly. Chill. Add the spinach leaves right before serving. Refrigerate leftover rice (remove spinach leaves first).

WALDORF SALAD

1 c diced celery

1 c diced apples (Granny Smith, Red or Gold Delicious, or Winesaps)

1 c seedless grapes, red or green

1/2 c chopped walnuts or pecans

3/4 c mayonnaise

Combine all ingredients and mix well. Refrigerate covered to prevent browning.

ITALIAN MARINATED VEGETABLES

SALAD:

8- or 16-oz pkg small fresh mushrooms, sliced

2 green peppers, sliced or chunked

3 carrots, blanched and cut into slices

1 head of cauliflower, cut into flowerets

13- to 14-oz can of artichoke hearts, cut in half

3- to 5-oz can of pimiento-stuffed sliced olives

13- to 14-oz can of hearts of palm, cut in half

19-oz pkg of frozen Brussels sprouts (or 2 c fresh), lightly steamed

Cherry tomatoes

6 green onions, chopped

MARINADE:

1/2 c red wine vinegar

1-1/2 tsp salt

2 tsp oregano

1 tsp sugar

1/2 tsp black pepper

1/2 c salad oil

1/2 c olive oil

Heat vinegar. Stir in seasonings. Add oils. Mix veggies in large bowl, then pour marinade over the veggies. Seal tightly in covered storage container. Refrigerate, allowing to marinate 2 to 4 days before serving. Drain and serve, garnish with tomatoes and parsley if desired. NOTE: Substitute large can of button mushrooms for fresh if you MUST.

MEDITERRANEAN CHICKPEA SALAD

1-1/2 c coarsely chopped tomatoes

  (Romas or Camparis work better than garden tomatoes, which get too soft and soupy)

1-1/2 c coarsely chopped cucumber

1 c cubed fresh mozzarella cheese

1/2 c sliced ripe olives (the quality of the brand makes a difference)

19-oz can of chick peas, drained, rinsed

1/3 to 1/2 c Wishbone or Newman's Own Italian Dressing

1/4 tsp dried basil, OR 4 large fresh basil leaves, minced

In a large bowl, combine all ingredients. Toss and serve immediately. *Yield: 6 servings.*

TEXAS CAVIAR (BLACKEYED PEA MARINATED SALAD)

This is our gentler Southeastern redneck version of Texas Caviar. Use your imagination for variations.

Two 15.5-oz cans of blackeyed peas, rinsed and drained

4-oz jar of diced pimientos, drained

2 large carrots, cleaned and sliced thin

1/4 to 1/2 c chopped bell pepper

1 medium sweet onion, chopped

1/4 c chopped fresh parsley

1/2 c chopped fresh mushrooms, OPTIONAL

2 c Wishbone Italian or Newman's Own Italian Dressing

Mix all ingredients well and cover with dressing. Let marinate in the dressing for at least 4 hours before serving. Serve with chips, toast, or as a side salad.

SOUTHWEST VERSION: Substitute a jar of sliced and pickled jalapeño peppers for the pimientos; substitute red onion for sweet onion.

BLACK BEAN SOUTHWEST CAVIAR VARIATION: Combine 2 cans black beans, drained, chopped red onion, 1 medium jalapeño deseeded and sliced, 1/2 c chopped green onion, 1/3 c chopped cilantro, 1 large green avocado, peeled, cored and diced. Chopped green bell pepper optional. Mix 2 T lime juice, 2 T olive oil, 1 T red wine vinegar, splash of Tabasco, 1 tsp salt and 1/2 tsp black pepper. Toss with veggies. Refrigerate overnight.

THREE-BEAN ROTINI SALAD

12-oz pkg rotini pasta

15-oz can green beans, drained (or 1-1/2 c fresh beans, cut into pieces)

15-oz can wax beans (or fresh wax beans cut into pieces)

14.5-oz can kidney beans, rinsed and drained

1 c chopped Vidalia onion (or Texas Sweet)

3/4 c apple cider vinegar

1/2 c salad oil (extra light olive or canola)

2/3 c white granulated sugar

1-1/2 c halved cherry tomatoes

Salt and pepper to taste

Prepare rotini according to package directions, then rinse with cool water. Set aside. Combine drained beans and chopped onion in a large bowl. In a separate small bowl, combine cider vinegar and salad oil; slowly add in sugar to dissolve. Add drained rotini pasta and vinegar mixture to the beans. Add in tomatoes, then salt and pepper to taste. Mix well. Refrigerate leftovers. *YIELD: 6 servings.*

MARINATED THREE-BEAN SALAD

15-oz can green beans

1 lb yellow wax beans

15-oz can kidney beans, drained and rinsed

1 medium-large white onion, sliced into thin rings and the rings cut into half

1 c sliced button mushrooms

1/2 c chopped bell pepper, red or green

3/4 c white granulated sugar

2/3 c white vinegar

1/3 c vegetable oil (extra light olive or canola)

1/2 tsp black pepper

1/2 tsp celery seed

1 T Dijon mustard, OPTIONAL

Mix first four ingredients together and whisk together the oil, sugar, vinegar and seasonings. Pour the sugar mixture over the bean mixture and mix well. Cover and refrigerate for at least 12 hours.

CANNED VS. DRIED BEANS

Canned or cooked from scratch, beans are rich in protein, fiber and essential vitamins and minerals.

Dried beans take more time to prepare than canned beans, obviously, but have a bit more nutritional value than canned beans. Dried beans give more food for the buck than canned beans. When prepared properly, dried beans provide more flavor than canned beans.

Canned beans are ready to use, which is especially important for kidney beans, which must be carefully prepared to remove toxins. Canned beans also don't cause as much gastrointestinal gas as poorly prepared dried beans. Canned beans contain preservatives, especially a color preservative. Canned beans usually contain a lot of sodium. Rinsing them helps remove the excess. Some purists are concerned about chemicals that might be leached from the can lining.

TOMATO-FIELD PEA SALAD WITH GARLIC MAYONNAISE

Fresh peas are one of the beauties of a Southern summer. I recommend a mixture of field peas, whiteacre (Lady) peas, and butter peas or blackeyed peas.

1-1/2 c shelled peas or 10-oz bag frozen peas (mix 2 to 3 kinds for best flavor)

6 c ripe summer tomatoes (mix heirlooms and cherry tomatoes)

6 green onions with tops, chopped

Kosher or sea salt to t taste

Black pepper to taste

1 small bunch fresh basil

2 to 3 T chopped fresh parsley

3 to 4 T extra virgin olive oil

Garlic mayonnaise (*see Garlic Mayo recipe, page 167*)

Blanch the fresh peas in a large saucepan of salted boiling water for 3-10 minutes. Drain the peas; plunge into a bowl of salted ice water to stop the cooking and set the color. When well chilled, drain thoroughly. Mix in bowl with chopped basil, parsley, and green onion. Dress with olive oil to coat. Refrigerate. Just before serving, cut tomatoes into wedges and halves, depending on size. Season generously with salt and fresh pepper. Add refrigerated peas. Toss salad in about 1-3/4 cup of garlic mayo. Serve immediately on bed of butter lettuce.

WHITE BEAN SALAD (PIYAZ)

2 c dried white beans

6 c cold water

Salt

One clove of garlic

2 small white onions

1/4 c lemon juice

1 T white vinegar

1/4 c olive oil

1/4 c good Italian salad dressing

1/4 c chopped fresh parsley

1 tsp chopped fresh mint

2 T chopped fresh dill

Wash beans, cover with cold water, and put on to boil. When boiling, remove from heat and leave aside until plump. Alternatively, beans may be soaked in cold water overnight in the fridge if warm outside. Return or bring plumped beans to a boil in their soaking water, cover and simmer gently over low heat until tender but still intact. Cooking time will vary according to beans used (usually about 2 hours). Add salt to taste after 1-1/2 hrs of cooking. When tender, drain well and turn into a bowl. Crush garlic with a little salt. Cut onions in half lengthwise and then slice thinly into semi-circles. Add to hot beans with lemon juice, vinegar and combined oils. Allow to cool. Gently mix in the chopped herbs and chill the salad for 1 to 2 hrs. Serve in a deep bowl garnished with sliced green pepper and sliced or quartered hardboiled eggs. *YIELD: 6 to 8 servings.*

BASIC PASTA SALAD

16-oz pkg Rotini or Penne or elbow pasta, cooked al dente

1/2 c chopped green bell pepper

1/2 c finely chopped white onion

1/2 c finely chopped celery, include some of the leaves

2-oz jar chopped pimiento, drained

2 c mayonnaise, more or less, to taste

2 T prepared yellow or spicy brown mustard

Toss all ingredients with the pasta noodles. Tightly cover and refrigerate until time to serve.

SALADS
& SOUPS

PASTA-VEGGIE SALAD

This dish was a Greensboro specialty of my late friend and colleague Bill Fones, and his wife Mary Jean. It's always a party favorite!

16-oz pkg of vermicelli, broken twice

16 oz of VIVA or Wishbone regular Italian dressing

1 pkg of Buttermilk Ranch Dressing mix

Salt to taste

3 Roma tomatoes diced into small chunks

4 celery stalks, sliced

1/2 c chopped onion

Large cucumber, halved, seeded, and sliced

12 radishes, sliced

Large green pepper, diced

3 medium carrots, sliced

1 head broccoli and/or cauliflower, broken into flowerets

Sliced water chestnuts

1 c sliced fresh mushrooms

2 to 3 tender young summer squash, peeled and sliced

Cook and drain noodles. Rinse in cool water. The day of serving, mix all ingredients together. Serve mounded in a large serving bowl or platter. Refrigerate up to 3 to 4 days. *YIELD: 10 or more servings.*

HAM SALAD

from Ruby White Thurmond, Mary Elizabeth Daltroff

Mom was a woman of her day: She kept her table-mounted grinder ever ready to crank out Cheddar for pimiento cheese, or ham for ham salad. Her classic ham salad calls for ground baked ham, mayonnaise, sweet pickle relish, chopped hardboiled eggs, diced celery, and an assortment of other condiments to taste, such as black olives, bell pepper and pimiento, and cubes of cheese. Some versions add mustard. Grandmother's Macaroni Ham Salad version below was designed to feed a crowd.

8 to 16 oz macaroni pasta, cooked
according to directions

6 hardboiled eggs, chopped

4 c baked ham, small cubes or diced

6 green onions, chopped fine

1/4 c white onion, chopped fine

1 c chopped celery, including leaves

1/4 c fine chopped bell pepper

8 oz sharp Cheddar cheese, sliced
1/4-inch thick; each cut
into three strips and cubed

15-oz jar Miracle Whip salad
dressing

1/4 tsp salt

Cayenne pepper to taste (1/8 tsp)

Combine ham and chopped eggs in bowl. Toss in onions, celery, pepper and cheese. Combine Miracle Whip, salt and cayenne in separate bowl; add to ham mixture and toss until completely blended. Add pasta and toss until blended. Add more Miracle Whip if needed. *YIELD: about 15-20 servings.*

MANDARIN TURKEY PASTA SALAD

This old recipe from Mom and Grandmother has variations. It makes a HUGE amount.

16-oz box of small pasta shells, cooked and drained

3 c cubed cooked turkey

1-1/2 c red or green seedless grapes, halved

1/4 c chopped green onions, with tops

1/4 c finely chopped green bell pepper

2 to 3 medium ribs of tender celery, chopped fine, including some leaves

2 Clementine or mandarin oranges or tangerines, sectioned (or 1 c canned, drained mandarins)

8-oz can pineapple chunks, drained, reserve juice

8-oz can water chestnuts, drained, chopped, OPTIONAL

1/4 c slivered almonds or toasted pecan halves

DRESSING:

1/2 c mayonnaise

1/4 to 1/2 c plain yogurt

1/2 sour cream

1/4 c orange juice

1/4 to 1/2 c pineapple juice

1 tsp soy sauce

1/2 to 1 tsp curry powder (I recommend less)

Dash of cayenne pepper

1/8 tsp white pepper (I prefer black pepper)

Mix first 10 ingredients together in large bowl. Combine next 9 wet ingredients and spices in small bowl and whisk until blended. Pour into bowl and toss to coat. If salad is soupy, add more pasta and turkey.

COOKING PASTA FOR SALADS:

If using dried pasta, make sure it's 100% semolina. Fill a large stock pot with cold water. Bring to a boil, add 2 T kosher salt and dump pasta in at once, stirring with wooden spoon. Do NOT add oil, which will prevent sauces from sticking to the pasta. Cook uncovered on a boil, stirring occasionally, for 4 to 8 minutes. Test at 6 minutes for doneness. If center of a pasta strand is whiter than the edges, it's not done. (Some shapes require longer to cook.) When done, pasta will be flexible but firm (al dente). Remove from heat; add a glass of cold water to halt cooking. Dump into colander to drain. Rinse pasta for salads in cold water to prevent sticking.

Gabrielle's former roommate, Lily Truong of Buras, LA, prepares chicken and pasta salad after Gabby's graduation from LSU.

CHICKEN SALAD

6 whole skinless, boneless chicken breasts

1 tsp thyme

1/8 tsp pepper

1 tsp salt

3 to 4 cloves garlic, peeled, OR 1 tsp garlic powder

1/4 c sweet pickle relish, plus juice

1/2 to 1 c mayonnaise

1/4 c celery, chopped fine

1/4 c sweet onion, chopped fine

Salt and pepper, to taste

Cayenne pepper to taste, OPTIONAL

Boil chicken breasts in next 4 spices, at least 1 hour. Cool in stock. Drain in sieve, chop or shred, then mix with mayo in large bowl, adding only enough mayo to blend. Add onion, celery and pickle relish. Add salt and pepper and cayenne to taste. If not sweet enough, add sweet pickle relish juice, being careful not to make it runny.

VARIATIONS: Add chopped hard-boiled egg, or slivered almonds.

CHINESE CHICKEN RICE SALAD

1 c brown rice

2-1/2 c water

2 T olive oil

3 T lemon juice

3 T reduced-sodium soy sauce

1 tsp minced fresh ginger

1 T teriyaki sauce

Salt and black pepper to taste

2 c cooked chicken breast

1 c diced celery

1 c sliced water chestnuts, drained

1 c fresh sliced mushrooms

1/2 c diced green onion

1/2 c diced red bell pepper

Bring rice and water to a boil in medium pan. Reduce heat to low, cover, simmer until water is absorbed (about 45 minutes). Set aside to cool. Whisk together oil, lemon juice, ginger, soy, and teriyaki sauce. Add salt and pepper. Mix cooked rice and chopped chicken in large bowl. Stir in celery, water chestnuts, mushrooms, green onion and red pepper. Add dressing; toss to coat. Cover. Refrigerate 8 hours or overnight. Toss gently before serving. *YIELD: 6 servings.*

HOT CHICKEN SALAD

from Louise Triplette

4 c cooked, chopped chicken

2 T lemon juice

1/4 c chopped celery

1 medium white onion, chopped

4 boiled eggs, chopped

10-3/4-oz can of cream of chicken soup

1 tsp salt

2/3 c mayonnaise

2-oz jar of chopped pimientos

1 c grated sharp Cheddar cheese

1-1/2 c crushed potato chips

2/3 c slivered almonds

Grease pan, sprinkle with small amount of cheese. Mix all other ingredients and put in pan. Add rest of cheese and then top with crushed potato chips and slivered almonds. Bake for 40 minutes at 350°F. Serve hot. *YIELD: 8 to 10 servings.*

HOT CHICKEN SALAD PASTRIES

from Louise Triplette

1 c plus 2 T all purpose flour

1 small egg (MUST be small and not medium or large)

1 stick (1/2 c) margarine or butter at room temperature

Put ingredients in a food processor and process until it forms a ball. This makes enough dough for 25 miniature pie pastries. Press dough into small pastry cups and bake at 400°F, until browned. Cool. Fill with hot chicken salad.

LAURIE'S CURRIED CHICKEN SALAD

SALAD:

6 boneless skinless chicken breasts

1 tsp thyme

4 to 6 good-sized peeled cloves of garlic

1 tsp salt

1/4 tsp black pepper

1/2 c sweet onion, diced fine

3 green onions, each halved and then diced fine

1 c seedless grapes, halved (Thompson green, or Red Flame)

1/2 c chopped toasted walnuts, cashews, almonds, or pecans

1/4 c chopped celery and leaves, OPTIONAL

DRESSING:

1 c mayonnaise

1/3 c plain yogurt

3/4 tsp curry powder

1 squirt or squeeze of lemon juice

1/2 tsp salt, to taste

1/4 tsp ground black pepper

1/8 tsp cayenne pepper, or less, to taste

Cover chicken breasts with water to about 2 to 3 inches above; add thyme, cloves, salt and pepper. Cook for about 1 hour. Let breasts cool in stock, then remove from stock to fridge to chill. (Freeze the stock for future use, including the stuff at the bottom of the pot.) Cube or chop the chilled breasts. Combine with next 5 ingredients in a large bowl. To make dressing, combine dressing ingredients in blender. Fold into chicken mixture until completely mixed. Refrigerate at least 3 hours before serving.

VARIATION: Add a pinch of turmeric and a tablespoon of pineapple juice.

EGG SALAD

from Louise Sherrill Triplette

6 to 8 large eggs

Mayonnaise

Prepared mustard

Dash of cayenne pepper

Apple cider vinegar

Place eggs in a 3-qt saucepan; just cover with cold water. Boil for 1 minute on medium-high; cover, reduce heat, boil 2 to 4 more minutes. Turn off heat; let sit 2 minutes. Cool under running cold water. Peel, cut eggs in half and mash yolks in mixing bowl to paste consistency. Add just enough mayo to blend. Mixture will be stiff. Add a few drops mustard (up to 1/2 tsp). Mix well. Coarsely chop eggs whites, mix into yolk paste. Add a few drops of cider vinegar to taste, continue mixing. Salad should be light yellow, and egg whites well blended, but fluffy Keeps 2 to 3 days, refrigerated, covered tight.

EGG AND OLIVE SALAD VARIATION: Mash the egg whites into the yolk paste. Mince 4 T chopped pimiento-stuffed olives, and stir into egg salad.

DEVILED EGG SALAD VARIATION: Mash the egg whites into thick yolk paste (use less mayo). Add 2 to 4 T of sweet pickle relish.

TUNA SALAD

1 regular size can of tuna, drained

Mayonnaise

Sweet pickle relish

1 to 2 hardboiled eggs, chopped

1 to 2 sticks of celery, chopped fine

In a medium sized bowl, mix the drained tuna, chopped egg, and celery. Use 1 egg and 1 stick of celery for a regular can of tuna, and use 2 eggs and 2 sticks of celery for a large can of tuna. Add enough mayo to moisten, but not to the soupy stage. Blend in 1 to 2 T of sweet pickle relish, along with some of the sweet pickle juice to taste. Refrigerate, covered. *YIELD: 4 servings.*

GARLIC DRESSING: Always remove sour-tasting green bud (germ) from garlic center. Grind 2 cloves garlic by rubbing over 1/2 tsp kosher salt with flat of a knife. Add juice of 1/2 lemon to the salted garlic to absorb garlic's indigestion-causing ingredient (allow to stand 10 minutes). Stir into 8 oz crème fraîche to make delicious dressing for greens.

Tuna Salad

SLAW

BROCCOLI SLAW

2 c shredded broccoli stems and red cabbage (or 2 c packaged broccoli slaw)

1 c shredded carrots

1/2 medium red onion, sliced thin

1 tart apple, peeled and diced, OPTIONAL

1/4 c toasted sunflower seeds, OPTIONAL

1 lime, zested and juiced

1/2 tsp kosher salt

2 T white sugar

1/4 c apple cider vinegar

1/2 tsp red pepper flakes

1/4 tsp fresh ground black pepper

2 T extra light olive oil

Mix broccoli slaw, carrots and onions in large bowl. In medium saucepan, mix lime juice and zest, salt, sugar, vinegar, red pepper flakes, and black pepper. Bring to a quick boil on medium-low heat to dissolve sugar, then remove and cool. Whisk olive oil into cooled vinegar mixture; pour over slaw, toss well. Add apples and sunflower seeds if desired. Keep refrigerated until serving.

VARIATIONS: Add ramen noodles or diced jalapeño.

CAROLINAS SWEET SLAW

from Laurie, learned from Louise Triplette

Make no mistake, once you've had THIS slaw, you'll not go back to Cole Slaw containing mayonnaise. Absolutely a must-have for pulled-pork barbecue and hot dogs all-the-way, beans or anything else. Lasts for weeks if not eaten first.

One cabbage, grated (in a chopper, or in a box grater)

2 to 3 large carrots, grated (adjust quantity so that the carrots are almost as much as the cabbage)

1 large bell pepper, grated

1 tsp of salt (or to taste, starting with the mixture being slightly salty)

1/4 tsp pepper, add more to taste if needed

White granulated sugar, to taste (1/2 to 1 cup)

1 c apple cider vinegar (adjust to taste)

Once the cabbage, carrots and pepper have been grated and mixed, the mixture should be multicolored. Mix in the salt and pepper. Taste it. If the mixture is slightly salty, then you're ready to add the sugar. NOTE: If your end result is too salty, simply rinse it under the tap in a sieve, drain, and start over.

Mix in 1/2 cup sugar. Adjust the sugar until the mixture has a sweet-and-salty taste. It's better to make it more sugary. Add apple cider vinegar until it is nearly visible as a liquid in the cabbage. Mix well, and refrigerate. Let the slaw sit at least overnight before serving. Pour out excess vinegar. Remix the slaw to blend.

LEXINGTON BBQ SLAW VARIATION: Add Polly's BBQ sauce to Carolinas Sweet Slaw.

MEMPHIS RENDEZVOUS-STYLE SLAW VARIATION: Add prepared yellow mustard, sweet pickle juice, and chopped sweet pickles to Carolinas Sweet Slaw.

MEMPHIS-STYLE COLE SLAW VARIATION: Add a dollop of mayonnaise, some grated onion, celery seed, and a squirt of prepared mustard to Carolinas Sweet Slaw. NOTE: Regular Cole Slaw omits the mustard.

RED CABBAGE SLAW VARIATION: Substitute red cabbage for green. Combine ingredients just as for Carolinas Sweet Slaw. Fold in 1 coarsely chopped red onion and 1/2 cup golden raisins.

VINEGAR TIP: Once opened, vinegar retains its flavor only about six months. Discard outdated balsamic and wine vinegars.

EVERLASTING (REFRIGERATOR) SLAW

from Mary Elizabeth Daltroff

This is one of those recipes that I have been given or found everywhere for the past 35 years. It was my favorite version of my mother's slaw. In some versions, the onions are chopped. It's fantastic with pork.

1 cabbage, chopped in the blender

2 sweet onions, sliced into rings

7/8 c white granulated sugar

1 c white distilled vinegar

3/4 c canola oil

2 T white granulated sugar

1 tsp celery seed

1 T salt

1 tsp dry mustard

Arrange cabbage and onions in layers in a 9-by-12-inch pan. Sprinkle 7/8 cup sugar over the top. Boil remaining ingredients in a saucepan. Once this mixture boils, remove from heat and allow to cool. Pour over layered cabbage and onions. Let it sit overnight in the fridge. This would last indefinitely, but gets eaten quickly. *YIELD: 10-15 servings.*

KRAUT SLAW

I was reintroduced to this regional favorite by Lee Uhlhorn, my choir director at Oxford-University United Methodist Church. It's great on hot dogs or with pork.

1-1/2 to 2 c granulated sugar

1/3 c apple cider vinegar

1/4 c extra light olive oil

Two 14.5 oz cans sauerkraut, rinsed well and drained

2 c celery, chopped fine

1 c red onion, chopped fine

1 medium green bell pepper, chopped fine

1/2 c julienned carrot

1/2 c sliced water chestnuts, drained and chopped

While stirring, bring vinegar, sugar and oil to a rolling (white) boil, only until sugar dissolves and loses its graininess, 1 to 2 minutes (color is clear amber). Do not over-boil. Cool pot in ice water bath, stirring to keep oil and sugar syrup mixed. Combine vegetables in a bowl. Add sugar syrup mixture; toss. Refrigerate at least 3 hours. Pour off excess syrup.

VARIATION: Add 1 tsp celery seeds and 1/2 c blanched frozen green peas.

SOUPS

BIGMAMMA ROSE'S MATZO BALL SOUP

Folks unacquainted with the Delta's Jewish flavors have missed out on one of the great ongoing culinary debates: Which matzo ball recipe is best. I love my family's version the best. This recipe descended from Rose Ackerman Daltroff through Florence and Freda's daughters, Rosalee Bloom Hyam and Rose Price May.

CHICKEN STOCK OR BROTH:

A chicken

3 to 6 cloves garlic, pressed

Thyme

Salt and pepper

1 c celery leaves, chopped

1 c carrots, chopped in big pieces

Bring to a boil; simmer for about 4 to 5 hours until chicken is falling apart. Strain the broth through a sieve. Pick out the chicken and save for other uses. Refrigerate broth until fat congeals on surface. Skim off fat, measure out 2 T chicken fat, freeze the rest. Measure out enough broth for soup; freeze rest in ice cube trays.

MATZO BALLS:

2 matzos

2 T rendered chicken fat (called schmaltz)

2 eggs, slightly beaten

1/4 c onion, chopped fine

1 tsp chopped fresh parsley

1/4 c matzo meal, more or less

1/8 tsp black pepper

1/8 tsp nutmeg

1/4 tsp ginger, OPTIONAL

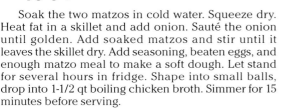
Shields and Rose Daltroff with grandson Louis

Soak the two matzos in cold water. Squeeze dry. Heat fat in a skillet and add onion. Sauté the onion until golden. Add soaked matzos and stir until it leaves the skillet dry. Add seasoning, beaten eggs, and enough matzo meal to make a soft dough. Let stand for several hours in fridge. Shape into small balls, drop into 1-1/2 qt boiling chicken broth. Simmer for 15 minutes before serving.

CHICKEN AND SAUSAGE GUMBO

There are numerous variations on this recipe. It can be made with or without the okra and/or the sausage and bell pepper. I omit the bell pepper but add lots of okra.

6 to 8 skinless, bones chicken breasts, or 1 chicken

3 qt water

3 T ground thyme

8 cloves garlic, peeled, sliced

1-1/2 tsp salt

1 tsp black ground pepper

4 to 6 links Andouille or Cajun style smoked sausage

Roux

1/4 to 1/2 c olive oil or 1 stick butter

3 celery heart ribs with leaves

1 onion, diced

2 to 6 T chocolate colored roux

2 c sliced fresh or frozen okra

Tabasco or hot pepper sauce of choice, to taste

Cayenne pepper and Tony's seasoning, to taste

Diced bell pepper, OPTIONAL

Gumbo filé, OPTIONAL

Boil 1 medium chicken, skinned, or 6 to 8 whole, skinless, boneless chicken breasts in 3 qt water with thyme or poultry seasoning, cloves of garlic, salt and pepper. Shred chicken and set aside (debone if needed). Sauté sausage in a skillet and set aside. Melt 1-2 sticks of butter or 1/4 to 1/2 cup of olive oil in a large stock pot or Dutch oven. Add onion and celery; cook until transparent. Stir in 2 to 6 T of Roux. Gradually whisk in chicken stock, including bits of cooked garlic from the stock. Simmer 15 minutes.

Add chicken, sausage, bell pepper (OPTIONAL) and okra, and more chicken stock. Add salt and pepper. Stir frequently; simmer 15-30 minutes. Add Tabasco, cayenne , and Tony's to taste. If gumbo needs thickening (which it shouldn't because of the roux and okra), add 1 tsp gumbo filé at the end. Serve in deep bowl over white rice. Works well with corn bread or muffins or French bread and salad.

TIP: When thickening a soup, gravy or gumbo with gumbo filé, add the filé at the end and stir well. Do not allow liquid to reheat to a boil, or the filé will become ropey. NOTE: One generally uses EITHER okra OR gumbo filé as a thickener.

CHICKEN NOODLE SOUP

The simplest, healthiest chicken noodle soup is built from the same base as chicken salad, chicken and dumplings, chicken pie and matzo ball soup. The stock base and the quality of chicken are the essentials.

4 to 6 chicken breasts, or 2 rotisserie chickens, deboned

2 to 4 cloves garlic

1 tsp thyme

1/2 tsp black pepper

1 tsp salt

1 large white onion, diced

2 to 4 large carrots, cleaned and diced

2 ribs celery, diced

1/2 c chopped celery leaves

1/2 c butter or light olive oil

Additional chicken stock as needed

1 to 2 c wide egg noodles

Place chicken in stock pot. Cover with water (2 to 3 inches above the chicken). Add garlic, thyme, salt and pepper. Boil about 1-1/2 hour. Remove chicken, strain stock through a sieve. Pick out garlic cloves, mash, and add back to stock. Shred or dice chicken, remove all bones and skin, and add back to stock. Sauté vegetables in butter or oil. Pour into stock pot and bring mixture back to a low boil. Simmer about 10 minutes. Add egg noodles and simmer until noodles are tender.

CORN CHOWDER

6 slices of bacon

1 large white onion, diced

1/2 c bell pepper (red or green), chopped

6 ears of corn, cut off cobs (or 6-7 c frozen corn)

6 c good chicken stock (homemade is preferred)

3 to 4 Russet potatoes, peeled and cubed

2 to 3 c half and half or heavy whipping cream

Fry bacon in skillet until crispy. Remove bacon to cool, then crumble and set aside. Sauté onion in bacon drippings until transparent, then add bell pepper and corn. Add butter if needed, to keep from scorching. Simmer about 5 minutes, then work in chicken stock. Stir in potatoes. Simmer 30-45 minutes until corn and potatoes are tender. Add crumbled bacon and cream, stir well, bring back up just to a boil. Serve.

VARIATION: Add shredded chicken to make corn and chicken chowder.

CHICKEN TORTILLA SOUP

I've enjoyed versions of this soup since we began going to Harlingen, TX, in the late 1950s. Little did we know back then that, by the 21st century, this would become one of the most widely shared and modified recipes in the United States.

1 medium white or yellow onion, chipped

4 garlic cloves, minced

1 medium jalapeño pepper, seeded and chopped

1/2 medium green or red bell pepper

4 to 6 boneless, skinless chicken breasts

1 to 2 c frozen corn

2 cans navy beans or black beans, drained and rinsed

1/2 c dry white wine or water

2 tsp to 1 T cumin

1 bay leaf

1 tsp chili powder

1/2 tsp cayenne pepper

10-oz can Rotel tomatoes and green chilies

Four 14-oz cans chicken broth

28-oz can crushed or diced tomatoes, to taste

Juice and zest of 1 lime

Kosher salt to taste

3 to 4 T chopped fresh cilantro

One firm avocado, peeled, chopped

Mexican Fiesta Blend cheese

Toasted tortilla strips

Sour cream

Chopped green onions

Sauté onion, garlic, jalapeño and bell pepper in olive oil in large stock pot until soft. Add next 14 ingredients to pot and bring to a boil. Remove chicken breasts after about 30 minutes and shred. Return chicken to pot; simmer additional 45 minutes. Ladle soup into bowls and top with chopped avocado, toasted tortilla strips and Mexican Fiesta blend cheese. Serve with sour cream and chopped green onion on the side for garnish.

TO MAKE TOASTED TORTILLA STRIPS: Cut stale tortilla into quarter-inch strips. Fry in hot cooking oil until crispy but not over-browned. Drain on paper towel.

CHILLED BERRY SOUP

When Gabrielle was in the Charlotte Symphony Youth Orchestra, we parents participated as volunteers during the annual fundraiser, the ASID Symphony Showhouse. We took turns waiting tables and dishing up luncheon fare prepared by participating local restaurateurs. One of my favorite dishes one year was a chilled raspberry soup. This is my facsimile interpretation of that dish. NOTE: Some versions I've tasted add ginger ale.

1 qt fresh raspberries (or strawberries)

1/3 c white granulated sugar

2 tsp fresh lemon juice

32-oz container of vanilla yogurt

1 c sour cream

Fresh mint leaves, OPTIONAL

Gently wash berries and pat dry. Puree berries in blender until smooth. Strain through sieve to remove seeds (essential if using raspberries). Add next three ingredients and process until smooth. Whisk in sour cream until smooth. Cover and refrigerate until chilled, about 4 hours. Serve in small cups with a dollop of sour cream and a mint leaf on top. *YIELD: About 8 servings.*

CUCUMBER SOUP

2 medium cucumbers, sliced and peeled

1 c buttermilk

1/2 c half and half light cream

1 small green onion, including 3 inches of top

2 to 3 sprigs of fresh parsley

1/2 tsp salt

1/4 tsp garlic salt

Dash of white pepper

1/2 tsp white wine tarragon vinegar

1/2 c sour cream

Puree the cucumbers in a blender with 1/2 cup buttermilk, the cream, green onion and parsley. Add garlic salt, salt, white pepper, with 1/2 cup buttermilk and vinegar. Blend a few seconds. Add sour cream and blend only long enough to mix. Refrigerate several hours or overnight to develop flavor. Serve thoroughly chilled and garnished with thin slices of cucumber or chopped parsley. *YIELD: 6 servings.*

GAZPACHO

I have tried variations and find this version I adapted from a Winston-Salem recipe is as good as any we might find in New York or L.A.

2 large tomatoes, peeled and seeded

1 large cucumber, peeled and seeded

1 medium white onion

1 medium green pepper

Two 12-oz cans tomato juice (I just use more tomatoes)

1/8 tsp garlic powder or 1 clove garlic, minced

1/3 c red wine vinegar

1/4 c olive oil (I use extra light)

Juice of one lemon or lime (I prefer lime)

1/4 tsp Tabasco or Louisiana Hot Sauce

Salt and pepper to taste (fresh-ground white pepper)

1/4 c chopped chives

Cilantro, OPTIONAL

In a blender or food processor, combine 1 tomato, half a cucumber, a fourth of a green pepper, half of the onion, garlic or garlic powder, and a half-cup of tomato juice. Blend at high speed for 30 seconds to puree. Add fresh cilantro if you like the flavor.

In a large bowl, mix the pureed vegetables with the remaining tomato juice, olive oil, vinegar, lemon or lime juice, Tabasco, salt and pepper. Cut remaining tomato, cucumber, green pepper and onion into bite-sized pieces and stir into mixture. Refrigerate mixture, covered, until well chilled, at least 2 hours. Top with fresh chopped chives and a dollop of sour cream when serving in chilled bowls.

VARIATION: Add 1/4 tsp Worcestershire sauce, fresh basil, and ground oregano. I think they muddy the flavor.

Gazpacho is the perfect summer luncheon soup, or prelude to a grilled dinner. Use only the freshest tomatoes and cucumbers.

LOBSTER BISQUE

from Mary Elizabeth Daltroff

This is a basic bisque, Southern style, and was a staple at elegant Memphis luncheons and dinners during the 1960s. The recipe adapts nicely to crab and shrimp.

1 large white onion, sliced

1 leek, cleaned thoroughly, then chopped

1 carrot, sliced

1 stalk of celery and celery leaves, chopped

1/2 tsp thyme

1 Bay leaf

1 tsp salt

2 small lobsters, shelled

1/2 c cognac

2 c white wine, or hot water

1 c cooked rice

2 T butter

3 T cream

2 egg yolks, beaten

Heat 2 tablespoons of butter in a 2-quart kettle, add onion, leek, carrot and celery, and brown lightly for 3 minutes. Add herbs, seasoning and lobster meat. Stir lightly over heat 5 minutes. Add 1/4-cup of cognac and the wine or hot water. Cover. Cook on low heat for 15 minutes. Remove lobster meat, put through a grinder, and return to cooking mixture. Mix in rice. Cover and boil 5 minutes. Strain mixture, then cook over low heat about 45 minutes until thick. Add butter, cream, egg yolks and remaining cognac. Do not boil. *YIELD: 4 servings.*

MANHATTAN CLAM CHOWDER

from Dr. Wilburta Daltroff

Auntie Doc was an Arkansas girl, born in Wynne before the turn of the (20th) century. Once she shook the black dirt off her shoes, she took to Yankee living like a duck to water. A practicing psychoanalyst at Central Park West in New York City for 42 years, Auntie Doc spent weekends at her country cottage in Sherman, CT, and lectured periodically at Yale. When age and heart disease caught up with her, Auntie Doc returned home to her family in Memphis. She was a cranky old dear, bless her heart, but we all benefited from her wisdom and her culinary skills.

2 to 3 dozen fresh clams

1/2 c boiling water

2 or 3 ribs of celery, diced

3 medium-sized onions, sliced

4 green peppers, sliced thin

4 slices of cubed salt pork, or bacon

2/3 c all-purpose flour

3 lb ripe tomatoes, peeled

1 tsp minced thyme

1 Bay leaf, crumbled

1 clove of garlic, chopped

6 medium potatoes, peeled

2 qts chicken broth (organic or homemade)

1 tsp salt

1/4 tsp pepper

3 T minced parsley

Scrub clams, rinse and drain. Put in a large stock pot or Dutch oven with a half-cup of boiling water. Cover pot, set it over heat until the steam opens the clams. Remove clams from shells; save all broth; chop clams. Sauté celery, onions and peppers with salt pork/bacon until the fat is melted and browning. Sprinkle flour over this and mix smoothly. Add broth from the clam pot with tomatoes, thyme, Bay leaf, garlic and potatoes. Stir in chicken broth. Cover. Simmer until vegetables are thoroughly cooked, about 30-45 minutes. Season, add the clams and parsley, stir and serve. *YIELD: 2 quarts.*

NEW ENGLAND CLAM CHOWDER

from Dr. Wilburta Daltroff

The old debate— Manhattan or New England. Everyone has their preference. Auntie Doc liked and made both.

2 to 3 dozen fresh clams

1/2 c boiling water

3 medium-sized onions, sliced

4 slices of cubed salt pork or bacon

2/3 c of all-purpose flour

1 Bay leaf, crumbled

6 medium potatoes, peeled

2 qts chicken broth (organic or homemade)

1 tsp salt

1/4 tsp pepper

3 T minced parsley

3 T butter

4 c whole milk or half and half cream

Scrub clams, rinse and drain. Put in a large stock pot or Dutch oven with a half-cup of boiling water. Cover pot, set it over heat until the steam opens the clams. Remove clams from shells; save all broth; chop clams. Sauté onions with salt pork/bacon until the fat is melted and browned. Sprinkle flour over this; mix smoothly. Add broth from the clam pot and bay leaf and potatoes. Add chicken broth and butter and stir. Cover and let simmer until potatoes are thoroughly cooked, about 30-45 minutes. Season, add the clams and parsley. Before serving, stir in 4 cups hot milk or half and half ((not boiling). Serve with oyster crackers. *YIELD: 8 to 10 servings.*

MAKE A SHRIMP STOCK:

Do not toss away those raw shrimp heads and shells. When making shrimp-based gumbos, jambalayas, or sauces, consider using shrimp stock where the recipe calls for water. The resulting flavor is more intense.

2 qts water

Heads and shells of raw shrimp

1 large onion, quartered

3 cloves garlic

6 ribs celery

Bring water to boil, and boil all ingredients for about 1-1/2 hrs (liquid will reduce; do not let liquid go below 1 qt). Strain stock, cool. Refrigerate or freeze in ice cube trays until needed.

OYSTER STEW

4 small white onions, chopped

4 hearts of celery

1/2 c chopped parsley

2 heaping T of all-purpose flour

6 T butter

2 dozen oysters with their liquor

2 c scalded whole milk

1 pt heavy cream

Salt and pepper to taste

Sauté the onions, celery, and parsley in 2 T butter in a frying pan until golden brown. Make a cream sauce in a double boiler by melting 2 T of butter, 2 heaping T flour and 2 cups scalded milk. Keep warm. Place oysters and oyster liquor in an enamel pan, with 2 T butter, freshly ground pepper and a little salt. When ready to serve, heat the oysters until edges curl. Add the oysters with some of their juice, and the heated cream to the basic cream sauce. Garnish with parsley. This makes a robust meal when served with crusty hot bread and a wedge salad. *YIELD: 6 servings.*

BASIC SEAFOOD GUMBO

1/4 c vegetable oil (extra-light olive or canola)

1/2 c bell pepper, chopped

1-1/2 c chopped white onion

4 cloves of chopped garlic

1/2 to 1 c chopped celery, including leaves if possible

1 c roux (between paper bag and milk chocolate colored)

3 qt water, boiling in a 5-qt stock pot

1 lb fresh or canned crabmeat (picked to remove shell)

1 lb raw shrimp, shelled, tails removed, and deveined

Tabasco Sauce

Tony's Creole seasoning, to taste

Cayenne pepper

Salt and black pepper, to taste

Gumbo filé

2 T green onion, chopped

Melt or heat the oil in a skillet, and sauté the vegetables until transparent. Remove from heat and immediately stir in 1 cup of hot roux. Pour this mixture into the boiling water. Cook for 1 hour. Add crab and shrimp. Season water with Creole seasoning, Tabasco, cayenne, salt, and pepper. Cook 30 minutes. Add gumbo filé and green onions. Cook on medium-low 10-15 minutes. Serve over steamed rice. *YIELD: 10 servings.*

JETTIES SEAFOOD GUMBO

This gumbo comes closest to what I remember eating in the 1960s at The Jetties, a restaurant located at the southern-most inhabited U.S. end of South Padre Island. This was long before South Padre became a National Seashore and collegiate Spring Break mecca.

4 lb shrimp, peeled and deveined

Extra light olive oil

Tony's Creole Seasoning

3 lb smoked sausage, sliced

1 lb Andouille or Cajun-style sausage, sliced

2 c chopped yellow onions

2 c chopped celery and celery leaves

2 c chopped green onions

106-oz can of whole tomatoes, cut into small pieces

2 c green bell peppers, chopped

1 qt homemade shrimp stock *(see recipe, page 153)*

1 tsp ground thyme

1 tsp garlic powder

1/2 tsp ground oregano

1/2 tsp cayenne pepper

Salt and pepper to taste

16-oz bag of frozen sliced okra (or 4 to 6 c fresh)

1 lb jumbo lump crabmeat (use Phillips fresh, if possible)

Roux

1/4 c gumbo filé, OPTIONAL (if not thick enough)

Steamed rice

Sauté shrimp in oil, sprinkle with Tony's. Set aside. Sauté sausage until done, add vegetables, and sauté until all are tender. Add cut-up tomatoes and continue simmering. In large stockpot, add shrimp stock, cooked sausage mixture, seasonings and okra. Add shrimp and crabmeat. Stir in dark Roux made of equal parts oil and flour, to thicken and to darken flavor. Reduce heat; simmer for 2 hours. Additional shrimp stock may be added if gumbo becomes too thick. Serve over steamed rice. *YIELD: 10-12 servings.*

SEAFOOD GUMBO, MEMPHIS STYLE

from Mary Elizabeth Daltroff

1 to 2 pieces of bacon

1 tsp bacon fat

16 okra pods (fresh or frozen), sliced

1 large onion, chopped

1 small green bell pepper, chopped

1 clove garlic, minced

2 T plain flour

4 c chicken broth or stock

1 stalk (a bunch) of celery, including the leaves

1/2 c canned tomatoes

1/2 tsp thyme

1 Bay leaf

1 tsp Worcestershire sauce

Salt and black pepper, to taste (1 tsp salt, 1/2 tsp pepper)

2 c cooked shrimp

15-oz can of crabmeat

1 T gumbo filé powder, OPTIONAL

Cut bacon into small pieces, put into pan with bacon fat, and fry for 2 minutes. Add okra, onion and bell pepper. Cook 5 minutes over low heat. Add garlic and flour and stir. Add chicken broth, chopped celery, tomatoes, thyme, Bay leaf, Worcestershire, salt and pepper to taste. Simmer for 1 hour, covered, then add the shrimp and crab. Cook 2 minutes. Stir in filé powder if thickening is needed (usually not when okra is used). Garnish servings with parsley. *YIELD: 6 to 8 servings.*

FAMILY MEMORY

PHOTO: Left to right, Mary Elizabeth Daltroff, Edith Gant of Richardson, TX, their children, and Rosalee Bloom Hyam, at the Jetties on South Padre Island, early 1960s.

SHE-CRAB SOUP

I became a she-crab soup fan in 1979, while coordinating a juried exhibition of North Carolina art photography for Charleston's Second Annual Spoleto Festival. During my stay, I sampled the variations offered by numerous Charleston-area cafes, fish shacks and restaurants. Each had its own twist on the basic recipe. All were delicious. Here's my interpretation.*NOTE BELOW: Vegetables are added for more chowder-like version. Omit veggies and start with a roux for smoother soup.

4 T butter

1 white onion, grated (about 1 c)

1 leek, sliced*

2 ribs celery, chopped fine*

1/4 c carrot, chopped fine*

2 T plain flour

1 qt fish stock (or half water with half fish base)

1/2 to 1 qt chicken stock

1 tsp Worcestershire sauce

1 tsp lemon zest (or 1/4 tsp of fresh lemon juice)

1/2 tsp ground white pepper

Salt to taste

1/4 tsp cayenne pepper

1/4 tsp ground mace or 1/8 tsp ground nutmeg

1 to 1-1/2 lb flaked blue crab meat (may substitute Dungeness)

2 c heavy cream

2 egg yolks, beaten

4 T fine sherry

1/4 c crab roe, to garnish

1 T finely chopped fresh parsley, to garnish

Melt butter. Add vegetables. Simmer until tender, stirring. Mix in flour, with more butter, if necessary, to start a roux. Stir well 5 minutes. Whisk in fish and chicken stocks. Boil 30 minutes, stirring occasionally. Add seasonings, Worcestershire, and lemon zest. Stir and simmer 5 minutes. Add crabmeat and sherry, stir, and simmer 5 minutes. Lower heat; whisk in beaten egg yolks and cream, stirring only until thickened. Remove at once and ladle into bowls. Add roe and sprinkle of parsley. Garnish with hard-cooked egg wedge, if desired. *YIELD: About 2 quarts.*

She-Crab Soup, shown here as a bisque rather than as a chowder.

ABOUT SHE-CRAB SOUP

Crab soup made with Atlantic blue crabs has been dished up in Charleston since the 18th century. According to local legend, Scottish settlers in Chucktown created it because they missed their traditional "partan-bree" crab and rice soup. The addition of orange crab roe is said to have occurred around 1912 when Charleston Mayor R. Goodwyn Rhett instructed his butler and cook, William Deas, to dress up the local crab soup for their VIP guest, President William Howard Taft.

True she-crab soup can be bisque-like or chowder-like, depending on whether the cook prefers to start with a roux or with fish stock and sautéed vegetables. Traditional versions include mace or nutmeg. Some versions include Old Bay seasoning instead of cayenne. One old recipe calls for adding a tablespoon of tomato paste during the broth-cooking phase. Sherry is either cooked in the soup or stirred in at the end. When no roe are available, the soup is served with wedged hardboiled eggs.

TIP WHEN USING FRESH CRABS: Bring 4 qt salted water to a boil in 8-qt stock pot. Drop in 12 live, good-size she-crabs (sooks). Return to a boil, cook 15 minutes. Drain. Clean and shell the crabs; save meat and roe for soup.

MINESTRONE SOUP

1-1/2 lb blade chuck roast or meaty soup bones

2-1/2 qts water

2 tsp salt

1 small white onion, sliced

1/2 c celery leaves, chopped

1 bay leaf

2 slices bacon, diced

1-1/2 c cooked or canned kidney beans

1/2 c cut-up fresh green beans

1/2 c diced celery

1/2 c fresh or frozen green peas

1/2 c thinly sliced zucchini

1/2 c thinly sliced carrots

1/4 c diced onion

1/4 chopped parsley

1 to 2 cloves of garlic, minced

1/2 c (approximately 2 oz) elbow macaroni

6-oz can of tomato paste

1 T olive oil

1 T Worcestershire sauce

1 tsp Italian seasoning

1 tsp salt

1/4 tsp black pepper

In a large pot, cover and simmer the first six ingredients for at least 2 to 3 hours, until meat is tender and falling apart. Strain broth; add ice cubes to harden the fat in the strained broth (or chill in fridge overnight). Remove fat from broth. Dice the meat, discarding fat and bones, and combine beef broth and meat in a 5- or 6-quart pot. Place over low heat.

Pan-fry or microwave bacon until crisp. Add the bacon, drippings, and all remaining ingredients to the meat broth. Cover and simmer for at least 30 minutes, until veggies and macaroni are tender. Sprinkle individual servings with fresh-grated Parmesan cheese.

VARIATION: Add 1 cup of Coca-Cola® while simmering. *YIELD: About 3 quarts.*

PASTA E FAGIOLI

This recipe reminds me of many sleepovers at the home of my childhood best friend, Dolly. Her mom was a terrific Italian cook. Something savory always simmered on the stove.

2 ounces small shaped pasta

1 lb extra-lean ground beef

Extra light olive oil

1 c chopped onion

1 T minced garlic

1 c sliced celery

1 c sliced carrot

Two 14.5-oz cans of Italian diced tomatoes

15-oz can navy beans, Northern or cannelloni white beans, rinsed and drained

15-oz can of tomato sauce

11.5-oz can V-8 juice (low sodium is fine)

3 c beef broth

1 c water

1 T white vinegar

1/2 c chopped fresh parsley

1/2 tsp dried thyme leaves

1 tsp basil flakes

1 tsp oregano flakes

Half fill a 3-qt sauce pan with water. Bring water to a rolling boil. Add pasta and follow directions on package until cooked al dente. Drain pasta and set aside.

Brown ground beef in extra light olive oil in large pan over medium-high heat. Add garlic when beef is crumbled and starting to brown. Cook, stirring, until completely browned. Add onion, celery, and carrot. Cook together for 5 minutes. Stir in all remaining ingredients except pasta, cover, lower the heat and simmer, about 45 minutes. Stir every 5 to 10 minutes to prevent mixture from sticking.

Mix in cooked pasta; simmer for additional 15 minutes before serving. *YIELD: 10 servings.*

THE SOUTHERN AND ITALIAN CONNECTION

Italian cuisine has specific significance for us Southerners, due to the Italian immigrants who came through New Orleans and Florida before and after both nations' civil wars, then again between 1880 and 1920. The later immigrants settled in Louisiana, the east Arkansas and Mississippi Delta, Memphis, the Ozarks, and Alabama. Their rice, hams, cheeses, sausage, garlic dishes, cured meats, mushroom and seafood dishes meshed nicely with our traditional Southern food ways.

MOM'S VEGETABLE BEEF SOUP

from Mary Elizabeth Daltroff

THE MEAT:

1 stick (1/2 c) butter, or 1/2 c olive oil

1 to 2 lb of uncooked chuck or stew beef*

Salt, pepper and garlic powder

1 pkg dry onion soup mix

10-3/4-oz can cream of mushroom soup +1 can water

Dust uncooked meat with salt, pepper and garlic powder, then sear all sides in hot oil or butter. Completely brown on stovetop set to medium-high heat. Drain grease. Add onion soup mix, and mushroom soup; lower heat to medium, simmer, and add 1 can of water after a few minutes. Simmer on stovetop until meat is thoroughly cooked. Chill overnight, remove congealed fat. (*OR use leftover pot roast.)

THE SOUP:

Two 32-oz cans crushed tomatoes

32-oz can tomato sauce

2 large Bay leaves

4 T butter or olive oil

3 ribs of celery, chopped, PLUS celery leaves chopped

1 large white onion, chopped

3 cloves of garlic, chopped fine

28- or 32-oz bag frozen butter peas or baby lima beans

28- or 32-oz bag of frozen white shoepeg corn

Two 15-oz cans cut green beans (or 1 bag of frozen)

1 to 2 c frozen green peas

1 c cabbage, chopped fine

3 to 5 large carrots, diced (or 1 bag frozen carrots)

1/2 to 1 tsp Worcestershire sauce

Tabasco, to taste

Salt and black pepper, to taste

1 tsp Italian seasoning

Cut meat into bite-size pieces. Place meat and gravy into a 6- or 8-qt pot. Add 3 to 4 qt of water. Bring to a rolling boil on medium-high heat, then lower heat to medium and cook for 1 hour. Add tomatoes, tomato sauce, and Bay leaves. Simmer until meat falls apart.

Sauté onion, garlic and celery in melted butter or heated oil. Pour into simmering soup stock with oil or butter from the skillet. Stir. Bring liquid back to a boil, then gradually add the cabbage and other vegetables. Add more water to cover completely. Stir until thoroughly mixed. Add seasonings. Raise to a boil, reduce heat; simmer 2 to 3 hours, stirring occasionally to prevent sticking. Add water if needed. Freeze leftovers.

CREAM OF BROCCOLI SOUP

Perfect use for leftover steamed broccoli and leftover homemade chicken stock. Ingredients are approximate.

1 stick(1/2 c) butter

3 T all-purpose flour

1 medium white onion, chopped fine

4 large steamed broccoli heads and tender stems, mashed

Salt and pepper to taste

Cayenne pepper to taste

4 to 6 c chicken stock

1 to 2 c light cream

1/2 to 3/4 c grated Monterey Jack or fiesta-blend cheese

Melt butter in a heavy large skillet or 10-inch saucepan. Sauté onions, add salt and pepper to taste. Gradually stir in flour. When flour mixture becomes crumbly and browning, whisk in warm chicken stock. Simmer, whisking, until the mixture thickens. Add the mashed broccoli, and stir, continuing to mash. Continue stirring with wooden spoon, about 5 to 7 minute; gradually add cream, cheese and cayenne. Stir well until completely blended and hot, but not boiling. Serve immediately.

VARIATION 1: Add a splash of sherry or cognac before the cream.

VARIATION 2: Add shredded chicken to transform it into chicken-broccoli soup.

CREAM OF MUSHROOM SOUP

Large pkg of fresh white mushrooms, chopped

1 large white or sweet onion

1 stick butter

2 to 3 c chicken broth (homemade, or packaged, but without MSG)

1 c heavy cream

2 T all-purpose flour

Sauté onions and mushrooms until onions are transparent, whisk in the flour to absorb the butter and start a roux; keep stirring for a few minutes, then whisk in heated chicken broth. Add cream; stir until thickened and hot but not boiling. Serve immediately. NOTES: If using canned broth, add dashes of thyme and garlic powder. If the soup lacks depth, add a splash of sherry or 1/4-cup of fiesta-blend shredded cheese; stir until melted.

CREAM OF PEANUT SOUP

The first time I ever had a version of this soup was in Williamsburg the summer after my junior year in high school, during our family's memorable journey toward the Montreal World's Fair, which we never reached. We visited relatives in Pennsylvania, Connecticut and New York along the way, and we drove by almost every college in six states. During a formal dinner in Williamsburg, Dad lit Mom's cigarette with a three-arm candelabrum, while my brothers put fake fly-embedded ice cubes in all the drinks. I was mortified. The colonial fare was yummy anyway.

1 medium white onion, chopped

2 ribs celery, chopped

1/4 c butter

3 T flour

2 qts chicken stock or broth

2 c smooth peanut butter

1-3/4 c light cream

1 c chopped peanuts

   Sauté onion and celery in butter until soft, but not browned. Stir in flour until well blended. Add chicken stock, stirring constantly, and bring to a boil. Remove from heat and rub through a sieve. Add peanut butter and cream, stirring to blend thoroughly. Return to low heat, but do not boil. Serve garnished with peanuts if desired. This also is good served cold. *YIELD: 10-12 servings.*

PUMPKIN SOUP

This soup is close to the Old Salem Tavern recipe, if cook omits the Bay leaf. A nice different flavor is achieved by omitting the lemon pepper and cayenne, adding 1/8 tsp nutmeg instead.

4 T butter

1 medium onion, chopped

1/2 c chopped scallions or green onions

16-oz can of plain pumpkin

5 c chicken broth

1 Bay leaf, OPTIONAL

1 tsp lemon pepper

Dash of cayenne pepper

2 c whole milk or half and half

Salt and pepper to taste

Parsley springs for garnish

Whipped cream or sour cream for garnish

   Sauté the onion and scallions in butter for 5 minutes. Puree this sautéed onion in a food processor, and add pumpkin, chicken stock, lemon pepper, and cayenne; whirl again in blender. Put into large saucepan with Bay leaf and parsley. Simmer for 15 minutes. Remove Bay leaf and parsley; stir in milk or Half and Half. Continue simmering until blended and thickened. DO NOT LET BOIL. Season with salt and pepper. Spoon into cups and top with whipped or sour cream and a green sprig from onions. *YIELD: 6 to 8 servings.*

TURKEY GUMBO AND GRADUATION

   At Joshua's Oxford High School graduation in the Ole Miss coliseum, the graduates' proud families raucously cheered, clapped and even blew a bullhorn once or twice. Our North Carolina relatives and Gabrielle's Louisiana friend, Ryan, were amazed by the exuberant behavior of the audience, which ignored officials' pleas for decorum.

   Ryan had spent half the previous day making turkey-bone gumbo for Joshua's post-graduation family gathering. Stuck at the stove, he'd suffered an estrogen overdose while Jeff's sisters Andrea and Dianne helped me recall Southernisms, and while we read aloud from Maryln Schwartz' *Southern Belle Primer.*

   As one soon-to-be-graduate approached the stage to the sound of particularly rambunctious cheers, Ryan muttered to me, "Well, I'll bet she doesn't cut the crusts off HER sandwiches."

   Our Triplette laughter rivaled the bullhorn.

Photo of Joshua Triplette by Ryan Russell

THE RECIPES

ABOUT OUR SOUTHERN SAUCES

Sauces form an essential component of everything Southerners cook, except perhaps baked goods and mixed drinks, although even those categories have exceptions (Mayonnaise Cake). Our stews, soups, and meat dishes contain a roux-based gravy. Many of our vegetable dishes are topped with a cream or cheese sauce. And, of course, our salads, sandwiches, and congealed concoctions are built from mayonnaise.

Southern sauce recipes derived primarily from French cookery. All Southern cooks of a certain age (born before JFK became president) know the five basic "mother" sauces from which so many wonderful sauce flavorings are derived.

Béchamel Sauce: (WHITE) Classic white *CREAM SAUCE* made by mixing scalded milk or cream into a flour-butter roux, whose thickness depends on the proportions of flour and butter to milk. Classic *CHEESE SAUCE* starts with cream sauce; *MORNAY SAUCE* specifically calls for cream sauce plus Parmesan and Swiss cheese.

Velouté: (BLOND) Pronounced veh-loo-TAY. Stock-based white sauce made from chicken, veal or fish stock, sometimes with egg yolks and cream added.

Espagnole: Classic Brown Sauce made from roasting veal or beef bones with mirepoix, the French trinity of onions, carrots and celery. It forms the basis for many gravies and for *DEMI GLACE*, the classic French sauce flavoring.

Hollandaise and Mayonnaise: Sauces made with an emulsion of egg yolks and fat. Classic hollandaise, served hot over vegetables, fish and egg dishes, is made in a double boiler with egg yolks, lemon juice and melted butter. Béarnaise is a variation of hollandaise with herbs. Mayonnaise, a cold dressing made by emulsifying vegetable oil with egg yolks, lemon juice or

vinegar, and seasonings, is served as a spread, a dressing and a sauce, and as the basis for numerous flavorful condiments such as tartar sauce and remoulade.

Vinaigrette: This sauce or dressing is made by combining vinegar and oil (usually three parts to one part) with salt and pepper, various herbs and seasonings. It is the basis for barbecue sauces and many relishes.

HOW TO MAKE ROUX

A roux is the basis for many soup and gumbo stocks, gravies and casserole fillings. Start with equal parts of flour and oil (butter heats too quickly and burns). Be prepared to stand over the stove for a while. A perfect roux requires 30-45 minutes to achieve. It's worth it.

2 c of all-purpose flour

2 c cooking oil (I prefer extra light olive oil, Wesson, or peanut oil)

Heat the oil in a heavy, well seasoned skillet over medium-high heat. Add flour, whisking continuously to blend. Continue whisking and cooking until roux begins to turn brown. Lower the heat, and continue cooking and whisking until roux reaches desired degree of doneness.

Perfect roux goes through four stages of cooking, and which roux to use depends on the recipe.

- *Blond* (when first mixed on the heat, used for some cream gravies)
- *Paper bag* (peanut-butter colored, and considered a light brown roux)
- *Milk chocolate* (generally what is known as a dark roux)
- *Dark chocolate* (borders on burned)

To keep the roux from burning, turn off the burner as soon as it becomes "milk chocolate" and set pan aside while preparing the ingredients that will be added to the roux. The heat from the cookware will continue cooking it darker for up to 5 minutes. Remove any remaining clumps with slotted spoon. If the roux becomes too dark, throw it away and start again. Otherwise, your dish will taste burned.

TIP FOR A SUCCESSFUL ROUX:
Roux-based sauces require constant stirring and whisking to prevent lumpiness. If lumps develop, force sauce through a sieve. If you must leave the stove in the midst of roux prep, remove pan from heat, or roux will scorch.

ROUX MEMORY

In 2008, I asked Gabrielle to stop by her local Baton Rouge grocery store for a jar of Bootsie's Cajun Roux on her way up to Oxford for the holidays. Gabrielle searched the vast Cajun section in Albertson's, but couldn't find any Bootsie's. She enlisted the store manager's help, and after 10 minutes, he concluded that the store had run out of Bootsie's. A Cajun through and through, the store manager looked down at her in exasperation and pointed. "You know, over here's the oil, and over there's the flour," he said. She knew she'd been told.

DEMI GLACE

Demi glace (pronounced deem uh glahs; translation = half-glaze) is an exquisite sauce and gravy flavorant. Sometimes called meat essence in old Southern recipes, it is the product of several reduction processes requiring few ingredients, but lots of time. Demi glace will transform the most ordinary meat gravy into an extraordinary sauce. To make demi glace, plan to be in the kitchen off and on for about two days. It's not hard ... just time consuming. Finding a source for the bones might be the most difficult part.

 Many classic recipes provide elaborate preparation steps that confuse all of us who weren't trained in culinary school. The best way I have found to accomplish demi glace, or a reasonable facsimile, is to combine some steps. But first, one should grasp the definitions of its ingredients.

- **Demi glace is made from:** Espagnole sauce, brown stock, herbs or combination of herbs.
- **Espagnole Sauce is made from:** Brown stock, mirepoix, bouquet garni, tomato puree, dark brown roux, additional vegetables (optional)
- **Brown Stock is made from:** Roasted and boiled meat marrow bones such as veal or beef (ask butcher for soup bones and knuckle bones), mirepoix.
- **Mirepoix is made from:** The French trinity of vegetables (50% onion, 25% carrots, and 25% celery).
- **Bouquet garni is made from:** Herbs wrapped in kitchen twine, including green leaves of leek, sprigs of parsley, sprigs of thyme, sprigs of marjoram (optional), bay leaves, sprigs of oregano (optional).

DEMI GLACE RECIPE

10 to 12 lb veal or beef bones, cut into 2-to-3-inch pieces

  (sometimes bundled by meat department as dog bones)

3 large carrots, scraped, cut into 2-inch pieces

2 large white onions, quartered or roughly chopped

White part of 1 leek, chopped, reserve the green leaves

Bouquet garni (2 outer green leaves from leek, wrapped around 15 flat-leaf parsley sprigs, 2 fresh thyme sprigs, 2 dried bay leaves, and tied with kitchen string; some purists add 2 whole cloves)

Dark brown roux

6-oz can of tomato paste

Water

Roasting pan

15-to-20-qt stock pot

Position bones in a single layer in roasting pan. Roast for about 1-1/2 hour in preheated oven set at 475°F. Remove pan from oven, and place the carrots, onions, leek and celery evenly around the bones. NOTE: Some modern chefs omit the celery because of its strong flavor, but it IS classic. Roast the bones and vegetables together for 45 minutes, or until deeply browned but not burned. Transfer bones and veggies to the large stockpot.

 Place roasting pan over two burners on the stove on medium heat, add 3 cups water to pan, and begin scraping up all caramelized bits with a wooden spoon. These browned bits are called fond (foundation). Simmer for about 3 to 4 minutes, then transfer liquid to pot of bones, making sure to get ALL the bits. Add Bouquet Garni to the pot, along with to-mato paste. Add 6 to 8 qt of COLD water. Turn heat to medium-high. When bubbles start to appear on surface of liquid, lower heat to medium-low. During the first hour, frothy foam, called scum, will rise to the top. Skim off as it rises. This may take up to a half hour.

 NEXT, Simmer for a minimum of 8 hours, up to 24 hours, adding a bit of water as needed during the cooking. During the first few hours, ladle off fat from the surface to keep it from clouding the stock. You may want to take a (sleep) break. If so, after 8 to 10 hours. Remove from stove. Refrigerate overnight, and in the morning, remove all the congealed fat from the surface before returning the stock to the stove. If you do this, simmer for about another 6 to 8 hours.

 Remove from stove, and strain the stock through cheesecloth stretched over another pot. Squeeze gelatin from the crumbly bones and veggies and add to stock. You should have 4 to 5 quarts of stock. Bring back to a boil. Continue until liquid reduces to half. At this point, you have Espagnole sauce. Strain once more through a cheesecloth to remove remaining particles. Refrigerate overnight and remove remaining congealed fat, if any. You may wish to freeze the Espagnole sauce and use it as you would use demi glace. NOTE: Recipes that call for working flour into the Espagnole sauce without further simmering and reduction tend to lack the intense flavor depth of a true demi glace.

 To proceed to demi glace, heat Espagnole stock with equal portion of plain meat stock (store-bought will work). Work in dark brown roux, and simmer on low until flour taste is absorbed and stock reduces to several cups. Pour sauce into ice cube tray, freeze; and then pop frozen cubes into a ziplock bag to use as needed.

INTENSE CHICKEN STOCK

2 stewing or baking hens (about 3 lb each)

Center part of a stalk of celery (all the heart ribs with leaves)

4 to 6 carrots, scrubbed, scraped

1/8 c whole black peppercorns

8 sprigs of fresh thyme

2 T salt

1 large head of garlic, roots trimmed, excess paper removed; cut in half between top and bottom to expose each clove

12-qt stock pot

Wash hens, clean cavities, and remove any remaining pin feathers. Do not remove skin. Drop into stock pot. Add remaining ingredients. Add water to 3 inches below pot rim. Simmer on stove 4 to 6 hours. Remove chickens; debone and set meat aside or freeze for other uses. Strain stock through a sieve. Store in freezable jars and ice cube trays for use as needed.

BARBECUE (BBQ) SAUCES

ALABAMA WHITE BBQ SAUCE

This is fantastic with fried green tomatoes!

1 c mayonnaise

1 c apple cider vinegar

2 T granulated sugar

1 to 2 T black pepper

1 tsp salt

1/2 tsp cayenne pepper

1/2 tsp smoked paprika

1 to 2 T lemon juice

1 tsp ground onion

Whisk ingredients together in a bowl. Refrigerate overnight to blend the seasonings. This north Alabama specialty is dynamite basted on chicken, turkey, and pork, as the sauce base for chicken-and-veggie pizza, and as a dipping sauce for everything else. When grilling, baste onto the meat during the last minutes of cooking. Top the grilled meat with more sauce when serving. NOTE: Burns easily.

CAROLINA MUSTARD BBQ SAUCE

This sauce is used for meats, including barbecue, and in slaw for a Down East flavor.

3/4 c yellow prepared mustard

3/4 c red wine vinegar

1/4 c white granulated sugar

1-1/2 T butter

2 tsp salt

1/2 tsp Worcestershire sauce

1-1/4 tsp ground black pepper

1/2 tsp Tabasco or Texas Pete hot sauce

Combine all ingredients in medium saucepan. Stir well to blend. Bring to a simmer on medium-low heat. Turn heat down to low, simmer 30 minutes. Let stand at room temperature 1 hour before using.

COLA BBQ SAUCE

Works well with pork chops, chicken, pork shoulder. NOTE This sauce contains natural sugars, which burn easily.

12-oz can cola soft drink (NOT diet; I prefer Coke Classic)

2 T orange juice

2 T soy sauce

1 T fresh minced ginger

1 clove minced garlic

Salt, pepper to taste

1/4 c vegetable oil

Combine all sauce ingredients and marinate meat overnight, reserving some of the sauce. Place meat on a well-oiled pan and bake at 350° until done, depending on type of meat and weight. Remove from oven, dredge the meat in unused sauce, baste with additional sauce and bake for 15 minutes or until done

WESTERN VARIATION: Add the following to original ingredients:

1/4 c Worcestershire sauce

1 tsp liquid smoke, or more, to taste

3 T steak sauce

1 tsp onion flakes

1 tsp garlic flakes

1/2 tsp freshly ground black pepper

LAURIE'S BBQ SAUCE

This sauce is terrific on chicken.

1 stick of butter

1 large onion, chopped

6 cloves garlic, minced

1 tsp cinnamon powder

1-1/2 tsp chili powder

1 to 2 T dry mustard

1 to 2 T Worcestershire sauce

2/3 c ketchup

2 c crushed tomatoes

1 c apple cider vinegar

2 T lemon juice

1/2 c brown sugar, packed

1/2 c molasses or dark Karo syrup

1/2 tsp paprika

1/4 tsp cayenne pepper

Dash (1 to 2 shakes) red pepper flakes

1 c water

1 tsp salt

Melt butter in a sauce pan on medium heat. Sauté the chopped onion and garlic in the butter. Mix in all remaining ingredients and bring to a boil. Reduce heat and simmer to half its volume, approximately 20-30 minutes. For smoother sauce, puree in blender. Use as a "mop" for basting during the last 15 minutes on the grill, or as a sauce after grilling. *YIELD: About 2 to 3 cups.*

MT. BETHEL BBQ SAUCE

from Louise Sherrill Triplette

Louise Triplette picked up this recipe from her friends in the Women's Society of Christian Service, Hickory, NC, who published the cookbook, **The Best Cooking in Mt. Bethel Church**.

1/4 lb butter (1/2 stick)

1/2 c ketchup

1 T Worcestershire sauce

3 T vinegar and lemon juice

1/2 c water

Melt butter and mix well with other ingredients. Use this to baste meats for grilling or baking. Makes a great marinade for oven-cooked or slow-cooked pork shoulder. *YIELD: 1+ cup.*

LEXINGTON-STYLE BBQ SAUCE

2 c of apple-cider vinegar

1/2 c water

1/2 c ketchup

2 T light brown sugar

1 T Louisiana Hot Sauce, Tabasco, or Texas Pete

2 tsp crushed red chili flakes

2 tsp kosher salt

1 tsp freshly ground black pepper

In a medium bowl, whisk the vinegar, water, ketchup, brown sugar, hot sauce, chili flakes, salt and pepper until the sugar and salt are dissolved. Store in an airtight container in the refrigerator for up to 4 weeks. Shake well. Use as a marinade and as a mop sauce. *YIELD: 3 cups.*

NC BOY SCOUTS BBQ SPLASH

This recipe is simple. It works as a marinade before grilling, as a mop during the grilling phase, and as a finishing splash on the finished pulled pork. Boy Scout troops such as Troop 355 at Sharon United Methodist Church in Charlotte include versions of this "Eastern Hot" Sauce with their pulled pork sales.

1-1/2 c distilled white vinegar

1 tsp Texas Pete hot sauce (or Louisiana or Tabasco)

2 T sugar (white, light brown, or dark brown)

1 T salt

2 tsp crushed red pepper

2 tsp ground black pepper

Pour all ingredients into a jar. Shake. Let sit at least 12-36 hours to allow the flavors to meld. Mop onto meat with basting brush once every hour while cooking.

NOTE: To prevent contamination by uncooked meat, make sure to use a clean brush dipped into mop sauce poured into a dish. Serve additional sauce in a cruet on the side. *YIELD: About 1-3/4 cup.*

HINT: Barbecued pork reheats nicely in a microwave. Heat, covered with waxed paper, about 3 minutes on medium power, then stir, and continue until completely heated. Another method is to put about an inch of water in a 3-quart saucepan and then insert a vegetable steamer. As the water begins to simmer and steam, pile the barbecue into the vegetable steamer and cover. Steam 5 to 10 minutes, until heated through. Mix with sauce to serve.

PHOTOS COURTESY OF THE NORTH CAROLINA STATE ARCHIVES, RALEIGH, NC. TOP: B's Barbecue and Grill, Pitt County, Greenville, NC, by Scott Power, February 1996. LOWER LEFT: Hardison House and BBQ Business, Jamesville vicinity, Martin County, NC, circa 1995. LOWER RIGHT: Barbecue in downtown Raleigh, 1926.

PREVENT SCORCHING

Rules of thumb to prevent scorching: Cook on medium or low, and stir frequently. Add the sugar or sugar-laden ingredients near the end of cooking because sugar has a low heat-point. If the recipe calls for adding milk or cream, stir it in when the dish is almost ready, and heat back up but do not boil.

POLLY MOORE'S BBQ SAUCE

from Polly Starnes Moore

Included in the original Grace Chapel Methodist Church Cookbook of the Women's Society, this is the recipe of Polly Starnes Moore, Louise Triplette's first cousin on her maternal side. Our family is convinced that this is the all-time best barbecue flavoring for cooked chicken or pork. Even if you want to add a heavier and sweeter sauce to the cooked meat, use this version as a marinade beforehand, and as a mop sauce during the cooking.

2 T Worcestershire sauce

2 T vinegar (I recommend apple cider vinegar)

1 T lemon juice

2 T butter, melted

3 T brown sugar

3 T ketchup

1 tsp salt

1 tsp dry mustard

1 tsp chili powder

1 tsp paprika

1/2 to 1-1/2 tsp red pepper flakes (amount determines fire of the flavor)

SIMPLE BBQ: Mix all ingredients and pour over the meat to marinate for at least an hour before cooking. For oven cooking, loosely wrap in aluminum foil and cook at 300-325°F until interior of pork reaches 145°F and chicken reaches 175-180°F. Pork will continue cooking for another 10 minutes after removal from the oven if left in the covered dish. *YIELD: About 1-1/4 cup.*

MAYONNAISE & HOLLANDAISE

CLASSIC MAYONNAISE

1 tsp dry mustard

1 tsp salt

1 tsp white granulated sugar

Dash cayenne pepper

2 egg yolks

1-1/2 to 2 c salad oil

1 T lemon juice

3 T tarragon vinegar

Chill bowl and all ingredients. Mix dry ingredients first in mixing bowl, then add egg yolks, beating well with rotary beater. Pour in 1/4 cup oil, drop by drop at first, then in a steady stream, beating constantly. Gradually add the lemon juice and vinegar, and the remaining oil.

Beat between each addition until mixture is thoroughly blended and thick. Keep very cold until serving. If mayo separates during mixing, beat 1 egg yolk with 1 T cold water, then beat the separated mayo mixture into it very slowly until thick.

BOILED MAYONNAISE DRESSING

2 T plain flour

2 T oil

1/8 c white distilled vinegar

1/8 c lemon juice

1 c boiling water

2 egg yolks, well beaten in a separate bowl

1/2 tsp dry mustard

1/2 tsp salt

Dash of cayenne pepper

1 c of vegetable oil

Flavoring such as ketchup, chili sauce, whipped cream

Mix first 4 ingredients in double boiler over boiling water. Add boiling water to mixture; boil for 5 minutes, stirring constantly. Pour at once over the well beaten yolks, whisking all the time. Stir in seasonings; cool. When cooled, but not cold, beat in oil. Before serving, add ketchup, chili sauce, or whipped cream for desired dressing flavor. Eggs won't curdle due to vinegar.

SOUR CREAM BOILED MAYO DRESSING

1 tsp white granulated sugar

1/2 tsp salt

Cayenne pepper to taste

1/2 tsp dry mustard

4 eggs, well beaten in separate bowl

1/2 c of vegetable oil

1 T white distilled vinegar

1 T lemon juice

1/2 c sour cream

Mix dry ingredients. Combine with well beaten eggs in a double boiler over boiling water, stirring constantly, about 5 minutes. While cooking, add alternately the oil, vinegar and lemon juice, stirring constantly. Add sour cream when ready to serve.

BASIL MAYONNAISE

from Missy Morrison

My wonderful Oxford neighbor, Missy Morrison, is always quick to share. This mayo of hers is tasty enough to eat like yogurt. NOTE: Never attempt to make mayo on a very humid or rainy day. The ingredients won't emulsify properly.

2 large eggs

1 c of canola oil (more or less)

1 T lemon juice, or white distilled vinegar if out of lemon juice

Salt and pepper to taste (about 1/4 tsp each)

Fresh basil, loosely chopped, about 1 T

1 to 2 cloves crushed garlic, OPTIONAL

Mix all ingredients together in a blender except the oil. While mixing, slowly add the oil until it completely emulsifies. Keeps 2 to 4 days, refrigerated. *YIELD: Two to three 10-oz jars.*

HINT FOR MAYONNAISE: Mayonnaise requires serious whisking and careful addition of the oil one drop at a time. Best oils for making mayonnaise are Canola, safflower or soybean. Olive oil's too flavorful.

GARLIC MAYONNAISE (AIOLI)

Garlic mayo is called aioli in France. It's terrific with tomato and field pea salad, with other summer salad veggies, and with grilled pork loin.

1 T cider or white wine vinegar

1 T freshly squeezed lemon juice

1 tsp kosher salt

1 tsp dry mustard

2 large egg yolks, either pasteurized, or organic and free range

1-1/2 c light olive oil

2 T boiling water

1 tsp garlic, chopped and rubbed to a very fine paste with a pinch of kosher salt

Combine vinegar, lemon juice, salt and dry mustard in a glass or stainless steel bowl. Whisk until the salt and mustard are dissolved. Add the egg yolks and beat until smooth. Add the oil, drop by drop, and then in a slow, steady stream, whisking constantly until all the oil has been incorporated into a thick emulsion. Pour the boiling water over the garlic paste and let stand for 2 minutes. Whisk the garlic mix into the mayonnaise. Lasts 3 days, refrigerated. *YIELD: 1-3/4 cup.*

QUICKIE VARIATION: For a super quick substitution for homemade, add the garlic paste to prepared mayonnaise (I only use Duke's or Hellmann's).

NO-YOLK MAYONNAISE

2 large egg whites

1 tsp Dijon mustard

1/8 tsp sugar

1/4 tsp salt

1/4 tsp black or white pepper

3/4 c corn oil

1 T fresh lemon juice

1 tsp white wine vinegar

Blend egg whites, mustard, sugar, salt and pepper in blender at slow speed, about 1 minute. With motor running, add oil in a thin stream. Turn off blender. Add lemon juice and vinegar and blend until mixture has combined and thickened. *YIELD: About 1 cup.*

SAUCES &
SEASONINGS

SUBSTITUTIONS

I always keep plain yogurt in the fridge as an emergency substitute for sour cream or whipping cream. Two-thirds of a cup of plain yogurt and one-third cup of mayonnaise make a flavorful sour cream substitution in chicken and Mexican dishes.

BLENDER HOLLANDAISE SAUCE

from Mary Elizabeth Daltroff

This quick, foolproof recipe has been used for more than 60 years by Southern Belle homemakers on their Eggs Benedict and steamed asparagus. A bit milder than the classic version, it gets my vote!

3 egg yolks

2 tsp lemon juice

1/2 tsp salt

2 dashes of cayenne pepper

1/2 c hot melted butter or margarine

Blend the egg yolks until light and fluffy, then add salt, pepper and lemon juice while still blending. Immediately blend in the hot butter and keep blending until mixture thickens. The lemon juice and hot butter are supposed to kill any bacteria. If in doubt, use pasteurized eggs. *YIELD: 1 to 2 cups*

MOCK HOLLANDAISE

2 T butter

8 T mayonnaise

2 to 4 drops of lemon juice

Fresh ground pepper to taste

Melt butter in double boiler over hot water. Mix with mayo and lemon juice. Add pepper. Beat rapidly.

Serve immediately.

FOR EGG-THICKENED SAUCES:

Cook egg-thickened sauces over low heat, or in a double boiler. Water must NOT touch the double boiler bowl, and must not come to a boil, or else the eggs will curdle. When adding the eggs, temper them with some of the warm liquid first, to ensure emulsification.

SAUCES

MOCK BÉARNAISE SAUCE

2 T tarragon vinegar

1/2 tsp dried tarragon

1/2 c mayonnaise or salad dressing

1 egg yolk

Salt to taste

Pepper to taste

Combine vinegar, tarragon, mayonnaise or salad dressing and egg yolk in top of double boiler. Place over hot, not boiling, water. Beat with wire whisk until mixture has thickened and is warm. Season to taste with salt and pepper. *YIELD: 3/4 cup.*

ME'S BÉARNAISE SAUCE

from Mary Elizabeth Daltroff

2 T minced shallots

3 T fresh chopped chervil, or 1 tsp dried chervil

1/2 tsp fresh crumbled thyme, or a pinch of ground thyme

2 oz dry white wine

2 T tarragon vinegar

1/4 tsp salt

2 or 3 twists of fresh ground black pepper

3 raw egg yolks

1 T cold water

4 oz (1/2 stick) butter, room temperature

1/2 tsp lemon juice

2 or 3 dashes of Tabasco

1 T tarragon

Combine chopped herbs, vinegar, wine, salt and pepper and simmer in a small saucepan until volume is reduced by one-third. Allow to cool ; transfer to a double boiler over hot but not boiling water. Use a whisk to stir in the eggs and water. Continue stirring until sauce begins to thicken. Then whisk in the butter about one tablespoon at a time. Stir in lemon juice and Tabasco last. Strain the sauce and return to the double boiler over heat just high enough to keep warm. Stir in additional fresh chervil and tarragon. If using dried equivalents, allow time for them to reconstitute in the wet mixture. Serve with filet mignon, crab, baked fish or baked chicken. Mom's company essential!

BORDELAISE SAUCE

1 large onion, chopped fine

2 T olive oil

1/2 tsp salt

1/8 tsp black pepper

1/2 c claret or red wine

2 T demi glace (meat essence)

1 T minced fresh parsley

Heat olive oil in small heavy skillet and add onion. Sauté gently until golden, stirring frequently. Add salt and pepper, stir in the wine. Cook gently 4 to 5 minutes. Add the demi glace (meat essence) and blend. Add parsley; serve over sliced meat. *YIELD: 1 cup.*

CHEESE SAUCE

1 egg yolk, beaten

1 c cream

1 tsp all-purpose flour

Dash cayenne pepper

Dash white pepper

1/4 tsp salt

1/4 stick (2 T) butter

1/8 c grated cheese

Put all ingredients except yolks in top of a double boiler over medium flame. Cook until slightly thickened, stirring constantly. Remove from heat and blend in the beaten egg yolks.

COCKTAIL SAUCE

1/2 c ketchup

3 T lemon juice

2 to 3 drops of Tabasco

1/4 tsp salt

1/2 c finely chopped celery

2 tsp Worcestershire sauce

Horseradish to taste

Combine all ingredients and use immediately or store in a jar in the fridge. A simpler version omits the celery and Worcestershire.

> **TIP FOR A SUCCESSFUL SAUCE:**
> Make a paste of the flour and luke-warm water before adding to sauce. This prevents lumps.

CREAM SAUCE

1 T all-purpose flour

   (2 T for medium sauce, 4 T for thick sauce)

1 T butter

   (2 T for medium sauce, 4 T for thick sauce)

1 c hot milk

Salt and pepper to taste

Heat butter and flour over a double boiler on medium flame, stirring, for 1 to 2 minutes. Stir in hot milk, whisking constantly. Add salt and pepper to taste, remove from heat when thickened.

SAUCES BASED ON CREAM SAUCE:

Mornay Sauce: Add equal measurements of grated Parmesan and grated Baby Swiss cheese.

Velouté Sauce: Substitute meat, fowl or fish broth for the milk.

Warm Mustard Sauce: Add 1 tsp dry mustard while cooking.

Fresh Herb Sauce: Add 1 tsp fines herbes while cooking the cream sauce.

CRÈME FRAÎCHE

This delicious European "fresh cream" is made by fermenting heavy cream with the bacteria in buttermilk. Crème fraîche won't curdle when boiled. It makes a great substitute for sour cream and bechamel sauce in dishes, and is delicious with desserts when sweetened.

1 c heavy cream (whipping cream)

2 T buttermilk

Shake ingredients in a clean glass container (I use clean pint canning jars). Cover and let stand at room temperature (60-85°F) for 12 to 24 hours. Mixture will appear very thick and velvety, having fermented. Stir well, cover and refrigerate at least 4 hours before using.

For dessert dishes: Beat in powdered sugar and vanilla extract. Keeps up to 10 days, refrigerated.

CREOLE SAUCE

from Mary Elizabeth Daltroff

Mom got this recipe from a New Orleans Public Service recipe flyer in the 1960s.

1/4 c chopped bell peppers

1/2 c chopped onion

2 stalks celery, chopped

1 clove garlic, minced

2 T butter

Large can of tomatoes

1 tsp chili powder

1/2 tsp white granulated sugar

1 Bay leaf

1 sprig fresh thyme

Salt and pepper to taste

Sauté bell pepper, onion, celery and garlic in butter. Add tomatoes and seasonings. Simmer 40 minutes, stirring frequently to prevent scorching. This is a basic sauce for many Creole dishes such as baked fish, shrimp, or veggies. *YIELD: 2-1/2 cups.*

DILL SAUCE

2/3 c melted clarified butter

2 T water

3 egg yolks

1/4 tsp salt

1/4 tsp white pepper

1 tsp lemon juice

2 tsp chopped fresh dill

1/4 c lightly whipped heavy cream

In a skillet, melt butter, and then skim froth from surface of melted butter and discard. Allow butter to cool slightly.

In a double boiler or bowl, whisk water and egg yolks together with salt and pepper for 30 seconds or until pale yellow and frothy.

Over barely simmering water, whisk mixture for 3 minutes or until it draws a ribbon for 5 seconds. Remove pan from heat, whisk in warm butter, 1 tbsp at a time, until sauce begins to thicken. Still whisking, pour remaining butter into sauce in a slow, steady stream. Stir in lemon juice and dill. Remove from heat, cool slightly. Gently fold in whipped cream. Adjust seasoning to taste. Keep warm by setting over a pot of warm water.

DRAWN (CLARIFIED) BUTTER

Drawn butter is called for when making many sauces, as a specialized baking ingredient, and as a dip for pieces of cooked lobster, shrimp, or crab.

1/4 c butter (1/2 stick)

You may start with any quantity of butter. Melt butter over low heat. When completely melted, remove from the heat, let stand for a few minutes, allowing the milk solids to settle to the bottom. Skim the clear butter fat from the top and place in a container. This is clarified butter, ready to use.

HORSERADISH SAUCE

1/2 c heavy sour cream

1 T tarragon vinegar

1/4 tsp salt

1/8 tsp white pepper

2 T freshly grated horseradish, well drained

Chopped chives

Tabasco, if desired

Combine all ingredients and chill. Serve cold with roast beef or prime rib.

HENRY BAIN SAUCE

This sauce is a spicy, sweet-and-sour salsa for strong meats. Developed by Henry Bain, who became the Louisville, KY, Pendennis Club maitre d' in 1881, the new beef sauce was an instant hit at the all-male club. Members also found it worked perfectly to tone down the gamey taste in their hunting spoils. Dad absolutely loved it.

17-oz jar Major Grey's chutney or peach chutney *(see recipe, page 83)*

1/2 of 9-oz jar of imported pickled walnuts, OPTIONAL

14-oz bottle of ketchup

11-oz bottle of A-1 Steak Sauce

10-oz bottle Worcestershire sauce

12-oz bottle Heinz Chili Sauce (or homemade like my grandmother's)

Tabasco or other Louisiana-style hot sauce, to taste

Fresh watercress, chopped fine, OPTIONAL

Use chopper to chop pickled walnuts. Mix with chutney, or puree if desired. Add other ingredients and stir well. Season to taste with Tabasco. Be heavy handed. *YIELD: About 9 cups.*

SAUCES & SEASONINGS

HOT PEPPER SAUCE

3 dozen large hot chili peppers

1 clove garlic

1/2 c spiced vinegar *(see recipe, page 173)*

Chop peppers (do not remove seeds) and chop garlic. Combine in small saucepan with just enough water to cover. Simmer until water has cooked almost away.

Press peppers and garlic through a fine sieve to remove seeds and stem parts. Add spiced vinegar, as needed, to bring puree to a thin creamy consistency. Bottle, cork and use as needed.

This pepper sauce is much more intense than the simple pepper sauce below. Both are great on greens.

SIMPLE PEPPER SAUCE VARIATION: Fill a cruet with cayenne or tabasco peppers. Add vinegar to top of bottle. Steep overnight. Voila! Add more vinegar as needed. The peppers stay good for a long time.

JEZEBEL SAUCE

The sauce name is a tongue-in-cheek reference to its lingering, piquant qualities. Like Queen Jezebel, who misled her husband, King Ahab of Israel, not a drop remains once our bold Jezebel is thrown to the dogs. The quantities of ingredients and "heat" can vary according to taste.

10-oz or 15-to-18-oz jar pineapple preserves

10-oz or 16-to-18-oz jar apple jelly

5 or 8 oz (around 1/2 c) fresh horseradish

2 or 3 T dry mustard (Dijon may be substituted)

1 to 2 tsp coarse ground black pepper (may substitute 1/4 tsp cayenne pepper)

Combine all ingredients, using whisk or processor. Put in clean airtight jars; store in fridge up to 2 weeks. Use as a dip with cream cheese and crackers, or as a sauce or side with pork or chicken. *YIELD: 4 to 6 cups.*

MADEIRA SAUCE

2 T butter

1 c leftover meat gravy

1/2 c sour cream

1 c fresh cream

1/4 Madeira wine

Sliced leftover veal, beef or lamb

Brown butter in skillet. Add remaining ingredients and pour over meat, either hot or cold.

KAYSEE SMITH'S MUSTARD SAUCE

Kaysee and Ed Smith were our neighbors in Memphis for more than 15 years, starting at the apartments near the old Fairgrounds in Midtown shortly after my birth. Their son Preston was born three days after me, and their daughter Marsha was born the same year as my brother Andy. When I was four, our families moved to the same neighborhood in East Memphis, and Ed served as Dad's lawyer until Dad's death. Kaysee came from Chicago, but we forgave her.

2 T dry mustard

1/2 c granulated sugar

2 eggs, beaten

1/2 c cream

1/2 c white distilled vinegar

Butter the size of an egg

SIZE OF AN EGG: My measuring indicates the size of an egg is equivalent to 3-1/2 to 4 T butter (almost half a stick).

Mix mustard and sugar, add rest of ingredients. Cook in saucepan until gently boiling, stirring constantly. Cool and use.

CLASSIC MINT SAUCE

There's nothing more classic than mint sauce with lamb.

1 c of lamb or veal drippings

1 T white distilled vinegar

1/4 c currant jelly

2 T fresh chopped mint

Cook drippings, vinegar and jelly together until jelly is melted, stirring with a whisk. Add fresh mint, finely chopped, just before serving.

SIMPLE VERSION

1-1/2 T confectioners sugar

3 T heated water

1/3 c fine-chopped mint leaves

1/2 c apple cider vinegar

Dissolve confectioners sugar in heated water. Cool, then whisk in the mint and vinegar. Serve immediately.

MISSISSIPPI COMEBACK SAUCE

Sometimes called Cumback or Kumback Sauce, this is the Magnolia State's answer to Remoulade, chili sauce and plain ol' ketchup. Serve with french fries, seafood, or as a dip or salad dressing.

1 c mayonnaise

1/4 to 1/2 c chili sauce

1/4 to 1/2 c ketchup

1/4 to 1/2 c vegetable oil

1 to 2 tsp prepared mustard (or 2 to 4 tsp dry mustard)

1 tsp to 1 T Worcestershire sauce

1 tsp to 1 T black pepper

2 cloves garlic, minced

1 onion, grated or minced

Juice of 1 lemon, OPTIONAL

1-2 T water to thin sauce, as needed

Dash paprika, OPTIONAL

Dash of Tabasco, OPTIONAL

Dash of cayenne pepper, OPTIONAL

Combine first three ingredients (to achieve a salmon-on-pink color). Adjust other ingredients to cook's personal taste. Puree ingredients in a blender. Refrigerate. *YIELD: About 2 cups.*

PESTO SAUCE

I fell in love with homemade pesto when my friend and academic advisor, Ray Pierotti, made it for a dinner.

2 large cloves of garlic

2 c packed fresh basil leaves

2/3 c grated Parmesan cheese

2/3 c chopped walnuts or pine nuts

1/4 c olive oil

In a food processor, process garlic until minced. Add basil, cheese and nuts; process until completely ground. Slowly add olive oil. Continue processing until mixture is a thick paste. Pesto may be refrigerated in an airtight container for up to 1 month. *YIELD: 2 cups.*

HINT: Be conservative when adding oregano, sage, cayenne, cilantro, tarragon, nutmeg, or ginger to a recipe. Tiny amounts of these spices can overpower other ingredients.

MOM'S REMOULADE SAUCE

from Mary Elizabeth Daltroff

This is the "white remoulade" version that was commonly used in Memphis during my childhood. I prefer the spicy version.

3 to 4 T fresh parsley, chopped fine

3 to 4 T kosher dill pickle, chopped fine

1 hard-cooked egg, chopped fine

3 to 4 T dry mustard

1 medium onion, grated

Juice of 1 lemon

Garlic salt to taste

1 pt mayonnaise

Grate onion on paper towel and let it stand until moisture is absorbed. Add to mayonnaise with remaining ingredients. If too thick, add juice from jar of dill pickles. Serve cold with seafood.

REMOULADE DRESSING: Combine 1/3 c Remoulade Sauce, 1/2 c ketchup, and 1 hard-cooked egg cut into coarse pieces. Serve over wedge lettuce.

SPICY REMOULADE SAUCE

2 c mayonnaise

2 T Creole mustard

3 T horseradish

1/4 tsp salt

1/4 tsp white or black pepper, to taste

1/4 tsp cayenne pepper

1 clove garlic, minced

1 T lemon juice

1 T white wine

Dash of Tabasco

1 c ketchup

2 T fine diced onion

2 T minced celery leaves

Combine first 11 ingredients in blender. Puree. Add in onion and celery. Tastes fantastic on shrimp, salmon and crab cakes, or fried green tomatoes. Store, refrigerated, in a covered canning jar for up to a week. *YIELD: About 3-1/2 cups.*

SPICED VINEGAR

1 qt white wine vinegar

1 tsp whole cloves

1 tsp whole allspice

1 tsp brown mustard seeds

1 blade mace

1 T granulated sugar

1 tsp salt

2 T brandy

Combine all ingredients in a crock or jar, cover tightly and let stand 3 weeks, stirring from time to time. At the end of that time period, strain and store the vinegar in a covered jar or condiment bottle. Use as needed.

LEMON-LIME AND SOY MARINADE

1 c lemon-lime carbonated soft drink such as Sierra Mist, Wink, or SunDrop (do NOT use diet versions)

1 T light brown sugar

3 T soy sauce

2 T olive oil

1 T Worcestershire sauce

2 cloves of garlic, pressed

3/4 tsp ground ginger

1/8 tsp ground cloves

Whisk together the soft drink and remaining ingredients until thoroughly blended. Use immediately as a marinade or basting "mop" on pork. Works great on pork loin roast. *YIELD: About 1-1/3 cups.*

WHAT IS A COULIS?

Pronounced koo-LEE. This French term traditionally refers to a thick sauce that is derived all or mostly from pureed fruits or vegetables. Example: cooked blackberry coulis. We Southerners call it Sauce! The term also refers to thick bisque sauce made from shellfish such as lobster, crawfish, or other crustaceans.

SWEET AND SOUR SAUCE

1/4 c brown sugar

1/4 c white wine vinegar

1/4 c ketchup

1 c water

1/4 c soy sauce

2 T cornstarch

3 T water

1 small green pepper, chopped fine

1/4 c canned crushed pineapple, drained

In a small saucepan, bring sugar, vinegar, ketchup, water and soy sauce to a boil. In a small bowl, mix cornstarch with water. Add to sauce. Bring sauce to a boil, stirring until smooth and thick. Stir in green pepper and pineapple. Serve with wontons, roast pork, or chicken. *YIELD: 3 cups.*

LOUISE'S TARTAR SAUCE

from Louise Triplette

1 c mayonnaise

2 T sweet pickle relish

1 T chopped white or yellow onion

1 T minced parsley

1 T chopped pimiento

Combine ingredients in the order listed. Chill. *YIELD: 1-1/4 cup.*

DOT'S ALABAMA TARTAR SAUCE

from Mary Elizabeth Daltroff

1 c mayonnaise

2 T dill pickle relish

2 T drained capers

2 T chopped fresh chives

1 T chopped fresh tarragon

1 T Dijon mustard

2 tsp fresh lemon juice

1/4 tsp black pepper

Stir together ingredients until blended. Cover and chill until ready to serve. *YIELD: 1-1/2 cup.*

TOMATO SAUCE

3 c chopped yellow onion

3 large cloves garlic, chopped fine or minced

1/3 c olive oil

2 c canned Italian tomatoes, OR 1 lb fresh Roma
tomatoes, blanched, peeled and crushed

Two 6-oz cans tomato paste

6 c water

2 bay leaves

1 tsp oregano

10 to 12 leaves fresh basil (or 1/2 tsp dried basil)

1-1/2 tsp salt

Fresh ground black pepper

Sauté onion and garlic in oil until onion is browned. Add tomatoes, paste, water, and Bay leaves. Simmer partly covered for 1 hour, stirring frequently. Add spices, continue cooking; stirring until sauce thickens, about 1 hour. Ladle into hot sterilized jars, seal; process in hot water canning bath, OR use fresh and store covered in fridge up to 3 weeks. *YIELD: About 9 cups.*

SEASONINGS

BOUQUET GARNI

3 sprigs parsley or chervil

Bay leaf

2 sprigs fresh thyme

1 leek, white portion only

2 cloves

1 to 2 leafy celery center ribs

Marjoram, OPTIONAL

1 sprig tarragon, OPTIONAL

A bouquet garni is a spray of fresh herbs tied together with kitchen string. Combine various herbs to suit the dish. One should position the larger items around the smaller items, in a tube-like roll formed by herb leaves. The bouqet garni is used as seasoning in a soup, stew or sauce during cooking. It must be removed before serving the dish. NOTE: Feel free to use other herbs than those listed here.

> **HINT:** Tabasco and other hot pepper sauces impart a vinegary spice flavor. Always start with one dash, taste the dish before adding more.

CHINESE FIVE-SPICE POWDER

2 T black peppercorns

3 star anise

2 tsp fennel seeds

2-to-3-inch cinnamon sticks, broken into small pieces

6 whole cloves

In a small, heavy dry skillet, toast peppercorns over medium heat until they become fragrant, about 1 to 2 minutes. Shake pan often to prevent burning. Remove to a bowl. Repeat toasting process separately with star anise, fennel seeds, cinnamon, and cloves.

Pour all of the toasted spices into a spice grinder (or clean coffee grinder) and grind to a fine powder. Let rest in the grinder for 1 minute, then transfer to a glass container and tighten lid. Store in a cool, dark place up to one month. *YIELD: About 1/4 cup.*

CREOLE SEASONING

Tony Chachere's Cajun Creole Seasoning is a store-bought version of this seasoning.

1/3 c salt

1/4 c granulated garlic

1/4 c fresh ground black pepper

2 tsp cayenne pepper

2 T ground thyme

2 T crushed oregano

1/3 c paprika

3 T minced dried onion or onion powder

Combine the ingredients, mixing thoroughly. Pour the mixture into a large glass jar and seal airtight. Keeps indefinitely. *YIELD: 2 cups.*

DUXELLES

1/2 lb mushrooms, chopped fine

1/4 c chopped onion or 2 T chopped shallots

2 T butter

3 T olive oil

1/4 tsp grated nutmeg

Duxelles is an intense mushroom seasoning for fish and meat dishes, stuffings, sauces and gravies. Squeeze mushrooms in paper towel to remove all possible liquid. Sauté onions in the butter and olive oil, until golden. Add mushrooms and grated nutmeg. Sauté on high until mushroom mixture is absorbed. Keep in covered jar, refrigerated, until ready to use.

FINES HERBES

This delicate blend of fresh herbs is for use in savory sauces, soups, all-cheese, and non-sweet egg dishes.

EQUAL MEASUREMENTS:

Fresh parsley

Fresh tarragon

Fresh chives

Fresh chervil

Mince the herbs together with a sharp knife, and add at the last minute to the cooking food. This retains and imparts the herbs' essential oils.

HERBES DE PROVENCE

Herbes de Provence, named for its French origin, may be added to stews, soups and cassoulets. Tastes best on roast fowl.

2 T dried savory

1 T crushed dried rosemary

2 T dried thyme leaves

1 T dried basil

2 T dried marjoram

1/2 tsp dried fennel seed

1 tsp dried sage

2 T dried, crushed lavender, OPTIONAL

2 T dried oregano, OPTIONAL

Combine all ingredients together in small mixing bowl and crush together. Spoon into a tightly lidded jar, and store in a cool, dark place up to 4 months. To season chicken, combine 1 to 2 T Herbes de Provence with olive oil, and rub over the bird before roasting.

MARTHA'S CHIMICHURRI RUB

from Martha Kroslak

This mixture originated in Argentina. Martha, a dear Argentinian-born friend in Charlotte, was a terrific and enthusiastic cook. Martha said dried herb leaves work better for this recipe than powdered or fresh.

3 T dried oregano leaves

3 T dried basil leaves

2 T dried parsley leaves

2 T dried thyme leaves

2 T kosher salt

1 T ground black pepper

1 T dried savory leaves

1 T smoked Spanish paprika

2 tsp garlic powder

1 to 2 tsp crushed red pepper flakes

Whisk all spices together in medium bowl. Transfer to airtight container. Use as a dry rub on beef or pork before roasting, or as a marinade sauce for grilled meats, especially for chicken.

MARINADE SAUCE: Whisk 1/4 c dry chimichurri rub with 1/2 c olive oil and 3 T red wine vinegar. Use as a mop when basting meat on the grill.

SOUTHWEST SEASONING

This seasoning works well on grilled beef, chicken and turkey. Serve the roasted meat with pico de gallo or a salad consisting of greens, sliced avocado, Serrano peppers and tomatoes. Chef Emeril Lagasse has developed his own packaged version, which has become as "necessary" as Tony's and Tabasco for Southern cooks.

2 T chili powder

2 T ground cumin

2 T paprika

1 tsp black pepper

1 T ground coriander

1/2 tsp cayenne pepper

1 T garlic powder

1-1/2 tsp crushed red pepper, OPTIONAL

1 T kosher salt, crushed

Combine all ingredients thoroughly. Store sealed in a jar in the fridge. *YIELD: 1/2 cup.*

TOPPINGS

SAUTÉED MUSHROOMS

1 lb fresh button mushrooms, chopped or sliced

Salt and ground black pepper

6 T butter

1 large white onion, chopped fine

1 clove garlic, crushed

1 tsp fine chopped parsley

Heat 4 T butter in skillet. Add mushrooms and cook until golden. Season with salt and pepper to taste. Remove mushrooms from pan, and add remaining butter to pan. Melt, and add onion, garlic and parsley; cook, stirring, about 2 minutes on high heat. Do not let get brown. Return mushrooms to pan, lower heat to medium, stir well until blended. Serve over beef or on toast points. *YIELD: 3 servings.*

Sautéed mushrooms are the perfect topping for filet mignon or a good hamburger.

CARAMELIZED VIDALIA ONIONS

These onions are to be used as topping on steak or hamburgers, mixed in with mashed potatoes, or as a garnish.

2 to 3 large or 4 to 5 medium-sized Vidalia onions

Three or four 8-oz bottles of cola soft drink

2 to 4 tsp liquid steak seasoning, to taste

Cut whole Vidalia onions vertically into wedges around 3/4-inch wide. Spread evenly in a 9-by-13-inch baking dish for oven-baking, or a 3-qt microwaveable casserole dish for microwaving.. Pour cola over the cut onions, adding more cola if necessary to cover all in the dish. Mix the steak seasoning into the liquid. Stir once to blend.

Place in preheated oven set to 400°F and bake about 1 hr to 1-1/2 hr; OR place in microwave covered with waxed paper, and cook for 20 minutes on high, or 30 minutes on medium setting. The coke should condense during cooking and the onions will turn dark as they absorb the sugar and cola. Cook longer if needed. Serve over Salisbury Steak, hamburgers, roast beef, or pork loin.

CROUTONS

Bread slices (Italian, French or loaf bread)

Butter

Parmesan cheese

Seasoned salt

Italian seasoning

Butter slices of bread. Sprinkle Parmesan over the bread, then seasoned salt, then Italian seasoning. Freeze slightly to make cutting easier. Cut into cubes and put into a pan, one layer thick. Preheat oven to 350°F. Turn oven off once heated. Place pan of bread cubes in oven. Allow to remain overnight. Place in airtight container the next morning. Keep indefinitely.

PLAIN CROUTONS VARIATION: Cut leftover bread crusts into cubes. Spread out in pan and bake on low heat, about 200°F for several hours. Cool, store in airtight container. These plain croutons crush well to make bread crumbs.

THE RECIPES

PIES, FRUITS & DESSERT

BAKLAVA

Baklava has become synonymous with Greek festivals around the United States. Our communities can't get enough of the fare. Even Costco and Sam's Club sell it in decorative gift boxes during the Christian holidays. But the best comes from the kitchens of our Southern Greek Orthodox neighbors, who became culinary lynchpins in most Southern communities during the past hundred years.

Today, most of the larger cities across the South offer annual Greek festivals featuring baklava and other Greek foods. New Orleans' Greek festival, Boon on the Bayou, was started in 1973 by Holy Trinity Cathedral, the oldest Greek Orthodox church in America. St. Paul's in Savannah, GA, has been offering baklava, spanikopita, and other Greek delicacies since 1951. The Memphis Greek Fest began

PHOTO: Courtesy of Angelo Politis, Holy Trinity Cathedral, Charlotte, NC

in 1958. Houston's Greek Fest was started in 1966, Richmond's in 1976, and Charlotte's Yiasou Greek Festival in 1978.

According to some scholars, baklava dates to the ancient Assyrians around the 8th century BCE. Many ethnic groups in the Middle East claim some authorship for baklava, which was carried back to Athens by Greek seamen returning from Mesopotamia. We have the Greeks to thank for inventing phyllo, the paper-thin dough used in today's baklava. The word phyllo in Greek means "leaf," referring to the thinness of the dough. The Turks, to this day, refer to baklava as a food for the rich. It's certainly rich in sweetness. The caloric content only runs about 55 calories per cubic inch, up to 335 calories for a wedge.

BAKLAVA RECIPE

16-oz pkg frozen phyllo dough, thawed in fridge

1 c (2 sticks) butter

1 lb chopped nuts (walnuts, almonds, or pistachios—or a walnut combination)

1 tsp ground cinnamon

1/2 c white granulated sugar

1 c water

3/4 c white granulated sugar

1 T lemon juice

1 tsp vanilla extract

1/2 c honey

1 cinnamon stick, broken into 3 pieces, OPTIONAL

Thaw phyllo dough according to package instructions, keeping sheets from sticking together. When ready to use, cover the dough with a clean, damp dish towel to maintain moisture, or the dough will dry out. Preheat oven to 350°F (as low as 300°F for a fast oven). Grease or butter bottom and sides of a 10-by-15-by-1-inch pan. Chop nuts, mix with cinnamon and 1/2 cup sugar in bowl. Melt butter in separate dish. Begin to layer 6 to 8 whole phyllo leaves or 12 to 16 half-leaves in the pan, brushing melted butter over the tops and allowing the edges to extend over the side. Sprinkle about 1 cup of the chopped nut mixture evenly over

the top, then begin layering again, this time with two buttered sheets topped by nuts until you have about 8 additional layers of phyllo and 4 additional layers of nuts. Many cooks prefer to add additional phyllo layers above the nuts. Don't forget to butter the top of the uppermost layer of dough. NOTE: Some cooks cut these top sheets in half and overlap them slightly to stagger the sheets' edges from corner to corner so the corners don't elevate above the middle.

Trim away any overhanging edges. Cut the prepared pastry into 2-inch diamonds (by cutting on a diagonal in the pan), using a sharp knife to cut down through the pastry. Again there's an option: Some cooks cut all the way through, and some only halfway down to the bottom, depending on whether they prefer the honey syrup to pool at the bottom.

Place a pan of water on the bottom rack below the rack of baklava. Bake for 50-60 minutes, until golden brown. While baking, prepare the honey syrup by boiling remaining sugar, lemon juice, cinnamon stick, and water about 15-20 minutes. Remove from heat, remove cinnamon stick; add vanilla and honey. Let cool while the baklava is baking, then pour evenly over the baked hot pastry. The syrup will penetrate the many layers. (NOTE: Some cooks boil the honey in the syrup from the start, and pour hot syrup over cooled baklava pastry.) Let pastry sit out to cool at least 2 hours, then re-cut in the pan. Loosely cover; let sit at room temperature 8 to 24 hours (not refrigerated). Serve in cupcake papers. Will keep about three weeks.

PHOTO, previous page: Gianna McCloud on her first birthday

BANANAS FOSTER

Mom and Dad always indulged at Brennan's when visiting the Big Easy. Everyone west of the Smokies and south of Chicago knows that this truly flamboyant dessert was created in 1951 at Brennan's in New Orleans by Chef Paul Blangé, and named for the crime commissioner, Richard Foster, a friend of Owen Brennan, the owner. The recipe below serves four.

1/2 stick butter (1/4 c)

1 c brown sugar

1/2 tsp cinnamon

1/4 c banana liqueur

4 bananas, sliced lengthwise, then halved

1/4 c dark rum

4 scoops vanilla ice cream

Combine butter, sugar and cinnamon in chafing dish or skillet. Place pan over low heat on alcohol burner or stovetop; cook, stirring, until sugar dissolves. Stir in liqueur. Place bananas in pan. As bananas begin to brown, carefully add rum. Continue cooking until rum is hot, then slightly tip pan to ignite rum. Lift bananas from pan when flames subside; place 4 pieces over each ice cream scoop. Spoon warm sauce over top. Serve immediately. SINGLE SERVING: 1 T butter, 2 T brown sugar, 1 banana, Dash of cinnamon, 1/2 oz banana liqueur, 1 oz rum, 1 scoop ice cream.

AUNT SHEILA'S CREAM PUFFS

from Rita Davidson Friend

My paternal grandmother, Eula May Daltroff, would make cream puffs for Papa, whenever he was out of sorts. After Eula May went into the Arkansas Tuberculosis Sanatorium in Booneville, Aunt Sheila learned to make them, first for Papa, then for her own family. They remain one of Cousin Rita's favorite dishes.

1 c water

1 stick butter

1 c all-purpose flour

4 eggs

Bring water and butter to boil. Add 1 c flour. Cook, stirring until it makes a ball. Remove from heat, cool. Add eggs, one at a time. Beat well. Place about 2 T onto ungreased pan 2 inches apart. Bake at 400°F for 35-40 minutes. Remove from oven, cool slightly, then cut off tops (like little hats, Aunt Sheila always said). Use teaspoon to scrape out any soft insides. Let tops and bottoms cool completely.

FILLING:

1-1/2 c whole milk

1/2 c evaporated milk

1/3 c flour

3/4 c white granulated sugar

2 eggs

1 tsp vanilla extract

Combine in saucepan. Cook until thick. Spoon filling into bottoms of pastries and place "top hat" over the filling.

Rita Davidson Friend prepares old-fashioned cream puffs the way her mother, Sheila Daltroff Davidson, taught her. She says the pearls and apron are essential accessories for baking the recipe.

CUSTARDS/ICE CREAMS

BOILED CUSTARD

from Ruby White Thurmond

Aunt Ruth Thurmond gave me Grandmother's origi-nal recipe, as recorded on site by my mother, Mary Elizabeth. There are many versions of this favorite treat that crossed the mountains from Virginia during west-ern settlement. Ours may be heavyweight, but ummm.

1 qt whole milk, scalded

6 eggs

2 c white granulated sugar

1 T vanilla extract

Beat eggs until thick. Add sugar, then gradually add scalded milk, stirring constantly. Place in sauce pan or double boiler and cook over low heat, stirring constantly, until mixture coats pan. Add vanilla and stir well. Refrigerate. FOR ICE CREAM: Add 1-1/2 qts of X cream (light half and half cream) and 1 pt XX cream (heavy whipping cream).

CARAMEL CUSTARD

from Ruby White Thurmond

1/2 c white granulated sugar

2 egg yolks

1 large egg

14-oz can sweetened condensed milk (I use fat-free)

12-oz can evaporated milk (I use fat-free)

3 oz cream cheese, softened (I use low-fat)

1 T vanilla extract

Cook sugar in an 8-inch round cake pan with 2-inch sides over medium heat, shaking pan occa-sionally, 5 minutes or until sugar melts and turns light golden brown. Remove pan from heat and let stand for 5 minutes. Sugar will harden. Process egg yolks and next 5 ingredients in a blender until smooth. Pour mixture over caramelized sugar in pan. Cover mixture with aluminum foil. Place cake pan in a broiler pan. Add hot water (150°F) to pan to dept of about 2/3 inch. Bake at 350°F for 1 hour or until knife inserted in cen-ter of custard comes out clean. Remove cake pan from water bath. Cool completely on a wire rack. Cover and chill at least 3 hours. Run knife around edge of pan to loosen; invert onto a serving plate with raised sides. The caramelized sugar will be a lovely glaze on top, like flan. *YIELD: 10 servings.*

CRÈME BRÛLÉE

2 c heavy whipping cream

4 well beaten eggs

2 T white granulated sugar

Light brown sugar

Heat the whipping cream in a double boiler mak-ing sure the water underneath does not touch the top bowl. When the whipping cream is hot but not boiling, pour it slowly over the 4 beaten eggs, beating constantly with a hand mixer while pouring. Return the mixture to the double boiler and stir in the 2 T of sugar. Heat until the eggs thicken and form a custard consistency, coating the spoon heavily. Remove from heat and immediately place the mixture in greased custard cups. Chill well, at least 4 hours.

When ready to serve, cover the chilled custard with a half-inch of light brown sugar. If the custard has been chilled for at least 12 hours, place the cups in a shallow pan, put the pan in a cold oven, and turn on the oven to 250°F, heating until the sugar on top caramelizes. If the custard hasn't been chilled for at least 12 hours, surround the custard cups with ice in the shallow pan, and put the pan under a hot broiler just long enough to melt the sugar.

NOTE: The easiest way to caramelize the sugar is to use a hand-held cooking blowtorch, of the variety available at a housewares specialty store. It's the most fun to torch the tops of the custard cups and watch the sugar caramelize instantly.

PUMPKIN FLAN

This is an easy and delicious autumn dessert.

1/2 c white granulated sugar

8 large eggs

2/3 c white granulated sugar

1/4 tsp salt

Two 12- to 13-oz cans of evaporated milk

2 tsp vanilla extract

1 c canned pumpkin

Heat oven to 350°F. In a heavy saucepan heat 1/2-cup sugar over medium heat until melted (caramelized) and golden brown. Pour into a 9-by-5-by-3-inch loaf pan. Whisk together the eggs, 2/3 cup sugar, salt, evaporated milk, vanilla and pumpkin just until blended, but not frothy. Carefully ladle the pumpkin mixture into the pan over the caramel layer. Set the pan into a larger shallow baking or roasting pan. Pour boiling or very hot water into the large pan so the level of water is 1 inch up the sides of the loaf pan. Bake for 1 hour or until a knife inserted into the center comes out clean. Cook on a wire rack.

Chill until cold. Just before serving, run a metal spatula around the edge of the flan to loosen from the sides. Place inverted plate over the flan and while holding both pans, carefully turn plate upright. The caramel should form a sauce dripping down the sides of the overturned flan. *YIELD: 8 sliced servings.*

PLAIN FLAN VARIATION: Caramelize 1/2 c sugar. Combine 3 whole eggs plus 3 additional yolks, pinch salt, 1 can sweetened condensed milk, 1 c whole milk, 1 tsp vanilla, 1/2 tsp almond extract. Add favorite liqueur if desired. Follow baking instruction above.

CHOCOLATE ICE CREAM

This is an old Delta recipe passed along throughout the region.

1-1/3 c sweetened condensed milk

Two 1-oz squares of unsweetened chocolate

2 c light cream (half and half cream)

1 c cold water

1 T vanilla extract

Combine the unsweetened chocolate in sweetened condensed milk in top of a double boiler, and cook, stirring frequently until thickened. In a large bowl, combine all ingredients, blend well, and refrigerate until well chilled. Pour into either a hand or electric ice cream freezer and freeze according to the ice cream freezer directions. *YIELD: About 1-1/4 quarts.*

ORANGE SHERBET

from Mary Elizabeth Daltroff

Mom loved sherbet; we children loved Orange Crush.

6 Orange Crush soft drinks

12- to 13-oz can of evaporated milk

20-oz can of crushed pineapple

10-oz bottle of maraschino cherries

Blend everything together and freeze.

PEACH ICE CREAM

1 c white granulated sugar

4 c fresh peaches, peeled, finely chopped

5 eggs, beaten

1-1/4 c white granulated sugar

1/2 tsp salt

1 qt whole milk

12- to 13-oz can of evaporated milk or 1 pt heavy cream

1 tsp almond extract

2 tsp vanilla extract

Pour first sugar over peaches. Mash a bit. Blend eggs, second sugar, salt, and milk in saucepan, cook slowly, whisking until slightly thickened. Cool. Combine with peaches, cream, and extracts, refrigerate overnight; freeze in churn. *YIELD: 1 gallon.*

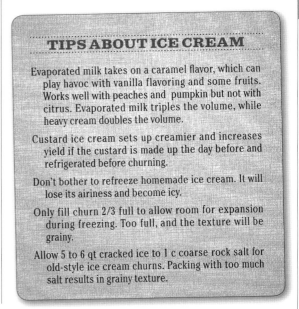

TIPS ABOUT ICE CREAM

Evaporated milk takes on a caramel flavor, which can play havoc with vanilla flavoring and some fruits. Works well with peaches and pumpkin but not with citrus. Evaporated milk triples the volume, while heavy cream doubles the volume.

Custard ice cream sets up creamier and increases yield if the custard is made up the day before and refrigerated before churning.

Don't bother to refreeze homemade ice cream. It will lose its airiness and become icy.

Only fill churn 2/3 full to allow room for expansion during freezing. Too full, and the texture will be grainy.

Allow 5 to 6 qt cracked ice to 1 c coarse rock salt for old-style ice cream churns. Packing with too much salt results in grainy texture.

PINEAPPLE ICE CREAM

from Ruby White Thurmond

2 c dairy sour cream

Two 14- to 15-oz cans of sweetened, condensed milk

4 c whole milk

2-1/2 c (# 2 can) crushed pineapple

Combine sour cream and sweetened condensed milk. Add the milk and stir well. Pour into gallon freezer can and churn it to freeze, using 6 parts ice to 1 part ice cream salt until mixture is partially frozen. At this point add pineapple, undrained. Freeze until firm.

RASPBERRY SORBET

I love raspberries in any form. As an alcohol-infused ice, they're delicious.

1 c white granulated sugar

16 oz fresh raspberries

2 T lemon juice

2 T raspberry liqueur such as Chambord

2 egg whites

Make a sugar syrup by combining 1 c sugar and 1 c water in a saucepan. Bring to a boil and simmer for 1 minute. Cool. Puree raspberries, lemon juice and liqueur in a food processor. Press through a sieve to remove seeds. Beat egg whites with a fork and add to the puree along with sugar syrup. Freeze in ice cream maker according to directions. Place in airtight container in coldest part of freezer to firm.

VANILLA CUSTARD ICE CREAM

from Butch Daltroff

2 c white granulated sugar

4 T all-purpose flour

1/4 tsp salt

3 c whole milk

4 eggs, well beaten

3 pt light cream (half and half cream)

6 to 8 tsp vanilla extract

Mix sugar and flour. Add salt, then milk. Cook in double boiler about 10 minutes, stirring constantly. Add some cooked mixture to the beaten eggs; whisk egg mixture into double boiler. Cook, whisking, for additional 2 to 3 minutes, until thickened. Remove from heat; cool 10 minutes. Add cream and vanilla; mix well. Cool. Pour into 1-gallon ice cream maker. Add additional milk if needed to fill the freezer can to within 3 inches of top. Freeze according to ice cream maker directions. *YIELD: 1 gallon.*

VELVET HAMMER

My parents' generation specialized in lengthy dinners followed by after-dinner liqueurs savored with cigarettes and cigars (it WAS a different, less enlightened time in some ways). This dessert combines ice cream and booze, and should be used as a substitute for after-dinner liqueurs. Serve with coffee, or expresso and benne wafers.

1 pt vanilla ice cream

2 jiggers B&B brandy

1 jigger Cointreau

1 jigger white crème de cacao

Blend all ingredients in a blender. Pour into parfait glasses. Freeze. To serve, top with a dollop of whipped cream and shaved chocolate. Yum! *YIELD: 4 servings.*

HINT FOR MELTING CHOCOLATE:
Never try to melt large bars or blocks; always chop into small, even pieces. Melt slowly over low heat, stirring frequently with rubber spatula. If using a microwave, melt on low (50% power) in 30-second increments, stirring, to avoid scorching or burning. If using a double boiler, make sure the chocolate bowl does not touch the water. Avoid all water contact, for even a few drops of water will render the chocolate unworkable. Same goes with cold liquids. If melting chocolate with liquid, use at least 1 T for every 2 oz of chocolate to prevent binding and lumping.

PIES, FRUITS & DESSERT

FRUIT AND FLUFFINESS

CHOCOLATE LOVERS SOUFFLÉ

My version is for die-hard chocoholics. If left in the oven too long before serving, it becomes grainy, but is still fabulous—if you like really sweet and really chocolate!

2 T whipping cream

1 generous c semi-sweet chocolate chips

6 egg yolks

1 c white granulated sugar

6 egg whites

Dash of salt

Melt chocolate chips and cream in saucepan on low (takes only a few minutes). Stir to blend and gather all the chocolate from pan sides; set aside. Beat egg yolks with sugar until light lemon colored. Use hand mixer to combine cooling chocolate and yolks. In chilled bowl, beat egg whites and salt until stiff. Fold into chocolate mixture, turning vigorously until blended. Pour into greased (cooking spray) 3-qt casserole dish. Place in a 9-by-13-inch pan containing 1-1/2 inch of hot water. Bake 1 hour in preheated oven set at 325°F. (May require a few extra minutes.) Turn oven off. Serve within 30 minutes—plain, or with whipped cream and tart berries. *YIELD: 6 to 8 servings.*

FLOATING ISLAND

from Ruby White Thurmond

1 pt whipping cream

1/2 c white granulated sugar

Pinch of salt

1/8 tsp vanilla extract

Angel food or sponge cake, or yellow cake

1 c tart jelly such as quince

1 qt boiled custard (*see recipe, page 180*)

Sprinkle of ground nutmeg

Whip the cream with the pinch of salt and sugar until it forms stiff peaks; whip in the vanilla. Refrigerate. Break the cake into large pieces into a large crystal or china bowl such as a punch bowl. Spread jelly over the cake pieces. Pour boiled custard over the jelly-covered cake. Spread whipped cream over the custard. Sprinkle with nutmeg. Cover and refrigerate at least 2 to 3 hours before serving in sherbet goblets or small fruit bowls. *YIELD: 10-15 servings.*

JILL'S CHERRY YUM YUM

from Jill Benfield

Jill brought many gifts to the family when she married Kurt. Her Cherry Yum Yum is one of them!

1/2 c sugar

Two 1.3-oz envelopes of Dream Whip topping mix

1 c cold milk

Two 21-oz cans of cherry pie filling

6 oz cream cheese

1-1/2 c graham cracker crumbs

1 stick (1/2 c) butter

Melt margarine and mix with the graham cracker crumbs. Cover bottom of an 8-by-14-inch pan with one-half of the crumb mixture. Meanwhile, have Dream Whip and milk mixing. When whipped, add sugar, then cream cheese. Mix well. Pour half the mixture over pan crumbs. Spoon both cans of cherry pie filling over the cream cheese mixture. Top cherry layer with remaining half of whipped cream mixture. Sprinkle remaining half of crumbs over pie for topping.

MOCHA MOUSSE

6 oz semi-sweet chocolate chips

5 T piping hot coffee

4 egg yolks from pasteurized or local organic eggs

2 T dark rum

4 egg whites from pasteurized or local organic eggs

1/4 c white granulated sugar

Whipped cream, OPTIONAL

Blend chips and hot coffee at high speed in blender for 10 seconds. Add egg yolks and rum. Blend on high for 5 seconds. In separate bowl, beat egg whites until stiff, and beat in sugar until glossy. Fold chocolate mixture into egg whites. Pour into individual sherbet dishes. Refrigerate at least 2 hours. To serve, top with a dollop of whipped cream. *YIELD: 6 servings.*

GRAPEFRUIT MEMORIES

Long before mail-order catalogues brought South Texas grapefruit to the attention of Americans everywhere, we Daltroffs lived for the fall season when the Texas grapefruit would start coming in. Ruby Red grapefruit, and now Star Rubies, straight from the orchard, are sweeter and juicier than any orange.

When Dad began going to The Valley each year, he arranged for the local orchards to ship boxes of grapefruit to his special customers, family and friends. Eventually, he invested in one of the orchards that fed their fruit into the commercial enterprise known today as Pittman & Davis. After Dad died in 1974, Jeff and I took up the mantle, and began sending Texas grapefruit to family

and friends. We have continued the tradition to this day.

A few years ago, one of those friends sent us a gift box from Pittman & Davis, apparently forgetting who first introduced the fruit to them. We never told them. After all, there's no such thing as too much Texas grapefruit. When that first box arrives from The Valley each year, it evokes strong memories of my childhood. The aroma of the ripe grapefruit also triggers my Christmas holiday spirit.

BROILED BRUNCH GRAPEFRUIT

Ruby Red Grapefruit

Light brown sugar

Ground cinnamon

Rum, brandy or cognac

Maraschino cherries, halved

Cut grapefruit in half. Loosen each segment with paring knife, but leave in place. Sprinkle light brown sugar over the grapefruit, dust with a pinch of cinnamon. Drizzle rum, brandy or cognac over the sugar.

Broil in oven until sugar melts, about 5 minutes. Remove from oven, top with a maraschino cherry in the center, and serve while hot.

> **PASTRY TIP:** Adding a few drops of white vinegar in ice water used for pastry will make it more flaky, which is desirable.

EASY LEMON FLUFF

from Andrea Benfield.

According to Andrea, Caroline Benfield McCloud always preferred this to birthday cake!

13-oz can evaporated milk

3-oz pkg lemon gelatin powder

1/4 c lemon juice

1-3/4 c hot water

1 c white granulated sugar

2-1/2 c of crushed vanilla wafers, reserve 1/2 c

Chill unopened can of milk in freezer until icy cold, about 30 minutes. Dissolve gelatin in hot water. Chill until partially set. Whip gelatin until light and fluffy. Add lemon juice. Whip the chilled milk with sugar in a small bowl and fold into the whipped gelatin mix. Line bottom of 9-by-13-by-2-inch pan with 2 cups crushed wafers. Pour in the fluff. Top with remaining 1/2 cup of crushed-wafer crumbs. Chill at least 8 hrs.

OLD-FASHIONED LEMON FLUFF

1 pkg + 1 tsp unflavored gelatin powder

1/2 c water

8 eggs, separated

1-1/4 c white granulated sugar

3 lemons, juice of 3 and zested rind of 2

10 marshmallows

1/2 pt whipped cream

12-16 lady fingers cookies, split (depending on size)

Dissolve gelatin in water, cream egg yolks and gradually add 3/4 cup of sugar. Combine both mixtures in double boiler adding lemon juice, lemon zest, and marshmallows. Cook until mixture is thickened, 20-25 minutes, stirring frequently. Cool custard. Whip egg whites and gradually add remaining sugar, about 1/2 cup. Fold custard into egg whites. Line sides of spring form pan with lady fingers (cut off rounded bottoms) and top with custard mixture. Refrigerate overnight. Top with whipped cream before serving.

PASTRY & MERINGUE

MERINGUE

Never try to make a meringue on a rainy day or a day with high humidity. It will fall flat every time. Use clean and dry bowl and utensils. NEVER use plastic bowls.

3 to 6 egg whites, room temperature (for more volume)

1/16 (large pinch) to 1/8 tsp cream of tartar

Pinch of salt

6 T to 1-1/2 c white granulated sugar

Beat egg whites in a mixer on medium until frothy Add cream of tartar and pinch of salt; beat until stiff enough to hold a soft point. Gradually beat in the sugar and continue beating until mixture is glossy and holds stiff peaks. DO NOT OVERBEAT. Fold onto hot pie filling with spatula, "seal" the edges by making sure the meringue touches and overlaps the crust. Brown at 300 to 325°F in preheated oven about 10 minutes.

SWISS MERINGUE VARIATION: Heat 6 egg whites and 1-1/2 c sugar in double boiler until 110-120°F (sugar grains have dissolved). Beat until stiff and glossy white. Pipe onto tarts, pies, or cookies. To brown, if desired, stick under broiler for a few minutes, or use chef's blow torch. OR, pipe as kisses onto parchment paper; bake at 200°F for 30-40 minutes until dry and hard to the touch.

PASTRY CRUST MIX

3 c all-purpose flour

1 tsp salt

2 tsp white granulated sugar

1 c shortening

Ice water

Mix dry ingredients together. Blend in shortening with knives or pastry blender until mixture is of pebbly consistency. Store in a covered container in the refrigerator. Measure these amounts to roll out pie crust(s):

Single-Crust 8-inch Pie............	1-1/4 cups
Double-Crust 8-inch Pie	2-1/4 cups
Single-Crust 9-inch Pie............	1-1/2 cups
Double-Crust 9-inch Pie	2-1/2 cups
Single-Crust 10-inch Pie..........	1-3/4 cups
Double-Crust 10-inch Pie........	2-3/4 cups
12 tart shells	2-3/4 cups

Moisten pastry mix with enough ice water to hold dough together when pushed lightly with a fork. Roll out on lightly floured board or pastry cloth. To make pre-baked shells, line the pans with dough, prick with a fork to prevent puffing, and bake at 425°F for 12-15 minutes or until golden brown. Some people place beans on the crust to keep it from puffing during baking.

SIMPLE PIE CRUST

SIFT TOGETHER:

2-1/4 c all-purpose flour

1 tsp salt

1 T white granulated sugar

Cut in 3/4 c shortening until the mixture forms beads

MIX IN SMALL BOWL:

1 egg yolk

1 T lemon juice

1/4 c whole milk

Beat these together and add gradually to the dry mix. Roll out between waxed paper and with floured surface to keep from sticking before rolling. *YIELD: 4 small pie crusts or 1 large pie crust.*

HINT: Meringue runny underneath? Beat in sugar more slowly to dissolve better; place meringue on filling while it's hot. Cool baked meringue in oven.

TRIPLETTE DOUGH

from Andrea Benfield, from Louise Triplette

5 c sifted self-rising flour

2/3 c of lard (or vegetable shortening)

2/3 c whole milk

Cut lard or Crisco into the flour with a fork or pastry blender. Work in milk with fingers. Knead until blended, and form a dough ball of medium consistency. Wrap and refrigerate at least 24 hours. Roll out very thin on lightly floured surface. Flip into pie plates and trim edges, crimping with finger. Use for apple pies.

AUNT DOROTHY'S TART PASTRY

from Fern Robertson Kerslake

2 c all-purpose flour

1/2 tsp salt

1/2 c confectioners sugar

1 tsp baking powder

7/8 c shortening

1 egg

1 T whole milk

Sift dry ingredients together. Use pastry blender or two forks to blend in shortening until crumbled. Mix in egg and milk. Makes a sticky pastry. Gently roll out between two sheets of waxed paper. Fit into tart pan or mini tart pans.

CREAM CHEESE PASTRY

from Mary Elizabeth Daltroff

1 c (2 sticks) butter

8 oz cream cheese, softened

2 c of all-purpose flour

1/2 tsp salt, OPTIONAL

Mix butter and cream cheese with electric beaters. Mix in flour until dough forms. Roll into ball, wrap in plastic; refrigerate overnight. Cut into two halves. Roll out between waxed paper. For two-crust pie, fit half the dough into pie pan and prick with a fork to prevent puffing. Fill pie and cover with second crust, folding edges under and crimping. Prick top. For pre-baked pie shells, heat oven to 450°F, bake 12-15 minutes until golden brown.

COOKIE PIE CRUSTS

Some of the best pies and tarts are made with crusts created from over-the-counter cookies. What would we do without graham cracker crust for cheesecake, or chocolate wafer crust for grasshopper pie?

CHOCOLATE WAFER CRUST

1-1/2 to 1-3/4 c chocolate wafer crumbs (24-28 wafers)

1/4 to 1/3 c white granulated sugar

3 to 4 T melted butter or margarine

Crush wafers in bag with rolling pin. Mix sugar and crumbs in bowl, add melted butter. Work with hands to mix, then use back of spoon to press on bottom and up sides of regular 8- or 9-inch regular pie plate. Use flat of hand and spoon to make top edges even and not too thin. Chill or freeze 5 to 15 minutes before filling.

GINGER SNAPS PIE CRUST

1-1/2 c crushed ginger snaps (about 24 cookies)

3 T white granulated sugar

1/2 tsp ground ginger, OPTIONAL

6 T butter, melted

1/3 c fine-crushed, toasted pecans, OPTIONAL

Preheat oven to 350°F. Lightly grease 9-inch pie pan with cooking spray. Combine ingredients in bowl. Press into pie pan, using flat of hand and back of spoon, bringing crumbs evenly to top edge of pan. Place pan on cookie sheet; bake 10 minutes, until crust is set. Cool, fill. This crust is excellent for black bottom pie, or various custard or chiffon pies, especially pumpkin.

GRAHAM CRACKER PIE CRUST

1-1/4 to 1-1/2 c graham cracker crumbs (24 crackers)

1/4 c white granulated sugar

1/3 c butter or margarine, melted

If using crackers, crush fine in bag with rolling pin. Mix crumbs with sugar in medium bowl; work in melted butter. Press crumb mixture evenly on bottom and up sides of regular 8- or 9-inch pie plate. Use back of large spoon to smooth crumbs evenly. Like a potter, press flat of hand against crust sides, flat of spoon resting on top edge; run around sides. Bake 6 to 8 minutes in preheated oven at 375°F to achieve crisp, firm crust. Cool 30 minutes; fill. OR, for frozen filling, chill or freeze crust 30 minutes before filling.

SHORTBREAD PIE CRUST

1-1/2 c shortbread cookie crumbs (10-oz pkg of cookies)

6 T unsalted butter, melted

Crush cookies in bag with rolling pin or pulse in food processor 8 to 10 times. Do not pulverize. Combine crumbs and butter. Press on bottom and up sides of 8- or 9-inch regular pie plate or six 4-inch tart pans with removable bottoms. Chill, then fill with pre-cooked filling. Do not bake this crust.

VANILLA WAFER CRUST

75 vanilla wafers

1/4 c confectioners sugar

1/2 c butter, melted

Preheat oven to 350°F. Spray pie plate(s) with cooking spray. Crush wafers in a bag with rolling pin, or pulse in food processor (I prefer the rolling pin). Combine crumbs with sugar in medium bowl. Work in melted butter. Press on bottom and up sides to top edges of 8- or 9-inch regular pie plate, or six 4-inch tart pans with removable bottoms. Bake 10-12 minutes, until lightly browned. (Bake tart pans on cookie sheet to prevent burning.) Cool completely, at least 1 hr.

MACAROON PIE CRUST

30 to 35 traditional coconut macaroons, crumbled

Macaroon cookies are sticky and loaded with butter and coconut. Press into pie pan and chill at least 1 hour before filling.

FRUIT PIES & COBBLERS

APPLE PIE

Pie crust for a covered pie

4 Granny Smith Apples

4 Jonathan, Braeburn, or Yellow Delicious apples

1/4 c all-purpose flour

1 T fresh lemon juice

1/2 tsp ground cinnamon

1/4 tsp salt

1/4 tsp ground nutmeg

1/3 c sugar

2 to 3 T butter, cut into pieces

Preheat oven to 450°F. Peel apples into salted water to prevent browning. Drain water, dice the apples. Mix flour, cinnamon, sugar, salt, and nutmeg together in a sifter. Add dry ingredients to the diced apples; mix well. The apple mixture will make juices in the bottom of the bowl; reserve about 1 T juice. Prepare pie crust for a 9-inch deep-dish pie. Prick lightly (but not completely through to the dish) around the sides and bottom to prevent puffing. Spoon apple mixture into the crust, heaping apples at center, leaving space around edges. Resembles a large mound. Work cut-up butter pieces evenly into the apple mound; top with the second pie crust. Crimp pastry edges, being sure to seal top to bottom so juices won't run. Make slits in top pastry for steam. Paint the top with the reserved apple juice mixture to make a dark shiny crust; or brush with beaten egg.

Place the pie dish on a foil-lined cookie sheet and loosely tent foil over the pie to prevent excessive browning of the crust while apples cook. Bake at 450°F on the bottom rack for 15-20 minutes. Lower temperature to 350°F; cook 30 minutes longer. Remove tented foil and continue baking until crust is browned and juices are bubbling. Test doneness of the apples by sticking a long wooden toothpick through one of the top crust slits. The apples are done if tender when pricked. Remove pie to a wire rack to cool about 2 hours. Pie needs to "set" before serving. Refrigerate leftovers.

CRUST VARIATION: Make a lattice top crust, or add decorative crust cutouts to top crust. Adjust baking times accordingly.

PIE VARIATIONS: Add raisins, berries or dried cranberries to the apples.

FRANKIE TEAGUE'S FRIED PIES

The Teagues were the Triplettes' neighbors and fellow church parishioners in Grace Chapel. Frankie was a terrific cook. When I wrote my original family cookbook in 2008, I had misinterpreted this recipe as a pie pastry recipe, when copying recipes from Louise's recipe box. We only learned something was wrong when I made up the pastry for a 10-inch Williamsburg Pecan Pie at Thanksgiving. Disaster! The pastry was thick and crumbly, almost like biscuit dough, rather than thin and flaky because it was meant to be fried. I'd only gotten HALF the recipe the first time. Louise set me straight during a 2010 visit to Grace Chapel.

FRIED PIE FILLING:

8 oz pkg dried fruit (apples, peaches, etc.)

2 T melted butter

1/2 to 1 c white granulated sugar

1 tsp cinnamon

Soak fruit overnight in a bit of water. Drain and rinse well. Cover with water and cook until soft. Drain. Add butter, sugar, and cinnamon; mash until smooth and blended.

BUTTERMILK FRIED-PIE PASTRY:

3 c all-purpose flour

1 T baking powder

1 egg

1/2 tsp baking soda

1/3 c shortening

1 c buttermilk

Combine flour, baking soda and baking powder (I always sift together in a sieve). Cut in shortening until it resembles coarse cornmeal. Combine egg and buttermilk; work into flour mixture. Knead until smooth. Separate into three pieces. Roll out pastry, and cut out circles, using a saucer as a template. Place about 3 T fruit filling in center of pastry circle. Dip fingers in water and run fingers around circle edges to moisten. Fold dough over evenly. Use a fork dipped in flour to seal edges together. Fry in hot cooking oil, turning one time. *YIELD: 18 fried pies.*

GRANDVIEW APPLE CRISP

from Cindy Thurmond Semple

Cousin Cindy says 3 T of bourbon drizzled over the apples before baking is an option for folks who like it.

1/2 c all-purpose flour

Pinch baking soda

1 tsp cinnamon

1/3 c packed light brown sugar

1/4 c white granulated sugar

1/2 c (1 stick) butter

1/2 c raw oatmeal

4 c sliced, peeled apples

Combine first 5 ingredients in food processor. Add butter and pulse. Remove blade and mix in oatmeal by hand. Place apples in a greased 8- or 9-inch square pan. Spoon flour mixture evenly over apples. Bake in preheated 375°F oven 40-45 minutes, until browned. Serve warm with ice cream or whipped cream.

LORETTA'S JAPANESE FRUIT PIE

from Loretta Phillips Triplette

2 eggs

1 T white distilled vinegar

1 stick (1/2 c) margarine or butter

1 c white granulated sugar

1/2 c pecans

1/2 c of shredded coconut

1/2 c of raisins

9-inch unbaked pie crust

Beat eggs and mix with sugar, raisins, coconut, nuts and vinegar. Melt butter and mix with the other ingredients. Pour into unbaked pie shell. Bake for 30 minutes at 350°F (until toothpick comes out clean).

NOTE: This pie can be very buttery. If desired, rather than reduce the amount of butter, consider increasing to 3 eggs and adding more pecans, coconut and raisins in equal amounts. For increased volume, use a 10-inch pie crust or a deep-dish 9-inch crust. *YIELD: 1 pie.*

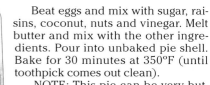

Joseph and Rachel Emma Link Sherrill, 1880s

NO-CRUST COCONUT PIE (IMPOSSIBLE COCONUT PIE)

I had five family versions of this pie!

4 eggs, well beaten

2 c white granulated sugar

1/2 c all-purpose flour

Pinch of salt

1/2 tsp baking powder

1 stick (1/2 c) butter, melted and cooled

1 tsp vanilla extract

7-oz can coconut

2 c whole milk

Mix all ingredients well and pour into two pie pans. Bake at 350°F in preheated oven for 30-40 minutes. *YIELD: Two 9-inch pies.*

VARIATION: The Grace Chapel UMW cookbook calls for 1/2-cup of self-rising flour instead of plain flour, 4 T butter (1/2 stick) and NO baking powder.

DIANNE'S SWEET POTATO PIE

from Dianne Triplette Poovey

4 c cooked sweet potatoes, mashed

1/2 stick (4 T) butter or margarine, melted

2 c white granulated sugar

4 eggs

1/2 cup evaporated milk

1 1/3 tsp salt

2 T vanilla

Mix all ingredients. Pour into 3 unbaked pie shells. Bake at 375°F in preheated oven until toothpick comes out clean. Let cool before serving. *YIELD: 3 pies.*

PUMPKIN PIE

This is the classic version that Libby's made famous on their canned pumpkin labels. My grandmother used sweetened condensed milk instead of evaporated milk for a much sweeter, more custardy pie. You might wish to substitute pumpkin pie spice for the individual spice ingredients listed below, but note that it contains nutmeg and less cloves.

3/4 c white granulated sugar

1/2 tsp salt

1 tsp ground cinnamon

1/2 tsp ground ginger

1/4 tsp ground cloves

2 large eggs

15-oz can pure pumpkin

12-oz can evaporated milk

9-inch deep-dish pie shell, unbaked

Mix sugar, salt, cinnamon, ginger, and cloves in small bowl. Beat eggs in large bowl; stir in pumpkin and sugar mixture, mixing on medium speed. Gradually stir in evaporated milk. Pour into pie shell. Bake at 425°F in preheated oven for 15 minutes, then reduce temperature to 350°F. Loosely tent with foil for first 20-30 minutes, while baking for 40-50 minutes. This prevents crust from burning. Remove when knife inserted in center comes out clean. Cool on wire rack for 2 hours. Serve with whipped cream. Refrigerate leftovers. Reheat to serve if desired. *YIELD: 1 pie.*

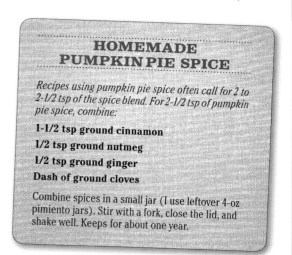

HOMEMADE PUMPKIN PIE SPICE

Recipes using pumpkin pie spice often call for 2 to 2-1/2 tsp of the spice blend. For 2-1/2 tsp of pumpkin pie spice, combine:

1-1/2 tsp ground cinnamon

1/2 tsp ground nutmeg

1/2 tsp ground ginger

Dash of ground cloves

Combine spices in a small jar (I use leftover 4-oz pimiento jars). Stir with a fork, close the lid, and shake well. Keeps for about one year.

STRABERRIES

West Tennessee strawberries were always the greatest. They still are, in my opinion. One can attend strawberry festivals all around the Volunteer State during strawberry season (late spring).

I vividly remember visiting Grandmother and Granddaddy Thurmond in Bells, TN, when Granddaddy was the preacher at the First Methodist Church. Bells is a picturesque town noted for its annual okra festival. More important to me, Bells was home to a strawberry packing plant, and its neighbor is Humbolt, home of the annual West Tennessee Strawberry Festival since 1936.

The sweet smell of strawberries permeated the air at the parsonage whenever I was lucky enough to visit. Grandmother would freeze as many strawberries as her freezer would hold; conserving and preserving dozens of jars with the leftover strawberries. Year round, whoever had the pleasure of visiting Grandmother and Granddaddy had the benefit of eating toast with strawberry preserves, and—even better—vanilla ice cream covered with slushy strawberries, straight out of the freezer.

Granddaddy always claimed that it was every citizen's responsibility to support our local farmers by buying their produce (such as strawberries). He always said, "When the farmer can't make it, America is in trouble."

Granddaddy was a very wise man.

Remembering his farm-boy roots, Granddaddy always kept a huge garden. Each year, he gave away more fresh produce than he and Grandmother kept, mostly to the "little widow ladies." When he died, Granddaddy and Grandmother had 12 freezer lockers full of frozen vegetables and fruit in rented storage at their local Halls, TN, grocery store. Strawberries accounted for much of the storage.

Mom always had a craving for those west Tennessee strawberries. I recall the time Mom drove to the Ripley (TN) area to self-pick strawberries on a hot, humid, May school day. By the time she arrived back home, well after dark, she had an un-air-conditioned Chevy full of over-ripe strawberries. It seems Mom got lost trying to find her way out of the strawberry patches in the Loosahatchie River Bottoms. She and I worked into the wee hours that night trying to salvage them.

Taking strawberries to market, Chadbourn, NC, circa 1907
PHOTO: Courtesy of the North Carolina State Archives, Raleigh, NC

FROZEN FLUFFY STRAWBERRY PIE

1/2 c lightly toasted flaked coconut

1/3 c margarine or butter

3-oz pkg cream cheese, softened

14-oz can sweetened condensed milk

1-1/2 c mashed or pureed unsweetened
    strawberries, either fresh or frozen

3 T lemon juice

1 c (1/2 pint) whipping cream, whipped

Additional fresh strawberries, optional

In large saucepan, melt butter, stir in toasted coconut. Mix well. Press into bottom and up sides of a 9-inch pie plate to form a coconut crust. Chill. In a large bowl, beat cheese until fluffy, beat in sweetened condensed milk. Stir in pureed strawberries and lemon juice. Fold in whipped cream. Pour into coconut crust and smooth out (will mound slightly in center). Freeze for 4 hours or until firm. Before serving, garnish with additional fresh strawberries, or on plates with individual slices. Keep leftovers frozen. *YIELD: One 9-inch pie.*

STRAWBERRY PIE

from Mary Elizabeth Daltroff, from Louise Perkins

I can remember all the moms in my neighborhood making furtive trips to Shoney's to eat a slice of strawberry pie, then attempting to recreate the glaze in their home kitchens. What a relief when the recipe was published!

1 c water

1 c white granulated sugar

2 T cornstarch

2 T lemon gelatin powder

1 drop red food coloring

1 pt fresh strawberries, rinsed, wiped and sliced

1 pie crust, baked

Boil the water, sugar, cornstarch until thickened, take off the stove and add the gelatin powder, stirring well, then adding the red food coloring. Layer the sliced strawberries into the baked pie crust, then top with the pie filling. Chill for several hours. Serve topped with whipped cream when ready. (NOTE: To really capture the nostalgia, use Reddi-whip topping!)

BERRY COBBLERS OR PIES

4 to 6 c berries (blackberries, blueberries, raspberries,
    or mixed)

1 to 1-1/2 c white granulated sugar

Juice of 1 lemon (or 3 T)

3/4 c plain flour

2 tsp corn starch, or use Clearjel® to thicken

1 tsp vanilla extract

Butter, cut into small pieces

Gently wash berries and drain (pat dry by hand if raspberries). Mix with sugar, lemon juice, flour and corn starch. Let sit 15 minutes. (Use the maximum amount of sugar if berries are tart.) Fold in butter pieces.

PIES: Spoon into 9-inch pie shell, mounding slightly in the center. Seal top with pierced crust, or leave uncovered. Tent foil over the pie plate on a lined cookie sheet. Bake at 350°F for 30-45 minutes, until bubbly. COBBLERS: Spoon berry mixture over thin biscuit dough or pie pastry in loaf pan. Dot top evenly with teaspoons of dough. OR, spoon into loaf pan, dot top only with bits of pie pastry. Bake at 350°F until bubbly.

MORE PIE CRUST TIPS: Pastry pie crusts tend to feel different every time we make them. It's because the humidity level in the air constantly changes, and flour absorbs moisture. Always keep a bit of extra flour on hand to sprinkle into the dough if too sticky. To prevent dough from becoming tough from too much flour, roll out pie crusts between sheets of waxed paper.

PEACH MEMORIES

Gabby and Joshua, like their seven Triplette first cousins, loved to spend the night with Mamaw and Papaw. Their stays with Louise and Lester reminded me of visiting my own grandparents, only for my children, it was Louise's juicy half-frozen peaches that they loved to eat over ice cream.

Peaches have always been a special delicacy in my opinion, but never more special than when I met the Clock Man. Our third Christmas together needed to be special, and I had determined that Jeff needed an antique mantel clock to make our house a home (never mind that we didn't have a mantel or fireplace in our doll-sized first home). I was referred to a fellow who had a passion for all clock things. He collected, repaired and sold old clocks. I called him, and he invited me to his clock studio behind his house on the outskirts of Winston-Salem. We spent almost three hours reviewing, studying and listening to more than a hundred clocks of all shapes and sizes.

Finally, we settled on a specific Seth Thomas mantel clock that suited both my aesthetic requirements and my limited budget. I suppose my enthusiasm inspired him because the Clock Man peered over at me and said "Do you like to take a drink?" I hesitated, then admitted that I certainly did. He reached behind a ruffled skirt covering the bottom-most clock shelf in the repair room, and pulled out a box containing a dozen pint jars. The Clock Man told me his auntie from near Mt. Airy put up jars of peach brandy every year for medicinal purposes and special occasions. We took a drink in convivial silence. It was a good thing. Once I could breathe and speak again, I told him it was the most wonderful peach brandy I'd ever had. Turns out it was a special family recipe involving homegrown peaches and white lightning (only the purest distillate, never made in a car radiator).

Like Rick and Louie when Lazlo and Ilsa flew away from Casablanca, that moment was the start of a beautiful friendship between the Clock Man and me. I hated it when I moved away.

MOM'S PEACH COBBLER

Mom got this recipe 45 years ago from the old Mrs. Snow family recipe notebook dating back to the 1850s.

2 to 4 c peaches
3/4 c white granulated sugar
3/4 c all-purpose flour
Pinch of salt
2 T baking powder
1 c white granulated sugar
1/2 c whole milk
1/4 tsp almond extract
1 stick (1/2 c) butter

Slice peaches; mix with 3/4 cup sugar. Let stand 2 hours. Preheat oven to 350°F. Sift together flour, salt, baking powder and then mix with 1 cup sugar. Stir in milk and almond extract. Melt butter in deep-dish baking pan; pour batter over melted butter. Do not stir. Pour peaches over the batter to form a layer. Bake for 50-55 minutes. It is important to have more unused pan on the sides above the portion containing batter to allow for the cobbler to rise. The cobbler will bubble over the sides. *YIELD: 6 servings.*

SOUTH CAROLINA PEACH COBBLER

1 stick margarine or butter
1 c whole milk
1 c self-rising flour
1 c white granulated sugar
4 c sliced peaches, sweetened to taste
1 tsp cinnamon, OPTIONAL

Melt margarine or butter in a 9-by-12-inch baking dish. Combine milk, flour, sugar, and optional cinnamon. Mix thoroughly. Add to the melted margarine or butter in the baking dish. Add peaches and do not stir. Bake at 375°F for approximately 40 minutes, or until browned.

CHESS & CHOCOLATE

BUTTERMILK PIE

from Ruby White Thurmond

3 T butter

1-1/2 c white granulated sugar

3 egg yolks, beaten

3-1/2 scant T buttermilk

3 egg whites, well beaten

1/2 tsp lemon juice, nutmeg or vanilla extract

Cream butter and sugar well. Add beaten egg yolks and then buttermilk. Fold in beaten egg whites. Flavor with lemon juice, nutmeg or vanilla. Pour into unbaked pie shell. Bake at 350°F in preheated oven until center is firm (30 minutes to 1 hour). Cool before serving. Top with whipped cream if desired.

CHESS PIE

from Mary Elizabeth Daltroff

1 c light brown sugar

1/2 c white granulated sugar

1 tsp all purpose flour

1 tsp vanilla extract

1/2 c (1 stick) butter

2 T whole milk

2 eggs, unbeaten

Mix white and brown sugar with flour. Break eggs into mixture, add milk and vanilla. Add melted butter. Bake in an unbaked pie shell in preheated oven at 350°F for 40 to 50 minutes. When it cools, the center of the pie falls slightly, and sets up rich and chewy. This recipe may be used for chess tarts, using one Tablespoon of filling in each uncooked tart shell.

TENNESSEE CHESS PIE

from Stella Thurmond Campbell

Stella's pretty sure this was one of Grandmother's pie recipes. At any rate, Tennessee Chess Pie is known for the cornmeal ingredient.

1 c white granulated sugar

1/2 c butter (1 stick)

3 egg yolks, beaten

1 T plain yellow cornmeal

1-1/2 T all-purpose flour

1/2 tsp nutmeg

1 tsp vanilla extract

1/2 c whole milk

Cream the sugar and butter until creamy-fluffy. Add the beaten egg yolks and other ingredients. Pour into an unbaked pie shell. Bake 35-45 minutes in preheated oven at 375°F. Remove from oven and let cool on a wire rack. Serve with whipped cream or fresh strawberries. Refrigerate any leftovers.

ANDREA'S LEMON CHESS PIE

from Andrea Benfield

Andrea shared this no-fail version at my Grace Chapel bridal shower. Hers is very similar to my mother's version, but not as tart.

1/4 c (1/2 stick) butter or margarine

1 c white granulated sugar

3 large eggs, well beaten

5 T lemon juice

1/2 tsp vanilla extract

Melt butter or margarine, add sugar and well beaten eggs and lemon juice until fluffy, then add vanilla. Pour into an unbaked 8-inch pie shell. Bake at 400°F for about 45 minutes in preheated oven, or until knife inserted in center comes out clean. *YIELD: 1 pie.*

PIE HINTS: To prevent crust from becoming soggy, sprinkle powdered sugar over bottom crust before adding the pie filling. OR, brush the bottom with egg white to seal the crust.

To prevent runny fruit pies and cobblers, use tapioca instead of cornstarch, or use Clearjel® Thickener, which works well with high-acid fruits.

MOM'S LEMON CHESS PIE

from Mary Elizabeth Daltroff

Mom's version is much more tart than Andrea's version, but contains more sugar.

3 eggs

1-1/2 c sugar

3 T lemon juice

1/2 tsp lemon extract

1 T white vinegar

Dash of salt

1/2 stick of butter

    This extra-sweet version also is extra-lemony. Beat eggs thoroughly and add sugar, lemon juice, extract, salt, and vinegar while beating. Mix well. Add melted butter, stirring until completely mixed. Pour into an unbaked pie crust. Bake in preheated 350°F oven for 35-40 minutes (until center appears set). Gently remove and cool on wire rack. Refrigerate for long-term keeping. *YIELD: 1 pie.*

CHOCOLATE CHESS PIE

This local favorite is VERY sweet. Must be served with whipped cream, fresh sliced peaches, and coffee!

4 T (1/2 stick) margarine or butter

1-1/2 squares of unsweetened chocolate

1-1/2 c white granulated sugar

1 T all-purpose flour

Dash of salt

2 eggs

1/2 c whole milk

1 tsp vanilla extract

9-inch unbaked pie shell

    Melt margarine and chocolate together in double boiler. Set aside. Mix next 6 ingredients together. Blend two mixtures for 5 minutes with mixer. Pour into unbaked pie shell. Bake at 350°F in preheated oven for 45-55 minutes, until knife cuts through clean in center.

CHOCOLATE FUDGE PIE

2 c milk

2 c white granulated sugar

2 squares unsweetened chocolate

4 T butter

6 egg yolks

2 T plain flour

2 tsp vanilla extract

9-inch baked pie shell

    Put milk, sugar, chocolate and butter in a double boiler and cook until almost at the soft ball stage. Beat egg yolks with flour and stir with other ingredients. Cook until thickened, and remove from stove. Add vanilla while still hot, stir, and pour into pie shell. Top with a meringue and brown in a 300°F oven for 15-20 minutes. Cool and refrigerate at least 4 hours. Keep refrigerated.

MISSISSIPPI FUDGE PIE

from Rose Price May

This pie is less custard-like than the chocolate fudge pie, but is extremely sweet and rich.

1/2 c (1 stick) butter

3 squares unsweetened chocolate

3 T white Karo corn syrup

1-1/2 c white granulated sugar

1/4 tsp salt

1 tsp vanilla extract

4 eggs

9-inch unbaked pie crust

    Preheat oven to 350°F. In top of double boiler, melt butter and chocolate. Cool slightly. In separate bowl, beat 4 eggs until light. Beat corn syrup, sugar, salt and vanilla into the eggs. Add the slightly cooled chocolate, and mix thoroughly. Pour into a 9-inch uncooked pie crust. Bake for 25-30 minutes, until top is crusty, and filling appears set. Serve with vanilla ice cream.

TIP FOR CHESS PIES: Classic Southern chess pies often contain white vinegar. They all are loaded with eggs and sugar. The aim is to create a smooth, tart-like custard pie. Chess pie is one of those recipes that should never be doubled. If you need more, make the recipe multiple times. Chess pie is done when it quivers when shaken lightly. Always keep chess pies refrigerated because they contain eggs.

PIES, FRUITS & DESSERT

ICEBOX

CHERRY CHEESECAKE PIE

This is an old and easy favorite that looks and tastes complicated. Cherry Yum Yum is a derivative of this.

1-1/4 c graham cracker crumbs

5-2/3 T melted butter (1/3 c)

1/4 c white granulated sugar

1-1/2 blocks cream cheese (8 oz + 4 oz)

14- to 15-oz can of sweetened condensed milk

1/4 to 1/2 c lime or lemon juice (I use 1/3 c lime juice)

1 tsp vanilla extract

21-oz can cherry pie filling

Make graham cracker crust by combining crumbs and sugar in clean bowl, then adding butter until completely blended. Press crumbs into 9-inch pie plate and up the sides. Bake crust 6 to 8 minutes in preheated oven at 350°F until lightly browned. Cool. While crust is cooling, mix cheese, milk, juice and vanilla until smooth. Do NOT use low fat or fat-free cheese or milk because the pie won't set. Pour into cooled pie crust and use spatula to smooth, with edges slightly higher than center. Cover top evenly with cherry pie filling, Refrigerate at least 4 hours before serving.

Ice cream vendor on the Outer Banks of North Carolina
PHOTO: Courtesy of Don and Charlotte Bradley

BANANA CREAM HEATH PIE

from Andrea Benfield

3.4-oz pkg instant banana pudding mix

1 c whole milk

2 bananas, sliced

3 Heath bars, chopped

8-oz container whipped topping, thawed

6-oz chocolate wafer crust

Combine pudding mix and milk. Whisk until thickened. Fold in 1-1/2 cup whipped topping. Arrange sliced bananas over pie crust. Sprinkle with half chopped toffee bars; spread half pudding mixture over the toffee. Sprinkle with remaining half of chopped toffee bars, reserving 1 T. Add remaining pudding. Chill 3 hours, until set. Spoon remaining whipped topping on pie just before serving; sprinkle with reserved toffee chips.

BLACK BOTTOM PIE

This traditional refrigerated sweet is a layered chiffon pie. The crust can be traditional pastry, or crushed graham crackers, chocolate wafers, or ginger snaps.

Chilled, prepared pie shell of choice

1/2 c white granulated sugar

1 T corn starch

2 c whole milk, scalded

4 egg yolks, beaten

6-oz pkg semi-sweet chocolate pieces

1 tsp vanilla extract

9-inch pie shell, baked and cooled

1 envelope unflavored gelatin

1/4 c cold water

4 egg whites

1/2 c white granulated sugar

1 to 2 T light rum, OPTIONAL

1 c sweetened whipped cream

Have eggs at room temperature. Combine first sugar and corn starch. Slowly add scalded milk to yolks, then stir in the sugar mixture. Cook over very low heat until custard coats wooden spoon. Add chocolate pieces to 1 cup of the hot custard. Stir until melted. Add vanilla. Pour into bottom of pie shell. Chill. Soften gelatin in water, add to remaining hot custard. Stir until dissolved. Chill until slightly thick. Beat whites, adding second sugar gradually until stiff. Add rum. Fold into custard-gelatin mixture. Pour over chocolate layer and chill overnight. Garnish with whipped cream.

CHOCOLATE ICE BOX PIE

from Mary Elizabeth Daltroff

1 baked pie shell

1 c evaporated milk

1/2 c water

1/4 tsp ground nutmeg

3 egg yolks from pasteurized eggs (reserve the whites)

1/2 c white granulated sugar

1/8 tsp salt

1 tsp unflavored gelatin

3 T cold water

1/2 tsp vanilla extract

3 egg whites (from pasteurized or safe organic eggs)

1 c sweetened whipped cream

1/4 c grated unsweetened chocolate

Heat milk, water and nutmeg in double boiler. Beat egg yolks with sugar and salt until light. Pour hot milk over egg mixture and return it to double boiler. Cook until it reaches the consistency of thick cream. Remove from heat, mix in grated chocolate till smooth. Soak gelatin in 3 T cold water, then add with vanilla to chocolate mixture. Whip egg whites until they form stiff peaks. When the custard has cooled almost to the point of setting, fold in the stiffly beaten egg whites. Pour into a baked pie shell and refrigerate at least 4 hours. Serve with whipped cream and grated unsweetened chocolate curls. *YIELD: 6 to 8 servings.*

COCONUT CARAMEL PIE

from Andrea Benfield

2 9-inch pie shells, baked

1 stick (1/2 c) butter

7 oz coconut (fresh or canned, toasted in oven)

1 c chopped pecans, toasted in oven

1 can sweetened condensed milk

8-oz pkg cream cheese, softened

16 oz Cool Whip

1 jar caramel ice cream topping

Saute the coconut and pecans in melted butter until golden brown. Beat the sweetened condensed milk and cream cheese until smooth, and fold in the Cool Whip. Spread half the cream-cheese mixture in each shell. Drizzle caramel topping, and then top with nuts and coconut mixture.

Repeat all 3 layers again, and drizzle caramel over the top. Refrigerate. *YIELD: 2 pies.*

EASY LEMON MERINGUE PIE

from Mary Elizabeth Daltroff

My mother made wonderful lemon icebox pies with homemade piecrusts prepared with traditional White Lily flour. This is a shortcut version due to the pie crust.

1 prepared graham cracker crust

3 eggs, separated

14-oz can of sweetened condensed milk

1/2 c lemon juice

1 tsp grated lemon rind

1/4 tsp cream of tartar

1/4 c white granulated sugar

Preheat oven to 350°F. Beat egg yolks in a medium bowl until fluffy, stir in the sweetened condensed milk, followed by the lemon juice and rind. When thoroughly blended, pour into the graham cracker pie shell. In a small clean bowl that has been chilled for a few minutes and very clean beaters, beat the egg whites with cream of tartar until foamy; gradually add in the sugar, beating until stiff but not dry. Spread meringue on top of the pie with a bowl scraper, sealing the edges to the edges of the pie shell. Bake on cookie sheet 15 minutes, until meringue is golden brown. Remove from oven and cool. Refrigerate 4 hours before cutting.

LEMON PUDDING VARIATION: Whisk together in sequence until smooth 3/4 c white granulated sugar, 1/4 c cornstarch, 2-1/2 c whole milk, 3 slightly beaten large egg yolks, 2 T lemon zest, punch of salt, 1/2 c lemon juice, 2 T softened butter. Cook, whisking, on medium heat until thickens and coats spoon. Pour into baked pie shell and chill, or use hot as cake filling.

KEY LIME PIE

from Andy Daltroff

1-1/2 c sweetened condensed milk

1/2 c Key lime juice

Grated zest of 1 lime

2 eggs, separated

9-inch baked pie shell or graham cracker crumb crust

4 T white granulated sugar

Blend condensed milk, lime juice and rind, then add the egg yolks. Mix well and pour into pie shell. Beat egg whites stiff but not dry. Gradually add sugar, beating constantly. Swirl meringue on top of filling. Bake at 350°F in preheated oven for approximately 35 minutes or until brown and sticky. Turn off and cool in oven. Chill about 3 hours before serving. Refrigerate any leftovers. *YIELD: 1 pie.*

PECAN PIE

CALLIE'S PECAN PIE

Another of Grandmother Thurmond's heirloom recipes, saved by Stella Thurmond Campbell. We're not sure who Callie was, although I seem to recall overhearing conversations about Callie. Was she one of Grandmother's church friends, or was she the family's part-time cook and housekeeper during the 1930s, rumored to have killed a man?

3 eggs

2 T melted butter

2 T all-purpose flour

1/4 tsp vanilla extract

1/8 tsp salt

1/2 c white granulated sugar

1-1/2 c dark corn syrup

1-1/2 c broken pecans

1 unbaked 8-inch pie shell

Preheat oven to 425°F. Beat eggs, blend in melted butter, flour, vanilla, sugar, salt and syrup. Sprinkle nut meats over bottom of pie shell. Gently pour the syrup mixture over the pecans, being careful not to disturb. Bake in oven set at 425°F for 10 minutes. Reduce to 325°F and continue cooking for about 40 minutes.

KARO PECAN PIE

1 c Karo light corn syrup

2 eggs, beaten

2 T butter, melted

1 tsp vanilla extract

3/4 c white granulated sugar

1 T all-purpose flour, rounded

1/2 c pecans

Beat eggs lightly, add flour and sugar. Beat well. Add Karo, butter and vanilla extract. Fold in nuts last. Put into unbaked 8-inch pie shell. Bake at 450°F for 15 minutes in preheated oven. Reduce heat to 350°F and bake about 30 minutes longer or until set. You probably will need to use pie rings to keep crust edges from overcooking. *YIELD: 1 pie.*

LOUISIANA PECAN PIE

I have seen other versions of this pie, calling for molasses instead of Karo syrup. The molasses version is always darker in color, and with a bit more edge to the bite. The southern Louisiana version calls for Steen's pure cane syrup instead of molasses. The flavor is different with cane syrup.

9-inch unbaked pie shell or pastry

1/3 c butter, softened

1-1/4 c white granulated sugar

1/2 c light molasses (or Steen's cane syrup)

3 eggs

1 tsp vanilla extract

1/4 tsp salt

1 c coarse chopped pecans

Sweetened whipped cream for garnish

Cream butter and sugar until fluffy. Add molasses or syrup; beat well. Beat in eggs, one at a time. Stir in vanilla, salt and pecans. Pour filling into pie shell. Bake on bottom rack of preheated oven at 375°F for 40-45 minutes, until just set. Cool on a rack. Serve with whipped cream or ice cream. *YIELD: 6 to 7 servings.*

FAMILY MEMORY

Beware of siblings with food cravings. Andrea once licked the entire top of a fresh apple pie to prevent brother Michael from getting any before supper. They were 11 and 9 at the time.

Lef to right, Michael and Dianne Triplette, cousin Willie June Keller, and Andrea Triplette rest on the back of a farm truck in Grace Chapel, NC. The Brushy Mountains are visible in the background.

ROSE'S MINIATURE PECAN PIES (PECAN TASSIES)

from Rose Price May

Rose noted that these pies freeze well.

1 stick (1/2 c) butter or margarine

3-oz pkg of cream cheese

1 c all-purpose flour

1 beaten egg

1 c packed brown sugar

1 T vanilla extract

1 T vegetable oil

3/4 c finely chopped pecans

Cream the butter and cream cheese. Blend in the flour and chill well. Pinch off small pieces of this pastry and press into party muffin tins, forming pastry shells. Mix pecan mixture until egg and sugar are completely blended. Pour scant teaspoon into crusts and bake at 350ºF in preheated oven for 30 minutes. Cool, remove from the tins. *YIELD: 24 miniature pies.*

WILLIAMSBURG PECAN PIE

6 eggs

1-1/2 c dark Karo syrup

1/2 c maple syrup

1 c sugar

2 T melted butter

1 tsp vanilla extract

2 c whole pecans

10-inch pie crust

Beat eggs and sugar together. Add vanilla to butter, then add to egg and sugar mixture. Add syrups. Position pecans in a pattern in pie shell, then pour mixture over the pecans. Bake at 300º to 325°F for 45 minutes, covering crust edges toward the end as needed. That little bit of maple syrup really alters the flavor in a tasty way. VERY RICH!

HINTS: Unlike raw egg yolks, raw egg whites do not readily support bacterial growth. That's why meringues, soufflés, frostings, and chiffons containing raw beaten egg whites are okay, especially if the cook beats the whites and sugar to soft peaks over hot water. Once created, refrigerate all foods containing raw egg whites, egg yolks or whole eggs and cream.

TARTS

ALMOND TARTLETS WITH FRUIT

TART DOUGH:

1-1/2 c all-purpose flour

1/4 c white granulated sugar

1/8 tsp salt

1 tsp finely grated orange zest

8 T (1 stick) chilled, unsalted butter, cut into 1/2-inch cubes

1 egg white, whisked until frothy

Preheat oven to 350ºF and position oven rack on lowest level. Use muffin tins or special 12-well mini-tart plaque. For miniature versions, use 24-count mini-muffin tin. To make dough, use pastry blender or processor to mix flour, sugar, salt and orange zest. Scatter butter over mixture; blend or pulse until it develops cornmeal consistency. Blend in egg white until dough forms a ball. Transfer dough to lightly floured surface; press with heel of hands until smooth and spongy. Measure 1 level tablespoon of dough for each tartlet; roll each into a ball. Press dough into greased wells, and evenly up the sides of each well.

ALMOND FILLING:

3/4 c almond paste

6 T (3/4 stick) unsalted butter

1 c confectioner's sugar

1 egg

1 egg yolk

1 tsp vanilla extract

1 tsp finely grated orange or tangerine zest

1/4 c apricot preserves or 24 large firm raspberries

Use food processor or mixer to soften almond paste, adding confectioner's sugar, egg, egg yolk, vanilla, and orange zest until smooth. Spoon 2 T into each dough shell. If shell won't hold it all, press the dough down further in the center. Spoon 1/2 tsp apricot preserves into center of each filled tartlet, OR press in 1 raspberry. Bake until filling and crust edges are golden, about 20-25 minutes. Cool on wire rack. Serve with fresh peaches or raspberries and whipped cream. *YIELD: 20-24 tartlets.*

GRASSHOPPER TARTS FOR TWO

These are miniature versions of grasshopper pie.

2/3 c of chocolate wafer crumbs

1 T butter or margarine, melted

1/2 c marshmallow cream

1 T green crème de menthe

1/2 c whipping cream, whipped

Combine chocolate wafer crumbs and butter; press onto bottom and sides of 6-ounce freezer-proof ramekins. Chill for 1 hour. Combine marshmallow cream and crème de menthe, stirring well. Set aside 2 T of whipped cream, and fold remaining whipped cream into the marshmallow mixture. Spoon into prepared crusts; top with reserved whipped cream. Cover loosely and freeze at least 8 hours. *YIELD: 2 servings.*

CHEESECAKE TARTS

1-1/2 c sugar

4 eggs

1 tsp vanilla extract

Three 8-oz pkgs cream cheese

Assorted fruit (sliced kiwi, starfruit, nectarines and berries), glazed, or 21-oz can of cherry pie filling

Tart-sized pie shells (*see page 185 for pie crust recipes*)

1/4 c apple jelly, melted, OR whipped cream, OPTIONAL

Combine the sugar, eggs, vanilla, and cream cheese until smooth. Grease tart pans well with butter. If not using premade crusts, form crust in each. Pour pans three-fourths full of cream cheese mixture. Bake at 375°F about 20 minutes until firm. Let tarts cool 20 minutes, then top with whipped cream and fresh fruit, or with sliced fruit brushed with apple jelly glaze. Refrigerate. *YIELD: A dozen 4-1/2-inch tarts.*

VARIATION: Assemble 24 baked tart shells, 8-oz cream cheese, 14-oz can of sweetened condensed milk, 1/3 c lemon juice, 1 tsp vanilla, assorted fruit and 1/4 c melted apple jelly. Beat cream cheese fluffy, mix in milk then lemon juice and vanilla. Spoon into crusts, top with fruit, and glaze. Refrigerate 2 to 4 hours. *YIELD: 24 tarts.*

Cheesecake tarts made with the Simple Pie Crust recipe on page 185. Double the pie crust recipe to make the full cheesecake tart recipe (12 tarts).

PUDDINGS

SEMI-HOMEMADE BANANA PUDDING

1 large pkg cook-and-serve vanilla pudding

3 c cold whole milk

1 bag or box of vanilla wafers

3 to 4 bananas, sliced

Follow package directions for making pudding (add pudding mix to 3 cups cold whole milk, bring to a boil, stirring constantly, then continue boiling for 5 minutes. Remove from heat). Line bottom of a bowl or 3-qt casserole dish with vanilla wafers. Add some of the pudding. Slice bananas over the pudding and add another layer of vanilla wafers. Repeat the layers, ending up with a layer of wafers over pudding. If desired, add a meringue topping *(see recipe, page 185)*.

Refrigerate 3 to 4 hours before serving.

OLD-FASHIONED BANANA PUDDING

2 eggs, separated

1/2 c white granulated sugar

Pinch of salt

1 T all-purpose flour

2 c whole milk

1 to 2 tsp vanilla extract

3 or 4 bananas, sliced

Vanilla wafers

3 T white granulated sugar

Cream eggs yolks and sugar, add salt, flour and milk. Cook over low to medium heat until thickened. Add vanilla. Pour into baking dish alternately with bananas and wafers. Beat egg whites with 3 T sugar until stiff. Spread egg-white meringue over pudding evenly; brown in preheated oven set to 350°F. Cool and refrigerate at least 3 hours before serving. *YIELD: 6 to 8 servings.*

BIGMAMMA ROSE'S DAIRY KUGEL

from Rose Ackerman Daltroff

I've listed Bigmamma's fruit cocktail kugel in the Bread and Breakfast section of the cookbook. This Dairy Kugel is more robust, and would be served in place of candied sweet potatoes, or as a dessert.

1/2 lb wide egg noodles

1/2 lb cottage cheese

1/4 lb cream cheese

3 eggs

1 c sour cream

2/3 c raisins

1 tsp vanilla extract

Salt

1/2 c granulated sugar

3 T sugar mixed with cinnamon

Butter

Cook noodles according to directions. Rinse and drain. In bowl, mix all remaining ingredients except cinnamon sugar. Combine with drained noodles. Pour into buttered casserole dish. Top with cinnamon sugar. Dot with butter and bake 1 hr and 30 minutes at 375°F in preheated oven, until firm in center.

PECAN VARIATION: Melt butter and brown sugar in dish, then stud with pecan halves, top-side down, before adding the noodle mixture. When baked, flip onto serving plate.

BREAD PUDDING

3 to 5 c diced fresh bread

3 c warmed whole milk

1/4 tsp salt

3 egg yolks, well beaten

1/3 to 1/2 c white granulated sugar

1 tsp vanilla

1/2 tsp nutmeg

Grated rind and juice of half lemon

1/4 c raisins

Trim off crusts before dicing bread; do not pack when measuring. Combine milk and salt, add bread; soak for 15 minutes. Stir in beaten egg yolks, sugar, vanilla and nutmeg. Add lemon juice, rind and raisins. Pour egg mixture over bread. Stir lightly with a fork to blend. Pour into bread pan. Set into larger pan of hot water; bake about 45 minutes in preheated oven set to 325°F. Serve with lemon sauce or hard sauce.

GRACE CHAPEL PERSIMMON PUDDING

from Louise Sherrill Triplette

This recipe is the one Louise always used for her family, and it came from Mrs. I.M. Starnes. I had never tasted persimmon pudding before marrying into the family, and fell in love with it. Louise faithfully made it for me (and others) every holiday. Shannon Triplette's wife, Katie, also fell in love with it, and juggled it by a sympathetic security guard after one Christmas holiday.

Good luck to anyone seeking a good persimmon tree. We were lucky; all the Grace and Clarence Sherrill descendants still have access to Grandma Sherrill's persimmon tree in the side yard.

2 c persimmon pulp

3 eggs

1-3/4 c sweet milk

2 c sifted all-purpose flour

1/2 tsp baking soda

1 tsp salt

1/2 tsp cinnamon

1/2 tsp nutmeg

1-1/2 c white granulated sugar

1 tsp vanilla extract

3 T butter

Gather the persimmons after the frost. If gathered before frost, they will be too tart to eat. Mix persimmon pulp, beaten eggs, and milk. Sift dry ingredients together. Blend in liquid mixture. Stir in melted butter. Pour into a pan 2 inches deep. Bake at 300°F until firm (toothpick comes out clean).

GRATED SWEET POTATO PUDDING

from Andrea Benfield

4 c coarsely grated shredded sweet potatoes

1/2 c light brown sugar

1/2 c white granulated sugar

1 c half and half cream, or whole milk

2 eggs, well beaten

1 tsp vanilla extract

1 tsp lemon flavoring

1 tsp cornstarch

1/4 tsp salt

1/3 c butter, melted

Mix all ingredients together and stir well. Pour into greased casserole dish. Bake 25-30 minutes at 350°F in preheated oven. Serve hot or cold, with cream.

OLD-FASHIONED RICE PUDDING

4 c whole milk

2/3 c white granulated sugar

1/4 c uncooked white rice

1/2 tsp salt

Dash of ground nutmeg

Dash of vanilla extract

1/2 c raisins

Put milk, sugar, rice, salt, vanilla, and nutmeg in a casserole dish and bake uncovered for 3 hours at 300°F in preheated oven. During the first hour, stir three or four times with a fork to keep the rice from settling. After the first hour, stir in the raisins and then finish cooking. Serve hot or cold with cream.

DESSERT SAUCES

FRESH PEACH DIP

from Andrea Benfield

2 c fresh peaches, peeled and chopped

1/2 c white granulated sugar

1 tsp fresh lemon juice

Dash salt

2 c whipped cream

Combine first 4 ingredients, mix well. Fold in whipped cream (or topping). Chill 2 to 4 hours, until serving time, but NO LONGER THAN 24 hrs. Serve over pound cake slices or with Moravian sugar cookies.

HARD SAUCE

1/4 c butter

1 c superfine granulated sugar

2 T brandy or rum

A few grains of nutmeg

Cream butter with mixer until fluffy. Gradually add sugar, beating continually. Add brandy; continue beating until light. Remove to a glass jar, sprinkle with nutmeg. Remove to a cool place to rest for several hours before serving on hot puddings or pies. Cover and refrigerate unused sauce. Potent flavor. NOTE: If you are unable to find superfine sugar, use a pestle and mortar to macerate regular sugar. *YIELD: 1 cup.*

LEMON SAUCE

from Ruth Callicott Thurmond

Aunt Ruth inherited this recipe from her mother, Lilla Callicott, and from her Aunt Alice Wall.

1 c white granulated sugar

2 T all-purpose flour

2 eggs

1-1/2 c boiling water

Juice and rind of 1 lemon

Pinch salt

Beat eggs well, blend flour and sugar, and beat into the eggs. Add boiling water gradually, stirring constantly. Add lemon juice and finely grated rind, cook until clear, about 10-15 minutes. Serve hot or chilled.

HOT LEMON SAUCE

The Helen Corbitt version

This was a Memphis favorite in the 1960s, brought back from Texas by our cotton people. Ms. Corbitt was the Yankee girl who made Texans fall in love with food during her many years of cooking up culinary creativity for the movers and shakers in Austin, Dallas and Houston.

1/2 c white granulated sugar

1/4 tsp salt

1 T cornstarch

1 c boiling water

1 tsp grated lemon rind (zest)

2 T butter

3 T lemon juice

Mix sugar, salt and cornstarch, add boiling water and cook until clear. Add lemon zest; continue cooking 1 minute. Remove from heat. Stir in butter and lemon juice. Serve hot over baked custard, puff pastry or fresh fruit. Makes a nice sauce for a Trifle with lady fingers.

CHERRIES JUBILEE:

Boil cherry juice from 16-oz can of Bing (dark sweet) cherries with 1 T cornstarch and 1/4 c sugar for 1 minute. Add cherries. Remove from heat. Add 1 T butter, 2 T kirsch and 2 T brandy. Pour cognac on top, and ignite. Serve hot over ice cream.

JUBILEE SAUCE

from Mary Elizabeth Daltroff

This sauce is a variation on a recipe that is found throughout the South at least back to 1939.

16-oz jar of dark cherry preserves

1/4 c port wine

16-1/2 oz can of Bing cherries

1/2 tsp almond extract

1 T Triple Sec

Vanilla ice cream

Thoroughly combine the cherry preserves, wine, Bing cherries, almond extract, and Triple Sec. Chill. Scoop ice cream into sherbet glasses and spoon the Jubilee sauce over the ice cream. Top each serving with a maraschino cherry.

RASPBERRY SAUCE

2 pts fresh raspberries (gently rinsed and drained)

1/2 c white granulated sugar

1 tsp cornstarch, OPTIONAL

Fresh lemon juice

Gently rinse and drain raspberries, taking care not to crush. Discard any that have gone soft. Puree in blender until completely smooth. Strain into a 3-qt sauce pan through a fine sieve, to remove seeds. A few seeds will get through the mesh. Combine cornstarch with sugar; stir into puree. Bring to a slow boil on medium-high heat, stirring to prevent scorching. Allow to boil, stirring, for several minutes. Add squirt of lemon juice and remove from heat, stirring until pan cools a bit. Strain again through sieve to remove remaining seeds. Store, covered, in fridge, until ready to use. Good hot or cold. Serve with chocolate cake, pound cake, cheesecake, almond squares, or baked custards.

COULIS VARIATION: Combine equal 1/2-lb weights of granulated sugar and blackberries, raspberries or blueberries in saucepan with 1/4 c blackberry, or raspberry liqueur, or with Amaretto for the blueberries. Simmer on medium about 10 minutes, until reduced by half to thick syrup. Strain through sieve to remove seeds. Cool, store covered in fridge.

Raspberry Sauce with Grandmother Thurmond's pound cake.

RED HOT (SPICED) APPLE SAUCE

from Mary Elizabeth Daltroff

1-1/2 c boiling water

1/4 c red hots candy

3-oz pkg of strawberry gelatin, dissolved in 2 T water

2 c of applesauce

Pour 1/2 c boiling water over the red hots. Stir well until candies are almost melted. Pour melted candies into gelatin and add remaining 1 c boiling water. Stir well until redhots are melted completely. Let cool slightly. Stir in applesauce. Chill. Serve with Grandmother Thurmond's pound cake, as shown in the photo above. It's fantastic for Valentine's Day.

SAUCY CHOCOLATE

This is a modified variation of quick fudge. It's best when aged from 4 hours to a day to blend the flavors.

1/4 c good quality cocoa powder

1-1/2 to 2 c of confectioners sugar

8 T cream or sweet milk

1 stick (1/2 c) salted butter, cut into 8 pieces

1 tsp vanilla or rum

Combine first four ingredients in saucepan. Heat on low, stirring, until melted. Just before serving, stir in vanilla or rum. Store at room temperature for up to 3 days. To reuse after it has cooled, microwave on medium (5 to 7) for 30 seconds and stir. Nuke again, if needed.

THE RECIPES

CAKES, COOKIES & CANDY

BARS

Mom's Lemon Squares; degree of gooiness depends on the lemons!

ALMOND SQUARES

2 c white granulated sugar

4 eggs

1 c (2 sticks) butter, melted

2 tsp almond extract

2 c all-purpose flour

Confectioners sugar

Preheat oven to 325°F. Grease a 9-by-13-inch baking pan with shortening. Beat on high speed the sugar and eggs in large bowl, until light lemon color. Mix in melted butter and almond extract until well combined. Add flour in three parts, beating until completely blended. Pour batter into pan and work knife over top to force out bubbles. Bake on middle rack 30-35 minutes until edges are light brown and toothpick inserted in center comes out clean. Remove to rack to cook. While cooling, use sifter to sprinkle powdered sugar evenly over top. When cool, cut into 30 squares. Serve with raspberry sauce or vanilla ice cream.

LAYERED ALMOND BARS VARIATION: Make a powdered sugar crust of 1-1/2 to 2 sticks butter, 2 heaping c plain flour, and 7 T powdered sugar; bake 20 minutes. Cool. Make filling by mixing 8 oz cream cheese, 4 eggs, 2 c white granulated sugar, 2 tsp almond extract. Pour filling over crust. Top with 1 c chopped salted almonds, lightly pressed into filling. Bake again at 325°F for 30-35 minutes.

BLONDIES

2-2/3 c sifted plain flour

2-1/3 tsp baking powder

1/2 tsp salt

2/3 c butter

1 lb light brown sugar

3 eggs

1 c chopped nuts

1 c semi-sweet chocolate chips

Sift dry ingredients together and set aside. Melt butter and blend in brown sugar. Allow to cool 10 minutes. Add eggs; mix well. Add flour, nuts and chocolate chips. Bake in 9-by-13-inch pan greased with cooking spray for 25-30 minutes in oven preheated to 350°F. Cool. Cut into 20-24 squares.

CARAMEL BROWNIES

from Ruby White Thurmond

One of Grandmother's favorites, this regional recipe was published in the 1964 cookbook of the Woman's Exchange of Memphis. These may be eaten plain, or frosted with Caramel Icing or Brown Sugar Icing.

2 c light brown sugar

1 stick butter, room temperature or softened

2 eggs

3/4 c plain flour

1 tsp baking powder

1 tsp vanilla extract

1/4 tsp salt

1 c fine-chopped pecans or shredded coconut

Blend softened butter and sugar. Add eggs and beat well. Add remaining ingredients and mix. Pour into an 8-by-10-inch baking pan greased with cooking spray or shortening. Bake for 30 minutes in a preheated oven set at 325°F. Remove from oven and cool. *YIELD: 16 brownies* (they're rich, so cut 'em small).

TIPS FOR CUTTING BARS:

- Lightly score with a knife or pastry knife as soon as they come out of the oven (use a ruler as a guide).
- Cool completely before cutting. Dip sharp knife in hot water and wipe with dry kitchen towel between cuts.
- Move knife across pan in sawing motion from one end to the other until cut. If pulling across, you will drag the goods and deform the cut.

DATE BARS

We made and sent these to Jeff during Operation Desert Storm and Desert Shield. They tended to survive the shipping and the heat.

3/4 c shortening

1-1/2 c white granulated sugar

1 egg

3 c cake flour

1 tsp salt

1 tsp baking powder

1/2 tsp baking soda

1 c sour milk (buttermilk)

1 c chopped pecans or walnuts

1 c chopped dates

Confectioners sugar

Cream shortening and sugar until fluffy. Add egg and beat thoroughly. Sift flour, salt, baking powder and soda together. Add alternately with the sour milk to the creamed mixture. Fold in pecans and dates. Pour into 2 greased shallow pans. Bake in oven at 350°F for 20 to 25 minutes. Remove from oven and cool. Cut into bars when still warm, and roll in or sprinkle on confectioners sugar. Store in a tightly covered metal container. *YIELD: 48 bars.*

CAKE MIX LEMON SQUARES

from Andrea Benfield

Andrea always takes these to her annual DAR New-Members Tea.

1 box lemon cake mix

1 egg

1 stick (1/2 c) melted butter, cooled

1 tsp lemon extract

8-oz pkg cream cheese, softened

2 eggs

2 T fresh lemon juice

2 c confectioners sugar

Mix first 4 ingredients until crumbly. Press into a sprayed 9-by-13-by-2-inch baking pan. Set aside. Mix last 4 ingredients with a mixer until smooth. Pour into the crust. Bake 35-45 minutes at 350°F in a preheated oven. Cool on wire rack. Slice when the pan has completely cooled.

MOM'S LEMON SQUARES

from Mary Elizabeth Daltroff

1/2 c butter

1 c all-purpose flour

3/4 c confectioners sugar

1 lemon

2 eggs

1 c sugar

2 T all-purpose flour

1/2 tsp baking powder

2 T lemon juice

1 c confectioners sugar

2 T lemon juice

Mix butter, 1 cup flour, and 3/4-cup confectioners sugar. Spread into 8-inch-square baking pan and bake at 350°F in preheated oven for 15 minutes. Grate 1 lemon and mix with 2 eggs, 1 cup sugar, 2 T flour, 1/2 tsp baking powder, and 2 T lemon juice. Pour over baked mixture. Bake 25 minutes at 350°F. Mix powdered sugar and 2 T lemon juice and spread over top while still hot. Cool on a rack. Cut into squares.

DREAM BARS

1/2 c butter or margarine

1/2 c brown sugar, packed

1 c unsifted all-purpose flour

2 eggs

1 c brown sugar, packed

1 tsp vanilla extract

2 T all-purpose flour

1/2 tsp salt

1 tsp baking powder

1-1/2 c shredded coconut

1 c chopped nuts

Cut sugar and flour into butter with pastry blender until crumbly. Pat dough into bottom of greased 8-by-12-inch pan. Bake in moderate oven at 375°F for 10 minutes. Cool.

Beat eggs, add brown sugar and vanilla. In a small bowl, mix flour, salt and baking powder. In another bowl, mix coconut and nuts. Sprinkle flour mixture over coconut-nut mixture to coat; add this to wet ingredients and blend. Pour on top of the baked crust. Spread evenly. Bake in preheated oven at 375°F for 20 minutes. Cool, cut into squares. *YIELD: 24 bars.*

GOOEY CHOCOLATE CASHEW BARS

from Andrea Benfield, from her friend Carol Bishee

1-1/2 c all-purpose flour

1/4 c packed light brown sugar

1/2 c butter, softened

1-1/2 c chocolate chips

3/4 c white granulated sugar

3/4 c dark corn syrup

3 eggs, slightly beaten

3 T melted butter

1-1/2 c salted cashews, coarsely chopped or pieces

Preheat oven to 350°F. Mix flour, sugar and soft butter until mixture resembles coarse crumbs. Press into bottom of ungreased 9-by-13-by-2-inch baking pan. Bake for 15 minutes, or until edges are slightly browned. Mix all remaining ingredients except nuts; spread over hot crust. Continue baking for 28-35 minutes, until set. Remove from oven and press cashew pieces into top. Cool completely before cutting. Keep refrigerated.

GINGER BREAD

from Mary Elizabeth Daltroff

1/2 c shortening

1/2 c white granulated sugar

1 c molasses

2 eggs

1 tsp ground cinnamon

1 tsp ground cloves

1 tsp salt

1 tsp allspice

1 tsp ground ginger

1 tsp baking soda

3/4 c hot water

3 c plain flour

Sift flour with soda, salt and spices. Set aside. Put sugar, shortening, molasses, eggs in mixing bowl and blend. Stir in hot water. Add flour mixture. Bake in greased shallow pan 30 minutes at 350°F in preheated oven. Cool before cutting. OPTIONAL: Glaze tops with a sugar glaze, or a dollop of whipped cream.

MAGIC COOKIE BARS

1/2 c (1 stick) butter or margarine

1-1/2 c graham cracker crumbs

14-oz can of sweetened condensed milk

6-oz pkg (1 c) semi-sweet chocolate chip morsels

3-1/2-oz (1-1/3 c) flaked coconut

1 c chopped pecans or walnuts

Preheat oven to 350° F (325 for glass dish). In a 9-by-13-inch pan, melt butter. Sprinkle crumbs over the melted butter in the pan, then pour sweetened condensed milk evenly over the crumbs. Top evenly in this sequence: chocolate chips, coconut, and nuts (last). Press the layers down gently. Bake for 25-30 minutes or until lightly browned. Cool thoroughly before cutting. Store loosely covered at room temperature. *YIELD: 24 bars.*

Michael Triplette on his birthday, circa 1947

HEIRLOOM CAKES

LOUISE'S APPLE LAYER TEA CAKE (APPLE STACK CAKE)

This is definitely a "girlie" recipe. This tea cake, called Apple Stack Cake in some Appalachian communities, probably dates from colonial times. Louise's version, while seemingly simple, ages best when kept wrapped in waxed paper and frozen in aluminum foil. Louise always slices the cake in segments around the circle, rather than in wedges. Louise also says filling made with homemade dried apples tastes the best. I like the apple butter version.

CAKE:

1 to 2-1/2 c white granulated sugar*

2 eggs

1 to 1-1/2 sticks melted butter or margarine*

1 tsp vanilla extract

4 to 5 c self-rising flour*

1/2 to 2/3 c whole milk

*Use all smaller or all larger quantities to make more or fewer layers. Mix eggs and sugar until fluffy. Add the butter, milk and vanilla, and then the flour gradually, beating until well blended. Squeeze mixture together, and knead and work the dough until firm. Refrigerate covered for at least 12 hours to allow this to stiffen. Spray cooking spray on a pastry board or surface, sprinkle with flour. Prepare 8-inch cake pans or pie pans by greasing and flouring, then fitting with parchment paper that you also spray with cooking oil and dust with flour. Measure out dough in balls the size of two extra-large eggs. Place dough balls one at a time on floured surface, sprinkle flour over top of dough, cover with wax paper and roll out pastry-thin into circles. Fit dough into bottoms of prepared pans. Prick the dough with a fork to prevent puffing during baking. Bake about 10-15 minutes at 350°F. Use fork to separate edges all around pan as soon as removed from oven. Turn out while hot onto baking cloth to cool. Makes about 10-12 layers.

LAYERING:

1 tsp vanilla extract

White granulated sugar to taste

Two 28-oz jars applesauce, apple butter, or dried apples)

Combine vanilla extract and jar of regular applesauce or apple butter. Sweeten applesauce with granulated sugar to taste, if not already sweet enough to suit. If using apple butter, mix in 1/4 cup of apple sauce. Place first baked pastry onto a cake plate, spread top

with 1/8-inch-thin layer of apple mixture . Repeat, adding pastry layer topped with sauce mixture, until all of pastry layers are used. Leave top and sides bare (no frosting and no applesauce). Refrigerate, wrapped. VARIATION: Use jams or cooked, sweetened fruit such as blueberry, or seedless raspberry or blackberry.

DRIED APPLES:

Wash, peel and core apples of choice (Red Delicious, Winesaps or Macintosh work well). Cut into rings or slices 1/8 to 1/4-inch thick. Spread slices on tray or screen. For sun-drying: place in direct sunlight, protected by netting to keep out insects. Move tray or screen to follow sun's path. Turn slices occasionally to allow even drying. Bring tray indoors overnight. Sun-drying takes 2 to 3 days, OR heat in oven set to 150°F for 4 to 6 hours. If apples still show moisture when cut or squeezed, extend drying time. Freeze in heavy-duty freezer bags. To make cake filling, cook dried apples with a small bit of water, brown sugar and cinnamon.

Evenly spread the dried apple, applesauce or apple butter mixture on top of each pastry-thin layer of cake. Apple Stack Cake tastes better after aging a few days in fridge or freezer, tightly wrapped.

Nora Dean White at home in Crockett County, TN, circa 1915

AUNT RUTH'S BANANA CAKE

from Ruth Callicott Thurmond

This was a Callicott Christmas cake tradition that Aunt Ruth has continued, even as a Thurmond!

6 over-ripe bananas

4 eggs

1/2 c vegetable oil

1/4 lb (1 stick) butter

2 tsp baking soda

1-1/2 tsp ground cinnamon

1 tsp ground cloves

Pinch salt

2 c sugar

3 c all-purpose flour

2 c raisins

2 c chopped walnuts or pecans

Preheat oven to 300°F; grease 2 loaf pans or 1 tube pan. Cream butter, sugar, oil and banana. Sift dry ingredients, then mix into batter, alternating with eggs, one at a time. Slow-bake in tube or loaf pans approximately 1 hour, 15 minutes. Cool on wire rack. Turn out onto serving platter.

BIGMAMA WHITE'S HICKORY NUT CAKE (1-2-3-4 CAKE)

from Ruby Thurmond, from Nora Dean White

Bigmama Nora Dean White, Mrs. Dick (Ernest E.) White, carried on a West Tennessee version of the 1-2-3-4 cake. She and Granddaddy White used walnuts, pecans, or hickory nuts from the native trees growing on the farm. Bigmama preferred hickory nuts. NOTE: Anybody who's ever tried to crack more than one hickory nut knows how much she must have loved this recipe.

CAKE

1 c (2 sticks) butter

2 c white sugar

3 c all-purpose flour

4 eggs, separated

1 c whole milk

1 tsp lemon juice

2 tsp baking soda

1/2 tsp salt

1 c chopped hickory nuts or pecans

1 tsp almond extract

Grease and flour a 10-inch tube pan. Preheat oven to 350°. Cream butter with 1 c sugar. Beat egg yolks until light. Beat in remaining sugar until light and lemon-colored. Add lemon juice, combine with creamed mixture. Sift together twice the flour, baking soda and salt. During the second sifting, sift dry ingredients alternately with milk into the wet mixture. Stir in nuts and flavoring. Beat egg whites until light but not dry. Fold in gently. Pour the cake mix into the pan and bake for about 1 hour at 325°F. Cool cake on a rack, then cut in half, making 2 layers before frosting.

ICING:

1 c white granulated sugar

1/2 c cold water

2 egg whites

1 tsp vanilla extract

1 c chopped hickory nuts or pecans

Make a syrup out of the sugar and water, cooking to the soft ball stage (238°F on a candy thermometer). Allow syrup to cool while beating egg whites. Pour the syrup in a thin steady stream onto the beaten egg whites, beating until thick enough to spread. Add flavoring. Spread between layers and over tops and sides of the cake. Sprinkle with more chopped nuts.

LOUISE'S 1-2-3-4 CAKE

Louise Triplette and Grandmother Thurmond each had a version of this cake, both inherited from their mothers. It forms the basis for coconut cakes, for wedding cakes, and for other desserts. It can be served with or without icing or hot sauce. Louise Triplette always made this version.

1 c butter

2 c white granulated sugar

3 c all-purpose flour

4 eggs

1 c whole milk or plain yogurt

1/2 tsp salt

1 tsp vanilla extract

1/2 tsp almond extract

2 tsp cream of tartar

1 tsp baking soda

Cream butter. Gradually add sugar, beat about 10 minutes with electric mixer until light and fluffy. Add salt and flavorings. Add eggs to the wet mixture, one at a time, beating after each. Sift cream of tartar and baking soda with flour twice. Add flour mix alternately with milk or yogurt to creamed butter, beating after each addition until smooth.

Bake in two greased, floured 8- or 9-inch pans, or in a Bundt pan, at 350-400°F in a preheated oven, about 20 minutes. Cover with Coconut Icing (*see recipe, page 235*) or Really Old Hot Sauce (*see recipe, page 236*).

Bigmama's 1-2-3-4 Cake with her Seven Minute Icing

DEPRESSION CAKE

1 c light brown sugar

1 c white granulated sugar

2 c hot water

2 tsp salt

4 T shortening

2 tsp cinnamon

1/2 tsp ground cloves

1/2 to 3/4 c raisins, OPTIONAL

2 tsp baking soda, dissolved in 1 T warm water

3 c plain flour

Boil sugars, hot water, salt, shortening, spices and raisins in saucepan for 5 minutes. Cool. Mix into the cooled batter the baking soda dissolved in warm water and the plain flour. Pour batter into greased 9-by-13-inch pan. Bake at 300°F in preheated oven for 1 hr and 15 minutes. Top with whipped cream when serving.

CLARA DOVER'S CORN BREAD CAKE

from Angela Kaiser

This vintage cake from the Cleveland County area of North Carolina has been handed down in Angela's family from her 5-great-grandmother Clara Dover (10 generations). The cake is known as a "basic" to which one might add different flavorings such as chocolate, fruits, and nuts. Over the years Angela's family has tweaked the written measurements to be understood by modern cooks. But never has the cake had any corn meal in it!

1 c white granulated sugar

1 c light brown sugar

1-1/2 c self-rising flour

1 c vegetable oil

4 eggs

1 tsp vanilla extract

Melted chocolate, or fruit of choice, OPTIONAL

1 c chopped pecans or walnuts

Mix all ingredients together by hand. DO NOT USE MIXER! Preheat oven to 350°F. Bake in a 9-by-13-inch greased pan for 30-35 minutes. The cake may be served plain, or it may be glazed or frosted.

GRANDMOTHER'S JAM CAKE

from Ruby White Thurmond

Grandmother always used blackberry jam. Seedless raspberry jam or strawberry jam also work well, producing very different flavors.

1/3 c cocoa

1-1/2 tsp baking soda

1 tsp cinnamon

1/2 tsp nutmeg

3 c plain flour

1-1/2 c butter

1-1/2 c white granulated sugar

3 eggs, beaten until light

1-1/3 c buttermilk

1-1/2 c jam

2/3 c coconut

1 T vanilla extract

1 c nuts (pecans or walnuts, chopped fine)

Sift all dry ingredients together and set bowl aside. Cream together the butter, sugar, beaten eggs, buttermilk, and jam. Fold in coconut, vanilla, and nuts. Gradually add the dry ingredients to the wet ingredients until completely blended. Bake in two greased and floured cake pans in a preheated oven at 375°F for about 25 minutes, or until toothpick inserted in center comes out clean. Remove to rack to cool, Turn out. To frost, use long serrated knife to even up the top side of one layer. Cut each of the two layers into thinner halves, using long serrated knife, in order to have four layers. Skim a thin layer of jam on the bottom of each layer. Frost top side of each layer with chocolate icing/filling as you stack the layers (jam-side facing down goes onto chocolate-filling-side facing up). Frost cake top and stacked sides with icing. Embellish with berries, mint leaves, chocolate curls, chopped nuts, or whipped cream.

CHOCOLATE ICING/FILLING FOR THE JAM CAKE:

10 T butter

6 T cream

4 T cocoa

Pinch of salt

1 tsp vanilla extract

16-oz box confectioners sugar

Mix butter, cream and cocoa (I always sift together the cocoa and sugar before adding to the butter). Add other ingredients and beat for 2 minutes. Let stand for 5 minutes and then frost the cake.

LADY BALTIMORE CAKE

There are numerous little variations on this favorite wedding cake, which was first known by its Lady Baltimore name around the turn of the 20th century. All versions are topped with a boiled or Seven-Minute Frosting, combined with nuts and fruits in the filling.

Family Tips: *Sift cake flour and baking powder together several times before adding to the mixture. Chill the bowl and make sure the beaters are clean before beating the egg whites stiff. Fold in a little of the egg whites first, then fold in remaining egg whites. Some of Mom's notes call for lining the cake pans with parchment paper and then greasing and flouring the paper.*

CAKE:

1 c butter (2 sticks)

2 c white granulated sugar

3-1/2 c cake flour, sifted

3 tsp baking powder

1 c whole milk

6 egg whites, beaten to stiff peaks

1 tsp vanilla or lemon extract

Cream butter. Beat in sugar until fluffy. Combine milk and extract, set aside. Sift together the flour and baking powder; add to wet mixture alternately with milk. Fold in stiff-beaten egg whites (stirring only in one direction). Bake in 2 or 3 greased and floured 8-inch cake pans in preheated oven at 375°F for 25 minutes, until center bounces back when pressed with finger. Cool and turn out. Cover with boiled frosting.

BOILED FILLING AND FROSTING:

2-1/4 c granulated sugar

1/2 c light corn syrup

1/8 tsp salt

1/2 c water

2 egg whites, beaten to stiff peaks

1 tsp vanilla extract

2/3 c seedless raisins, cut fine

2/3 c walnuts or pecans, chopped

Cook sugar, syrup, salt, and water to thread stage, 246°F. Slowly beat the hot syrup into stiffly beaten egg whites. Add vanilla. Put aside 1 c of frosting for top of cake. Add fruit and nuts to remaining frosting. Beat briskly. Spread layers and top of cake with filling. Cover cake top with thin layer of the withheld frosting.

FRUIT-NUT FROSTING VARIATION: Some of our recipes call for adding 1/4 c fine-cut raisins, 1/4 c figs cut into strips, 1/4 c chopped candied cherries, and 1/2 c chopped nuts.

LANE CAKE

The Lane Cake first appeared in the South in the 1830s. It was popularized in the late 19th century by Mrs. Emma Rylander Lane, of Clayton, Barbour County, AL, at a county fair in Columbus, GA. Lane Cake is a rich, sponge-type white cake, built in three or four layers with brandy- or whiskey-laced raisin, pecan, coconut, and custard filling. Mrs. Lane baked her four layers of cake in pie tins lined with brown paper. The classic Lane Cake top and sides are slathered with fruit custard filling. Some folks nowadays cover the top with seven-minute white icing, like a Lady Baltimore Cake.

CAKE:

1 c salted butter, softened

2 c white granulated sugar

1 tsp vanilla extract

3-1/4 c all-purpose flour

1 T baking powder

3/4 tsp salt

1 c whole milk

8 egg whites

Preheat oven to 350°F. Line three to four 8-inch cake pans with parchment paper, then lightly grease and flour the parchment linings. Cream 1 c butter with 2 c sugar and vanilla until creamy. Combine flour, salt and baking powder. Add to butter mixture in three parts, mixing in alternately with milk added in two parts, beginning and ending with flour mixture. Beat egg whites until stiff; gently fold into batter. Spread batter evenly into the four prepared cake pans. Tap pans lightly on counter to burp out air bubbles. Bake at 350°F for 25 minutes, or until toothpick inserted in center comes out clean. Cool pans on rack, then turn out and continue cooling. Peel off parchment paper.

Lane Cake filling and frosting is weepy, but delicious.

OPTION 1, FRUIT CUSTARD FILLING:

1/2 c butter

1-1/4 c white granulated sugar

8 egg yolks

1/2 c water

1 tsp brandy or whiskey, or rum

1 c chopped pecans

1 c raisins

1/2 c candied cherries, chopped

1/2 c flaked coconut

Cream butter and sugar until fluffy, then beat in egg yolks until well mixed. Stir in water and brandy or whiskey. Place in double boiler over boiling water. Cook, stirring constantly until thickened. Add pecans, raisins, cherries and coconut. Stir filling until all ingredients are well mixed. Remove from heat. Cool before spreading evenly between cake layers, reserving some for top. Frost sides of stacked cake with Seven Minute Frosting or Colonnade Icing *(see recipes, page 236)*. Spread remaining fruit filling over iced top of cake.

OPTION 2, FRUIT CUSTARD FROSTING:

1-1/2 c raisins

12 egg yolks

1-3/4 c white granulated sugar

1/2 tsp salt

3/4 c salted butter

1/2 c brandy or whiskey

1-1/2 c coarsely chopped pecans

1-1/2 c shredded fresh coconut

1-1/2 c quartered candied cherries

Cover raisins with hot water, let stand a few minutes, then drain and dry (to plump). Combine egg yolks in top of double boiler and beat slightly. Add sugar, salt and butter and blend. Put double boiler over simmering water and cook, stirring, until sugar is dissolved, butter melts, and mixture begins to thicken, Do NOT overcook or let egg yolks appear scrambled. Mixture should become almost translucent. Remove from heat and add brandy or whiskey. Beat 1 minute with hand mixer. Add nuts, cherries, and coconut. May need to expand into a larger bowl. Cool. To frost cake: spread first between layers, then on top and last on sides. Frosting may start to slide off sides. Lift with spatula and keep spreading back. Cover loosely with foil or plastic wrap, tucking under plate. Store in cool place for several days before serving, or freeze.

TIP: Let Lane Cake age a day before cutting. This allows flavors to blend.

MARDI-GRAS KING CAKE

King cake is made for celebrating the Feast of the Epiphany (12th Night) honoring the three kings who brought gifts to the Christ Child. The European tradition surrounding this bread-like cake has been popular in New Orleans since the 1870s, and in recent years has spread upriver as far as Memphis, and eastward across Alabama. Usually a brioche bread, the cake is shaped like a ring or "crown." The older traditions called for hiding a bean in the cake. The New Orleans King cake contains a plastic baby Jesus. The person who gets the slice containing the baby is responsible for the next party or cake, and will have a year of good luck. The cake is decorated in traditional New Orleans Mardi Gras colors: Green for faith, gold for power, and purple for justice. The cake filling varies according to family tradition.

BRIOCHE:

1 pkg dry yeast

2 T warm water (115°F)

1 tsp salt

2 T white granulated sugar

1/4 c whole milk

2 tsp orange zest, minced

2 c plain flour, sifted

1 tsp cinnamon

2 eggs, beaten

1-1/4 sticks cold unsalted butter, cut into very small dice

1 egg beaten with 2 T water for the egg wash

1 plastic baby trinket

FILLING:

1 c pecan halves, broken up, roasted until fragrant

2/3 c brown sugar

1 tsp vanilla extract

1 tsp ground allspice

Pinch salt

4 T cane syrup (Steen's)

Raisins, OPTIONAL

GLAZE:

1 c confectioners sugar

1 T water

3/4 c white granulated sugar, separated into 3 parts (1/4 c each)

Green, gold and purple food coloring (mix blue and red for purple)

Dissolve yeast in warm water in bowl of a stand mixer fitted with dough hook. Let stand until frothy. Dissolve salt, sugar, orange zest and milk in small bowl, then combine with yeast mixture. Mix cinnamon with flour. Add eggs one at a time with mixer on low speed, then add flour gradually. Knead on low for 10 minutes or until a smooth elastic dough forms. May need to add more flour. Quickly work unmelted butter into dough a bit at a time with mixer. Turn dough into oiled bowl, loosely cove with plastic wrap; let riser about 1 hr in warm spot. When doubled in bulk, remove wrap, pinch down, cover again, and place in fridge overnight.

Make pecan filling by combining all ingredients. Preheat oven to 350°F. Roll dough out to 6-by-8-inch rectangle. Spread pecan filling out in middle of rectangle along whole length, leaving a 1-1/2-inch border on each side. Fold length of dough over the filling and roll up tightly, leaving seam side down. Turn roll into a circle, seam side down; put one end inside the other to hide seam; seal circle. Place on baking sheet and let rise, loosely covered with plastic wrap about 45 minutes, or until doubled. Brush lightly with egg wash. Place in oven and bake about 25-30 minutes until golden brown. Remove to wire rack to cook, and while warm, make a slit and insert baby.

While baking cake, dye the 3 parts of white sugar with food coloring. Make glaze by combining confectioners sugar and water. NOTE: Some diehards add a splash of Bourbon to the glaze. Before cake cools, brush or drizzle glaze over top of cake. Sprinkle colored sugars on glaze, alternating colors. *YIELD: 10-12 servings.*

QUICKIE KING CAKE

1 can cinnamon rolls with icing

3 parts white granulated sugar, dyed purple, gold and green (*see instructions, previous page and below*)

Separate cinnamon rolls; roll out by hand to look like hot dogs. Shape each into an oval, pinch the rolls together, end to end. Place on cookie sheet. Cook as directed. While cooking, dye the 3 parts of white sugar with food coloring. When cinnamon-roll ring is done, remove from oven and ice with white icing. Sprinkle with sugar while hot, alternating colors on each roll.

TIPS FOR MIXING FOOD COLORING:

· Purchase food coloring in squeeze bottles that allow you to measure one drop at a time.

· To make purple, add one drop of red to four drops of blue. Too much red will make burgundy.

· To make green, add one drop of blue to three or four drops of yellow. Too much blue will make a blended color muddy.

MAYONNAISE CAKE

2 c plain flour

1-1/2 tsp baking soda

1-1/2 tsp baking powder

4 T cocoa

1 c white granulated sugar

1 c mayonnaise

1 tsp vanilla

1 c cold water

2 c confectioners sugar

1 c cocoa

3 T hot coffee

Sift together first five ingredients. Add mayo, vanilla and cold water; mix well. Bake in prepared loaf pan at 350°F in preheated oven for 25 minutes or until toothpick comes out clean. Cool and turn out onto plate. For topping, blend confectioner's sugar and cocoa. Beat in hot coffee until smooth. Add more liquid to thin topping if needed when spreading over cake.

SPICE CAKE

from Mary Elizabeth Daltroff

Spice cake is my favorite cake. Mom had two recipes; this one is her old recipe that I've adapted with several ingredient alternatives. Do not overbake.

2-1/2 c sifted cake flour

2 tsp baking powder, OR
　　　　1-1/2 tsp baking powder + 1/2 tsp baking soda

1/2 tsp salt

1/4 tsp ground cloves

1/4 tsp ground nutmeg or mace

1/2 tsp allspice

1 tsp cinnamon

1/2 c vegetable shortening, OR 3/4 c (12 T) unsalted butter, OR 1 c applesauce

1-1/2 c brown sugar, packed

3 eggs

1 c buttermilk

Sift flour, baking powder, soda, salt and spices. Cream shortening and sugar until light and fluffy. Beat in eggs, one at a time. Add flour mixture alternately with buttermilk. Pour batter into two greased, floured 9-inch cake pans. Bake at 350°F in a preheated oven for 30 minutes, until center springs back to touch. ***Do not over-bake.*** Remove from pans. Cool on racks. Frost with Cinnamon Icing (*see recipe, page 234*).

ROBERT E. LEE CAKE

I first encountered this cake while a student at Salem College, then pursued it avidly during my many years in Winston-Salem. The cake appeared in the 1879 cookbook, **Housekeeping in Old Virginia; Contributions from Two Hundred and Fifty of Virginia's Noted Housewives, Distinguished for their Skill in the Culinary Art and Other Branches of Domestic Economy,** *edited by Marion Cabell Tyree. The ingredients were measured in pounds and egg weight. Here's my version.*

2 c pre-sifted plain flour

1/2 tsp cream of tartar

1-1/2 tsp baking powder

8 large or 10 medium eggs, room temperature, separated

1 lb white granulated sugar (2 c)

1 T grated lemon zest

1/4 c fresh lemon juice

Two 10-oz jars of lemon curd

Lemon-Orange Frosting

Preheat oven to 350°F. Grease and flour two 9-inch cake pans. In medium bowl, sift together the pre-sifted flour, with cream of tartar and baking powder. Set aside. In large bowl, beat egg yolks until thick and creamy. Add in sugar, a little at a time, beating until smooth and pale yellow. Stir in lemon zest and lemon juice. Gently fold in the dry ingredients until well mixed, using a wooden spoon and folding only in one direction.

Beat egg whites in chilled bowl with clean beaters until stiff peaks form. With wooden spoon, fold 1/3 of the egg whites into batter, then fold in remaining egg whites, folding only in one direction, until batter is uniform in color. Spoon batter into prepared pans.

Bake about 20-25 minutes, until cake begins to pull away from pan sides. Remove from oven. Cool pans on rack about 10-20 minutes. Loosen edges with knife if needed, turn out onto wire cooling racks to completely cool. Make frosting while cake cools.

When completely cooled, use long serrated-edge knife to cut each layer in half, for a total of four layers. Spread lemon curd between each layer. There will be some left over. You may wish to secure the 4 layers with 1 to 2 wooden skewers inserted near middle (avoid cracking the layers). Spread lemon-orange frosting on sides and top of cake. Refrigerate, covered until use.

LEMON-ORANGE FROSTING:

1/2 c (1 stick) butter, room temperature

1 T grated lemon zest

3 to 4 T grated orange zest

2 T lemon juice

6 c sifted confectioners sugar

4 T fresh orange juice

Beat butter until creamy, beat in the zest and lemon juice. Stir in powdered sugar and orange juice, in 4 segments. Continue beating until smooth If too thick, add more orange juice. Use spatula to cover sides and top of cake.

STRAWBERRY SHORT CAKE

Traditional strawberry shortcake was made either as a sheet cake, layered, or as sweetened drop biscuits, sliced and filled with the strawberries.

1/2 c butter (1 stick)

1 c white granulated sugar

2 eggs

1/2 c whole milk

1-3/4 c cake flour

1/4 tsp salt

3 tsp baking powder

3/4 tsp vanilla extract

Ripe strawberries

Whipped cream

Cream butter, slowly beat in sugar. Add 1 egg at a time; beat briskly until light in color. Sift dry ingredients together. Add sifted dry ingredients to butter mixture alternately with milk. Add vanilla. Blend well. Pour into buttered square 8-inch baking pan. Bake in preheated oven at 350°F about 40 minutes. Test for doneness. Split while warm, place sweetened, sliced strawberries between layers and on top. Cut into squares, serve with sweetened whipped cream.

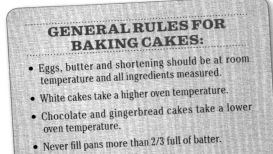

GENERAL RULES FOR BAKING CAKES:

- Eggs, butter and shortening should be at room temperature and all ingredients measured.
- White cakes take a higher oven temperature.
- Chocolate and gingerbread cakes take a lower oven temperature.
- Never fill pans more than 2/3 full of batter.

CAKES, COOKIES & CANDY

WHITE CAKE

from Ruby White Thurmond

This recipe was on a torn sheet of paper written by Grandmother Thurmond in pencil. No title, no notes.

3 c of all-purpose flour

1 tsp baking powder

1/4 tsp salt

2/3 c vegetable shortening

2 c white granulated sugar

1 tsp vanilla extract

1 c water

4 egg whites

1 tsp baking powder

Sift flour before measuring, then measure out 3 c sifted flour, and sift two times with 1 tsp baking powder and salt. Cream shortening and sugar. Add vanilla. Mix in water, alternating with the dry ingredients. Beat egg whites stiff, add baking powder, and gently fold into the cake mix, going only in one direction. Bake in two greased 9-inch cake pans at 350°F in preheated oven for 30 minutes. Cool on rack before turning out.

EASY SPONGE CAKE

from Rosalee Bloom Hyam

7 large eggs, separated

Juice of 1 lemon

1 c white granulated sugar, divided

1 c Swansdown cake flour

Zest from the lemon rind

Beat egg yolks until light, add 1/2 cup sugar and lemon juice. In a separate bowl, beat egg whites; mix in 1/2 cup sugar until stiff. Fold into the egg yolk mixture. Lightly blend in flour and lemon zest. Pour into an ungreased 10-inch tube pan and bake 45-50 minutes at 350°F. Invert pan over rack until cake is cool. Loosen sides of cooled cake with spatula. Gently remove to a cake plate. Sift powdered sugar over top.

SOMETHING YOU NEED TO KNOW:

Aunt Sheila always said the trick to making angel food and sponge cake is to use a clean stainless steel whisk, and gently fold together the dry ingredients, flavoring, and beaten egg whites, STIRRING ONLY IN ONE DIRECTION. It's important not to lose the air bubbles in the beaten egg whites.

Robert E. Lee Cake

ANGEL FOOD CAKE

from Mary Elizabeth Daltroff and Sheila Daltroff Davidson

Sponge cakes and angel food cakes are made without shortening. They are made light with beaten egg whites, which must be beaten stiff, but not overbeaten. Angel food cakes omit the yolks, which is why they are so white.

1-1/4 c granulated sugar

1-1/2 c egg whites

1 c confectioners sugar (12 or 13 eggs)

1-1/4 c Swansdown cake flour

1 tsp cream of tartar

1/4 tsp salt

1 T lemon juice or vanilla extract

Preheat oven to 350°F. Sift sugars and flour together two times (I use a sieve over a large bowl). In a large bowl, add salt to egg whites and beat until foamy. Add cream of tartar and continue to beat only until stiff enough to fold. Do not overbeat to stiff peaks. Fold in dry flour mixture gradually, add flavoring, and pour into an ungreased 10-inch tube pan. Bake about 50 minutes. To test for doneness, press top of cake with finger. If it springs back without a dent, it's done. Invert pan over a soft drink bottle to cool completely. Loosen sides with spatula to remove to a plate.

Clarence and Grace Sherrill, late 1930s, with older childrn Paul, Hugh, Willie Sue, Louise, son-lin-law Lester Triplette, and youngsters Alline and Rebecca.

CREAM CAKES

FRESH COCONUT CAKE

Every family cook has inherited at least one coconut cake recipe. Grandmother and Aunt Emily could make wonderful ones, but Aunt Ann Thurmond made the best in our family. Louise Triplette has always made a pretty fair coconut cake as well.

1 c (2 sticks) butter, softened

2 c white granulated sugar

4 eggs

3 c all-purpose flour

2 tsp baking powder

1 tsp salt

1 c milk or buttermilk (my preference)

1 tsp vanilla extract

Coconut filling

Cream butter and sugar until light and fluffy. Add eggs, one at a time, beating well after each addition. Sift flour with baking powder and salt. Add to creamed mixture alternately with milk, beating well after each addition. Blend in flavorings. Pour batter into 3 greased and floured 9-inch cake pans lined with greased and floured parchment. Bake at 350°F for 18 minutes, until done. Cool completely. Spread coconut filling between layers. Frost top and sides of cake with Seven-Minute Frosting or Classic Coconut Icing (*see both recipes, page 235*); sprinkle with coconut.

COCONUT FILLING:

1/2 c coconut milk from 1 coconut

1/2 c heavy whipping cream

4 c white granulated sugar

2 T cornstarch)

1 fresh coconut, grated

Combine coconut milk and whipping cream with sugar and cornstarch in saucepan. Bring to a boil. Cook until slightly thickened to soft ball stage, about 5 to 10 minutes, stirring constantly. Remove from heat. Add 2 cups of grated coconut, reserving remainder for topping the cake. Sugar will crystallize if over-boiled.

VARIATION: In cake, reduce vanilla to 1/2 tsp and add 1/2 tsp lemon extract. Make lemon pudding (*see recipe, page 196*). Use long knife to cut cake layers into thin halves. Spread lemon pudding filling between cut halves, and coconut filling on center, top, and sides.

THREE-DAY COCONUT CAKE

from Louise Sherrill Triplette

This was Louise's best coconut cake. Trust me, you won't get enough of it.

FIRST DAY, COMBINE; STORE IN FRIDGE 3 DAYS:

16 oz sour cream

2 c white granulated sugar

18 oz frozen grated coconut

EVENING OF SECOND DAY:

1 c butter

2 c white granulated sugar

3 c plain flour

3 tsp baking powder

4 eggs

1 tsp vanilla extract

1 c buttermilk

Cream butter and sugar. Add eggs, one at a time, beating lightly after each addition. Combine dry ingredients and add alternately with buttermilk to butter mixture. Add vanilla. Bake in 3 greased and floured 8-inch cake pans at 350°F in preheated oven about 30 minutes. Cool, turn out, cover overnight.

THIRD DAY:

Make Seven-Minute Frosting *(see recipe, page 236)*

Split each cake layer in two. Position one layer on cake plate, and begin building layers, spreading refrigerated coconut mixture between layers. Frost cake top and sides with Seven-Minute Frosting. Sprinkle coconut all over. Refrigerate, wrapped. Freezes well.

TIPS ABOUT COCONUTS:

- Choose a coconut that feels heavy for its size (fresh and full of coconut meat).
- Shake the coconut to hear liquid sloshing inside (not dried out or fermented).
- Avoid nuts with mold around the coconut eyes, eyes that leak, or eyes that feel soft when pressed.
- Store whole coconuts in the fridge for up to two months.
- Store grated coconut tightly wrapped in the freezer up to 10 months.
- Store open bags of packaged sweetened coconut in the fridge up to a week.
- Throw away old open bags or cans of coconut, which will taste sour or musty.

DUTCH COCOA CREAM CAKE

from Louise Sherrill Triplette

3 c pre-sifted all-purpose flour

2-1/2 c white granulated sugar

6 tsp baking powder

1-1/2 tsp salt

1/2 c cocoa

1 c (2 sticks) butter or margarine

1-1/2 c evaporated milk

4 eggs

1/4 c whole milk

2 tsp vanilla extract

1 pt heavy cream (whipping cream)

1/2 c white granulated sugar

Sift all dry ingredients together. Cream butter and evaporated milk, continue beating 2 minutes. Beat in the eggs, whole milk and vanilla extract, continuing another 2 minutes. Gradually add the dry mixture to the beaten wet mixture and beat for about 2 minutes until thoroughly mixed. Pour into 4 greased and floured cake pans (8-inch or into 9-inch pans for thin layers). Bake in preheated oven at 375°F for about 33 minutes. Whip 1 pint of whipping cream with 1/2 cup of sugar until stiff; spread between the 4 layers. Frost top and sides of stacked layers with favorite chocolate frosting.

Dutch Cocoa Cream Cake iced with Aunt Annie's no-fail chocolate frosting that has been beaten for 10 minutes before applying, then smoothed out after refrigeration overnight.

HUMMINGBIRD CAKE

from Mary Elizabeth Daltroff

This cake has been around the Carolinas, Georgia, Alabama, and parts of Tennessee for a long time. It started off as a banana cake (see my Aunt Ruth's Banana Cake), but cooks fueled up the recipe by adding pineapple, pecans and cream cheese icing.

CAKE

3 c all-purpose flour

1 tsp baking soda

1/2 tsp salt

1 tsp ground cinnamon

2 c white granulated sugar

3 large eggs, lightly beaten

1 c vegetable oil

1-1/2 tsp vanilla extract

1 c toasted pecans, finely chopped

8-oz can crushed pineapple, with juice

2 c overripe bananas, mashed

PECAN CREAM CHEESE FROSTING

1/4 c unsalted butter, room temperature

8 oz cream cheese, room temperature

16 oz (1 lb) confectioners sugar, sifted

1 tsp vanilla extract

1 c fine-chopped pecans, divided

Preheat oven to 350°F. Line two or three 9-inch cake pans with parchment paper; grease paper. In a larger bowl, whisk together flour, sugar, baking soda, salt and cinnamon. In second bowl, mix eggs, oil, vanilla, fruit and pecans (in this order). Add batter to flour mixture, stirring until combined. Evenly divide batter between two or three 9-inch cake pans. Bake 25-30 minutes on center rack of oven until toothpick inserted in center comes out clean. Remove, cool on wire rack 10-15 minutes, then invert cakes and remove parchment. Cool completely.

Cream butter, vanilla and cream cheese with mixer. Add powdered sugar gradually until completely blended. Mix in 1/2 cup of pecans. Place one cake layer, top-side down, on cake plate. For three layer cake, spread with 1/3 of the frosting. If only using two layers, place second cake layer, top-side up, onto frosted first layer. If using three layers, place second layer top-side down, cover with frosting, the place third layer, top-side up. Spread remaining frosting over top and sides of cake. Garnish top with additional 1/2 c chopped pecans. Refrigerate covered until ready to serve.

ITALIAN CREAM CAKE

from Alline Sherrill Annas

This recipe was given to me by Jeff's Aunt Alline at my Grace Chapel bridal shower. My mother used the same recipe, which came from our Memphis neighbor, Louise Perkins. Andrea and my grandmother also had similar versions of this ever-popular cake. NOTE: This cake is not suitable as a sheet cake.

CAKE

1 stick (1/2 c) margarine or butter

1/2 c shortening

2 c granulated white sugar

5 egg yolks

2 c all-purpose flour

1 tsp baking soda

1/2 tsp salt

1 c buttermilk

1 tsp vanilla extract

1 c chopped nuts (pecans or walnuts)

1 c coconut

5 egg whites, beaten until fluffy

Cream the first 4 ingredients. Sift together flour, soda and salt, and add to wet mixture. Pre-mix and add in the buttermilk, vanilla, nuts and coconut. Fold in beaten egg whites. Grease and lightly flour two 9-inch cake pans. Pour mixture into prepared pan(s) and bake at 350°F in preheated oven about 20 minutes. Cool cake completely. Coat cake with the icing, using a spatula or large flat knife. Refrigerate, covered.

CREAM CHEESE ICING:

8-oz pkg cream cheese, softened

1/2 c butter (1 stick)

16-oz box confectioners sugar

1 tsp vanilla extract

Cream cheese and butter together, fold in confectioner's sugar and vanilla. *YIELD: 4 cups.*

MASCARPONE SUBSTITUTE FOR FROSTING AND FILLING

12 oz cream cheese

4-1/2 T sour cream

3 T unwhipped heavy cream

Mix ingredients together and measure out amount required in recipes calling for mascarpone.

LEMON TIRAMISU CAKE

from Rosa Lee Morton, modified by Laurie Triplette

You may need to stake the layers with two wooden picks to prevent them from cracking or sliding.

CAKE:

Two French vanilla cake mixes

1-1/3 c water, each

1/4 c extra light olive oil, each

3 large eggs, each

1 tsp lemon extract, each

FILLING:

3/4 c whipping cream

1-1/2 tsp white granulated sugar

12 oz Mascarpone cheese substitute, 6 T reserved
     (see recipe, page 218)

3/4 c confectioners sugar

1-1/2 c ricotta cheese

1-1/2 tsp vanilla extract

3 T grated lemon zest

15 oz lemon curd, divided into 10 oz and 5 oz

GLAZE AND GARNISHES:

1/2 c lemon liqueur (limoncello)

1 c prepared lemonade (Crystal Light or Minute Maid)

Confectioners sugar

Lemon peel curls

Shaved semi-sweet chocolate

Preheat oven to 350°F. Grease and flour four 9-inch cake pans. Prepare cake mixes in two separate batches, following directions EXCEPT mix the water and oil for 2 minutes, THEN beat in eggs for 30 seconds. Add lemon extract, stirring just to blend. Ladle batter equally into the pans. I use a 1-cup measure and alternate until each pan contains the same amount of batter. Thump gently against counter to remove bubbles.

Bake for 30 minutes or until a wooden toothpick inserted in center comes out clean. Do not over-bake. Remove pans to wire rack to cool 20-30 minutes. Gently jiggle to loosen from sides and bottom, them, carefully slide onto waxed paper, top-side facing up. Cool 30 more minutes.

Beat whipping cream and granulated sugar with a mixer at high speed, until stiff peaks form. Refrigerate.

Combine Mascarpone substitute with confectioners sugar. Beat well with mixer at medium speed. Blend in ricotta cheese. Add vanilla, lemon rind and 10 oz (1 jar) lemon curd. Mix well. Fold in whipped cream. In a separate bowl, spoon 4 to 6 T Mascarpone mixture into the remaining 5 oz of lemon curd.

Combine limoncello and lemonade in a small bowl to make glaze. When ready to assemble cake, use large serrated knife and carefully slide through tops of each layer to make tops even and porous. You will use 3 of the 4 layers; the 4th is for emergency use as a replacement if one layer cracks. Place one layer on serving plate. Brush or spoon top evenly with about 1/4 c glaze. Use paper towel to wipe excess liquid from plate after each application. Spread about 1-1/2 cup of the Mascarpone filling. Repeat with second layer. Top with third layer and brush with remaining glaze. Spread with remaining lemon curd. Frost sides of cake with remaining Mascarpone filling. Refrigerate several hours or overnight. Before serving, dust top of cake with confectioner's sugar and shaved chocolate. Garnish with lemon slices or peeling swirls. Serve with fresh strawberries or raspberries. Cake will be jiggly, so slice carefully! Freezes well.

TIRAMISU CAKE

Tiramisu is an increasingly popular Italian layer cake that could be considered a cousin to English trifle. Afficionados disdain mascarpone substitute made with American cream cheese. But hey, it works in a pinch.

6 egg yolks

1-1/4 c white granulated sugar

1-3/4 c heavy whipping cream

1-1/4 c mascarpone cheese or mascarpone substitute

Two 3-oz pkgs ladyfingers (12 split fingers in each pkg)

1/3 c Kahlua or Tia Maria

1 tsp cocoa powder

1-oz square of semisweet chocolate, shaved into curls

Separate eggs. Set whites aside. Combine egg yolks and sugar in top of a double boiler over boiling water. Reduce heat to low. Cook about 10 minutes, stirring constantly, until mixture coats spoon. Remove from heat. Beat with mixer until yolks become thick and lemon colored. Add mascarpone, beating until mixed. Whip cream to stiff peaks in separate, chilled bowl. Fold whipped cream into beaten yolks. Set aside. Line bottom and sides of trifle dish or large glass bowl with the split ladyfingers, the curved sides facing out along the sides of the dish. Brush ladyfingers with coffee liqueur. Spread half the cream filling over the ladyfingers lining dish bottom. Repeat process until all has been used, with filling on top. Garnish with cocoa and chocolate curls. Refrigerate 4 hours or overnight before serving

VARIATION: Soak lady fingers in espresso laced with rum and sugar. Layer in a loaf pan lined with plastic wrap. Refrigerate, then turn out and slice.

Cousin Bradley Cooke and little sister Caroline help
Kurt Benfield blow out his birthday candles.

POKE CAKE

from Andrea Benfield.

This cake is a good one for those little pre-school help-ers, who can poke the holes and pour in the gelatin.

1 box yellow cake mix

1-1/4 c water

1/3 c vegetable oil (canola)

3 eggs

3-oz pkg flavored gelatin, your choice

1-1/2 c boiling water

6 oz cream cheese, softened

8 oz frozen whipped topping, thawed (*I use Cool Whip*)

1/4 c confectioners sugar

1 tsp vanilla extract

Combine cake mix, water, eggs and oil in bowl. Beat 2 minutes. Pour into a greased and floured 9-by-13-by-2-inch baking pan. Bake at 350ºF in preheated oven for 30-35 minutes. When cake is done, prepare gelatin with boiling water. Poke holes in top of cake with a wooden dowel or large fork. Pour liquid gelatin over cake. Mix cream cheese, topping, sugar and va-nilla until smooth. Spread over cake. Refrigerate.

HINT ABOUT YOUR WATER:

If you don't have a water purification system filtering the tap water in your home, you may need to use distilled or bottled water when baking. The chemical additives in many municipal water systems can kill yeast and otherwise alter the chemistry of baking ingredients.

TIPS FOR IDENTIFYING CAKE PROBLEMS AFTER THE FACT:

Cake is Heavy:
Too much mixing
Too much fat or liquid
Not enough sugar, baking powder or baking soda (or old)
Baking temperature not right

Cake is too flat:
Not enough baking powder or soda
Pan too large for amount of batter
Baking temperature not right

Cake is tough:
Too little fat or sugar
Too much flour
Batter was overmixed
Oven was too hot
Cake was baked too long

Cake ran over:
Too much batter in pan
Oven wasn't hot enough
Too much baking powder or soda
Too much sugar

Crust color uneven:
Ingredients not well blended
Oven temperature is uneven
Oven was overcrowded
Cake was placed too close to edge of oven

Cake crust is sticky:
Too much sugar
Not baked long enough
Not cooled properly

Cake is coarse:
Not enough fat and sugar
Oil was used instead of shortening
Plain flour used instead of cake flour
Too much baking powder or soda
Oven not hot enough

Cake fell:
Too much sugar, fat, liquid, or baking powder or soda
Not enough flour
Eggs were overbeaten
Oven not hot enough
Cake pans jarred

Cake top too rounded or cracked:
(NOTE: Loaf cake should be cracked.)
Too much flour
Not enough liquid
Batter was overmixed after flour addition
Oven was too hot at beginning

CHEESE CAKES

CLASSIC NEW YORK CHEESECAKE

FILLING

Four 8-oz pkgs cream cheese, softened

1-1/3 c sugar

2 T cornstarch

1 tsp vanilla extract

3 eggs

1 c sour cream

CRUST

2 c graham cracker crumbs

1/2 c (1 stick) butter, melted

2 T sugar

Mix crumbs, sugar and butter. Reserve 2 T of crumb mixture; press rest of crumbs into 9-inch spring-form pan and 2 inches up pan sides. Chill in freezer while preparing filling. Beat cream cheese until fluffy. Add 1-1/3 cup of sugar, cornstarch and vanilla, beating until combined, then add eggs, one at a time. Do not overbeat. Stir in sour cream and pour into chilled crust, sealing the edges. Bake at 325°F, about 1 hour and 15 minutes, up to 1 hour and 30 minutes, until center is almost set. Remove from oven; cool on wire rack 15 minutes. Loosen sides, cool 45 more minutes. Remove to serving plate. Sprinkle reserved crumbs on top. Refrigerate. Serve with chilled raspberry sauce and curls of shaved chocolate.

VARIATIONS: Add Amaretto, Kahlua, or rum to filling.

CHOCOLATE SWIRL CHEESECAKE

CRUST:

1-1/4 c crushed chocolate wafers

2 T confectioners sugar

2 tsp unsweetened cocoa powder

1/2 c finely chopped walnuts

5 T unsalted butter, melted

Preheat oven to 350°F. Lightly butter 8-inch spring form pan. For crust, mix all ingredients except butter in a mixing bowl. Drizzle butter over the mixture and stir until crumbs are moistened. Press over bottom and halfway up the sides of the buttered pan. Bake 6 minutes. Let cool on a wire rack, then refrigerate until cold.

FILLING:

1 c semisweet chocolate chips

Two 8-oz packages cream cheese, room temperature

1/2 c white granulated sugar

4 large eggs

1 tsp vanilla extract

1 c sour cream, divided into 1/3 and 2/3

3 T firmly packed light brown sugar

Heat oven to 425°F. Melt chocolate in top of a double boiler over simmering water. Beat cream cheese and granulated sugar in a mixer bowl until light and fluffy. Beat in eggs one at a time, then beat in vanilla. Divide batter in half. Beat 1/3 cup sour cream, the brown sugar, and melted chocolate into half the batter. Beat remaining 2/3 cup sour cream into second half. Pour chocolate batter into chilled crust. Gently pour white batter on top. Swirl the batters together using a thin knife careful not to over-mix. Bake cake for 12 minutes. Reduce heat to 250°F and bake until 1-inch circle in center of cake is barely soft, which will be around 55-60 minutes. Turn oven off, open oven door slightly, and let cool for several hours. Refrigerate overnight. Remove sides of spring form pan and serve.

PUMPKIN CHEESECAKE

from Mary Elizabeth Daltroff

1/4 c graham cracker crumbs

Four 8-oz pkgs of cream cheese, softened

1-1/2 c white granulated sugar

5 large eggs

1/4 c of all-purpose flour

1/4 tsp salt

16-oz can of pumpkin

2 tsp pumpkin pie spice

1/2 c heavy cream, whipped

Butter bottom and sides of a 9-inch spring form pan. Sprinkle with cracker crumbs. Shake pan to coat all sides. Let excess crumbs remain on bottom. Preheat oven to 325°F. In large mixing bowl, beat cream cheese with the mixer until fluffy. Beat in sugar gradually. Add eggs, one at a time, beating well after each addition. Sift together flour, salt, pumpkin and spice and beat into batter. Pour into prepared pan. Bake 1 hour and 30 minutes, until firm around sides but soft in center. Turn off heat. Open oven door a crack; let cake cool in oven for 30 minutes. Top of cake will have cracked during baking. Remove cake from oven after 30 minutes. Cool completely, remove sides of pan. Chill. Top with whipped cream to serve.

RED VELVET CHEESECAKE

1-1/2 c chocolate graham cracker crumbs

1/4 c (4 T) butter, melted

1-1/2 c white granulated sugar, PLUS 1 T sugar, divided

Four 8-oz pkgs of cream cheese, softened and divided

4 large eggs

3 T unsweetened cocoa powder

1 c sour cream

1/2 c buttermilk (not light version)

2 tsp vanilla extract

1 tsp white distilled vinegar

Two 1-oz bottles of red food coloring

1/2 c (1 stick) butter, softened

1 tsp vanilla extract

16-oz box of confectioners sugar

Stir together the graham cracker crumbs and 1/4-cup melted butter, with 1 T sugar. Press mixture into bottom of a 9-inch spring form pan. Beat three of the 8-oz pkgs cream cheese with 1-1/2 cups sugar on medium speed. Add eggs and next 6 ingredients, and beat until completely mixed. Pour into prepared crust. Bake at 325ºF in preheated oven for 10 minutes. Reduce heat to 300º; bake 1 hour and 15 minutes, until center is firm. Turn off oven. Leave cheesecake in oven for 30 minutes. DO NOT OPEN BEFOREHAND. Remove cheesecake and run knife along outer edge. Cool on a wire rack for 30 minutes. Cover and chill for 8 hours.

Beat remaining 8-oz pkg of cream cheese and butter until smooth; gradually add confectioners sugar and vanilla, beating until smooth. Spread evenly over top of cheesecake. Chill again before serving. Refrigerate unused leftovers. *YIELD: 8 to 12 slices.*

Mississippi Mud Cake

CHOCOLATE

CHOCOLATE ÉCLAIR CAKE

1 box of graham crackers

Two small pkgs French vanilla instant pudding mix

3 c whole milk

Large container of Cool Whip

Two 1-oz squares of semi-sweet baking chocolate

6 T butter

3 T milk

1-1/2 c confectioners sugar

Line bottom of 9-by-13-by-2-inch baking pan with whole graham crackers. Mix 2 pkgs of pudding with 3 cups cold milk. Beat together. Add Cool Whip; stir but do not beat. Pour over graham cracker layer. Place second layer of graham crackers over Cool Whip. In a double boiler, melt 2 squares of chocolate, stir in butter and 3 T milk. Beat in confectioners sugar with mixer. Pour chocolate over graham crackers. Refrigerate 3 hours. Cut like regular cake.

MISSISSIPPI MUD CAKE

1 stick (1/2 c) butter

1/2 c cocoa powder

5 extra large, or 6 large eggs

1-1/4 c sifted self-rising flour

2 c white granulated sugar

1 generous c chopped, roasted walnuts or pecans

2 tsp vanilla extract

16-oz bag of mini-marshmallows

1 box (16 oz) confectioners sugar

1 stick (1/2 c) butter, softened

1/3 c cocoa powder

1/2 c evaporated milk

Chopped nuts, OPTIONAL

Melt first butter, mix in cocoa, eggs, sugar and flour. Stir in nuts and vanilla, pour into greased 13-by-9-inch baking pan. Bake at 350ºF for 30 minutes, until top springs back when touched (do not overbake). Combine second sugar and butter, beating in 1/3 cup cocoa and evaporated milk until creamy. Remove cake from oven. Cover with marshmallows, return to oven for 5 minutes to melt marshmallows, then pour frosting on top, swirling frosting over and into the marshmallows to blend. Sprinkle with optional nuts.

CHOCOLATE COLA CAKE

from Mary Elizabeth Daltroff

CAKE:

1 c (2 sticks) butter

1/4 c unsweetened cocoa powder

1 c cola soft drink (NOT diet)

2 c all-purpose flour

2 c white granulated sugar

1 tsp baking soda

1/2 c whole buttermilk

2 eggs

1 tsp vanilla extract

1-1/2 c miniature marshmallows

Heat butter, cocoa, and cola to boiling stage. Remove from heat and add flour, sugar, and baking soda; then mix gently. Stir in buttermilk, eggs, vanilla and marshmallows. Pour into greased 13-by-9-inch pan. Bake at 350°F in preheated oven for 30 to 35 minutes. Cake can be frosted while warm.

COLA ICING:

6 T regular cola soft drink (NOT diet)

3 T unsweetened cocoa powder

1/2 c (1 stick) butter

4 c confectioners sugar

1 c chopped walnuts

1 tsp vanilla extract

Bring to a boil the butter, cocoa, and cola. Remove from heat. Stir in confectioners' sugar, chopped nuts, and vanilla. Frost top of cake while icing is still hot. *YIELD: 10-12 servings.*

FLOURLESS CHOCOLATE CAKE

1 T cocoa powder

1/2 c (1 stick) butter, softened

1 c plus 2 T white granulated sugar, divided

1 c ground almonds

8 oz semisweet chocolate, melted in double boiler

4 eggs, separated

1 c whipping cream

1 tsp vanilla extract

2 c strawberries

Preheat oven to 350°F. Coat a 9-inch spring-form pan with cooking spray or butter and cocoa. Shake off the excess. Beat butter until smooth. Add 1 cup sugar and beat until creamy. Add the ground nuts, chocolate and egg yolks, beating thoroughly. Beat egg whites until they form soft peaks. Stir 1/3 of the egg whites into chocolate mixture and then gently fold in the remaining egg whites. Scrape batter into prepared pan. Bake 35 to 45 minutes or until toothpick inserted in center comes out nearly clean. Let cool in pan for 30 minutes, then release the sides and slide cake onto a serving plate. Combine cream, vanilla and 2 T sugar, beating until soft peaks form. Top cake with whipped cream and strawberries. *YIELD: 12 servings.*

LOUISE'S CHOCOLATE SHEATH CAKE

from Andrea Benfield

CAKE:

2 c white granulated sugar

2 c self-rising flour

1 stick (1/2 c) butter or margarine

1/2 c vegetable oil

4 T cocoa powder

1 c water

1/2 c buttermilk

2 eggs

1 tsp cinnamon

1 tsp baking soda

1 tsp vanilla extract

Sift sugar and flour together in large mixing bowl. Bring to a rapid boil in a medium saucepan the oil, butter, cocoa and water. Pour this over the flour-sugar mixture, beating well. Mix the buttermilk, eggs, cinnamon, soda and vanilla together and add to the flour mixture, beating well. Pour into a greased, floured 10-by-15-1/2-by-1-inch baking pan. Bake at 400°F in preheated oven for 20-25 minutes, or until toothpick comes out clean.

ICING:

16-oz box of confectioners sugar

4 T cocoa powder

6 T milk

1 stick (1/2 c) butter or margarine

1 tsp vanilla extract

1/2 c nuts

Five minutes before cake is done, start the icing. Put all ingredients except confectioners sugar into a saucepan and bring to a boil. Pour the hot ingredients over the confectioners sugar in a mixing bowl and beat well. Remove cake from oven and spread warm icing on hot cake.

HERSHEY BAR CHOCOLATE CAKE

from Mary Elizabeth Daltroff

This cake was one of Mom's favorite recipes. Many variations on this recipe have floated around over the years, some calling only for Hershey chocolate syrup, others calling for varying quantities of the Hershey Company's best known chocolate bar.

CAKE:

2 sticks butter or margarine, softened

2 c white granulated sugar

4 eggs

2 small cans Hershey Syrup (equivalent of 2/3 c)

2-1/2 c of all-purpose flour, sifted

1/4 tsp salt

1/2 tsp baking powder

1 tsp vanilla extract

1/4 tsp baking soda

1 c buttermilk

Seven 5-cent Hershey's Milk Chocolate Bars (the current NEAREST equivalent would be the 1.55-oz bars)

Preheat oven to 350°F. Grease and line the bottom of a tube pan with waxed paper. Cream the butter and sugar at high speed until fluffy. Add 4 eggs, one at a time on low speed. Add the Hershey's syrup, sifted flour, salt, baking powder and baking soda, vanilla and buttermilk. Melt 7 Hershey Bars in double boiler; fold into the batter. Pour into the tube pan and bake 1 hour and 30 minutes, until toothpick inserted in center comes out clean. Cool on wire rack and turn out onto cake plate. Top with icing.

ICING:

4 T (1/2 stick) melted butter or margarine

Dash salt

1 T cocoa powder

Confectioners sugar

Whole milk

Use mixer to blend butter, salt and cocoa. Add confectioners sugar and moisten with milk, to reach spreading consistency over top of cake. To drizzle rather than ice, thin the frosting with additional milk.

ME'S GERMAN CHOCOLATE CAKE

from Mary Elizabeth Daltroff

CAKE:

4 oz of sweet baking chocolate, melted in double boiler

1/2 c water

1 tsp vanilla extract

1 c butter (2 sticks)

2 c white granulated sugar

4 eggs, separated

3 c sifted all-purpose flour

1 tsp baking soda

1/2 tsp salt

1 c buttermilk

Combine chocolate and water, cool. Add vanilla. Cream butter and egg yolks, beating well after each. Add chocolate mixture. Combine all dry ingredients and add to chocolate mixture alternating with buttermilk, ending with the flour mix. Beat egg whites until stiff. Fold into batter. Pour into three 9-inch round cake pans. Bake at 350°F in preheated oven for 30-35 minutes, until toothpick comes out clean. Cool 10 minutes; remove from pan. Spread coconut-pecan frosting as a filling between layers, and over the top.

COCONUT-PECAN FROSTING:

1-1/3 c evaporated milk

1-1/3 c white granulated sugar

4 egg yolks

2/3 c butter

1-1/2 tsp vanilla extract

1-1/3 c coconut

1-1/3 c pecans

Combine milk, sugar, egg yolks, and butter in a saucepan. Boil, cook over medium heat for 12 minutes, stirring constantly. Add vanilla, coconut and pecans; stir until frosting is cool and of spreading consistency. Frost the cake as directed above.

Red Velvet Cake may be made in two large or three thinner layers, adapted to cupcakes (see page 225).

RED VELVET CAKE

from Andrea Benfield

CAKE:

1-1/2 c shortening

2 eggs

1 T butter

1-1/2 c white granulated sugar

1 tsp vanilla extract

3 T cocoa powder

1-1/2-oz bottle red food coloring

1 T white distilled vinegar

1 tsp salt

1 tsp baking soda

1 c buttermilk

2-1/2 c cake flour, sifted

Preheat oven to 350°F. Grease and flour three 8-inch round cake pans. Cream together the shortening, sugar, eggs, vanilla and butter. Combine cocoa and food coloring in a small bowl. Mix into a paste and add to creamed mixture. Mix salt, vinegar and soda together and add to buttermilk in a small bowl. Add flour and buttermilk mixture alternately into the creamed mix, beating well after each addition. Pour into prepared cake pans. Bake for 20-25 minutes. Cool on wire rack for 10 minutes, then turn out onto floured cloth on rack. Cool completely before frosting with Snow White Frosting.

SHORT-CUT VARIATION: Use French vanilla cake mix, follow directions for preparation; add 3 T cocoa powder and 1-1/2 oz red food coloring.

SNOW WHITE FROSTING:

3 T all-purpose flour

1/2 tsp salt

1 c white granulated sugar

1/2 tsp butter flavoring

1 c vegetable shortening

1 c milk

2 tsp vanilla extract

Cook the flour, salt and milk in a saucepan, stirring until thick. Let cool completely. Cream sugar and shortening in bowl until smooth. Add vanilla and butter flavoring. Stir the cooled flour mixture into the creamed mixture. Beat until smooth. Frost between layers, on sides and on top of Red Velvet Cake.

FROSTING VARIATIONS: Use Cream Cheese Frosting or Butter Cream Frosting.

MARY ELIZABETH'S FAVORITE RED VELVET CAKE RECIPE

from Mary Elizabeth Daltroff

This was a handwritten note in Mom's recipe files.

CAKE:

3 oz unsweetened chocolate, chopped

2 c white granulated sugar

4 large eggs

1-1/2 c vegetable oil

1-1/2 tsp vanilla extract

2 c all-purpose flour

2-1/4 tsp baking soda

1/4 tsp salt

1-1/2 lb canned beets, drained and pureed

1 tsp red food coloring

Preheat oven to 350°F. Butter three 9-inch round cake pans and line with parchment paper. Melt unsweetened chocolate in a double boiler over boiling water. Mix sugar, eggs, oil and vanilla with electric mixer paddle attachment, on low speed for about 2 minutes. Sift dry ingredient together and add to the wet mixture a bit at a time, continuing to mix on low speed. Scrape down sides with bowl scraper while mixing. Blend in melted chocolate on low speed. Add the pureed beets and food coloring, continuing to mix on low speed until completely blended.

Evenly divide batter among the three prepared cake pans. Bake in the middle of the oven for 20-25 minutes, or until inserted toothpick comes out clean. Remove pans from oven; cool on rack 10-15 minutes; turn out to finish cooling.

ICING:

2 c heavy cream

12 oz cream cheese at room temperature

12 oz mascarpone cheese (or mascarpone substitute)

1/2 tsp vanilla extract

1-1/2 c powdered sugar, sifted

Pour heavy cream into a small bowl and whip it into soft peaks. Set aside in the fridge.

Mix softened cream cheese with electric mixer on low speed until smooth. Add the mascarpone cheese and continue mixing until the two cheeses are combined. Add the vanilla extract and the powdered sugar, mixing until all are combined and smooth. Fold in the whipped cream by hand with a spatula. Refrigerate the icing until ready to assemble.

Sarah Yancey, left, and her fellow docent Mabel play an 18th century board game at Monticello, Thomas Jefferson's home in Charlottesville, VA. Sarah was the docent who transcribed the Monticello music.

POUND CAKES

EVIE'S BROWN SUGAR POUND CAKE

from Evalyn Yancey Lipoff

This is a classic pound cake recipe. Eve, my college roommate and singing partner, passed it along to me from her mother, Sarah, a wonderful Virginia cook.

1 c solid shortening

1 stick salted butter

1 c white sugar

1 box light brown sugar, sifted through a sieve

5 large eggs, added one at a time

1 scant c whole milk

3 c sifted flour

1/2 tsp baking powder

2 tsp vanilla extract

Preheat oven to 350°F. Mix shortening, butter, white and brown sugars in a mixer on high until fluffy, reducing to medium speed as the eggs are added one at a time. Fold in the dry ingredients and the vanilla extract until blended thoroughly but not overbeaten. Bake in a well greased and floured angel food cake pan for 1 hour and 35 minutes, until toothpick comes out clean. Cool on rack; gently loosen sides and slide out. Serve unglazed or with glaze of choice.

GRANDMOTHER'S POUND CAKE

from Stella Thurmond Campbell

1-3/4 c white granulated sugar

2 sticks (1 c) salted margarine or butter, softened (Stella uses one of each)

5 eggs

1-3/4 c all-purpose flour

1 tsp vanilla extract

1 T lemon juice, OPTIONAL

Cream the butter and sugar until fluffy, and add the eggs, one at a time. Add the flour until mixed, then add the vanilla and optional lemon juice. Pour into a well greased loaf pan and bake for 45 minutes to 1 hour at 350°F in preheated oven, or until toothpick inserted in center comes out clean. NOTE: Do not open oven door to test with toothpick until sides of the pound cake start coming away from the pan.

VARIATION 1 (ALMOND): Add 2 tsp almond extract; add 3 T applesauce; omit lemon juice.

VARIATION 2 (CHOCOLATE): Reduce flour to 1-1/4 cup, sugar to 1-1/4 cup; add 1/4 cup cocoa powder, and 6 oz chocolate chips; omit lemon juice.

POLLY'S COLD OVEN POUND CAKE

from Polly Starnes Moore

This recipe was given to me at my Grace Chapel bridal shower by Louise Triplette's cousin, Polly Starnes Moore. The Memphis version listed separately was in Mom's files. Neither recipe works if oven is preheated.

2 sticks salted butter (1 c)

1/2 c vegetable shortening

3 c white granulated sugar

1 c milk

5 eggs

3 c all-purpose flour

1/4 tsp baking powder

1 tsp lemon extract

1 tsp vanilla extract

Cream butter, shortening and sugar. Add eggs, until light and fluffy. Sift flour and baking powder. Add flour mixture and milk to the creamed sugar mixture in thirds until well blended. Add flavorings and mix well. Pour into tube pan lightly greased; put into cold oven. Turn oven on to 325°F, and bake 1 hour and 25 minutes; OR at the end of 1 hour, raise temperature to 350°F and continue baking additional 20-30 minutes. DO NOT OPEN OVEN DURING BAKING.

MEMPHIS VERSION COLD OVEN POUND CAKE

from Mary Elizabeth Daltroff

2 sticks (1 cup) unsalted butter, softened

Additional butter for buttering the tube pan

3 c cake flour; sift before measuring

Additional flour for dusting the tube pan

3/4 tsp salt (sifted 2 times with the flour, bringing flour sifting to 3 times)

3 c sugar

7 large eggs, at room temperature 30 minutes, added 1 at a time

2 tsp vanilla, mixed in after the flour

1 c heavy cream, added alternately with the flour to the butter mixture

Cream butter, shortening and sugar. Add eggs, until light and fluffy. Sift flour and baking powder. Add flour mixture and milk to the creamed sugar mixture in thirds until well blended. Add flavorings and mix well. Pour into tube pan lightly greased; put into cold oven. The oven is set to 350°F for this version after placing the pan on center rack. The cake is baked for 1 hour and 25 minutes. DO NOT OPEN OVEN DURING BAKING.

SUNDROP POUND CAKE

This pound cake is a favorite in east Tennessee and the Carolinas, where SunDrop citrus soft drink is readily available. It's a ringer for the traditional Seven-Up Pound Cake. The SunDrop Bottling Company is headquartered in Pulaski, TN, and also makes RC Cola.

2 sticks salted butter

1/2 c shortening

3 c white granulated sugar

5 eggs

1 tsp vanilla extract

1 tsp lemon extract

3 c plain flour

7 oz Sun Drop

Cream butter and shortening with sugar until fluffy. Add eggs, one at a time. Add extracts. Add flour and SunDrop alternately, beating after each addition. Bake in a greased, floured tube pan at 325°F for 90 minutes in a preheated oven. Cool on rack before turning out. Glaze, if desired, with 2 cups powdered sugar mixed with 2 T softened butter and 4 T of SunDrop.

SOUR CREAM COFFEE CAKE

from Mary Elizabeth Daltroff

Mom always made this for her UMW circle meetings. She had to hide the cooling cake from my brothers, who would pick off the yummy topping.

1/2 c shortening

3/4 c white granulated sugar

1 tsp vanilla extract

3 eggs

2 c sifted plain flour

1 tsp baking powder

1 tsp baking soda

1 c sour cream (1/2 pint)

6 T salted butter, softened

1 c firmly packed light brown sugar

2 tsp cinnamon

1 c finely chopped nuts (walnuts or pecans)

Cream shortening, sugar and vanilla until fluffy. Add eggs, one at a time, beating well after each. Sift flour, baking powder and soda in small bowl. Add flour mix to creamed mixture, alternating with sour cream; blend well. Batter will be thick. Spread half in a greased and floured, or wax paper-lined 10-inch tube pan. Cream butter, brown sugar and cinnamon. Add nuts and mix well. Dot half the nut mixture on top of batter in pan. Cover with remaining batter. Dot with remaining nut mixture. Bake at 350°F in preheated oven for about 50 minutes. Cool about 10 minutes on rack. Flip out of pan onto plate, then flip again onto serving plate so that crusty topping is on top again. No need for icing or glaze.

Sour Cream Coffee Cake is always a winner with coffee.

FRUITS AND NUTS

AUNT ALLINE'S CHERRY FRUIT CAKE

from Alline Sherrill Annas

1 lb (4 sticks, equaling 2 c) margarine or butter

16-oz box light brown sugar

6 eggs, yolks and whites separated

4 c all-purpose flour, divided

1/2 lb candied pineapple

1 lb candied cherries

1 tsp baking powder

1-1/2 oz lemon extract

12-oz jar pineapple preserves

2 c pecans

Cream butter and sugar; add egg yolks one at a time. Mix 2 cups flour with the fruit. Mix remaining flour with baking powder. Mix floured fruit, flour-baking powder combo, preserves, and nuts into batter. Fold in egg whites, lightly beaten. Pour into greased, floured tube pan, lined with greased, floured parchment. Bake 3-1/2 hours at 250°F in preheated oven.

APPLESAUCE CAKE

This is an old recipe used by everyone up and down the Mississippi for as long as I can remember.

1/2 c vegetable shortening

1 c white granulated sugar

1 c natural applesauce

1 c raisins

2 c sifted all-purpose flour

1 tsp ground cinnamon

1 tsp ground nutmeg

1-1/2 tsp baking soda

1/2 tsp ground cloves

1/2 tsp salt

1/2 c chopped nuts, pecans or walnuts

Cream shortening and sugar. Heat applesauce, add with raisins to the sugar mixture. Cool. Sift dry ingredients together and gradually beat into the sugar mixture. Add nuts. Pour into a greased 9-by-5-by-2-3/4-inch loaf pan. Bake at 325°F in preheated oven for 1 hour, until toothpick comes out clean. Cool for 10 minutes on a wire rack, then turn out onto a cloth-covered rack to continue cooling.

FRESH APPLE CAKE

This cake was ever-popular in Winston-Salem and the surrounding counties at the foothills of the mountains. We had access year round to wonderful homegrown apples, ranging from commercially grown Red and Gold Delicious, to special heirloom varieties.

3 c white granulated sugar

1-1/2 c vegetable oil

2 eggs, beaten

3 c of all-purpose flour

1 tsp baking soda

1 tsp salt

2 tsp vanilla extract

3 c peeled, diced apples (Red Delicious or Winesap)

1/2 to 1 c chopped nuts (I prefer walnuts to pecans)

Beat first 3 ingredients until fluffy. Sift next 3 ingredients, add gradually to the wet mixture. Mix in vanilla; gradually fold in apple and nuts. Pour into greased, floured 9-by-13-inch pan. Bake at 350°F in preheated oven for 1 hour.

ICING ON THE CAKE

1-1/2 c butter

1 c light brown sugar (packed into measuring cup)

1/2 c canned evaporated milk

Boil these ingredients for 4 minutes. While cake is still warm, drip the boiled mixture over the cake. Leave cake in the pan and cut when serving. The icing penetrates and retains the moisture of the cake.

Grace and Clarence Sherrill at their 60th anniversary party

Grace Kirby and Clarence Sherrill wedding portrait, circa 1915

SUE'S APPLE-COCOA CAKE

from Louise Sherrill Triplette

There are several versions of this cake, which remains popular in the Carolinas. This one calls for cocoa and raisins, and is baked in a Bundt pan.

1/2 c all-purpose flour

2/3 c golden raisins

3 eggs

1 c light brown sugar

3 c all-purpose flour

1 tsp baking soda

1 tsp salt

1/4 c cocoa

1 tsp cinnamon

1 tsp allspice

1-1/2 c vegetable oil

2 T vanilla extract

1 c chopped walnuts

3 c chopped Golden Delicious apples

Preheat oven to 350°F. Mix first flour with the raisins and walnuts to coat, shake off excess flour; set aside. Cream eggs and sugar. Combine all dry ingredients. Add to batter, alternating with oil. Mix in vanilla, nuts and apples. Pour batter into one large or two small greased and floured Bundt tube pans. Sprinkle floured raisins over top of the batter in the pan(s). Bake until toothpick comes out clean.

CARROT CAKE

1-1/4 c vegetable oil (canola or extra light olive oil)

2 c white granulated sugar

4 eggs

3 c grated carrots

2 c all-purpose flour

2 tsp cinnamon

2 T baking powder

2 T baking soda

1 tsp salt

1/2 c chopped pecans

Mix well the oil, sugar, eggs and carrots. Mix all dry ingredients together, and add to the batter gradually, stirring well. Add nuts. Bake in three 9-inch greased cake pans for 30-40 minutes at 350°F in preheated oven. Frost with cream cheese icing after cooled.

CARROT-PINEAPPLE CAKE

2 c white granulated sugar

1-1/2 c canola oil

3 eggs

8-oz can of crushed pineapple

2 c ground carrots

1 c chopped walnuts or pecans

2-1/2 c all-purpose flour

1 tsp vanilla extract

1 tsp salt

1 tsp baking soda

1 tsp cinnamon

Pre-heat oven to 350°F. Lightly grease and flour cake pans. Cream sugar, oil and eggs until fluffy. Add pineapple (drained), carrots and nuts, and vanilla. Sift together the flour, salt, cinnamon and baking soda. Gradually add to wet mixture until completely blended. Pour into the two cake pans, shaking out the bubbles. Bake for about 40 minutes or until toothpick comes out clean.

CREAM CHEESE ICING:

1/2 c (1 stick or 8 T) butter

4 oz cream cheese

1/2 tsp vanilla extract

1 to 2 c powdered sugar

1 c chopped nuts

Mix all together and spread on the cake. Keep refrigerated when not serving.

CAKES, COOKIES & CANDY

DAD'S CHRISTMAS POUND CAKE

from Fern Robertson Kerslake

Fern's father, Bill Robertson, whose ancestors traveled to Canada from Wisconsin, loved this version of a fruitcake. It's a terrific compromise between fruitcake and pound cake for the holiday season. They may not be from around here, but I consider Fernie's people "Southern" Canadian, especially since Fern and her husband Graham hooked up with us Tar Heels and Vols almost 30 years ago. They've even made pilgrimages to Grandfather Mountain, Opryland, Graceland, Charleston, and New Orleans.

2 c butter

2 c white granulated sugar

1 tsp grated lemon rind

2 T lemon juice

8 large eggs

3-1/2 c all-purpose flour

1/2 tsp baking powder

1/4 c of all-purpose flour

2 c red and green candied cherries, cut in half

1 c sliced, blanched almonds

Grease and flour regular tube pan. Cream butter until fluffy, add sugar gradually until creamy. Mix in lemon rind and juice. Beat in eggs one at a time. Sift in flour and baking powder; beat only until smooth. Combine 1/4-cup of flour with fruit and nuts. Fold in. Bake in prepared tube pan at 300°F for 85-95 minutes. Turn off, do not open oven. Leave cake in oven about 10 more minutes. Remove to rack to cool. Store in covered tin. Cake keeps about 2 weeks.

CANDIED CITRUS PEEL FOR GARNISH

2 c white granulated sugar

2 c water

Fresh oranges or grapefruit

Slice peels off the fruit in strips, starting at the top and slicing downward, following curve of the fruit, and retaining white pith. Place peel slices in a pot of cool water, bring to a rolling boil, then remove from heat and drain peel in a colander. Repeat the blanching process two more times for oranges, and seven more times for grapefruit (which are more tart). When the peel is completely tender, place it in a pot of simple syrup made from boiled water and sugar. Simmer 15-30 minutes until peel becomes translucent. Remove from heat, Cool. Remove peels from syrup and roll in granulated sugar. Store in tight container, refrigerated.

Grace Sherrill plays organ during church for the 100th anniversary celebration of Grace Chapel United Methodist Church, in 1977.

GRANDMA SHERRILL'S FRUIT COCKTAIL CAKE

from Andrea Benfield, from Grace Kirby Sherrill

This was one of Grandma Sherrill's favorite recipes.

CAKE:

2 c of all-purpose flour

1-1/2 tsp baking soda

Dash of salt

1-1/2 c white granulated sugar (may reduce to 1 c)

2 eggs

15-oz can of good quality fruit cocktail in heavy syrup

ICING:

1 stick (1/2 c) butter

1 c water

1 c evaporated milk

1/2 c coconut

1/2 c pecan pieces

1 tsp vanilla extract

Preheat oven to 350°F. Mix dry ingredients in large bowl. Beat in eggs and fruit cocktail with syrup. Bake in a greased 9-by-13-by-2-inch pan for about 30 minutes or until toothpick comes out clean in center. For icing, bring first three ingredients to a boil on medium heat in medium saucepan; boil for 10 minutes. Remove from heat, stir in remaining ingredients. Pour over warm cake. Let soak. Refrigerate before serving.

NO-FAIL FRUITCAKE

2-1/2 c sifted all-purpose flour

1 tsp baking soda

2 eggs, lightly beaten

28-oz jar of ready-to-use mincemeat

1-1/2 c (15-oz can) of sweetened condensed milk

1 c walnuts, coarsely chopped

2 c mixed candied fruit (pineapple and cherries)

Preheat oven to 300°F. Butter a 9-inch tube- or spring-form pan. Line bottom with waxed paper. Butter again over the waxed paper. Sift flour with baking soda. In a separate bowl, combine eggs, mincemeat, condensed milk, chopped walnuts, and candied fruits. Fold dry ingredients into this. Pour into prepared pan. Bake in slow oven about 2 hours, until center springs back (top is golden). Cool on a rack; turn out onto plate, remove paper. Decorate top with walnut halves and candied cherries.

HOMEMADE CANDIED FRUIT

2 c white granulated sugar

1 c water

1 c fresh or canned cherries, pineapple, mandarin oranges, or citrus peel

Make a simple syrup by combining equal parts water and granulated sugar in a medium saucepan. Bring to a boil and stir to dissolve sugar. Remove syrup from heat and cool slightly. Cut fresh cherries in half, and remove pits. For pineapple, cut slices or chunks, or used canned chunks. With a slotted spoon, lower fruit into the syrup in pan. Simmer on low 20-30 minutes (less for canned fruit). Remove from heat. Let fruit soak in pan overnight, covered. Remove with slotted spoon and place in large bowl. Cover and roll in granulated sugar. Preheat oven to 200°F at least 25 minutes. Place candied fruits on baking sheet or cake rack. Bake 10-15 minutes to let fruit become dry and firm. Cool then store in tight container. Refrigerate.

FRUITCAKE MEMORY

One of my only miserable holiday memories is of the year Mom made me help her make sticky, brick-like no-bake fruitcake logs. To this day any fruitcake log entering my house ends up as a doorstop.

WHITE FRUITCAKE

I always loved our Daltroff family's Christmas fruitcake tradition. Uncle Louie would give everyone a Hostess fruitcake packaged in Christmas-season golden tins. He worked for Hostess, and we all were glad. This white fruitcake recipe is a much loved 20th century interpretation of an heirloom Southern recipe.

1 c white granulated sugar

1/4 lb butter

4 egg whites

1/2 tsp salt

2 c cake flour

1 tsp baking powder

1 tsp vanilla extract

1 lb golden raisins

1/4 lb citron

1 fresh coconut, grated

4 c pecan meats, chopped

1/4 lb red candied cherries

1/4 lb crystallized pineapple

1/2 c orange or pineapple juice

1/4 c brandy

Cream butter and sugar, beat in egg whites until fluffy. Sift dry ingredients; add alternately with fruit juice. Sprinkle finely chopped fruits with a half-cup of extra flour, add this to cake batter. Bake in a large tube pan which has been greased and then lined on the bottom with greased brown paper. Bake at 325°F in a preheated oven about 3 hours. If cake begins to brown too rapidly, place shallow pan of water in oven and reduce temperature to 300°F for 15-20 minutes. When done, remove from oven. Pour about 1/4-cup of brandy over top. Store in tightly closed tin after it is cooled.

Homemade Candied Fruit

LOUISE'S FIG CAKE

from Louise Sherrill Triplette

CAKE:

2 c all-purpose flour

1 tsp salt

1 tsp baking soda

1-1/2 c white granulated sugar

1 c vegetable oil

3 eggs beaten

1 c buttermilk

1-1/2 c fig preserves

1 tsp vanilla extract

1 c chopped nuts

Sift flour, salt, baking soda, and sugar together. Add oil, figs, buttermilk and beat well. Add eggs gradually, then add the nuts and vanilla, and pour into a greased and floured tube pan or loaf pan. Bake at 325°F in a preheated oven for 1 hour, or until toothpick comes out clean. Remove from oven, and while hot, pour glaze over the cake.

GLAZE:

1 c white granulated sugar

1 stick (1/2 c) butter or margarine

1 T light corn syrup

1 T vanilla extract

1/2 c buttermilk

1/2 tsp baking soda

Bring these ingredients to a boil in a saucepan and stir until slightly thick. Pour over cake while still in pan. Let cool before serving.

Pineapple Upside-Down Cake

LOUISE'S PECAN AND RAISIN CAKE

from Louise Sherrill Triplette (Helen Fowler's recipe)

2 c (1 lb = 4 sticks) butter

2 c white granulated sugar

6 eggs

1 T lemon juice

1 tsp grated lemon rind

1 T vanilla extract

1-1/2 c golden raisins

4 c chopped pecans

3 c all-purpose flour (reserve 1/4 of this for the raisins)

1/4 tsp salt

1 tsp baking powder

Cream butter and sugar. Beat in eggs, one at a time. Add lemon juice, rind and vanilla. Sift together the dry ingredients. Shake the raisins in the reserved flour then mix with the nuts and remaining dry ingredients. Fold into the wet ingredients, mixing thoroughly. Pour into prepared greased and floured angel food pan. Bake 1 hour and 50 minutes at 300°F in preheated oven. Remove when toothpick comes out clean. Turn out as soon as cake cools enough. GLAZE: Mix 1/4 cup orange juice, 1/4 cup lemon juice, and 1/4 cup of white granulated sugar. Pour over still-warm cake.

FOR FREEZING CAKES

- Any type of cake may be frozen.
- For best preservation, wrap the layers separately; fill and frost after thawing.
- If freezing a completed cake, wrap first in waxed paper to prevent sticking. Then wrap in plastic wrap to keep out air, followed by a layer of foil.
- When thawing, remove the foil and plastic wrap. The thawed cake will be very moist.
- Banana bread, pumpkin muffins, zucchini bread, and coconut cake all taste better after having been frozen.

PINEAPPLE UPSIDE-DOWN CAKE

from Mary Elizabeth Daltroff

3 T butter

1/2 c light brown sugar, packed firm

9 slices canned pineapple, drained

5 maraschino cherries

1-1/2 c sifted all-purpose flour

2 tsp baking powder

1/4 tsp salt

1/3 c shortening

2/3 c granulated white sugar

1 large egg

3/4 tsp vanilla extract

2/3 c milk

Preheat oven to 350ºF. Place the butter in an 8-by-8-inch pan and place in the oven to melt. When the butter has melted, remove pan from the oven. Tip around to spread the melted butter evenly across the bottom of the pan. Sprinkle the brown sugar evenly over the melted butter. Arrange the pineapple rings over the butter, making three rows. Cut each cherry in half and place one half of each in center of each pineapple ring, cut-side up. Set aside.

Over a sheet of parchment paper, sift together the flour, baking powder and salt. Sift again. Set aside. In a large bowl, use an electric mixer to cream the shortening and sugar until light and fluffy. Add the egg and beat until fully combined. Mix in the vanilla.

Starting and ending with the flour mixture, blend in the dry ingredients and milk, alternating between the two. After each addition, stir only enough to combine. Carefully pour the batter into the pineapple-lined pan. Bake for 40 minutes or until toothpick inserted in center comes out clean. Remove and run a knife around the edges of the pan, then place a serving plate upside down over the top of the pan.

Invert the cake onto the serving plate carefully. Let sit for several minutes to allow the syrup to soak into the cake, then carefully remove the pan, making sure all the pineapple and syrup remain on top of the inverted cake.

PINEAPPLE FACT: Fresh pineapple contains enzymes that react with baking and congealing ingredients, preventing the desired results. That's why most recipes call for canned pineapple instead of fresh.

PUMPKIN PIE CAKE

from Aline Thurmond Miller, from Ruth Thurmond

Nothing quite says Thanksgiving like pumpkin. To embellish this cake, serve with a dollop of whipped cream flavored with Kahlua.

16 oz canned pumpkin

3 eggs, beaten

3/4 c white granulated sugar

3/4 c light brown sugar

1 T pumpkin pie spice

1 tsp salt

1 can evaporated milk

1 box yellow cake mix

2 sticks (1 c) butter

1 c chopped nuts

Mix first 7 ingredients and pour into 9-by-13-by-2-inch pan. Sprinkle box of yellow cake mix on top of this. Sprinkle melted butter over cake mix, top with nuts. Bake at 350ºF in preheated oven for 1-1/2 hour (90 minutes). Cool, cut into squares.

STRAWBERRY CAKE

from Aline Thurmond Miller

CAKE:

1 box white cake mix

1/2 c vegetable oil

4 eggs

3-oz pkg strawberry gelatin

1 c frozen sweetened sliced strawberries with juice

Mix oil and eggs with cake mix. Dissolve gelatin in 1/4 c of warm water, then blend into cake mix. Add strawberries. Bake at 350ºF in preheated oven for 1 hr 30 minutes in tube pan or in a 9-by-13-by-2-inch pan.

ICING:

16-oz box of confectioners sugar, sifted

1 stick (1/2 c) butter

8 oz frozen strawberries

Mix all icing ingredients together until fluffy. Spread over warm cake. This cake freezes well.

Coconut cake made with Classic Coconut Icing is the perfect dessert for a poolside tea party.

FROSTINGS

BROWN SUGAR ICING

from Ruby White Thurmond

Grandmother and Mom used this recipe frequently, as did many Memphis-area homemakers in the 1950s and 1960s. It was included in recipes issued by the Woman's Exchange of Memphis in 1964, and was republished by the Exchange in **Tearoom Treasures** *in the 1990s.*

3/4 c light brown sugar

2/3 c white granulated sugar

2-1/4 tsp dark corn syrup

1/2 c heavy cream

1/4 c (4 T) butter

Mix all ingredients together and bring to a boil in a saucepan. Cook for 15 to 20 minutes to the soft ball stage (230°F on a candy thermometer). Stir several times. Pour over cooled caramel brownies or cake. Allow to cool before cutting. YIELD: Enough for an 8-by-10-by-2-inch pan of brownies or cake.

BUTTERCREAM CHOCOLATE ICING

1 stick (1/2 c) butter or margarine

1/4 c cocoa

6 T milk

16-oz box of confectioners sugar

Cream the butter and milk, mix the cocoa and confectioner's sugar together and add to creamed butter. Add more milk if needed to achieve spreading consistency.

CLASSIC CINNAMON FROSTING

16-oz box of confectioners sugar

1 T ground cinnamon

1/4 c melted butter

1 egg white from pasteurized or local, organic egg

Dash of salt

3 T whole milk

Sift sugar and cinnamon together. Add about 1/3 of the sugar-cinnamon mixture to the butter, creaming with mixer. Beat in the egg white and salt. Add remaining sugar and enough milk to get to spreadable consistency. Makes enough to frost the top and sides.

CLASSIC COCONUT ICING

3 c white granulated sugar

1 c whipping cream (1/2 pt)

1-1/2 c half-and-half cream, divided into 1 and 1/2 cups

2 lb grated fresh coconut (use bagged coconut in a pinch)

1 tsp cornstarch

1/2 c sour cream, OPTIONAL

Put sugar in saucepan with whipping cream and 1 cup half-and-half, along with grated coconut. Blend well; allow to reach a rolling boil. Mix cornstarch into remaining half-and-half; add to coconut mixture. Stir constantly until mixture thickens (usually less than 5 minutes). Stir in sour cream. Put filling, while still hot, between layers, on top and sides of three-layer cake. Cover well and refrigerate. Remains fresh refrigerated for up to 3 weeks if wrapped well. Freezes well.

CREAM CHEESE ICING

16-oz pkg or box of confectioners sugar

8-oz pkg of cream cheese

1-1/2 to 4 T milk or cream

1 tsp vanilla extract

Sift the confectioners sugar and set aside. Mix the cream cheese with milk or cream, adding the vanilla on medium speed in a mixer. Gradually add confectioners sugar to the creamed cheese mixture. Add more milk or cream if too dry.

VARIATION 1: Add lemon extract instead of vanilla.

VARIATION 2: Add 1/2 tsp cinnamon with the vanilla.

ANDREA'S VARIATION: Add 1 tsp rum flavoring and 1 c chopped pecans, toasted (for Italian Cream Cake).

STRAWBERRY CHEESECAKE GLAZE

1 lb frozen sliced strawberries

2 T cornstarch

2 T white granulated sugar

1/4 tsp red food coloring, OPTIONAL

Thaw 1 lb of frozen sliced strawberries. Drain well, saving 2/3 cup of the strawberry juice. Blend 2 T cornstarch with 2 T sugar in a small saucepan. Gradually blend in the 2/3 cup of strawberry juice and 1/4 tsp red food coloring. Cook and stir over medium heat until mixture is thickened and clear. Stir in the drained strawberries. Cool before spreading.

GRANDMOTHER'S CARAMEL ICING

from Stella Thurmond Campbell

This is another of Grandmother Thurmond's recipes, saved and passed along by Cousin Stella Thurmond Campbell.

1 stick butter (1/2 c)

1-1/2 c light or dark brown sugar, to taste

1/3 c whole milk

8 oz confectioner's sugar (use more as needed)

1 tsp vanilla extract

Additional milk as needed

Melt 1 stick of butter over medium heat. Add brown sugar; bring to a boil, stirring constantly. Add the milk and stir well. Bring back to a boil, and boil for 1 to 2 minutes. Remove from heat. Add confectioner's sugar, stirring constantly until shiny and smooth and of spreading consistency. Blend in the vanilla. Add more sugar if too thin; more milk if too thick.

MOCHA BUTTER FROSTING

1/2 c (1 stick) butter or margarine

1/4 c of cocoa powder

4 tsp instant coffee

4 c (approximately 1 lb) confectioners sugar, sifted

1/4 c evaporated milk

1 tsp vanilla extract

Blend until fluffy butter or margarine, cocoa, and instant coffee. Add sugar, 1/2 cup at a time, alternating with the milk, and beating smooth after each addition. Stir in vanilla. If too thin, work in additional confectioners sugar. If too thick, work in a bit more milk.

FROSTING VS. ICING VS. GLAZE:
The terms frosting and icing are used interchangeably in the South and other American regions. Technically, icing is thinner and glossier, and hardens. (Royal Icing includes egg whites that enable it to hold a shape when applied with a pastry bag.) Frosting is thick and fluffy, usually made with buttercream, and retains its softness. Glaze is a thin icing made with powdered sugar, flavorings, and milk or citrus juice, and is drizzled over the top.

NEVER-FAIL CHOCOLATE ICING

I learned this recipe from my mother. I also got it from Great-Aunt Anne Thurmond (Uncle Gene's wife), who was noted for making this. You might need to double the recipe for a big two-layer cake.

2 c white granulated sugar

2 squares unsweetened chocolate (or 1/2 c cocoa)

1 stick margarine or butter

1/2 c whole milk

1/2 tsp vanilla extract

Combine all ingredients except vanilla. Stir over medium heat in a heavy saucepan until sugar dissolves. Bring to a hard boil and boil for 2 minutes, not stirring if using cocoa, or for 1 minute, stirring once, if using squares. Remove from heat and let cool to lukewarm. Do not stir BEFORE lukewarm. Add vanilla and beat with mixer until smooth and stiff enough to spread. If frosting begins to harden, add about 1 T hot water and remix. Aunt Annie always said the success depends on not stirring until mixture is lukewarm.

REALLY OLD HOT SAUCE RECIPE (ALTERNATIVE TO ICING)

from Ruby White Thurmond, from Bigmama White

1 c reserved cake batter

2 eggs

1 c sugar

2 T plain flour

3 c whole milk

1/2 c butter

1 tsp vanilla extract

Nutmeg

Add eggs to reserved batter while beating. Mix flour into the sugar, then add to batter. Slowly add the milk and cook in double boiler over boiling water. Add butter once liquid becomes warm, and add vanilla as sauce thickens. Continue stirring with whisk until sauce becomes thick. Serve warm over warm cake. Sprinkle nutmeg over sauce upon serving.

HINT: Cream-cheese and powdered-sugar icings may be frozen for up to a month. Brown sugar icings and boiled icings should not be frozen.

SEVEN-MINUTE FROSTING

From Ruby White Thurmond

This is one of several variations of the classic 7-minute frosting. Colonnade Icing is another (see below).

3 egg whites

3/4 c sugar

3/4 c light corn syrup

1 T water

1/2 tsp vanilla extract

Combine all ingredients except vanilla in a double boiler, place over boiling water (make sure the top of the water does not touch the bottom of the double boiler bowl). Cook about 7 minutes, beating constantly with an electric mixer. Remove from heat and stir in vanilla. *YIELD: Frosting for a 9-inch cake.*

COLONNADE ICING

4-1/2 c white granulated sugar

1 c water

6 T corn syrup

6 stiff-beaten egg whites

1/3 c confectioner's sugar

Mix first three ingredients in saucepan to soft ball stage (238°F). Use candy thermometer and also test by dropping a drop into a glass of cold water. Add sugar syrup to the stiff-beaten egg whites. Mix in powdered sugar. Do not add vanilla. *YIELD: Enough icing to use as filling between layers of a three-layer cake plus sides and top of cake.*

TWELVE-MINUTE CHOCOLATE ICING

Three 1-oz squares of unsweetened chocolate

1-1/2 c white granulated sugar

1/2 c whole milk

3 rounded T butter

Pinch of salt

1 T vanilla extract

1 c broken pecans, OPTIONAL

Stir and heat on a slow flame first three ingredients until all are mixed well. Time as soon as all three ingredients are dissolved, adding 3 heaping T butter. Simmer for 6 more minutes. Remove from heat. Add pinch of salt, 1 T vanilla extract. Add 1 cup broken pecans if desired. Stir with the pan in cold water, beating until slightly thick. Quickly pour onto cake while soft.

WEDDING CAKE MEMORIES

Jeff and I were married in 1973, during the waning days of Flower Power. A week of parties had been planned by family and friends. Our rehearsal dinner was scheduled to be held at the most popular French restaurant in Memphis. When planning the actual wedding ceremony, I told my mother I wanted it to occur in a large tent in the garden, with white doves on the altar.

Mom snorted and looked at me. "You're getting married in MEMPHIS in JUNE. Your 82-year-old grandfather is one of the ministers. And there will be NO livestock on the altar," she said.

The subject was closed.

The wedding went off without a hitch at Mullins United Methodist Church, followed by a lively reception at the Petroleum Club in the Peabody Hotel. After hours of partying, my parents insisted that Jeff and I leave so the guests could depart.

Dad never once complained about the costs for the wedding decorations, for the reception liquor, for the seafood and prime rib buffet, or for the musicians. But he never let me forget the cost of the out-of-season wildflower spray atop the simple wedding cake.

He was not amused when I pointed out that at least he didn't have to pay for doves.

CANDIES

BENNE BRITTLE

1-1/4 c raw sesame seeds

2 c white granulated sugar

2 T water

1 tsp vanilla extract

Thickly grease a cookie sheet with butter. Toast seeds in heavy skillet on medium heat, shaking and stirring until seeds begin to turn brown, 7 to 9 minutes. Remove from skillet at once and set aside. Cook sugar and water in skillet on low heat, stirring until the sugar dissolves, about 10 minutes. While hot, stir in the toasted sesame seeds, then the vanilla. Quickly pour onto greased sheet and spread thin with metal spatula to about 1/8-inch thickness. Cool (about 20-30 minutes). Break into pieces. Store in airtight metal container.

CARAMELS

from Rita Davidson Friend

2 c white granulated sugar

A few grains of salt

2 c light corn syrup

1/2 c (1 stick) butter

2 c evaporated milk

1 tsp vanilla extract

Stirring occasionally, boil the sugar, salt and corn syrup to 245°F to a very thick syrup. Add butter, then gradually add milk. Don't let mixture stop boiling. Stir constantly and cook rapidly to firm ball stage (242°F). Add vanilla, pour into greased 9-by-13-inch pan. Cool thoroughly. Cut into cubes with heavy sharp knife greased with butter, using a sawing motion.

CHOCOLATE TRASH

24 oz chocolate almond bark (candy coating)

24 oz white chocolate

4-oz bar German chocolate

12-oz bag milk chocolate chips

2 c thin stick pretzels or mini-twist pretzels

24-oz jar dry-roasted peanuts, or 2 c roasted pecans

Layer ingredients in order listed in crock pot. Cook on low 1 hour; stir just to swirl; cook 1 more hour. Drop by the teaspoon onto wax paper to cool.

DIVINITY

from Mary Elizabeth Daltroff

Do not EVER try to make divinity on a damp, humid or rainy day. Also note: Divinity is wonderful, but like a cloud, its goodness doesn't last long. So eat up.

1/2 c water

2-1/2 c white granulated sugar

1/2 c light corn syrup

2 large egg whites, at room temperature

Pinch of cream of tartar

1 c chopped walnuts

1-1/2 tsp vanilla extract

Cook the water, sugar, corn syrup until the sugar is dissolved (about 5 minutes) in a 2-qt heavy saucepan over medium heat. Stir constantly with wooden spoon (*important to use spoon that doesn't transmit heat). Brush down the sides of the saucepan with a pastry brush dipped in warm water to prevent the sugar from crystallizing as it splashes up the sides during boiling. Increase heat to medium high, place sugar thermometer in the saucepan, and cook without stirring until candy thermometer registers 256°F (about 10 minutes). Brush down sides of the pan with pastry brush dipped in warm water two more times during the cooking process.

While the sugar syrup is cooking, beat the egg whites on medium speed in the bowl of a stand mixer fitted with a whisk attachment. Beat on medium until frothy. Add the cream of tartar, increase mixer speed to medium-high, and beat the egg whites until they hold firm peaks like a meringue (about 3 to 5 minutes).

Remove the pan with the sugar syrup from the heat. Reduce mixer speed to medium and pour the sugar syrup slowly into the egg whites, being careful not to drip the syrup down the sides of the bowl. Increase mixer speed to high and beat until the mixture is firm and no longer shiny (10-15 minutes). Blend in the chopped walnuts and vanilla.

Line 2 baking sheets with waxed paper. Drop 1-1/2-inch-wide spoonfuls of the mixture onto the paper, leaving 1 inch between them. Let the candy set at room temperature until firm, about 30-40 minutes. tore in a tightly covered container between sheets of waxed paper. Keeps for about 4 days.

LOUISE TRIPLETTE'S VARIATION: Fold in 1/4-cup of candied cherries and 1/4-cup of chopped crystallized pineapple with the chopped nuts and vanilla. *YIELD: 50 pieces.*

RIPPLE DIVINITY

3 c white granulated sugar

1/2 c water

1/2 c light corn syrup

2 egg whites, beaten until stiff

1 tsp vanilla extract

1 c semi-sweet chocolate chips or pieces

Combine sugar, water and corn syrup in a 2-qt saucepan. Cook over high heat to boiling stage; reduce heat and continue cooking until mixture reaches 240°F on a candy thermometer.

Slowly pour one-third of the mixture over the egg whites, beating constantly. Cook remaining syrup to 265°F; add gradually to the first mixture. Beat with a hand-held mixer until mixture will hold its shape when dropped from a spoon.

Add vanilla; fold in the chocolate pieces, which will partially melt and give the ribbon-like rippled appearance. Drop from teaspoon onto a greased baking sheet. *YIELD: About 4 dozen.*

ENGLISH NUT TOFFEE

from Mary Elizabeth Daltroff

1 lb butter

1 lb (2 c) white sugar

1/2 c coarsely chopped almonds

6 regular size Hershey bars (1.55-oz size bars)

Heat butter and sugar in pot to boiling at 305°F until mixture turns golden brown. Turn off heat. Stir in almonds. Pour out into buttered cookie sheets. Melt Hershey bars in double boiler and spread over toffee. Let cool.

CHOCOLATE NUT CLUSTERS

2 bags of MILK chocolate chips

One can of Planter's Spanish Peanuts (with the skins on)

Melt chocolate chips in microwave in a microwave-able dish. Stir until smooth. Pour in the peanuts and mix together until peanuts are covered with chocolate. Drop by spoonfuls onto aluminum foil or wax paper. Let harden overnight.

HOMEMADE MARSHMALLOWS

This is a recipe that has kicked around for generations. It's a bit of trouble for someone who wants to save time, but the results are a delight! Homemade marshmallows are lighter, fluffier, and purer in flavor than store-bought.

Three 1/4-oz pkgs unflavored gelatin powder

1/2 c cold water

2-1/2 c white granulated sugar

3/4 c light corn syrup

1/2 c hot water (I boil it to get it hot enough)

1/2 tsp salt

2 tsp vanilla extract

Confectioners sugar

Pam cooking spray

Line a 9-by-13-inch pan with parchment paper. Coat with cooking spray. In a large metal or Pyrex bowl, combine unflavored gelatin and cold water. In a heavy medium saucepan, combine sugar, corn syrup and hot water with salt. Cook on medium-high heat, stirring until it boils. Stop stirring but continue boiling. Use a candy thermometer to let the boiling mixture reach 240°F.

Once mixture reaches 240°F, pour it into the gelatin mixture. Use mixer to whip until mixture doubles in size. Fold in vanilla with mixer.

Use rubber bowl scraper (spatula) to pour mixture into prepared pan. Spread evenly. Set on rack to cool and set up overnight. To cut into half-inch squares, use serrated knife dipped in warm water. Once cut, toss squares in confectioners sugar to coat. Store in airtight metal container up to 2 weeks. *YIELD: About 48 marshmallows.*

NO-FAIL MARSHMALLOW FUDGE

3 c white granulated sugar

3/4 c butter (1-1/2 sticks) or margarine

2/3 c evaporated milk

12-oz pkg of semisweet chocolate chips

1 jar of marshmallow cream

1 c chopped pecans or walnuts

1 tsp vanilla extract

Combine butter, sugar and milk in a sauce pan and bring to a boil. Boil for 5 minutes. Remove from heat and stir in the chocolate chips and marshmallow cream until melted, then mix in the vanilla extract and nuts. Pour into a greased (with butter) 8-inch pan and let set before cutting into pieces.

QUICK FUDGE

I double the recipe and spread out in an 8-by-8-inch buttered pan. It's thicker, so I cut it into slivers 1/4-inch cubed, and then cut the slivers in half. When done properly, it melts in your mouth.

1 lb confectioners sugar

1/2 c cocoa powder

1/4 tsp salt

6 T butter or margarine

4 T milk

1 tsp vanilla extract

1 c chopped pecans or walnuts

Sift together the powdered sugar and cocoa with the salt. In the top of a double boiler, combine dry and wet ingredients, except nuts and vanilla.

Place over simmering water and stir constantly until smooth. Add vanilla and stir some more. Just at the point of bubbling, remove from stove, add nuts, and mix thoroughly.

Spread out quickly in a buttered 9-by-5-inch loaf pan. Cut into small squares after cooling. *YIELD: 2 dozen small pieces.*

HOMEMADE MOUNDS BITES

from Mary Elizabeth Daltroff

This is an old recipe Mom would make for Christmas company.

Two 16-oz boxes confectioners sugar

12-oz can evaporated milk

3 sticks (1-1/2 c) butter

Four 7-oz cans of flake coconut

3 c chopped pecans

12-oz bag of chocolate chips

Stick of Paraffin wax

Mix milk and confectioners sugar. Melt butter, mix with the sugar. Add coconut and pecans. Form into small balls.

Melt paraffin in top of double boiler; add chocolate chips and cook until dissolved, blending well.

Dip each ball in the chocolate Paraffin melt and cover completely.

Place on waxed paper to cool. Store in a tightly covered metal container. *YIELD: 2 to 3 dozen.*

GORP (TRAIL MIX)

This is a fun snack that can be as healthful or unhealthful as you wish to make it. For a tropical version, add shredded coconut, candied pineapple pieces, and other dried fruit to taste. To make any variation, combine all ingredients together. Store in tightly covered glass jars.

GORP TRAIL MIX 1:

16-oz box granola without raisins

6-oz package mini chocolate chips

1 c peanuts (dry salted)

1 c sunflower seeds

1 c raisins

1/2 c finely diced dried apricots, apples, or cranberries

GORP TRAIL MIX 2:

Large pkg of M&M's

Large pkg of M&M peanuts

15-20 oz dry salted peanuts or almonds

Jar of sunflower seeds

Regular box of raisins

HEAVENLY HASH

12 marshmallows, diced

1 c pecans or walnuts, chopped

1 lb milk chocolate

Boil water in the bottom of a double boiler. While the water is coming to a boil, line a tray or cookie sheet with waxed paper. Place the milk chocolate in double boiler bowl over boiling water (not touching bowl); stir until it melts. When completely melted, pour half onto the waxed paper. Cover with the chopped marshmallows and nuts. Pour the rest of the chocolate over this layer. Cool. Break into pieces. *YIELD: About 1-1/4 lb.*

HOMEMADE SWEETENED CONDENSED MILK

Every homemaker born before 1940 has this recipe.

1 c instant nonfat dry milk

2/3 c white granulated sugar

1/3 c boiling water

3 T melted butter or margarine

Combine all ingredients in a blender and process until smooth. Store in refrigerator until ready to use. *Yield: 1-1/2 cups, which is equivalent to 1 can.*

PEANUT BRITTLE

from Verlee Triplette Mull

Jeff's Aunt Verlee always made him her peanut brittle for Christmas. Uncle George entertained on his ukulele.

4 T unsalted butter

2 c white granulated sugar

1/2 c water

1 c light corn syrup

1 T baking soda

1 T vanilla extract

2 c toasted, salty peanuts (OR add raw peanuts during cooking stage)

Coat a baking sheet with 2 T butter. Set aside. Cook sugar, water and corn syrup in a 3-quart heavy saucepan over high heat. Do not stir until mixture reaches 300°F on a candy thermometer (10-15 minutes). Brush down pan sides two times with a pastry brush dipped in warm water to prevent sugar crystallization. Remove saucepan from heat. Use long wooden spoon to quickly stir in 1 T butter, baking soda, vanilla and peanuts. The mixture will bubble and foam fast. Immediately turn out onto the buttered baking sheet. Quickly spread out thin with the wooden spoon.

Let brittle cool 5 minutes, then loosen from the pan with a spatula (flexible blade version is best). Butter your fingertips with remaining 1 T of butter, and stretch the brittle as thin as possible. Let cool completely, about 30 minutes, then break into pieces. Watch for the sugar to turn light amber-colored. When the sugar has caramelized light amber, stir the nuts in quickly. Pour out. Store in tightly covered metal container(s). Keeps 1 to 2 weeks. *YIELD: 4-1/2 cups.*

TURTLES

72 fresh pecan halves

24 caramels, unwrapped

6 oz almond bark

6 oz semisweet chocolate chips

Preheat oven to 300°F. Grease a baking sheet. Arrange pecan halves in groups of three, end to end, flat side down, on the baking sheet. Place a caramel on top of each cluster of pecans. Place in oven until caramels soften, about 5 to 8 minutes. Remove from oven. Flatten each caramel with buttered wooden spoon. Cool slightly. Place almond bark and chocolate chips in microwave-safe dish and heat on low at 2-minute intervals until melted. Dip turtles into chocolate to coat. Cool on waxed paper. Store in tight covered container in a cool place. *YIELD: 24 turtles.*

PECAN PRALINES

Never attempt to make stovetop pralines on a really humid, rainy day. Always stir with a wooden spoon. "Soft-ball stage" and "hard-ball stage" refer to the crystallization stage of the cooked sugar. At soft-ball stage, when a drop of sugar syrup is dropped into cold water, the sugar forms a soft ball that flattens. At hard-ball stage, the drop retains its shape but can be reworked with your fingertips. NOTE: It is very easy to undercook or overcook the sugar mixture. Either way, the pralines will not harden properly. Just keep practicing.

1 c evaporated milk

1-1/2 c light brown sugar

1-1/2 c granulated white sugar

1 T butter or margarine

1 tsp vanilla extract

1-1/2 to 2 c pecans

In a heavy saucepan combine the sugar, brown sugar and milk, until creamed. Cook on medium heat and bring to a boil, cooking until reaches the soft-ball stage (238-240°F). Use a candy thermometer to measure temperature.

Add pecans and butter and stir well, just long enough to reach the hard-ball stage (245°F). Remove from heat, add vanilla, and mix thoroughly. If mixture becomes too thick, add 1 to 2 T evaporated milk and mix thoroughly.

Spoon dollops of the mixture onto waxed paper sprayed with cooking spray. Mixture will spread. Allow to cool and harden. *YIELD: 20-24 pralines.*

POPCORN BALLS

This is an old fashioned treat that the children loved to make with Mom.

3 qt popped corn (plain)

1-1/2 c light corn syrup

1/4 tsp salt

1 tsp white vinegar

2 T butter

Pop plain corn and spread evenly in large pan. Cook syrup slowly to medium brittleness (about 270-280°F). Add salt, vinegar, and butter. When mixed, pour slowly over pan of corn stirring with wooden spoon so all the kernels will be evenly coated with syrup. Grease fingers with butter, and shape corn into balls. Lay balls on waxed paper. Wrap each individually in waxed paper.

COOKIES

APPLE BUTTER FILLED COOKIES

from Rita Davidson Friend

2 c light brown sugar

1 c butter or lard

1 large egg

1 c sour milk (buttermilk)

1 level tsp baking soda

1 level tsp salt

6 c plain flour (more or less)

Apple butter

Cream brown sugar with butter or lard and eggs. Combine buttermilk with baking soda and salt, then mix into batter. Add enough of the flour to make a soft dough. Roll dough to 1/8-inch in thickness. Cut out round shapes with cookie cutter. Place 1 tsp pure apple butter on center of each cookie and cover with another cookie of equal size. Press edges together to seal. Sprinkle with granulated sugar. Bake on parchment-lined cookie sheets in moderate oven (about 350°F) until brown, about 15 minutes.

COOKIE TIPS

Always combine dry ingredients together before adding to wet ingredients. (I sift them in a sieve.)

When in doubt about flour quantity, err on the side of too little. Too much flour makes cookies harder.

Measure your liquids in a liquid measuring cup. Measure your dry ingredients in dry measuring cups.

Recipes calling for brown sugar generally mean for it to be packed into the spoon or cup.

Oven should be preheated at least 15 minutes before baking, unless recipe calls for cold oven.

If dough starts to spread for drop cookie, chill it in the fridge.

No need for greased cookie sheets when cookie dough contains large amounts of butter or shortening.

Do not place two sheets of cookies on different racks in the oven. The cookies will bake unevenly.

Cool sheets between batches of cookies, or the cookie dough will start to spread improperly.

Benne wafers are made with toasted sesame seeds.

BENNE WAFERS

Benne Wafers are a rich cookie dating back to the Carolinas Low Country of the 17th century. Like many of our favorite Southern foods that originated with the West African cultures, the sesame seeds traveled to the region with the African peoples who were brought over as slaves. Benne seeds contain nutritious protein, calcium, iron, zinc and vitamins B and E. The Olde Colony Bakery of Charleston has been making their version of the benne seed wafer since 1919. Here's mine.

1/2 to 1 c sesame seeds, lightly toasted

3/4 c salted butter (1-1/2 sticks)

1-1/2 c light brown sugar, packed

2 eggs (some versions call for 1 egg)

1 tsp vanilla extract

1-1/2 c all-purpose flour

1/4 tsp baking powder

1/4 tsp salt (some older recipes exclude the salt)

Preheat oven to 375°F. Spread raw seeds evenly on ungreased cookie sheet; bake until lightly browned (watch carefully, do not over-brown), turning two or three times. Cream butter and sugar, add egg and vanilla; mix until fluffy. Add in dry ingredients, then benne seeds. Line cookie sheets with parchment paper. Drop dough by scant teaspoon onto sheet, 2 inches apart; flatten slightly with knife dipped in ice water to prevent sticking. Bake 4 to 10 minutes until lightly brown. Adjust cooking time and heat according to your oven (325 to 375°F). *Yield: 5 to 7 dozen small cookies.*

BETTY FEEZOR'S OATMEAL COOKIES

Betty Feezor was the home economist who presented foods on WBTV in Charlotte, starting in the 1950s. Her recipes became household staples.

3/4 c all-purpose flour

2/3 c white granulated sugar

1/2 tsp salt

1/2 tsp baking soda

1 tsp ground cinnamon

1-1/4 c rolled oats (not instant)

1 c chopped pecans

1 c raisins, OPTIONAL

1/3 c vegetable oil

2 unbeaten eggs

3 T dark Karo syrup

Sift dry ingredients except oats, into a mixing bowl. Add remaining ingredients and beat on medium speed until well blended. Drop onto ungreased cookie sheet and bake at 350°F in preheated oven for 10-12 minutes. Do not overbake. Cool 5 minutes, then remove from pan to a cloth to finish cooling. Store in airtight metal container. NOTE: If omitting the raisins, reduce the oil. *YIELD: About 1 dozen.*

GRANDMA GEIL'S OATMEAL RAISIN AND COCONUT COOKIES

from Fern Robertson Kerslake

1 c butter

2 eggs

2 c light brown sugar

2 c plain flour

1 tsp baking soda

1 tsp baking powder

Pinch of salt

1 tsp vanilla extract

2 c oatmeal (NOT instant)

1 c shredded coconut

1 c raisins

Sift dry ingredients together. Set aside. Cream butter and brown sugar. Mix in eggs until creamy. Add dry ingredients, gradually, then add vanilla. Add oatmeal, coconut and raisins, mixing after each. Roll into 1-1/2 inch balls and press with fork onto parchment-lined cookie sheets. Bake at 350°F in preheated oven 8 to 10 minutes, until lightly browned. *YIELD: About 4 dozen.*

PLAIN OATMEAL COOKIES

1 c butter, softened

1 c white granulated sugar

1 c packed brown sugar

2 eggs

1 tsp vanilla extract

2 c all-purpose flour

1 tsp baking soda

1 tsp salt

1-1/2 tsp ground cinnamon

3 c quick oats (not instant)

Sift dry ingredients together. Set aside. Cream butter with white and brown sugars. Mix in eggs until creamy. Add dry ingredients, gradually, then add vanilla. Add oatmeal. Chill at least 1 hour. Preheat oven to 375°F, roll dough into balls and place 2 inches apart on cookie sheets lined with parchment paper. Bake 8 to 10 minutes. Cool on sheets. *YIELD: 3 to 5 dozen soft cookies.*

OATMEAL CHOCOLATE CHIP COOKIES

This is the oatmeal cookie version for all the chocaholics.

1 c butter

1-1/2 c light brown sugar, packed

1 large egg

1-1/2 c plain flour

1 tsp baking soda

1/2 tsp salt

1 tsp vanilla extract

2 c rolled oats (quick or old fashioned, NOT instant)

2/3 to 1 c semi-sweet chocolate chips

1/4 to 1/2 c pecans, fine chopped, OPTIONAL

Cream butter and sugar until fluffy. Add egg. Sift together dry ingredients, then add to wet mixture gradually until well blended. Beat in vanilla. Add oatmeal and mix. Use spoon to fold in chocolate chips and nuts. Drop by the rounded teaspoon onto parchment-lined baking sheet. Bake at 350°F in preheated oven about 10 to 15 minutes, until lightly browned. Cool on rack. *YIELD: 3-1/2 to 4 dozen.*

VARIATION: Reduce oats to 1 c, add 1 c shredded coconut.

Mississippi Mud Cookies without the marshmallows.

CHOCOLATE CHIP COOKIES

Always everybody's favorites, chocolate chip cookies were created by Ruth Wakefield and named Toll House Cookies. Various versions, such as this one, now abound.

1 c (2 sticks) butter, softened

3/4 c granulated sugar

3/4 c packed brown sugar

1 tsp vanilla extract

2 eggs

2-1/4 c plain flour

1 tsp baking soda

1 tsp salt

Two 12-oz pkg semisweet chocolate chips

1 c chopped nuts, OPTIONAL

Sift and measure out flour, then re-sift with baking soda and salt in a small bowl. Cream butter, sugar and brown sugar. Set aside. Add vanilla and eggs, beating well after each addition. Mix dry ingredients into wet, then stir in chocolate chips and nuts. Chill, covered.

Preheat oven to 375°F. Drop dough by the teaspoon onto parchment paper-lined baking sheets, leaving about 1 inch between each cookie. Bake 8 to 12 minutes, until golden brown. Cool 5 minutes on wire rack, lift cookies with spatula, remove to a pastry cloth to finish cooling. *YIELD: About 5 dozen.*

CHOCOLATE NO-BAKE COOKIES

*This regional sweet can be found for sale beside the cash registers of NC gas-and-shop quick-stops. *NOTE: Ingredients are listed below for both smaller and larger batches; use all smaller or all larger amounts.*

1/2 c (1 stick) of butter

2 c white granulated sugar

3 T to 1/3 c unsweetened cocoa*

1/3 to 1/2 c whole milk*

Pinch of salt

3 T to 1/3 c smooth peanut butter*

2 to 2-1/2 c old-fashioned oatmeal (NOT Instant)*

1 tsp vanilla extract

Melt butter in saucepan. Add sugar, cocoa, milk, vanilla and salt. Mix and cook on low heat until comes to a boil. Set timer and boil 1 minute more. Remove from heat, add peanut butter and oatmeal.

Mix well; drop immediately by the tablespoon onto waxed paper. Flatten into "patties." Cool several hours. Wrap cookies individually in plastic wrap to keep them fresh. *YIELD: 15-24 cookies.*

MISSISSIPPI MUD COOKIES

1 c semisweet chocolate morsels

1/2 c (1 stick) butter, softened

1 c white granulated sugar

2 large eggs, room temperature

1 tsp vanilla

1-1/2 c plain flour

1 tsp baking powder

1/2 tsp salt

1 c chopped roasted, salted pecans

1/2 c milk chocolate morsels

1 c plus 2 T mini-marshmallows

Prep cookie sheets with parchment paper. Preheat oven to 350°F. Sift together flour, baking powder, and salt. Set aside. Microwave semisweet chocolate morsels in microwavable glass bowl on high, 1 minute or until smooth; stirring every 30 seconds. May take longer, but only do 30 seconds at a time. Beat butter and sugar with mixer until creamy. Mix in eggs, one at a time, until smooth. Add flour and vanilla. Gradually add melted chocolate, mixing until well blended. Mix in pecans, then milk chocolate morsels.

Drop dough by mounded tablespoon onto parchment-lined sheets. Bake 10-12 minutes. While still hot, immediately press 3 marshmallows into top of each cookie, flattening slightly. Remove to wire racks to cool. *Yield: 3 dozen.*

DIANNE POOVEY'S PEANUT BUTTER COOKIES

from Dianne Triplette Poovey

The whole family made these and shipped them to Iraq and Saudi Arabia when Jeff was stationed there during the Persian Gulf War 1990-1991.

1 c peanut butter (smooth or crunchy)

1 large egg

1 c white granulated sugar (may reduce to 2/3 c sugar)

Mix all ingredients and roll into small balls. Slightly flatten on cookie sheet to achieve large cookies, or leave as little balls to achieve rounded bites such as those depicted in the photo on page 244. Bake at 350°F in preheated oven for about 10 minutes, or until slightly browned. Remove from pan immediately and cool on waxed paper. Store in tightly sealed metal container lined with wax paper.

PEANUT BUTTER CRINKLES

from Mary Elizabeth Daltroff

This is a standard version of peanut butter cookies used by Mom for many years. The trick was to keep all of us from picking off the kisses.

1 c margarine

1 c smooth peanut butter

1 c white granulated sugar

1 c firmly packed brown sugar

2 eggs

1 tsp vanilla extract

2-1/2 c unsifted flour

1 tsp baking powder

1 tsp baking soda

12 tsp salt

Pecan or walnut half, or Hershey's Kiss for garnish

In a bowl, beat the first 6 ingredients on medium speed until fluffy. Then at low speed, beat in the next four ingredients until blended. Drop 1/2-tsp of beaten mixture in a small bowl containing granulated sugar and roll into 1-inch balls coated with sugar.

Place the sugar-coated balls 2 inches apart on a greased cookie sheet. Bake at 350°F in preheated oven for 12-15 minutes until brown.

Remove from oven and immediate press nuts, candies or jam into the tops of the cookies. Cool, and store in airtight containers. *YIELD: 6 dozen.*

VARIATION: Dab jelly or jam in depressed center instead of nuts and kisses.

COOKIE MEMORIES

Today's elementary school students select their own lunches in the school cafeteria. During the 1950s, children in grades 1 through 6 purchased assigned lunches that followed the then-accepted food pyramid. Only dessert was flexible. I've loved oatmeal cookies since first grade, when we were allowed to spend a penny on a cookie for dessert at lunch. By the time I reached high school, the cookies had risen to 2 cents.

BILLY GOATS COOKIES

from Mary Elizabeth Daltroff

Without a doubt, these are my absolute favorite cookies. They never last more than a couple of days, no matter how many I make.

1 c butter

1-1/2 c white granulated sugar

3 egg yolks

1 tsp vanilla extract

2-1/2 c pre-sifted plain flour

1 tsp baking soda

1/8 tsp salt

1 tsp cinnamon

1/4 tsp cloves

2 T sour milk

1 c chopped nuts

1 c chopped dates

1-1/2 c red candied cherries, each cherry cut into half

Blend butter, sugar, egg yolks, and vanilla on medium speed 2 to 3 minutes. Sift dry ingredients together three times. Add to wet batter. Blend in the milk, then fold in the nuts, dates and cherries. Drop by the teaspoon onto cookie sheet lined with parchment paper. Bake at 325°F in preheated oven about 12 minutes. Cool on rack. Store in sealed metal container. *YIELD: 4 dozen.*

CHRISTMAS CHERRY COOKIES

1 c butter, softened (2 sticks)

1/4 c sifted confectioners sugar

2 c all purpose flour

1 c chopped pecans

1 tsp vanilla extract

36 red or green candied cherries

Confectioners sugar

Cream butter and 1/4 cup sugar; beating well at medium speed of an electric mixer. Add flour, pecans and vanilla; mix until well blended. Shape dough into 1-inch balls and place on ungreased cookie sheets. Press a cherry into the center of each cookie. Bake at 325°F for 30 minutes. Remove to wire racks to cool slightly. One at a time, roll cookies in remaining powdered sugar. Cool completely on the cookie sheets on wire racks. *YIELD: 3 dozen.*

COCONUT MACAROONS

2 egg whites

1 c white granulated sugar

1 c shredded coconut

2 c corn flakes, crushed

1/2 tsp salt

1 tsp vanilla extract

Beat egg whites with sugar, salt and vanilla until stiff. Fold in coconut and corn flakes. Drop onto well greased or parchment-lined baking sheet, about 3 inches apart. Bake in preheated oven at 325°F about 12 minutes, until light brown. Cool on rack. Store in covered container.

CREAM CHEESE COOKIES

1/4 lb butter, melted (1 stick)

3 oz cream cheese

9 T white granulated sugar

1 c sifted all-purpose flour

9 to 12 walnut or roasted pecan halves

Cream the cheese, melted butter and add sugar and then the sifted flour. Take a dollop of the cookie dough and spread out with a wet finger onto cookie sheet (lightly greased), making the cookie as thin as possible. Press nut into top. Bake at 350°F for about 10 minutes or until lightly browned. *YIELD: 9 to 12 cookies.*

DATE BALLS

from Louise Triplette

1 stick butter or margarine (1/2 c)

1 c brown sugar

1 c chopped dates

1/2 c flaked coconut

1 c pecans, crushed

2 c Rice Krispies

Combine butter, sugar and dates in a sauce pan. Cook on medium or medium-low until well blended, approximately 5 minutes. Combine the coconut, pecans and Rice Krispies in a bowl. Fold in the melted date mixture. Let cool. Shape into small balls. Roll the balls in powdered confectioners sugar. Store in tightly covered tin.

FRUITCAKE COOKIES

from Mary Elizabeth Daltroff

1/2 c butter or margarine

1 c brown sugar

4 eggs

1 tsp baking soda

3 c cake flour

3 T buttermilk

1/2 tsp nutmeg

5 oz rum, cognac or booze of choice

1 tsp vanilla extract

1 lb candied cherries

1 lb candied pineapple

1-1/2 lb small pecans

Roll fruit and nuts in 1/2-cup of the flour. Cream sugar and butter, add eggs, soda, nutmeg, booze, vanilla and buttermilk. Mix. Add flour, then fruit and nuts. Drop on lightly greased cookie sheet. Cook 10-15 minutes at 350°F until risen and browned. *YIELD: 4 to 5 dozen cookies.*

CHOCOLATE ALMOND SNOWDROPS

1 stick butter (1/2 c)

3 T confectioners sugar

2/3 c sifted all-purpose flour

1/3 c dry cocoa beverage mix

1 c finely chopped almonds

Confectioners sugar

Cream butter or margarine with the 3 T of confectioners sugar until fluffy in a medium sized bowl. Stir in the flour and cocoa mix, then add the almonds. Chill until stiff enough to handle. Preheat oven to 325°F. Roll chilled dough, a teaspoonful at a time, into marble-sized balls. Place 2 inches apart on ungreased cookie sheets. Bake in the slow oven at 325°F for 20 minutes, or until firm. Remove carefully from the cookie sheets while still warm, and roll in the additional powdered sugar to coat generously. Cool completely on wire racks. *YIELD: About 4 dozen.*

WHITE CHOCOLATE AND MACADAMIA NUT COOKIES

1 stick (8 T) butter, softened

4 oz cream cheese, softened

1/2 tsp light brown sugar

1/2 c white granulated sugar

1 egg

2 tsp vanilla extract

2 c all-purpose flour

1 tsp baking soda

1 c white chocolate morsels

1/2 c macadamia nuts

Cream the butter, cream cheese and sugars until fluffy. Add the egg and vanilla. Add the dry ingredients and mix on low speed until just combined. Do not over-mix, or the cookies will become dense and hard. Bake at 300°F in preheated oven for 18-20 minutes until lightly browned and puffed. Remove from oven and cool on rack. After 15 minutes, remove cookies from cookie sheet and place on waxed paper to continue cooling. Store in a covered metal container.

ALTERNATE RECIPE FOR LARGER QUANTITIES:

1 lb (4 sticks) butter

1-1/2 c white granulated sugar

16-oz box of light brown sugar

3 eggs

2 T vanilla extract

5-1/2 c all-purpose flour

1-1/2 tsp baking soda

1-1/2 tsp salt

4 c white chocolate morsels

2-1/2 c macadamia nuts.

Cream the butter and sugars for 3 minutes. Add eggs and vanilla. Mix an additional 1 minute. Add flour, soda, and salt. Mix well. Add white chocolate chips and nuts. Make cookies large, dropping onto ungreased cookie sheet and baking at 350°F for 12-15 minutes. Do not overbake. Remove from oven and cool on rack. After 15 minutes, remove cookies from cookie sheet and place on waxed paper to continue cooling. Store in a covered metal container.

GRAHAM CRACKER COOKIES

from Andrea Benfield and Dianne Poovey

Andrea got this recipe from Dianne, and now makes it annually for her Christmas Open House.

1 sleeve of graham crackers (out of a box of 3 sleeves)

1 c butter (2 sticks)

1 c brown sugar

1 c chopped pecans, and/or sliced almonds

Place graham crackers in a jelly-roll pan lined with foil. Mix and boil butter and brown sugar for 2 minutes, to hard boil, then add nuts and stir. Spread over crackers. Bake at 350°F in preheated oven for 10-15 minutes. Cool about 5 minutes on a rack, then break apart at cracker seams.

MEXICAN WEDDING COOKIES

1 c (2 sticks) butter, softened

1/2 c confectioner's sugar

1 T vanilla extract

2-1/4 c all-purpose flour

1/4 tsp salt

3/4 c finely chopped pecans

Confectioners sugar

Heat oven to 400°F. Mix thoroughly the butter, sugar and vanilla. Work in flour, salt and pecans until dough holds together. Shape dough into 1-inch balls. Place on ungreased baking sheet. Bake 10 to 12 minutes or until set, but not brown. While warm, roll in confectioners sugar. Cool. Roll in sugar again. Store in tightly sealed metal container.

Coconut Macaroons, page 246

OLD-FASHIONED TEA CAKES

from Rose Price May

Rose gleaned this traditional recipe from a lady in north Mississippi during the 1950s. The recipe, popular throughout the state, is based on English shortbread cookies.

1-1/4 c sugar

2 c all-purpose flour

1/2 scant c buttermilk

1 tsp baking soda

1 tsp baking powder

1 egg

2/3 c shortening

Salt

Vanilla extract

Mix sugar and shortening. Sift flour, soda, salt, and baking powder together; add to sugar mixture along with the buttermilk. Add egg and vanilla extract. If more flour is needed, add it to make the dough stiff enough to roll out thin.

Cut with a cookie cutter and bake the cutouts in a fairly hot oven (375-400°F, depending on how your oven heats). You'll know when they are done by the aroma and slight darkening of the dough.

SCOTCH SHORTBREAD

Great with morning coffee or tea. Better than Lorna Doones.

1/2 c confectioners sugar

1 c butter (2 sticks)

1 tsp vanilla extract

2 c cake flour

1/4 tsp salt

1/4 tsp baking powder

Sift confectioners sugar. In large bowl, beat the butter, gradually adding sugar. Mix until fluffy, add vanilla. Sift flour, salt and baking powder into a separate bowl. Beat into the wet mixture, blending thoroughly. Chill the dough, covered.

Preheat oven to 350°F. Roll chilled dough into 1/4-inch-thickness. Prick dough all over with a fork to prevent puffing. Cut into squares. Cover a cookie sheet with foil; place the squares on sheet. Bake 20 minutes until light golden.

BROWN SUGAR COOKIES

1 c pre-sifted plain flour + 1 cup more or less, as needed

1-1/2 tsp baking powder

1/3 tsp salt

1/2 c (1 stick) butter

1/2 light brown sugar, packed

1 egg

1 T heavy cream

1-1/2 tsp vanilla extract

Confectioners sugar

Sift together 1 cup pre-sifted flour, baking powder and salt. In large mixing bowl, cream butter, beat in sugar. Add in egg, vanilla and cream. Stir in flour and enough more to make dough stiff enough to roll. Wrap in waxed paper, chill several hours.

Place on boards lightly dusted with confectioners sugar, and roll out to 1/8 inch in thickness. Use floured cookie cutter to cut out cookies. Place on ungreased baking sheet, sprinkle with granulated sugar.

Bake about 8 minutes in 375°F preheated oven until lightly browned. Cool on rack. Store in covered metal container. If cookies tend to burn on bottom, bake on parchment-lined sheets.

SUGAR COOKIES

2 sticks butter (1 c), softened

1-1/2 c confectioners sugar

1 egg

1/2 tsp almond extract

1 tsp vanilla extract

2-1/2 c all-purpose flour

1 tsp baking soda

1 tsp cream of tartar

1/4 tsp salt

Cream butter and sugar, add egg and extracts. Sift dry ingredients and add to batter. Measure out by the teaspoon; form the dough pieces into small balls and place on greased cookie sheets.

Bake at 375°F in preheated oven about 7 to 8 minutes. The dough spreads on the cookie sheet. *YIELD: about 4-1/2 dozen.*

WHOOPIE PIES

from Louise Sherrill Triplette

This is a home-made variation of every Southerner's favorite snack, the MoonPie®, a graham cracker sandwich with marshmallow filling and chocolate coating, which was created around 1917 by Chattanooga Bakery. MoonPies teamed up with RC Cola in the 1950s as a 10-cent snack combo. Today, MoonPies are thrown instead of beads by krewes at the Mobile Mardi Gras parades.

COOKIES:

1 c white granulated sugar

2 c all-purpose flour

1 egg

1 c sweet milk

5 T cocoa

1-1/2 tsp baking soda

1/2 tsp salt

5 T shortening

1 tsp vanilla extract

Mix together all ingredients and beat well. Drop onto lightly greased cookie sheet by small spoon or scoop. Space far apart. Bake at 450°F in a pre-heated oven for 7 minutes. Makes 40-48 cookies. Spread Snow frosting filling between two cookies to make a cookie sandwich. The classic filling would be marshmallow cream, first melted in a double boiler. Our Carolina variation calls for the following filling.

SNOW FROSTING FILLING

5 T self-rising flour

1 c sweet milk (whole milk)

1/4 c margarine or butter

1/2 c shortening

1 c white granulated sugar

1 tsp vanilla extract

Combine flour and 1 cup whole milk in saucepan; cook over medium heat until thick, stirring constantly. Cool completely. Cream together the butter, shortening, sugar and vanilla. Beat well until fluffy. Spread between cookies.

RED VELVET VARIATION: Make cookies with 3 c flour, 1/3 c cocoa, 1 tsp baking powder, 1/2 tsp baking soda, 1/2 tsp salt, 1/2 c salted butter, 1/2 c shortening, 1/2 c light brown sugar, 1 c granulated sugar, 2 large eggs, 3 tsp food coloring and 1 c buttermilk. Bake at 350°F for 7-10 minutes. Fill with cream cheese frosting.

WONDERFUL COOKIE SANDWICHES

These sandwich cookies are versatile, and can be stuffed with whipped cream, cream-cheese-based filling, preserves, or flavored frostings. Use your imagination. Prepare the cookies in advance, and stuff them the day of serving. The cookies are very sweet. Keep refrigerated.

THE COOKIES:

1/2 c (1 stick) UNSALTED butter, softened

1-1/2 c white granulated sugar

3 large eggs

2-1/3 c plain flour (if using White Lily, add 4 rounded T extra)

1/3 c cocoa powder, sifted

1 tsp baking powder

Pinch of salt

Cocoa powder for dusting

Preheat oven to 325°F. Line two to four baking sheets with parchment paper. (You will be making 48 cookies.) Sift together all dry ingredients, including 1/3 c cocoa, flour, baking powder and salt. Set aside.

Combine butter and sugar, mixing until creamy and fluffy. Add eggs one at a time, beat thoroughly. Beat in dry mixture, adding in three parts, until well mixed. Dough will be sticky. Chill in fridge about 15 minutes.

Remove dough from fridge. Dust hands with extra cocoa powder. Spoon out 2 tsp of dough at a time; roll into balls. Place on cookie sheets, flattened slightly, about 1 inch apart (up to 12 cookies per sheet). Bake 15-20 minutes, until cookies are set. Cool before filling.

THE FILLING:

3/4 c unsweetened whipping cream, whipped

8 oz semisweet chocolate, chopped or grated

1/4 c frozen strawberries, thawed

1/4 c confectioners sugar, OPTIONAL

Whip cream and set aside. Melt chocolate in double boiler or in microwave and fold into whipped cream. Beat in strawberries. Pour into small bowl and chill until thickened to icing consistency.

To assemble, spread filling on bottoms of 24 cookies. Top with remaining cookies. NOTE: If filling is slightly runny, beat in confectioners sugar. *YIELD: 24 cookie sandwiches.*

VARIATION: For less chocolatey, less gooey cookies, beat 8 oz cream cheese with sweetened whipped cream and strawberries; omit the chocolate.

RANDOM BAKING TIPS

Have all ingredients out at room temperature, and measured.

Even if flour is pre-sifted (like White Lily), when recipe calls for sifting, do so.

Baking soda will increase the browning of cookies. Be sure not to over-measure.

Check expiration dates on baking powder and baking soda. Test to see if still good:

- *Baking soda should bubble when added to vinegar*
- *Baking powder should bubble added to hot water*

To measure flour, spoon flour into measuring cup. Use knife across top to level. Do NOT scoop flour with the measuring cup; it over-packs the flour.

Be sure to note whether recipe calls for butter chilled, softened, room temp or melted. Butter can't be too hot or too cold, or it won't emulsify properly with the sugar.

Check your oven temp with an oven thermometer. If too hot or too cold, the cooking time and texture will be off.

THE RECIPES

ASPARAGUS

ASPARAGUS CASSEROLE

Ingredient quantities are flexible according to size of anticipated crowd. This is like a soufflé.

1 to 2 cans of asparagus spears or asparagus tips, drained and mashed

1 to 2 c sharp Cheddar cheese, grated

1 to 2 c milk

2 to 4 c saltine cracker crumbs

4-oz jar diced pimiento

3 to 6 eggs, well beaten

1/4 to 1/2 c butter or margarine, melted (1/2 to 1 stick)

1/2 to 1 tsp salt

1/4 to 1/2 tsp black pepper

1 c shredded Cheddar cheese

Bread crumbs

Mix first nine ingredients well, making sure asparagus is mashed thoroughly. Pour into a well greased casserole dish in which the wet ingredients do not cover more than half the height of the dish (casserole size depends on whether making the larger or smaller quantity). Bake at 350°F in preheated oven for 30 minutes. At about 25-minute time, after casserole is bubbling, remove long enough to sprinkle shredded Cheddar cheese and bread crumbs over top. Return to oven. Bake until cheese melts and casserole bubbles through crumbs.

ASPARAGUS TART

This recipe adapts well to similar cheeses, and is an elegant addition to a company dinner. Experiment until you find the cheese you like best.

1 lb fresh asparagus, trimmed

1 sheet frozen puff pastry, thawed

1/2 lb Fontina or Gruyere cheese, shredded and divided

2 T lemon juice

1 T olive oil

1 tsp grated lemon peel

1/4 tsp salt

1/4 tsp black pepper

Bring 1 inch of water to a boil in a large skillet. Add asparagus to boiling water. Cover and cook for 3 to 5 minutes or just until crisp-tender. Drain. On floured surface, roll out pastry into 12-by-16-inch rectangle.

Transfer to a parchment paper-lined baking sheet. Bake at 400°F in preheated oven for 10 minutes, until golden brown. Sprinkle 1-1/2 c shredded cheese over the pastry. Arrange asparagus on top in a linear pattern, all spears pointing the same direction. Sprinkle remaining cheese evenly over the asparagus. Combine lemon juice, oil, lemon peel, salt and pepper. Sprinkle over asparagus. Bake additional 10-15 minutes until tender, and cheese melted. Slice and serve warm. *YIELD: 6 servings.*

GRILLED ASPARAGUS WITH GARLIC

I got this recipe from my Charlotte friend, Jean Hogsed. I've tweaked it a bit, Jean.

Bunch of asparagus

3 to 4 cloves garlic, minced

2 limes

Extra virgin or extra light olive oil

Fresh sea salt and black pepper

Select freshest asparagus available, breaking off any woody ends of stems. Gently wash; avoid crushing tips. Drizzle a bit of olive oil in the bottom of a 7-by-9-inch pyrex dish. Place a single layer of asparagus in the dish. Sprinkle garlic over the asparagus, and season with fresh-ground salt and pepper. Squeeze lime juice over, then drizzle lightly with olive oil. Add second layer, repeating. Bake 15-20 minutes at 350°F. *YIELD: 4 to 6 servings.*

STEAMED ASPARAGUS

Bunch of asparagus

1 lemon

4 T butter, melted

Select fresh asparagus whose stems are still tender, and tips are still crisp with no mushiness. Gently wash. Peel the stems with a vegetable scraper; trim off woody bottoms of stems. Place in a steamer basket over boiling water, Season lightly with salt. Cover and steam about 5 to 10 minutes. Remove from steamer to asparagus plate. Drizzle with lemon juice and melted butter or with Hollandaise sauce. Garnish plate with parsley and lemon slices.

VARIATION: Boil asparagus for 4 minutes, then plunge in ice water for 1 minute before serving. *YIELD: 6 servings.*

VEGETABLES & SIDES

BEANS

OLD-TIME BAKED PORK AND BEANS

from Ruby White Thurmond

1 lb dried navy beans

1 large yellow onion, sliced

1 Bay leaf

1/2 lb salt pork, sliced (or bacon)

1 c or one 8-oz can of tomato sauce

2 T of dark brown sugar, packed tight

1 T Worcestershire sauce

2 tsp salt

2 T white distilled vinegar

1/4 tsp ground cloves

1/4 tsp ground cinnamon

Soak beans overnight to plump. Wash and add enough new water to cover, then add onion, Bay leaf, and salt pork. Simmer until tender—do not boil. Drain water, reserving 1 c of the liquid to add as needed. Add remaining ingredients, top with more sliced onion. Bake in a greased 2-qt. casserole dish or bean pot for about 1-1/2 hours at 350°F. *YIELD: 8 to 10 servings.*

LAURIE'S BAKED BEANS

Two 20-oz cans pork & beans, drained

1 large yellow or white onion, diced

1/4 c diced green bell pepper

1 tsp dry mustard

1-1/2 tsp Worcestershire sauce

1 dash of Tabasco sauce

1/2 c dark brown sugar

1/4 c maple syrup

1/4 to 1/2 c medium chow-chow

6 slices of cooked bacon

Mix all ingredients except the bacon. Pour into a large greased casserole dish or baking pan. Allow plenty of room in dish for overflow. Crumble 2 of the cooked bacon slices and mix into the beans. Top with remaining bacon slices, either whole or crumbled. Bake at 350°F in preheated oven for 1 to 1-1/2 hours. *YIELD: 10+ servings.*

BASIC CALICO BEANS

2 lb ground beef

2 large white onions, chopped

1 lb bacon, cut into half-inch pieces

40-oz can pork and beans

Two 15-oz cans kidney beans, drained

Two 15-oz cans butter beans, drained

8 oz ketchup + 8 oz BBQ sauce, OR 14 oz hot ketchup

1-1/4 c light brown sugar, packed

1 green bell pepper, chopped

3 T liquid smoke

3 T white vinegar

1/2 c water

2 cloves garlic, minced

Brown beef and drain; place in slow cooker. Brown bacon, remove from pan with slotted spoon to place into slow cooker. Sauté onions and bell pepper in bacon drippings. Drain and add to cooker Add remaining ingredients. Stir well. Cover; cook on medium 6 hours. Makes a one-dish meal. NOTE: To bake in oven, put ingredients in Dutch oven; bake covered at 350°F for 1 to 1-1/2 hour. *YIELD: Feeds an army.*

BARBECUE LIMA BEANS

from Ruth Callicott Thurmond

Aunt Ruth inherited this recipe from her mother, Lilla Callicott, who made it for cookouts. So does Aunt Ruth.

1 lb dried lima beans

1/4 lb salt pork, diced

1 medium onion, chopped

1 clove garlic

1/4 c bacon grease

1-1/2 tsp prepared mustard

2 tsp steak sauce (A-1 is fine)

1 tsp chili powder

Salt to taste

10-1/2-oz can tomato soup

1/3 c vinegar (distilled or apple cider)

Crisp bacon slices

Soak beans in water overnight or cover and bring to a boil, then let sit 1 hour to plump. Sauté the onion and garlic, add with other ingredients to the beans. Bring to a boil and lower heat to medium, simmer for 30 minutes to 1 hour. Serve in a 9-by-12-inch dish, topped by bacon slices. *YIELD: About 10-12 servings.*

RED BEANS AND RICE

1 lb dried red beans (not kidney beans)

1 large white or yellow onion, chopped

3 stalks celery, chopped

6 cloves garlic, chopped

2 Bay leaves

1 piece of bacon or pork salt meat

1/2 stick butter (4 T)

1 lb Cajun smoked sausage, cut into 1-inch slices

1/2 lb chunks or chopped ham

Salt and pepper to taste

Tabasco to taste

2 c cooked rice

Rinse beans, cover with water in a large saucepan and soak for 30 minutes or longer. (I soak them overnight.) Rinse again and cover with new water. Add onion, celery, garlic, Bay leaves, and salt meat or bacon. Bring to a medium simmer and cook for 2 hours, stirring often. When beans begin getting soft, take out about 1 cup of the beans (not water, just beans). Mash this cup of beans. Add back into the bean pot, stirring completely. Add butter and stir until melted. Cook another 2 hours. Add water if needed during this time. Cut sausage and ham and add to the beans, add Tabasco and add salt and pepper as needed. Simmer for another 30-40 minutes. Serve over white rice.

GREEN BEAN BUNDLES

I had never had this tasty side dish until I moved to Oxford, MS. It is standard fare at local pot luck gatherings.

Three 15-oz cans whole green beans (or fresh ones, steamed briefly)

1 lb regular-cut bacon (about 16 slices)

1 c brown sugar

1/2 c white distilled vinegar

Salt and pepper to taste

Put 8 to 10 beans together in a bundle and wrap with a strip of bacon. Secure with a toothpick. Place bundles in a casserole dish. Mix brown sugar, vinegar, and seasonings together. Pour mixture over beans. Bake about 50 minutes at 350°F.

SOUTHERN STYLE GREEN BEANS

This is one of our must-have home-cooking dishes. Anyone who didn't learn how to make this at someone's knee can't be called a Southerner. NOTE: It really is better if NOT cooked limp and NOT standing in fatback grease and sugar.

1 qt fresh green pole beans, snapped, strung and rinsed

2 to 4 T bacon grease (or extra-light olive oil), enough to moisten and sear beans

1 fresh whole cayenne pepper, OPTIONAL

1-1/2 tsp salt

1/4 tsp black pepper

1 to 2 T white granulated sugar

Dash of cayenne pepper, to taste

Melt bacon grease or oil in large pot set on medium-high. Add beans and the whole cayenne pepper. Stir to shock the beans, lower heat to medium and cook, covered, for 2 to 3 minutes. Stir beans with slotted spoon to coat evenly. Cover again for 2 to 3 minutes. Repeat a few times, adding a very small amount of water if needed to start the steam-related cook-down process. When beans begin to change color, add salt, pepper and cayenne; stir. Cook another few minutes, then stir again, adding just enough sugar to bring out the flavor. Toss with a dash of ground cayenne pepper if you did not add a whole pepper. Cover, cook 2 to 4 more minutes on low. Turn off heat and do not remove lid until time to serve.

VEGETABLES & SIDES

BROCCOLI AND BRUSSELS SPROUTS

BROCCOLI

Steamed broccoli is just that—steamed, not boiled. Prepare the broccoli right before serving the meal.

1 bunch of fresh broccoli, stems and florets

1 tsp kosher salt

2 T butter, cut into small pieces

To prepare, wash broccoli, trim off woody stems. Place broccoli into vegetable steamer over pot containing 2 inches of water. Sprinkle with kosher salt, dot with bits of butter. Cover. Bring water in pot to full boil and let steam for 5 minutes. Turn off heat, drain off water to prevent further steaming; keep covered another 5 minutes, then uncover when ready to serve. Serve with cheese sauce, Hollandaise, or slice of lemon.

BROCCOLI CASSEROLE

This recipe works with frozen or fresh veggies, baked or in the slow cooker. I like to combine broccoli and cauliflower.

Two 10-oz pkg frozen chopped broccoli, partially thawed

   OR 4 c fresh broccoli and cauliflower, chopped

1 can condensed cream of celery soup

1-1/2 c (6 oz) shredded sharp Cheddar, divided

1/4 c white onion, chopped fine

1/2 tsp Worcestershire sauce

1/4 tsp black pepper

1 c crushed Ritz crackers (about 25)

2 T butter

Combine vegetables, soup, 1 cup of cheese, onion, Worcestershire, and pepper. Pour into greased 3-qt casserole dish or slow cooker. Sprinkle crackers evenly across top, dot with butter. Loosely tent with foil and bake at 350°F in preheated oven 30 minutes to 1 hr. Remove from oven, sprinkle remaining cheese; cook until cheese melts. In slow cooker, cook 2-1/2 to 3 hrs; sprinkle remaining cheese; cook 10 more minutes, covered, until cheese melts. *YIELD: 8 to 10 servings.*

VARIATION: Combine the listed ingredients with 2 c steamed, julienned carrots, 1/2 tsp Italian seasoning, 1/8 tsp salt, 1 cup shredded mozzarella, and 8 oz cooked elbow macaroni before baking. Yum!

BROCCOLI, RICE AND CHEESE-WHIZ CASSEROLE

This is the casserole used by every Methodist woman of my childhood acquaintance for gatherings of any sort.

1-1/2 c minute rice (or regular white rice, cooked fluffy)

2 pkgs frozen chopped broccoli

8-oz jar of Cheese Whiz

1 can cream of mushroom soup

3 T butter or margarine

1/2 c chopped onion

1/2 c milk

Prepare rice according to package directions. Cook broccoli. Mix the rice and broccoli and put into a greased 9-by-12-inch casserole dish. Sauté onion in butter. Add milk and cheese to the onion. Mix well. Stir in the soup. Pour soup mixture over the broccoli and rice. Bake at 350°F in preheated oven for about 40 minutes.

SAUTÉED BRUSSELS SPROUTS

from Aline Thurmond Miller

1/2 c slivered almonds

2 T butter

4 large garlic cloves, slivered

30 oz of Brussels sprouts, trimmed; each cut lengthwise into quarters

1/3 c water

Salt to taste

In nonstick 12-inch skillet, cook almonds over medium heat 4 to 5 minutes, until browned, stirring frequently. Transfer to a cup; set aside. In same skillet, melt butter over medium heat. Stir in garlic, sprouts, water and 1 tsp salt. Cover, cook 10-12 minutes, stirring. Transfer sprouts to serving bowl. Sprinkle with skillet-toasted almonds. *YIELD: 5 cups.*

VARIATION: Sprinkle crisp-cooked, crumbled bacon into the skillet while stirring the sprouts.

HINT: To cook green beans or Brussels sprouts but not to the soft point, steam them just to cook, then immerse in iced cold water to stop the cooking process. Drain. They will be crunchy but cooked and will retain the fresh green color.

CABBAGE

CABBAGE AND BACON SAUTÉ

1 head of cabbage

1 T kosher salt

4 T extra light olive oil

1 T white granulated sugar

4 pieces cooked bacon, crumbled

Wash and dry cabbage head. Core the cabbage and remove loose outer leaves. Chop. Cabbage will fill a large bowl. Heat olive oil in sauté pan or large skillet. Add cabbage, stirring and tossing with large slotted spoon. Sprinkle salt to taste. Cabbage leaves will begin to change colors, becoming more translucent. Add a small amount of sugar to bring out flavors. Continue to toss in hot skillet, adding crumbled bacon.

MOM KERSLAKE'S RED CABBAGE

from Fern Robertson Kerslake

My friend Fern gave me her mother-in-law's family recipe for red cabbage. I ate it as a child, but couldn't find it in Mom's or Grandmother's recipe files. NOTE: Use 1 onion per 1 head of cabbage.

1/3 chopped white onion

1/2 c butter

1/2 c vinegar

1/2 c water

1/4 c light karo syrup

1 T salt

1/4 tsp pepper

1 head of red cabbage, shredded

Sauté onions in butter in large pan, Combine vinegar, water, syrup, salt and pepper and add to onions. Add shredded cabbage. Toss with wet mixture until coated, and stir while cooking until cabbage is soft, about 1/2 hour. Once cabbage has wilted, bring to boil, cover; simmer 1-1/2 to 2 hours until very tender or until all liquid is cooked out. *YIELD: 4-1/2 cups (8 servings).*

GLAZED CARROTS

Some cooks steam the carrots to a semi-soft cooked stage before glazing, and omit the orange juice.

4 to 6 large carrots, scraped and washed

2 c orange juice

3 to 6 T butter

Salt to taste

1 to 2 T granulated white or light brown sugar, to taste

Julienne the carrots into strips 2 to 3 inches long, but not too thin. Melt butter in skillet on medium, add carrots. Sauté, add about 2 to 3 shakes of salt. Add orange juice and simmer until carrots are soft and liquid cooks down. When the carrots have softened, remove from skillet. Add sugar. Use wooden spoon to pull drippings off sides; blend with sugar and butter. Add carrots back into pan; gently stir. Cook on medium-low 2 to 3 more minutes. Glaze should be smooth and should adhere to the carrots. *YIELD: 4 to 6 servings.*

Maggie Clark Triplette in front of a bean pole at home, circa 1915

CORN

To this day everyone I know gets excited when the fresh corn starts arriving at the local grocery stores and farmers markets. Nothing has ever been as sweet as the silver queen corn grown by Lester and Louise in their garden. They taught me what all the folks in Grace Chapel already knew how to do, which was to freeze corn so it would taste fresh when boiled during the winter.

I really loved those days up at the farm shucking and silking the corn right out of the field. We'd blanch it, ice it, and wrap it in Saran wrap. It's the only time during the year I would use that sticky plastic wrap, which just seemed to work best on the corn.

Every fall, when I see spent fields of corn, I'm reminded of my Uncle Enos, the country doctor. Uncle Enos maintained a large summer garden that some years included corn stalks he set aside for popping corn. I can recall riding up to Martin, TN, with Mom to get popcorn out of Uncle Enos' field. We'd develop sore thumbs from pushing the hard kernels off the cobs.

Corn Shucking at the Jim Franklin Farm in western North Carolina, October 27, 1910
PHOTO: Courtesy of the North Carolina State Archives, Raleigh, NC

CORN

CORN ON THE COB

Fresh ears of corn, shucked, silked (quantity to suit)

Stock pot of water

1 to 2 tsp salt, OPTIONAL (salt may toughen the corn)

Bring pot of salted water to boil, if you use salt. Drop in fresh ears of corn (shucked and silked). Cover, boil about 3 to 7 minutes. Serve immediately.

CREAMED SWEET CORN

6 to 12 ears of fresh corn, shucked, silked

4 T butter

1 to 2 T water

1/2 to 1 c cream

Salt and pepper, to taste

Cut 6 to 12 ears of corn off cob (position cob in center hole of bundt pan to cut). Put into heavy saucepan. Add 4 T butter and 1 to 2 T water. Bring to a simmer on medium heat, stirring to keep from sticking. When butter has melted, reduce to medium-low and cover for 5 minutes. Add 1/2 to 1 cup of cream, salt and pepper. Bring just to boil, turn off and serve.

CLASSIC CORN PUDDING

from Ruby White Thurmond

This was one of Grandmother Thurmond's sure-fire standards. Corn pudding came over the mountains from Virginia. Variations of the recipe are found throughout the Mid-South. Jeff's North Carolina mountain family never ate it, but our friends on the Eastern Shore eat it regularly.

1/4 c white granulated sugar

3 T all-purpose flour

2 tsp baking powder

1-1/2 tsp salt

6 large eggs

2 c whipping cream

1/2 c butter (1 stick), melted

6 c fresh corn kernels (12 ears white corn preferred)

OR 6 c canned or frozen corn kernels

Combine first 4 ingredients. Whisk eggs, whipping cream and butter together. Gradually add sugar mixture, whisking until smooth. Stir in corn. Pour mixture into a lightly greased 13-by-9-inch baking dish. Bake at 350°F for 40-45 minutes, or until golden and set (toothpick comes out clean). Remove from oven and let it set for 5 minutes before serving. *YIELD: 10-12 servings.*

PAN-FRIED CORN (CONFETTI CORN)

from Butch Daltroff

8 ears of fresh corn, shucked and silked

1/2 tsp salt

1/4 tsp pepper

4 T butter

1/4 c chopped green bell pepper, OPTIONAL

2 oz jar chopped pimientos, drained, OPTIONAL

3 slices cooked bacon, crumbled, OPTIONAL

1/2 c whole milk or cream

2 eggs, OPTIONAL (for a full-bodied meat substitute)

Cut corn from cob. Melt butter in skillet and add corn when hot. Mix in salt and pepper, bell pepper and crumbled bacon. Cook until tender, add milk; stir until creamy and hot but not boiling. NOTE: I always add the peppers to this dish. Just before taking up off the stove, if eggs are desired, break 2 raw eggs into skillet and toss well, which breaks up the eggs as they cook, much like in stir-fried rice. Omit the milk if eggs are added. Serve hot. *YIELD: 6 servings.*

SUCCOTASH

2 c fresh corn cut off cob

1-1/2 to 2 c butter peas or baby limas

3 to 4 c homemade chicken broth (canned will do in a pinch)

1 T butter

Salt and pepper to taste

1/4 to 1/2 c chopped white onion

3 strips bacon

Simmer fresh cut corn and butter beans in chicken broth. Add butter, and add salt and pepper to taste. Fry bacon in skillet until crisp, remove bacon and cool, then crumble it. Use bacon drippings to sauté onions until transparent. Add with drippings and crumbled bacon to corn mixture. Simmer 10-20 more minutes until ready to serve. *YIELD: 6 servings.*

OKRA VARIATION: Add 1-1/2 c fresh, sliced okra, plus 1 tsp Tony's and 2 c diced fresh tomatoes when adding drippings and bacon. Simmer as noted above.

HINT: Lightly oil foil with cooking spray before using it to cover a hot casserole so the topping won't stick.

EGGPLANT

ANDREA'S EGGPLANT PARMESAN

from Andrea Benfield

Andrea says the eggplant and toppings may be layered if a more casserole-texture is preferred. Either way: YUMMY!

1 purple eggplant, peeled; sliced about 1/4-inch thick (or 2 long Chinese eggplants)

2 eggs

2 c Italian bread crumbs

Olive oil

26- to 28-oz jar spaghetti sauce

1/2 c fresh grated Parmesan

1/2 c grated mozzarella

Mix 2 beaten eggs with 1 T water. Dip eggplant slices in the beaten egg mixture; roll in Italian bread crumbs to coat. Brown both sides of the battered eggplant in a slight amount of oil on medium heat—about 2 to 3 minutes on each side.

Spray a 7-1/2-by-9-inch baking dish with cooking spray, or use a larger pan if needed. Arrange eggplant in one layer. Cover with favorite prepared spaghetti sauce. Top with grated Parmesan, then with mozzarella. Bake at 350º F in preheated oven for 20-25 minutes, until bubbly and browned. *Yield: 8 to 10 servings.*

Eggplant Parmesan is colorful and tasty.

CAJUN STUFFED EGGPLANT

3 medium eggplants, about 1 lb each

2 slices bacon

1 c chopped white onion

1/2 c chopped celery

1/2 c chopped green bell pepper

2 cloves garlic, minced

1/2 lb ground pork

1/2 lb ground beef (85-93% lean)

16-oz can diced tomatoes

1 T Tabasco

1 tsp dried oregano

1 tsp dried thyme leaves, crumbled

1 tsp salt

1/2 c day-old bread crumbs

3/4 c grated Parmesan cheese, divided

Preheat oven to 350°F. Split eggplants in half lengthwise. Place cut-size down on racks over sheet pans filled with water. Bake for 35-40 minutes or until tender but still firm. Cool slightly and carefully scoop out pulp, leaving shells intact. Chop the pulp and set aside. Cook bacon in a large skillet on medium heat until lightly browned. Remove bacon and set aside.

Add onion, celery, green pepper and garlic to bacon drippings; cook on medium for 5 minutes, stirring. Add pork and beef and cook, stirring to break up, until browned, about 5 to 10 minutes. Stir in the tomatoes, eggplant pulp, herbs, and salt. Cook 5 minutes, until most liquid is evaporated. Remove from heat to cool.

Stir in bread crumbs, 1/2 cup of cheese and crumbled bacon. Spoon the mixture into eggplant shells. Sprinkle tops with cheese. Place on baking pan and bake until heated through. *YIELD: 6 servings.*

DELMONICO CREOLE EGGPLANT

from Butch Daltroff

Daddy got this recipe from "Dot Dear" in Darlington, SC. I wish I could remember Dot's surname. This creole recipe is similar to versions that appear in various Mississippi cookbooks, and is loosely based on the old Delmonico Restaurant version from New Orleans.

2 eggplants, peeled and the pulp diced into cubes

1 white onion, chopped

2 ribs of celery, chopped

1 c small raw shrimp, cleaned, peeled and de-veined

4 T butter

1 large Roma tomato, skin remaining, diced

Dash of Tony's Creole Seasoning

Dash of Tabasco

Dash of Worcestershire sauce

1 Bay leaf

1/4 c seasoned bread crumbs

Parboil the eggplant. Sauté the onion, celery and shrimp in butter, about 3 minutes. Add tomato and Tony's. Cook several more minutes. Add Tabasco sauce, Worcestershire, and bay leaf. Cook until thickened as a sauce. Fold in the eggplant. Place in greased baking dish. Top with seasoned bread crumbs. Bake at 350°F approximately 20 minutes. *YIELD: 4 to 6 servings.*

EASY BAKED EGGPLANT

1 large eggplant, peeled, cut into 3/8-to-1/2-inch slices

Mayonnaise

Lemon pepper

Grated Parmesan cheese

Spread mayo over both sides of each eggplant slice. Dust with lemon pepper and grated Parmesan. Place on baking pan that has been sprayed with Pam. Bake at 450°F for 8 to 10 minutes. Serve immediately.

EGGPLANT-OYSTER CASSEROLE

from Butch Daltroff

I found this recipe in Mom's card file, written by Dad on the back side of a cotton inventory sheet dated 12/16/70, from Federal Compress & Warehouse in Walnut Ridge, AR, home of his good buddy, Bill Conley. Dad loved eggplant in all guises.

1 medium eggplant, peeled

1 c shredded or grated American or Cheddar cheese

1 c bread crumbs (plain)

4 to 5 strips of bacon

1 large can of oysters

1 large egg, beaten

LOUISIANA TRINITY (start with 3 celery ribs with leaves, 1/2 c chopped onion and 1 diced bell pepper)

Cook eggplant until tender in salted water, then drain and cool. Cook bacon strips until crisp and crumble them. Set crumbled bacon aside.

Cube the cooked eggplant and put into the bacon drippings in pan to brown slightly. Add the chopped Louisiana Trinity to the eggplant in skillet; continue cooking until celery is clear. Add the can of oysters, juice and all.

Combine the beaten egg and bread crumbs, then add to the skillet mixture and simmer for a few minutes. Pour skillet mixture into an unbaked 9-inch deep-dish pie shell, OR in a greased, buttered casserole dish without crust. Sprinkle bread crumbs and bacon over top. Bake for about 30 minutes at 350ºF.

EGGPLANT SEAFOOD LAGNIAPPE

A Cajun acquaintance recently confirmed that lagniappe means "that little something extra—The OOMPH!" I believe Dad got his version of this recipe from one of the New Orleans restaurants.

2 large eggplants

Olive oil

6 T butter, plus 2 T butter

1 c chopped green onions

1/2 c diced white onion

3 cloves garlic, minced

1/2 c chopped bell pepper

1/2 c chopped celery

Chopped parsley

Salt and pepper to taste

1 lb lump crabmeat

1/2 lb shrimp, cooked, deveined, chopped, or butterflied

Italian breadcrumbs (without cheese)

Grated Parmesan cheese

Cut eggplants in half lengthwise. Rub cut surface with olive oil and place cut-side-down in roasting pan. Bake 30 minutes at 350ºF. Remove from oven, and scrape cooked eggplant away from skin, leaving shell intact. Chop eggplant meat coarsely and reserve it. Melt 6 T of butter in a skillet, and sauté the onions, garlic, bell pepper, celery and generous amount of parsley. Season mixture with salt and pepper and cook for 4 minutes. Add eggplant and sauté for another 6 minutes. Remove from heat and add crabmeat and shrimp. Mix well. Stuff eggplant shells with the mixture; sprinkle each with bread crumbs, dot with pieces of the 2 T of butter, and sprinkle with Parmesan cheese. Bake at 350ºF for 20 minutes. *YIELD: 4 to 6 servings.*

Butch Daltroff classes cotton at his office on Front Street, circa 1968.

HAM AND EGGPLANT CASSEROLE

from Butch Daltroff

1 large eggplant, peeled and cut into small chunks

3 medium tomatoes, peeled, seeded, chopped, drained

1/2 c bread crumbs

1 tsp salt

1/2 tsp black pepper

1 tsp Worcestershire sauce

2 T butter

2 T finely chopped green bell pepper

1 medium white onion, chopped fine

1 c chopped cooked ham

Buttered bread crumbs

Grated Cheddar cheese

Soak eggplant chunks in salt water for about 20 minutes after cutting. Drain to just cover the eggplant in pot; cook until almost done. Drain completely. Sauté the onions and bell pepper in 2 T butter. Mix in with the eggplant, tossing gently. Add the bread crumbs, salt and pepper, Worcestershire, ham and tomatoes in this order, tossing gently with each addition.

Put into a buttered casserole dish and top with buttered bread crumbs. Use fork to punch some of the crumbs into the eggplant below. Bake at 350°F in preheated oven for about 40 to 45 minutes, or until the breadcrumbs are golden brown. Remove from oven long enough to sprinkle grated cheese over the top. Return dish to oven and cook 5 more minutes until cheese begins to melt. Serve at once while hot.

GREENS AND THINGS

TURNIP, COLLARD, MUSTARD, MIXED GREENS

I'm the only person in my immediate family who loves greens. Louise has always gone out of her way to save me a mess of greens when they're in season. Bless her heart! Jeff had a hard time understanding my joy the day I brought home an entire bushel basket of Spring turnip greens at the end of a Saturday farmer's market. He didn't realize that a whole lot of greens cook down to a little bit of heaven.

12-quart stock pot

3-1/2 to 4-1/2 lb of raw greens

1/2 lb lean salt pork or smoked ham hock (or 1/4 c bacon drippings)

1 T white granulated sugar

Salt and pepper to taste

4 to 8 shakes of hot pepper sauce *(see recipe, page 171)*

Tabasco to taste afterward

Remove stems. Rinse greens in sink thoroughly, drain in colander and rinse again 2 more times (or more, if particularly sandy). Put de-stemmed, washed greens in large stock pot, fill with water, and bring to a boil.

Drain and start over, filling with water at least to the pot half-way mark to more than cover the blanched greens. This time, add bacon drippings or pork, Tabasco, salt and pepper, and hot pepper sauce. Bring to a boil, then lower to medium-low, and cook until liquid almost cooks away (usually takes a couple of hours to cook to tender point).

Taste. If a bit bitter, add 1 T sugar and more hot pepper sauce.

NOTE: A batch of cooked greens is called "a mess of greens." The liquid in cooked greens is what we old-timey Southerners always call "potlikker." Ummmm, good. Freeze in pint- or quart-sized freezer bags.

HINT: Dishes calling for sausage or ham taste much better when the cook uses high quality sausage, ham, or ham hock. Greens, beans, and gumbos aren't worth making, in my opinion, if the sausage and ham ingredients are not up to snuff.

LORETTA'S VEG-ALL CASSEROLE

from Loretta Triplette

1 stick butter (1/2 c)

2 cans of Veg-All, drained

1 can cream of chicken soup

1 c chopped white onion

1 can sliced water chestnuts, drained

1-1/2 c or more of grated sharp Cheddar cheese or mixed blend

1 roll of Ritz crackers, crushed with a rolling pin

Mix vegetables, chopped onion, water chestnuts and approximately 1/2-cup of cheese. Place in a greased 3-qt casserole dish. Sprinkle 1 cup of the grated cheese over the mixture. Melt the butter and combine with the roll of crushed crackers. Sprinkle this over the cheese layer. Bake at 350°F in preheated oven for 30 minutes.

MAC & CHEESE & MORE CHEESE

What can be said about the American classic, macaroni and cheese? I never met an American, native-born or newcomer, who doesn't like some version of this most comforting of comfort foods. In researching variations on the mac'n cheese recipes, I learned that Thomas Jefferson is credited with bringing the first version to America from France. Mr. Jefferson's cousin Mary Randolph, has a simple recipe in her 1824 cookbook entitled *The Virginia Housewife*. Macaroni and cheese as we know it became popular in the 19th century, but really became a household staple after Kraft introduced the Kraft dinner of macaroni and cheese in 1937.

I have listed three variations in my cookbook, including the version used by my mom, as well as the Ronald Reagan family. In concession to evolving tastes, I recommend adding at least 2 T of Velveeta or other processed cheese to your version just to enhance the creaminess.

CLASSIC MACARONI AND CHEESE

from Mary Elizabeth Daltroff

Mom usually omitted the onion and Worcestershire.

6 T butter, divided

1/4 c all-purpose flour

1 tsp salt

1/2 tsp dry mustard

1/4 tsp pepper

3/4 tsp Worcestershire sauce, OPTIONAL (*I don't use it*)

3 c whole milk, heated but not boiled

1 small onion, grated, OPTIONAL (*I don't use it*)

3/4 lb (3 c) shredded sharp Cheddar cheese

2 T Velveeta cheese

9 oz large elbow macaroni, cooked and drained (or ziti)

1 egg, beaten

3/4 c soft bread crumbs or crushed crackers

Dash of paprika, OPTIONAL

In saucepan over medium low heat melt 4 tablespoons butter; blend in flour and seasonings, stirring until smooth and bubbly. Gradually stir in milk; cook and stir until thick and smooth. Stir in grated onion and 2-1/2 cups Cheddar and the 2 T Velveeta. Place cooked drained macaroni in a buttered 3-quart casserole. Mix in beaten egg. Pour sauce over macaroni and gently mix to blend. Melt remaining 2 tablespoons of butter; toss with the bread crumbs. Sprinkle bread crumbs and remaining cheese over macaroni. Sprinkle with dash of paprika if desired. Bake at 375°F for 30-45 minutes, until golden brown. *YIELD: 6 to 8 servings.*

SLOW COOKER MAC AND CHEESE

12-oz can evaporated milk (or 12 oz of cream)

1/4 tsp white ground pepper

2 tsp salt

1/4 tsp dry mustard

2 c sweet milk

2 c fresh-grated sharp Cheddar cheese

1 c grated medium Cheddar or Monterey Jack

4 T butter, melted

2 eggs, beaten

8-oz pkg elbow macaroni, cooked al dente, drained

Combine first 9 ingredients in large bowl. Add pasta and blend well. Pour into greased crock pot. Cook 3 hours on low temperature. *YIELD: 6 to 8 servings.*

LAURIE'S ULTIMATE MACARONI AND CHEESE

16-oz pkg of large elbow macaroni or ziti

1 c shredded mozzarella cheese

1 c shredded sharp Cheddar or Swiss cheese

1 c grated Parmesan cheese

1 c shredded Monterey Jack cheese

1/2 c ricotta cheese

2 T Velveeta cheese

1 to 2 eggs

2 T butter

2 T WONDRA gravy flour

1 to 1-1/2 c whole milk

1 tsp dry mustard

1 tsp salt

1/8 tsp white pepper

1 c buttered bread crumbs (1 to 2 T melted butter)

Prepare macaroni noodles according to package directions. Rinse and drain, put into large mixing bowl, and set aside. In a separate bowl, combine ricotta, Parmesan, mozzarella and Monterey Jack cheeses with 1 to 2 eggs to create a thick but workable paste. Fold the salt and pepper into this cheese mixture.

Make a white sauce by melting the butter, mixing in flour, dry mustard, and milk. Melt 2 T Velveeta and sharp Cheddar or Swiss cheese into this. It should be creamy and not too thick. If too thick, add more milk. Pour over the noodles, and mix thoroughly. Stir in pepper and the mozzarella-Parmesan-Monterey Jack-ricotta mixture. Fold into a large, greased casserole

dish. Pat down to remove air pockets. Sprinkle top with buttered crumbs, or sprinkle plain crumbs over the top, poke holes, and drizzle melted butter over the crumbs. Bake in preheated oven at 400°F for 30-45 minutes, until bubbling.

VARIATIONS: Substitute low-fat versions of all cheeses. Substitute with Italian seasoned panko crumbs.

CHEESE SOUFFLÉ

*This is one of those dishes that work well for a brunch or light luncheon. Mom found it 40 years ago in **The Commercial Appeal**. It was said to have originated at the Women's Athletic Club in Chicago.*

1/4 c (2 T) butter

1/4 c all-purpose flour

1 c whole milk

1/2 tsp salt

3/4 c shredded sharp Cheddar cheese

4 egg yolks, beaten

4 egg whites, beaten stiff

2 T Parmesan cheese

Preheat oven to 375°F. Prep 4 individual 10-oz ramekins or soufflé dishes with butter or cooking spray. Melt butter and blend in the flour, cooking 2 to 3 minutes to remove the raw flour taste. Heat milk separately, and add slowly to the butter-flour mixture, stirring with a whisk. Add salt and continue stirring, until thick. Add Cheddar and stir until cheese is melted. Remove from heat and stir in the egg yolks. Cool (about 20 minutes). Fold in beaten egg whites. Spoon into individual ramekins. Sprinkle grated Parmesan over the tops. Bake the ramekins in a pan of water for 25 to 30 minutes. Serve immediately.

VIDALIA® ONIONS

(References: Vidalia Onion Committee, University of Georgia Agriculture Department, and **New Georgia Encyclopedia)**

Vidalia onions are the delicate, sweet onions grown in Georgia. Vidalias as we know them were first grown by Mose Coleman in 1931 in Toombs County, Georgia, where the soil's sulfur content is extremely low.

The secret to sweetness apparently lies in a combination of the low-sulfur soil, mid-50s winter temperatures, mid-70s spring temperatures, and average rainfall of 3-1/2 inches.

Coleman didn't know this when his first crops came in sweet. He managed to sell his first crops in 50-lb bags. The state of Georgia started a farmer's market in Vidalia by the 1940s, specializing in the new onions. The Vidalia onion festival began in 1977, and "Yumion," the Vidalia onion mascot, was created in 1980.

Today, Vidalias are grown by approximately 130 registered growers on 15,000 acres in the official Vidalia region. Only 13 Georgia counties and portions of seven other Georgia counties officially grow Vidalia® onions, named the Georgia state vegetable in 1990. The Vidalia season runs between April and June. Sweet onions from other locales such as Texas or Mexico are NOT the same as Vidalias, which are much milder.

OKRA

BOILED OKRA

Gently wash a mess of fresh okra. Slice off caps and any tough parts such as tips. Place in medium saucepan with just enough water to cover. Add salt and pepper to taste. Bring to a boil on medium-high heat; cover, lower heat to medium, and simmer for about 10-15 minutes.

FRIED OKRA

1 mess of fresh okra, washed, caps removed, sliced

2 c buttermilk

1 to 2 eggs, beaten

Dash of cayenne or Tony's Creole seasoning, to taste

1 c to 2 c yellow cornmeal, to taste (I prefer more)

1/2 c to 2 c plain flour to taste (less is best, or no flour)

Salt and pepper, to taste

NOTE: cornmeal and flour proportions are to taste. Whisk buttermilk, egg and seasoning. Soak okra 5 minutes in egg bath. Lift okra with slotted spoon to drain; dredge in a large plastic bag of combined cornmeal, flour, salt and pepper. Shake off excess; gently lower into deep fryer. Do not crowd in fryer. Lift out when okra rises to top. Drain on paper towel in pan, keep warm in oven set at 275°F until ready to serve.

ONIONS

STUFFED VIDALIA ONIONS

I remember when Vidalia onions first became readily available in western North Carolina. What a treat for making blooming (fried) onions and stuffed onions. Nowadays, folks round here start asking for Vidalias as early as March. We can always hope!

4 large Vidalia onions

3/4 lb ground regular pork sausage

3/4 c sliced mushrooms

4 oz herb stuffing crumbs

1/8 tsp ground thyme

1/8 tsp sage

2 to 4 tsp mayonnaise

1 c shredded Cheddar cheese

Cut off Vidalia root to flatten bottom. Peel and core, retaining 2 to 3 outer layers. Steam in a steamer until slightly soft (not translucent). Drain, set aside. Chop cores, and sauté with sausage and mushrooms. Drain, then drain again on brown paper bags. Combine sausage mixture with stuffing crumbs, herbs and enough mayo to moisten (do NOT overdo). Heap stuffing into onions. Place filled onions in greased baking pan. Bake in preheated oven at 350° 20-25 minutes. Remove temporarily, sprinkle with cheese; bake additional 5 minutes or until cheese melts. *YIELD: 4 servings.*

PEAS

CHICKPEA SUCCOTASH

This recipe can be adapted to lady peas or red beans. The peas or beans must be crunchy and the corn fresh.

1 T extra light olive oil

1/4 c diced andouille or Cajun-style smoked sausage

1/4 c crisp-cooked, crumbled bacon or bacon bits

1/2 c diced white onion

1/2 c diced green or red bell pepper

3/4 c fresh corn cut off cob

3/4 c canned chickpeas, rinsed and drained

1 T light brown sugar

2 T chopped parsley

1/4 c sliced green onions, including green parts

1 tsp Tabasco

1 tsp Worcestershire sauce

1/4 c heavy whipping cream

Dash of cayenne pepper, to taste

Salt and fresh-ground black pepper to taste

Combine oil, sausage, bacon and onion to large skillet on high heat. Sauté, stirring frequently until onions start to brown. Add peppers, corn and peas. Reduce heat slightly; sauté 4 to 6 more minutes. Add brown sugar, parsley, green onions, hot sauce, Worcestershire, cayenne, and heavy cream. Cook until sauce forms. Add salt and pepper. Remove and let set up for 5 minutes (sauce thickens as it cools).

VARIATION: Add bread cubes and bake as a stuffing.

Ruby White Thurmond at the White farm with Jimmy and baby Bill, 1925

FRESH PEAS

Blackeyed peas, purple hull peas, and lady (whiteacre) peas take longer to cook than green peas. They will start to ferment if left raw in the fridge for more than a few days. NOTE: Like fresh beans, peas will become tough if salt is added before they soften from cooking.

1 pt fresh peas

2 c water

1 T bacon drippings

1/2 tsp salt

1/4 tsp black pepper

Hot pepper sauce or Tabasco, OPTIONAL

Rinse fresh peas well. Let sit in cool water for several minutes, then rinse again through a colander. In 3-qt sauce pan, bring about 2 cups water to a boil. Add enough peas to boiling water for water to cover the peas by about 1 inch. Bring water back to boil; skim off scum that forms on top. Lower heat to medium or simmer and continue cooking, adding small amounts of water to keep peas covered as needed. Simmer about 30-45 minutes. Add 1 T bacon drippings if desired; simmer another 30 minutes on low. About 10 minutes before serving, add salt, pepper and optional seasonings.

HOPPIN' JOHN

This was originally a Low Country dish. Now it's a pan-Southern staple on New Year's Day, or at any other time.

2 cans blackeyed peas, or 4 to 5 c cooked dried peas

6 slices bacon, fried and crumbled (reserve drippings)

1 medium onion, chopped

1 bunch green onions, chopped (tops too)

Dash of hot sauce (Tabasco)

1/2 to 1 c of chopped ham, OPTIONAL

2 c cooked rice

Salt and pepper to taste

Sauté onion in bacon drippings. Mix onions and drippings with peas, bacon, hot sauce and optional ham. Bring to a boil and simmer in saucepan 15 minutes. Add cooked rice plus extra water, salt and pepper to taste. Lower heat, cover, and simmer 15 more minutes. Garnish with green onions upon serving. *YIELD: 6 to 8 servings.*

BLACKEYED PEA CASSEROLE

This casserole feeds a crowd. It's a Mississippi twist on dirty rice. Add 1 T butter or extra-light olive oil if you use extra-lean ground beef.

6-oz pkg long grain and wild rice mix

1 lb ground chuck or 85%-lean ground beef

1 medium white onion, chopped

1 small green bell pepper, chopped fine

2 cans blackeyed peas, rinsed and drained

1 small jalapeño pepper, seeded, diced fine

1 can condensed cream-of-mushroom soup

1/2 to 2/3 c shredded sharp Cheddar mixed with fiesta-blend cheese, to taste

Cook rice according to pkg directions. In large skillet, brown beef, onions and bell pepper; drain. In large bowl, combine peas, jalapeño, soup, rice and beef. Put in greased 2-1/2 qt baking dish. Cover. Bake 20-25 minutes at 350°F, until hot. Uncover, sprinkle cheeses. Bake until cheese melts (5+ minutes). *YIELD: 10-12 servings.*

PINEAPPLE

VIRGINIA NICHOLS' PINEAPPLE CASSEROLE

David Nichols' mother, Virginia, made this for Jeff and me during one of our visits to the Eastern Shore. It was the first time I had pineapple casserole. I love it with the bread cubes.

#2 can (20 ounces) of crushed pineapple, drained

4 to 5 slices of white bread, cubed and browned in butter

2 large eggs, beaten

2 T all-purpose flour

3/4 c white granulated sugar

1/2 tsp salt

Mix all ingredients together except bread cubes. Spread cubes over top of the mixture in a greased or buttered casserole dish. Bake at 350°F for about 45 minutes.

VARIATION: Work 1/2-cup of shredded sharp Cheddar cheese into mixture before turning it out into the casserole dish.

LORETTA'S PINEAPPLE AU GRATIN

from Loretta Phillips Triplette

Loretta's version of the pineapple casserole depends heavily on the cheese and flour to create a soufflé-type casserole. It is chunkier than Virginia's version.

2 large eggs

2 large cans pineapple (chunked or tidbits) drained

3/4 stick melted margarine

3/4 c sugar

5 T self-rising flour

1 sleeve of low-fat Ritz crackers, crushed with rolling pin

2 cups of shredded sharp Cheddar cheese

Mix together and pour into 9-by-13-inch baking dish. Top with one stick of melted margarine mixed with crushed Ritz cracker crumbs. Bake at 350°F for about 20 minutes, until cheese has melted and cracker topping is turning brown.

POTATOES

BAKED POTATOES

4 Russet potatoes

Select firm potatoes without black spots or greenish skin (which indicates they are starting to turn). Preheat oven to 375°F. Scrub the potatoes, pat dry, and pierce with fork 2 to 3 times to allow pressure to escape during baking. Bake for 30-45 minutes, or until completely done. To tell if done, gently press a side. It will give if completely cooked.

Candied Sweet Potatoes with topping of cornflakes, pecans, and cranberries.

TWICE-BAKED POTATOES

2 to 3 large Russet potatoes

Whole milk

Cream or sour cream

2 T butter

Salt and pepper, to taste

Grated sharp Cheddar cheese

Also called stuffed potatoes. Scrub the potatoes, pat dry, and pierce with fork 2 to 3 times to allow pressure to escape during baking. Bake at 350°F for 30 minutes, or until completely done. Remove from oven, slice potatoes in half longwise. Scoop out potato, leaving skin intact. Mash potatoes, adding butter, salt and pepper to taste, along with equal parts milk and cream, until smooth. Spoon back into potato skins. Top with grated cheese, bake again until cheese has melted.

VARIATION: Combine potato stuffing with chives, crumbled bacon, and cheese before baking. May be frozen before second baking.

CANDIED SWEET POTATOES

from Ruby White Thurmond

Grandmother's candied sweet potatoes were always the lightest and fluffiest, like a soufflé. After playing around with the sweet potato casserole of my sister-in-law Dianne, I realized that Grandmother's version would positively sing with a little bit of tweaking in the way of topping.

4 to 6 medium to large sweet potatoes, peeled and sliced

2 to 6 T butter

1 to 2 T maple syrup

1/2 to 1 c light brown sugar, packed (depending on quantity of sweet potatoes)

Dash of orange juice or pineapple juice

1 egg, beaten, OPTIONAL

1/2 c crushed corn flakes

1/2 c fine-chopped roasted pecans

Additional brown sugar

1/4 to 1/2 scant c chopped fresh cranberries

Miniature marshmallows

Cover sliced sweet potatoes with water and boil until soft. Drain the boiled yams in a sieve, then put back into still-warm pot. Add 2 to 6 T of butter and stir well, then mash with a ricer or fork until smooth, and butter is completely blended. Add 1 to 2 T of maple syrup, and up to 1 cup of light brown sugar, a dash of orange or pineapple juice, and continue mashing and stirring until creamy smooth. Add egg for soufflé texture.

Pour into greased casserole dish, or into hollowed orange halves set into large muffin cups. Sprinkle pecans and crushed corn flakes over the tops, followed by a light dusting of additional brown sugar. Bake 30-45 minutes at 350°F in preheated oven. About 10 minutes before done, remove dish from oven; top with cranberries and miniature marshmallows. Bake until marshmallows have browned and started to bubble.

DIANNE'S SWEET POTATO CASSEROLE

from Dianne Triplette Poovey

1 c cornflakes, crushed

2 T butter, melted

1/4 c brown sugar

4 medium sweet potatoes, boiled and peeled

4 T butter

1/2 c chopped nuts

1/2 c coconut

3/4 c brown sugar

4 bananas, mashed

Combine cornflakes, 2 T melted butter and 1/4 cup brown sugar to form topping. Set aside. With mixer, blend sweet potatoes, butter, nuts, coconut, brown sugar and bananas. Pour into greased casserole dish. Evenly spread cornflake topping over mixture. Bake at 350°F in preheated oven for 20 minutes.

GARLIC SMASHED NEW POTATOES

This is fantastic with fish dishes or with simple baked chicken. VERY SPICY!

8 to 10 medium red potatoes, scrubbed, skins on

1 bag of Crab Boil

3 to 4 cloves garlic, crushed and minced

Salt and pepper, to taste

2 to 4 T butter

Milk, to taste

Place potatoes in a 3-qt saucepan with water and bag of crab boil. Boil on medium heat until potatoes are soft. Remove from heat, remove crab boil, and drain but reserve about 1 cup potato water. Mash the potatoes,with skins; add garlic, salt, pepper and butter. Mix in reserved potato water and milk to thin to consistency of ice cream and to heighten the flavor.

MASHED POTATOES

4 Russet potatoes, peeled and sliced

Salt and pepper to taste

4 T butter

Milk or half and half cream

Place the sliced potatoes in a 3-qt saucepan. Just cover with water. Add salt (about 1 tsp). Boil on medium heat until soft, about 10-15 minutes. Remove from heat, drain water, and add butter, salt and pepper to taste. Mash with a ricer or potato masher. When lump-free, add enough milk or cream while mashing to make creamy but not runny or stiff.

ROASTED POTATO SALAD

This is a Mississippi version of German-style potato salad.

4 lb unpeeled red potatoes, washed and cut into 1-inch pieces

2 T olive oil, divided

2 tsp black pepper

1/2 tsp sea salt

1/3 c bacon bits (or crisp-cooked bacon, crumbled), divided

2 c Vidalia onions, diced (about 2 medium onions)

1 garlic clove, minced

3 T Dijon mustard

2 T mayonnaise

1-1/2 T honey

1-1/2 T balsamic vinegar

2 T fresh parsley, divided

1/4 c grated Parmesan cheese

Preheat oven to 400°F. Combine potatoes, 1 T olive oil, salt, and pepper in a large bowl. Toss to coat. Arrange the potatoes in a single layer on a jelly-roll pan. Bake for 40 minutes or until the potatoes are tender, stirring once. Transfer potatoes to a large bowl. Heat 1 T olive oil and add onion. Cook 15 minutes, or until the onions are golden brown and caramelized, stirring frequently. Add garlic to pan, and cook 30 seconds. Add onion mixture and half of the bacon bits to the potatoes, and toss gently. Let stand for 15 minutes. Combine mustard, mayo, honey, and vinegar in a small bowl, and stir with a whisk. Add the mustard mixture and half the parsley to the potato mixture. Toss gently. Sprinkle with Parmesan cheese, remaining parsley, and remaining bacon bits. Serve immediately. Keep unused salad refrigerated. *YIELD: 8 servings.*

SOUTHERN POTATO SALAD

In the South, as elsewhere in the United States, there are two basic types of potato salad: The German-based kind served hot with bacon, onion and vinegar dressing; and what we Southerners just call Potato Salad (and everyone else calls Southern Potato Salad), served cold, with mayonnaise as a base ingredient. Variations in ingredients contribute to the differences in family recipes, with some people preferring to add chopped egg or crumbled bacon, tarragon or dill to their salad.

This is the standard Southern version that I was taught during Reform-Laurie Sundays. Omit the eggs, bell pepper and pimiento if you wish. Do not serve at pot-lucks on hot days, as it will spoil, unless you keep it on ice or refrigerated.

4 to 8 large red, white or Yukon potatoes, boiled in their skin, then peeled (any waxy potato that will not become soft and mushy)

1-1/2 c chopped celery

2 to 4 chopped hardboiled eggs

1/2 c sweet onion, chopped fine

1/4 c green bell pepper, chopped fine

4-oz jar diced pimientos, drained

1 c sweet pickle relish

1 to 2 c mayonnaise

1/4 c mustard

Dash of cayenne pepper to taste

Salt and pepper to taste

Chop the peeled potatoes into cubes and place into a large mixing bowl. Add the chopped celery, onion, bell pepper, pimiento, and pickle relish. Toss well. Mix in chopped egg, being careful not to mash the egg. Combine mayo and mustard; blend into potatoes. Add cayenne, salt, and pepper to taste.

ABOUT POTATOES

When shopping for potatoes, we must determine whether we will be baking, mashing or boiling. The best baking and mashing potatoes have a coarse thick skin, are high in starch, and have a mealy texture. Think Russet or Idaho (same thing). The best boiling potatoes have thin, smooth skin, and are high in moisture and sugar, but low in starch. They tend to hold their shape when boiled, and are best for soups, stews, potato salad, casserole, and roasting. Think red or white, or think yellow, such as Yukon Golds.

KUGEL

This is a traditional eastern European Jewish dish served with chicken or brisket—a soufflé version of hashbrown potato casserole. Some kugel variations add carrots or zucchini, or fruit and sugar (breakfast variations).

8 medium potatoes (Russet) or 2 pkg refrigerated hash brown potatoes

2 white onions

6 large eggs

1/2 c oil

4 T plain flour

1 rounded T salt

1/2 to 1 tsp black pepper

Preheat oven to 400°F. Mix eggs, oil, flour, salt and pepper in a large bowl. Coarsely grate potatoes and the onion, let stand 3 to 5 minutes, and squeeze out excess liquid. Add potato-onion mixture to egg-flour mixture and stir by hand until smooth. Pour into greased 9-by-13-inch baking dish.

Bake uncovered 1 hour, or until golden brown on top and knife inserted in center comes out clean. *YIELD: 12 servings.*

HASH BROWN POTATO CASSEROLE

To reduce this company-sized recipe, keep the can of soup, use 1 cup of cornflakes, reduce other ingredients to half. Bake in a greased 9-by-13-inch dish.

Two 30-oz pkgs frozen hash browns (country style or shredded), thawed

3/4 c butter (1-1/2 sticks), melted and divided in half

4 c (32 ounces) sour cream

10-3/4-oz can of cream-of-chicken soup

1 c green onions, chopped

4 c shredded sharp Cheddar cheese

1 tsp salt

1/4 tsp black pepper

1-1/2 c cornflakes, crushed

In a large bowl, combine potatoes, half the melted butter, sour cream, soup, onions, cheese, salt, and pepper. Transfer to two greased, shallow 3-qt baking dishes or one 10-by-15-inch deep baking dish.

Combine cornflakes and remaining butter. Sprinkle evenly over tops of casseroles. Bake uncovered at 350°F in preheated oven for 55-60 minutes, or until bubbly. *YIELD: 20-30 servings.*

Roasted Potatoes Provençal

ROASTED POTATOES PROVENÇAL

2 to 3 large Russet potatoes, coarsely cut into wedges

3 to 4 T olive oil

Salt and pepper to taste

1 packet of herbs seasoning (or equivalent made up of 2 tsp garlic salt, 1 tsp dried basil, 1 tsp dried thyme leaves, 1/2 tsp rosemary and 1/2 tsp marjoram)

Preheat oven to 425°F. Coat the potato wedges in olive oil. Sprinkle the herb seasoning over the wedges and toss to coat. Spread out on baking sheet. Bake for about 10 minutes, turn once, reduce heat to 400°F. Continue baking 5 to 10 minutes, until tender.

VARIATION: Add large slices of yellow squash, zucchini, large mushrooms, red or green bell pepper, and red onion; increase olive oil and spices.

HINT: YAM OR SWEET POTATO? If the skin is smooth, it's a sweet potato, even if called a yam. A vine native to South America, the sweet potato comes in two types—lighter in color, more starchy, and less sweet; and more colorful, more moist, sweeter, and softer when cooked. Folks often call the latter yams, after the African tuber of a different genus.

RUSSET POTATO LATKES

This essential Hanukkah potato pancake dish is a favorite any time of year, for breakfast or dinner. The best latkes are not greasy, and are crunchy on the outside but soft on the inside. Serve latkes hot with sour cream and applesauce on the side. Russet potatoes contain the essential starch needed to hold the pancakes together during frying. BEWARE: Too many eggs will overwhelm the potato taste. Allow about 1/2 cup flour per pound of potatoes. Less is better than too much.

2 lb Russet potatoes, peeled and placed in ice-cold salted water to prevent browning

1/3 c grated onion

2 eggs, lightly beaten (1 egg per lb of potatoes)

1 c of all-purpose flour or 1/2 c matzo meal

1 tsp salt, plus more to taste

Fresh ground black pepper to taste

Peanut or vegetable oil for frying

Line a large baking sheet with paper towels. Preheat oven to 200°F. Fill a large bowl halfway with iced cold water. Grate the peeled potatoes, using hand box grater or food processor fitted with medium shredding disc. For lacy latkes with rough crispy edges, shred coarsely. Use fine side of the grater for denser latkes with smooth edges.

Transfer grated potatoes immediately to iced water. When all potatoes are grated, set aside for 5 minutes, then drain in large colander, rinsing with cold water. Place potatoes into a piece of cheesecloth and squeeze. When you can't squeeze any more liquid, use fork to open up and stir potatoes around, then squeeze again. Empty the potatoes into a clean bowl. Mix in remaining ingredients. If using matzo meal, let stand a few minutes for the matzo to soak up remaining liquid.

Pour oil 1/4-to-1/2-inch deep in heavy frying pan and heat to about 350°F. Form the latkes by using two tablespoons from regular flatware set. Scoop generous spoonful with one spoon, then flatten with the other spoon. Slide from spoon into the heated oil. Repeat until pan is full but not crowded. Cook until browned at the edges, then turn over and cook until fully browned. Transfer to lined baking sheet to drain. Keep warm in oven until ready to serve. To freeze for future use, cool the latkes to room temp before freezing. Remove from freezer. Reheat in oven at 350° F; drain again on paper towels.

SOUTHERN VARIATION: Add chopped green onion, grated sharp Cheddar cheese, 2 T of chopped green chilies or bell pepper, and a teaspoon of mayonnaise to the shredded potato mixture before forming into patties. I doubt this could be considered kosher on so many levels, but it's certainly tasty!

SWEET POTATO LATKES

Here is a really Southern version of latkes.

2 sweet potatoes, peeled and shredded

2 eggs, lightly beaten

1 T light brown sugar

2 T all-purpose flour

2 tsp ground cloves

2 tsp ground cinnamon

1/4 c peanut or vegetable oil

Prepare potatoes the same way as for Russet potato latkes. Combine grated and drained sweet potatoes with other ingredients. Heat oil to 375°F in heavy frying pan or skillet. Form with two tablespoons and slide into oil. Flip after 2 to 3 minutes when bottom is browned. Remove when browned and drain on paper towels. Serve piping hot.

POTATOES AU GRATIN

Whenever you see the word au gratin, look for cheese.

6 raw Russet potatoes

1-1/2 c white sauce (béchamel)

1/2 c grated sharp Cheddar cheese

Peel and slice potatoes. Layer slices into buttered baking dish, sprinkle each layer with salt and cheese. Continue until potatoes are all used. Pour hot white sauce over all. Cover with buttered bread crumbs. Bake at 350-375°F about one hour, until done. Test doneness by inserting a straw or toothpick.

SCALLOPED POTATOES

4 Russet potatoes, scrubbed and peeled

All purpose-flour

8-oz pkg sharp Cheddar cheese, grated

2 medium white onions, sliced thinner than the potatoes

Cream and/or whole milk

Butter or margarine

Preheat oven to 350-400°F. Spray 9-by-13-inch pan or large casserole dish with cooking spray. Slice the peeled potatoes about 1/4- to 1/2-inch thick. Soak in salted cold water to prevent browning and add moisture. Sprinkle flour, salt and pepper on bottom of dish. Layer potatoes over this flour mixture, trying not to overlap the potatoes too much. Sprinkle flour, salt and pepper over the potato layer, then dab butter, and cover with a layer of onion slices. Top with evenly sprinkled cheese. Repeat layers, with a topping of onion slices. Sprinkle cheese over the top onion layer.

Scald 1 qt of cream or cream-milk mixture. Do not boil. Pour the scalded milk over casserole, filling dish at least half-way. Bake 45 minutes to 1 hour, or longer if needed. The potatoes should be tender but not mushy, and the liquid absorbed. Prior to serving, sprinkle more grated cheese on top, and continue baking 5 more minutes. *YIELD: 12 servings.*

VARIATION: Add crumbled bacon to topping.

TANTE IDA'S TZIMMES

from Randy Rosen

Potato and carrot tzimmes can be considered a German Jewish version of our Southern sweet potato casserole. Randy shared her Aunt Ida's recipe, which is quick to prepare, and similar to Bigmamma Rose's tzimmes.

2 lb sweet potatoes

1 lb washed prunes

2 medium carrots, parboiled

Brown sugar to taste

1 tsp salt

#2 can (20-oz can) pineapple slices, drained and cut into 1-inch pieces

Peel sweet potatoes, cut into 1-1/2-inch slices. Cut carrots into 1-inch pieces. Arrange potato slices, carrots, prunes, and pineapple pieces in oblong pan. Sprinkle with salt and sugar; pour pineapple juice over all. Bake at 400°F in preheated oven, basting veggies periodically with pan juices. Remove from oven when potatoes and carrots are soft, about 30-45 minutes.

RICE

ABOUT RICE

Like grits, rice is a staple starch of our Southern cuisine. As a child, I always loved driving past the exotic-looking rice fields whenever my family crossed the old Mississippi River Bridge from Memphis into Arkansas on our way to North Little Rock to visit Aunt Sheila and Uncle Herschel. To this day, Stuttgart, Arkansas, is the rice-growing capital of the U.S.

Jeff fusses at me for cooking too much rice too often (Dump Method). I point out to him that rice is an important part of my Mississippi River Valley heritage, which includes Cajun, Creole, Lebanese, Delta Chinese, and Tex-Mex rice recipes. The Triplette family used to eat sweetened rice for breakfast, which I always found to be one of the more peculiar foodways of Tennessee-North Carolina mountain people. Perhaps that's why Jeff isn't a big rice fan. Gabby, on the other hand, eats hers almost daily. With chopsticks.

COOKED RICE

There's a trick to cooking rice properly if you don't have a rice cooker. If you prefer your rice fluffy, rinse raw rice several times to remove excess starch. Drain in a sieve. Do not rinse if you prefer your rice sticky.

Coat the bottom of a saucepan with cooking spray, then cover the rice in the pot with at least 1-1/2 inches of water above the rice level. On medium-high heat, bring to a boil, and lower the heat to medium. Leave the pot alone for several minutes, stirring once to keep the rice from sticking to the bottom as the water cooks down. Add salt and pepper, cover, and turn off the heat. Let sit undisturbed for about 10 minutes.

CHINESE FRIED RICE

1/4 c peanut oil

3 c cooked, one-day-old fluffy rice

4 chopped green onions

3/4 tsp salt

1/2 chopped roasted pork, OPTIONAL

1 c cooked and diced shrimp, OPTIONAL

3 eggs

1-1/2 T soy sauce

1/4 c Chinese parsley, minced

Podded peas (sugar snaps or snow peas)

Heat the peanut oil in a heavy skillet and when "dancing" hot, toss in the rice and fry, turned occasionally, until hot and golden. Add in soy sauce, toss several times, then add green onion, salt and meat or seafood. Mix well. When completely mixed and heated, hollow a space in the center of the rice. Break 3 eggs into the hollow and scramble until semi-cooked, then stir quickly into the rice mixture. Stir in trimmed, podded peas such as snowpeas or sugar snaps, until warmed and remove from heat. Do not over-stir or the rice will become mushy.

DIRTY RICE

1/2 lb ground hot pork sausage, such as Jimmy Dean

1/2 lb 90% lean ground beef

2 bunches green onions, chopped, including the greens

1 medium white onion, chopped

1-1/2 c long grain rice, uncooked

3 c water

Salt and pepper to taste

Tony's Creole Seasoning

Tabasco or Louisiana Hot Sauce, to taste

In a large skillet brown the sausage (or sausage and ground beef) with the onions. Work in the seasonings as the meat starts to brown. When completely browned, drain all but 2 T of the grease from the skillet, add the rice and the water. Bring to a boil. Turn down heat and simmer for 15 minutes (5 minutes covered, after 10 minutes uncovered), or until rice is tender. *YIELD: 4 servings.*

VARIATION: Use all ground beef and omit sausage.

EASY RISOTTO

You can purchase arborio rice for risotto, but I use whatever I have in the pantry—long-grain, basmati or arborio. This dish must be made quickly and without distraction in order to avoid gumminess.

1/2 to 1 stick butter

1 medium sized white onion, chopped fine (minced)

2 c rice

8 to 10 c hot chicken stock or broth

Salt and white pepper, to taste

Melt butter in heavy large pan; add onion and sauté until golden. Add rice; stir with wooden spoon until butter is absorbed. Stir in 1 cup of hot stock, adding additional stock gradually, over a 10-minute period. To make it more authentic, add a tiny pinch of saffron or 1/2 tsp fennel seed while cooking. Continue to stir and cook 5 to 10 minutes longer, until all liquid has been absorbed and the rice has fluffed. Season with salt and pepper to taste. Pour into hot serving dish. If desired, sprinkle fresh grated Parmesan over the top. Serve immediately. *YIELD: 8 to 10 servings.*

SIMPLE RICE PILAF

3 c basmati rice

1 stick butter

1 white onion, chopped

Salt and pepper to taste

6 c meat broth (chicken, beef or lamb)

Sauté onion in butter, add dry rice and braise until butter begins to bubble. Add broth and seasoning. Mix well. Pour into casserole, lightly greased, and bake at 400°F in preheated oven for 30 minutes. Remove from oven, mix again; bake 20 additional minutes.

Spanish rice

Sautéed Spinach

SPANISH RICE

3 slices bacon, chopped

1/2 c uncooked rice

1/2 c thinly sliced onion

1-1/4 c canned diced tomatoes

1/2 tsp salt

1 tsp paprika

1 seeded and finely chopped green bell pepper

1 clove garlic, minced, OPTIONAL

1/2 tsp Emeril's Southwest Seasoning, OPTIONAL

Sauté bacon until brown. Remove the bacon to drain, add rice to drippings and cook, stirring, until brown. Add and brown the onion. Return bacon to dish, and add remaining ingredients. Pour into double boiler bowl set over 3-qt saucepan of simmering water. Cook for about 1 hour, stirring frequently. Add hot water or hot chicken stock to moisten while cooking.

MEXICAN RICE VARIATION: Mix in a can of Rotel. Simmer until liquid evaporates. Very spicy!

SPINACH

CREAMED SPINACH SOUFFLÉ

Growing up, my generation ate spinach a lot. Popeye was our role model.

2 lb spinach, washed very well, or two 10-oz pkg frozen

2 T butter, olive oil or bacon grease

1 c grated onion

1/4 c seasoned bread crumbs, divided

1/2 tsp salt

1/8 tsp pepper

Dash or two of of nutmeg (do not omit this)

1 c medium white sauce *(see recipe, page 169)*

Grated Parmesan or sharp Cheddar cheese, to taste

Cook spinach in pot of water until tender. Drain well and chop fine. Sauté onions in butter, oil or grease, add crumbs and seasonings, brown lightly. Mix with spinach. Add white sauce; mix in some cheese. Pour into greased casserole dish. Serve immediately if preferred, or sprinkle top with grated cheese topped with more bread crumbs, and brown in oven at 350° for 15 minutes. *YIELD: 4 servings.*

SAUTÉED SPINACH

8 to 12 oz fresh spinach leaves

2 to 3 cloves garlic, minced or crushed

3 T extra light olive oil

1/2 tsp kosher salt

Fresh ground black pepper, to taste

Fresh grated Parmesan cheese, OPTIONAL

Gently rinse and drain a mess of fresh spinach. Heat olive oil in skillet and add spinach leaves. Cover briefly, then remove lid and toss leaves to coat in oil. Mix in garlic, toss until spinach wilts. Add salt and pepper. Serve with fresh grated parmesan cheese. *YIELD: 4 servings.*

HINT: Spinach is a delicate green, crushing and wilting easily. When ready to use, rinse fresh spinach carefully in a pan of vinegar water to remove soil and contamination. Drain in colander, and dry in a salad spinner. It will only keep one or two days in the fridge before wilting.

SQUASH

ANDREA'S SQUASH CASSEROLE

from Andrea Benfield.

There are a variety of squash casserole recipes in our families. Andrea's favorite has a Mediterranean twist.

4 c sliced young yellow (summer) squash

1 medium white onion, sliced

1 clove garlic, crushed (or 1/2 tsp garlic powder)

1/2 to 2/3 c water

1/2 tsp salt

1 tsp white granulated sugar

1/4 c sour cream

1/4 c mayonnaise

1/4 c Italian bread crumbs

1/3 c grated cheese (Cheddar, Monterey Jack or Colby)

1 tsp Greek seasoning (Cavender's)

4 T melted butter

Mix together the squash, onion, garlic, water, salt and sugar. Cook in a saucepan over medium heat 10-15 minutes until just tender. Remove from heat and add sour cream, mayo, bread crumbs, grated cheese and Greek seasoning. Pour into casserole dish. Sprinkle with 1/3 cup grated cheese and 1/4 cup Italian crumbs. Drizzle butter over top. Bake 15-20 minutes at 350°F in preheated oven, or until bubbly and brown.

AUNT ALINE'S ZUCCHINI SAUTÉ

from Aline Thurmond Miller, from Ruby Thurmond

1-1/2 small zucchini squash, unpeeled

3 T margarine or butter

1 medium onion, sliced

1 green pepper, diced

1 tsp sugar

1 tsp salt

1/4 tsp pepper

1/4 lb okra, sliced

Slice zucchini. Melt margarine in large skillet. Cook zucchini and onion, pepper and seasoning, covered, over medium heat, stirring often. Add okra when tender, and cook 10-12 minutes or longer, until okra is tender. *YIELD: 6 servings.*

CAROLINA SOUR CREAM SQUASH

Dad brought this squash casserole version home one winter after being invited to the old Southern Railway hunting camp in South Carolina. It's very close to his standard recipe, only with sour cream and store-bought or homemade dressing crumbs added.

2 lb yellow squash and/or zucchini, peeled and sliced

1 medium to large white onion, chopped

4 T butter, divided

3/4 c grated sharp Cheddar cheese

1 c sour cream

1 tsp salt

1/2 tsp black pepper

1 egg, beaten

1/2 c stale bread crumbs seasoned with 1/4 tsp poultry seasoning (or sage stuffing mix)

1 T paprika

Cover the squash and zucchini with water in a pan and boil until tender. Drain completely, and mash with a fork or ricer. Let stand until cool. Sauté onion in 2 T of butter until transparent and not browned. Mix the squash, onion, cheese, sour cream, salt, pepper and egg. Gently pour into a greased casserole dish (about a 3-quart). Sprinkle stuffing mix on top and dot with 2 T of butter. Sprinkle paprika on top of this and cook uncovered for 30 minutes at 350°F or until bubbly. Cooked leftovers freeze well.

DAD'S SQUASH CASSEROLE

from Butch Daltroff

This is the version that started it all for me. It can be modified with Italian bread crumbs and chopped bell pepper. I like it just the way it is—it is still my favorite!

Dad's Squash Casserole

2 lb summer squash (yellow)

1 large white or yellow onion, chopped

4 T butter, divided

1 tsp salt

1/4 to 1/2 tsp black pepper, to taste

2 eggs, beaten

8 oz grated extra-sharp Cheddar cheese

Bread crumbs or crushed potato chips

Peel and slice squash into a large stock pot. Add the chopped onion, salt and pepper. Use some of the butter to butter casserole dish.

Fill with water to cover tops of the squash. Boil until squash is soft, then drain through a sieve. Put drained squash and onion mixture back into warm pot and mash with a ricer or potato masher. Stir in 2 T butter plus eggs. Add all but 2 oz of the cheese mixture. If too soupy, add some bread crumbs. Pour into dish. Top with remaining cheese and sprinkle crumbs evenly over the cheese. Dot with remaining butter. Bake at 350°F in preheated oven until firm in center. It has the consistency of a soufflé.

STUFFED MIRLITONS (SHRIMP-STUFFED SQUASH)

from Mary Elizabeth Daltroff

This recipe came from Bennie and Lemée Bargas, Cajun friends of Mom's in Memphis. The handwritten recipe included no quantities except for the shrimp. Quantities of ingredients depend on the size of the squash and shrimp. This recipe is called Stuffed Mirlitons when made with chayote squash (pronounced cho-cho), also known as green vegetable pear.

White squash, halved, insides scooped out and cubed

3 to 4 slices of bacon

3 to 4 ribs of celery PLUS celery leaves, chopped fine

1 green bell pepper, diced

1 to 2 cloves of garlic, minced

Dash of cayenne pepper

3 to 4 slices of stale bread, soaked in a bit of water

2 to 3 T butter or margarine

1 lb raw shelled shrimp

Fry bacon in skillet, then remove bacon and crumble, and set aside. Add the celery, bell pepper, garlic and cayenne pepper to bacon drippings and cook until soft and transparent. Add the shrimp and some of its "shrimp juice." Stir in the butter and cook about 10-15 minutes, or until the shrimp are cooked. Add salt, cayenne and bacon and squash cubes. Continue cooking until thoroughly mixed and heated. Add about 3 pieces of the soaked bread, break up the bread as you stir it in. Simmer some more until all ingredients are well mixed.

The mirliton, a chayote squash indigenous to the Caribbean, was almost wiped out in the U.S. in 2005 by Hurricane Katrina.

This cooked mixture can be scooped into the hollowed squash, the squash placed in a pan in 1/2-inch of water, and baked in the oven for 15 more minutes. Squash mixture can be put into a greased casserole and served with or without baking as a dressing.

SUBSTITUTIONS: Yellow, zucchini or chayote squash, deseeded, may be substituted in place of the white squash. This recipe is NOT suitable for acorn or butternut squash.

DRESSING
(STUFFIN'S FOR YANKEES)

CORNBREAD DRESSING

Cornbread dressing is another one of those dishes that each Southerner prepares slightly differently. Some cooks like their dressing to be firm enough to slice it. Most of us prefer it to be the consistency of mashed potatoes. Successful cornbread is airy but not gummy. NOTE: Homemade cornbread contains egg; the dressing may not need egg added. It's a judgment call.

10-inch cast-iron skillet of yellow cornbread, baked the day before (absolutely no sugar in the cornbread)

10 stale white or whole wheat bread heels

2 tsp poultry seasoning

1/2 tsp rubbed sage

1/2 tsp ground black pepper

3 to 4 large ribs of celery, chopped fine
PLUS the celery heart and leaves, also chopped fine

1 large white onion (2-1/2 to 3 c), chopped

1-1/2 to 2 sticks butter (3/4 to 1 c)

4 to 6 c chicken stock, heated

1 c turkey pan drippings from the cooked turkey

1 to 2 eggs, lightly beaten, OPTIONAL

Crumble the cornbread and grate the white bread into a very large baking pan (Use the large turkey roasting pan lid).

While the turkey is cooking, in a large skillet, sauté the celery and onion in butter over medium heat until transparent. Combine the sautéed celery and onion with the bread crumbs and mix well (pour the butter drippings into the crumbs with the vegetables. Add 2 tsp poultry seasoning, 1/2 tsp rubbed sage, black pepper, and mix thoroughly. This can be set aside until ready to assemble the ingredients and bake.

When ready to bake the dressing, add the beaten eggs, heated chicken stock and turkey drippings, and stir. You may need to add more chicken stock in order to render the uncooked dressing to the slushy state. The uncooked dressing should be very moist, and jiggly when the pan is lightly shaken. It is better to be too moist than too dry. Pour uncooked dressing into the pan in which it will be cooked. Preheat oven to 375°F. Total cooking time of the dressing should be about 30-40 minutes. Do not overcook. Feeds a whole family.

VARIATIONS: Add apples, roasted pecans, cracklins.

Sol and Eula May Daltroff, 1928

CAJUN-STYLE CRAB AND EGGPLANT DRESSING

4 large eggplants

2 T bacon fat

Salt and cayenne pepper to taste

2 large onions, chopped (Vidalia or white)

1 large bell pepper, chopped

2 ribs of celery, chopped

2 pounds lump crabmeat or fresh shrimp or ham

Seasoned bread crumbs

1/2 c fresh grated Romano cheese, plus more for garnish

Peel and cube eggplants. Soak in cold salted water. Drain and cook in large Dutch oven in bacon fat for 1 hour over medium heat, then add salt, red/cayenne pepper, onions, bell pepper and celery. Continue cooking until thoroughly done. Use a potato masher to break up eggplant while cooking. If using fresh shrimp add and cook an additional 10 minutes. If lump crabmeat or ham is used, stir in without cooking. Add enough seasoned bread crumbs to absorb liquid. Stir in 1/2-cup Romano cheese. Place in 2-qt casserole and top lightly with more crumbs and cheese. Bake at 350°F in preheated oven for 30 minutes. *YIELD: 6 servings.*

VEGETABLES & SIDES

CAJUN CRABMEAT DRESSING

7- to 8-oz can of crab meat

10-3/4-oz can of cream of mushroom soup

1/2 c seasoned stuffing mix crumbs (sage or cornbread)

1/2 c chopped bell pepper

1/2 c chopped celery

1/2 c mayonnaise

Tabasco to taste

Creole Cajun seasoning to taste (see recipe, page 174)

Combine all ingredients. Pour into a lightly greased 1- to 1-1/2-qt casserole dish. Bake at 350°F in preheated oven for 45-55 minutes, or until hot and bubbly. *YIELD: 4 servings.*

OYSTER DRESSING

Southern cornbread dressing, unbaked

1 dozen raw oysters with liqueur

Add a dozen raw oysters and at least 1-1/4 cup of oyster liqueur to cornbread dressing mixture after eggs have been folded into the mixture. Bake in a lightly greased baking dish at 325°F in preheated oven for approximately 50-60 minutes.

MCGEHEE ARKANSAS DRESSING

from Rita Davidson Friend, from Aunt Sheila

Rita says that this version of rice dressing was the favorite of the family when living in McGehee. Arkansas and rice. Of course!

1 pan of day-old skillet cornbread (yellow meal, made without sugar)

4 slices of stale white bread

1 cup COOKED WHITE RICE (not minute rice)

2 eggs

Celery

Onion

Butter

Salt and pepper

Sage

Chicken broth

Cook celery and onion in about 2 tablespoons of butter until tender. Crumble cornbread into a large bowl. Add bread after it has been soaked in water. Then add the rest of the ingredients. Season with sage to desired taste. Add chicken broth until the consistency of a thick soup. Bake at 350°F in preheated oven uncovered until set.

Rock Island Raiload Bridge over the Arkansas River at the William J. Clinton Presidential Center and Park, Little Rock, AR

PUMPKIN DRESSING

from Laurie Triplette

As a lover of pumpkin muffins, I had to include my version of pumpkin dressing. You can leave it lumpy, or mix it smooth before baking. I think it's better with lumpy texture.

DRESSING:

1 stick of butter

1-1/2 c of coarsely chopped yellow onion

1 butternut or zucchini squash, peeled, coarsely chopped

1 to 2 c coarse chopped apple (McIntosh, Rome, Empire)

1 fresh Bay leaf

2 c chopped celery and celery leaves (use center ribs)

Salt and pepper to taste

About 2 T poultry seasoning

1/2 c crumbs from grated stale 12-grain bread

1/2 c dried cranberries

4 to 8 stale Old Salem pumpkin muffins containing
golden raisins, toasted (*see recipe, page 112*)

Chicken stock (use homemade or organic)

TOPPING:

1 c roasted pecans, chopped

4 T butter

Sauté onion, zucchini, apples, and celery in butter, with poultry seasoning and Bay leaf. In a large bowl or pan, combine sautéed mixture and bread crumbs. Mix thoroughly and add cranberries. NOTE: Add 1/4 chopped nuts if omitting nutty topping. Crumble pumpkin muffins and gently fold into mixture with hot chicken stock to moisten, until dressing reaches consistency of stiff and chunky mashed potatoes. Pour into a greased casserole or pan.

Make a butter-pecan topping by chopping 1 c roasted pecans, then sautée-ing in a pan of 4 T melted butter for about 1 minute. Spread over the dressing before baking. Bake at 350°F in preheated oven for about 30 minutes. Loosely tent with foil halfway through to prevent the nuts from burning. Serve with pork tenderloin or roasted turkey.

WILD RICE

1 c wild rice, soaked at least 1 to 2 hrs

4 c water or chicken broth

Bring to a boil on medium-high heat in a saucepan; lower heat and simmer 45 to 60 minutes, covered. Check periodically for doneness. Add more water or broth if needed.

ABOUT WILD RICE

We Mississippi River watershed Southerners love the expensive delicacy called wild rice. Wild Rice isn't really rice—it's a marsh grass, native to the Great Lakes region. Like brown rice, its Asian cousin, wild rice is full of protein and energy-boosting complex carbohydrates, minerals and vitamins.

The cooking time will vary according to color and amount of cooking liquid. The darker the color, the longer the wild rice takes to cook. It is recommended to soak the wild rice grain in water for several hours before cooking. When cooked, the grains should have split (crunchy and nutty tasting) or "butterflied" fully open and become rounded (tender). But don't cook it too long or it will become mushy and starchy. Never add salt during cooking; it makes the rice tough.

Cooked wild rice is a flavorful addition to veggies, salads, and soups, stuffed in a bird, or mixed with basmati or jasmine rice in a pilaf. NOTE: A little wild rice goes a long way, as 1 cup expands to 3 cups of cooked rice.

WILD RICE DRESSING

Chicken, duck, game hen, or other poultry giblets

4 c water

1 tsp salt

1 c wild rice

1/4 c butter

2 T chopped shallots

1 T chopped green bell pepper

1/4 c chopped celery

1 c sautéed mushrooms

1/2 c sliced water chestnuts, drained

1/2 c chopped pecans

Boil the giblets in the water with 1 tsp salt for about 15 minutes. Remove from the water, and chop the giblets. Bring the giblet water back to a rolling boil, and add the rice. Lower heat to medium-low and simmer until the rice is nearly tender, about 30 minutes.

Melt the butter in a skillet and sauté the shallots, pepper and celery. Add the hot rice and chopped giblets, along with the sautéed mushrooms, pecans and water chestnuts. Mix thoroughly. Use this to stuff the game after the game has been cooked to all but the last 10-20 minutes, or add a bit of hot chicken stock or water to thin the mixture slightly, and pour the mixture into a casserole dish.

Bake in the oven for about 15 minutes at 350°F in preheated oven before serving.

TOMATOES

Daddy usually was already in the Valley by the time tomato season started in the Delta. He occasionally would sneak a quick trip home to Memphis just to get fresh okra, corn, tomatoes and purple hull peas (the vegetable-growing season in South Texas occurs in the winter, not the summer).

Mr. Bistolfi, the East Memphis grocer who was our back-fence neighbor, came from Lake Village, Arkansas, a tomato-growing district and an enclave of Italian immigrants. Mr. Bistolfi would haul in Lake Village tomatoes just for Daddy, a bushel at a time. What we didn't consume, Mom would make up into a tomato chili-sauce relish for use on meats, using Grandmother's old recipe. I recall the house smelling of tomatoes and onions for days afterward.

BACON AND TOMATO TARTLETS

12-oz can buttermilk biscuits

8 slices bacon, cooked, drained and crumbled

1 medium Roma tomato, seeded and chopped

3 oz mozzarella cheese, shredded

1/2 c mayonnaise

1 tsp Italian seasoning

3/4 tsp garlic salt

Preheat oven to 350°F. Split each biscuit into 3 pieces. Press dough into greased mini muffin tins. For filling, mix together the bacon, tomato, cheese, mayo and seasonings. Stir well. Fill each biscuit cup and bake for 10-12 minutes or until golden brown.

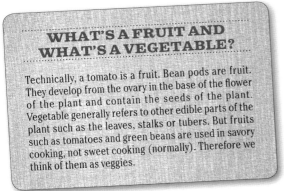

WHAT'S A FRUIT AND WHAT'S A VEGETABLE?

Technically, a tomato is a fruit. Bean pods are fruit. They develop from the ovary in the base of the flower of the plant and contain the seeds of the plant. Vegetable generally refers to other edible parts of the plant such as the leaves, stalks or tubers. But fruits such as tomatoes and green beans are used in savory cooking, not sweet cooking (normally). Therefore we think of them as veggies.

FRESH TOMATO TART

1 refrigerated pie crust (or homemade, if preferred)

1-1/2 lb thinly sliced, ripe tomatoes

1/4 tsp dried thyme, or less, to taste (*I use less*)

1/4 tsp salt

1/8 tsp pepper

1 tsp olive oil (Bertolli extra light)

1/2 c chopped sweet onion

1 T Dijon mustard

1-1/2 c shredded Cheddar, Monterey Jack cheese, mixed

Let dough thaw enough to handle. Press into a tart pan with removable bottom, or into a 9-inch pie plate. Trim and crimp edge. Refrigerate 30 minutes. Pierce bottom and sides of chilled dough to keep from puffing. Bake, unfilled, in preheated oven at 425°F for 5 minutes or until pale gold. Remove from oven and cool. Place tomato slices between sheets of paper towel to absorb moisture; let stand for 20 minutes. Heat oven to 375°F. In a small bowl, combine thyme, salt and pepper, set aside. In a medium skillet, set burner on medium and heat the olive oil. Add onion and cook and stir for 5 minutes or until softened. Spread mustard on bottom of tart shell. Sprinkle half the cheese and all the cooked onion evenly over the mustard. Top with half the tomato slices. Sprinkle with half the thyme mixture and remaining cheese. Cover with remaining tomato slices and coat with olive oil cooking spray and remaining thyme mixture. Bake 30-35 minutes or until pastry is golden brown. Serve hot. *YIELD: 8 to 10 slices.*

FRIED GREEN TOMATOES

1 egg

2 T water

3 green tomatoes

1/2 c plain cornmeal

1/2 c of all-purpose flour

Salt and pepper to taste

Cooking oil or shortening

Mix egg and water. Soak peeled and sliced tomatoes in egg mix while combining yellow cornmeal and flour. Heat oil in skillet, or deep fryer; heat. Dredge soaked tomatoes in cornmeal mix. Fry in hot skillet or deep fryer, turning once, until just brown. Drain on paper towels. Salt and pepper to taste. Serve with spicy remoulade sauce, Alabama white sauce, or dill sauce. *YIELD: 4 servings.*

SPINACH-STUFFED TOMATOES

This recipe calls for ripe but firm slicing tomatoes. Prop them upright for baking in muffin tins greased with cooking spray and lined with strips of parchment paper long enough to use for lifting out the baked tomato.

8 medium-large firm tomatoes

8 pkgs thawed Souffers Spinach Soufflé or creamed spinach with bread crumbs *(see recipe, page 273)*

Grated Parmesan cheese

Scoop out the 8 tomatoes, leaving as much of the tomato meat as possible inside the skin. Lightly salt the interiors. Fill each tomato with one package of Stouffer's Spinach Soufflé or 1 cup of prepared creamed spinach seasoned with breadcrumbs. Sprinkle each with Parmesan. Bake at 350°F in preheated oven for 20-25 minutes. *YIELD: 4 to 8 servings.*

Laurie's Tomato Tart, recipe page 279, will make up three to six small tarts, depending on the tart pan size.

THE
RECIPES

FISH & SEAFOOD

FISH AND OTHER WATERY THINGS

Every grandchild who spent any time with Granddaddy Thurmond eventually picked up a bamboo fishing pole and went fishing with him. The Thurmond men of his generation were serious hunters and fishermen, but we kids just loved sitting on the water in silence with Granddaddy.

Fish market in New Bern, NC, circa 1903
PHOTO: Courtesy of the North Carolina State Archives, Raleigh, NC

CRAPPIE: Depending on where you live, this little fish is pronounced crap-ee or crop-ee. We have whole festivals in May honoring crappie in Mississippi and Arkansas. Daddy wasn't much of a fisherman (too static for him), but from time to time he'd go crappie fishing. For a few mornings after each crappie foray, we would enjoy a breakfast feast of fried fish, fresh tomatoes, and grits. His Arkansas childhood made him do it.

CARP: An essential component of certain Asian food dishes. When Mom was battling lung cancer, we followed a completely macrobiotic diet. Mr. Kushi, of the Kushi Institute of Macrobiotics, had prescribed a carp recipe as part of the regimen to help Mom fight off the cancer. We couldn't find any carp in or around Winston-Salem, so Lester, being the Good Samaritan he always was, set out to find some for her at a Caldwell County farm with a carp pond. On his way home, he was severely injured when a runaway farm truck broadsided Lester's pickup. I have never forgotten his efforts, nor loved him more.

FROG GIGGING: I went out with Daddy and Uncle Herschel late one night in a flat-bottom boat. I didn't much care for the dark, the spooky black water, or the mosquitoes, but the resulting fried frog legs were mighty good. Tasted like chicken.

SHRIMP: I have a great memory of arising with Mom around 4:30 am., and driving the 38 miles from Harlingen to Port Isabel to watch the seasonal blessing of the shrimp fleet. Nowadays, Gabrielle visits her friends in the Louisiana Bayou country whose families are shrimpers. Like all fishermen everywhere, they too have the blessing of the fleet.

PREVIOUS PAGE PHOTO: Charlotte and Don Bradley with their haul of blue crabs

FISH

(See Soups *for gumbo recipes.)*

BAKED FILLET (ANY TYPE)

1 egg, beaten

3 lb fillet of flounder, sole, whiting or other white fish

1 c bread crumbs combined with crumbled cornbread or crushed cornflakes

1 stick (1/2 c) butter

Salt and pepper to taste

Do not use margarine in this recipe. Preheat oven to 375°F. Dip fish in the beaten egg. Press crumbs onto fish. Brown butter in oven in a shallow baking pan. Dredge both sides of fish in the butter, seasoning both sides. Bake 15-20 minutes, basting the tops while baking (do not turn). Serve with lemon wedges or slices. *YIELD: 6 servings.*

Aunt Emily Thurmond and my Granddaddy,
Rev. Enos C. Thurmond, with their fishing spoils in Halls, TN

BEER-BATTERED FISH

There are many versions of this batter recipe used for frying pan fish of all sorts, from crappie, bluefish, and flounder, to catfish and tilapia. I have used and found some that call for ratios of 1-1-1-1 for the flour, salt, beer, and seasoning such as Old Bay or cayenne. Some tempura versions call for an egg white to be beaten in just before adding the beer. All versions call for baking powder or self-rising meal to cause the batter to puff during frying. And all require a darker beer or ale than the generic American light beer.

1 c plain flour

1 c plain yellow cornmeal

1 T baking powder

1 T kosher salt

1/2 tsp cayenne pepper (or Old Bay seasoning)

12-oz bottle Amber beer or Ale

1 T salt

1 T cracked black pepper

2 T garlic powder

Red pepper flakes, OPTIONAL

4 to 6 fish fillets, cut in strips

Mix first 5 ingredients well, then whisk in beer until thickens. Let sit for about 1 hour to cure. Combine last 4 seasonings in large bowl, and pat into both sides of dried fillets. Dip each seasoned fillet into batter, let excess drip off, then gently wiggle each battered piece into fryer preheated to 350°F. Do not overcrowd in the oil. Ready in about 3 to 4 minutes. Repeat until all are done. Squeeze fresh lemon over the fish.

SELECTING FRESH FISH

- Do the smell test: Fresh fish smell mild, not fishy.
- Gills are bright and shiny.
- There's no darkening or discoloration.
- Firm flesh springs back when pressed with fingers.
- Eyes are clear and slightly bulged.
- Visible ice crystals inside the package indicate freezer burn or prior thawing.
- Fresh shellfish such as oysters or mussels are closed; avoid open or cracked shells.
- When in doubt about when you plan to use fresh fish, freeze it immediately.

FISH & SEAFOOD

COMPANY FISH ROLL-UPS

1 T butter or margarine

2 T all-purpose flour

1/4 tsp paprika

1/8 tsp salt

1-1/4 c lowfat milk

3/4 c shredded Cheddar cheese, divided

6 c (10-oz pkg or a 1-lb bunch) of fresh spinach leaves,
     rinsed, coarsely chopped, cooked and well
     drained

2 T thinly sliced green onions

6 fillets of sole, flounder or haddock (about 1-1/2 to 2 lb)

Grated zest and juice of half a large lemon

Preheat oven to 350°F. Make cheese sauce in a small saucepan: Melting butter, remove from the heat and stir in flour, paprika and salt. Whisk in milk. Cook over medium heat, whisking, until thickened. Remove from heat. Stir in 1/2-cup of cheese. Combine cheese sauce with spinach and green onion.

Douse both sides of fish fillets with lemon juice. Place about 1 to 2 T of spinach mixture on fillets, and roll up around the spinach, seam side down. Place in 9-inch baking dish on a small amount of spinach-cheese mixture. Sprinkle lemon peel zest over roll-ups. Bake 30-35 minutes, or until fish flakes easily with a fork. Sprinkle remaining grated cheese over the roll-ups, return to oven and bake until cheese melts. Remove from oven and garnish with additional green onion. Serve with hot rice. *YIELD: 6 servings.*

CLASSIC POMPANO EN PAPILLOTE

This was one of the fun grownup dishes attempted by Mom and her friends. Paper-bag baked fish dates from 19th century Creole cooking. Antoine's restaurant in New Orleans created Pompano en Papillote for visiting dignitaries to celebrate hot-air ballooning. Antoine's original version featured pompano in a wine-flavored velouté sauce with shrimp and crab.

3 green onions and tops, chopped; OR 2 shallots, chopped

3 oz fresh mushrooms, chopped

1 T butter

2 T flour

2 c chicken stock

Salt and pepper, to taste

1/3 c white wine

2 lb fillet of pompano, red fish, flounder, drum, or catfish

1 c crabmeat

4 T butter, divided

1 T white wine

1/2 T white wine

1 egg yolk, slightly beaten

1 lemon, sliced thin

Paper lunch bags, or 12-inch lengths of parchment paper

Brown mushrooms and onions in butter. Whisk in flour, add stock, salt and pepper; boil 5 minutes. Add wine. Sauté fish fillets in butter and 1 T of wine 5 minutes, set aside. Sauté crabmeat, stir in wine, salt and egg yolk; cook, stirring, until thickened.

Spoon crab on each fillet. Fold each fillet over crab filling. Spray insides of bags with cooking spray (or top sides of parchment lengths), place fillets inside oiled paper bags or on oiled sides of parchment paper (fold lengthwise around fish and twist long ends). Secure ends of bags or pouches with kitchen twine. Bake at 425°F about 10-15 minutes. Place each package with lemon wedges on plates. The paper will be puffy. Instruct guests to cut slit in the paper to get to the steaming fish.

The Thurmond men of West Tennessee were die-hard fishermen and hunters. Left to right, 1930s, Rev. Enos C. Thurmond, his sons Bill, Norman, and Jim, and his brother, Rev. Eugene E. Thurmond

PECAN-CRUSTED FISH

Four 6-to-8-oz fillets of fish such as rainbow trout, halved, about 1/2-inch thick, or catfish

1 c fine chopped roasted pecans (roasted at 350°F for 5 to 7 minutes, until deep brown and glossy)

1/4 c homemade French bread crumbs

2 tsp grated lemon zest

2 T water

1/2 tsp kosher salt

1/4 tsp black pepper

2 tsp chopped rosemary

1 egg

1/3 c flour

4 T butter, melted

Combine pecans, crumbs, lemon zest, and spices. Rinse fillets, pat dry. Salt and pepper each side. Dredge in flour, then dip in egg wash, dripping off excess. Dredge in pecan mixture. Press crumbs into fish.

Place fillets skin-side down on greased cookie sheet lined with parchment paper. Drizzle fillets with melted butter. Bake at 450°F in preheated oven for 10-12 minutes, until fish is flaky. Serve with rice pilaf, salad, and Quick Tiny Rolls (*see recipe, page 123*).

BAKED OR GRILLED SALMON

1 to 1-1/2 lb salmon fillets

2 to 4 shallots, peeled and chopped

Fennel and celery, chopped, about 1/4 cup

1/2 c dry white wine

1/2 c water

Cooking spray and parchment paper

Place salmon skin-side down in a baking pan that's been oiled with cooking spray. Cover with shallots, fennel and celery, then pour over this the white wine and water. Butter one side of a grease-proof parchment paper cut to pan size, and cover salmon, butter-side down. Bake at 375°F until salmon changes color and becomes opaque, about 30 minutes. Serve topped with fresh corn relish (*see recipe, page 82*). *YIELD: 2 to 4 servings.*

GRILLING VARIATION: Place salmon on large sheet of foil. Sprinkle with salt, pepper, and garlic powder, and position sprig of dill or rosemary on top, with dots of butter. OR, brush fish with a marinade of extra light olive oil, salt and pepper, garlic powder, and Tuscan herbs. Fold foil over and seal, tented. Bake on charcoal or gas grill about 30 minutes.

Poached Salmon tastes divine with Creamy Dill Sauce (see recipe, 170).

POACHED SALMON IN WHITE WINE

from Dr. Hugh Crawford and Pat Daltroff

1 to 1-1/2 lb salmon fillets

1/2 c dry white wine

1/2 c water

2 to 3 thin slices of yellow onion

1 shallot, sliced

2 to 3 sprigs of fresh dill, or a sprinkle of dried dill

Fresh ground black pepper to taste

Sprig of fresh parsley

Put wine, water, parsley, dill, onion and shallot in sauté pan and simmer on medium heat. Add the salmon fillets, skin side down in the pan. Continue to simmer for 5 minutes or until salmon reaches flakey stage. Do not overcook or it will become rubbery. Remove salmon from pan and serve with fresh ground pepper and dill sauce (*see recipe, page 170*).

VARIATION: Wrap large salmon fillet in cheesecloth to hold it together. Place it in a large sauté pan on top of the stove. Add 1 tsp peppercorns and 1 tsp salt, cover the wrapped salmon in water, and squeeze the juice of 2 lemons or limes into the water and over the salmon. Bring to a slow boil and cook for 20 minutes. Deceptively simple! *YIELD: 4 or more servings.*

HINT: Always place skin- or scale-side down when baking or grilling fish.

SALMON CROQUETTES

14.5 to 16-oz can of salmon

2 T lemon juice

1 to 1-1/2 T Dijon mustard

3/4 c to 1 c dry bread crumbs (or crushed saltine cracker crumbs, or Italian-seasoned bread crumbs)

1/2 c green onions, chopped with green tops

1/4 tsp black pepper

Salt to taste, if needed

1 egg, slightly beaten, or 3 egg whites, beaten

Drain the salmon and flake it by removing all bones and skin, and crumbling the fish in a large bowl. Mix in the green onions, and add lemon juice and mustard. Blend well and add the bread crumbs. Mix in the egg or egg whites, and combine until entire mixture is eggy. Form into 4 to 6 patties.

Deep-fry, turning once, until golden brown and floating; or sauté in a skillet until golden brown on each side (about 5 minutes per side), or bake 30 minutes at 350°F. Serve with spicy Remoulade sauce. Yum!

MOM'S TUNA NOODLE CASSEROLE

from Mary Elizabeth Daltroff

Andy, Dad and Jeff always hated tuna in any form. Mom, Pat and I didn't care. We loved Mom's tuna-noodle casserole. Pat and I would even eat it cold for breakfast. None of us ever liked the version with peas and pimientos. Humorist Garrison Keillor once noted that we Methodists think they add too much color.

1/4 c (4 T) butter or margarine

1/2 c celery chopped fine

1/4 c white onion, chopped fine

1 can cream of mushroom soup

1 small pkg egg noodles

1 tsp salt

2 T all-purpose flour

1/2 tsp paprika, OPTIONAL

1 c half and half cream, or whole milk

8 oz grated sharp Cheddar cheese

Two 6-oz, or one 12-oz can(s) light tuna, drained

Crushed potato chips

Cook noodles in salted water until al dente (not too soft or they become mush when baked). Drain and set aside in colander over hot water. Make sauce: Melt butter over medium-low heat, sauté the onions and celery

(if added) until transparent but not browned. Add flour to butter and onion mixture, stirring well. Season with salt, pepper, and paprika (if used). Keep stirring over medium heat until mixture begins to change. Add the half and half cream or whole milk, stirring well with a whisk until it thickens to a cream sauce. Do NOT boil. At this point add the cream of mushroom soup and mix well. If too thick, add more milk.

Place noodles into a casserole dish. Break up the tuna and fold into the cream-soup mixture. Fold the tuna and sauce mixture into the noodles until completely blended. Add shredded cheese and mix through the noodle mixture gently. Top with crushed potato chips. Bake at 375°F for about 45 minutes. Just before the cooking is completed, remove dish from oven long enough to sprinkle Cheddar cheese over the top. Return dish to oven until cheese topping has melted but not browned. Serve immediately.

CATFISH

BLACKENED CATFISH

4 farm-raised American catfish fillets

1 tsp paprika

1/2 tsp dried sage

1/2 tsp ground cumin

1/2 tsp garlic powder

1/2 tsp white granulated sugar

1/2 tsp salt

1/4 tsp onion powder

1/4 tsp cayenne pepper

1 tsp olive oil

Lemon slices

Nonstick cooking spray (PAM)

Mix the spices in a 1-gallon plastic food storage bag. Close and shake until all spices are completely blended. Rinse and pat dry the fish, then place one at a time in the bag and shake until lightly coated. Coat large nonstick skillet with PAM. Add olive oil and heat over medium-low heat until hot. Add the catfish, skinned side up, and cook 4 to 5 minutes, until lightly blackened. Carefully turn with a spatula, trying not to break the fish or the coating on the fish. Continue cooking for 4 to 5 minutes on the second side, until fish becomes opaque at its thickest part and feels firm but not spongy. Remove from the skillet and arrange on plates with lemon slices as garnish.

ABOUT CATFISH

I'm from Tennessee, lived in North Carolina and came back to roost in Mississippi. It is understood by my fellow Volunteers, Tar Heels and Magnolia-staters that catfish are among God's many gifts to Southerners.

What could be more perfect? Catfish will survive when other fish can't. They eat garbage, keeping the ponds and lakes and rivers clean, but taste like Heaven, especially when breaded and fried up with hushpuppies and served with sweet tea and slaw. The first "farm" ponds for catfish were developed in Arkansas, and quickly spread to Mississippi, Alabama, Louisiana, Tennessee and the Carolinas. The biggest commercial catfish ponds in the world today are in these states. And at its annual ode to catfish, The World's Biggest Fish Fry in Paris, TN, serves up more than five tons of catfish each April.

When a Southerner refers to eating at the "fish camp" down the road, he or she means eating fried catfish with hushpuppies, sweet tea, slaw and some sort of pie or cobbler (preferably apple or peach). A person could and should draw up a map of fish camps around the South. Taylor, MS, will be near the top of the list.

A Saturday morning view of the A-rated Taylor (MS) Grocery and Restaurant, before opening-up time. The wait to be seated can be almost an hour long. It's worth it, for the peach cobbler and the entertainment alone. And then there's the catfish...

FRIED CATFISH WITH HUSHPUPPIES

4 farm-raised catfish, cleaned and filleted

4 c yellow cornmeal (plain or self rising)

1 T all-purpose flour

1 pint buttermilk

2 tsp salt

1/2 tsp black pepper

Dash of cayenne pepper

1 onion, chopped fine

1/2 c chopped bell pepper, OPTIONAL

1 to 2 eggs

Shortening or cooking oil

Old Bay dry seasoning

Rinse the catfish and pat dry. Mix the cornmeal, flour, salt and pepper in a large bowl or pan. Marinate the catfish in the buttermilk about 30 minutes. Beat eggs in a bowl and set aside.

Begin heating oil in a deep fryer or large iron skillet. Dredge catfish in the cornmeal mix. Dip into beaten egg, then dredge a second time in the cornmeal.

Gently wiggle each piece of fish into the hot oil. Do not crowd it. The catfish will rise to the surface of the oil in the pan or deep fryer when done. If skillet frying, use tongs and spatula to gently turn one time.

Remove to a wire rack over a paper towel-lined pan. Then put the drained catfish in warm oven set at 175-225°F to keep hot until ready to serve.

THE HUSHPUPPIES: Mix remaining buttermilk, onion, bell pepper and egg with the remaining cornmeal mix. Add a dash of Old Bay for extra flavor. Work it with fingers and make small hushpuppy balls out of the dough. Drop into the fryer and cook, turning them to brown all sides equally until they rise to the top. Drain on paper towels. If not making hushpuppies, bag the cornmeal mix and freeze for future use.

SEAFOOD

BOUILLABAISSE

A bouillabaisse originally was a Mediterranean fisherman's stew. A true bouillabaisse combines several fish varieties, sliced or diced, along with shellfish in their shells. Our Gulf Coast version adapted the original Mediterranean spices, fish and shellfish to Creole tastes. New Orleans-style bouillabaisse requires two fish (usually red fish and red snapper).

Fish bones and heads

1 sliced onion

1/4 c olive oil

3 medium to large onions, chopped

2 green bell peppers, chopped

2 potatoes, peeled, sliced (Yukon or large red potatoes)

2 T salt

2 cloves garlic, minced

Bouquet garni (2 bay leaves, sprigs of thyme, parsley)

1/4 c tomato paste, or 2 c diced tomatoes, drained

2 large carrots, pared and cubed

1 qt boiling fish stock

1-1/2 lb fish fillets cut into 1-inch chunks
    (white fish, red fish, snapper, flounder, catfish, drum)

1/2 lb shrimp, shelled and deveined

1/2 lb fresh crabmeat

Fresh parsley, minced, for garnish

2 c white wine

Prepare fish stock by simmering fish heads and bones with 1 sliced onion and Bouquet Garni (See *Sauces and Seasonings*) in 2 qts water until liquid reduces by half. Strain, discard bones and garni; reserve liquid and bring back to a slow boil.

Heat oil in a large Dutch oven, sauté onion, add green peppers, potatoes, and carrots. Cook for several minutes. Add the salt, garlic, Bay leaf, tomato paste or tomatoes, and boiling fish stock. Cover and simmer for 20 minutes. Add fish fillet chunks. Cook 10 more minutes. Add the shrimp and crabmeat, and simmer for 15 minutes. Serve in deep bowls, garnished with chopped parsley. NOTE: Frozen cooked shrimp may be substituted for fresh. *YIELD: 6 to 8 servings.*

COQUILLE ST. JACQUES

from Butch Daltroff

Coquille means shell. Dad loved Low Country cooking, and spent a lot of time in South Carolina on cotton business. He brought back this scallop-and-oyster dish, which is a favorite appetizer or main meal in the Low Country.

12 shrimp, cooked, peeled, diced (about 1 lb)

4 plump scallops (about 1 lb)

1/2 c dry white wine or cognac

Bouquet Garni made of parsley, chives, dill, tarragon,
    Bay leaf, thyme)

Salt and pepper, to taste

8 to 10 oysters (may substitute 1 lb lobster)

1/2 c sliced fresh mushrooms

4 T butter

2 T plain flour

1/2 c grated Parmesan cheese

2 T whipping cream

1 egg yolk

4 to 6 thin slices large tomato, peeled

4 to 8 oz Cheddar or Baby Swiss cheese, grated

1/2 to 1 c bread crumbs

2 T parsley, minced

Put scallops, wine, Bouquet Garni, salt and pepper in sauce pan. Bring to a boil, then lower heat and simmer for 8 minutes. Turn off heat. Remove scallops and slice thin. Set aside with shrimp. Strain stock from saucepan in strainer over bowl, then return stock to pan. Add oysters, bring to a boil for 2 minutes. Set aside oysters with shrimp and scallops. Reserve stock.

Brown mushrooms in 2 T butter. Spoon cooked mushrooms into seafood mixture along with parsley, but reserve mushroom pan liquid. Melt remaining 2 T butter in skillet. Remove from heat; add 2 T flour, stirring well. Add mushroom and shellfish stocks, stirring in Parmesan. Bring just to a boil. Beat 1 egg yolk with 2 T cream. Stir into mixture. Simmer several minutes, until velvety. Add seafood and mushrooms. Remove from heat. Put into large scallop shells or ramekins. Cover top of each serving with a tomato slice. Top with grated cheese and bread crumbs. Dot with butter. Bake 20-30 minutes at 350°F; or broil until brown and bubbly. *YIELD: 6 servings.*

ÉTOUFFÉE

2 lb medium raw shrimp, peeled, scallops, or crawfish, peeled; or a combination of these

1/4 c (1/2 stick) butter

3 T white all-purpose flour

1 to 3 cloves of garlic, minced

2 T dried dill weed

2 T green onions, chopped fine

1 white onion, chopped fine

1/4 c green bell pepper, chopped fine

3/4 c celery, chopped fine

1/2 c water

1/2 tsp salt

1/2 tsp cayenne pepper

Tabasco to taste

1 T lemon juice

Melt butter in large frying pan. Blend in the flour. Add garlic, dill, green onion, green peppers, celery, and onion. Cover and cook 8 minutes or until tender. Add water and stir. Add salt, pepper, Tabasco, and lemon juice. Push veggies to the side; drop in raw shrimp, scallops or crawfish. Spoon veggies over them.

Cover and cook on low heat until pink and tender. Serve over rice. NOTE: One family version calls for adding cream of mushroom soup to the vegetables before the shellfish. I don't.

Oysters Rockefeller, yummm.

OYSTER CASSEROLE

1 c crumbled saltine crackers (coarse)

1 qt shucked fresh oysters (30 to 40 count), drained

1/4 c chopped scallions or green onions

1/4 c fresh parsley, chopped fine

1 T fresh lemon juice

Salt to taste

1/2 tsp black pepper

1 tsp Worcestershire sauce

1/2 c butter, cut into small pieces

1 c light cream

1/2 c whole milk

Dash Tabasco

Dash cayenne pepper

Paprika

Grease 1-1/2 qt shallow casserole dish with butter or Pam. Sprinkle half the cracker crumbs evenly over bottom. Place 15-20 oysters evenly over crumbs. Mix onions and parsley together; add dash of cayenne. In a separate bowl, combine next 4 ingredients. Layer over the oysters half the onions and parsley, and half the seasoning mix. Dot with butter. Cover with half the cream and milk. Repeat layering with remaining oysters, onion mix, seasonings, cream, and milk. Splash Tabasco over top, then cover with crumbs. Dot more pieces of butter over crumbs. Sprinkle surface generously with paprika. Bake 30 minutes at 400ºF in preheated oven. Serve hot. *YIELD: 6 servings.*

DOWN-HOME OYSTERS ROCKEFELLER

6 oysters in shells per serving (or bulk oysters and store-bought shells)

Creamed spinach *(see recipe, page 273)*

Cream sauce *(see recipe, page 169)*

Cayenne pepper and lemon juice to taste

Grated Parmesan cheese

Crumbled bacon bits

Rock salt

Preheat oven to 475˚F. Shuck oysters, and drain. Rinse shells and pat dry. Doctor cream sauce with cayenne and a few drops of lemon juice. Fill half of each shell with creamed spinach, and position one oyster on top. Spread 1 tsp seasoned cream sauce over each oyster. Sprinkle with 1 tsp Parmesan and top with 1 tsp crumbled bacon. Embed shells in rock salt in pans. Bake about 10 minutes until oysters are plump, then run under hot broiler to brown. Serve at once.

FRIED OYSTERS

12 large shucked oysters, drained

1 egg

2 T water

1-1/2 to 3 c seasoned bread crumbs*

*Season crumbs with salt, pepper, and Old Bay, Zatarain's, or Tony's, to taste. Preheat fryer to 375°F with shortening or peanut oil. Dry oysters in paper towels. Beat egg with water. Spearing each oyster with fork, dip in egg, then in crumbs. Repeat. Place dredged oysters on rack to dry 15 minutes. Ease into hot oil; fry about 4 minutes. Remove with slotted spoon and drain grease on paper towels. Serve on po-boy sandwiches or on a platter with dipping sauce and slaw.

PAELLA

The Spanish conquistadors' influence remains strong up the Mississippi Valley, and along the Florida and Gulf coasts. The classic Mediterranean version has become popular once again at our fancy buffet receptions.

2 c cooked chicken, cut into 1 to 1-1/2-inch pieces

4 c hot chicken stock

1/4 c olive oil

2 cloves garlic

2 c uncooked rice

Saffron (from a pinch up to 2 tsp)

1 c green peas

2 slices of sweet red peppers

6 artichoke heart

8 thin slices of chorizo sausage

Salt and pepper to taste

8 raw large shrimp

16 well-scrubbed clams in their shells

Preheat oven to 350°F. Have ready either a paellero cooking dish, or a very large lidded casserole dish (such as a 15-quart Dutch Oven). Heat olive oil and garlic in the dish. Remove the garlic. Add rice, stirring on moderate heat until lightly browned. While rice is browning, add saffron to the hot stock. Pour hot stock over rice; stir well. Mix in peas, red pepper, artichoke hearts, chorizo, salt and pepper. Stir well. Add chopped chicken, arranging it toward the top of the mixture. Cover. Bake about 15 minutes. Remove from oven. Arrange the shrimp and clams in their shells on top. Cover and bake about 10-15 more minutes to cook shrimp and clams. Serve at once *YIELD: 8 servings.*

SEAFOOD CASSEROLE

from Mary Elizabeth Daltroff

For many years, my mother made this seafood casserole as a special company dish. I developed my own crabmeat casserole as a variation of this.

1/2 c diced lobster

1/2 c lump crabmeat

1/2 c diced boiled shrimp

1/2 c chopped fresh mushrooms

1/2 stick (1/4 c) butter

1 c thin cream sauce (*see below*)

1 T sherry

1/2 c grated American or Cheddar cheese

Sauté the mushrooms in butter. Mix seafoods together. Combine with 1 c of cream sauce and the sautéed mushrooms. Pour into casserole dish. Top with grated cheese. Bake 30 minutes at 350°F. Serve with cheese sauce.

CREAM SAUCE:

1 T all-purpose flour

1 T butter

1 c hot milk

Salt and pepper to taste

Heat butter and flour over a double boiler on medium flame, stirring, for 1 to 2 minutes. Stir in hot milk, whisking constantly. Add salt and pepper to taste, remove from heat when thickened.

CHEESE SAUCE:

1 c cream

1 tsp all-purpose flour

Dash of cayenne pepper

Dash of white pepper

1/4 tsp salt

2 T butter

1/8 c grated cheese

1 egg yolk, beaten

Put all ingredients except egg yolks in top of a double boiler over medium flame. Cook until slightly thickened, stirring constantly. Remove from heat and blend in the beaten egg yolk.

LOW COUNTRY BOIL

This dish is universal to the Gulf and Atlantic low country areas, particularly the Eastern Shore along the Chesapeake Bay, where they use crabs (CRAB BOIL); the Louisiana Bayou Country, where they use crawfish (CRAWFISH BOIL); and the Carolina-Georgia Low Country, where they use shrimp and call it either a SHRIMP BOIL or FROGMORE STEW. Diehards in the Bayou and in the Low Country will "make do" a pot of potatoes, sausage, and corn, even without the shrimp or crawfish—as long as they have hot spices.

3 T Old Bay seasoning

3 T salt

1-1/2 gal water

2 lb Keilbasa, Andouille, or smoked sausage

12 ears shucked corn, broken into pieces

4 lb shrimp or 8 lb crawfish or crabs in shells

1 lemon

12 small red or white potatoes, scrubbed, unpeeled

1 qt fresh button mushrooms, OPTIONAL

2 celery ribs, cut up, OPTIONAL

In large stock pot, combine Old Bay seasoning and salt with water. Cut lemon in half and squeeze juice into the water. Add rinds. Bring to rolling boil. Cut sausage 1-to-3-inches long; add to pot with potatoes. Boil uncovered, 5 to 10 minutes. Break ears of corn in half, add to pot with mushrooms and celery. Cook five more minutes. Add shrimp, crawfish, or crabs, and cook until they just turn pink and start to rise to top, about three to five minutes for shrimp and crawfish, longer for crabs. Pour out into colander. Dump into large platter or onto newspaper-covered table. Eat while hot. *YIELD: 8 servings.*

WARNING: Mushrooms and celery soak up the pepper heat. Eat at your own risk. Ice-cold beer helps.

Traveling crawfish companies service neighborhood low country boils

RICE COOKER SEAFOOD JAMBALAYA

1 lb peeled raw shrimp

1 pint oysters

15-oz can of crabmeat, picked clean

4-oz can mushroom pieces

1 can beef broth

1-1/2 c uncooked rice

1 medium white onion, chopped

1 medium green bell pepper, chopped

1 stick margarine or butter, softened

Salt and pepper to taste

Dash of Louisiana Hot Sauce or Tony's, OPTIONAL

Add all ingredients into rice cooker, mix well, and turn it on. Takes approximately 30 minutes to cook.

VARIATIONS: Add 2 pounds peeled crawfish tails instead of the shrimp, oysters and crabmeat; OR substitute smoked sausage for the seafood.

CRAB IMPERIAL

1/3 c green bell pepper, diced fine

2 T diced pimiento

1-1/2 tsp dry mustard

1/2 tsp salt

1/4 tsp white pepper

1 egg

3/4 c mayonnaise

1-1/2 lb picked crabmeat, chopped

Mix green pepper, pimiento, mustard, salt and pepper. In separate bowl, beat egg and add mayo. Combine the two mixtures, then carefully fold in crabmeat. Spoon into individual scallop shells and bake 15 minutes at 350°F; OR in casserole dish for 35 minutes.

CRAB CAKES

Jeff and I fell in love with crab cakes when visiting the Bradleys and Nichols in Hurlock, MD, on the Eastern Shore of the Delmarva Peninsula. This recipe is a healthy variation on the traditional fried Chesapeake Bay version. You could fry these if you prefer. Just make sure the oil is hot enough, or the cakes will soak up too much oil and might fall apart.

2 lb fresh crabmeat, picked clean

1/2 c mayonnaise

1/2 c fresh parsley, chopped

1/4 c fresh lemon juice

1 large egg

1 T Dijon mustard

1 T Old Bay dry seasoning (buy the canned loose seasoning instead of bagged version)

1 tsp salt

1/4 tsp black or white pepper

1 c fine saltine crumbs (about 30 crackers, crushed in a bag with a rolling pin)

4 T unsalted butter, melted

Heat broiler, with rack 4 inches from heating elements. Line a baking sheet with aluminum foil and set aside. In a large bowl, mix the mayo, chopped parsley, lemon juice, egg, mustard, Old Bay, salt, and pepper. Add crumbs and crabmeat to the mayonnaise mixture and stir well. Dividing evenly, loosely form mixture into 8 cakes. Place cakes on prepared baking sheet, drizzle with melted butter. Broil until golden brown and warmed throughout, about 12-15 minutes. Move to lower shelf if tops brown too quickly. Serve with spicy Remoulade sauce. *YIELD: 8 servings.*

Spicy Remoulade Sauce, see page 172, is a must for Crab Cakes.

LAURIE'S CRABMEAT CASSEROLE

from Laurie Triplette

I developed this high-test variation in the early 1970s. It's always a hit with company. Leftovers actually can be frozen for up to one month. Requirement for consuming: Veggie and fruit diet before and after eating this.

1 stick (1/2 c) butter (not margarine)

1 to 2 c of chopped sweet onion

1 to 2 c of finely chopped celery and celery leaves

16-oz pkg fresh white mushrooms, chopped

Dash cayenne pepper (about 2 to 4 shakes)

Dash Worcestershire sauce , OPTIONAL

1 tsp salt (to taste)

2 to 6 T plain flour

12 to 16 oz drained lump crabmeat (I prefer Phillips)

UP TO 12 oz (one pkg) shredded sharp Cheddar, to taste

About 2 c cream

8 to 12 oz of lowfat cream cheese

1/4 c sherry or cognac, or up to 2 cups dry white wine

1 to 4 egg yolks (the amount of egg yolk to use as a thickener depends on crabmeat density and the wine volume — use more yolk to make thicker)

Sauté onions, celery and mushrooms in melted butter until onion is transparent. Add flour, and alternate adding rest of flour and cream, stirring constantly as it thickens. Add cayenne, optional Worcestershire and salt, and sherry/wine, stirring constantly. As mixture begins to bubble again, add crabmeat, stirring constantly, then add cream cheese. Depending on how dense the mixture is at this point, stir in egg yolk (it may be omitted completely if mixture is very thick). Fold in half of grated cheese and pour mixture into greased casserole dish (use Pam spray). Top with grated cheese (do NOT omit this part). Bake 20-30 minutes at 350°F, depending on your oven.

Keep same proportions of onion and celery. May omit salt and grated cheese. May also add bread crumbs as a topping. Serve with toast points or crusty bread and steamed rice. *YIELD: 8 to 12 servings.*

SOCK-EM CRAB IMPERIAL

Combine 1/2 c mayonnaise, 1/2 tsp salt, 1/4 tsp white pepper, 1/2 tsp Worcestershire sauce, 8 T melted butter, 1 T horseradish, 1 T sherry. Beat in 1 egg. Fold in 1-1/2 lb picked crabmeat. Sprinkle 1 c grated sharp Cheddar cheese on top. Bake at 350°F 35 minutes in casserole dish. YIELD: 4 servings.

CRAB SOUFFLÉ

This is like a strata, only with crab. Great for luncheons or brunch.

8 slices white or 7-grain bread

2 c fresh crabmeat, picked clean

1/2 c mayonnaise

1 sweet onion, chopped

1 c finely chopped celery

1 c finely chopped green pepper

3 to 4 large eggs

3 c whole milk

10-1/2-oz can cream of mushroom soup (no msg)

1/2 to 1 c grated sharp Cheddar cheese

Paprika (not smoked)

Cube 4 slices of bread and place bread cubes in greased or buttered 3-qt casserole dish. Mix crabmeat, mayo, onion, celery and bell pepper and spread over the diced bread. Trim crust from remaining 4 bread slices; place slices over mixture. Beat eggs, milk and soup together. Pour over mixture. Refrigerate, covered, overnight. When ready to bake, top dish with grated cheese and sprinkled paprika. Bake, uncovered, in preheated oven set to 350°F for about 1 hour.

DEVILED CRAB

12- to 16-oz can crabmeat, drained, picked clean

1 medium white onion, minced

Dash of garlic salt

2 eggs, beaten well

1/2 tsp yellow or Dijon mustard

6 to 8 drops of hot sauce (Tabasco, etc)

1 slice of toast, buttered and crumbled fine

1/2 tsp Worcestershire sauce

Salt and pepper to taste

Mix all ingredients and spoon into four oven-use clam shells or ramekins. Dot with butter. Sprinkle lightly with paprika. Bake at 375°F until light brown and bubbly. *YIELD: 4 servings.*

LOBSTER NEWBURG

Louise bought a batch of salvaged frozen lobster tails when Jeff and I were newlyweds. For a year we all ate like royalty.

4 lobsters, each 1-1/2 lb

2 tsp salt

1/2 tsp paprika

1/2 c sherry or Madeira

1-1/2 c cream

4 egg yolks, beaten

1 T cognac

4 T butter

Cook lobsters in boiling salted water for 20 minutes. Remove meat from shells, cut into half-inch slices, and refrigerate until needed. Melt butter in top pan of double boiler, add lobster meat, and sauté over direct flame until outside membrane becomes a bright red. Sprinkle with paprika. Add wine and cook until wine is almost completely cooked away. Place over hot water, add cream blended with egg yolks. Stir gently until thick. Add cognac. Keep hot until ready to serve on fresh toast with touch of paprika. *YIELD: 6 to 8 servings.*

LOBSTER THERMIDOR

Two lobsters, 1-1/2 to 2 lb each, boiled

1/4 c butter

1/2 tsp paprika

1/2 c sherry

2 T all-purpose flour

2 c thin cream (half and half)

2 egg yolks

1-1/2 c sliced mushrooms, sautéed

1/2 c grated cheese

Split lobsters lengthwise of shell and remove all lobster meat. Clean shell and wash well. Cut meat into good size pieces. Melt butter in saucepan, add paprika, sherry and lobster meat. Cook for a minute or two, then sprinkle with flour and fold together. Add egg yolks to cream and beat together, then add to lobster mixture. Add 1 cup of the mushrooms and cook over low heat, folding over and over until well blended, thickened and smooth. Fill lobster shells with the mixture, top with mushrooms and cheese. Brown well under broiler in oven. *YIELD: 4 servings.*

CHARLESTON SHRIMP AND GRITS

I have numerous versions of this Low Country favorite, and all contain the same ingredients, with variations on the grits preparation. ALL Charleston Shrimp and Grits recipes call for bacon, lemon juice, onion and bell pepper in the shrimp sauce.

1 c stone-ground or quick grits, NEVER instant

4 c water

1 tsp salt

1/4 tsp pepper

1/8 tsp cayenne pepper

Dash Tabasco

2 c shredded sharp Cheddar cheese (or less, to taste)

1 to 1-1/2 lb large (16-20 count) raw shrimp

1 to 2 large clove(s) garlic, minced

2 T chopped fresh parsley

4 to 6 T fresh lemon juice

2 T all-purpose flour

6 slices of bacon, cooked and chopped into tiny pieces

2 to 4 T butter

Small onion, chopped fine

2 T up to 1 whole green bell pepper, seeded, chopped fine

Salt and pepper to taste (1-1/2 tsp salt + 1/4 tsp pepper)

1-1/2 c chicken broth + shrimp stock
     (see shrimp stock recipe, page 153)

3 T all-purpose flour

2 to 4 T chopped green onion

Clean, peel and devein the shrimp. Bring 4 c water to boil in large saucepan. Add the grits, salt and pepper. Stir continuously with a whisk to keep from spattering, reducing heat to low as it thickens. Cook, whisking, until all the water is absorbed. Be careful not to scorch the grits. Stir in butter if desired, and the shredded cheese until melted. Whisk in cayenne and Tabasco and set aside.

Place shrimp in a bowl. Sprinkle with lemon juice, salt and pepper, garlic, chopped parsley, and 2 T flour. Stir to mix and set aside.

Fry or microwave bacon in a large skillet until crisp and then drain the bacon on a paper towel. Chop into tiny pieces when cooled. Add the butter to the bacon grease. When the butter begins to sizzle, sprinkle 3 T of the flour over it and reduce heat to low, stirring with a whisk for about 12 minutes until dark brown— but NOT scorched. You are making a roux. Once the roux achieves chocolate brown, increase the heat to medium-high and add the chopped onion and bell pepper. Cook and stir until softened. Add the chopped bacon and shrimp mixture to the roux-onion-pepper and whisk briskly for about 1 minute, then add the chicken or shrimp stock, stirring and reducing the heat to low. Cook for just 2-3 minutes until centers of shrimp become pink and gravy thickens. Remove skillet from the heat.

To serve on a large platter, or in four individual plates: Spoon hot grits onto plate(s). Top with the shrimp gravy mixture. Sprinkle chopped green onion as garnish.

CREOLE SHRIMP AND GRITS

This Creole recipe for shrimp and grits reminds me of the old clam chowder battle.

2 to 3 cloves garlic, minced

3 c water

1/2 tsp salt

1 T butter to sauté, plus 1/2 stick (4 T)

1 c grits

2 c sharp Cheddar cheese

1 T butter to sauté

1 small green bell pepper, diced

1 c tomatoes, diced

1/2 c white wine

1 T chili powder

1/4 tsp black pepper

1 small onion, diced

1 c diced Andouille sausage

1 c V8 or tomato juice

2 to 3 cloves garlic, minced

1 tsp ground thyme

Dash of Tabasco or to taste

1-1/2 to 2 lb (16 to 20-count) shrimp, cleaned, deveined

Chopped fresh parsley to garnish

Heat butter in a heavy-bottomed skillet. Add Andouille sausage and brown on all sides. Add onion and peppers, sauté for a few minutes. Add garlic, chili powder, and thyme. Deglaze with wine and let reduce by half. Add V8 or tomato juice, diced tomatoes, and black pepper. Simmer 15-20 minutes. Season to taste with Tabasco.

Sauté shrimp in a hot skillet with butter and more garlic if desired. Add to sauce. Keep warm.

Sauté garlic in 1 T butter. Add water; bring to a boil. Add salt and 1/2 stick of butter. Whisk in raw grits. Reduce heat to low and stir until grits are tender. Whisk in cheese and remove from heat. Divide grits over 4 plates. Ladle sauce on the plates next to grits, dividing shrimp evenly. Garnish with chopped parsley.

Shrimp Scampi is delectable served with toast points or over fresh pasta.

SIMPLE SHRIMP CREOLE

3 lb shrimp, boiled and peeled

1 T olive oil

1 green bell pepper, chipped

3 stalks celery with leaves, chopped fine

1 large white onion, chopped

28-oz can of diced tomatoes

1 to 3 cloves of garlic, minced

Chopped parsley

Bay leaf

1/4 to 1/2 tsp ground thyme

1/2 T white granulated sugar

Salt to taste

Dash of Tabasco or other hot sauce

Dash of Tony's Creole seasoning

Heat olive oil in skillet. Sauté onion, green pepper and celery. Add the other ingredients except shrimp, and simmer uncovered until thick, about 40 minutes. Add shrimp at the last and simmer about 10 minutes. Serve over a bed of rice. *YIELD: 6 servings.*

SHRIMP SCAMPI

1 lb large raw shrimp

1/2 to 1 c butter

1/2 tsp salt

6 to 8 cloves crushed garlic

2 T chopped parsley

1 T grated lemon peel

1 T lemon juice

Lemon wedges or slices

Preheat oven to 400°F. Shell, devein, and wash shrimp, leaving on the tail shells. Pat dry. Melt butter in a 9-by-13-by-2-inch baking dish in oven. Add salt, garlic and 1 T parsley. Mix well. Arrange shrimp in a single layer over butter layer in the baking dish and bake uncovered for 5 minutes. Turn the shrimp. Sprinkle with lemon peel, lemon juice and remaining parsley. Bake 8 to 10 minutes, until tender. Arrange in a serving platter or chafing dish with lemon slices. Drizzle with garlic-butter drippings. Excellent with angel hair pasta, or alone. To multiply, make up in separate batches. *Yield: 4 servings.*

BOILED SHRIMP

The easiest way to boil shrimp is to use Old Bay (East Coast) or Zatarain (Gulf Coast) seasoning with lemons, vinegar, salt, pepper, cayenne, Bay leaf, and sometimes with beer. The old-fashioned way is to combine spices into a bag and make your own seasoning, using the recipe listed below

1 large square of cheesecloth, folded double

4 large Bay leaves

20 peppercorns

1 tsp mustard seeds

1/2 tsp whole basil leaves

12 whole cloves

1/8 tsp cumin seeds

1 tsp crushed red pepper

1/8 tsp celery seeds

1/8 tsp light fennel seeds

1/8 tsp caraway seeds

1/4 tsp ground marjoram

1/4 tsp whole thyme

1 tsp salt

1 lemon, cut in half

2 cloves of garlic

2 tsp dehydrated onion flakes

5 lb medium or large shrimp

Lemon slices, OPTIONAL

Place the first 12 spices in the doubled cheese-cloth, tying it up as an herb packet with kitchen twine. Bring 4 to 5 quarts of water to a boil. Add salt, lemon halves, onion flakes, and herb bag; return to a boil and cook for 2 to 3 minutes. Drop the shrimp into the boiling water and return to a boil, cooking for 3 to 5 minutes. The shrimp will turn pink and start to float. Remove from heat and drain immediately to prevent overcooking. Serve immediately hot, or chill and serve cold. *YIELD: 8 to 10 servings.*

TIPS ON FRYING FISH, ETC.

- Fill cooking oil or shortening only to half-full level in fryer.
- Do not let fryer heat to the smoking point. If you do, the crust that forms on the food will over-brown and the food won't be cooked through.
- To test for readiness, stick the handle of a wooden spoon into the hot grease. It's ready (at least 350°F) if bubbles form around the wood.
- To put out a grease fire, cover quickly with pan lid, or cover with salt to smother the fire. NEVER use water, which makes grease fire spread.
- Do not over-crowd the food in the fryer, which causes uneven cooking.
- While frying, remove crackling bits from the grease with a slotted spoon.
- To reuse grease, strain it through cheesecloth while still warm (not hot). Store in metal container covered, in cool dark place. It is recommended to reuse it only for frying the same food, such as fish or chicken.

THE RECIPES

MEATS, POULTRY, MAIN DISH

Chopping pulled pork, Sept., 1944, photo by John Hemmer.
COURTESY OF THE NORTH CAROLINA STATE ARCHIVES, RALEIGH, NC

BARBECUE, AMBROSIA OF THE SOUTH

B arbecue is one of those topics about which Southerners are apt to draw their weapons. Every American region has its own preferences as to type of meat for barbecuing. We Southerners use pork, but debate ad infinitum how the meat has been cooked, whether it's whole hog, ribs, or shoulders only, what type of sauce or rub has been used to flavor the meat, and WHEN it was applied to the meat. Even the slaw choices are hotly debated—with some justification.

Vinegar-based. Tomato-based. Mustard-based. Wet or dry. I haven't the patience to go into the nuances. In my opinion, there IS no bad barbecue. I'll even eat Kansas City and Texas barbecue, where it's all about the sauce (Kansas City) or the beef (Texas!). However, I limit my favorites to Carolina-style pulled pork and Memphis ribs because I know them best.

North Carolina is recognized worldwide as the cradle of American BBQ (although Big Daddy George Washington was known to attend a pig-picking in Virginia once in a while). Carolina barbecue starts with a commitment to slow-cook the pig (whole hog or shoulder only, depending on locale) either in a pit, on a spit, or in a large covered cooker, over a combination of hickory or fruitwood and charcoal briquettes. Once completely slow-cooked, the pig is removed from its pit, spit or cooker, the fat removed from the outside, and the meat pulled apart and chopped or shredded. The best part, in everybody's opinion, is the crusty, charred-looking exterior meat (called bark). Barbecue sauce is almost an afterthought.

Jim n Nick's Bar-B-Q comptroller John Bakkegard serves pulled pork at the 2010 Southern Foodways Alliance Symposium in Oxford, MS, October, 2010.

The Memphis barbecue tradition also includes some bodacious pulled pork (Leonard's, Tops, Payne's, Central, Germantown Commissary, etc. and etc.). However, to think "Memphis barbecue" is to think "ribs, wet or dry." In recent years, many great rib joints have contributed to the Bluff City's BBQ fame, including Corky's and Jim Neely's Interstate 51. But Memphis ribs are world famous thanks to the persistence of that great institution, The Rendezvous, with a bit of help from that little Memphis company called FedEx.

Rendezvous dry-rub ribs have been smoking since 1948 in Charlie Vergos' basement in a downtown back alley just a few streets away from Cotton Row. My father and his cotton buddies regularly frequented Mr. Charlie's basement in the early days, bequeathing to my generation a rib-loving legacy that we've worked hard to uphold. (I'm convinced my brothers have a house account.) After Al Gore invented the internet, the Vergoses discovered they could sell their ribs online, and ship them overnight via FedEx to rib-lovers far, far away. They also now market a version of their Rendezvous mop sauce and dry rub online and in regional grocery stores.

The Rendezvous reputation is well deserved. Their lip-smacking ribs are mopped with the thin vinegar-based sauce, and dusted (not rubbed) with Mr. Charlie's special spices before going into a fiery charcoal-fueled oven to flash-roast in their own juices. Basted only once more during cooking, the ribs are scored and liberally coated with rub as soon as they come off the fire. The Rendezvous serves no coffee, no hard liquor, no butter with the rolls, and no dessert with their barbecue. And like their dad before them, Mr. Charlie's kids John, Nick and Tina will gladly show you the door if you disrespect the ribs or the institution.

RENDEZVOUS-STYLE RIBS

When it comes to cooking ribs, one has to make a number of choices. It's all about the rub, the cooking method (charcoal versus wood), and length of time cooking (flashed over high heat, or slow-roasted in low heat).

The Memphis dry-rub tradition originated with the city's Greek and African-American communities. Charlie Vergos put it on the map at the Rendezvous. All Memphis cue-ers have personal dry-rub recipes, with spice ingredients ranging from the basic four (salt, pepper, chili powder and paprika) to more than 15. I've listed two standard dry-rubs below, along with my personal variation. To make each recipe, combine spices in a large bowl, then let age for at least a day before using.

RENDEZVOUS MOP SAUCE

from The Rendezvous Restaurant, with permission

4 c white distilled vinegar

4 c water

1/3 c Rendezvous seasoning rub

Combine in a jar and shake to blend. Advice from Nick Vergos: Keep the mop sauce beside the grill to keep it warm. Use clean brush and "clean" sauce to mop the meat when it's done to avoid contamination.

NICK VERGOS' PUBLISHED RENDEZVOUS RUB

from The Rendezvous Restaurant, with permission

1/2 c salt

1/4 c black pepper

1 T garlic powder

1 T crushed oregano leaves

1 T celery seed

1 T paprika

1 T chili powder

Meat Prep Instructions:

To barbecue ribs, you'll want to get short ribs or spare ribs (my favorite), or cut-up country-style backbone. A slab of ribs contains 12 to 14 bones. Each slab should be enough to feed up to 2 people. Allow 2 to 3 country-style ribs per person. Rinse meat, pat dry. If going with the traditional closed-heat approach, apply dry rub liberally to the meat, cover, and refrigerate several hours or overnight before cooking. NOTE: True Rendezvous ribs are dusted, not "rubbed" with seasoning before cooking, unlike most barbecue. PERSONAL NOTE: I brine the meat in Polly Moore's BBQ sauce, refrigerated, for a few hours before patting dry, rubbing with spices, and refrigerating overnight.

To Cook:

Rendezvous ribs are cooked differently than most barbecue, which is slow cooked in a closed environment such as a smoker. The Rendezvous approach to cooking ribs is to flash cook them at high heat, starting with the bone side down to prevent charring. Place meat rib-side-down, about 18 inches above fire. Baste top side twice with mop sauce or apple cider vinegar when meat begins turning color. Flip the ribs; repeat on the other side. MINIMUM flash-cooking time: 30 minutes per side. In the smoker, longer is better. Baste once more about 10 minutes before they are done. Remove from heat; sprinkle with rub seasoning. When mopping sauce near the end, be sure to use a clean mopper and reserved sauce that hasn't been "double-dipped."

The Vergoses say the flash-roasted ribs are done when so hot you can't touch them. I say they're done when the meat pulls away from the bone.

CRAIG GOLDWYN'S RENDEZVOUS-STYLE RUB:

(see http://www.amazingribs.com)

Craig Goldwyn hosts a blog dedicated to the art of barbecueing. He and his readers have analyzed the Rendezvous dry rub, and concluded that the published Rendezvous Rub recipe might have omitted a few ingredients. Here's Craig's rub version, with his permission.

8 T paprika

4 T garlic powder

4 T mild chili powder

3 T black pepper

3 T kosher salt

2 T celery seed

1 T crushed celery seed

4 T whole yellow mustard seed

1 T crushed oregano

1 T ground thyme

1 T whole coriander seed

1 tsp ground coriander

LAURIE'S TWEAKS TO CRAIG'S RUB:

Add 1/4 tsp cayenne pepper

Add 1/4 tsp ground cinnamon

Add 1/2 tsp dry mustard

Reduce celery seed to 1-1/2 tsp

Omit coriander (both ground spice and seeds)

Families share pit-cooked pulled pork barbecue at Tom Pearson's annual worker barbecue at Braswell Plantation, NC, 1944. Photo by John Hemmer.
PHOTO: Courtesy of the North Carolina State Archives, Raleigh, NC

SLOW COOKER BBQ

This extremely slow method of cooking a pork shoulder until it's falling apart will come closest to the real thing without the pit fire. Add a bottle of your favorite BBQ sauce and a dash of liquid smoke to fake it!

1 pork shoulder

1/4 c water

Salt and pepper

Barbecue sauce (I prefer homemade such as Polly's)

1 tsp Liquid Smoke, to taste

Marinate pork shoulder in Polly's BBQ sauce (*see recipe, page 166*) for 1 to 3 hours, refrigerated. Warm slow cooker for 15 minutes before placing pork shoulder inside. Season the meat with salt and pepper before adding 1/4-cup of water to the slow cooker. Turn cooker temperature to high for 1 hour, then lower heat to cook for 7-9 hours.

Do not lift lid unnecessarily during slow-cook stage. Each peek adds 20 minutes to cooking time! However you might need to add additional water periodically. At the end of the cooking cycle, while pork is still extremely hot, carefully remove from crock pot and discard fat and juices that remain in the slow cooker. Once the meat has had a few minutes to cool, use a knife and fork to chop, or shred by hand. Once the chopping is complete, return shredded pork to slow cooker. Mix in desired amount of BBQ sauce and Liquid Smoke; cook on low for another hour.

VARIATION: 1 c of apple cider instead of water, plus 1 T sugar and 1 T salt.

PULLED PORK SHOULDER

10 lb pork shoulder

1 gal of Polly Moore's BBQ sauce (*see recipe, page 166*)

Laurie's version of Dry Rub (*see recipe, page 300*)

12-oz can or bottle of Coca-Cola® Classic

Rinse meat and pat dry. Brine overnight in Polly's sauce or homemade vinegar-based brine. Place in roasting bag in a pan. Remove pork from brine, pat dry. Sprinkle liberally all over with dry rub.

To oven-cook, preheat oven to 215° or 250°F. Place pork in roasting pan and pour cola in the bottom of the pan (not over the roast). Cover pan with aluminum foil, shiny side out (not with pan lid which would steam the meat). Slow-roast about 10-11 hours.

When ready, remove from heat and let rest 5 to 10 minutes. Use two forks to shred meat. Chop if desired once shredded.

If roasting in a charcoal-and-wood-chips smoker grill, cradle the meat in open foil containing cola; cook slowly over smoke heat about 5 to 6 hours.

If cooking in a slow cooker, set cooker to 10 hours.

NOTE: For smaller shoulder, adjust ingredients accordingly.

Silver Moon Barbecue Restaurant, curb service, 1937, probably Greensboro, NC
PHOTO: Courtesy of the North Carolina State Archives, Raleigh, NC

BEST BARBECUE I EVER ATE

I love Lexington Barbecue #1, NC Boy Scout barbecue, and the barbecue presented by the hundreds of joints dotting every town and two-lane road in both Carolinas. I've been known to drive 600 miles to get to some of those joints. But the best pulled pork barbecue I ever ate was on a Saturday in October, 1998. It was one of those perfect, crisp, clear autumn days, the memory of which always keeps Tar Heels going during the scorching weeks of July and August.

The occasion was a surprise pig-picking honoring Louise Triplette's 80th birthday. (The oldest of six siblings, she had never been thrown a birthday party.) The pig-picking was to be held at the Sherrill family farm now owned by Louise's brother, Paul Sherrill, located a mile from Louise and Lester's farm on Grace Chapel Road outside Granite Falls, NC. More than 75 kinfolk and friends were invited and all came—with friends.

Friday morning, Dianne Triplette's husband, Gary Poovey, and his friend, Scott Beam, set up a hickory smoke pit behind Grandma and Grandpa Sherrill's farm house, and began tending pork shoulders drowned in Polly Moore's thin, vinegar-based mop sauce.

On Saturday, the exquisite smoky aroma of hickory-roasted pork struck me as soon as I turned onto Grace Chapel Road from Highway 321. I drove 4-60 the remaining three miles to the farm, drooling in anticipation.

It was a day to remember, as we feasted on savory pulled pork, along with 27 barbecued chickens, thrown on the pit Saturday morning as culinary backup. Dessert wasn't bad either. We ate homemade chocolate sheet cake made from Louise's family recipe.

If ever a group could have floated straight up to Heaven, fat, dumb and happy, that was us, and that was the day.

BEEF

BEEF KEBAB MARINADE

2 tsp water

2 tsp red wine vinegar

2 T coarse Dijon mustard

2 tsp vegetable oil

2 cloves garlic, minced

1/2 tsp black pepper (fresh ground is best)

Combine ingredients in a small bowl. Pour over cubes of tenderloin or lean beef stew meat in a sealable bag and cover. Shake occasionally. Refrigerate the beef-marinade mixture for at least 6 to 8 hours, turning over or shaking at least once or twice. String the kebabs onto skewers, alternating with veggies if desired. Discard marinade. Grill.

BEEF STEW

1 stick (1/2 c) butter or 1/4 c light olive oil

2 lb of beef stew meat, cut up

1 large white onion, chopped

2 to 3 ribs celery with leaves, chopped

2 to 3 cloves garlic, crushed and minced

1-1/2 tsp salt

1/2 tsp black ground pepper

2 to 3 c sliced carrots

2 Russet potatoes, peeled and cubed

1 to 2 Bay leaves

1 tsp Italian seasoning blend

28-oz can crushed tomatoes

Large can tomato sauce

1 T Worcestershire sauce

Splash of red wine, OPTIONAL

Sauté onions and garlic in a large skillet in melted butter or olive oil. Add the beef and continue simmering to brown the meat, folding from time to time to brown on all sides. Drain the grease and turn the ingredients into a large stock pot. Add remaining ingredients and bring to a boil on medium heat. Cook on medium for about 10-20 minutes, stirring occasionally. Reduce heat to low, continuing to cook until meat and carrots are tender, about 20-30 more minutes. Be careful not to let potatoes stick to bottom of pot.

BEEF POT PIE

from Mary Elizabeth Daltroff

This was very popular when I was a child, before frozen pot pies were edible. The Wondra flour is my later conversion from plain flour. The optional addition of cola came later. NOTE: Cola is favored by Southern cooks for marinating tougher cuts of meat to break down the connective tissues and render the meat more tender. It also imparts an additional subtle flavor.

1-1/2 lb beef round steak, cut into 1-inch cubes

2 T unsalted butter

1-1/2 c diced Russet potatoes

3 carrots, peeled and sliced

3/4 c diced celery

1 medium onion, chopped

1 c sliced mushrooms

1/4 c Wondra flour

1/2 c no-msg beef broth

1/2 c fresh or frozen baby peas

1 T dark brown sugar

Salt and freshly ground black pepper to taste

10-piece, regular-size can of biscuit dough, OR
          homemade pie crust pastry

1 egg, beaten

12-oz cola soft drink, OPTIONAL

Preheat oven to 350°F. Melt butter in large skillet over medium-high heat. Sauté beef, until it begins to turn brown. Add potatoes, carrots, celery and onion; continue until celery and onions are translucent, about 10 minutes. Stir in mushrooms, cook 5 minutes. Lower heat to medium, whisk in flour, and cook, stirring constantly, 2 minutes. Stir in broth, peas, and brown sugar. Add salt and pepper to taste. Simmer 15 minutes.

Equally divide beef mixture in 4 round oven dishes. Roll out pie pastry, use biscuit cutter to cut out 4 rounds to fit over the top of each dish. OR, roll out biscuit dough and cut out 4 rounds. Position pastry over the dishes. Brush with beaten egg. Bake until filling is bubbling and crust is browned, about 30 minutes. Loosely tent with foil to prevent crusts from browning too soon.

VARIATION: Before cooking, marinate beef in coke for at least 30 minutes, up to 24 hrs, in fridge. Drain, reserving 1/2 cup of cola. Pat meat dry. Proceed with cooking the meat and veggies as stated above. Add reserved cola during the step when adding the beef broth, peas and brown sugar.

SALISBURY STEAK

10-1/2-oz can French onion soup

1-1/2 to 2 lb ground beef (combine 85% and 93% lean)

1 pkg dried French onion soup mix

1/2 c plain bread crumbs

1 to 2 eggs, beaten

1/4 tsp salt

1/8 tsp black pepper

1/2 tsp dry mustard

3 T extra light olive oil

2 T butter

1 T plain flour

1/4 c ketchup

1/4 c water

1 T Worcestershire sauce

6- or 7-oz jar or can of sliced mushrooms, drained

Combine 1/3 can of soup, beaten eggs, and dry spices. Break up beef into the bowl, add bread crumbs, and mix well with hands. Form into oval patties no more than 3/4-inch thick. Brown patties on both side in olive oil in skillet, about 4 to 5 minutes. Remove and set aside. Discard grease. Melt butter in skillet, add flour, whisk in water, ketchup and Worcestershire, scraping drippings. Add remaining soup and mushrooms. Bring to a boil, stirring, and add patties back to skillet. Cover, simmer 15 minutes.

COUNTRY-FRIED STEAK

from Butch Daltroff

1/2 c all-purpose flour

1/4 c white cornmeal

3/4 tsp salt, divided

1 tsp ground black pepper, divided

Pinch of cayenne pepper

1/8 tsp garlic powder

1 lb cubed sirloin steak

2 T bacon drippings

2 T WONDRA (or plain) flour

2 c whole milk

Stir together the first flour, cornmeal, 1/2 tsp salt, pepper, cayenne, and garlic powder in a shallow dish. Cut steak into 4 pieces and dredge in the flour mixture. Heat bacon drippings in a large skillet until hot, and add the steak. Cook 3 to 5 minutes until browned, turning once. Cover, reduce heat; cook 15 additional minutes. Uncover, and cook 10 minutes or until crisp, turning once. Drain on paper towels, reserving the drippings in the skillet. Transfer steak to a serving plate. Heat the skillet drippings, whisk in 2 T of flour and cook, stirring constantly, until browned. Gradually whisk in milk, stirring constantly until thickened, about 3 to 5 minutes. Whisk in remaining 1/4 tsp salt and 1/2 tsp pepper. If too thick, add more milk. If too thin, keep on cooking. Serve this gravy with the steak. *YIELD: 4 servings.*

CHICKEN FRIED STEAK VARIATION: Dredge in beaten egg and seasoned flour to coat before frying.

HAMBURGERS

2 lb ground turkey, OR combine 85% + 93% lean ground beef

Splash of Worcestershire sauce

1-1/2 T garlic powder

1-1/2 tsp salt

1/2 tsp black pepper

1 egg, beaten

1 pkg French onion soup mix, OPTIONAL

In a large bowl, combine ground meat with minced onion, spices and Worcestershire. Mix well with hands. Work in beaten egg (important for lean cuts of meat). Use hands to shape 6 large burgers or 12 mini-burgers (around 3-1/2 inches wide). Make dimple in center of patties with thumb to prevent puffing. Place burgers on low flame or low coals; grill slowly until springy.

VARIATION 1: Add barbecue sauce while grilling; OR, sprinkle with Southwest seasoning and serve with avocados and red onion.

VARIATION 2: Form thin patties. Spread light amount of Creole mustard over one, top with thin-sliced red onion, then position second patty on top. Pinch sides together all around. Grill. These "stuffed burgers" are delicious.

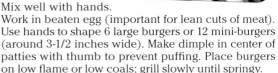

HAMBURGER TIP: To enhance moistness of hamburgers, add 1/4 cup evaporated milk per pound before shaping.

MEAT LOAF

There are numerous variations on the basic meat loaf recipe. The key ingredient is top quality ground beef.

2 lb ground beef (85% lean; needs some fat content)

1 egg, lightly beaten

1/2 c fine bread crumbs (or 10 crushed saltine crackers)

1 pkg of Lipton French onion soup mix

1 tsp of Italian seasoning

1/2 tsp salt

1/4 tsp black pepper

1 tsp Worcestershire sauce

Tomato soup (1 can, plus 1 can of water)

Ketchup to taste

32-oz can or jar of tomato sauce or tomato, mushroom and pepper spaghetti sauce, OPTIONAL

Combine all ingredients in a bowl, mixing by hand. Shape into a loaf or ball, flattened, and set up to bake in pan using Option 1, Option 2, or Option 3.

OPTION 1: Pack into a 9-by-5-by-3-inch loaf pan and cover with ketchup or canned tomato soup, undiluted. Bake in preheated oven at 350°F for about 1 hour and 15 minutes. Turn out onto platter after loosening sides.

OPTION 2: Form into a loaf as if it were going into a loaf pan, but position the loaf in a 9-by-13-inch pan sprayed with Pam. Criss-cross top and sides with ketchup. Surround the loaf with sliced mushrooms, and with pre-steamed cut carrots and baby potatoes. Pour diluted tomato soup, tomato sauce, or spaghetti sauce over the ketchup-decorated loaf.

Bake in preheated oven at 350°F for about 1 hour and 15 minutes. Spread top with a little barbecue sauce or ketchup about 5 or 10 minutes before done. Let rest a few minutes before slicing.

OPTION 3: Mix 1 can of medium Rotel into the ground beef instead of onion soup mix. Bake in preheated oven at 350°F for about 1 hour and 15 minutes.

LOUISE'S SOUR CREAM BEEF CASSEROLE

from Andrea Benfield (Louise Triplette's recipe)

1 c chopped white onion

2 T butter or olive oil

1 lb ground beef (lean)

3 c uncooked medium egg noodles

2 c tomato juice

1 T salt

1-1/2 tsp celery salt

Dash pepper

2 tsp Worcestershire sauce

1/2 c frozen green peas

1/4 c chopped green bell peppers

1 c sour cream

3 to 6 oz canned mushrooms, drained

Cook onions in butter or oil until transparent. Add beef and brown, stirring continuously. Place uncooked egg noodles over the meat. Combine tomato juice and seasonings, and pour over the noodles. Bring to a boil, cover, reduce heat, and simmer for 20 minutes. Add green peas and green bell peppers. Cover again and cook 10 more minutes, or until noodles are tender. Stir in sour cream and mushrooms. Heat again to boiling and add additional seasonings to taste.

James Thurmond family farm, west Tennessee, early 20th century

LIVER AND ONIONS

Liver and onions is an acquired taste, especially for the post-Baby Boom generations who never HAD to eat organ meats to avoid starving. My advice regarding this dish: Only use calf liver. Beef liver is a whole different animal, so to speak. Calf's liver is available in the freezer section of most stores nowadays.

2 lb calf liver, sliced 1/2-inch thick

All-purpose flour

Salt and pepper (about 1/2 tsp salt, 1/8 tsp pepper)

Spices, crushed together:

- **Marjoram**
- **Thyme**
- **Dry mustard**

Ice cold milk

8 T (1 stick) butter, divided

Parsley

2 Vidalia onions (sweet)

1 c fresh, or 4- to 7-oz can or jar of sliced mushrooms

Rinse liver in cold water, then pat dry. Soak in cold milk for 1 hour in fridge. Remove from milk and pat dry. Combine salt, pepper, and blended spices, sprinkle on all sides of liver. Dredge in flour. Melt 4 T butter in skillet (stainless or cast iron). Sauté mushrooms with onions until transparent, then remove mixture from skillet, leaving drippings. Add 4 T butter, turn heat to medium-high, and add liver. Braise about 1 to 2 minutes on each side, turning no more than twice. Remove liver to serving plate, return onions and mushrooms to skillet, lower heat, mix well, add a bit of water or chicken stock, and stir only a few minutes until pot residue combines to make sauce; smother liver with onion sauce; serve immediately.

MARINATING TIPS: One marinates meat for three reasons: To add flavor, to add moisture, and to tenderize it. Vinegars and soy-based marinades such as soy sauce, teriyaki sauce or Worcestershire sauce break down connective tissues in tougher cuts of meat. Marinades containing olive oil seal in moisture and bind the seasonings to the meat. For safety, always reserve some of your marinade at the start in a clean dish. Use clean utensils to apply it to the completely cooked meat.

ORIENTAL PEPPER STEAK

from Ruth Callicott Thurmond

This is one of Aunt Ruth's favorites. She recalls Granddaddy Thurmond visiting one day and scrutinizing her efforts as she cut up the meat (he never thought anyone could cook except Grandmother). According to Aunt Ruth, Granddaddy "lapped it up" when served.

1-1/2 lb beef (sirloin, or rib or round), cut into thin strips

1-1/2 tsp Accent, divided

1/4 c salad oil (Wesson)

1 c beef bouillon

1/2-tsp white granulated sugar

1/4-tsp ginger

1 tsp soy sauce

2 green peppers, cut into strips

1 medium white onion, sliced

2 tomatoes, peeled and cut into wedges

2 tsp cornstarch

2 T water

Sprinkle beef with 1 tsp Accent. Brown beef in hot oil in skillet. Add bouillon, sugar, ginger and soy sauce. Bring to a boil, reduce heat and simmer 15 minutes. Add vegetables, sprinkle with remaining 1/2 tsp Accent. Cook 5 more minutes. Combine cornstarch and water, stir until smooth. Gradually add to beef mixture and cook, stirring constantly, until thickened and boiling. Serve with rice. *YIELD: 6 servings.*

MOM'S VARIATION:

2 lb sirloin

1/2 c soy sauce

3 cloves garlic

1 bunch broccoli

1 sliced bell pepper

2 medium onions, sliced

2 T sherry

2 T cornstarch

1 c water

1/2 c peanut oil

Cut meat into strips. Stir-fry ingredients in 1/2 c peanut oil, beginning with browning the meat, after marinating the meat for 30 minutes.

POOR MAN'S BEEF STROGANOFF

from Louise Sherrill Triplette

Louise got this recipe from Emma and Wayne Nichols. Lester, Louise, Uncle Lawrence and Aunt Hilion all became great friends with the Nichols, who were farmers in Nebraska. They spent time together every year during Lester and Lawrence's pheasant hunting trips in Nebraska. This recipe is included in their family cookbook, **Nichols Family Recipes and Remembrances. Seasoned with Love,** *1954, published in Kearney, NE, by Morris Press. Wayne and Emma visited our family in Grace Chapel several times, and came down to keep Louise company after Lester's death.*

1-1/2 lb ground beef

1/4 c butter

2 white onions, sliced

16-oz can mushrooms, drained, divided, and liquid reserved

2 T plain flour, dissolved in 2 T water

2 tsp salt

1/4 tsp black pepper

1/4 tsp paprika

1 can cream of chicken soup

1/2 c sour cream

Chopped fresh parsley for garnish

Preheat frying pan. Melt butter and sauté the ground beef until lightly browned. Add onion, brown slightly. Place mushroom liquid, half the mushrooms, soup and sour cream in a blender. Blend, then pour over the meat. Add remaining mushrooms, dissolved flour, and spices to pan. Stir and heat on medium for 15 minutes. Serve with rice or the traditional flat noodles.

VARIATION: I find this recipe a bit bland unless I add a dash each of cayenne and Tabasco, and also increase the black pepper to 1/2 teaspoon.

PORCUPINE MEATBALLS

from Willie Sue Keller

1-1/2 lb lean ground beef

1/4 c diced onion

1 tsp salt

1/4 tsp pepper

1 large egg, fork beaten

2/3 c of uncooked rice

1/2 c fine bread crumbs

2 T milk

3 c tomato juice

1 c water

1 tsp white granulated sugar

1/2 tsp liquid gravy browner

Willie Sue and June Keller

Combine first 8 ingredients, mix well, and shape into 1-1/2-inch balls. Place in 3-1/2 qt slow cooker. Mix tomato juice, water, sugar, salt and gravy browner. Pour over meatballs. Cook on low 8 to 10 hrs, or on high 4 to 5 hrs. This is an adaptation of the pressure cooker recipe. *YIELD: 36 meatballs.*

Delicious Pot Roast

POT ROAST

from Mary Elizabeth Daltroff

Everyone has a version of this recipe. The leftovers make great second and third meals, such as beef and rice, or vegetable soup starter.

3 to 5 lb chuck roast (boneless preferred)

Garlic powder

Salt and pepper

1 stick (1/2 c) butter or margarine (olive oil can be substituted)

2 pkgs French onion soup mix

1 can cream of mushroom soup

Garlic powder

Salt and pepper

Rinse and pat dry the meat, then coat with garlic powder, salt and pepper. Be generous with all the seasonings. Melt butter, or heat oil in large skillet or pan on stovetop. When hot, sear the meat, approximately 2-3 minutes on each side. Use a large meat fork to hold the edges against the heat. When meat has properly browned, with some juices running, remove from heat, pour off the grease.

Sprinkle contents of 1 onion soup mix pkg all over the top and sides of the seared meat. Mix the other pkg in a bowl with the can of mushroom soup and a soupcan of water. *YIELD: 4 to 6 servings (more if larger).*

TO COOK ON STOVETOP: Pour the soup mixture over the meat in large pan, Dutch oven or stock pot, and bring to a slow boil on medium to medium-high heat. Stir, then reduce to medium low and let simmer for about an hour. Stir and turn meat occasionally.

TO BAKE IN OVEN: Place seared meat in roaster, cover with soup mixture, place new potatoes and peeled, sliced carrots around the roast, cover, and bake at 350°F for about an hour.

TO COOK IN SLOW COOKER: Place seared meat in cooker, cover with combined spices and soup mixture, and set to cook 4, 6, or 8 hours. Pot Roast is better if allowed to cook at least 6 hours.

HINT: Bone-in roast cooks faster than boneless roast. The bone conducts heat. This applies to standing rib roast as well as chuck, rump, or round. (See cooking times, page 363.)

REUBEN CASSEROLE

from Andrea Benfield

This is a great substitute for a Reuben sandwich.

1 can sauerkraut, well drained

1/2 lb sliced corned beef

1/2 lb sliced Swiss cheese

1 c Thousand Island dressing

3 c cubed rye bread

1/2 stick (4 T) butter

Spread kraut in casserole. Layer corned beef over it, and then spread with dressing. Layer Swiss cheese on top. Melt butter and mix with rye bread cubes. Spread over the cheese. Bake at 350°F for 30 minutes.

SIMPLE BEEF BRISKET

from Rosalee Bloom Hyam

Every good cook needs a basic brisket recipe. Brisket cooks well in a slow cooker, which provides the same closed environment as foil wrapping in the oven.

1 large beef brisket

Extra light olive oil

Garlic salt

Black pepper

2 large white or yellow onions

Worcestershire sauce

Tabasco sauce

Rinse beef brisket and pat dry. Rub with oil to moisten. Season with garlic salt, pepper, Worcestershire, and Tabasco. Slice the onions. Lay out 2 large sheets of heavy-duty aluminum foil, and place the brisket in the center. Put the onion slices on top of the brisket and sprinkle a bit more spices, Worcestershire and Tabasco over the top. Bring the 2 sheets of foil up across the roast, sealing it by double folding the 2 edges together, then sealing each end by folding several times and crimping those edges so the juices won't leak out.

Put the foil-wrapped roast in a baking pan with the foil seam right-side-up. Bake 8 hours or overnight in a 250°F oven. When ready to serve, pour the broth out of the aluminum foil into a sauce pan. Dissolve cornstarch in cold water and stir into the hot brisket broth, cooking until mixture bubbles and thickens.

VARIATIONS: (1) Season the brisket with BBQ dry rub before cooking and add BBQ sauce to the broth; or (2) add minced garlic and red wine to broth.

SLOPPY JOES (LOOSE MEAT SANDWICHES)

from Mary Elizabeth Daltroff

4 T butter or olive oil

1 lb lean ground beef

1/2 c chopped onion

1/3 c chopped green bell pepper

12-oz bottle of chili sauce (Mom's recipe calls for Heinz)

1/4 c water

1 to 2 T brown sugar

1 T Worcestershire sauce

1/4 tsp salt

1/8 tsp black pepper

Hamburger buns

In a large saucepan brown the ground beef with salt and pepper in butter or olive oil. Add onion and bell pepper and stir, simmering until onion is transparent and bell pepper is tender. Drain grease. Stir in chili sauce, water, sugar, Worcestershire and additional salt and pepper if needed. Stir, simmer for about 10 minutes until liquid has been absorbed and ingredients blended. Serve on hamburger buns.

Uncle Harold (LT. Col. Harold Hoffman, USAF, Rebecca Thurmond's husband), at Sherman Air Force Base, early 1960s

SURE-FIRE SPAGHETTI MEAT SAUCE

In today's fast-paced world, nobody has to make anything completely from scratch. However, I am offering both the all-the-way-homemade and the semi-homemade versions in my spaghetti meat sauce recipe.

2 to 3 lb ground beef, combined 85% and 92-96% lean

2 to 3 medium white onions, chopped

3 heart-ribs of celery, with leaves, chopped fine

1 clove elephant garlic, or 4 cloves regular garlic, minced

1 tsp salt

1/4 tsp black pepper

1/2 to 1 stick butter, or 1/4 c olive oil

1 bell pepper, chopped fine

1 bunch fresh basil, chopped fine (or 2 T dried basil)

1 to 2 generous T Italian seasoning, made up of:

- 1/2 tsp oregano
- 1/4 tsp marjoram
- 1/4 tsp ground
- 1/2 tsp thyme
- 1/2 tsp rosemary (or 1/4 tsp rosemary + 1/4 tsp of dried basil)

1 large pkg fresh white button mushrooms, chopped

Two 28-oz cans of crushed tomatoes

Two 6-oz cans of tomato paste, dissolved in 1-1/2 c water

1 T white granulated sugar

Chopped Italian sausage, OPTIONAL

Brown onions, celery, and ground beef in butter or olive oil on medium heat, keeping the ground beef broken up by stirring. Drain grease. Add garlic, salt, pepper, bell pepper, basil, mushrooms, and Italian seasonings. Stir well and continue simmering for about 10-15 minutes, stirring frequently. Add crushed tomatoes and tomato paste and stir until thoroughly blended. Add sugar (this blends all the salty and spicy tastes and helps the sauce cook down), and lower heat to medium-low or simmer, depending on your stove. Add Italian sausage if desired. Continue to simmer for about 30 minutes to 1 hour, stirring occasionally to prevent sticking or burning on pan bottom.

SEMI-HOMEMADE SHORTCUT: After browning and draining the ground beef and onions, add 2 commercially prepared jar(s) of spaghetti sauce. I recommend one jar with chunky mushrooms and bell peppers, and one jar with roasted garlic.

STUFFED BELL PEPPERS

MEAT FILLING:

4 T (1/2 stick) butter or margarine, or 3 T olive oil

1-1/2 to 2 lb ground beef

1 medium onion, chopped

1-1/2 tsp salt

1/4 tsp pepper

1 T Italian seasoning

14.5-oz can of tomato sauce

6-oz can tomato paste

1/2 c water

1 c bread crumbs (I prefer Italian-seasoned crumbs)

3 T white granulated sugar (to taste)

Brown the ground beef. Add in the onion, and spices, and continue cooking, stirring frequently, until onion is transparent and ground beef is completely broken up. Add tomato sauce and tomato paste, with water as needed to cause a thick paste when stirring. Add more water to keep from getting too thick. Stir in bread crumbs and sugar, to taste.

PEPPERS:

Clean bell peppers and either cut into equal halves or leave whole, with hole in top (smaller peppers). Drop into a stock pot of boiling water and cover. Blanch for 1 to 2 minutes, then remove the peppers from the water and drain. Position blanched peppers in a deep casserole dish, baking pan, or greased muffin tin. Spoon meat filling into and around the peppers. Bake at 350°F for about 20 minutes. These freeze well.

SLOW COOKER VARIATION: Skip the pepper-blanching stage, and spoon filling into deseeded halved or whole peppers. Place filled peppers in slow cooker, add additional filling or tomato sauce around the peppers. Set to cook 4 to 6 hours.

AUNT ROSIE'S CABBAGE ROLLS

from Rosalee Bloom Hyam

I've listed two versions of stuffed cabbage rolls. Both were classics in my parents' day, and both were regulars in my father's family. Cook the prepped rolls in a slow cooker for 8 hours if you have a busy day ahead.

Large cabbage leaves

1 lb ground beef (or lamb)

1/2 c cooked rice

1/2 c bread crumbs

1 small onion, grated & sautéed

1 to 2 eggs

Salt and pepper

1-1/2 c tomato sauce

Cut out and discard cabbage core. Put in large pot; pour boiling water over cabbage; let steep until leaves are flexible and easily removed. Select 8 large leaves. Combine meat, eggs, salt, pepper, rice, bread crumbs, and onion. Roll meat mixture in each leaf. Fasten with toothpicks. Dredge the prepared cabbage rolls in flour. Brown them in olive oil in a skillet. Place cabbage rolls in an oiled Dutch oven, folded side down. Pour tomato sauce over the rolls. Add a cup of water. Cover, and bake in slow oven at 300°F about 2 hours; or simmer, covered, on low on stovetop about 1 hour.

TANTE IDA'S STUFFED CABBAGE ROLLS WITH FRUIT SAUCE

from Randy Rosen

2 onions, chopped

6 dried apricots

6 prunes

1/4 c golden raisins

Juice of 1 lemon

1-1/2 c tomato sauce

28-oz can tomato sauce

Sauce-can full of water

1/2 c light brown sugar

Remaining cabbage, chopped

Prepare cabbage rolls as described in Rosalee's version. Set aside. Sauté onions in a Dutch oven. Stir in 1-1/2 cup tomato sauce, brown sugar, lemon juice and fruit. Simmer 1 hour. Stir in 28-oz can of tomato sauce and 28 oz of water. Dice remaining cabbage leaves; add to sauce. Place cabbage rolls on sauce, folded side down. Cover. Cook 2 hours in a slow oven.

LAMB

LEG OF LAMB WITH HUNTER SAUCE

from Mary Elizabeth Daltroff

LAMB:

5 to 6 lb leg of lamb, or larger

6 cloves of garlic, thinly sliced

3 T Dijon mustard

1 T chopped fresh rosemary

1 T garlic powder

2 tsp cracked black pepper

Hunter Sauce

Cut small slits in the lamb with a sharp knife or skewer. Insert garlic slices into the slits. Place the lamb into a large shallow dish. Combine the mustard, rosemary and pepper, and spread over the entire lamb. Cover and refrigerate for 2 days to allow the spices to soak into the meat. On the day of cooking, remove lamb from fridge and place in a roasting pan. Let stand at room temperature for 30 minutes. Place meat uncovered in roasting pan in preheated oven at 475°F for 15-20 minutes. Reduce heat to 325-350°F and bake 1 hour or until meat thermometer inserted into thickest portion registers 145° (about 20 minutes per pound). Baste occasionally during cooking. Remove lamb from oven and loosely cover with foil. Let stand for about 20 minutes or until thermometer registers 150° (which is medium rare). For a well done roast, cook until meat thermometer registers 160°F. Serve with Hunter Sauce; OR ladle off fat, and use pan drippings to make gravy or mint sauce if desired.

HUNTER SAUCE (CHASSEUR SAUCE):

1/2 c brown sugar

1/2 c ketchup

1/4 c butter or margarine

1/4 c apple jelly

3 T lemon juice

1 tsp ground cinnamon

1/2 tsp ground allspice

1/2 tsp pepper

1/4 tsp ground cloves

Combine all these ingredients in a medium saucepan. Cook over low heat, stirring until smooth.

YIELD: 1-1/3 cups.

CROWN ROAST RACK OF LAMB

A crown roast of pork, beef or lamb is made by standing two loin rib sections on end, bones facing out, and curving the two sections end-to-end to form a circle, then binding the two sections together around the middle with kitchen twine. Before tying the crown, season the meat side and the bone side with salt, pepper, and garlic powder. Stand the prepared crown rack in an open roasting pan. Cover rib tips with aluminum foil to prevent charring during roasting. Sear for 10-20 minutes in a very hot oven at around 475°F, then lower heat to 300°F, and roast until done, allowing 30-35 minutes per pound. Meat temperature should read 175-180°F when ready to serve and meat will be somewhat pink or medium rare. Before serving, remove foil tip covers and replace with paper frills. Fill center of the crown with mashed potatoes, peas, or dressing.

SHISH KABOBS (KEBABS)

from Mary Elizabeth Daltroff

Leg of lamb, deboned by butcher, cut into cubes (approximately 1-1/2 inches square)

Juice of 2 lemons

4 T olive oil

2 T grated onion

2 T chili peppers

1 tsp coriander

1 tsp powdered ginger

1 clove of garlic

1 tsp turmeric

3 T salt

2 large white onions, cut into large chunks for skewering

Cherry tomatoes

Fresh button mushrooms

Green bell pepper, cut into cubes for skewering

Mix the spices, olive oil and lemon juice well. Marinate the lamb for at least 2 hours. Skewer the marinated cubes on wood or metal grilling skewers, alternating meat with onions, tomatoes, mushrooms and pepper cubes. Cook over charcoal fire until lamb reaches at least 170°F on a meat thermometer (medium doneness).

WHOLE LEG VARIATION: After deboning, tie up leg with butcher string. Marinate as above. Roast in preheated oven at 475°F for 15 minutes. Reduce heat to 350°F and bake, basting, until thermometer registers 160°F. Remove from oven and cover with foil to set up 15 minutes before carving. Serve with rice or rice pilaf.

LASAGNE

CHICKEN LASAGNA FLORENTINE

This dish is one of the old standards for Methodist get-togethers. Everyone uses the same recipe, tweaking the nutmeg and sliced mushrooms. Works great as a main dish with a green salad and a light fruit dessert.

PECAN TOPPING:

2 T salted butter

1 c chopped pecans (packaged pecan bits work well)

Melt butter in saucepan over medium heat. Add pecans and cook, stirring for up to 3 minutes, or until just before pecan oil darkens (smell is nutty but not burnt).

11-BY-7-INCH CASSEROLE DISH

6 uncooked lasagna noodles (NOT precooked noodles)

10-oz pkg frozen spinach, thawed

2 c cooked chicken, chopped (about 3 breasts)

2 c shredded sharp Cheddar cheese

1/3 c white onion, chopped fine

1 to 2 dashes ground nutmeg

1/2 tsp salt

2 tsp white pepper

1 T soy sauce

1 can of cream of mushroom soup

1 jar sliced mushrooms, drained

8-oz carton sour cream

1/3 c mayonnaise (homemade is best)

1 T corn starch

3/4 c fresh grated Parmesan cheese

Pecan Topping

Preheat oven to 350°F. Cook noodles according to package directions, drain, set aside on paper towels. Squeeze water out of spinach, drain. Press dry between paper towels. Combine spinach, chicken, Cheddar cheese, onion, sliced mushrooms, nutmeg, salt, pepper, soy sauce, soup, sour cream, corn starch, and mayonnaise in large bowl. Stir well.

Arrange half the noodles in lightly greased baking dish. Spread half the chicken mixture over noodles. Repeat, alternating layers of chicken mixture and noodles, ending with thin layer of chicken mixture on top. Sprinkle with Parmesan cheese. Top with butter-pecan topping. Bake, loosely covered, 55-60 minutes or until hot and bubbly. Let stand 15 minutes before cutting. NOTE: For a 9-by-13-inch casserole, double the recipe.

3-QUART CASSEROLE VERSION

9 lasagna noodles

3 c cooked chicken, chopped (6 breasts)

3 c shredded sharp Cheddar

1/2 c onion

4 shakes of nutmeg

1-1/2 T cornstarch

1 tsp salt

1/2 tsp white pepper

1-1/2 T soy salt

2 cans cream of mushroom soup

12 oz sour cream

2 jars sliced mushrooms, drained

1/2 c mayonnaise

1 c fresh grated Parmesan cheese

Pecan Topping

Prepare casserole as instructed in version above. Arrange noodles in dish, cutting to fit if dish is round.

POTLUCK ETIQUETTE

Always carry enough food to feed your own family when attending a potluck gathering. Upon moving to Charlotte, NC, from Winston-Salem, we could tell we'd landed in a part of town populated by folks not from around here. My family attended a church potluck luncheon where half the attendees came empty-handed. The organizers had to run out for Bojangles chicken and biscuits.

MEAT LASAGNA

This dish requires more prep time than actual assembly. Prepare ahead of time, refrigerate, then place in the oven two hours before serving.

6 c homemade spaghetti sauce, more or less as needed (or 1 lb ground beef, pork, turkey, or sausage meat browned and combined with two 26-oz jars of prepared sauce)

2 large eggs, beaten

15-oz container of ricotta cheese

4 c shredded (16-oz pkg) of mozzarella, divided

1/2 c (2 oz) grated Parmesan cheese

Homemade spaghetti meat sauce (OR commercially prepared marinara or spaghetti sauce combined with 1 lb browned ground beef + two 26-oz jars of sauce)

9-oz box of No-Boil Lasagna noodles

FILLING:

Beat the eggs in a medium bowl. Stir in the ricotta, 2 c of the mozzarella, and the Parmesan. If not using homemade spaghetti sauce, add 1/2 tsp salt and 1/8 tsp pepper to the cheese mixture and stir well. Omit the salt and pepper if using homemade sauce. Preheat oven to 375°F. Spray a deep-dish 9-by-13-by-3-inch baking pan with Pam. If using a less-deep dish, plan to make fewer layers of the lasagna.

ASSEMBLY:

Spoon a small amount of the sauce on the bottom of the cooking dish, spreading evenly. Layer 4 to 6 of the noodle sheets over this, with the noodles slightly overlapping. Spread 1/3 of the ricotta cheese mixture over the noodles, followed by spaghetti sauce, followed by 1 cup of the mozzarella. Repeat this layering process for a total of 4 layers in a deep dish, or three layers in a 2-inch-high dish. Use the remaining mozzarella to cover the top layer.

Spray one side of a long sheet of foil with cooking spray. Tent foil, sprayed-side down, loosely around lasagna to prevent casserole from sticking to the foil. Bake, covered with the tented foil, for at least 1 hour.

Remove foil, and continue cooking for another 30 minutes. Remove pan from oven and let rest for at least 15 minutes before cutting or spooning to serve. The lasagna will continue cooking during those 15 minutes, but will set up, so that the juices don't run once cut. *YIELD: 12 or more servings.*

VEGETARIAN LASAGNA

1 large onion, chopped

3 cloves garlic, minced

1 tsp olive oil

28-oz can of tomato puree

14.5-oz can of whole tomatoes, undrained, chopped

2 c fresh sliced mushrooms

1 zucchini, peeled and diced

1 large green bell pepper, chopped

2 tsp fresh basil, crushed

1 tsp salt

1 tsp sugar

1/2 tsp crushed red pepper flakes

1/2 tsp crushed oregano leaves

2 c (15 oz) light ricotta cheese

10-oz pkg of frozen chopped spinach, thawed and squeezed dry

2 egg whites

2 T shredded Parmesan cheese

1/2 lb lasagna noodles (ready-to-use)

3/4 c shredded mozzarella cheese, divided in half

3/4 c mild Cheddar cheese, divided in half

Spray large skillet with nonstick vegetable spray. Add onion, garlic and olive oil. Cook over medium heat until tender, stirring occasionally. Add tomato puree, tomatoes, tomato liquid, mushrooms, zucchini, bell pepper, basil, salt, sugar, pepper flakes and oregano. Heat to a boil. Reduce heat, then cover and simmer for 10 minutes or until veggies are crisp-tender.

Combine ricotta cheese, spinach, egg whites and parmesan cheese, and mix well. Spread 1 c sauce in bottom of a 13-by-9-inch baking dish. Layer 3 lasagna noodles over sauce. Top with half of ricotta cheese mixture and 2 cups remaining sauce. Repeat layering with 3 more lasagna noodles, remaining ricotta mixture and 2 cups of sauce. Combine mozzarella and Cheddar cheeses. Sprinkle 3/4-cup cheese mixture over sauce. Top with remaining lasagna noodles and sauce. Cover with foil. Bake at 375°F for 30 -60 minutes. Uncover, bake 15 minutes more. Sprinkle with remaining 3/4 cup of cheese mixture. Let stand 15 minutes or longer, to "set up" before serving. *YIELD: 12 or more servings.*

TAMALES — HEART OF THE DELTA

I've been eating homemade tamales since I could walk. They are a specialty of the Mississippi Delta, that region divinely defined by David Cohn in 1948 as "beginning in the lobby of the Peabody Hotel in Memphis and ending at Catfish Row in Vicksburg."

Today, there's an official Mississippi Tamale Trail running from Vicksburg to Tunica, with segues eastward to Corinth in the north, Natchez and Lumberton in the south, and Jackson in the middle. Greenville is the heart of the Tamale Trail.

This meat-filled delicacy is thought to have been introduced to the Delta's African-American community during the early 20th century by Mexican laborers brought in to work in the cotton fields. Tamales may have been introduced even earlier. The Delta's African-American workers took favorably to tamales, obtained recipes from the Hispanic workers, and tweaked the ingredients to suit their Southern taste. As early as the 1930s African-American entrepreneurs were selling tamales from vendor's carts and

Martha White Tamale Luncheon at the 2010 Southern Foodways Alliance Symposium in Oxford, MS

street stands. Scott's in Greenville, and Rhoda's in Lake Village, AR, are among the best known of the old-style vendors still cooking. Over time, Caucasian entrepreneurs got hold of some of those closely guarded tamale recipes. Doe's is the best known of these establishments, but Honest Abe's has made inroads Delta style — selling tamales and donuts.

Traditionally, the tamales were sold by the threes, sixes, dozens, or 3-dozens, wrapped in paper to go, or in old coffee cans that could be reheated right on the stove. Today, Delta tamales are sold in bundles of three, six or a dozen. Delta tamales usually contain more meat than traditional Hispanic versions, and are simmered in hot pepper sauce. Local connoisseurs know to ask for their tamales wet, Delta style, not dry, Mexican style. We eat them with saltine crackers.

One of my most vivid early childhood memories is of riding with Daddy back to Memphis from Greenville, after he stopped to buy a large coffee can packed with tamales. Even as a toddler, I noticed the sawdust on the tamale shack floor and the newspapers covering the plain wooden picnic tables.

After Aunt Rosalee's funeral in Greenville (the one where Cousins Frank and Marian and Richard and I failed to hide the bottle of Black Jack in her coffin), Frank made a run to Doe's for tamales, and sent me back to North Carolina on Piedmont Airlines with a Styrofoam cooler containing the mother lode.

MISSISSIPPI TAMALES

MEAT FILLING:

6 to 8 lb pork shoulder, chuck roast or chicken (leftover pot roast or stewed chicken, shredded, work well)

3/4 c vegetable oil

1/4 c chili powder

2 T paprika

2 T salt

2 tsp black pepper

1 tsp cayenne pepper

1 T onion powder

1 T garlic powder

1 tsp cumin

If not using leftovers, cut the meat into large chunks and place in a heavy large pot. Cover with cold water and bring to a boil over high heat. Cover the pot, reduce the heat to medium low and simmer for about 2-1/2 hours, until the meat is very tender and falling apart. Remove from heat, remove the meat to cool and reserve the broth. Let cool. Remove all fat and skin, then shred or dice the meat into very small pieces. You should have 14 to 16 cups of diced or shredded meat. Heat the vegetable oil in a large heavy pot on medium heat. Stir in the chili powder, paprika, salt, pepper, cayenne, onion powder, garlic powder and cumin. Add the meat to this and stir to coat with the oil and spices. Cook about 7 to 10 minutes, stirring often, until meat has been completely heated again. Set aside.

CORN HUSKS PREPARATION:

While the meat is cooking, soak corn husks in a large bowl or sink of very warm water until they become soft, about 2 hours. Separate the husks into individual leaves, being careful not to tear them. Discard corn silks and other debris. Keep the split shucks to use (overlapping to make up one after all the unsplit husks have been used).

CORN MEAL DOUGH:

8 c yellow corn meal or masa mix, your preference

4 tsp baking powder

2 tsp salt

1-2/3 c lard (!) or vegetable shortening

6 to 8 c warm meat broth (reserved from boiled meat)

Stir the cornmeal or masa, baking powder, salt and shortening in a large bowl until well blended. Gradually stir in enough warm liquid to make soft dough with the consistency of thick mashed potatoes. The dough should be moist but not wet. If too wet, add more corn meal or masa. If too dry, add more broth. Cover the bowl with a damp cloth.

ASSEMBLY AND COOKING:

Remove a softened corn husk from the water and pat dry on a work surface. Spread about 1/4 scant cup cornmeal or masa dough in an even layer across the wide end of the husk, stopping about 1 inch inside each edge. Place about 1 tablespoon of the meat mixture down the center of the dough in an even line. NOTE: Less dough and more meat is best. Roll the husk so the dough surrounds the meat filling and forms a cylinder or "package." Fold bottom of husk to close up the bottom and to complete the package.

TO SIMMER: Place the completed tamales in a single layer on a baking sheet. Repeat until all dough and filling is used. Stand the tamales upright in groups of 3 or 6, and tie together with kitchen string, making sure to prevent the bottoms from coming open or the husks from falling apart. Stand tied groups of tamales upright, closed sides down, in a large stock pot. Place enough groups to prevent them from falling over or coming unrolled. Carefully fill the pot with enough water to barely cover the open tops of the tamales but not to swamp the filling inside. Add generous amounts of Tabasco sauce, chili powder and cumin to the water, to taste. (NOTE: I premix and use about 1 c of Tabasco, 2 T chili powder, and 2 tsp cumin.) Bring the water to a boil over high heat. Cover the pot at this point, reduce heat to medium low and simmer for about 1 hour, until dough becomes firm and pulls away from the husk easily.

TO STEAM: Stand grouped tamales upright, closed sides down, in a large steamer basket, being careful to place enough groups to prevent them from falling over. Cover the top of the steamer basket with a damp towel or additional corn husks that have been soaked. Steam the tamales over simmering water for up to 1-1/2 hour, until the dough pulls away from the husks. Serve warm with extra Tabasco Sauce. YIELD: 7 to 8 dozen.

MEXICAN

BEEF ENCHILADAS

15-oz pkg large flour or corn tortillas (about 10 tortillas)

3 to 4 c homemade ground beef chili without beans

1 tsp chili pepper

Cayenne pepper to taste

1 to 2 large yellow onions, chopped

Two 4-oz cans of diced green chili peppers

4 c of fiesta-blend grated cheese, divided

1 bunch green onions, chopped, including some green

Two 10-oz cans of enchilada sauce

Sour cream

Diced tomatoes

Combine chili with chili pepper and cayenne. Soften corn tortillas in hot oil (white flour tortillas don't need it). In each tortilla, layer cheese, spiced meat, about 1 T chopped onion, green chilies, and enchilada sauce, then roll filled tortilla, tucking the ends inside. Place, edge-down, in greased 9-by-13-inch pan. Pan should allow 8 rolled tortillas. Cover with remaining cheese, onions, chilies and second can of enchilada sauce. Sprinkle evenly with green onions. Bake in preheated oven at 350°F for 35-45 minutes. Remove from oven and let sit 5 minutes before dishing up. Top each serving with a dollop of sour cream and diced tomatoes. Serve with guacamole, shredded lettuce, and heated nacho chips. *Yield: 6 to 8 servings.*

QUICK CHILI-TAMALE CASSEROLE

This version of tamale pie was born out of desperation.

Two 15-oz cans of commercially canned tamales

15-oz can of chili with beans

1/2 to 1 c chopped white onion

1/2 c grated Cheddar cheese

1/2 c Mexican fiesta blend cheese

1 c minced green onion

Two 4-oz cans of chopped green chili peppers

Drain and remove paper covering each tamale. Place 1 layer of tamales in an 8-by-14-inch pan, lightly greased, covering with a layer of chili, then chopped onion and cheese. Add a second layer of tamales, chili, onion and cheese, with top layer being cheese. Garnish with green onion and green chilies if desired. Bake at 350°F for 35-45 minutes.

CHEESE CHILES RELLENOS

8 large poblano or Anaheim peppers

8-oz pkg Monterey Jack cheese with peppers

2 large eggs

1/4 c whipping cream

3/4 c all-purpose flour

3/4 c yellow cornmeal

1/4 tsp salt

Peanut oil

Place peppers on a foil-lined baking sheet. Broil the peppers 5 inches from the broiler heat for about 5 minutes on each side, or until the pepper skins look blistered. Leave oven door partially open.

Place broiled peppers in a bowl or zip-lock bag, cover bowl with plastic wrap or seal the bag. Let stand for 10 minutes, then refrigerate to cool to prevent from falling apart. This will cause the skins to loosen on the peppers. After cooling, peel off skins. Carefully cut them lengthwise on one side, leaving the stems attached. Remove the seeds.

Cut the Monterey Jack-and-pepper cheese into 8 long pieces. Place 1 strip of cheese into each pepper cavity. Secure with long wooden picks to keep closed.

Combine eggs and whipping cream, mix thoroughly. Combine the flour, cornmeal and salt in a shallow dish. Dredge the peeled, deseeded, broiled peppers in the cornmeal mixture and then dip into the egg-cream mixture. Dredge again in the cornmeal mixture to coat. Let rest on a cookie sheet.

Pour 1-inch depth of peanut oil into heavy frying skillet. Heat the oil to 325°F and fry 2 peppers at a time, cut-side up, for 2 minutes, turning once. Drain the peppers on paper towels and remove wooden toothpicks before serving.

ABOUT MEXICAN CUISINE

True Mexican cuisine is considered one of the world's original cuisines (along with Indian cuisine, Chinese cuisine, Italian cuisine, and French cuisine).

Traditional Mexican cookery relies on a combination of beans, peppers, tomatoes and corn to build nutritious and healthful dishes. Popular seasonings include cilantro, cumin, lime, garlic, onions, chili powder, oregano, and cinnamon. Cocoa also is a traditional spice for seasonings and sauces. (Mexicans introduced Europeans to chocolate!)

In the United States, we often think of Mexican food in terms of the Tex-Mex or Arizona-New-Mex dishes that evolved through the interactions of European-descended settlers and the indigenous peoples along the American and Mexican border. But it's so much more….

CHICKEN ENCHILADAS

16-oz container light sour cream

7-oz can diced green chilies

4 to 8 large green onions, chopped

1/2 c chopped fresh cilantro

1-1/2 tsp ground cumin

2 c diced cooked chicken

2 c packed grated sharp Cheddar cheese

Salt and pepper, to taste

Eight large flour tortillas

8-oz pkg of cream cheese, cut lengthwise into strips

24 oz (about one and a half 16-oz bottles) mild picante sauce or salsa

Additional chopped cilantro

Butter a 13-by-9-inch glass baking pan. Mix 1-3/4 cup sour cream, chilies, green onions, 1/2-cup cilantro, and the cumin in a large bowl. Mix in the chicken and 1 cup Cheddar cheese. Season filling to taste with salt and pepper. Spoon generous 1/2-cup of filling down the center of each tortilla. Top filling with cream cheese strip. Roll up each tortilla, enclosing the filling and tucking in ends of tortilla. Arrange enchiladas seam-side down in prepared dish. (Prepare up to 3 hours ahead, cover, and refrigerate until time to cook).

Preheat oven to 350ºF. Pour picante sauce over the enchiladas. Loosely cover with tented foil. Bake until sauce bubbles and enchiladas are heated through, about 45 minutes. Uncover, and sprinkle with remaining 1 cup of Cheddar cheese. Bake uncovered 5-10 minutes, until cheese melts. Remove from oven, let sit 5 minutes before serving with remaining sour cream and cilantro garnish.

CHILI CON CARNE

There are almost as many fanatics about chili as there are about barbecue. Many of the best recipes call for shredded beef and/or pork rather than ground beef. I am listing the simple, basic chili recipe that can be expanded or otherwise modified to suit the cook. Ground turkey may be substituted for beef, if one adds 1 to 2 T butter to offset the dryness.

2 lb ground beef, combining 90-95% lean with 85% lean

1/2 c olive oil or 1 stick butter

3 green bell peppers, chipped fine

3 large yellow onions, chopped

6 cloves of garlic, minced

Four 28-oz cans of chopped or died tomatoes

6-oz can of tomato paste

1 c water

3 T chili powder

1 T ground cumin

Dash of cayenne pepper

1 to 1-1/2 tsp salt

1/4 tsp black pepper

Tabasco to taste

2 Bay leaves

1 T cocoa powder, OPTIONAL

3 cans light red kidney beans, OPTIONAL

Fiesta-blend cheese, OPTIONAL

Brown ground beef in hot olive oil or melted butter on medium heat. Work the ground beef to keep it from clumping. Drain off the oil and fat. Work in the onion, garlic and peppers. Continue cooking until the onions are transparent. Add the tomatoes, Bay leaves and spices, and lower the heat to medium-low once temperature brings the mixture back up to a simmer. Simmer for about 2 hours, stirring occasionally to prevent sticking. Fold in the drained kidney beans and cook for another 30 minutes. Serve in bowls or mugs. Top with grated cheese.

TO SOFTEN PACKAGED TORTILLAS:

Warm in hot, ungreased skillet or griddle about 30 seconds to 1 minute. I prefer to wrap packaged tortillas three at a time in a dampened microwaveable paper towel and microwave them for 15 to 20 seconds, or wrap up to six at a time in a dampened white cotton dish towel, and place in oven at 250°F for 15 minutes.

RULES OF THUMB TO PRODUCE BETTER MEXICAN FOOD:

- Use Mexican cheeses when appropriate; they are creamier and more flavorful than Cheddar cheeses.
- Try to incorporate Mexican fruits such as jicama, papaya, mangos, guayabas, guava, and avocados into your Mexican dishes.
- Try combining toasted, spiced pumpkin and squash seeds, or roasted walnuts in your Mexican dishes.
- Try using tomatillos in your salsa recipes. Select tomatillos with the husk still tightly drawn around the fruit. To use, husk and rinse off the sticky residue.

MOM'S IMPOSSIBLE TACO PIE

from Mary Elizabeth Daltroff

1 lb ground beef

1/2 c chopped yellow onion

1-1/4-oz envelope of taco seasoning mix

4-oz can of chopped green chilies, drained

1-1/4 c milk

3/4 c Bisquick

3 large eggs

2 medium slicing tomatoes, sliced

1-1/2 c shredded Monterey Jack or Cheddar cheese

Heat oven to 450°F and grease a 10-inch pie plate. Brown ground beef and onion. Drain off grease. Stir in taco seasoning mix. Sprinkle the beef mixture into the prepared pie plate. Evenly top with chilies. Beat Bisquick with milk and eggs until smooth (about 15 seconds in a blender on high, or 1 minute with a hand mixer). Pour over meat mixture. Bake for 25 minutes. Remove from oven to sprinkle top with cheese and tomato slices. Return pie to oven, baking until knife inserted in center comes out clean (about 8-10 minutes). Cool 5 minutes before serving with sour cream, chopped tomatoes, shredded lettuce and shredded cheese on the side. YIELD: 6- to 8 servings.

SWEETER VARIATION: Replace the Bisquick, 1-1/4 c milk and 3 eggs with 1 pkg of Jiffy corn muffin mix, 1/3 c +2 T milk, and 2 eggs. Poke the batter through to the meat layer before baking. Bake at 350°F in preheated oven for about 30 minutes. *YIELD: 4 servings.*

ROSE'S TAMALE LOAF CASSEROLE

from Rose Price May

Rose was the first person I knew to use this recipe in the 1960s. Over the past 30 years I have seen variations around the U.S. It's always great with a salad and pico de gallo.

4 large yellow onions

1 cup olive oil

2 pounds lean ground beef

Two 28-oz cans of tomatoes

6-oz can of tomato paste

14-1/2 to 15-oz can of yellow cream-style corn

1 large can of black olives, drained

Two 4-oz cans or jars chopped or sliced mushrooms, juice and all

2-oz jar of pimientos, drained

15-oz can of early English peas, including the juice

2-1/2 c corn meal

2 tsp salt

2-1/2 T chili powder

1 c milk

5 beaten eggs

Chop the onions and sauté in the 1 cup of olive oil until clear. Add 2 lb ground beef and keep stirring until the beef is browned and not clumped. Add tomatoes, tomato paste, corn, olives and mushrooms. Mix in corn meal, salt, chili powder, milk and the 5 beaten eggs. Continue stirring and cooking over a low flame for 15 minutes or until the mixture begins to thicken. Pour into a greased 3-qt casserole dish. Bake in a 350°F pre-heated oven for 30-40 minutes, until mixture firms up and is browned on top. *YIELD: 6 to 8 servings.*

ROASTED CHILIES

Roasted chilies are more flavorful than raw, and the heat is somewhat dispersed. Clean. Deseed them. To roast, place cleaned chilies on hot grill, on broiler, or on stovetop over an open flame in a steamer basket. Turn every minute for 5-10 minutes, until 50% of the skin has blackened. Remove from heat and place in plastic baggie 10-20 minutes. The steam released in the baggie continues the cooking and makes the skins easier to remove (see chiles rellenos). Rub skin off chilies and use knife to scrape any stubborn skin. Chop or slice to use as appropriate in recipes.

KNOW YOUR HAM FACTS

Ham is a technical term referring to the hind leg of a pig. A whole ham weighs between 10 and 20 pounds. Hams generally are cured, or cured and smoked. The curing process is either wet, involving brines, or dry, involving salt or sugar rub and smoking to remove all the moisture. Wet-cured hams are called city hams. Dry-cured hams are called country hams. A "picnic ham" is not really ham. It is a cut from the lower portion of the pig shoulder cured like ham. Boiled ham has been boned, cured and cooked in a boiling process. It is ready to eat without further cooking.

One may select a whole or half ham. The half ham is offered as a butt half or as a shank half. The butt half comes from the top half of the hind leg. The shank half comes from the lower half of the hind leg. The butt half has more fat but generally is meatier than the shank half. The shank half is harder to carve because it is less fatty, but the flavor is sweeter than the butt half.

Moreover, one may select the ham with bone-in, or boneless (de-boned). Bone-in hams serve two to three people per pound. We old-fashioned cooks prefer bone-in because it adds flavor when cooking the ham. The leftover ham bone is also essential for cooking our beans and greens. Boneless hams serve four to five people per pound. Either way, if you intend to feed fewer than 10 people, buy half a ham.

Ready-to-eat ham is fully cooked. Partially cooked ham or "cook before eating" is ham that has been cured but requires cooking. Fresh ham is completely uncured (and they must be special-ordered). To prepare any partially cooked or fresh ham for eating, the internal temperature must be cooked to 160°F. Allow 17 to 20 minutes per pound. Fully cooked hams should be heated to an internal temperature of 140-150°F to achieve maximum flavor.

When buying partially cooked or fully cooked city ham, look for a ham that is bright grayish pink in color, with firm texture. Avoid ham that appears slimy or iridescent. If it smells, don't buy it (or throw it away). The fat on the outside of the ham should be white. If it has yellowed, the ham is probably spoiled.

Uncooked pork of any sort should be used within 3 days of purchase, and should be stored in the fridge at a tem-

Country ham biscuits from G&W Hamery, Murfreesboro, TN
PHOTO: Courtesy of G&W Hamery

perature below 40°F. An unopened fully cooked ham will keep in the fridge for several weeks. Freezing it is not recommended. Once cooked, leftovers from a whole or half city ham remain good for 3 to 5 days, wrapped, in the fridge.

Country ham is dry-cured in a mixture of salt and other ingredients such as sugar (I do not recommend hams containing sodium nitrate). NOTE: Prosciutto is the Italian version of our Southern country ham. Westphalian ham is the German equivalent. American country hams are hung to "cure" in a smokehouse in changing temperatures of the seasons. The temperature and humidity level are carefully controlled to reflect those seasons. They are cured for a minimum of three months, and are offered cured six months one year, and longer than 12 months. Country hams cured for a minimum of 12 months are considered the most desirable. Whole country hams are sold unrefrigerated as whole bone-in hams. They usually are packaged in cotton bags. Country ham sold in ready-to-cook pre-sliced packages already has been scrubbed and soaked. Uncooked country ham, once cut, will keep for two to three months in the refrigerator. Once cooked, it will keep only seven days in the fridge.

Whole country hams have a thick crust of mold. They must be washed in hot or very warm water and scrubbed with a stiff vegetable brush to remove the mold. The mold must be carefully discarded and prep-area surfaces disinfected. The scrubbed ham is then soaked for 4 to 12 hours to remove the salt cure and remaining mold. The ham remains salty. A proper country ham smells fresh and is firm to the touch. If the smell is really powerfully sour, the ham may have gone bad.

Southerners are fond of slicing country ham thin and pan-frying the slices. But cooked whole country ham is a real treat. To cook a whole country ham after cleaning and soaking it, one places it skin side up in a very large pan, and fills the pan with water. There are two schools of thought about how much liquid—completely covering the ham, or halfway up. One then simmers the ham tightly covered on low, either on stovetop or in the oven set to 300°F. The ham is done when the bone comes loose, and when the internal temperature registers 160°F. Remove from the pan, remove the fat and skin, and glaze the ham like a city ham. Brown at 400°F at least 15 minutes.

PORK

EASTER BAKED HAM

7- to 12-lb shank or butt ham, rind removed

Whole cloves

1 lb of dark brown sugar

14-oz can pineapple rings, drained; juice reserved

2 c of orange juice

10 to 12 maraschino cherries

Fresh Bay leaves, for garnish

Preheat oven to 325°F. Using a sharp knife, lightly score surface of ham fat layer in cross-hatch diamond pattern. Place a clove in center of each intersected line of hatching. Place ham, scored fat-side up, in a roasting pan lined with foil. Pat brown sugar onto the ham surface, allowing excess to fall into the roaster. I always place about 1 cup water in the pan. Transfer to oven, and bake until sugar begins to melt, about 30 minutes.

Remove ham from oven. Combine pineapple juice with orange juice, and pour over ham, letting it blend with melted sugar. Baste with melted sugar mixture. Return to oven, and bake 20 more minutes. Baste with pan juice. Continue baking for about 16 minutes per pound if the ham is not pre-cooked, basting every 20 minutes with pan juices. During last 20 minutes of baking time, decorate ham with pineapple rings, using toothpicks to hold in place. Fix a cherry in the middle of each ring with a toothpick. Transfer ham to platter, removing all toothpicks. Garnish presentation with fresh Bay leaves. *YIELD: 10-12 servings.*

VARIATION: Substitute a 12-oz cola soft drink in the place of the fruit juices.

BAKED HAM MEMORY

Mom and Dad in the kitchen carving leftover ham, circa 1970.

There are two kinds of ham for us Southerners: Country ham and baked ham. Depending on preference and the consumer's place of birth, one means Christmas and the other means Easter.

Mom and Dad, on behalf of the Memphis Cotton Exchange and the American Cotton Shippers Association, played host to a visiting group of Eastern-bloc cotton industry representatives one Christmas season while I was home from college. I say group, but they were two men—one from Romania and the other from Bulgaria. We knew the Second Man, the Bulgarian, was KGB. Being Dad, and being Mom, they opened our home to these Communists, and being good Southerners, they shared our food.

True Southerners relish life's ironies. Irony was never more obvious than that evening in Mom and Dad's living room, as the Second Man lectured Daddy on how the West just must recognize the superiority of Communism. All this, while drinking Dad's Cutty Sark and Drambuie, and single-handedly consuming half a baked Christmas ham AFTER a lavish meal.

BAKED OR GRILLED PORK LOIN ROAST

1 boneless pork loin roast, trimmed (4.5 to 6 lb)

Kitchen string

2 to 3 cloves of garlic, or 1 clove elephant garlic, crushed, minced fine

2 tsp kosher salt

1 tsp black pepper

1/4 to 1/2 c extra light olive oil

1 T fresh ground Tuscan herb mix, store-bought or measured from the following mixture:

- **1 T finely chopped fresh rosemary**
- **1 T finely chopped fresh thyme**
- **1 T ground thyme**
- **1/2 tsp sage**
- **1/2 tsp marjoram**

Pinch of dried basil, crushed

Rinse and pat dry the pork roast, then if using a whole loin, using the kitchen string, tie it together at about 2-inch intervals. Make a paste by crushing the fine-minced garlic with salt in a small bowl. Whisk in olive oil, add herbs and pepper. Rub garlic paste all over roast, wrap in foil, refrigerate overnight.

TO BAKE: Place roast in pan, uncovered, in an oven set to 350-400°F. Bake about 1 hour, or until thermometer inserted into thickest part registers 145-150°F. Remove and let stand for about 10 minutes. The pork will continue cooking but will "set" before slicing.

TO GRILL: Keep roast wrapped in foil. Place in hot charcoal smoker grill (prepped with pan of water but no wood chips). Grill wrapped and covered, about 1-1/2 hr. Open foil at top, re-cover smoker, continue cooking 30 more minutes. Uncover, temporarily set aside the roast, carefully lift out foil package and pour out juices. Place roast directly on grill, remove water pan, and grill, covered, 1 hour, turning at 30 minutes to brown each side. Remove roast from grill and let set for 30 minutes before slicing.

HINT: I prefer to purchase a pork loin roast that contains no additives or injected juices. A good pork roast will be firm to the touch and the grain of the meat will be even and dense, with little or no marbling. Pork roasts will easily become dried-out when cooked on open heat. It is imperative to marinate the roast with olive oil and spices before slowly roasting the meat, preferably, over a pan of water.

CHINESE GROCERY STORE ROAST PORK

This is a popular pork dish developed by the Mississippi Delta's Chinese grocers early in the 20th century. I ate it as a child and rediscovered it upon moving to Mississippi. It tastes like pulled pork, Asian style. I prefer homemade Chinese 5-Spice seasoning to store-bought. The most difficult part of making the seasoning for this dish will be finding a source for star anise.

3-lb picnic shoulder or Boston Butt pork roast

1 tsp canola or peanut oil

4 green onions, white and green parts, chopped

2 garlic cloves, minced

1 tsp grated and peeled fresh ginger

1 c dark soy sauce

1/2 c dry sherry

1/2 c rice vinegar (I suggest red)

1 T honey

2 T dark brown sugar

1 T hoisin sauce

1 star anise

2-inch piece of cinnamon stick

1/4 tsp Chinese 5-spice powder (*see recipe, page 174*)

Preheat oven to 325°F. In a large Dutch oven, or roasting pan, heat oil over medium heat. Add onions, garlic, and ginger, and cook for 1 minute. Add next 9 ingredients and simmer for 1 minute. Add 1 c water and bring to a boil. Reduce heat so mixture simmers. Loosen the skin from the meat in several places, but do not remove it. Place the meat in liquid, turning it several times to coat with sauce. Transfer pan to oven and cook for 30 minutes undisturbed. Baste with cooking liquid. Repeat every 20 minutes until internal temperature of the meat is 185°F. This will be around 4 to 4-1/2 hours.

Remove pork to cutting board and let it rest for 10 minutes. Slice thinly, or chop. Pour pan juices over the meat, removing the star anise and cinnamon.

COLA MARINATED COUNTRY HAM

This recipe works particularly well for Tennessee country ham, or for any country ham that's been cured at least 12 months.

1 whole country ham, about 18-20 lb

Four 16-oz bottles of regular cola soft drink (NOT diet)

Whole cloves

Scrub mold and scum off the ham with a soft bristle scrub brush (disinfect brush afterward). Put ham in a large roasting pan. Add cola to cover entire ham. Soak refrigerated for 48 hours. Remove ham from cola brine, pat dry, and cross-hatch the top, adding whole cloves studs about every 1 to 2 inches along hatch marks. Loosely wrap in tented foil with an opening at the top. Slow-roast the ham at about 300°F to 325°F for 3 to 7 hours, depending on weight, allowing about 30-40 minutes per pound. Ham is ready when internal temperature reaches 160°F.

COLA PORK CHOPS

We Southerners have always liked our Co-cola. We could produce (and have) entire cookbooks using this medicinal nectar as a recipe ingredient.

8 pork chops (center cut)

1 c regular cola soft drink (NOT diet)

1 c ketchup

4 T light brown or dark brown sugar

Preheat oven to 350°F. Place pork chops in a 9-by-13 or 10-by-15-inch baking dish. In a small bowl, mix together the cola and ketchup. Pour over chops and sprinkle with brown sugar. Bake uncovered for about 1 hour, or until pork is cooked completely and internal temperature has reached 160°F.

Pork Loin Roast is an elegant entrée for company.

COUNTRY HAM MEMORIES

Andrea Benfield, Louise and Lester Triplette, and Dianne Poovey, with Jeff Triplette, holding Gabrielle, at Fort Eustis, VA, after his return from the Persian Gulf in April, 1991

Country ham has regional distinctions much like our barbecue. Tennessee country ham is different from Johnston County (NC) Smithfield ham, which is different from Smithfield (VA) ham. It's all good.

When Jeff returned stateside from his tour of duty in the Persian Gulf, Louise, Lester, Andrea, Dianne, Gabrielle and I went up to Fort Eustis, VA, to meet him. Louise took a North Carolina country ham with us. Every morning during our weekend visit in the little army-base motel kitchenette, she made him homemade country ham with redeye gravy, grits and eggs. Jeff knew he was finally back home in heaven after nine months in hell. The entire motel smelled like country ham by the time we left.

My Uncle Enos always had a trick with a Tennessee country ham. He would soak the ham for a couple of days in ginger ale to remove some of the salt brine and to tenderize the cured meat. Then he would place the ham in a cooker, and slow-roast it. The resulting tenderness and flavor were unlike anything I've tasted in a ham before or since.

PORK CHOPS WITH RICE

from Willie Sue Keller, at my bridal shower

4 pork chops

2 T fat, butter or olive oil

1 c uncooked rice

2 c canned tomatoes

1 medium onion, chopped

3 tsp salt

1/4 tsp black pepper

Brown pork chops with fat in a pressure-cooker saucepan. Remove chops from pan; add tomatoes, chopped onions, salt, pepper and uncooked rice. Lay pork chops over the top. Cover and bring to 15 pounds of pressure. Cook 15 minutes, A covered frying pan may be used instead by adding 1-1/2 cup of water, and increasing cook time to 35 minutes. The only way to adapt this recipe to a slow cooker is to omit the rice from the slow cooker, and add cooked rice the last 15 minutes to prevent mushiness.

SKILLET PORK CHOPS

4 pork chops

Salt

Garlic powder

Black pepper

4 T butter

1/2 c water, divided

1-1/2 T plain flour (or Wondra)

Rinse chops and pat dry. Dust with seasonings, starting with salt. Melt butter in skillet on medium-high heat. Add chops, not touching or overlapping. Brown on both sides, then turn again and before drippings burn, add 1/4 cup of water all around the chops. Cover immediately to hold in steam. Let simmer until water evaporates, turn chops over and repeat process. Remove lid, simmer a few more minutes until juice and drippings cook down. Remove chops to plate. Whisk drippings, adding a shake of gravy flour to thicken. Add small amount of water and whisk sides and bottom to gather all drippings. When gravy has thickened and begun bubbling, turn off, add chops back to pan, and cover until ready to serve.

HAM-STUFFED PEPPERS

from Ruth Callicott Thurmond

This is one of Aunt Ruth's Callicott family recipes.

2 c ground ham

2 large green bell peppers

1 medium onion, chopped

1 medium can (14.5 to 15.5-oz) tomatoes (OR 6-oz can of tomato paste)

2 slices bread, wet and squeezed dry

2 eggs

Cook ham and onions together until onions are transparent, about 5 minutes. Add water to prevent sticking as needed. Break up 2 bread slices into mixture while stirring to thicken. Break eggs into mixture and stir well. Split peppers, remove seeds; pour boiling water over them in a saucepan. Cook for 2 to 3 minutes to blanch. Remove and pat dry. Put in baking dish and fill with ham mixture. Pour small amount of pepper water into baking dish to prevent scorching. Bake at 350°F for 20-30 minutes, until browned and bubbly. *YIELD: 4 servings.*

MOM'S HAM PIE

from Mary Elizabeth Daltroff

9-inch unbaked pie shell or fresh pie pastry

3 T butter

3 T all-purpose flour

1 c whole milk

1 medium onion, chopped

1 green bell pepper, chopped

1 T butter

3 to 4 c cooked ham, diced

Saltine cracker crumbs (made with a rolling pin)

Grated sharp Cheddar cheese

Pinch of cayenne pepper

Make a white sauce by melting the butter and blending with flour and milk. Cook over low heat, stirring, until thick and smooth. Sauté chopped onion and pepper in butter. Add to cream sauce with diced cooked ham. Pour into unbaked pie crust, smooth out top. Sprinkle with sharp cheese, a pinch of cayenne, and cracker crumbs. Bake at 350°F about 30 to 40 minutes. Serve hot. *YIELD: 6 to 8 servings.*

Thurmond men prepare hogs in West Tennessee, 1920s-1930s. This process always requires extremely cold weather.

POULTRY

BRUNSWICK STEW HISTORY

I first encountered Brunswick Stew by that name when I went to North Carolina in 1969. It was served in the rural areas at barbecue gatherings around Madison, Mayodan, Danbury and Belews Creek, northwest of Winston-Salem. Over the years, I learned more about this most colonial of stews. The Virginia version and the Georgia version might differ some, but they all originated as backwoods comfort food using whatever game was available.

According to one story I read, Brunswick Stew was named for Brunswick County, VA, where a Dr. Creed Haskins of the Virginia State Legislature asked in 1828 for a special squirrel stew to feed folks at a political rally. There's also a Brunswick, GA, which claims to be the origin of the stew. I think it probably originated with the Native Americans, then got "stewed" when introduced to the colonials and their slaves. Brunswick stew is most commonly made with chicken or a combo of meats that might include pork, rabbit, or squirrel. Onions, corn and tomatoes usually are included, along with lima beans and okra.

CATAWBA COUNTY (NC) BRUNSWICK STEW

from Louise Sherrill Triplette

Louise got this recipe from a friend in the Women's Society of Christian Service, Hickory, NC.

2 c cooked fresh pork (tenderloin)
2 c cooked chicken, deboned
3 c frozen corn
2-4 c of ketchup
1 small bottle of Worcestershire sauce
1 T dry mustard
1 T white vinegar
Salt and pepper to taste
3 to 4 c chicken broth or stock

Cook and then grind the pork and chicken. Also grind the frozen corn. Pour into large pot and cook together with remaining ingredients for several hours.

OLD-FASHIONED BRUNSWICK STEW

4 to 5 lb of chicken, either whole chicken parts, skinned, or legs, thighs and breasts
1/3 c all-purpose flour
1 tsp salt
1/2 tsp fresh ground black pepper
1/2 tsp dried leaf thyme
1/8 tsp cayenne
3 T vegetable oil
1 c chopped onion
6 oz lean smoked ham, diced (I get mine from the deli)
Splash of Tabasco, OPTIONAL
4 to 6 c chicken broth
28-oz can whole tomatoes, drained and cut up
1/2 c chopped green bell pepper
1/4 c chopped red bell pepper
1 medium Bay leaf
2 c fresh shelled lima beans or 10-oz pkg frozen limas, thawed
2 c fresh corn kernels, or thawed shoepeg frozen corn
2 to 3 c peeled and cubed red potatoes

Cut chicken into pieces: 2 drumsticks, 2 thighs, 2 wings, and cut the two breast halves in half again. You should have 10 pieces. Trim away as much fat as possible. Rinse and let drain. In a shallow bowl, mix the flour, salt, pepper, thyme and cayenne. Dredge the damp chicken pieces in the seasoned flour.

In a large skillet, heat 2 tablespoons of the oil over medium-high heat. Dredge the chicken again if the coating looks damp; shake any excess back into the bowl. Reserve the excess seasoned flour. Add the chicken pieces to the pan in a single layer without crowding, in batches if necessary, and cook, turning, until golden brown, about 7 minutes per batch. Lower the heat if necessary about half-way through, so the fat doesn't burn.

Remove the chicken to a large Dutch oven. In skillet, cook onions and peppers in chicken drippings plus 1 T oil until soft, about 3 minutes. Add the ham and cook until lightly browned, about 2 to 3 minutes longer. Sprinkle the reserved seasoned flour over the ham and onions and cook, stirring, just to blend in, about 30 seconds. Add a splash of Tabasco if desired. Pour into Dutch oven over chicken. Add remaining ingredients to Dutch oven. Bake in moderate oven at about 325°F for about 2 to 3 hours. NOTE: Leftovers from this version freeze well, if potatoes are removed.

VARIATION: Add game such as rabbit or squirrel.

CROCK POT BRUNSWICK STEW

14.5-oz can of diced tomatoes

6-oz can of tomato paste

3 c cooked, cubed chicken (light and dark)

1-1/2 c sliced okra (frozen but thawed, or fresh)

1 c cut corn, fresh or thawed from frozen

1 c baby limas or butter peas, fresh, or thawed from frozen, OPTIONAL

1 c chopped white onion

1 Bay leaf

1 tsp salt

1/4 tsp dried crushed rosemary

1/4 tsp crushed oregano

1/2 tsp ground black pepper

Dash of ground cloves

2-1/2 c chicken stock

In slow cooker, combine tomatoes and tomato paste; stir to blend. Add chicken, vegetables and spices. Stir in chicken broth. Cover; cook on LOW for 5 to 6 hours, or for 8 hours if pot doesn't allow low setting. Before serving, remove Bay leaf and stir well. *YIELD: 6 servings.*

ROASTING WILD POULTRY

Dad had a very rudimentary sheet of cooking instructions from William Ross, dated December 1960, that told how to cook duck, chukar, pheasant and quail. There were no ingredient quantities except those as listed below. The cook must use his or her own judgment, depending on quantities of birds being cooked.

DUCK:

Ducks, prepared for cooking

Salt

3 small white onions

Celery ribs

3/4 c white distilled vinegar (I like red wine vinegar)

Plain flour

Place ducks in roaster, breast-side up. Add salt, three small onions, and celery ribs. Place top on roaster and cook, covered, for one hour at 350°F. Remove roaster lid, and pour off stock and drippings. Baste ducks with vinegar to brown them. Make a roux, using duck drippings and flour. Add roux to duck, and baste while braising, until done.

CHUKAR AND PHEASANT:

Chukar or pheasant, prepared for cooking

Salt and pepper

Ground thyme

Plain flour

1/2 c Dry Sack wine or sherry

Bake like chicken, seasoned with salt and pepper and a bit of ground thyme, in a roaster pan. Bake with top off roaster. Make a golden-brown roux with pan drippings and flour, and then make a gravy, adding 1/2 c dry sack wine or dry sherry. Pour gravy over the chukar or pheasant and baste often, about every 15 minutes until done.

SMOTHERED QUAIL:

Quail, prepared for cooking

Cooking oil

Salt and pepper

Plain flour

Worcestershire sauce, to taste

Combine flour, salt and pepper. Dredge the birds in flour mixture. Fry like chicken only until browned. Do not fry until done. Place browned quail in roaster in oven set to 325°F. Use part of the skillet grease to make a golden brown roux. Add Worcestershire sauce to the roux (about 1 T per bird) to make gravy. Pour gravy over the quail in roaster, and bake, basting every 15 minutes until done. (*See poultry cooking chart, page 365.*)

Butch Daltroff and golden retriever Chatwood, after a successful duck hunt in 1957. Chatwood was run out of Shelby County, TN, by the dog catcher. No fence could contain him when he smelled water.

Trail Jordan, left, and Andy Daltroff, after a successful day of duck hunting

TRAIL'S TOTALLY DELICIOUS GRILLED DUCK BREAST

from Henry H. (Trail) and Ann Jordan

Trail Jordan of Kosciusko, MS, developed this recipe for duck and dove. My brother Andy and his lifelong buddies Jimmy and Skip Clark go duck hunting with Trail at a hunt camp north of Yazoo City, MS, owned by Skip, Trail and several other Jackson-area businessmen. The men hunt all morning and cook all afternoon.

6 duck breasts, deboned (12 pieces)
Wishbone Italian Dressing
1 stick butter (1/2 c)
1/4 c Worcestershire sauce
1 T lemon pepper
Garlic salt to taste
1 lemon
12 strips of bacon

Place duck breasts in zip-lock freezer bag; cover with Wishbone dressing. Refrigerate overnight or 6 hours. Combine butter, lemon pepper, Worcestershire, and garlic salt in small saucepan. Squeeze lemon juice into pan and throw in rind. Cook until butter melts, and ingredients are well mixed. Wrap duck breasts in bacon strips, securing with toothpicks. Baste with lemon butter sauce. Grill over hot coals about 10 minutes, turning frequently. Baste after every turn. Remove from grill. Let rest 5 minutes. Serve as entree with wild rice and veggies; or in quarter-inch slices as hors d'oeuvres. NOTE: Sauce also works well with steak such as filet mignon.

COMPANY CORNISH HENS

2 Cornish hens, about 1-1/2 to 2 lb each, split lengthwise
Garlic salt
Salt and pepper
1 medium white onion, chopped
4-oz can sliced mushrooms, drained
3 T melted butter or margarine
1/2 c dry white wine
1/3 c sour cream

Wash the hens and pat dry. Sprinkle with garlic salt, salt and pepper, and place them cut side down in a lightly greased 9-by-13-by-2-inch baking pan. Cover with aluminum foil and bake at 350°F for 30 minutes. Remove the foil, and bake an additional 30 minutes. Sauté onion and mushrooms in butter over medium heat for 5 minutes. Stir in the wine while simmering and mix well. Pour the onion-mushroom mixture over the hens. Bake an additional 25 minutes or until juice runs clear when thigh is pierced with a fork. Place hens on a serving platter. Stir sour cream into the pan drippings and pour over the hens. *YIELD: 4 servings.*

ROAST CORNISH HEN AND BACON

This is my variation of Trail Jordan's Totally Delicious Grilled Duck Breasts. Omit the bacon and sprinkle with a bit of salt and thyme, if you prefer simple, roasted Cornish hens.

4 Cornish hens, rinsed

Olive oil as needed

Fresh ground pepper to taste

12 to 16 bacon slices

2 T fine-diced shallots

1 tsp plain flour

1/2 c white wine

2 T chicken demi glace, OR pan juices

1 c chicken broth

1 tsp minced fresh thyme

2 T cold unsalted butter, cut into 2 pieces

Preheat oven to 450°F. Blot hens dry. Rub with oil; season all around with pepper. Place breast-side up on rack in roasting pan, tucking wings behind breasts. Wrap four bacon slices around each hen, tucked-side down. Roast hens until thighs register 170°F, about 1 hour to 1-1/4 hour. Tent with foil if bacon becomes too dark. Transfer hens to carving board, tent with foil until ready to carve.

Discard all but 2 T fat from pan. Reserve juices. Set pan on burner over medium high heat, Add shallots and saute 2 minutes. Add flour; cook 30 seconds. Add wine, whisk in juices or demi glace and broth. Simmer 3 to 5 minutes. Remove from heat, and whisk in thyme and butter. Carve hens. Drizzle with sauce and pass remaining sauce alongside. Serve with wild rice medley. *YIELD: 8 servings.*

Coq Au Vin

ALLINE'S BARBECUED BAG CHICKEN

from Alline Sherrill Annas, at my Grace Chapel bridal shower

3 lb fryer

2 T Worcestershire sauce

2 T vinegar

1 T lemon juice

4 T water

2 T butter or margarine

3 T packed brown sugar

3 T ketchup

1 tsp salt

1 tsp dry mustard

1 tsp chili powder

1 tsp paprika

1/2 tsp red pepper flakes (or 1/8 tsp cayenne pepper)

Mix ingredients thoroughly. Grease inside and outside of brown paper bag with butter or margarine. Dip chicken in sauce and put in paper bag. Pour remaining sauce over chicken in the paper bag. Place bag in a Dutch oven and bake 15 minutes at 500°F. Turn oven down to 350°F, and bake for 1 hour and 15 minutes.

COQ AU VIN

4 bacon slices, cut into 1/2-inch pieces

6 chicken thighs, skinned

Salt and pepper to taste

3/4 tsp ground thyme

Large white onion, coarse-chopped

4 cloves garlic, minced

8 small red potatoes, quartered

10 medium mushrooms, quartered

14 to 15 oz Italian-style stewed tomatoes

1-1/2 c of red wine

Fry bacon pieces in Dutch oven over stovetop, just to brown. Sprinkle seasonings over chicken. Add chicken to frying bacon, and brown on medium-high heat, both sides. Add onion and garlic, stirring and tossing. Cook 2 minutes. Drain grease. Add veggies and wine. Cook, covered, about 25 minutes, until potatoes are tender and sauce has thickened. Stir occasionally. Pour into serving dish or individual plates and garnish with fresh parsley.

THE CHICKEN KILLING

The first year of my marriage to Jeff, the little community of Grace Chapel, NC, started a volunteer fire department. To raise money for the building and the first fire truck, the community held chicken and dumpling suppers. Acknowledged as the best chicken and dumpling maker in three counties, Louise Triplette was chief cook for these fundraising suppers. Under her direction, volunteers prepared the food in the kitchen at Grace Chapel United Methodist Church, fondly known by our family as "OUR church." Next door to Louise and Lester's farm, the church had been built with James B. Duke Endowment church money. The Sherrills and their kin were founding members.

Jeff was scheduled to attend his monthly National Guard drill in West Jefferson the weekend before the first fund-raising supper. I rode up with him from Winston-Salem to stay with Louise and Lester. As usual, they welcomed me right into their weekend activities.

Saturday morning dawned bright and breezy. We went next door to the church, where Michael and Grandpa Sherrill and Uncle Paul and Aunt Alline and Uncle Red and Aunt Willie Sue and Uncle June and dozens of neighbors already had gathered. Mr. Henry Lee Satterwhite, the nearby chicken and egg farmer, had donated almost 30 chickens for the fundraiser. It was up to the volunteers to prepare the chickens for the following week. It was time for the chicken killing.

Every participant had his or her preferred method of killing: Neck wringing, head snapping, or decapitation. They'd each brought their preferred implement for doing the deed, and vociferously compared notes on the best way to kill a chicken, sneaking peeks at me to see if and when I, the City Slicker from Memphis, might gag.

To this day, when recalling that event, I can smell the odor of scalded chicken feathers. With photographic clarity, I still see the white church steeple jutting upward into the Carolina-blue sky, the bird carcasses dangling from a clothesline, dancing in the breeze.

Grace Chapel United Methodist Church, Granite Falls, NC

CHICKEN AND DUMPLINGS

from Louise Sherrill Triplette

Bar none, Louise Triplette was the best chicken and dumpling cook in America. Over the years, the family sometimes requested her chicken and dumplings instead of turkey for holiday meals. Folks in three counties used to pay Louise to make pots of her dumplings for their events. Louise always made her dumplings by "feeling" the dough.

COOK THE CHICKEN:

6 to 10 boneless skinless chicken breasts

Water

1 to 2 tsp thyme

4 to 6 peeled cloves of garlic

1 tsp salt

1/4 to 1/2 tsp black pepper

Place chicken in a large stock pot (quantity depends on the frozen-breast package size and how much you want to make); cover with water to about 4 inches below top of pot.

Add spices, and bring to a boil for 15-20 minutes. Lower heat and simmer until the chicken falls apart in the broth. Add water back up to within 4 inches of top of pot. This will make enough broth for the dumplings.

LOUISE'S DUMPLINGS:

Plain flour, as much as feels right (3 to 4 c in a dough bowl)

Salt and black pepper to taste

A tiny bit of shortening, about 1 T for 3 to 4 c of flour

Boiling water, added a little bit at a time

Mix ingredients all at one time. Begin working the dough by hand. The boiling water will make it too hot to do more than caress and fold the flour with fingertips at first. It will start out sticky, but keep working it until stiff and fully blended. Add more flour as needed. When dough reaches stiff stage, roll into two balls and refrigerate 1 to 2 days in mixing bowl covered with waxed paper. I flatten wax paper against the sticky dough in the bowl, covering all exposed dough to keep out air. Then I stretch additional waxed paper over the rim of the bowl and secure with a rubber band.

Dough should be very supple when rolled out on a floured pastry cloth or board. Roll very thin (no more than 3/8-inch thick) between two sheets of waxed paper. Cut into strips about 1-1/2 inches wide by 3 inches long and drop one at a time into boiling broth, letting come to a full boil between drops. Simmer covered for about 30-45 minutes, making sure to stir to prevent sticking to bottom of pot.

BAKED STUFFED CHICKEN BREASTS

from Andrea Benfield

This recipe came to Andrea from Chris Angelo English.

BREASTS:

4 chicken breasts, bone-in, washed and patted dry

1/4 c all-purpose flour

1/2 tsp salt

1/2 tsp paprika

1/4 to 1/2 tsp ground black pepper

1/2 c (4 T) melted butter

1/2 pint whipping cream (or half and half)

STUFFING:

2 c fresh bread cubes

2 T butter

Salt and pepper to taste

1/4 tsp poultry seasoning

2 T finely minced celery

2 T chopped white onion

1/4 c hot water

Combine first 4 dry ingredients in a paper bag. Dredge chicken breasts in the seasoning bag by shaking. Mix stuffing ingredients together and fill cavity of chicken breasts, closing with toothpicks. Dip sealed breasts into melted butter. Place in baking dish. Drizzle any remaining butter over the breasts. Bake uncovered for 30 minutes at 325°F. Turn breasts over and bake additional 30 minutes. Remove from oven and pour half-pint of cream over the chicken. Return to oven and heat for 10 additional minutes. When serving, baste each serving with the cream-broth drippings.

ANDREA'S STUFFING VARIATION: Fill chicken cavities with spinach-artichoke dip (*see recipe, page 77*), and continue with original instructions. OMG!

ABOUT THOSE DUMPLINGS... ADVICE FOR YOUNG COOKS:

Apprentice to a master like Louise. Practice two or three times before serving to your family. In a pinch, buy Anne's or Mary B's frozen dumplings at the grocery store. Drop them one at a time into the boiling broth, allowing the broth to rise to a boil again between drops. Cover, and simmer much longer than stated in the package directions.

CHICKEN BREASTS SUPREME

3 whole chicken breasts, split, skinned and boned

6-oz pkg frozen crab meat, thawed, drained and flaked

1/4 c small bread cubes

1/4 c diced celery

1/2 tsp lemon juice

2 T butter or margarine

1 can (10-3/4 oz) cream of chicken soup

1/3 c water

2 T chopped parsley

Cooked rice

Flatten chicken breast half with flat side of a knife. Combine crabmeat, bread cubes, celery, lemon juice. Place 1/4 cup of mixture on the center of each breast. Roll, tucking in the ends, and fasten with toothpicks or skewers. Brown chicken in butter or margarine, add remaining ingredients except the rice. Cover, cook over low heat around 30 minutes, until done. Baste with sauce to keep moist.

CHICKEN CACCIATORE

3 lb chicken cut into eighths

3/4 cup olive oil

Salt to taste (about 1-1/2 tsp)

1 tsp ground black pepper

6 to 10 cloves unpeeled garlic, mashed

1 tsp rosemary

1 tsp oregano

1/2 c dry white wine

1-1/2 c tomato sauce

Heat olive oil in large skillet. Add chicken pieces, turning often to brown on all sides. Sprinkle with salt and pepper while browning. As chicken finishes browning, add garlic oregano and rosemary, stirring to mix well. Remove skillet from stove. Pour wine over the chicken, shaking pan a bit to blend. Add tomato sauce, stir well, return to stove and simmer 15 minutes until wine and sauce have blended and thickened. *YIELD: 4 servings.*

CHICKEN FLORENTINE WITH HERBED CHEESE SAUCE

6 split boneless, skinless chicken breasts

1/2 c low-calorie Italian dressing

1/4 c onion, chopped fine

40 saltine crackers, crushed with rolling pin

10-oz pkg frozen chopped spinach, thawed, well drained

2 T butter or margarine, melted

1-1/4 c thin cream sauce *(see recipe, page 169)*

1/3 c grated Swiss cheese

2 T chopped parsley

Pound chicken thin, and place in a baking dish. Add Italian dressing. Turn chicken to coat. Cover and chill for 2 hours. To prepare for baking, remove from fridge. Make stuffing using Italian dressing from the chicken pan, combining with the spinach and cracker crumbs, reserving enough crumbs to dredge the chicken. Divide stuffing evenly among the breasts, spreading in a line down center of each breast. Roll each breast around the stuffing, secure each roll with toothpicks. Dredge the rolled breasts in reserved cracker crumbs to coat; then return to the dish. Drizzle melted butter or margarine over the breasts. Bake at 375°F in preheated oven, uncovered, for about 40 minutes. Remove toothpicks to serve.

Make a white cream sauce from scratch, adding cheese and parsley while still warm. Stir well. Pour over the chicken and serve. *YIELD: 6 servings.*

COMPANY CHICKEN OR TURKEY DIVAN

Two 10-oz pkgs frozen broccoli, or 4 bunches of fresh broccoli, trimmed; cooked in steamer

4 to 6 c cubed chicken or turkey breast (about 1 lb sliced thin)

2 c Hollandaise sauce *(see recipe, page 168)*

1/2 pt heavy whipping cream, whipped (unsweetened)

5 T sherry

Grated Parmesan cheese

Add whipped cream and sherry to Hollandaise sauce. Set aside. Arrange poultry over layer of broccoli in small individual Pyrex pie plates: Pour Hollandaise over the layers. Cover sauce with grated Parmesan cheese. Brown casserole under flame. *YIELD: 6 servings.*

CHURCH SUPPER CHICKEN DIVAN

This down-to-earth version of Chicken Divan can be multiplied to bake in a 9-by-13-inch casserole dish. I increase the amount of chicken or turkey by 2-1/2 times rather than doubling.

1 lb fresh broccoli cut into spears, or a 10-oz pkg of frozen spears

1-1/2 c cubed cooked chicken or turkey

1 can cream of broccoli soup

1/3 c milk

1/2 c shredded Cheddar cheese

1 T butter, melted

2 T dry bread crumbs

Cook and drain broccoli. Arrange in shallow dish. Top with the meat. Combine soup and milk, pour over the chicken. Sprinkle with cheese. Combine butter and bread crumbs, sprinkle over cheese. Bake at 450°F about 15-20 minutes in conventional oven; or 6 minutes on high in microwave oven. *YIELD: 4 servings.*

CHICKEN AND RICE CASSEROLE

3 c cooked chicken, cut in large pieces or shredded, according to taste

1 can cream of mushroom soup

1/2 c mayonnaise

1 c chopped celery

4- to 8-oz can or jar of sliced mushrooms, reserve liquid

1-1/2 tsp chopped onion

1 T lemon juice

1/2 c sliced almonds or 1 can water chestnuts, sliced

Buttered bread cubes made from white or French bread

1 c rice cooked in 2 c chicken broth with juice drained from canned mushrooms

Sauté celery, onions and mushrooms first. Set aside. Combine mayo, soup and lemon juice, mix into the veggies and cooked rice. Combine with chicken and almonds or water chestnuts. Pour into 3-qt casserole dish.

Prepare buttered bread cubes by cubing regular white bread or stale French or Italian bread, and toasting in skillet with a few tablespoons of butter (amount varies according to bread). Top casserole with buttered bread cubes. Bake at 350°F in preheated oven about 30 minutes, or until bread cubes are brown.

To reheat, add some chicken broth to rehydrate the rice. Stir and heat.

CHICKEN TETRAZZINI

48 oz of skinless chicken breasts, cooked and chopped

2 green bell peppers, chopped

2 white onions, chopped

1 small bunch celery, chopped fine

One 5- to 7-oz can or jar of sliced mushrooms

3 slices bacon

3 c of medium cream sauce *(see recipe, page 169)*

2 c grated Cheddar or mild blend cheese

3/4 of a small pkg of vermicelli

6 oz toasted, slivered or sliced almonds

Fry bacon, using grease to sauté the onion, green peppers, celery and mushrooms until tender. Add the bacon to these ingredients. Make medium-consistency cream sauce; add the grated cheese to sauce. Cook vermicelli, drain. Mix vermicelli with all ingredients except nuts. Put into lightly greased casserole. Bake at 400°F until hot. Sprinkle hot, toasted slivered or sliced almonds over the top and serve. *YIELD: 10 servings.*

CHICKEN À LA KING

from Mary Elizabeth Daltroff

1/2 c butter

1/2 c plain flour

Paprika

2 c chicken stock or canned broth

1/4 c milk

1/2 c cream

2 egg yolks, beaten

1/2 c whole pimientos, cut into strips

1 c sautéed fresh mushrooms (or canned)

1/4 c boiled green bell pepper strips, OPTIONAL

1 tsp salt

White pepper to taste

2 T sherry or cognac

2 c cooked chicken or turkey, cubed

Melt butter, add flour and a few grains of paprika. Cook 5 minutes. Add chicken stock, milk, and cream. Bring to a boil, put in double boiler over hot but not boiling water and cook 15 minutes. Remove from heat and add beaten egg yolks, pimientos, mushrooms and cooked bell peppers. Season with salt, pepper and sherry. Add 2 cups cooked chicken (or turkey) cut into cubes and mix well. Serve immediately over toast points or in puff pastry shells.

Lester Triplette loved to go pheasant hunting in Nebraska.

CHICKEN JAMBALAYA

from Butch Daltroff

1 whole chicken, cut into pieces, skinned

1 stick (1/2 c) butter or 1/4 to 1/2 c extra-light olive oil

1/3 to 1 c chopped white onion

15.5-oz can of diced tomatoes

1 green bell pepper, diced

1/2 c celery, diced, with leaves

1 c uncooked rice

1 Bay leaf

1/4 tsp ground thyme

1/4 c chopped fresh parsley

1 tsp salt

1/4 tsp pepper

Tabasco sauce to taste

Creole seasoning (Tony Chachere's) to taste

Boiling water

Cajun-style sausage, sliced

Sauté the chicken pieces in the olive oil or melted butter for about 5 minutes in a large heavy skillet or pan. Remove the chicken and sauté the sausage. Add the onion and tomatoes to sautéed sausage, stirring well into the drippings for about 3 to 5 minutes. Add the bell pepper, celery and uncooked rice. Stir well to mix.

Return the chicken to the pan, stirring to combine with the sausage, onion and tomato mixture. Cover with boiling water, then add the Bay leaf, thyme, parsley, salt and pepper.

Simmer for about 20-30 minutes, until the rice is almost done. At this time add Tabasco and Tony's, along with additional meat or seafood of choice (usually chopped cooked ham or sausage, and shrimp).

Correct the seasoning if more salt and pepper is needed. Put skillet or pan into oven and bake for about 5 to 10 minutes at 350°F to dry out the rice.

> **HINT:** When transporting unlockable crock pots and covered dishes in the car, use a laundry basket; stuff towels around the containers to prevent spills.

CHICKEN FRICASSEE

from Butch Daltroff

3- to 4-lb stewing chicken, cut up or disjointed

1 c of all-purpose flour

2 tsp salt

2 tsp paprika

1/4 tsp black pepper

1 c water

3 T all-purpose flour

Whole milk

Soak chicken in water-and-salt brine overnight as if to prepare for fried chicken. When ready to cook, remove chicken from water and pat dry. Mix in a bowl 1 cup flour, the salt, paprika and pepper. Coat chicken with flour mixture. Heat a thin layer of shortening or peanut oil in a 12-inch skillet or Dutch oven until hot, about 325-250°F. Cook chicken in hot oil until browned on all sides. Drain fat, but reserve for later use. Add chopped onion, lemon juice or herbs such as thyme and/or rosemary. Add water. Cover and cook over low heat, adding water as necessary until thickest pieces are tender, about 2-1/2 to 3-1/2 hours.

Remove chicken, but keep warm. Drain liquid, but reserve. Heat 3 T of reserved fat/oil in skillet, and stir in 3 T flour. Cook over low heat, stirring until mixture is smooth and bubbly. Remove from heat. Add milk to reserve liquid to measure 3 cups. Pour this milk chicken-stock mixture into the skillet. Heat to boiling, stirring constantly. Boil, stirring 1 minute; return chicken to the pan and coat with the gravy. Simmer no longer than 5 minutes just to allow gravy to soak into meat. Serve immediately.

MUSTARD CHICKEN

2-1/2- or 3-lb fryer chicken, cut into serving pieces

3 T melted butter

2 to 3 T Dijon style mustard

1-1/2 c plain bread crumbs

Ground black pepper

Mix crumbs and pepper in large bowl. Rinse chicken and pat dry. Combine melted butter and mustard, then slather over chicken, to coat. Dip chicken into bread crumbs and place in a shallow baking pan. Do not overlap pieces. Bake at 350°F for 40 minutes. *YIELD: 4 servings.*

COMPANY CHICKEN AND BROCCOLI

from Andy Daltroff

This recipe is an uptown variation on church supper chicken divan. Unlike many casseroles, the dish even looks beautiful when presented on individual plates with each sauce-covered breast over broccoli spears.

6 chicken breasts

3 pkgs frozen broccoli spears (or 2-3 bunches fresh broccoli florets

Three 10-3/4-oz cans cream of chicken soup

1-1/2 c mayonnaise

2 tsp lemon juice

6 T sherry or cognac

3/4 c sharp Cheddar cheese

3/4 c soft bread crumbs

2 tsp melted butter

Boil chicken breasts with salt, pepper, garlic powder and poultry seasoning. Steam broccoli until just done and not overcooked. Lay out broccoli in a 9-by-13-inch casserole dish, pre-greased lightly with cooking spray. Place each chicken breast over broccoli. Mix soup, mayo, lemon juice and sherry, then pour over the chicken breasts. Sprinkle cheese, then top evenly with crumbs. Drizzle melted butter over the crumbs. Bake uncovered at 350°F for one hour. *YIELD: 6 servings.*

VARIATION for a large group: 4 c fine-chopped chicken and 48- or 64-oz pkg frozen broccoli crowns, steamed. Increase cheese and crumbs to 1 cup, and increase butter to 4 T. Spread broccoli across bottom of dish, then layer as usual. They'll eat every bite.

CURRIED CHICKEN AND RICE

from Mary Elizabeth Daltroff

1-1/2 to 2 c uncooked rice

2 T curry powder, divided

1 tsp salt

1/8 tsp black pepper

15-oz can of chicken broth

1 c water

6 whole chicken breasts with or without bones

Grease bottom and sides of a 9-by-13-inch pan. Spread uncooked rice evenly across bottom of pan. Sprinkle curry powder, salt and pepper evenly across the rice. Place uncooked chicken breasts over the rice, and sprinkle the breasts with additional salt, pepper and curry powder. Pour chicken broth and water into pan without disturbing the breasts. Loosely cover with aluminum foil and bake at 375°F for approximately 45 minutes to one hour, until chicken is done and rice has soaked up all the liquid.

TERIYAKI CHICKEN

1 lb skinless, boneless chicken breasts, cut into strips (or trimmed wings)

1 c soy sauce

1/2 c cola soft drink

2 T orange juice

1 T fresh ginger, minced

1 clove garlic, minced

Salt, pepper and chili powder to taste

1/4 c vegetable oil

Combine all marinade ingredients. Marinate chicken overnight. To cook, place chicken on oiled pan and bake at 350°F about 30 minutes. Remove from oven, slide chicken around in pan to sop up the caramelized sauce, baste with additional marinade and return to oven for another 15-20 minutes. Serve over steamed rice.

IT'S ALL RELATIVE: You can invite the relatives with all the cats to the family reunion. Just don't tell them to bring food to the potluck picnic.

DIANNE'S EASY CHICKEN PIE

from Dianne Triplette Poovey

This is the pan-pot-pie recipe that Louise and Dianne have used to everyone's cheers over the years, It's an easy crowd pleaser.

10-3/4-oz can of cream of chicken soup

10-3/4-oz can of chicken broth or water

1 c all-purpose flour

1 c whole milk

1 stick (1/2 c) butter

Cooked chicken, diced

Cook and cut up the chicken into bite-size pieces. Place in a greased 9-by-13-inch baking dish. Combine the soup and broth/water, and add to chicken in pan. In a saucepan, melt butter or margarine. Remove from heat and add flour and milk. Beat until smooth. and pour over chicken. Bake 45 minutes at 350°F in a preheated oven, until bubbly and golden. *YIELD: 6 servings.*

POPPYSEED CHICKEN PIE

I got this recipe from our Winston-Salem babysitter, Kate Misenhimer, when her daughter and son-in-law worked for RJR's Winston NASCAR program. They got it from Flossie Johnson, Mrs. Junior Johnson.

4 to 6 chicken breasts, boiled in spices

Two 10-3/4-oz cans cream of chicken soup

3 tsp poppy seeds

1 c sour cream

1 to 2 c of onion plus butter

1/2 c grated, mixed mild and sharp cheese (I use Mexican fiesta blend)

1-1/2 to 2 rolls Ritz crackers, crushed

1-1/2 sticks butter, melted (3/4 c)

Boil chicken until tender, seasoned with salt, pepper, thyme and garlic powder. Shred chicken. Mix with onion sautéed in butter. Stir in grated Mexican fiesta cheese. Pour into a 9-by-13-inch pan prepared with cooking spray. Combine soup, sour cream and poppy seeds in a separate bowl. Pour over chicken. Sprinkle cracker crumbs over top, then drizzle with melted butter. Bake 40-60 minutes at 350°F in a preheated oven. *YIELD: 6 to 8 servings.*

LAURIE'S MORAVIAN CHICKEN PIE

Traditional Moravian chicken pie from North Carolina is typically a pastry dream chock full of chicken and gravy, with a subtle hint of nutmeg, and no veggies added. It usually is baked as a two-crust, crimped 9-inch pie in one of our local potters' lovely stoneware pie dishes. It also can be made in a 9-by-13-inch casserole dish. If baking in a casserole dish, do not line the bottom with crust. The pie can be frozen, wrapped in foil, unbaked, then removed from the freezer, loosely tented, and baked. It's the best of all emergency-food gifts.

CHICKEN:

6 to 10 skinless chicken breasts

Large stock pot full of water

1 to 2 tsp thyme

4 to 6 peeled, sliced garlic cloves

1 tsp salt

1/2 tsp black pepper

Boil chicken breasts in pot of water with spices added. Cook for 2 hours. Remove breasts from stock, chop or shred and set aside.

CHICKEN GRAVY:

1 to 1-1/2 stick(s) butter (8 to 12 T)

1/4 scant c plain flour or Wondra flour (not quite 1/4 c)

3/4 c water

1 c finely chopped sweet onion

1 tsp salt

1/8 tsp black pepper

3 shakes of cayenne pepper

Sprinkle of nutmeg

Chicken stock from boiled chicken

4 to 6 oz grated/shredded sharp Cheddar cheese, OPTIONAL

In this instance, I break the cardinal rule of avoiding butter when making a roux. Melt butter in a large sauté pan. Combine flour and water to form a paste, removing all lumps. Add flour paste to melted butter in pan, whisking until it starts to thicken and darken. If too thick, add warm water. ONLY AFTER the flour and butter mixture darkens to a golden brown, start adding chicken stock; stirring with a whisk. In a separate pan, sauté the onions until transparent. Dump into the roux base in larger pan, and continue whisking. Add salt and pepper , continuing to whisk. Add chicken stock, stirring vigorously as it thickens. Continue, adding stock as desired until you have the desired amount of gravy broth— thickened and creamy, but not too thick and not soupy. This takes about 10-15 minutes for a big

batch in a 13-inch skillet. Once thoroughly simmered and blended, add nutmeg and cayenne and whisk some more. When thoroughly mixed and simmered, remove from heat. Fold chicken into the gravy and mix thoroughly. Add more black pepper to taste. If it needs more depth of flavor, stir in cheese until melted. Don't add so much cheese that you can taste it!

THE PIE:

Four 9-inch unbaked pie crusts (I prefer homemade)

If using frozen pie crusts, I suggest allowing them to thaw, then re-roll on lightly floured surface. This brings back original flavor and allows you to use two to cover the two pies. If baking in a casserole dish, it allows you to reconfigure the crust to conform to the dish.

Pour the chicken mixture into pie shell(s) or into a greased 9-by-13-inch cooking dish. Top with crust, crimp the sides, and poke a pattern of knife holes in the center of the crust topping. A decorative embellishment of additional crust may be added to the top.

If baking in pie dishes, place on cookie sheet to catch spillage. Bake in a preheated oven at 350°F for at least an hour, less if oven heats hot. Loosely tent foil over the pie(s) to prevent the top from burning. After 30 minutes, remove the tented foil and return pie to oven for about 30 more minutes, or until it becomes bubbly. Remove and let it rest for 5 to 10 minutes to set up before slicing and serving. *YIELD: Two 9-inch pies, or a 9-by-13-inch pan.*

VARIATION 1: Add English peas and carrots.

VARIATION 2: Instead of pie crust, pour filling onto divided refrigerator biscuits, patted down on dish.

SOUTHERN FRIED CHICKEN

There are as many recipes for Southern Fried Chicken as there are Southerners, and then some. My Aunt Sheila Daltroff Davidson was a master at frying. She always told us to get the cooking oil hot enough before adding the chicken, and then "not mess with it." She also advised us never to crowd the chicken in the pan in order to prevent irregular cooking. Aunt Sheila was adamant that the cook should "disjoint" a whole chicken, and not rely on store-bought chopped chicken.

3 lb whole chicken, disjointed (or chicken breasts, thighs, wings, and/or legs)

1 large bowl of iced water containing 1/4 c table salt

3 to 5 large eggs

2 c to 1 qt milk or buttermilk

1/4 to 1/2 tsp cayenne pepper or hot pepper sauce

1 to 2 tsp salt

1/8 to 1 tsp black pepper (I like a lot of black pepper)

1/2 tsp ground thyme

1 to 2 tsp paprika

1/4 to 1/2 tsp garlic powder

1 to 2 T cornstarch

2 to 4 c all-purpose flour

Shortening or peanut oil (about 1 qt or up to fill line)

Sheila Daltroff, in McGehee, AR, circa 1928

CLEAN IT, BRINE IT, BATHE IT:

Clean chicken, remove skin, and soak overnight or several hours in a large bowl of iced water brined with salt. This clears out any blood vessels and softens the chicken tissue to prevent over-drying during frying. To fry, remove chicken from brine, pat dry, and place in buttermilk bath in fridge for at least 30 minutes, preferably several hours. Prior to frying, beat eggs with cayenne or hot pepper sauce in large bowl.

DREDGE IT:

In a large pan, sift together flour, salt, black pepper, garlic powder, paprika, thyme, and cornstarch. Set up wire rack over shallow pan to hold dredged chicken prior to frying. Set up another shallow pan lined with brown paper bags or wire rack to hold fried chicken. Remove chicken from buttermilk and dip into egg bath. Hold up with tongs to let excess egg drip back into bowl. Dredge in seasoned flour mix. Dip again into egg bath and repeat dredging in flour mixture. Place onto holding rack, not touching, to set up.

FRY IT:

While the chicken is resting, heat shortening or peanut oil. NOTE: Use enough cooking oil to cover chicken pieces when frying if in skillet, or to fill up to appropriate level, if in deep fryer. Use tongs and carefully lower prepared chicken pieces into hot oil, not touching. It will take 2 to 3 batches to cook all the chicken.

SKILLET FRYING: Use tongs and spatula to flip pieces after 8 to 10 minutes. Fry 8 to 10 more minutes.

DEEP FRYER: Chicken will rise to top when done.

For either method of frying, remove chicken from oil to prepared pan when done, and keep in oven set at 275-300°F while cooking remaining chicken. The extra bit of oven time seals in the juices.

To make sure chicken is done, pierce with a fork. Clear juices indicate it's done; reddish juices indicate it needs more cooking.

TIPS FOR GREAT FRIED CHICKEN

Several factors are fundamental to ALL variations of Southern fried chicken:

- Cooking grease/oil that gets hot enough on a high temperature (Do not use butter or corn oil for frying); heat the oil to 365 degrees before adding chicken);

- Cooking in a cast iron skillet or Dutch oven—or deep fryer (my preferred method);

- Soaking the chicken in a saltwater brine, and a buttermilk bath;

- Resting the chicken after dredging and before frying;

- Never over-crowding the chicken in the fryer.

ROAST TURKEY AND CHICKEN

It doesn't take a rocket scientist to properly prep a bird for roasting uncovered in an oven. To prevent over-browning the bird, loosely tent aluminum foil over it (without any part sealing or touching the bird). Or, after the first hour of roasting, soak a cloth with melted butter and drape this over the bird to continue self-basting. NOTE: A bird sealed in foil or a bag in the oven is a bird that's being steamed or stewed, not roasted. Uncovering the bird during the last half hour to brown the top will merely dry out the meat. To ensure a moist, tasty bird, inject broth and spices into the carcass before cooking.

Preheat oven to 450°F.

Remove the giblets and neck from the cavities.

Wash the bird and pat it dry. Place it in roaster.

Coat the bird with melted butter.

Sprinkle poultry seasoning (or ground thyme and sage) evenly all over the bird, including around the legs and wings, and inside the cavity.

Repeat this with salt, pepper, and garlic powder.

Place 2 T of butter inside the cavity.

Add 1 to 2 c of water (less for a smaller bird, and more for a larger bird) to the roaster to form a cushion for the bird, and to absorb the drippings.

Put roaster in the oven and cook for 15-20 minutes. Lower the heat to 350°F and continue cooking, allowing about 20 minutes per pound for an unstuffed bird, and 25-30 minutes per pound for a stuffed bird. Large turkeys should be roasted at a slightly lower temperature for a longer time (around 300-325°F) allowing 13-18 minutes per pound) to prevent over-drying. After the first hour of roasting, baste the bird with its pan drippings about every 15 minutes (or cover with a butter-soaked cloth). If self-basting with butter-soaked cloth, remove the cloth for the last half hour to allow the bird to brown. Length of cooking time depends on size of the bird. Internal temp should be 190°F.

BASIC ROAST TURKEY TIMETABLE Oven set at 325°F:	
6 – 8 lb	3-1/2 to 4 hrs
8 – 12 lb	4 to 4-1/2 hrs
12-16 lb	4-1/2 to 5-1/2 hrs
16-20 lb	5-1/2 to 6-1/2 hrs
20-24 lb	6-1/2 to 7 hrs

Early 1960s, Butch Daltroff holds Tim Thurmond, while Aunt Aline and Great Uncle Gene help themselves to more turkey.

HOLIDAY GIBLET GRAVY

3 T butter

3 T all-purpose white flour

1 c pan drippings from the roasting pan, skimmed of fat

1 c chicken broth or stock

Salt and black pepper, to taste (don't skimp on the pepper)

1 to 1-1/2 c turkey giblets, cut up (chopped pieces of cooked liver and neck)

1 hardboiled egg, chopped, OPTIONAL

Boil the neck and liver in a pan of lightly salted water with some ground thyme. Some cooks prefer to include the gizzard, which "darkens" the flavor. When boiled, cut up liver and pull the meat away from the neck bone, discarding the bones.

Over medium heat, melt the butter in a large saucepan or skillet to the bubbly stage, then sprinkle flour over the butter and stir quickly until blended. Let cook to the crumbly stage, just before burning, and slowly stir in the turkey drippings, stirring or whisking constantly, to blend the flour-butter with the drippings. Let simmer for about a minute, then slowly add more turkey or chicken stock, stirring constantly. Cook over medium heat, stirring constantly, until the gravy has become smooth and thickened. Reduce heat to low, and add salt and pepper to taste. Add the giblets and stir. NOTE: It's sometimes easier to do this part in the roasting pan set onto the stovetop over two flames.

VARIATION: Cook chopped celery and onion until transparent, then whisk into gravy base. Simmer, whisking. Stir in 1 c chopped hardboiled egg, just before serving, if you like egg in your giblet gravy. Keep gravy warm until ready to serve; reheating and stirring gently if needed.

GRANDMOTHER'S TURKEY ROYALE

from Ruby White Thurmond

Granddaddy was a complete teetotaler, so I don't know what Grandmother used as a substitute for the white wine! I'd like to think she slipped it in without Granddaddy's knowledge, but I doubt it.

2 T butter

1/2 lb fresh mushrooms, sliced

1/4 c butter

3 T all-purpose flour

Dash of cayenne pepper

1/2 tsp dry mustard

3/4 c turkey/chicken broth

3/4 c light cream

1/2 c dry white wine

4-oz jar of pimiento, drained and chopped

1 c shredded sharp Cheddar cheese, divided

5 c cooked, sliced or chopped turkey

Melt the 2 T of butter in saucepan; add mushrooms and sauté over medium heat for 10 minutes. In another pan, melt the 1/4-cup of butter and stir in flour, cayenne, and dry mustard; stir until blended. Stir in broth, light cream and wine, using a whisk if desired. Add pimiento and 1/2-cup grated cheese once the other ingredients have simmered. Cook over low heat until the cheese has melted.

Butter a 2-qt casserole and in bottom arrange a layer of sliced, cooked turkey, using about 2-1/2 cups of the meat. Top the turkey layer with half the sautéed mushrooms, and pour half the sauce over the top. Make a second layer of the second half of the turkey, mushrooms and remaining sauce. Top with 1/2-cup shredded cheese. Bake at 300°F for 1 hour. Serve over hot buttered cornbread. *YIELD: 6 to 8 servings.*

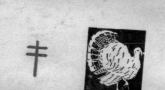

Arkansas Tuberculosis Sanatorium
Thanksgiving 1928
DINNER

Roast Turkey — A-La-San-Roasting
Sea Coast Dressing — Giblet Gravy
Cranberry Sauce
Potatoes Triturate — Bride Peas
Snowflake Salad
Indian Bread — Southern Butter
Ark-San-Milk — Eden Fruits
Jack-O-Lantern Pie

"BETTER THANK YOU"
MY DINNER GUEST *Mrs Herring*

PROGRESS PRINTING CO., BOONEVILLE, ARK.

THANKSGIVING MEMORY

My paternal grandmother, Eula May Stewart Daltroff, contracted tuberculosis and spent years battling the disease. She first went into the Arkansas TB sanatorium when Dad was just past infancy. Unfortunately for her and her family, most of her Thanksgivings were not spent at home between 1927 and her death in 1938. Nevertheless, her journal and photo albums from that time remained upbeat and full of observations about the professionals caring for her, and about her fellow patients.

MEATS, POULTRY, MAIN DISH

FRIED TURKEY

TURKEY FRYING EQUIPMENT:

Special 30- to 40-qt vessel with lid on stand

Basket

Lifting hook

Burner

Propane gas tank

Meat thermometer

Injector (plastic or metal, from the grocery store, home repair store or dollar store)

3 to 5 gallons peanut oil

TURKEY PREPARATION:

8 to 15 pound turkey (10-to-12 lb size is best)

Salt and pepper to taste

Homemade Creole seasoning, Slap Ya Mama, or Tony's or Emeril's Essence, OPTIONAL

Prepare turkey by washing, removing giblets from cavity, and clipping off wing tips and bit of tail to prevent turkey from sticking in the fryer. Pat dry, rub with salt, pepper, and Creole seasoning.

INJECTION MARINADE:

1 c good chicken stock or organic chicken broth

1 tsp garlic powder

1 tsp onion powder

1 tsp homemade Creole seasoning, Slap Ya Mama, or Tony's, or Emeril's Essence

1 T kosher salt

1/4 tsp black pepper

2 T Louisiana Hot Sauce, OPTIONAL

Mix dry spices together in a bowl. Whisk in wet ingredient(s) until spices are dissolved. Fill turkey injector with the liquid. Inject each breast at three different points; inject thighs, legs and the wings. It might be easier to inject the thighs through the interior of the cavity. Place turkey in roaster in fridge to marinate. Massage two to three times over two hours to spread the marinade. Remove turkey from roaster and let excess marinade drain off.

FRY THAT SUCKER:

Gently lower turkey basket into hot oil that has reached 350° to 375°F. Everyone has a different opinion about this temperature. Fry larger turkeys hotter. Allow 3 to 3-1/2 minutes per pound for turkey larger

Wes Russell, Keith Espedron, and Ryan Russell fry a turkey Bayou Style.

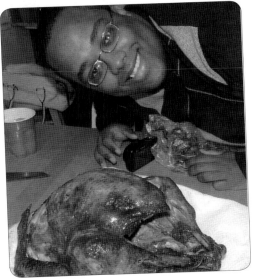

than 12 pounds, allow 2-1/2 minutes per pound for smaller turkey. A 15-pound bird should take about 45 minutes at 375°F, a 12-pound bird should take about 36-40 minutes. If frying a large turkey breast, place it breast-side down in basket; allow as much as 7 to 8 minutes per pound. When ready, carefully raise basket on hook, allow oil to drip off, and test internal temperature. Internal breast temperature should be 165° to 170°F, thigh should be 175° to 180°F. Remove cooked bird from hot oil; drain on paper towels spread over paper bags. Let bird rest 15 to 20 minutes before cutting to serve. Refrigerate leftovers within two hours. I doubt this will be an issue.

TIPS FOR FRYING A TURKEY

The art of frying a turkey is relatively recent in the lexicon of what we Southerners acknowledge as manly man outdoor grilling and cooking. This technique originated in Louisiana, swept the South like Sherman's troops marching through Georgia, and rapidly spread nationwide. Nowadays, some folks as far away as South L.A. and South Bend prefer their turkeys fried, not roasted or stewed. The cook must adhere to a few basic rules in order to be successful.

- Have the proper frying equipment.
- Place the fryer in an open area on grass, not on a wooden deck (which WILL burn, just ask Jeff Triplette), and not concrete (which will stain from the oil).
- Use peanut oil, which heats to a higher temperature without burning or smoking (no peanut allergies allowed).
- Make sure the turkey is the proper size. Fry more than one if needed.
- When lowering turkey basket into the hot oil, turn off burner temporarily to prevent fire from spilled or splattering oil.
- Have containers for proper storage or disposal of used oil.
- Disinfect all areas that have come into contact with raw bird; thoroughly wash hands and turkey-prep utensils.
- Keep fire extinguisher handy just in case.
- After frying, allow oil to cool completely before disposing or storing.
- To store oil for reuse, strain through cheesecloth, and store in cool place or in fridge, or it will turn rancid.

QUICHE

CHEESY SPINACH QUICHE

from Mary Elizabeth Daltroff

9-inch deep-dish pie crust

10-oz pkg frozen spinach

8-oz pkg Swiss cheese slices

2 T all-purpose flour

3 eggs, beaten

1 c whipping cream

1/2 tsp salt

Dash of pepper

Thaw spinach, drain well. Line pie pan with pastry, prick with a fork to keep from puffing, and bake at 425-450°F for 5 minutes. Cut cheese into half-inch-long strips. Toss with the flour. Combine eggs, whipping cream, salt and pepper, beating well. Stir in spinach and cheese, Pour mixture into partly baked pastry. Lower preheated oven to 350°F; bake for 1 hour. Cover crust edges if necessary to prevent over-browning.

MUSHROOM QUICHE

9-inch deep-dish pie crust

1 T butter

1 c shredded Swiss cheese

4 eggs, beaten

1 c whipping cream

3/4 tsp salt

Dash of pepper (white or black)

4 T butter or margarine

1 sweet onion, chopped fine

1/4 c chopped green onion

1/2 lb fresh mushrooms, very thinly sliced

1/4 tsp salt

1/8 tsp black pepper

Line pie pan with pastry, prick with a fork to keep from puffing, and bake at 425-450°F for 5 minutes. Mix the eggs, cream, cheese, salt and pepper with a wire whisk and set aside. In a 10-inch skillet melt the butter over high heat. Add green onion and mushrooms, salt and pepper. Cook until tender, about 5 minutes. Ladle into the cream mixture. Pour into partly baked pastry. Bake for 15 minutes at 425-450°F, then lower oven to 325°F. Bake additional 35 minutes to 1 hour, until knife inserted in center comes out clean.

QUICHE LORRAINE

from Mary Elizabeth Daltroff

9-inch uncooked pie crust

4 strips of bacon

1 onion, thinly sliced

1 c Gruyere or Swiss cheese, cubed

1/4 c Parmesan cheese

4 eggs, lightly beaten

2 c heavy cream, or 1 each of milk and cream

1/4 tsp ground nutmeg

1/2 tsp salt

1/4 tsp white pepper

Preheat oven to 450°F. Line a 9-inch deep dish pie plate with pastry and bake for 5 minutes. Cook bacon until crisp; remove from skillet. Pour off all but 1 T of the bacon grease. Cook onion in the bacon drippings until transparent. Crumble bacon; sprinkle with onion and cheeses over partly-baked pie crust. Combine eggs, cream, nutmeg, salt and pepper. Strain over the onion-cheese mixture. Bake pie for 15 minutes, then reduce temperature of oven to 350°F. Continue baking until a knife inserted 1-inch from pastry edge comes out clean (about 10 more minutes). Serve immediately.

VIDALIA ONION-BACON QUICHE

9-inch unbaked deep-dish pie crust

3 T butter

4 c Vidalia onions, chopped

1/2 tsp salt

1/4 tsp pepper

6 slices bacon, cooked and crumbled

1 c light cream

1 c sour cream

4 eggs, lightly beaten

2 c Swiss cheese, grated

2 T grated Parmesan cheese

Preheat oven to 350°F. Bake the pie crust to point of very light golden color (not completely baked). In a large skillet, sauté the onions in butter until transparent. Add the salt and pepper. In a large bowl, beat the eggs, stir in cream, sour cream and cheese. Add the onions and bacon, and pour into the partially baked pie shell. Bake in preheated oven for 20 minutes, until toothpick comes out clean. Remove from oven and let set for about 2 to 5 minutes before cutting.

SHERRIED CRAB QUICHE

Pastry for a 9-inch deep-dish pie pan

1 c shredded Swiss cheese

4 eggs, beaten

1 c whipping cream

3/4 tsp salt

Dash of pepper (white or black)

3 T butter or margarine

2 T minced green onions

Two 6-oz pkgs of frozen snow crab, thawed, well drained

2 T dry sherry

1/4 tsp salt

1/8 tsp cayenne pepper

Line pie pan with pastry, cover bottom with 1/4 to 1/2 c dried beans or ceramic beans to keep pastry from puffing. Bake at 425-450°F in preheated oven for about 5 minutes. Mix the eggs, cream, cheese, salt and pepper with a wire whisk and set aside.

In a 1-qt sauce pan, melt the 3 T of butter, add the green onion and cook until tender, about 5 minutes. Stir this into the cream mixture, along with the crab meat, sherry, additional salt and cayenne. Remove beans from empty pie crust. Pour mixture into partly baked pastry. Bake for 15 minutes at 425-450°F, then lower preheated oven to 325°F. Bake for 35 minutes to 1 hour until knife inserted in center comes out clean. Cover crust edges if necessary to prevent over-browning.

ABOUT VEAL

Veal is the tender meat from a calf no more than 5 to 6 months old. One generally creates light dishes from veal chops (similar to a lamb chop), veal medallions, or veal cutlets, which are thin slivers of prime meat. The most popular dishes are Veal Parmesan and various versions of Veal Scaloppini. Scaloppini refers to the veal being prepared by pounding it thin, breading it and gently frying it before adding sauce. The sauces range from mushroom sauce to lemon sauce, to capers or a tomato sauce.

VEAL SCALOPPINI PICATTA

2 lb veal cutlets (in our Oxford store they are packaged as veal scaloppini)

Salt and black pepper

1/2 tsp garlic powder

1/4 to 1/2 c plain flour

2 eggs, beaten with a splash of water

Italian seasoned breadcrumbs

3 T olive oil

1/4 c white wine

1/4 c lemon juice

1 to 2 c chicken broth

2 to 3 cloves garlic, minced

1/2 tsp chives, chopped

1 T butter

1 c heavy cream or 2/3 c whole milk +1/3 c crème fraîche

1 T lemon zest

Wondra flour for thickening

2 T fresh parsley, minced

Prepare the cutlets by placing between two sheets of waxed paper and pounding even thinner. Pat dry, sprinkle with salt and pepper. Dredge in flour and shake off excess. Dip into egg, then dredge in seasoned bread crumbs. Heat olive oil in skillet. Drop in the cutlets. Brown on both sides; remove to a warm plate. Use whisk or wooden spoon to scrape pan drippings, adding wine, lemon juice and chicken broth. Stir until color turns, then whisk in garlic, chives, butter and cream, stirring as it blends. Whisk in Wondra if needed. Return cutlets to the sauce, spooning some over meat. Sprinkle in lemon zest; simmer 5 minutes. Plate the cutlets over fettuccine or linguine. Ladle sauce over the cutlets and sprinkle with fresh parsley.

VARIATION: Add 1 c sliced fresh Portobello mushrooms when adding the garlic and chives.

VEAL SCALOPPINI ALLA MARSALLA

2 lb veal cutlets

Salt and black pepper

Plain flour for dredging

1 to 2 eggs, beaten

Homemade bread crumbs, made from Italian bread

3 T butter

1/4 c Marsala wine

2 T concentrated beef base or 2 beef bouillon cubes

Pound the veal between sheets of waxed paper until very thin. Season flour with salt and pepper. Dredge the veal in the seasoned flour. Heat butter in skillet, add veal, and brown on both sides. Add the Marsala and simmer one to two minutes longer on medium high heat. Transfer meat to a warm platter. Add beef base or bouillon to the Marsala sauce in pan, and scrape pan drippings into the liquid. Bring to a boil. Pour sauce over the veal and serve with pasta or toast points.

VEAL KALV OSKAR

from Mary Elizabeth Daltroff

This was one of Mom's more exotic company entrees. SO Sputnik!

Six 1/4-inch-thick veal cutlets, pounded

Salt and pepper

All-purpose flour

4 T butter

2-1/2 T chicken stock

Fresh asparagus tips, steamed but crisp

30 crab legs, steamed and shelled

Butter

Béarnaise Sauce (*see recipe, page 168*)

Rinse and pat dry the veal cutlets before flattening. Season both sides with salt and pepper, then dredge in flour. Sauté in melted butter until completely done. Add chicken stock and bring to a boil, then reduce heat to a simmer. Place 4 asparagus tips and 5 shelled crab legs that have been dipped in melted butter on top of each cutlet. Pour pan juices over, turn off heat, and cover. Serve with Mary Elizabeth's Béarnaise Sauce (*see recipe, page 168*).

VEAL PARMESAN

1-1/2 to 2 lb veal cutlets

Salt and pepper

Plain flour for dredging

2 eggs, beaten

1 c Italian seasoned bread crumbs (I prefer Panko)

1/2 c extra light olive oil

1 medium zucchini, diced

4 cloves garlic, minced

2 c white onion, chopped fine

1/4 c white or red wine

Two 8-oz cans tomato sauce

Small can tomato paste

1/2 tsp ground thyme

1/4 tsp ground oregano

1 T dried basil or 2 T fresh chopped basil

Grated Parmigiano-Reggiano cheese

Preheat oven to 400°F. Pound the cutlets between sheets of wax paper until very thin. Pat dry. Dredge in seasoned flour. Dip in egg, then dredge in seasoned bread crumbs. Set aside to rest. Heat olive oil in skillet. Add vegetables and sauté until onions are transparent. Move veggies to outer edges of pan, and fry the cutlets about 4 minutes each side, until brown. Place cutlets in warm baking dish. Add wine to pan, scraping pan drippings from sides. Combine tomato sauce and paste, gradually add to pan while stirring on medium-high heat until everything is blended. Mix in spices and stir another 5 minutes. Spoon sauce over cutlets in baking dish. Top with grated Parmigiano-Reggiano cheese. Bake about 10 minutes to melt the cheese.

VARIATION: Boil pasta of choice. Spoon sauce over pasta, place cutlets over pasta and ladle a bit of sauce over the cutlets. Top with grated cheese.

SHORTCUT VERSION: Prepare cutlets as stated above. Instead of homemade sauce, use prepared Marinara Sauce and slices of Mozzarella cheese.

IT'S TABLE ETIQUETTE, PRECIOUS

Gimme Some Sugar, Darlin' was created to serve as a one-stop primer for my children, their many cousins, and other readers who might never bother to consult encyclopedic cookbooks.

This section is dedicated to all of you who never pledged Greek in school, never attended the Sears Charm School, Junior Cotillion, or Miss Manners' classes, and whose grandparents never schooled you in proper table etiquette when your parents weren't around. Good table manners are essential in business, or if you wish to be invited into the Junior League, or if you hope to be invited BACK to your Rotary, DAR or Benevolent Society meetings. For further instructions, my darlings, refer to Amy Vanderbilt's or Emily Post's etiquette books.

INDIVIDUAL COVERS (SETTINGS)

Individual place settings include plates, glasses, cutlery, and napkin, positioned one inch from the table edge and about 25 inches between plates.

TABLECLOTH VS. PLACE MAT

Breakfast, luncheon, or informal supper do not require a tablecloth. Place mats will do. Use trivets and place mats under hot dishes. A formal seated dinner always requires a tablecloth covering the table. If the table is wood, one should use table pads underneath the cloth to protect the finish.

GLASSES

The water glass is positioned directly above the knife, with the iced tea glass to the right, and wine glass on the outside. The water glass should only be filled 1/2 to no more than 3/4 full. A person may decline to be served wine by placing one's hand over the wine glass as the server approaches. The server removes the wine glass. Glasses are filled from the right, and should never be lifted by the server when pouring.

When a guest in someone's home, NEVER NEVER NEVER put your glass on a surface without a napkin or coaster underneath. The host neither expects nor wants to gain water rings on the furniture from your thoughtlessness.

PLATE PLACEMENTS

The bread and butter plate is positioned directly above the forks, with spreader straight across the top of the plate, handle to the right. Very formal dinners exclude the spreader. When time to serve coffee, the empty coffee cup and saucer are positioned to the right of the plate, and coffee spoon placed on the saucer away from the diner, parallel to the cup handle, which is positioned to the right on the saucer.

A decorative charger plate may be placed at the individual seats before the meal. The charger remains in place until the first hot course is served on a dining plate. It is permissible to place onto the charger the plate or bowl containing the fruit or seafood appetizer, or the cup or bowl containing bouillon or soup.

SILVER PLACEMENT

Silver is placed around the central plate, which may be positioned on a charger. The silver is positioned in the order of intended use, outermost used first, to innermost used last. Fork tines are turned up. Knife blades always point toward the plate. Spoon bowls are turned up. To the left are the fish or salad fork and dining fork. To the right are the dining and fish knife with the spoons outside the knives, starting with the soup spoon, iced tea spoon, coffee spoon, and with the seafood or cocktail fork or spoon angled at the far right. The order inward of the forks, knives and spoons depends on the order of service, whether salad, fish or soup are served before or after the entree.

Silver for the dessert course is not put on the table with the other silver at a formal dinner. Additional silver is brought in with the dessert and coffee, either on the plate, or placed at the right of the dessert plate.

At informal luncheons or dinners, the dessert silverware is positioned above the place plate, parallel, with the fork facing right, tines up, and spoon or knife facing left.

When finished with the meal, position the knife and fork centered on the place plate, facing inward from the right side, knife above (to the right) of the fork.

NAPKINS

When the first course is on the place plate during seating, the napkin is placed to the left of the forks, with fold at the top, or hemmed edges parallel with the forks and table edge. At formal dinners, the napkins may be placed on the service plate or charger. Informal service allows for the napkin to be folded decoratively in a water glass.

FINGER BOWLS

I actually have Auntie Doc's crystal finger bowls. They make great ice cream dessert bowls (the confession of which forever eliminates me from Southern Belle-hood). If attempting a very formal dinner, with servants, the finger bowls are brought in before dessert. They are served to the diners on a plate containing a linen doily and the dessert silver. The diner should remove the doily to the left of the place setting, place the bowl on the doily, and the dessert silver to the right. Generally, one merely dips the fingers of one hand and then the other in the bowl, then quietly pats dry on the napkin. The finger bowls should be three-fourths filled with tepid water and contain a thin slice of lemon or flower petals. The finger bowls and doilies should be removed from the table before dessert is served.

SERVING AND SEATING TIPS

Use your serving table or sideboard to hold the water and iced tea pitcher, the wine cooler, all the silver for serving, and all extras which may be needed during the meal.

The host sits at the head of the table, and the hostess opposite the host. The guest of honor, if a man, is seated to the right of the hostess. If a woman, the guest of honor is seated to the right of the host. If being served by servant helpers, the lady guest of honor should be served first and service continues toward the right. The next course should be served toward the left, so that no side is always served last. The server should serve from the left and remove from the right of the individual. However, the server should not reach across the dinner plate; this means pouring from the right, and removing glasses from the right.

A formal dinner requires two servers, one from the hostess to the right, the other from the host to the right. Plates are usually removed from the right, and placed or passed from the left. When seated at a dinner, luncheon or supper with no servant, the host starts service by carving and passing plates counterclockwise, to the right.

TABLE DECORATIONS AND CENTERPIECES

Table decorations should never obstruct the diners' view. They either need to be low and sweeping or tall enough in clear containers that diners can see around and through the arrangements. In the modern world, the host/hostess can be creative about decorations. For very formal occasions, two candelabra or four candlesticks are placed at each side of a floral centerpiece. Compote dishes containing nuts and/or mints may be placed at the ends of the table. No candles are used for a luncheon.

BUFFET SERVICE

When serving a large crowd buffet-style, it is convenient to have the plates, napkins and cutlery at one end, with the food laid out in the order in which it should be served. Only offer the cutlery pieces that will be needed during the buffet meal. I recommend keeping the dessert cutlery with the desserts on a separate table. Try to avoid buffet food requiring knives. Serve the dessert and coffee from a separate table or sideboard. Buffet table decorations can be tall and dramatic.

CLEARING THE TABLE

At a seated meal, remove all plates and dishes containing food first, then platters, vegetable dishes and smaller serving dishes.

Do not remove cutlery from the dishes at the table. Also do not stack dishes at the table.

Before serving dessert, remove all relishes and condiments such as salt and pepper. At a formal meal with servants, the servants should "crumb" the table before dessert, by sweeping the crumbs onto a plate or butler's tray with a folded napkin.

STOCKING A SOUTHERN KITCHEN

My children, their cousins, and their friends have asked what tools and food stuffs they should have in a well stocked kitchen. In my day, the pressure cooker and the blender were the must-have kitchen tools. Nowadays, it's all about the food processor and the slow cooker.

KITCHEN TOOLS:

6-qt bowl

Biscuit cutter (Mom used an old potted meat can)

Bottle opener

Box grater

Bowl scraper (soft spatula)

Candy thermometer

Colander

Commercial spoon with holes

Cutting board

Dough or pastry scraper

Garlic press

Hand grater

Juicer (manual version is fine)

Ladle

Manual can opener

Meat fork

Meat thermometer

Melon baller

Microwavable 2-cup Pyrex measurer

Nut cracker and pick

Pastry blade

Pastry cloth (for rolling out dough)

Pepper mill

Ricer/masher

Rolling pin

Set of good knives, including the following:

·   boning knife

·   bread knife

·   carver

- chef's chopper
- meat cleaver
- paring knife

Set of measuring cups

Set of measuring spoons

Set of nested mixing bowls (PLUS over-size bowl**)**

Sifter (sieve for dry ingredients)

Spatula (also called a flipper)

Spice grinder and/or pestle and mortar

Strainer (sieve for wet ingredients)

Vegetable peeler

Whisks (one large, one small)

Wine opener

Wooden spoons, various sizes

POTS AND PANS:

Omelet pan

Frying pan

Cast iron skillet

Sauce pot

1-qt pot w/ lid

2-qt pot w/ lid

3-qt pot w/ lid, double boiler and steamer inserts

8-qt stock pot with lid

Dutch oven

Turkey roaster

9-by-13-inch baking pan

8-by-8-inch baking pan

7-by-11-inch baking pan

8.5-by-4.5-by-2.5-inch Pyrex baking dish w/cover

Loaf pan (2 preferred)

Two 9-inch or 8-inch cake pans

Muffin/cupcake pan

Springform pan

9-inch pie plate (freezable)

SUPPLEMENTAL APPLIANCES:

Blender

Food processor (at least a small one)

Microwave

Mixer (at least a good hand mixer)

Rice cooker

Slow cooker

PANTRY ESSENTIALS:

Cooking spray such as Pam

Shortening

Cooking oil (vegetable, olive, peanut)

Flour (all-purpose and self-rising)

Corn meal (plain and self-rising)

Packaged yeast (watch out for expiration date)

Rice (long grain, basmati, arborio, brown)

Rolled oats

Baking powder (watch out for expiration date)

Baking soda

Cream of tartar

Corn starch

Cocoa powder

Vanilla extract

Corn syrup (both light and dark)

Distilled white vinegar

Cider vinegar

Rice wine vinegar

Balsamic vinegar

Sugar and sugar-like sweeteners (white granulated, light brown, dark brown, confectioners sugar; Splenda, Truvia)

Honey

Molasses

Packaged crumbled bacon or bacon substitute

Raisins and dried cranberries

Walnuts and pecans

Diced pimientos

SPICES:

Allspice

Basil

Black, Cayenne and White pepper

Chili powder

Dry ground mustard
Garlic powder
Ground cinnamon
Ground cloves
Ground cumin
Ground ginger
Ground nutmeg
Ground thyme
Marjoram
Onion powder
Oregano
Paprika
Red pepper flakes
Rosemary
Sage
Salt (table, Kosher, and sea)
Turmeric

CONDIMENTS:

Hot pepper sauce
Ketchup
Lemon juice
Mayonnaise
Mustard (regular, Dijon, Creole-style)
Pickles and sweet pickle relish
Soy sauce
Stuffed olives
Worcestershire sauce

CANNED AND PACKAGED GOODS:

Canned or dried beans, including:
· Blackeyed peas
· Cannellini white beans
· Kidney beans or red beans
· Pintos
· Pork and beans
Canned chicken
Canned pineapple (crushed, chunk, sliced)
Canned salmon

Canned salsa
Canned soups (low sodium, no MSG):
· beef broth
· chicken broth
· cream of celery
· cream of chicken
· cream of mushroom
· tomato
Canned tomatoes (one each):
· crushed
· paste
· sauce
· whole
Canned tuna
Evaporated milk
Powdered milk
Sweetened condensed milk

FROZEN AND/OR REFRIGERATED INGREDIENTS:

Broccoli
Butter or margarine
Celery and carrots
Cheese (Cheddar, fiesta-blend, processed, Parmesan)
Chicken breasts
Cut corn
Dinner rolls or biscuits
Garlic
Green peas
Ground turkey
Ground beef
Milk
Onions
Potatoes
Spinach

COOKING GLOSSARY

Add: To add the ingredient into the mix; does not imply mixing method.

Bake: To cook in an oven.

Baste: To spoon or brush liquid over cooking food to retain moisture and enhance flavor while cooking.

Beat: To stir or mix until smooth, using a wire whisk, spoon, hand beater or mixer.

Blanch: To immerse in boiling water briefly for the purpose of loosening the skin or to pre-cook to set color and flavor, and deactivate enzymes prior to freezing or drying.

Blend: To thoroughly combine two or more ingredients, usually in a blender or food processor.

Boil: To cook at 212°F or higher.

Braise: To slowly cook in a covered pan or baking dish in a small amount of liquid. Interchangeable with "simmer, covered."

Brown: To cook in fat until browned on all sides.

Caramelize: To cook until sugar content is melted and liquid begins to bubble.

Chill: To refrigerate until cold, or let stand in ice or ice water until cold.

Coat: To dip or cover with a substance such as flour, until surface of food is covered all over.

Cream: To mix with spoon or mixer until smooth and soft and lighter in color.

Deglaze: To work meat drippings off the bottom and sides of a pan by adding boiling liquid and stirring, usually with a slotted spoon.

Dice: To cut into small pieces.

Dollop: A small portion, spooned over food.

Dredge: To coat or cover a food with flour, sugar or other coating by patting or tossing the food in the coating substance.

Fold: To combine ingredients with a spatula or spoon by cutting vertically downward with one stroke, then sliding across the bottom and upward to turn the mixture over.

Frothy: Whisked or beaten until the ingredients expand with air bubbles.

Glaze: To coat with a glossy mixture such as sauce to impart a sheen and outer layer of flavoring.

Level and rounded: Measurement is flat in the cup or spoon (level), or heaped above the rim (rounded).

Lukewarm: Temperature is approximately 95°F; feels neither hot nor cold against the inside of the wrist.

Marinate: To soak in a marinade, which usually is a liquid mixture based on vinegar or wine seasoned with spices and herbs.

Mix: To combine ingredients evenly with a mixer.

Parboil: To boil until partially cooked.

Reduce: To decrease quantity by rapidly boiling uncovered, to evaporate moisture and concentrate the liquid flavor.

Reserve: To hold out for later use in recipe.

Rolling boil: To fully boil to the point where bubbles form rapidly and break the surface of the liquid all over, not just around the edges.

Sauté: To cook in a small amount of fat or oil.

Scald: To heat to just below the boiling point, when tiny bubbles form at the edge of the liquid. Scalding also can be accomplished by pouring boiling liquid over a food.

Scant: An amount not quite up to the level measure.

Score: To cut shallow gashes before cooking.

Sear: To brown over high heat to seal in the juices.

Shell: To remove the outer covering of nuts, peas, beans, and eggs.

Shred: To grate, using the large hole on a grater.

Shuck: To remove shells or husks of corn.

Simmer: To cook slowly, below boiling, over low heat.

Skim: To remove fat or foam from the surface.

Steep: To let food stand in liquid that was poured when boiling in order to extract flavor.

Stir: To combine with a circular or figure-eight motion until all components of a mixture are uniform.

Tent: To cover loosely with a piece of aluminum foil to prevent over-browning.

Toss: To mix lightly with a lifting motion, which is why salad is tossed with two implements.

Water bath (bain-marie): The food container is set either into a larger pan of water, or on a rack above a tray or pan of water. Purpose is to keep the bottom of the food from scorching while cooking, and achieve uniform heating of dense ingredients (such as flan or cheesecake).

Wet and dry: Wet ingredients contain liquid, dry ingredients do not contain liquid.

Whisk: To beat with a wire whisk until smooth.

Zest: Citrus peel grated on small hole of a grater.

PRESERVING, CANNING AND FREEZING

PRESERVING AND CANNING

The jelly, preserves, relish and pickle recipes contained in this cookbook are all heirloom recipes. I have updated the processing instructions to reflect modern opinions about safety.

What I know about home canning could fit into Tom Thumb's thimble. But I have learned that ALL vegetables, meats, soups, stews, jellies, jams, pickles, preserves and relishes should be processed in a hot water canning bath to deactivate enzymes, bacteria, yeasts and other ingredients that can grow into contaminants over time.

In other words, forego the paraffin and forget about the simple hot sealing of the jars. If in doubt about what you've done, freeze or refrigerate it. Preserves and jams freeze nicely. Pickles and relishes should go in the fridge, not the freezer.

After sealing the jars, all low-acid foods (pH higher than 4.6) such as veggies, meats, soups and stews must be heat processed in a pressure canner at a temperature of about 240ºF for a specified period of time. All high-acid foods (pH at or lower than 4.6) such as fruit jams, preserves and jellies, pickles and relishes containing vinegar, should be processed in a boiling water canning bath at 212ºF in a large covered pot or special canner for a specified time. NEVER DOUBLE A CANNING RECIPE.

NEVER process with the following:
- Microwave
- Oven
- Dishwasher

STEP 1.

Thoroughly wash the home-canning jars, new SNAP lids, and screw bands in soap and hot water. Boil the jars and bands (but not the lids) for 5-10 minutes, then drain, upside down on a clean canning rack. Keep lids in clean hot water that has cooled down from boiling.

STEP 2.

Prepare recipe according to recipe directions. Funnel recipe into the hot jars, leaving about 1/8 inch of space from top of rim. Shake or bump lightly on counter to "burp" out the air bubbles. Wipe off rim and screw threads with clean damp cloth to remove all stickiness. Using tongs, remove lid from hot water, shake and pat dry with clean cloth, then center on jar. Loosely screw on lid band. Press down on center of lid to secure it.

STEP 3.

Place jars upright in boiling water canner or pressure cooker, with at least 1-2 inches of water above the jar tops. Boil 5-10 minutes according to instructions. Remove jars with canning tongs. Keeping jars upright, dry off, then let sit undisturbed for 24 hours. DO NOT RE-TIGHTEN LIDS. After 24 hours, check seals. Jars are properly sealed if lids don't pop when pressed. Reprocess unsealed jars, or refrigerate and use immediately.

For expert advice, read **Bernadin Guide to Home Preserving**, or contact the following:
- www.homecanning.com (Ball Jar site)
- www.freshpreserving.com
- www.pickyourown.org
- Your local home extension service

FREEZING FRUITS AND VEGETABLES

CORN: Use vegetable brush, toothbrush, terry-cloth towel, or paper towel to remove silk from shucked corn as soon as picked. Brush in a downward motion. Wash. Bring large stock pot of water to a boil and drop in the corn. Blanch the corn for 3 minutes (timed), then remove and immediately submerge in large pan of ice water for 3 minutes to stop the cooking process. Remove from ice water, pat dry, cool completely, then roll each ear in Saran wrap. Immediately place into freezer. Freezer corn usually will last in a good freezer through the winter.

PEACHES: Peel and slice into a large glass or metal bowl. Sprinkle with Fruit Fresh and sugar. Toss to coat all the slices. Let sit for a few minutes, then use slotted spoon to spoon into pint bags or freezer pint jars. Freeze immediately. Pint bags can be double bagged in gallon bags and stored in coldest part of freezer. Will last for months.

STRAWBERRIES: Cap and rinse, then pat dry. For sliced strawberries, slice into a bowl and sprinkle with sugar. Toss to coat. Spoon into pint freezer bags or freezer jars. For whole strawberries, place onto a wax paper-covered cookie sheet and put into freezer until frozen. Remove long enough to put frozen berries into freezer bags. Return to freezer.

BLACKBERRIES, BLUEBERRIES, RASPBERRIES: Best frozen on wax paper-lined cookie sheets, then placed in freezer bags for long-term freezing.

HOT PEPPERS: I confess, I have been known to take a freezer bag out to the garden and pick jalapeño peppers, toss them into the bag, and then walk the bag straight to the freezer. I have kept some jalapeños and Tabasco peppers for over a year in the freezer.

GREEN or RED BELL PEPPERS: When fresh, or even when they are about to start getting soft, go ahead and dice them, put into freezer bags, and freeze until needed for soups, stews or gumbos.

QUANTITIES FOR 100 PEOPLE

found this list in some of Grandmother's notes. It might prove useful the next time you're in charge of the food for a church Lenten luncheon, a wake, a tailgate extravaganza, a family reunion, a Presidential debate, or an inaugural picnic!

Food Item	Quantity
Coffee	3 pounds
Cream	3 quarts
Iced tea	8 gallons + 16 cups sugar
Fruit cocktail	2-1/2 gallons
Soup	5 gallons
Chili, stew, gumbo	9 gallons
Main dish casseroles	10-12 each, 9x13-inch pans
Ham	40 pounds
Beef	40 pounds
Roast pork	40 pounds
Hamburger	30 to 36 pounds
Fried chicken	75 pounds
Potatoes	35 pounds
Scalloped potatoes	5 gallons
Vegetables	4 No.10 cans (26 pounds)
Baked beans	5 gallons
Cabbage for slaw	20 pounds
Carrots	33 pounds
Bread	10 loaves or 9 dozen rolls
Butter	3 pounds
Potato salad	12 quarts
Congealed salad	17 small packages of gelatin
Vegetable salad	20 quarts
Salad dressing	2-1/2 to 3 quarts
Heads of lettuce for tossed salad	20 heads
Pies	18 pies
Cakes	8 cakes
Ice cream	4 gallons
Cheese	3 pounds
Olives	1-3/4 pounds
Pickles	2 quarts
Assorted nuts	3 pounds

KITCHEN PREP HINTS

BACON:

Low sodium bacon will not keep as long as regular bacon. To store a partial package of bacon, roll it into a tube lengthwise and secure with a rubber band. It stores better and stays fresh longer.

Prevent bacon from over-curling when skillet frying by dipping it in cold water before putting it into the frying pan.

If you don't have a microwave for thawing frozen bacon, heat your metal spatula in boiling water or the stovetop flame and then run it under the bacon strip desired.

BEANS:

Cook pintos or other gas-producing beans with a potato. Remove the potato when cooked and throw it away. It removes much of the gas-producing ingredients.

To prevent pot from boiling over, place a wooden spoon across the top.

Add salt near the end of cooking. If added before half way finished, the salt will cause the beans to cook up tough.

EGGS:

Fresh eggs' shells are rough and chalky; old egg shells are smooth and shiny. The fresher the egg, the more difficult it is to peel when boiled. Brown eggs have thinner shells than white eggs; otherwise, there is no major difference in the eggs.

To test eggs for freshness, place in a bowl of cold water. If eggs float, do not use them.

Allow eggs to come to room temperature before beating them into bakery recipes. They'll fluff better.

To boil eggs, put the eggs into a pan and add cold water to cover. Add a bit of vinegar to the water to prevent the egg whites from running and to aid in peeling when done. Bring pan to a boil for about 1 (soft-boiled) to 3 minutes (hard-boiled). Turn off the heat and cover. Let sit for 2 minutes.

Egg shells are more easily peeled from hard-boiled eggs if the eggs are quickly rinsed in cold water after boiling.

For fluffier omelets or microwave-scrambled eggs, whisk in water instead of milk.

FREEZING LEFTOVERS:

MEATS

Leftover pot roast or pork tenderloin may be frozen, but refrigerate first and remove fat, then wrap tightly in foil and plastic freezer bags, To thaw and reheat, thaw overnight in the fridge, and add additional stock liquid to pan, covering loosely with foil when baking in the oven.

SOUPS AND STOCK

Stocks should be simmered until they become concentrated in volume. Refrigerate overnight to remove fat and grease, then freeze. May be frozen in ice cube trays to provide equivalent of "cubes" of broth flavor.

Soups and other items having a milk base do not freeze well because the milk is likely to curdle during the freezing and thawing process. If you know you intend to freeze a milk-based liquid, freeze it at the stage just before adding the milk or cream, then when you thaw it, you can continue cooking by adding the milk.

Vegetable soup freezes well as long as no potatoes are in the soup. Potatoes do not freeze well. Chowders in general do not freeze well: they contain both potatoes and milk products.

FRYING:

To prevent splatter when frying in an 8- or 9-inch skillet, use a turned-over metal colander as a splatter guard.

Always preheat the pan or pot before adding the grease, butter or oil. Peanut oil can go hotter than shortening, and butter will burn at a fairly low temperature.

A little salt sprinkled into the frying pan will prevent or reduce spattering.

Vinegar brought to a boil in a new frying pan or sauté pan will prevent foods from sticking.

GRAVIES:

Add a pinch of salt with plain flour before mixing with water to form a thin paste that is stirred into the hot broth or grease with a whisk. The pinch of salt prevents lumpiness.

A different way of browning the flour for gravy is to put it in a custard cup beside meat roasting in the oven. Once the meat is done, the flour will be properly browned, and can be added to stock or oil to form the basis of the gravy.

A very small pinch of baking soda added to gravy will eliminate grease.

Pale gravy may be darkened by adding a bit of instant coffee straight from the jar. No coffee taste remains.

GREASE AND FAT REMOVAL FROM A DISH:

Drop a lettuce leaf into a pot of homemade soup to absorb excess grease from the top.

Ice cubes will cause fat in a pot to cling to the cubes. Remove before the cubes melt.

Dish can be refrigerated overnight with a covering of waxed paper. After overnight chilling, the waxed paper can be removed and the congealed grease will come off with the paper.

MAYONNAISE:

Never attempt to make mayo on a very humid or rainy day. The ingredients won't emulsify properly.

MERINGUE:

Never attempt to make meringue (or divinity) on a very humid or rainy day.

For never-fail, never-weep meringue, add 1 tsp of cornstarch to the sugar before beating it into the egg whites.

Always "seal" the edges of the pie crust with the edge of the meringue before baking, to prevent separation of meringue from the edges.

Once baked, cut meringue cleanly using a knife coated in butter.

To store meringue pie covered in the fridge, first grease the waxed paper or plastic wrap with margarine to prevent sticking.

MILK:

Thaw frozen fish in milk to eliminate the frozen taste.

Small cartons of milk can be frozen and then thawed in the refrigerator.

Whole milk can be converted into buttermilk by stirring 1 T of white vinegar into each cup of whole milk. Allow to sit for at least 10 minutes to clabber the milk.

SPICE STORAGE:

Store spices in a cool, dry space, away from any windows. Sunlight, heat and moisture will damage or ruin the spices.

Throw out herb leaf spices every 12 months because they lose their flavor.

Store red spices in the fridge to prevent weevils. This includes paprika, cayenne, red pepper, chili powder.

STARCHES AND COOKING OILS:

Adding a few drops of lemon juice to simmering rice will keep the grains separate.

Adding a few teaspoons of oil to the water will prevent noodles from boiling over.

It's also helpful to pre-rub the insides of the cooking pot with vegetable oil to prevent noodles, rice, or fresh peas and beans from boiling over.

Oil your measuring cup before measuring honey or syrup so all of the sweet will end up in the recipe and not inside the cup.

SUGAR:

If your brown sugar has become brick hard, grate it with a cheese grater, or place the sugar brick in a plastic bag with a slice of soft bread. It will soften within 2 to 3 hours.

Lumpy white sugar will lose its lumps if you place the sugar bag in the refrigerator for 24 hours.

WHIPPED CREAM:

Always pre-chill the mixing bowl in the fridge or freezer, and take the cream out of the fridge right before mixing it. The cream will mix faster and fluffier.

If you must whip the cream well ahead of time, add 1/4 tsp of unflavored gelatin per cup of cream to prevent it from separating and becoming soupy.

VEGETABLE AND FRUIT TIPS

COCONUTS:

To remove coconut milk from the coconut, pierce the two eyes with an ice pick and work the pick until one hole is big enough to allow the coconut juice to drain out when upended over a measuring cup.

One method for removing the coconut meat from the shell is to place the drained coconut in a pan and heat at 325-350ºF in the oven for 15-20 minutes or until you hear the shell crack. Time varies according to size of coconut.

Another way to remove coconut from the shell: Before cracking open a coconut, firmly tap the shell all over with a hammer. Don't hammer too hard. After a few minutes of firmly tapping around all areas, the sound will change from a tap to a thud, indicating the coconut meat has broken loose from its lining. This will make it much easier to remove the meat.

To flake fresh coconut, break coconut meat into smaller pieces once removed from shell, and freeze overnight. The next day, drop the coconut, piece by piece, into a whirling blender. Empty blender as necessary when blades become covered with finely flaked coconut. Keep repeating process until all the coconut has been flaked.

CORN:

Corn silk can be removed more easily from fresh corn by brushing downward with a dampened paper towel or terry cloth.

The best way to cut corn off the cob is to notch the corn cob into the center of a bundt cake pan and then cut. The corn is held firm and the kernels fall into the pan.

LEMONS AND LIMES:

You can extract more juice from a lemon or lime if you bring it to room temperature, or even warm it for a few minutes in a low-heat oven, then roll the lemon or lime under your palm on the counter before cutting. Juice of one average sized lemon equals about 1/4 cup. Juice of one average sized orange equals about 1/3 cup.

Use lemon juice, orange juice, or Fruit Fresh mixed in with cut peaches, apples, pears and/or bananas to retard darkening caused by oxidation.

LETTUCE:

Hit the core of a head of lettuce against the counter, which will break the core loose from the leaves for easy removal without using a knife.

MELONS:

Cantaloupe and watermelon can be frozen in scooped balls when mixed with sugar and lemon juice.

NUTS:

For easier removal of nuts from shells, such as pecans or walnuts, drop into boiling water and blanch.

ONIONS:

Cut the root end off an onion last and you'll shed fewer tears. If the onion has spent a few minutes in the freezer first, there will be virtually no tears upon chopping.

Raw onion and raw bell pepper can be frozen if chopped and tightly wrapped in plastic wrap then inserted into freezer-grade baggies.

PEELING:

For peeling quantities of tomatoes, pears or peaches, blanch in boiling water briefly, and skin will peel away.

PEPPERS:

Raw jalapeño and Tabasco peppers can be picked in the garden and stuck right into a freezer bag and frozen for later cooking use.

POTATOES:

Boil potatoes in their skins and then peel away the skins. You save more potato this way.

A leftover baked potato can be rebaked if you dip it in water and bake it again in a 350°F oven for 20 minutes. But it's better to convert it to a "twice-baked potato" by cutting in half, mashing the pulp with butter, cream, salt and pepper, filling the two halves of skin with mashed potato, and topping with cheese. These may be frozen for future use, or baked immediately.

RIPENING FRUITS AND VEGGIES:

Ripen green fruits by placing in a perforated plastic bag or one of the new special ripening bags. The holes allow air movement, yet retain the odorless gas which fruits produce to promote ripening.

To hasten ripening of tomatoes or avocados, place them in a closed brown paper bag for a few days. This works with not-yet-ripe tomatoes saved just before the autumn frost.

SALT AND SWEET:

For over-salted soup or vegetables, add a cut raw potato and discard once the dish has finished cooking. The potato absorbs the salt.

One tsp of cider vinegar plus 1 tsp of sugar added to an over-salted dish will balance the saltiness.

Add salt or 1 tsp of cider vinegar to balance over-sweetened vegetables or meats.

Put raw rice in the salt shaker to prevent clumping in humid weather.

PERK UP SOGGY VEGGIES:

Wilted or blemished fresh vegetables should be picked over to remove the brown edges, then sprinkled with cool water, wrapped in a paper towel, and refrigerated for one to two hours.

Soggy lettuce can be perked up by adding lemon juice to a bowl of cold water and soaking the lettuce in this liquid for an hour in the fridge. Lettuce then should be removed from the lemon water and patted dry, then wrapped in paper towels.

Keep lettuce and celery longer by storing them in paper bags instead of plastic wrap. I always wrap lettuce in paper towels and store in the fridge in a salad crisper. I also clean and trim celery and store in fridge in a jar of water until ready to use.

OVEN CHART AND CAN SIZES

GENERAL OVEN CHART

Very slow oven	250-300° F
Slow oven	300° to 325° F
Moderate oven	325° to 375° F
Medium hot oven	375° to 400° F
Hot oven	400° to 450° F
Very hot oven	450° to 500° F

CAN SIZES AND CONTENTS

Size	Average Contents
8 oz	1 cup
Picnic	1-1/4 cups
No. 300	1-3/4 cups
No. 1 tall	2 cups
No. 303	2 cups
No. 2	2-1/2 cups
No. 2-1/2	3-1/2 cups
No. 3	4 cups
No. 10	12 to 13 cups

VOLUME CONVERSIONS

You know:	Multiply by:	To get:
Milliliters	0.2	Teaspoons
Milliliters	0.07	Tablespoons
Milliliters	0.03	Fluid ounce
Liters	4.23	Cups
Liters	2.1	Pints
Liters	1.06	Quarts
Liters	0.26	Gallons
Teaspoons	5	Milliliters
Tablespoons	15	Milliliters
Fluid ounces	30	Milliliters
Cups	0.24	Liters
Pints	0.47	Liters
Quarts	0.95	Liters
Gallons	3.8	Liters
Dry ounces	28.35	Grams
Pounds	0.45	Kilograms

LIQUID SUGAR SUBSTITUTIONS

One must reduce the amount of liquid called for in a recipe when using these liquid substitutes for granulated sugar. Fruit juice is not recommended as a substitute because of the enzymatic chemical reactions caused by the fruit acids. Candies and baked goods have precise chemistry; the cook may have to experiment when using agave, honey, or maple syrup in traditional candy and baking recipes.

LIQUID SWEETENER SUBSTITUTIONS FOR ONE CUP OF WHITE GRANULATED SUGAR

Ingredient	Liquid Sweetener Amount	Reduce this Amount of Liquid in Recipe
Strained honey	3/4 cup	Reduce 3-1/3 T liquid for each 1 c honey
Molasses	1-1/2 cups	Reduce 1/4 cup liquid for every 1 c molasses
Sorghum	1-1/2 cups	Reduce 1/4 cup liquid for every 1 c sorghum
Corn syrup	2 cups	Reduce 1/4 cup liquid for every 1 c corn syrup
Maple syrup	1-1/2 cups	Reduce 1/4 cup liquid for every 1 c maple syrup
Agave nectar*	2/3 cup	Reduce 1/4 to 1/3 cup liquid for every 2/3 c of agave nectar

Agave nectar will not crystallize (same as corn syrup). It also browns baked items more quickly, so the oven temperature should be reduced by 25˚F, and baking time increased.

MEASUREMENTS AND CONVERSIONS

This amount:	EQUALS	This amount:
Baking powder, 1 cup		5-1/2 ounces
8-10 egg whites		1 cup
12-14 egg yolks		1 cup
4 cups sifted plain flour		1 pound
4-1/2 cups cake flour		1 pound
3-1/2 cups unsifted whole wheat flour		1 pound
2 cups white sugar		1 pound
1 jigger		1-1/2 fluid oz (3 Tablespoons)
1 large jigger		2 fluid ounces
5/8 cup		1/2 cup + 2 Tablespoons
7/8 cup		3/4 cup + 2 Tablespoons
Smidgen		1/32 tsp, or 1-1/2 drops
Pinch		1/16 tsp, or 3 drops, or 2 smidgens
1 Dash		6 fluid drops, or 1/3 tsp, or 2 pinches
1 tsp		1/8 ounce
3 teaspoons		1 Tablespoon
4 Tablespoons		1/4 cup
5-1/3 Tablespoons		1/3 cup
8 Tablespoons		1/2 cup
10-2/3 Tablespoons		2/3 cup
12 Tablespoons		3/4 cup
16 Tablespoons		1 cup
12 cups		1 gill
2 cups		1 pint
4 cups		1 quart
4 quarts		1 gallon
8 quarts		1 peck
4 pecks		1 bushel
Level measures		**Equivalent**
16 ounces		1 pound dry
32 ounces		1 quart dry
8 ounces liquid		1 cup
1 ounce liquid		2 Tablespoons
4 ounces liquid		1 glass or 1 wineglass
1 split		6 ounces

(for additional information, see www.accuracyproject.org/measurements.html)

MEAT ROASTING GUIDE

Cut of Meat	Weight in pounds	Approx. Time at 325°F	Internal Temperature
BEEF			
Standing Rib Roast *(10 inch ribs)* *Allow 30 more minutes for 8-inch*	4 8	1-3/4 hr. 2 2-1/2	140° (rare) 160° (medium) 170° (well done)
Rolled Ribs	4 6	2-1/2 hr. 3 4-1/2 3 3-1/4 4	140° (rare) 160° (medium) 170° (well done) 140° (rare) 160° (medium) 170° (well done)
Rolled Rump *(Roast only if high quality; otherwise, braise it.)*	5	2-1/4 3 3-1/4	140° (rare) 160° (medium) 170° (well done)
Sirloin Tip Roast *(Roast only if high quality; otherwise, braise it.)*	3	1-1/2 2 2-1/4	140° (rare) 160° (medium) 170° (well done)
Leg of Lamb	6 8	3 3-1/2 4 4-1/2	175° (medium) 180° (well done) 175° (medium) 180° (well done)
VEAL			
Leg *(piece)* **Shoulder** **Rolled Shoulder**	5 6 3 to 5	2-1/2 to 3 3-1/2 3 to 3-1/2	170° (well done) 170° (well done) 170° (well done)
PORK			
Pork Tenderloin	1/2 to 1 lb	45 min. to 1 hr.	170°
Boston Butt or Blade	3 to 5 lb	2 to 3-1/2 hr.	170°
Fresh Picnic	5 to 8 lb	2-1/2 to 3-1/2 hr.	170°
Fresh Spareribs, Backribs and Country-style Ribs	1 rack	1-1/2 to 2-1/2 hr.	Cooked well done
Fresh Ham *Whole (bone-in)* *Boneless* *Half (bone-in)*	12 to 14 lb 10 to 14 5 to 8	4-1/2 to 6 hr. 4 to 6-3/4 hr. 3 to 5 hr.	170° 170° 170°

Pig farm, NC mountains.
PHOTO COURTESY OF THE NORTH CAROLINA STATE ARCHIVES, RALEIGH, NC

POULTRY ROASTING GUIDE

Type of poultry	Weight	Oven temperature	Roasting time
Turkey	6 to 8 lb 8 to 12 lb 12 to 16 lb 16 to 20 lb 20 to 24 lb	325° 325° 325° 325° 325°	2-1/2 to 3 hr 3 to 3-1/2 hr 3-1/2 to 4 hr 4 to 4-1/2 hr 5 to 6 hr
Chicken	2 to 2-1/2 lb 2-1/2 to 4 lb 4 to 8 lb	400° 400° 325°	1 to 1-1/2 hr 1-1/2 to 2-1/2 hr 3 to 5 hr
Duck	3 to 5 lb	325°	2-1/2 to 3 hr
Cornish Hen	1-1/2 to 2 lb	350°	1 to 1-1/2 hr

Internal temperature should read 175-180°F minimum, and thigh juices should run clear. These times are for unstuffed birds. NOTE: Small chickens brown better if roasted in a medium hot oven. Increase cooking time by 15 to 30 minutes for stuffed chicken and duck.

Memphis, Mississippi, and Arkansas cotton men were passionate hunters in the 1950s and 1960s.

RUBY THURMOND'S
HOUSEKEEPING RECEIPTS

PHOTO: Ruby Adell White, circa 1914

RUBY THURMOND'S HOUSEKEEPING RECEIPTS

WALL PAPER CLEANER

3 turkish towels

1 or 2 T Naphtha gas per towel

Crush towel into jar, adding gas until all 3 towels are in. Seal and let stand several hours or overnight. Wrap around mop sponge head, and wipe walls. Hang towels in air before washing to remove the gas.

STARCH FOR RUFFLED DOILIES

This recipe actually came to Grandmother from my Great-Aunt Annie Thurmond.

1/4 c dry starch, mixed with 1/2 c cold water

Add 1-1/4 c boiling water, and cook until clear.

Immerse the doilies into the wet cooked starch, wring out excess. Pin them into shape on a sheet of cardboard, allowing some air between the doilies and the cardboard. Allow to dry, but not in full sun, which will discolor the starched cotton. No ironing needed.

REMOVING TARNISH FROM STERLING OR SILVERPLATE

Large roasting pan lined with heavy-duty aluminum foil

1 T baking soda

1 T table salt

1 gal water

Bring ingredients to a boil in the lined pan. Boil the silver in this bath until tarnish comes off. Hand-wipe or polish dry to prevent spotting, This formula is fantastic for heavily tarnished silver. But BEWARE: Do not use this chemical bath process for antique sterling: Joints and soldered spots could become discolored.

CLEANING CORNINGWARE

Fill stained Corning dish with water. Drop in two denture cleaning tablets. Rinse and wash after soaking.

POLISHING COPPER

Make a paste of table salt and white vinegar. Coat the copper and rub vigorously. Wipe clean.

Pat Daltroff and Betsy Thurmond, circa 1960

HOMEMADE FURNITURE POLISH

1/3 c boiled linseed oil (do NOT boil your own)

1/3 c turpentine

1/3 c white vinegar

Mix well in a jar. Shake each time before using. Pour a small amount onto a soft cloth and apply in long strokes, going with the grain of the furniture. Wipe completely dry with a separate clean cloth (old cotton t-shirts work best). NOTE: boiled linseed oil may be purchased at a craft, paint or hardware store.

KITCHEN CLEANUPS

Keep your can opener clean by brushing the cutter with a toothbrush and soapy water.

To cleanse a blender's blades, fill blender part way with hot water and a drop of detergent, cover and turn it on for a few seconds. Rinse and drain dry.

To remove lime deposits from teakettles and coffee pots, fill with equal parts vinegar and water, bring to a boil (teakettle) or run the coffee pot, and allow the vinegar-and-water to stand overnight. Do a clean-water run-through.

To remove scorched and caked-on food from sides and bottom of a pot or pan, fill half way with water and add about 1/4 cup of baking soda. Bring this to a boil and keep boiling until the burned portions break loose.

To remove dark cooking stains in aluminum pots, boil a solution of vinegar containing a bit of cream of tartar.

Line the bottom of your oven with aluminum foil before baking "spill-over" foods such as fruit pies or lasagna. Do NOT do this when using the convection oven.

For food spillovers in the oven, sprinkle salt over the spill immediately to prevent smoking and odor. Later, after oven cools, gently wipe away and clean oven according to appliance directions.

To remove coffee and tea stains and cigarette burns from fine china, rub with a damp cloth dipped in baking soda.

To unclog a drain clogged with grease, pour in a cup of salt and a cup of baking soda followed by a kettle of boiling water.

To otherwise clear a sink or basin drain, pour 1/2 cup of baking soda followed by a cup of white vinegar and additional 2 Tablespoons of baking soda into the drain. Let this mixture foam, then run hot water into the drain.

To reduce or remove white water ring on wood, rub vigorously with mayonnaise immediately after the occurrence. Let sit overnight before buffing off excess mayo.

To reduce a white scorch mark on wood (the result of varnish or lacquer being raised by excess heat), place a bar towel over the mark, then gently run a hot iron over the towel to press down the separating sealant. This may or may not work, depending on the severity of the scorch.

STAIN REMOVAL

DO NOT WASH AND DRY before treating stains. Once heated, the stains are set. NEVER USE BAR SOAP. It will set in the stain.

BLOOD, URINE, FELT PEN, ACID BASED STAINS

Non-sudsy, unscented household ammonia. Sponge stain, wearing gloves, in a well ventilated space. Rinse with cold water. NEVER mix bleach and ammonia: fumes are toxic.

Urine stains: To remove urine smell from fabrics and carpeting, sponge with vinegar, let dry completely. Rinse with water. To remove urine stains from mattress or fabric, either use an enzyme cleanser such as the ones available at pet stores, or mix a solution of 8 oz hydrogen peroxide, 3 T baking soda, and a drop of liquid hand soap. Mix well; spray onto stain immediately while still mixed (the baking soda separates from the peroxide within 5 minutes). Let sit on the stain until it dries. Vacuum any residue. Mixture must be made fresh for each use and applied within 20 minutes.

PROTEIN STAINS

Sweat and antiperspirants: Three crushed aspirin in 1/2 cup of warm water. Saturate the stains; let sit 2 to 3 hours. Launder as usual. Soak longer if stains are really bad. OR, add 1 T white vinegar to 1 c cold water; soak discolored area, and allow to sit a while before rinsing in cold water. OR, soak stain 1+ hour in 3 T salt dissolved in 1 qt cool water.

Egg: Scrape off as much as possible. Make paste of crushed aspirin and water. Spread paste over reverse side of the fabric. Work it with a toothbrush. Rinse with warm water. Repeat as needed.

Andrea Triplette Benfield cleans up at Grace Chapel United Methodist Church.

Joshua Triplette, Louise and Lester's youngest grand-child, at Dianne and Gary Poovey's cabin in Vale, NC

CHOCOLATE, BIRD DROPPINGS, FECES

3% hydrogen peroxide, followed by boiling water.

COFFEE, TEA ON CLOTHING

Run under cold water as soon as possible. Soak in white vinegar, rinse and apply stain remover. If still stained, repeat.

COOKING OIL OR GREASE

Dawn Original dishwashing detergent. Spread Dawn over oil stain and work with the tip of the Dawn bottle. Let sit about 5 minutes, then throw in the washing machine with regular load. Waterless hand cleaner, wet wipes, and WD-40 might be used to remove fresh oil or grease (test first).

PHOTO, RIGHT: Louise and Lester Triplette with grandchildren, 1990; second row, left to right, Kurt Benfield, Brad and Matthew Cooke, Shannon Triplette; and front row, left to right, Weston Triplette, Lauren Triplette, Gabrielle Triplette, and Caroline Benfield.

GRAPE JUICE, OTHER FRUIT JUICES

Rub salt on the stain (re-wet with water if completely dry). If fabric is white, add lemon juice to salt. Rub gently, and let sit. Keep damp. Pour boiling water over the stain until it dissolves. May take several attempts. Hydrogen peroxide also works (using a fingernail brush to scrub the peroxide). Test for color-fastness first.

INK PEN ON COTTON

Aerosol hair spray or carbon tetrachloride worked into the stain on both sides of the fabric, then washed with cold water.

PENCIL, MASCARA, CANDLE-WAX RESIDUE

Rubbing alcohol, even on drycleaning. Wet Wipes sometimes work. NOTE: Waterproof mascara needs special care. Allow to partially dry, then soak smear with Shout. Use a knife to scrape saturated stained area, scraping up excess Shout and mascara. Work gently until the stain disappears. Rinse in running cold water, working with toothbrush, and repeat if necessary.

CHEWING GUM

Remove chewing gum from clothing, rugs, or upholstery by rubbing with ice and then scraping while cold. Remove chewing gum from skin and hair by rubbing with peanut butter. It really works. Ask my daughter.

THE INDEX

Recipes
Here's what's cookin'
serves:
Soup's
WEIGHT:
R. R. Pays
We Pay
TOTAL
Grand Total
To Lining on
To Patching on
To Marking on
POST CARD

THE RECIPES

APPETIZERS

BREAD & BREAKFAST

Biscuits

Breakfast Grains

Muffins & Breads

Griddle

Eggs, Meat, Casseroles

Breakfast Gravies

Corn Meal

Rolls

CAKES, COOKIES & CANDIES

Bars

Heirloom Cakes

Cream Cakes

Cheesecakes

Chocolate

FISH & SEAFOOD

See Soups for Gumbo Recipes

Fish

Seafood

MEATS, POULTRY & MAIN DISH

Barbecue

Beef

PIES, FRUITS & PASTRY

SALADS & SOUPS

See Veggies & Sides for Potato Salad Recipes

SAUCES & SEASONINGS

VEGGIES & SIDES